"This book forms a substantial contribution to literary studies and is likely to be the standard work on the subject for a decade or two.... The chapters are densely detailed, the vocabulary elevated."

Reference Reviews

"The long eighteenth century is well represented in Blackwell's A Companion to Satire: Ancient and Modern, edited by Ruben Quintero, which contains nine full essays and parts of several others devoted to the period.... This sturdy volume should be of use to a variety of readers from advanced undergraduates to scholars seeking refresher (or crash) courses on either major satirists... or less familiar topics and subtopics."

Studies in English Literature 1500–1900

"Offering a valuable contribution to the critical study of satire, Quintero has assembled insightful essays by an impressive roster of scholars... This book serves as a cogent, instructive overview of satire."

Choice

"This book obviously brings to readers a dazzling variety of topics relating to satire. There is a rich abundance of material here, surely something for everyone. Indeed, the quality of these essays is uniformly high. All are well-written, well-researched, thoughtful, and insightful examinations of an assortment of satiric expressions. The array of subject matter is compelling. Primarily, we are given thorough, informative overviews of the major players, issues, eras, and types of satire. This book... makes an invaluable contribution to the study of that form."

Notes and Queries

Blackwell Companions to Literature and Culture

This series offers comprehensive, newly written surveys of key periods and movements and certain major authors, in English literary culture and history. Extensive volumes provide new perspectives and positions on contexts and on canonical and post-canonical texts, orientating the beginning student in new fields of study and providing the experienced undergraduate and new graduate with current and new directions, as pioneered and developed by leading scholars in the field.

Published Recently

59. *A Companion to the Modern American Novel 1900–1950*	Edited by John T. Matthews
60. *A Companion to the Global Renaissance*	Edited by Jyotsna G. Singh
61. *A Companion to Thomas Hardy*	Edited by Keith Wilson
62 *A Companion to T. S. Eliot*	Edited by David E. Chinitz
63. *A Companion to Samuel Beckett*	Edited by S. E. Gontarski
64. *A Companion to Twentieth-Century United States Fiction*	Edited by David Seed
65. *A Companion to Tudor Literature*	Edited by Kent Cartwright
66. *A Companion to Crime Fiction*	Edited by Charles Rzepka and Lee Horsley
67. *A Companion to Medieval Poetry*	Edited by Corinne Saunders
68. *A New Companion to English Renaissance Literature and Culture*	Edited by Michael Hattaway
69. *A Companion to the American Short Story*	Edited by Alfred Bendixen and James Nagel
70. *A Companion to American Literature and Culture*	Edited by Paul Lauter
71. *A Companion to African American Literature*	Edited by Gene Jarrett
72. *A Companion to Irish Literature*	Edited by Julia M. Wright
73. *A Companion to Romantic Poetry*	Edited by Charles Mahoney
74. *A Companion to the Literature and Culture of the American West*	Edited by Nicolas S. Witschi
75. *A Companion to Sensation Fiction*	Edited by Pamela K. Gilbert
76. *A Companion to Comparative Literature*	Edited by Ali Behdad and Dominic Thomas
77. *A Companion to Poetic Genre*	Edited by Erik Martiny
78. *A Companion to American Literary Studies*	Edited by Caroline F. Levander and Robert S. Levine

A COMPANION TO
SATIRE
Ancient and Modern

EDITED BY **RUBEN QUINTERO**

A John Wiley & Sons, Ltd., Publication

This paperback edition first published 2011
© 2011 Blackwell Publishing Ltd except for editorial material and organization
© 2011 Ruben Quintero

Edition history: Blackwell Publishing Ltd (hardback, 2007)

Blackwell Publishing was acquired by John Wiley & Sons in February 2007. Blackwell's publishing program has been merged with Wiley's global Scientific, Technical, and Medical business to form Wiley-Blackwell.

Registered Office
John Wiley & Sons Ltd, The Atrium, Southern Gate, Chichester, West Sussex, PO19 8SQ, United Kingdom

Editorial Offices
350 Main Street, Malden, MA 02148-5020, USA
9600 Garsington Road, Oxford, OX4 2DQ, UK
The Atrium, Southern Gate, Chichester, West Sussex, PO19 8SQ, UK

For details of our global editorial offices, for customer services, and for information about how to apply for permission to reuse the copyright material in this book please see our website at www.wiley.com/wiley-blackwell.

The right of Ruben Quintero to be identified as the editor of the editorial material in this work has been asserted in accordance with the UK Copyright, Designs and Patents Act 1988.

All rights reserved. No part of this publication may be reproduced, stored in a retrieval system, or transmitted, in any form or by any means, electronic, mechanical, photocopying, recording or otherwise, except as permitted by the UK Copyright, Designs and Patents Act 1988, without the prior permission of the publisher.

Wiley also publishes its books in a variety of electronic formats. Some content that appears in print may not be available in electronic books.

Designations used by companies to distinguish their products are often claimed as trademarks. All brand names and product names used in this book are trade names, service marks, trademarks or registered trademarks of their respective owners. The publisher is not associated with any product or vendor mentioned in this book. This publication is designed to provide accurate and authoritative information in regard to the subject matter covered. It is sold on the understanding that the publisher is not engaged in rendering professional services. If professional advice or other expert assistance is required, the services of a competent professional should be sought.

Library of Congress Cataloging-in-Publication Data
A companion to satire : ancient and modern / edited by Ruben Quintero.
     p. cm.—(Blackwell companions to literature and culture ; 46)
  Includes bibliographical references and index.
  Hardback ISBN: 978-1-4051-1955-9 (alk. paper); Paperback ISBN: 978-0-470-65795-9
1. Satire—History and criticism.   I. Quintero, Ruben, 1949–   II. Series.

PN6149.S2C66 2006
809.7—dc22
                                                          2005034702

A catalogue record for this book is available from the British Library.

This book is published in the following electronic formats: ePDFs 9781405171991; Wiley Online Library 9780470996959; ePub 9781444395662

Set in 11/13pt Garamond 3 by SPi Publisher Services, Pondicherry, India.

1   2011

Contents

Illustrations	viii
Notes on Contributors	ix
Acknowledgments	xiv
Introduction: Understanding Satire *Ruben Quintero*	1
Part I Biblical World to European Renaissance	**13**
1 Ancient Biblical Satire *Thomas Jemielity*	15
2 Defining the Art of Blame: Classical Satire *Catherine Keane*	31
3 Medieval Satire *Laura Kendrick*	52
4 Rabelais and French Renaissance Satire *Edwin M. Duval*	70
5 Satire of the Spanish Golden Age *Alberta Gatti*	86
6 Verse Satire in the English Renaissance *Ejner J. Jensen*	101
7 Renaissance Prose Satire: Italy and England *W. Scott Blanchard*	118

Part II	**Restoration and Eighteenth-century England and France**	137
8	Satire in Seventeenth- and Eighteenth-century France *Russell Goulbourne*	139
9	Dramatic Satire in the Restoration and Eighteenth Century *Jean I. Marsden*	161
10	Dryden and Restoration Satire *Dustin Griffin*	176
11	Jonathan Swift *Frank Boyle*	196
12	Pope and Augustan Verse Satire *Ruben Quintero*	212
13	Satiric Spirits of the Later Eighteenth Century: Johnson to Crabbe *James Engell*	233
14	Restoration and Eighteenth-century Satiric Fiction *Joseph F. Bartolomeo*	257
15	Gendering Satire: Behn to Burney *Claudia Thomas Kairoff*	276
16	Pictorial Satire: From Emblem to Expression *Ronald Paulson*	293
Part III	**Nineteenth Century to Contemporary**	325
17	The *Hidden* Agenda of Romantic Satire: Carlyle and Heine *Peter Brier*	327
18	Nineteenth-century Satiric Poetry *Steven E. Jones*	340
19	Narrative Satire in the Nineteenth Century *Frank Palmeri*	361
20	American Satire: Beginnings through Mark Twain *Linda A. Morris*	377
21	Twentieth-century Fictional Satire *Valentine Cunningham*	400
22	Verse Satire in the Twentieth Century *Timothy Steele*	434
23	Satire in Modern and Contemporary Theater *Christopher J. Herr*	460
24	Irish Satire *José Lanters*	476

Part IV The Practice of Satire — 493

25 Modes of Mockery: The Significance of Mock-poetic Forms in the Enlightenment — 495
Blanford Parker

26 Irony and Satire — 510
Zoja Pavlovskis-Petit

27 Mock-biblical Satire from Medieval to Modern — 525
Michael F. Suarez

28 The Satiric Character Sketch — 550
David F. Venturo

29 The Secret Life of Satire — 568
Melinda Alliker Rabb

Index — 585

Illustrations

16.1	William Hogarth, *A Harlot's Progress*, Plate 1, 1732	294
16.2	James Gillray, *Smelling out a Rat*, 1790	295
16.3	James Gillray, *An Excrescence*, 1791	296
16.4	William Hogarth, *The Lottery*, 1724	297
16.5	William Hogarth, *A Harlot's Progress*, Plate 4 (detail), 1732	300
16.6	Albrecht Dürer, *Flagellation* (detail), c.1500	301
16.7	William Hogarth, *Gin Lane*, 1751	303
16.8	William Hogarth, *Characters and Caricaturas*, 1743	311
16.9	James Gillray, *The Plumb-pudding in Danger*, 1805	313
16.10	Thomas Rowlandson, *Comparative Anatomy*, c.1800	315
16.11	Thomas Rowlandson, *Modern Antique*, 1811	320
16.12	Thomas Rowlandson, *The Anatomist*, c.1800	321
27.1	Artist unknown, *The New Coalition*, 1784	532
27.2	Artist unknown, *Idol-Worship or the Way to Preferment*, 1740	536
27.3	Steve Bell's "IF..." cartoons from the *Guardian*, September 15–17, 1997	539
27.4	Artist unknown, *Fox and North as Herod and Pilate*, 1783	541

Notes on Contributors

Joseph F. Bartolomeo is Professor of English and Chair of the English Department at the University of Massachusetts, Amherst. He is the author of *A New Species of Criticism: Eighteenth-century Discourse on the Novel* (1994) and *Matched Pairs: Gender and Intertextual Dialogue in Eighteenth-century Fiction* (2002), as well as several articles on eighteenth-century fiction and criticism. He has served as a member of the executive board of the Northeast American Society for Eighteenth-century Studies, and as a field editor for the Twayne English Authors Series.

W. Scott Blanchard is Professor of English Literature at College Misericordia in Pennsylvania. He has published a book on satire in the European Renaissance, *Scholars' Bedlam: Menippean Satire in the Renaissance* (1995), and is the author of numerous articles on both satire and Renaissance humanism. He is currently working on a project involving the satires of the Italian humanist Francesco Filelfo.

Frank Boyle is the author of *Swift as Nemesis: Modernity and its Satirist* (2000). He is Associate Professor of English at Fordham University and chair of the New York Eighteenth Century Seminar.

Peter Brier is Professor Emeritus of English at California State University, Los Angeles. He is the author of *Howard Mumford Jones and the Dynamics of Liberal Humanism* (1994) and co-author (with Anthony Arthur) of a descriptive bibliography, *American Prose and Criticism 1900–1950* (1981). He has published articles on Romantic and modern writers in *The Denver Quarterly*, *The Huntington Quarterly*, and *The Southwest Review*.

Valentine Cunningham is Professor of English Language and Literature at Oxford University and Senior Fellow in English Literature at Corpus Christi College, Oxford. His publications include *Everywhere Spoken Against: Dissent in the Victorian Novel* (1975), *British Writers of the Thirties* (1988), *In The Reading Gaol: Postmodernity, Texts, and History* (1994), and *Reading After Theory* (2002). He has edited *The Penguin Book of Spanish Civil War Verse* (1980), *Spanish Front: Writers on the Civil War* (1986), George Eliot's *Adam Bede* (1996), and *The Victorians: An Anthology of Poetry and Poetics* (2000).

Edwin M. Duval is Professor and Chair of French at Yale University. His books include *Poesis and Poetic Tradition in the Early Works of Saint-Amant* (1981) and a three-volume study of form and meaning in the works of Rabelais: *The Design of Rabelais's Pantagruel* (1991), *The Design of Rabelais's Tiers Livre* (1997), and *The Design of Rabelais's Quart Livre* (1998). He has published many articles on Rabelais and other French Renaissance authors, including Marot, Marguerite de Navarre, Scève, Montaigne, and d'Aubigné. His current research is devoted to echoes of Virgil's *Aeneid* in French Renaissance literature.

James Engell has written and edited numerous books and articles on eighteenth-century and Romantic studies. His most recent volume, *Saving Higher Education in the Age of Money* (2005), co-authored with Anthony Dangerfield, examines how colleges and universities – and the humanities in particular – can address the challenges and pressures that have developed in the past four decades. He is co-editor of a forthcoming interdisciplinary reader in environmental studies. Currently, he chairs the Department of English and American Literature and Language at Harvard University.

Alberta Gatti is an Associate Professor of Spanish at Saint Xavier University, Chicago, where she directs the Foreign Languages Program. Originally from Buenos Aires, Argentina, she received a PhD in Hispanic Language and Literature from Boston University. Her research work has focused on Spanish satire of the Golden Age (sixteenth to seventeenth centuries).

Russell Goulbourne is Senior Lecturer in French at the University of Leeds. A specialist in seventeenth- and eighteenth-century French literature, he is the author of *Voltaire Comic Dramatist* (2006) and the translator for Oxford World's Classics of Diderot's *The Nun* (2005). He is also a member of the editorial board of *The Complete Works of Voltaire*, published by the Voltaire Foundation in Oxford.

Dustin Griffin is Professor of English at New York University and the author of *Satires against Man: The Poems of Rochester* (1974), *Alexander Pope: The Poet in the Poems* (1978), *Regaining Paradise: Milton and the Eighteenth Century* (1986), *Satire: A Critical Re-introduction* (1994), *Literary Patronage in England, 1650–1800* (1996), and *Patriotism and Poetry in Eighteenth-century Britain* (2002).

Christopher J. Herr is Assistant Professor of Theater at Missouri State University, where he directs the graduate program and teaches theater history, dramatic theory, and modern drama. His book, *Clifford Odets and American Political Theater*, was published in 2003. He has also taught in the English Department at California State University, Los Angeles, and in the Theater Department at Bowling Green State University.

Thomas Jemielity is Professor Emeritus of English at the University of Notre Dame. Besides his *Satire and the Hebrew Prophets* (1992), he has published essays on Alexander Pope's use in satire of biblical material (a technique he calls mock-biblical), on satire and irony in Edward Gibbon, Samuel Johnson, and Evelyn Waugh, and on the Johnson–Boswell tour, in 1773, of the Highlands and Western Islands of Scotland. The Lilly Endowment supported his proposal for introducing a course in comedy at Notre Dame, where he has for more than three decades taught satire as well.

Ejner J. Jensen is Professor Emeritus of English Language and Literature at the University of Michigan, where he taught for over forty years. He has published widely on topics in Renaissance drama and on satire, poetry, and current issues in higher education. He is the editor of *The Future of Nineteen Eighty-four* (1984) and author of, among other works, *Shakespeare and the Ends of Comedy* (1991).

Steven E. Jones is Professor of English at Loyola University, Chicago. He is the author of a number of articles and books on satire of the Romantic period, including *Shelley's Satire* (1994) and *Satire and Romanticism* (2000), and the editor of *The Satiric Eye: Forms of Satire in the Romantic Period* (2003). He has just completed a book entitled *Against Technology: From the Luddites to Neo-Luddism*.

Claudia Thomas Kairoff is a Professor of English at Wake Forest University. She is the author of *Alexander Pope and his Eighteenth-century Women Readers* (1994) and co-editor, with Catherine Ingrassia, of *"More Solid Learning": New Perspectives on Alexander Pope's Dunciad* (2000). She has also written numerous articles on eighteenth-century women writers and is currently working on a book reappraising the writings of Anna Seward.

Catherine Keane received her PhD in Classical Studies from the University of Pennsylvania and is currently Assistant Professor of Classics at Washington University in St Louis. She is the author of *Figuring Genre in Roman Satire* (2006) and of several articles on ancient Roman satiric poetry and related comic traditions. Her current work in progress is a book on Juvenal's personae and poetics.

Laura Kendrick, Professor at the Université de Versailles, is the author of *Chaucerian Play: Comedy and Control in the Canterbury Tales* (1988) and of several articles on medieval satire and comedy in both verbal and visual forms. She is currently finishing an edition of Eustache Deschamps' late fourteenth-century *Mirror of Marriage*, a text noteworthy for its satire of women.

José Lanters is Professor of English at the University of Wisconsin–Milwaukee, where she also serves on the Advisory Board of the Center for Celtic Studies. She has written numerous articles on Irish fiction and drama, and she is the author of two books, *Missed Understandings: A Study of Stage Adaptations of the Works of James Joyce* (1988) and *Unauthorized Versions: Irish Menippean Satire, 1919–1952* (2000).

Jean I. Marsden is Professor of English at the University of Connecticut. She is the author of *The Re-imagined Text: Shakespeare, Adaptation, and Eighteenth-century Literary Theory* (1995), *Fatal Desire: Women, Sexuality and the English Stage, 1660–1720* (2006), and of numerous articles on Restoration and eighteenth-century theater.

Linda A. Morris is Professor of English at the University of California, Davis. Her books include *Women Vernacular Humorists in Nineteenth-century America: Ann Stephens, Frances Whitcher, and Marietta Holley* (1988), *Women's Humor in the Age of Gentility: The Life and Works of Frances Miriam Whitcher* (1992), and *American Women's Humor: Critical Essays* (1993). She is currently completing a book entitled *Gender Play in Mark Twain*. She regularly teaches courses in American humor, American satire, and Mark Twain.

Frank Palmeri, Professor of English at the University of Miami, is the author of *Satire in Narrative* (1990) and *Satire, History, Novel: Narrative Forms 1665–1815* (2003), and the editor of *Humans and Other Animals in Eighteenth-century England: Representation, Hybridity, Ethics* (forthcoming). He is currently working on a volume on the eclipse and re-emergence of satire in the long nineteenth century (1790–1910) and writing a book on the afterlife of Enlightenment conjectural history in early anthropology and psychoanalysis.

Blanford Parker teaches Restoration and eighteenth-century poetry, philosophical prose, and the history of literary criticism at The College of Staten Island and The CUNY Graduate Center. He has previously taught at Iowa, NYU, and the Claremont Graduate School. His book, *The Triumph of Augustan Poetics* (1998), maps the intellectual and cultural changes from the Baroque period to the eighteenth century that made Augustan poetry possible. He is now completing a book on the European genre system.

Ronald Paulson is Professor Emeritus of English at The Johns Hopkins University. He is author of *The Fictions of Satire* (1967) and *Satire and the Novel in Eighteenth-century England* (1967), and editor of *Satire: Modern Critical Essays* (1971). His major work is a series of books on William Hogarth and English art, including *Hogarth's Graphic Works* (1965; 3rd edn, 1989) and the three-volume *Hogarth* (1991–3), *Emblem and Expression: Meaning in English Art of the Eighteenth Century* (1975), *Literary Landscape: Turner and Constable* (1982), *Representations of Revolution, 1789–1820* (1983), *Breaking and Remaking: Aesthetic Practice in England: 1700-1800* (1989), *The Beautiful, Novel, and Strange: Aesthetics and Heterodoxy* (1996), *Don Quixote in England: The Aesthetics of Laughter* (1998), and *Hogarth's Harlot: Sacred Parody in Enlightenment England* (2003).

Zoja Pavlovskis-Petit is Professor of Comparative Literature and Classics at Binghamton University. Her research is mainly concerned with irony and with Latin poetry of the late Roman empire, and her main publications on irony are *The Praise of Folly: Structure and Irony* (1983), "Aristotle, Horace, and the Ironic Man," *Classical Philology* 63 (1968), 22–41; and "The Voice of the Actor in Greek Tragedy," *Classical World* 71 (1977), 113–23. She is currently working on the uses of irony in Nabokov.

Ruben Quintero is Professor of English at California State University, Los Angeles, and teaches Restoration and eighteenth-century literature. His book *Literate Culture: Pope's Rhetorical Art* (1992) received a University of Delaware Press Manuscript Award.

Melinda Alliker Rabb is an Associate Professor of English at Brown University. She has published on a wide range of Restoration and eighteenth-century writers and topics, including Swift, Pope, Manley, Sterne, Richardson, Fielding, Scott, Godwin, satire, the canon, and women writers. Currently, she is completing a book on satire and secrecy from the Restoration to the postmodern era.

Timothy Steele is the author of several collections of verse, including *Sapphics against Anger and Other Poems* (1986), *The Color Wheel* (1994), *Sapphics and Uncertainties: Poems 1970–1986* (1995), and *Toward the Winter Solstice* (2006). He has also published two books of literary criticism – *Missing Measures: Modern Poetry and the Revolt against Meter* (1990) and *All the Fun's in How You Say a Thing: An Explanation of Meter and Versification* (1999) – and has edited *The Poems of J. V. Cunningham* (1997). He is a Professor of English at California State University, Los Angeles.

Michael F. Suarez, S.J. is University Professor, Professor of English, and Director of the Rare Book School at the University of Virginia. The co-General Editor of *The Oxford Companion to the Book* (OUP, 2010) and *The Collected Works of Gerard Manley Hopkins* (8 vols, OUP, 2005–13), his other projects include a two-volume study of scriptural satires from Cromwell to George IV, to be published by Oxford University Press.

David F. Venturo, Associate Professor of English at the College of New Jersey, is author of *Johnson the Poet: The Poetic Career of Samuel Johnson* (1999) and editor of *The School of the Eucharist with a Preface Concerning the Testimony of Miracles* (forthcoming), and has written extensively on British literature and culture, 1640–1830. He helps edit *ECCB: The Eighteenth Century: A Current Bibliography* and *The Scriblerian,* and is writing a book, *Fall'n on Evil Days: Alienation and Protest in Milton, Dryden, and Swift.*

Acknowledgments

I editorialize here my gratitude to our authors for their intellectual commitment and gifts of time, expert knowledge, and critical insight. This volume would not exist without such individual generosity. Our collective references should also serve as a general expression of gratitude to all scholars of satire. Satire is an indispensable art form, and scholarship helps keep satire of the past in memory and accessible. The critical comments and suggestions made by my anonymous readers were invaluable. Blackwell's editors Emma Bennett and Karen Wilson at each stage were helpful without fail, and Sue Ashton is a fine copy editor. My gifted colleague Timothy Steele read my scribbling and offered excellent advice, as did James Engell, to whom I am also indebted for suggesting this project. I also want to thank Michael Shinagel for his support and liaison. I appreciate the assistance of all of these splendid people. In the muse department, special thanks must go to Elena, Evelia, and Isabella for their support of the non-institutional kind in advancing the completion of this volume, which I regret my father did not live to see.

The editor and publisher gratefully acknowledge the permission granted to reproduce the copyright material in this book:

A Harlot's Progress, Plate 1, etching and engraving, 1732. *The Lottery*, etching and engraving, 1724. *A Harlot's Progress*, Plate 4 (detail), 1732. *Gin Lane*, etching and engraving, 1751. *Characters and Caricaturas*, etching, 1743. By William Hogarth. Reprinted by courtesy of the British Museum, London.

Comparative Anatomy, drawing, c.1800. By Thomas Rowlandson. Reprinted by courtesy of the Huntington Library, Art Collections, and Botanical Gardens, San Marino, California.

Countee Cullen, "For a Lady I Know," from *Color* by Countee Cullen (New York: Harper & Bros, 1925). Copyright © 1925 Harper & Bros, NY. © Renewed 1952 by Ida M. Cullen. Copyrights held by Amistad Research Center, Tulane University. Administered by Thompson and Thompson, Brooklyn, NY. Reprinted with permission.

Acknowledgments

"Eastern Europe," from *Boss Cupid* (Farrar, Straus and Giroux, 2000) by Thom Gunn. Reprinted by permission of Faber and Faber Ltd and by Farrar, Straus and Giroux, LLC. Copyright © by Thom Gunn.

"Engineers' Corner," from *Making Cocoa for Kingsley Amis* (1984) by Wendy Cope. Reprinted by permission of Faber and Faber Ltd and Farrar, Straus and Giroux LLC. Copyright © by Wendy Cope.

"IF..." cartoons from the *Guardian*, September 15–17, 1997. By Steve Bell. Reprinted by courtesy of Steve Bell. Copyright © 1997 by Steve Bell.

"Literary Theorist," from *Taken in Faith: Poems* (2002) by Helen Pinkerton. Reprinted by permission of Ohio University Press and Swallow Press. Copyright © 2002 by Helen Pinkerton.

"Movie Stars" and "Social Darwinism," from *Deeply Dug In* (2003) by R. L. Barth. Reprinted by permission of the University of New Mexico Press. Copyright © 2003 by R. L. Barth.

The New Coalition, etching, 1784 (BM 6568). Artist unknown. *Idol-Worship or the Way to Preferment*, etching and engraving, 1740 (BM 2447). Artist unknown. *Fox and North as Herod and Pilate*, etching, drypoint and roulette with hand coloring, 1783 (BM 6194). Artist unknown (sometimes attributed to James Gillray). Reprinted by courtesy of the Lewis Walpole Library, Yale University.

"Overture," from *The Collected Poems of Henri Coulette* (1990) by Henri Coulette. Reprinted by permission of the University of Arkansas Press. Copyright © 1990 by Henri Coulette.

Roy Campbell, "On Some South African Novelists." Jonathan Cape Ltd.

"They," from *Collected Poems of Siegfried Sassoon* by Siegfried Sassoon. Reprinted by permission of Mr George Sassoon and by permission of Viking Penguin, a division of Penguin Group (USA) Inc. Copyright © 1918, 1920 by E. P. Dutton. Copyright © 1936, 1946, 1947, 1948 by Siegfried Sassoon.

"This be the Verse," from *High Windows* (1974) by Philip Larkin. Reprinted by permission of Faber and Faber Ltd and by Farrar, Straus and Giroux, LLC. Copyright © by Philip Larkin.

"This Humanist whom no Beliefs Constrained," from *The Poems of J. V. Cunningham* (1997) by J. V. Cunningham. Reprinted by permission of Ohio University Press and Swallow Press. Copyright © 1997 by J. V. Cunningham.

"To Someone Who Insisted I Look Up Someone," from *Emily Dickinson in Southern California* (1973) by X. J. Kennedy. Reprinted by permission of the author. Copyright © 1973 by X. J. Kennedy.

"Visiting Poet," from *Selected Poems* (1982) by John Frederick Nims. Reprinted by permission of the University of Chicago Press. Copyright © 1982 by John Frederick Nims.

"Which the Chicken, Which the Egg?" from *The Old Dog Barks Backward* (Little Brown and Company, 1972) by Ogden Nash. Reprinted by permission of Curtis Brown, Ltd and by permission of André Deutsch Ltd. Copyright © 1972 by Ogden Nash.

Every effort has been made to trace copyright holders and to obtain their permission for the use of copyright material. The publisher apologizes for any errors or omissions in the above list and would be grateful if notified of any corrections that should be incorporated in future reprints or editions of this book.

Introduction: Understanding Satire
Ruben Quintero

> But still, despite our cleverness and love,
> Regardless of the past, regardless of
> The future on which all our hopes are pinned,
> We'll reap the whirlwind, who have sown the wind.
> (Timothy Steele, "April 27, 1937")

The Satirist

If, at the end of Nathaniel Hawthorne's short story "Young Goodman Brown" (1835), the "darkly meditative," aging, and "distrustful" protagonist, believing he once saw his Salem neighbors and newlywed wife ("Faith") cavorting in a witches' Sabbath one wild night in the forest, had chosen to take up the quill instead of bitterly retreating from life, he would have written satire. For satirists do not wither in despair but, on the contrary, feel compelled to express their dissent. Juvenal is as typical a satirist as he is a great one for being so singularly dissatisfied and wanting to tell others about it. Living in an imperial Rome that has thoroughly surrendered its former republican glory, he tells his readers from the outset that it is difficult for him *not* to write satire (*difficile est saturam non scribere*; *Satires* 1.30). Indignant, he must speak out against the decadence and corruption he sees all about him. Thus satirists write in winters of discontent.

And they write not merely out of personal indignation, but with a sense of moral vocation and with a concern for the public interest. In his second "Epilogue to the Satires" (1738), Alexander Pope's poetic speaker is called "strangely proud" by his adversarial friend, who would have him stop writing satire altogether. The poet agrees that he is "odd" – for "my Country's Ruin makes me grave" – and that he is "proud" – "proud to see / Men not afraid of God, afraid of me: / Safe from the Bar, the Pulpit, and the Throne, / Yet touch'd and sham'd by *Ridicule* alone." The poet's satire is a "sacred Weapon! Left for Truth's defence, / Sole Dread of Folly, Vice, and Insolence!" and that prosecutorial weapon of words has been entrusted only to his "Heav'n-directed hands" (*Dialogue II*, 208–15). As in the formative Roman verse satires of Horace and Juvenal, Pope's poetry creates a people's court of blame and shame, and his satirist litigates and adjudges misconduct that, though not restrained by legislated law, is subject to the unofficial law of satire (*lex per saturam*).

Such sanction for scorn or ridicule, however, does not mean that the satirist can lash out or laugh at just anything. Not only must a boundary between truth and libel be respected, but also a socio-ethical boundary regarding satirical subject matter. It may be true, as Ronald Paulson observes, that punishment is "the most extreme, and at the same time most common, consequence in satire" and "conveys a definite admonition: this is the consequence of your foolish act, this is the effect of X's evil act; or, beware! This is what you could look like or what X in fact looks like" (1967: 10, 14). But, in order to be laid bare and satirized, X's "evil act" must be an evil of error, not pure evil, nor can X be hypothetically incorrigible, that is, beyond punishment. The immutably divine or demonic cannot be made satiric, except through a humanizing or a thoroughly iconoclastic perspective, such as we find, for example, in *Paradise Lost* (1667), in which John Milton ridicules a foolish, despairing Satan by presenting him as a parody of Christ, or in Mel Brooks's film *The Producers* (1968), in which Hitler indirectly becomes the butt of comedy when a vulgar theater-going public makes a hit of *Springtime for Hitler* – mistaking this tasteless, morally objectionable play, intended as a flop, for a mock-musical satire on the Third Reich. Hitler, *qua* genocidal monster, cannot be dressed down, satirized, though it appeared possible before full disclosure of his atrocities, as in Chaplin's cinematic satire *The Great Dictator* (1940). As another example of the limits of satire, Joseph Conrad first drafted *Heart of Darkness* (1902) with the expressed intent of writing a political satire of colonial exploitation in the Congo, but when he added and then developed the character Kurtz into an "unlawful soul" who went "beyond the bounds of permitted aspirations," Conrad's novel became more of an exploration of the mystery of human evil than a satiric condemnation of institutional misconduct. Similarly in political rhetoric, when one national leader demonizes another, calling him a Hitler or a devil, satire ends and propaganda begins. Satire requires the inclusion, not the exclusion, of human failing.

Not only concerned with what has happened but also with what may happen, the satirist, through an historical logic of inference and extrapolation into the future, may also serve as a cautionary prophet or an idealistic visionary. The satirist is fundamentally *engagé*, as Patricia Meyer Spacks states:

> Satire has traditionally had a public function, and its public orientation remains. Although the satirist may arraign God and the universe... he usually seems to believe – at least to hope – that change is possible. Personal change, in his view, leads to social change; he insists that bad men make bad societies. He shows us ourselves and our world; he demands that we improve both. And he creates a kind of emotion which moves us toward the desire to change. (1971: 363)

So pervasive is the satiric "public function" remarked by Spacks that we might suspect satire to be, at bottom, a product of our biological grammar. Robert C. Elliott, perceiving a deeply rooted impulse within the art of satire, declares that magical satire, a ritual form present in the earliest of cultures, sprang "from one primordial demand – a demand that out of the fears and confusions engendered by a hostile world man shall be able to impose some kind of order" (Elliott 1960: 58). Satirists were our first utopians.

Satirical Purpose

The satirist attempts more than visceral laughter or corrosive spite. Surely, a satire may fall dully flat, and the satirist may appear unfairly prejudiced or sanctimonious; or a satire may be vacuously humorous, playful, witty, or ridiculous without point. But any satirist deserving the name must be more than a partisan advocate or a clownish entertainer, for a true satirist must be a true believer, a practicing humanitarian, responsible even in his or her own subjective indulgence or personal indignation. "The satirist, in short, demands decisions of his reader, not mere feelings"; he "wishes to arouse [the reader's] energy to action, not purge it in vicarious experience" (Paulson 1967: 15). Through either mimetic or discursive art, the satirist provokes mirth or sadness, a concern for the innocent or the self-destructive fool, or a revulsion for the deceitful knave, and always either laughter or scorn at the anatomized subject. As with the agon of tragedy and comedy (the conflict of characters), satire also moves heart and mind through building tension and provoking conflict, but, unlike tragedy and comedy, stops short of any reconciliation with its subject. And as the prism does to light, it leaves its subject refracted and disharmonized. Satire remains militantly rhetorical and hortatory.

Satire cannot function without a standard against which readers can compare its subject. We praise with delight what we admire, enjoy, or profit from, and we censure with indignation the despicable or what causes ill because we have an acquired sense of what the world should or might be. How could we perceive something as ridiculous, monstrous, wicked, or absurd without having a comparative sense of what would *not* be the case? How could we believe that something is wrong with the world without some idea of what the world should be and of how it could be righted? The satirist, either explicitly or implicitly, tries to sway us toward an ideal alternative, toward a condition of what the satirist believes should be. It is assumed that the satirist has our best interests at heart and seeks improvement or reformation. Whether that standard is incontrovertibly right does not really matter. But what does matter is that the satirist and the reader share a perception of that standard.

Yet, the satirist is not obligated to solve what is perceived as a problem or replace what is satirically disassembled or unmasked with a solution. It is missing the mark to claim, as some have done, that Joseph Heller's World War II novel *Catch-22* (1961) is not satirical because it offers no alternative to the self-defeating logic of an inescapable Catch-22, which not only victimizes the main character, Yossarian, but everyone else except the advantageously situated military bureaucrats who profit from the death and destruction of the war. Absurdity in itself, even if it permeates a literary universe, does not undermine the possibility of satire, unless, of course, the reader obdurately subscribes to a larger belief in a world completely subversive of all human intention. The satirist's responsibility is frequently that of a watchdog; and no one expects a watchdog to do the double duty of alarming others that the barn is on fire and of putting out the blaze. Satirists, that is, rouse us to put out the fire. They encourage our need for the stability of truth by unmasking imposture, exposing fraudulence, shattering deceptive illusion, and shaking us from our complacency and indifference. Philip Wylie, author of the once highly controversial *Generation of Vipers* (1942), a satiric tour de force, expressed his pleasure at the response of one reader who wrote to his publisher: "PUT OUT THE LANTERN OF DIOGENES FOR HERE BY GOD IN THE PLAIN LIGHT OF DAY IS AN HONEST MAN" (Wylie 1970: xi). Honesty promulgates criticism, and, as Wylie himself explains, "Criticism . . . and the *doubt* out of which it arises, are the prior conditions to progress of any sort" (Wylie 1970: xiv).

If satirists are sometimes prophets and idealists, they are also artists, even or especially when they conceal their art. For instance, the satiric films of Michael Moore – *Roger & Me* (1989), *Bowling for Columbine* (2002), and *Fahrenheit 9/11* (2004), among others – are cleverly crafted *faux* documentaries that through the eye of a camera employ radical juxtaposition, visual metaphor, ironic debunking, selective compression for dramatic effect, a carefully positioned naïve narrator, and other techniques commonly utilized in literary satire. Moore's skilful cinematography and editing, and the journalistic character of his work, create a cinematic realism not unlike the literary realism and detailed verisimilitude of Swift's *Gulliver's Travels* (1726). In Moore's films, we travel as Lemuel Gullivers through an all-too-familiar world, at first happy in being well deceived, then seeing things from disruptively new but believable angles. We see how we and our world are manipulated by powerful industries, lobbies, and government officials. We see, or think we see, behind the curtain that conceals the cruelty, deceit, or folly of the corporations and government administrations. Yet, we who are being enlightened may sometimes fail to perceive that artifice plays as great a role in this process as fact. By the same token, those who see themselves as being attacked, as suffering the brunt of Moore's satire, for example, see only artless and unfounded invective or diatribe in his films: Moore is not funny, they protest, and he is not honest; he is the knave, and anyone who takes him at his word is the fool. As occurred in Swift's time, when a purblind Irish bishop proclaimed that he for one did not believe a word of the *Travels*, today we have critics, perhaps, imperceptive, humorless, or apologetic defenders, maybe blinded by partisan politics or an exuberant sense of patriotism, scoffing at Moore's veracity, making lists of his deceits, and wholly misunderstanding his objective of finally promoting more criticism and open inquiry of perceived injustice. In the plain light of public scrutiny, the satirist would contend, there should appear nothing wrong if, really, there is nothing wrong.

Such confusions between literal fact and the truth of art remind us that satirists must ultimately rely on audiences to share a common ground of reason and, as far as literary satire is concerned, of belief. Readers of satire are expected to suspend disbelief, to play along with the game, but not ever to surrender sanity or sound judgment. And satirists may employ fiction for seeking truth but not establishing falsehood. The satirist, in seeking a re-formation of thought, expects readers to engage the satire by applying their reasoning, moral values, and taste to the subject. Through an aggressive strategy of distortion or defamation that demands our critical judgment, the satirist seeks to affect our attitude or perspective, and often through the indirection of a narrator purposely designed to befuddle and obscure whatever exact direction the satirist would probably have us go. As Wayne Booth notes, "Since the rhetorical intent of these works [innumerable satires and burlesques, from Rabelais through Erasmus and Swift] is evident to every reader, the function of the dramatized spokesman, whether fools, knaves, or sages, is usually quite clear; no one accuses them of mad incoherence" (1961: 229). The unreliability of the narrator's position observed in Swift's *A Tale of a Tub* (1704), which may confuse our understanding of Swift's latent attitude at any one time, does not disqualify the work as a satire. From a distance of time, the work may now appear more pointless in its ridicule than the topical blunderbuss it once was. Yet, despite the seemingly ludicrous narration, the larger satire remains palpable because we, poised outside the text, are not giddy inhabitants of an absurd, material, and godless world. Swift's satiric purpose, in the playful humanist spirit of Erasmus' *Praise of Folly* (1511) and consistent with his other satire, may have been simply to illustrate how contemporary examples of scholastic intellectualism may be reduced to absurdity. A similar cautionary function may also have been the thrust of Swift's parodies of actual science in Gulliver's third voyage.

Finally, satire castigates the representative bad behavior or thought of an individual, but not any one individual who misbehaves or errs. In his *Dictionary* (1755), Samuel Johnson makes a broadly applicable distinction between *satire* and *lampoon* while defining the genre of formal verse satire: "[Satire is a] poem in which wickedness or folly is censured. Proper *satire* is distinguished, by the generality of the reflections, from a *lampoon* which is aimed against a particular person; but they are too frequently confounded." The same disavowal of personal attack is expressed by Swift's apologist, who defends his satire:

> Yet, Malice never was his Aim;
> He lash'd the Vice but spar'd the Name.
> No Individual could resent,
> Where Thousands equally were meant.
> His Satyr points at no Defect,
> But what all Mortals may correct.
> ("Verses on the Death of Dr Swift," 459–64)

Satire has a wide range of strategies. At one extreme is *invective*, only a scant shade away from gross individual insult of unequivocal censure or condemnation. Though some form of attack or ridicule is necessary for something to be satiric, without intentioned art there is no satire. A direct, unregulated insult, for example, is not satiric – as, for example, "That guy is an SOB!" Reviving the clichéd language of dead metaphor to serve a purpose of ridicule, on the other hand, may make insult satirical. In retirement, US President Harry Truman was asked if he had once called Richard Nixon an SOB. Truman replied that that could hardly be true because he had understood Nixon to be "a self-made man." Tonally ironic and metaphorically playful, Truman's wit had transformed a common insult into satire by mocking a linchpin of Nixon's Republican Party politics – self-reliance.

Problems of Origin and Definition

Questions remain about the origin of *satire* or *satyr* (a popular alternative spelling during the English Renaissance), probably because no literary genre has a lexicon with more nominal red herrings. The classicist G. L. Hendrickson modestly understates the case: "Few of us I imagine are conscious that in using the series 'satire,' 'satiric,' 'satirist,' 'satirize,' we are dealing with words unrelated etymologically" (1971: 49). If this is not enough, add further the consanguineous confusion of trying to define satire with the help of similarly pettifogging critical terms, such as "parody," "irony," "comedy," and "humor." We are better able to circumscribe than define satire, though we continue to try.

Renaissance satirists, in believing that the poetic genre of satire had descended from ancient Greek *satyr* plays, availed themselves of a dramatic license for a crude, animated, and hostile language appropriate to the coarse but wise woodland creature; as Alvin Kernan explains, "The idea that poetic satire had its origin in a dramatic form distinguished for its viciousness of attack and spoken by rough satyrs was the basis for nearly all Elizabethan theories of satire" (1959: 55). On the other hand, critics (such as Mikhail Bakhtin) claim that popular cultural festivals, such as Roman *Saturnalia* and the public spectacle and free-for-all of medieval carnivals, spawned satire. For Matthew Hodgart, "The essence of the carnival and saturnalia is the glorification of irresponsibility, even to the point of anarchy," and from such festive eruptions flowed a magma of demotic transgression into the tradition of satire, for "there are strong elements of travesty and anarchistic parody in *all* good satire" (1969: 24).

Formal verse satire, our name for a discernible tradition of poetical refinement that evolved in the genre-conscious Roman period, was more precisely called *satura*, which suggests a medley or a hodgepodge. In this tradition, the satirical poet provides a virtuoso offering of theme, fable, tone, parody, and figurative expression, something like a platter or a bowl displaying mixed fruits or food dishes (*lanx satura*) in a variegated but artful composition. For the highly influential first-century Roman rhetorician Quintilian, *satura* was a generic creation totally Roman (*Institutio oratoria* 10.1.93) in that it was a relatively newer kind of poetry, becoming metrically disciplined into hexameters and stylistically purified into an identifiable verse genre by the Roman poets Lucilius, Horace, and Persius (as well as Juvenal, who later, true to his iconoclastic spirit, will mock Quintilian's authority in *Satires* 7.186–94). In formal verse satire, a first-person poet-persona typically attacks forms of vanity or hypocrisy, those vices of "affectation" that satiric novelist Henry Fielding compactly called "the only source for the true Ridiculous" (Author's Preface, *Joseph Andrews*, 1742). Ronald Paulson, in examining modern fictions of satire from the perspective of classical satire and rhetoric, perceptively observes: "As a structure of exposition, *satura* is like a house of mirrors in which one theme (or vice) is reflected over and over, with distortion and variations but without essential change" (Paulson 1967: 43). How a subject is presented (arrangement, design, patterning) and with what expression (style, tone, diction, figures) for the purpose of positioning an audience and promoting an opportunity for persuasion (*kairos*) – what we may more simply call "the rhetorical form" – is constitutive of satiric content in classical *satura*.

Quintilian recognizes other types of satire. He briefly praises the poetic style of the Greek Archilochus (10.1.59), the iambographer famous for his vindictive satires against Lycambes, and also mentions the satiric power of Aristophanes and Attic Old Comedy (10.1.65). The comedies of Aristophanes will supply us with our earliest assembly of stock characters: the imposter, the self-deceiving braggart, the buffoon, the rustic, and, of course, the ironist. More cosmopolitan character types will become satiric fodder for the dramatic or narrative undercutting of foolish or knavish behavior (Frye 1957: 172–6). Quintilian also refers to an older and more diffuse sense of *satura* among Greek and Latin writers (10.1.95), such as Terentius Varro, who mixed his verse with prose, as did Varro's model, the Cynic philosopher Menippus (not mentioned by Quintilian), whose prosimetric work has been lost to time. Today, we loosely classify generically mixed works as *Varronian* or *Menippean* satire, or, less often, as "anatomy." Two extant classical examples of Menippean satire are Seneca's *Apocolocyntosis* and Petronius' *Satyrica*. This form of indirect satire uses narrative to lambaste, parody, or make ironic fun of its satiric objective, usually through dialogue between fools, knaves, or ironists. An obtuse fool or naïf may also narrate. This branch of ancient satire, which has grown into our most popular type by becoming so inclusive, is even more difficult to define than formal verse satire, and without clearly delineated generic features one may wonder what is in a name.

Even though a universal definition of Menippean satire may be a will-o'-the-wisp (as, perhaps, the physicist's dream of a unified field theory), scholars continue to enlighten us about this especially complex art form. Northrop Frye preferred to use the term "anatomy" (Frye 1957: 308–12), which classicist Joel C. Relihan finds particularly appropriate:

> Frye's anatomy is not a genre in the classical sense but a much broader classification, and his sensible renaming of the genre indicates that we ought not to identify it immediately with the peculiarities of ancient texts, which are, as it were, a subset of it. Anatomy therefore tends to blur distinctions that classical literary criticism would prefer to maintain. (Relihan 1993: 5)

Not surprisingly, W. Scott Blanchard begins his authoritative study of Menippean satire in the Renaissance with a caveat, "Menippean satire is amongst the most elusive genres to define" (Blanchard 1995: 11), but tries nonetheless. Among Renaissance humanists:

> Menippean satire is a genre for and about scholars; it is an immensely learned form that is at the same time paradoxically anti-intellectual. If its master of ceremonies is the humanist as wise fool, its audience is a learned community whose members need to be reminded, with Paul, of the depravity of their overreaching intellects, of the limits of human understanding. (Blanchard 1995: 14)

"Menippean satire refuses to allow an ideal type to emerge from its chaotic sprawl, whereas Roman satire achieves its effect by contrasting the debased world of the present to models of human behavior that are acceptable" (Blanchard 1995: 18–19). Howard Weinbrot, a scholar of the eighteenth century, offers his own well-researched reconsideration of this genre from antiquity to the eighteenth century. He desires a more precise generic definition because "[c]urrent theories of Menippean satire based on Frye and, largely, Bakhtin allow too many texts at too many times to be Menippean" (2005: 296), and, through a critical review of available classical texts, discovers that "much of Bakhtin's theory of the Menippea is alien to actual events in literary history so far as we can reclaim them" (2005: 39). He provides a concise definition:

> Menippean satire uses at least two other genres, languages, historical or cultural periods, or changes of voice to oppose a threatening false orthodoxy. In different exemplars, the satire may use either of two tones; the severe, in which the angry satirist fails and becomes angrier still, or the muted, in which the threatened angry satirist offers an antidote to the poison he knows remains. (Weinbrot 2005: 297)

Alas, however successful Weinbrot may be in trimming this unregenerate, "swallowing" trans-generic genre, he fairly accepts "that we can never be precise and never should be rigid when dealing with the products of licentious imagination" (2005: 303).

Another dimension often overlooked in the origin and generic development of satire is the leapfrogging influence of the Bible on a Christianized satirical tradition. Recalling Shakespeare's words in *King Lear*, "Jesters do often prove prophets," Thomas Jemielity notes how "[t]his implied equivalence of jest and prophecy, of ridicule and preaching, appears throughout the Hebrew Scriptures, where prophets do often prove jesters. They taunt, gibe, scoff, mock..." He further explains: "[t]he nature and characteristics common to both prophecy and satire explain their frequent intermingling and shared identity [in the Scriptures]. The message of biblical prophecy is pervasively and predominantly criticism, and criticism is always the content of satire. Things as they are profoundly dissatisfy prophet and satirist alike" (Jemielity 1992: 84, 85). As one example of a fructifying combination of biblical and classical texts, we might recall Samuel Johnson's poem "The Vanity of Human Wishes" (1749), which, while an imitation of Juvenal's *Satires* 10 on the same topic, recalls also Ecclesiastes and the preacher's dark lament about the vanity of vanities.

Thus, satire, as if it were equity interminably disputed in chancery, comes down to us as an enduring creative product of a jumbled and sometimes specious genealogy – rhetorically assertive, concretely topical, and palpable as an art form but with its title and pedigree as a genre perpetually in question. Competing views of the generic origin of satire may be why, as Dustin Griffin observes, "[m]ost satiric theory, at least since the Renaissance, is polemical, ranging itself against previous practice or claim and attempting to displace it" (Griffin 1994: 6). For readers of the twenty-first century, it should be no surprise that such an adaptive genre, somewhat existentialist in nature (i.e., in practice, one might argue that its existence precedes its essence), has found so many niches in popular culture and has become a favored vehicle for assuming a critical posture of a less powerful but contentious underdog or of a selflessly interested, shrewd observer. Satire has come a long way from John Dryden's witty allegory and royalist defense of monarchy in "Absalom and Achitophel" (1681); as George Test asserts, "satire is by no means confined to written forms":

> It is found in other art forms from the graphic arts to music to sculpture and even dance. Therefore, works by Gillray, Daumier, Gilbert and Sullivan, Erik Satie, Moussorgsky, sculpture out of the Dada and Pop Art movements, and the dances of the late Myra Kinch and much else must be assimilated into the concept of satire. The mass media teems with satire from such stand-up comics of the 1950s as Mort Sahl and Lenny Bruce (Hendra) to newspaper columnists Art Buchwald and Art Hoppe, from rock music to cartoon strips, and films from around the world too numerous to mention. Despite their ephemeral nature, folk expressions in graffiti, almanacs, office memoranda, and mock festivals ought not to be excluded from consideration. In many preliterate cultures satire occurs in trickster tales and oral poetry. (Test 1991: 8)

Such open-ended inclusion is daunting. Surely no omnibus definition can ever pigeonhole all types of satire. It has an unparalleled facility at cuckoo nesting in different media and genres old and new.

This anthology of essays is for new as well as advanced students of satire. There are unavoidable gaps of coverage as one might expect in any attempted study of such a leviathan subject within a single volume, but it is hoped that readers will be pleased by how much ground actually has been covered and with probity. Satire in the English language flowers most completely during the seventeenth and eighteenth centuries, and more satires were written during these centuries than any others. Greater focus, therefore, has been given to this productive period, which provides many of the classics in the language. Our coverage of modern literary developments is necessarily selective, yet I hope illustrative. With such a wide-angle lens, students of satire may begin to see for themselves how tradition and individual talent have combined catalytically in more recent works of satire. As with other Blackwell *Companions*, our authors, with deference to the more general reader, purposely avoid theoretical jargon and potentially distracting scholarly apparatus, such as routine references to primary texts and the critical use of numbered notes.

Since satire assumes a reasonably sound judgment of its audience, we might expect audiences, however removed, to share a predictable common sense by which a satire may be, at least broadly, understood. But very often the immediacy of a work is not evident to readers, because a satire, in varying degrees, has been rooted within a context of expectation, convention, and local understanding shared by its originally intended audience. Detailed references of satirical subjects are not always accessible or even clear to different audiences across place and across time; as Northrop Frye comments on this all-too-mortal topical nature of satire: "To attack anything, writer and audience must agree on its undesirability, which means that the content of a great deal of satire founded on national hatreds, snobbery, prejudice, and personal pique goes out of date very quickly" (1957: 224). This *Companion* attempts to situate its satiric subjects within a particular time and place and within identifiable domains of ideas and of social life. As the essays that follow demonstrate, the history of satire is as rich as its forms are varied, and its evolutionary ramifications suggest that its future will feature the same lively diversity that has characterized its past.

References and Further Reading

The beginning student of satire would do well to locate handy authoritative definitions of satire: Robert C. Elliot in the *Princeton Encyclopedia of Poetry and Poetics* (Princeton, NJ: Princeton University Press, 1974) and Alvin B. Kernan in the *Dictionary of the History of Ideas*, ed. Philip P. Weiner, vol. 4, pp. 211–17 (New York: Scribner's Sons, 1973), two foremost scholars in the field, offer especially informative and insightful synopses of "satire"; M. H. Abrams's *A Glossary of Literary Terms*, 8th edn, pp. 284–8 (New York: Harcourt Brace, 2005) is always a useful reference for critical terms. Simon Dentith's *Parody* (London: Routledge, 2000) contains useful discussion of various definitions of parody and further bibliography (pp. 9–21), and D. C. Muecke's *Irony and the Ironic* (London: Methuen, 1982) thoughtfully surveys "the almost cancerous growth of the concept of irony since the 1790s" (pp. 33–55). "Theorizing Satire: A Bibliography," created and maintained by Brian A. Connery, continues to be a valuable, somewhat comprehensive bibliographical resource available on the Internet (search by title).

Blanchard, W. Scott (1995) *Scholar's Bedlam: Menippean Satire in the Renaissance*. Lewisburg: Bucknell University Press.

Booth, Wayne C. (1961) *The Rhetoric of Fiction*. Chicago: University of Chicago Press.

Dentith, Simon (2000) *Parody*. London: Routledge.

Elliott, Robert C. (1960) *The Power of Satire: Magic, Ritual, Art*. Princeton, NJ: Princeton University Press.

Freudenburg, Kirk (2005) Introduction: Roman satire. In Kirk Freudenburg (ed.), *The Cambridge Companion to Roman Satire*, pp. 1–30. Cambridge: Cambridge University Press.

Frye, Northrop (1957) *Anatomy of Criticism: Four Essays*. Princeton, NJ: Princeton University Press.

Griffin, Dustin (1994) *Satire: A Critical Reintroduction*. Lexington: University Press of Kentucky.

Hendrickson, G. L. (1971) Satura tota nostra est. In Ronald Paulson (ed.), *Satire: Modern Essays in Criticism*, pp. 37–51. Englewood Cliffs, NJ:

Prentice-Hall (originally published in *Classical Philology* [1927] 22, 46–60).

Hodgart, Matthew (1969) *Satire*. New York: McGraw Hill.

Jemielity, Thomas (1992) *Satire and the Hebrew Prophets*. Louisville: Westminster/John Knox Press.

Kernan, Alvin (1959) *The Cankered Muse: Satire of the English Renaissance*. New Haven, CT: Yale University Press.

Muecke, D. C. (1982) *Irony and the Ironic*. London: Methuen.

Paulson, Ronald (1967) *The Fictions of Satire*. Baltimore, MD: The Johns Hopkins University Press.

Relihan, Joel C. (1993) *Ancient Menippean Satire*. Baltimore, MD: The Johns Hopkins University Press.

Spacks, Patricia Meyer (1971) Some reflections on satire. In Ronald Paulson (ed.), *Satire: Modern Essays in Criticism*, pp. 360–78. Englewood Cliffs, NJ: Prentice-Hall (originally published in *Genre* [1968] 1, 13–20).

Steele, Timothy (2006) April 27, 1937. In *Toward the Winter Solstice*. Athens: Swallow Press/Ohio University Press.

Test, George A. (1991) *Satire: Spirit and Art*. Tampa: University of South Florida Press.

Weinbrot, Howard D. (2005) *Menippean Satire Reconsidered: From Antiquity to the Eighteenth Century*. Baltimore, MD: The Johns Hopkins University Press.

Wylie, Philip (1970) *Generation of Vipers*. Marietta: Larlin Corporation (originally published in 1942).

Part I
Biblical World to European Renaissance

1
Ancient Biblical Satire
Thomas Jemielity

Ancient Biblical Laughter

He that sitteth in the heavens shall laugh: the Lord shall have them in derision.
(Psalm 2: 4, *Authorized Version*)

Asked to name the world's funniest book, few would mention the Bible. Yet, somewhat perversely perhaps, I have for many years thought that one of the funniest scenes I have ever read occurs in the Gospel of John when Jesus has a lengthy conversation with the Samaritan woman at a well where she has come to draw water (John 4: 4–42). The woman is amazed that Jesus should ask her for a drink, since, as John notes, "Jews and Samaritans ... do not use vessels in common" (4: 9). When Jesus asks her to get her husband and return, she says, "I have no husband" (4: 17). Jesus agrees, but adds, with an intense look most likely, "although you have had five husbands, the man with whom you are now living is not your husband" (4: 18). To which the Samaritan woman replies, "Sir ... I can see that you are a prophet" (4: 19). From my high-school days, I have always found that a very funny response, an apparently thorough *non sequitur* covering an embarrassing moment in a talk that has turned decidedly personal and intimate.

At an older period of my life, I know now that the woman's comments were not as off the point as I had once thought. Like many readers of the Bible, I had assumed that a prophet was in the business of prediction, foretelling the future. What could the Samaritan woman have meant by calling Jesus a prophet, a designation frequently applied to him by those who heard his message? What I had not realized was that prophets, at least their Hebrew incarnation – or their contemporary embodiments, like Mahatma Gandhi or Martin Luther King – rarely, if ever, predict. The future they envision is the likely consequence of present behavior. Conduct and consequence are causally related. Prophets criticize that conduct: they judge, and, in an almost strictly legal sense, they render sentence, God's sentence, a sentence of built-in, coming disaster for current misbehavior. Prophets disparage their society. They have unflattering things to say about their hearers. So Jesus is indeed speaking as a prophet when he talks with the Samaritan woman. However many husbands the woman might have had, the man she is currently involved with sexually is not her husband. Later illumination notwithstanding, I still think it is a funny exchange, even if the Gospel of John does not intend it that way.

Whatever my enjoyment in the remark, the Samaritan woman was not likely amused by the observation. That awareness highlights a needful caution about the laughter that Scripture can induce in us. We easily assume that laughter is always the sign in us of an agreeable emotion, a response that puts us in a most complimentary light. Psychologists, physicians, and therapists, to name but a few, tell us repeatedly of the mental and even physical benefits of laughter. To understand much of the laughter evoked in Scripture, and especially in the Hebrew Scriptures, however, we must admit that laughter does not always reveal our most attractive side. We reveal another face of laughter, a most unsympathetic one, which many of these same psychologists, physicians, and therapists warn about. Enjoy the laughter of comedy, they urge, but beware the laughter of satire. Yes, in the laughter of comedy, we laugh *with*, we laugh sympathetically and identifiably. We cheerfully recognize others in situations like our own, and we enjoy our common fallibility. But in satire, we laugh *at*. We laugh with hostility. We imply a superiority in our laughter because our laughing *at* implies that we do not share in the object of derision. The laughter of comedy is a *we* laughter. We participate in what amuses us. The laughter of satire is a *you* laughter, mocking, malicious, finger-pointing, and gloating.

Jonathan Swift once disturbingly reminded us in an adaptation of a maxim of Rochefoucauld that he much admired that there is something in the misfortune of our friends that does not displease us. How much more satisfaction must there be in the misfortune of our enemies, in seeing them brought down for behavior we find reprehensible and which, by implication at the very least, we do not discover in ourselves? We stand apart from what we deride. We are not implicated in what we mock. It is important to bear this distinction in mind because the laughter of Scripture, and especially of Hebrew Scripture, is prevailingly satiric and especially so in the text of the fifteen canonical prophets, often in the narratives of other prophets to whom a text has not been assigned, and in the so-called wisdom writings, conduct books of a sort that place a premium on one's social standing and how that status can be maintained or damaged.

Two examples. Elijah meets on a mountain top the priests of Baal, a false god, of course (1 Kings 18: 17–40). As the priests, in increasing fury and fever, seek a response from their unresponsive divinity, Elijah offers help – sarcastically. Baal, he suggests, might be "engaged," that is, attending to his bodily needs (18: 27), urinating or defecating and hardly in a position to respond at once. The scene reminds one of the Phantom Poet Contest in Alexander Pope's *Dunciad* (1743), when the contemptible and thieving publisher Edmund Curll, momentarily at a loss in the exercise, sends up a prayer to a Jove likewise engaged. More helpfully than with the priests of Baal, Jove can assist Curll, signaling his help with a tissue-like note wafting down to Curll and "signed with that Ichor which from gods distills." So for a believing Israelite, contemptuous of the worship of false gods, this passage about Elijah has to have been quite funny indeed. It vindicated, and it amused. Only the priests of Baal and their cronies would have recoiled at the insult. This joke is told at the expense of the non-believer.

Or take the famous Psalm 23, "The Lord is my Shepherd." A favorite, for example, at the internment of a deceased person, the psalm evokes most pleasant pastoral images, the security of being in the hands of a loving, providing shepherd. The psalm envisions satisfaction and plenty. What could be more innocent, innocent in a root sense: devoid of harm? Yet, as the psalm anticipates the various pleasures of pastoral protection given by the Lord, it revealingly celebrates as one of the divine bounties a table that will be spread before the psalmist in the presence of his enemies. The psalmist's satisfaction also anticipates the dissatisfaction of his enemies witnessing, for themselves, a most galling sight. What biblical readers might be disinclined to realize is the pervasiveness with which the Scriptures speak of a divinely granted satisfaction that comes as the consequence of divinely granted punishment. The bystanders and onlookers denied heaven-sent satisfaction in the Scriptures are very often consumed with jealousy, envy, impotent rage, and humiliation, all of which underscore a key feature in the enjoyment of divine satisfaction. The lesson, sometimes mockingly enforced, is clear: don't fool around with God. He can have a nasty sense of humor.

The believing Israelite himself, however, may become the target of chastisement or ridicule, a victim of that divine nastiness and malice, for the examples drawn from Elijah and the Psalter present, thus, only one side of a picture that appears equally often in the Hebrew Scriptures. From the point of view of the Israelite believer, the episodes such as those with the prophets of Baal or the reassurances of Psalm 23 are encouraging. The Israelite will rejoice in the discomfiture of his enemies. In a society and culture as keenly attuned, however, to the pain of humiliation, embarrassment, and ridicule, a considerable part of Hebrew Scripture speaks of the humiliation felt by the just at misfortune or embarrassment. Indeed, the sanctions cited for misbehavior on the part of the just highlight, and sometimes keenly, the humiliation, ridicule, and embarrassment that will be felt by those who misbehave or whose misfortune, as in the Book of Job, is seen to be a deserved punishment for wrongdoing.

The Book of Psalms is a particularly useful source for bringing out the power and pain of humiliation and ridicule because the psalms, as passed on and as written, span at least a millennium of Israel's history and testify throughout that time to the power of shame and ridicule. Psalm 23 is by no means unique. Psalm 137, set in the Babylonian captivity, brings out the humiliation sharply felt by Israelites in captivity and closes with a hair-raising curse on their Babylonian captors. Psalm 109 speaks of the malicious tongues of those who speak against the psalmist and, like Psalms 35 and 73 (and, of course, Psalm 137), curses those responsible for this situation. Since satire originated from the curse, the proximity to satire of these violent feelings is clear.

In addition, biblical narrative and those conduct writings known as wisdom literature provide more instances of the keen sense of ridicule felt in Scripture. Sarah, in Genesis (16: 1–6), becomes jealous of the successfully pregnant Hagar and demands that Abraham send her away. The Philistines, "when they grew merry," call for the blinded and impotent Samson "to make sport for us" (Judges 16: 25). (To escape humiliation at the hands of the victorious Philistines, Saul asks his armor-bearer to run him through "so that these uncircumcised brutes may not come and taunt me and make sport of me" [1 Samuel 31: 4].) Despite his suicide, Saul is regarded as one of the heroes of Israel. David rejects the advice of Ahitophel, which is a public humiliation, and the counselor returns immediately to his home and hangs himself (2 Samuel 17: 23). In Ecclesiasticus, in Proverbs, and even in Ecclesiastes, counsels of conduct are reinforced by the threat of shame that will accompany misbehavior – in oneself, in one's wife, or in one's children. Proverbs can reinforce its catechism of avoidable shame with humor, as for example, in dramatizing the hallucinations of the drunkard as part of its endorsement of sobriety (23: 29–35). The writer of Ecclesiasticus is so convinced of the efficacy of shame as a spur to righteous behavior that he carefully and extensively delineates "proper shame" so that his attentive and presumably obedient listener "will be popular with everyone" (Ecclesiasticus 41: 14–24).

No biblical writing speaks more powerfully of the power of shame than the story of Job, who, like his friends, believes that he has been cursed by God, but who, unlike his friends, feels that the curse and shame of misfortune are undeserved. Job's intense response to what he believes to be unjustifiable misfortune leads to self-imprecation – cursing the day of his birth – that parodies Psalm 8. He nastily calls God the "man watcher" (7: 17), spying on his creatures to find them at fault, ironically reducing God to the role of the overseer or Satan who prompted God to test Job in the first place. Job repeatedly expresses his sense of shame at his misfortune. As the exchange with his friends continues, the sarcasm and the satire of the four increase, because Job's three friends cannot admit the theology-shattering possibility for them that the innocent might indeed suffer. To suggest the vacuous and the insubstantial, the disputants trade deprecating wind imagery back and forth among themselves anticipating by centuries the same Swift-like image that courses through *A Tale of a Tub* (1704) to picture the inane and the unconvincing (a basic image in Ecclesiastes as well). The intensity of these exchanges concludes with Job's self-imprecation and demand that God appear as witness to respond. However much the Book of Job restores and increases Job's good fortune, it is well to remember that the God who appears in Job neither answers Job's questions nor even informs him that his test has been the result of a wager on his justice. In *Satire and the Hebrew Prophets*, I observed: "If the lexicon of the Hebrew Scriptures does not include *satire* and *irony*, it certainly includes innumerable instances of many words associated with both: *byword, contempt, hate, humiliate, laughingstock, reproach, scoff, shame, taunt*, and related terms like *honor, regard,* and *repute*" (Jemielity 1992: 37). These words are certainly central to the lexicon of Job.

When the Hebrew Scriptures give us such humor, they create disgust or dismay in the audience that is its target or believes that it is being unjustifiably targeted. Consciously or not, this is satire, that is, criticism, judgment, or censure that amuses. It is not a conscious literary artifact, written, as in Horace, to entertain. In the Hebrew Scriptures, as diverse as the writings are, the moral purpose, the instruction, is always primary and close, one assumes, to exclusive. These diverse writings instruct, uplift, reassure, and criticize. They do not entertain, except peripherally. Ancient biblical satire is satire, but not intentionally so. It is not a deliberately designed literary artifact. While it can amuse and entertain those who share, say, the prophet's viewpoint, it discomfits those who do not. The laughter of the Hebrew Scriptures is frequently hostile and aggressive toward those who stand outside of or neglect the faith of Israel or, as in the Psalms and in wisdom writings, feel the humiliation directed at them by enemies or by the consequence of their own misbehavior. The laughter directed at the enemy or at unethical conduct simultaneously reinforces and amuses anyone who shares the same point of view. Like satire, consequently, ridiculing passages in the Hebrew Scriptures are directed at a twofold audience: one whose behavior is being criticized and one who agrees with the prophet or wisdom writer or storyteller that such behavior deserves to be criticized. Ancient biblical satire is thus punitive and persuasive.

A simple comparison. Husband and wife argue in the presence of the wife's friend. The wife insults her husband with a remark that her friend finds amusing. Here, in a nutshell, we find the double audience of satire: the target, whose reformation the critic (the wife) might genuinely desire, and the friend who agrees with the wife's point of view. The wife's remark discomfits one hearer and amuses another. In the Book of Amos, for example, Amos utters judgments against the nations of Damascus, Tyre, Edom, Ammon, Moab, and the Northern Kingdom. Amos' targets there were not amused. Amos' supporters, on the other hand, those whose faith Amos sought to reinforce, were amused. Amos was directing God's laughter at the unbelievers of the North. Those who agreed with him shared in God's laughter at the expense of the Northern Kingdom. These are the two audiences of all satire: the targeted and the reinforced. The same comparison, moreover, illustrates two criteria of effectiveness. If every critical statement – prophecy, satire, or editorial – speaks to a double audience, it speaks with two criteria of effectiveness as well: the rhetorical and the historical. The wife's friend, who laughs at the insults directed at her friend's husband, has no way of knowing how effective her friend's chastisement will be, what the insult in fact or in history will effect. She laughs because she enjoys the language skill of the censure, how it is crafted rhetorically. Effectiveness can thus be rhetorical and historical. Judged by the latter, the Hebrew prophets, for example, were colossal failures. Not one single catastrophe they threatened was avoided. But, the same may be said about the historical effectiveness of most satire. Did, for example, Jonathan

Swift's *A Modest Proposal* (1729) alleviate Irish poverty? If the potato famine in Ireland a century later is any indication, *A Modest Proposal* must be regarded as a failure.

What becomes a common denominator between prophetic satire in particular and its classical and later equivalents is their frequent complaint about the ineffectiveness of their criticism. Alexander Pope's concluding note to *Dialogue II* (1738) threatens to abandon satire because it is useless: "Ridicule was become as unsafe as it was ineffectual." Jeremiah frequently complains about the indifference of his listeners, and the Christian gospels are studded with Jesus's frequent complaints about the refusal of those who have ears to hear. But, aside from a shared perception of historical ineffectiveness, these satires, biblical, classical, and modern, also share a quality of rhetorical effectiveness, by which we may evaluate how well the language has been put together. As we leave church on Sunday and comment on the excellence of the sermon, we surely are not speaking historically or empirically. Did the sermon change hearts? We don't know. The excellence we speak of pertains to an effectiveness of language: a sermon coherent, well organized, effectively illustrated and the like, a sermon worth our time to listen to.

The analysis that follows is concerned with the rhetoric of ancient biblical satire, its uses of language that make biblical censure often funny. What I propose to do here is to examine the language of ancient biblical satire as it appears especially in Hebrew prophecy and in wisdom writings. The language and strategy of the Hebrew prophets, for example, bear striking and pervasive resemblances to satire, however unconscious those resemblances. The Hebrew prophets did not speak to entertain: they spoke to proclaim the judgment of the Lord. The basic similarity that prophecy has to satire is that both are criticism, both are judgment. The rhetorical strategies of prophecy bear remarkable and sustained similarities to the rhetoric, that is, to the language fashioning, of satire. Any biblical writing that ridicules is treading in the domain of satire.

This chapter on ancient biblical satire, therefore, pursues a limited, but accessible focus as a study of the historical effectiveness of any satire might not. It will draw on relevant material from several of the texts in the Hebrew canon (what Christians somewhat colonially call the Old Testament), especially from the canonical Hebrew prophets, from prophetic narrative within and without these texts (for example, Elijah), and from biblical narrative and wisdom writing. Although Jonah is also listed among the prophetic writings, Jonah is a narrative, a parable and, significantly, a satire on the reluctant prophet. All the other prophetic books present the so-called oracles or preaching of the prophets. The narrative component is sometimes more extensive, as in the case of Jeremiah, or sometimes non-existent. In the prophetic books we read primarily not the story of the prophets, but their preaching. Earlier in the Hebrew Scriptures, as mentioned, we have long narratives of earlier prophets, prophets like Samuel and Elijah, but no extensive account of their oracles forms any part of the text. Theirs is essentially a narrative. Before considering those extensive similarities with satire, however, an important question arises: what do we mean by satire?

What is Satire?

Ridentem dicere verum
(Horace, *Satires* 1.1)

Satire, prophecy, conduct books, sermon, editorial – what do they have in common? A content comprised of criticism or judgment. As Northrop Frye observes in his analysis of satire in the *Anatomy of Criticism*: "essential to satire... is an object of attack." What distinguishes satire from the attack or judgment that might appear in an editorial or the like is a second essential feature: "wit or humor founded on fantasy or a sense of the grotesque or absurd" (1968: 224). Satire seeks to make its criticism funny and does so by employing the empirically impossible or unlikely. The world of satire calls to mind an infinite host of the fantastic: the Lilliputians, Brobdingnagians, and Flying Island of *Gulliver's Travels*; the sylphs of *The Rape of the Lock*; Juvenal's sexual gymnast, the Empress Messalina; Mr Joyboy in Evelyn Waugh's *The Loved One*; the talking animals in Horace and in George Orwell; Philip Roth's Trick E. Dixon, in *Our Gang*, in hell and campaigning against the devil for the leadership of the underworld. Even Philip Roth's recent *The Plot Against America* rewrites past history to allow for the election of the anti-semitically inclined Charles Lindbergh as president. The improbabilities and impossibilities of satire call to mind the unbroken, empirically improbable sequence of catastrophes in *Candide*; the unbroken sameness of the cycle of disappointment in *Rasselas*; the stripping away of any certainties in the Howard Campbell of Kurt Vonnegut's *Mother Night*. Satire's humor, however disturbing it might be, derives from fantasy: from the weird, the improbable, the grotesque, or the impossible.

This fantasy-like quality of criticism that is satire finds frequent expression in the Hebrew Scriptures whose mocking is often couched in the fantastic or the grotesque. Jealous of David's recent success against the Philistines, for example, and hoping for David's death in the venture, Saul demands as a bride-price from David "the foreskins of a hundred Philistines" (1 Samuel 18: 25). David slays two hundred Philistines, returns with their foreskins, and counts them in the presence of Saul. This Parade of the Philistine Foreskins cannot be without a strong element of deeply and grotesquely enjoyed satisfaction at the discomfiture of a legendary enemy of Israel and amusement as well at the continuing discomfiture of a king made uneasy by the unending triumphs of the rival of whom he is insanely jealous. The Saul who earlier rankled at the songs that celebrated the havoc David made "among tens of thousands," compared to Saul's "havoc among thousands" (1 Samuel 18: 7), now witnesses a second installment of David's version of "Anything You Can Do I Can Do Better."

Perhaps the most shocking and certainly very extensive use of the critical fantasy in prophecy that is satire occurs in Ezekiel 16, the longest single unit in the prophecy and one so offensive it is not used in public Jewish worship. Ezekiel plays on the theological and sexual meanings of infidelity, terms whose relationship appears in the sexual license that often accompanied the worship of the false gods denounced by the prophets. Israel is unflatteringly compared to Samaria and to Sodom, reminded of the care bestowed on her by Yahweh before she undertook her career of cosmic whoredom, and hears the resumé of her career as a sexual exhibitionist who could rival Juvenal's later Empress Messalina. Her depravity shocks her infidel Philistine neighbors, and Ezekiel piles on graphic images and ever-increasing outrages until Yahweh, in a terrifyingly cathartic moment, concludes the vignette with a threat: "I will spend my fury against you and my rage at you shall subside; I will grow calm and not be vexed any more" (16: 42). Yahweh's admonition is a paralyzing and fearful but finally satisfying release of pent-up fury. This passage can rank with anything in Swift or in Juvenal for the violent pleasure it registers in successful and obscene scorn.

In addition to providing a most useful and seminal definition of satire as critical fantasy, Northrop Frye also provides a basis for understanding the kinds of satire and irony that do and do not appear in ancient biblical texts. He introduces, first of all, a basic distinction: satire is explicit criticism, irony implicit. What does Umbricius dislike about Rome in Juvenal's third *Satire*? His dissatisfactions are many and detailed. In Samuel Johnson's 1738 adaptation of Juvenal's poem, what Thales dislikes about London Johnson's poem also makes abundantly and specifically clear. But, when the text does not make that criticism explicit, we are dealing with irony, irony as a device of satire. Edward Gibbon's *Decline and Fall* (1776–88) alludes to the fact that Origen, bothered by a different limb, was moved to self-castration because he read literally the text about cutting off a hand or foot should it prove an occasion of sin. Gibbon states only that it seems a shame that the prominent theologian and intellectual, famous for allegorical readings of Scripture, should have read this text literally (Matthew 18: 8). Frye's basic distinction is between explicit and implicit criticism, that is, between satire and irony. The viewpoint of satire is explicit and unmistakably clear; that of irony, on the other hand, is implicit and often mystifying. Was there irony in the Hebrew Scriptures? Like *satire* that word does not appear in the lexicon of biblical writing. Anyone, however, reading the contribution of the Yahwist, perhaps writing in the Davidic monarchy, can answer that question with a confident and resounding "Yes!"

The Phases of Ancient Biblical Satire and Irony

> A mighty maze! but not without a plan.
> (Alexander Pope, *An Essay on Man*, I, 1733)

Especially seminal for an analysis of ancient biblical satire, however, is Northrop Frye's paradigm of the three phases of satire and the corresponding and parallel phases of irony. At first glance, Frye's analysis is very off-putting: the terminology is cumbersome and inconsistent (for example, irony is also a device of comedy, romance, and tragedy); not all of the phases are descriptively titled. Not surprising, therefore, is Terry Eagleton's short shrift of Frye's *Anatomy* as a whole – along with his parenthetical warning that "Frye is a clergyman." (Eagleton, by the way, is *still* a Marxist.) But Frye focuses on satire as a literary artifact, as a verbal construct designed to amuse. Used flexibly, with no suggestion of mutual exclusion – that is, no assignment to a "slot," as Eagleton dismissively calls it (1983: 93) – and with some addition of descriptive phraseology, Frye's patterning of satire provides a useful paradigm for describing the various kinds of ancient biblical satire. Frye offers an insight into the panorama of satire that can and does include writers as diverse as Horace and Juvenal, Pope and Swift, Orwell and Vonnegut – and the panorama of ancient biblical satire that appears in texts as diverse as Genesis and Amos, 1 Samuel and Job, or Ecclesiastes and Hosea.

One example. Horace would appear to be the paradigm of the genial satirist, lightly mocking the follies of human behavior, a first-phase satirist Frye would term him, writing satire of the low norm. Yet, when Horace takes on the rationalizations of the well-named Cupiennus for adulterous relationships (*Satires* 1.2), he uncharacteristically uses the obscenity most often associated with Juvenal. Cupiennus' rationalizations about desiring a married woman for this or that apparently sophisticated or chic reason are brutally destroyed by Horace's statement of what Cupiennus really wants, *cunnus*. Against those rationalizations Horace posits his alternative, of enjoying whatever fantasy about his partner that comes to mind "*dum futuo*" (1.2.127) – that is, while he fucks her (*futuo* having no polite translation). In Frye's terminology this would be an exception to Horace's pervasive use of first-phase satire, a laughing at avoidable human folly, with this emphatic burst of third-phase satire: namely, the use of scatological and obscene language and associations most often banished from polite conversations, as pervasively present in Swift and Juvenal and, by the way, in Jeremiah and Ezekiel. At issue here is the critical stance taken by the text, the degree to which the text allows for accommodations within an admittedly flawed context, social, political, or what have you, or the degree to which such adaptations, as in Juvenal or in Jeremiah, are not morally possible.

Like comedy, satire focuses on the individual in society, as opposed to the focus on the individual as individual in tragedy and romance (the other two main story forms in Frye). In satire, as in comedy, we will always be made aware of the conventions, patterns, systems, theories, and the like which operate in any society and quite often operate without awareness on the part of those living by those norms. Where we marry, what subject we major in, what political ideas we subscribe to, how we are educated, what we believe – the answers to these and like questions are the conventions we live by. In the critical laughter generated by satire (and irony), these conventions in their many, many forms will be the target. What determines the quality and tone of satire and irony is the attitude the satirist or the satire takes toward these conventions. Always critical, but critical in varying degrees of intensity, that attitude underlies the three phases of satire and their corresponding phases of satiric irony. Ancient biblical satire runs virtually the full gamut of these satiric and ironic possibilities.

Let us look at what Frye calls first-phase satire or satire of the low norm. The satire asks whether a constructive life is possible within the admittedly limited conventions of the society at issue. This is, obviously, non-revolutionary satire: it does not call for the overthrow of institutions, political, marital, economic, or whatever; it looks for a way to live advantageously within those conventions or systems however flawed they might be. Orwell's severe questioning of totalitarian societies and their utopian fantasies hardly qualifies as first-phase satire, for the system cannot be accommodated; it must be overthrown. Ezekiel's denunciation of Israel's religious whoredom allows for no accommodation.

Satire of the low norm seeks no displacement of the satirized society. Here the satire emphasizes discretion or an unillusioned central character who recognizes the limitations of the context but works perceptively and shrewdly within them. Jane Austen's Elizabeth Bennett will not allow her mother's ga-ga attitude toward any suitor to become her own. This shrewd, cheeky, early-twenties heroine turns down two proposals of marriage before finally, and only at the second bidding, accepting Darcy. She will not allow desperation to dictate her choice, as it does in the case of her best friend, Charlotte Lucas. Elizabeth is clear-headedly aware as well that her six years junior status vis-à-vis her friend gives her no small advantage in treading warily on the road to marriage. Elizabeth, furthermore, has a sense of moral responsibility, something she sees sadly lacking in her father, an awareness she keeps to herself. In an ironic parallel – what I might term as the irony of the avoidable – Horace, in *Satires* 2.3, does not tell Damasippus that he is a fool, that his supposed wisdom about everyone's being mad is morally useless without differences of degree. His laconic concluding remark to the garrulous, long-winded, pseudo-philosopher asks only that the greater madman spare the lesser. Horace keeps his wisdom to himself in the second book of the *Satires* and affirms the possibility that a constructive way of living is possible within admittedly limited contexts by maintaining an unillusioned view of what is going on. What is recommended is a street savvy that recognizes the less-than-ideal quality of the neighborhood but knows how to survive there without relocating.

Ecclesiastes repeatedly exhibits a good deal of this approach. Its narrator does not, for example, claim that the edicts and wishes of the king are without fault. What is said is that the king is the king, and it is well to be circumspect in his presence and to do what he orders: "For the king's word carries authority" (Ecclesiastes 8: 4). The king might not be right, but he is powerful. Much of Proverbs pursues the same sort of advice, about the supposedly beneficial life that will be enjoyed by the discreet and the sensible. Frye's term for this is "flexible pragmatism." The frequent emphasis in Ecclesiastes and Proverbs on propriety, on the seasonableness of behavior, implies an awareness of the social context within which an individual arrives at the street savvy for surviving the king's presence regardless of limitations seen there. Keep your eyes open, analyze the situation discreetly, and know when to make your move and what kind of move to make if any. If satire of the low norm, first-phase satire, is, admittedly, not a prominent component of ancient biblical satire, the reason is clear. In matters of faith, there is but one God: "You shall have no other god to set against me. You shall not make a carved image [of the kind Hosea ridicules in 4: 12] for yourself or the likeness of anything in the heavens above, or on the earth below, or in the waters under the earth. You shall not bow down to them or worship them; for I, the Lord your God, am a jealous god" (Exodus 20: 3–5).

This attitude pervades the prophets and explains why no first-phase satire appears there. Ecclesiastes and Proverbs, like other wisdom writings, however, focus very much on such worldly behavior in contexts where bedrock religious attitudes are not an issue. One can be flexibly pragmatic with the world. One cannot be flexibly pragmatic, however, in the face of false gods. Even the narratives of exemplary Israelites, like Daniel or Mordecai in Esther, reinforce this awareness of the non-compromising quality of faith in Yahweh. Daniel is a success even in captivity. But called upon to worship a false god instead of or in addition to Yahweh, Daniel refuses. His steadfastness is, of course, rewarded. Daniel, like Mordecai, will not compromise his faith. Nor is Mordecai's steadfastness without its grimly humorous component, as the treacherous Haman is hanged on the very gibbet he had prepared for his Israelite enemy. The humor is reminiscent of David's foreskin triumph in 1 Samuel.

The corresponding and first phase of irony, irony of the avoidable, pursues the insight that much of the trouble we suffer as human beings is not determined at all but the product of our own folly. In the climax of *Pride and Prejudice* – Darcy's second proposal – Elizabeth Bennett realizes that she, who has always prided herself on good judgment, has been suckered by George Wickham's account of his controversy with Darcy and not even considered the possibility of another point of view. As much as she resents Darcy's unflattering comments about her family, she must admit her own opinions are no different. The story of Oedipus seems to present us with ritual or tragic inevitability: a man doomed to kill his own father and marry his own mother. A comic or satiric ironist might have much fun with that story and suggest that a forewarned man, after all, who kills a man old enough to be his father and marries a woman old enough to be his mother isn't doomed, he's foolish. Perhaps there's a Woody Allen movie in there somewhere. In the Hebrew Scriptures, Jonah, although a narrative and parable, might satisfy the expectations of the irony of the avoidable. Simply, had Jonah accepted God's commission, he might have avoided all the troubles that followed from his seeking to refuse it.

What happens, however, when the satirist's attitude challenges the very conventions themselves because they are worthless and must be discarded? This is Frye's second-phase or quixotic satire (are we to think of the unconventional Don Quixote?). We do not find a *modus vivendi* with the conventions – we challenge them head on. Austen, as noted, works out in her fiction how a woman might marry advantageously despite the limitations for women in getting and in being married. Part of her toughness is the awareness she leaves us with that even where a woman is successful, at least on her own terms, the price can be high, as in the case of Charlotte Lucas Collins.

However, what if the satirist challenges the sources, the bases, the values of the conventions themselves, ridicules the systems or theories, and points out their inadequacy? Any convention, any theory, system, ideology, or pattern assumes it has the answers: capitalism, Marxism, Roman Catholicism, Mormonism, the worship of Baal – these are all systems, and all claim the truth. The satirist sets theory against practice to show the inadequacy of the theory. In Part 3 of *Gulliver's Travels* (1726) the theorizing of the academicians at the Grand Academy of Lagado – where Progress is not the most important product – is constantly set against the catastrophic and ludicrous practical consequences of their theorizing.

Driving home one day, I saw an accidental combination of a building sign and a bumper sticker that brought out unmistakably for me the difference between these two satiric approaches, these two phases of satire or irony. A sign on a building across from me confidently asserted: "A helping hand is as near as the end of your elbow." The point was clear: just make the effort, and you will be a success. Glancing over at a car next to me at the light, I read: "If you think the system works, ask someone who doesn't." The first buoyantly affirms a cardinal tenet of capitalism: effort brings reward. The second challenges that view: the system does not work. No theory, pattern, system, or the like has all the answers. In *Candide* (1759), Doctor Pangloss, Doctor Explain Everything, becomes more and more ridiculous as he insists on his theory despite the catastrophic quality of his experiences and that of all those others in the tale. *Rasselas* (1759) explodes the myth of perfect happiness on this earth, but acknowledges that the itch to find it will not disappear. The unresolved dialectic of human life is unsatisfied desire always desiring. The satirist in this kind of satire prefers experience to theory.

Ecclesiastes and Job are the finest examples in Scripture of this continuing challenge to the optimism of systematic explanation. An irony pervades Ecclesiastes as a whole, the irony experienced by a believer in God who nonetheless realizes that his behavior among men is capable of no convincing intellectual explanation. The just suffer, the evil are honored, a situation Ecclesiastes finds senseless (Ecclesiastes 8: 6). The viewpoint, consciously or not, challenges the buoyant optimism of Proverbs (or the optimism of Job's three friends) that God works in the world according to identifiable norms. Ecclesiastes counters, however, that if we saw God punishing evildoers, we would stop doing evil. We don't stop because we don't see God doing that: "I perceived that God has so ordered it that a man should not be able to discover what is happening here under the sun. However hard a man may try, he will not find out." Then, with the cocky theorist perhaps in mind, Ecclesiastes cautions: "the wise man *may think* that he knows, but he will be unable to find the truth of it" (Ecclesiastes 8: 17, emphasis added). I know what the theory is, Ecclesiastes says, but the theory doesn't work. God's behavior in this life has no rational explanation. This is not to deny God – Ecclesiastes does not do that – but to deny a human capability to fathom the ways of God. The day-to-day world answers the theorizing. The relentless turning of the inexplicable cycle of life and experience, a cycle prominent in second-phase irony (the irony of the cycle?), pervades Ecclesiastes. In a way, the wisdom of Ecclesiastes to enjoy the life that is life's one certainty for as long as one will have it parallels the final wisdom of *Candide*, itself a relentlessly ironic exposure of inane and unconvincing rationality: skip the theory, and cultivate the garden. The inside knowledge that would resolve these inexplicabilities is denied to human ken. Like *Candide*, the irony of Ecclesiastes is not simply a literary device but a mirror of the irony that is the condition of human life itself.

Northrop Frye observes that in second-phase satire or irony, the conventions of art can themselves be ridiculed. The complete title and author identification of Kurt Vonnegut's *Slaughterhouse-Five* (1969) – over two dozen lines long – is certainly one such instance, as is his division of the less than two hundred pages of *Cat's Cradle* (1963) into one hundred and twenty-seven chapters. The designation of chapter becomes hilariously meaningless. In ancient biblical satire, no artistic conventions are ridiculed. But Amos allows himself to parody the call to worship by satirically urging those in the Northern Kingdom to seek out their places of worship for sinfulness: "Come to Bethel – and rebel!" he taunts. "Come to Gilgal – and rebel the more!" (Amos 4: 4). Isaiah provides a lengthy mock-lamentation for the departed King of Babylon (14: 12–21). The shades of the forgotten dead mockingly review the pretensions of this tyrant and his final doom, "brought down to the depths of the abyss." In a culminating indignity, the shades describe the king's dishonorable burial and the slaughter of his sons. He is "unburied, mere loathsome carrion," of a "breed of evildoers [who] shall never be seen again." Throughout this passage, the text of Isaiah ironically and mockingly uses the form of the funeral lament. Elijah, as noted, makes fun of a busy Baal, defecating or urinating, and hence too busy to answer the call of his priests. This is hardly the way we would expect liturgy or a divinity to be treated. In this kind of satire, the satirist or ironist overturns conventional forms with parody. The upside-down formulas embody the thrust of experience over theory like Socrates' idiotic experiments and theories in Aristophanes' *Clouds*, the oldest surviving literary fun that parodying writers have had with theorizing academics and philosophers. The jump between Aristophanes' *Clouds* to Tom Stoppard's *Jumpers* (1972) is a short jump indeed.

Satire, thus, can argue the possibility of a constructive life within admittedly limited conventions or challenge the conventions themselves as unworkable and unreasonable. In Frye, these are the first two phases of satire (with corresponding phases in irony). In challenging whatever conventions are at issue, the satirist, of course, assumes that sensory data provide a reliable basis upon which to challenge conventions: that we can rely on what we see, hear, feel, smell, and taste. What if we can't? After all, at this very moment, I am assuming a stationary position. I am not moving. Actually, I am, at a speed so fast I cannot even begin to fathom it, being whirled around in a circle around a circle. From a different perspective, physical stability or immobility is an illusion. Third-phase satire, satire of the high norm, challenges the very bases of our sense perception. It casts doubt on the reliability of sensory experience. Such satire repeatedly places us in singularly uncomfortable, threatening situations, situations that force us to see ourselves in ways that overturn conventional experiential associations. We see ourselves sexually and scatologically, naked and diseased, insignificant and transitory, without value, without dignity. This satire at its most disturbing is the cattle car stuffed with human beings who must urinate, defecate, and copulate, treated as herded animals for whom, of course, private facilities are hardly provided – *Schindler's List* as Nazi satire. Such a context does not disturb a cow; it profoundly disturbs a human being. This is, as Frye observes, critical fantasy at perhaps its most critical and most intense, breaking down all those customary associations we unconsciously assume in order to maintain our dignity as human beings.

The satirist who has concentrated a great deal on the upsetting assumptions of modern science is Kurt Vonnegut. *Slaughterhouse-Five*, with its Tralfamadorians profoundly amused by human questions about purpose and meaning, relentlessly undermines the stability we assume in order to maintain our place in the universe. How does one deal with the possibility that human beings are an accident in what might be more than one universe, and that human pride in human dignity is as ludicrous as Lilliputian claims to cosmic importance? While Horace encourages us with the possibility that life can be constructively lived in the world as we know it, Vonnegut profoundly upsets us with the possibility that any such plans for constructive living are meaningless in a wider picture of which we have no sure knowledge. Gulliver, as he arrives in Brobdingnag, speculates on the relativity of human greatness. Throughout Part II, in fact, Gulliver behaves like a pet, a human on a leash, entertaining his owners. Likewise, this is Horace's momentary use of obscenity in *Satires* 1.2 to strip away Cupiennus' rationalizations about his supposedly high-quality, tasteful, sexual desire for the Roman matron. Swift's *Modest Proposal* presents one-year-olds as a market commodity. Even architecture can adopt the satirist's use of the sexual and the scatological to break down the taboos we observe to maintain our dignity. Presented with an opportunity to construct a fountain outside the headquarters of the Dominican Order he despised, Renaissance architect Giovanni Bernini obliged by having the Piazza della Minerva prominently feature an elephant whose hindquarters are the first thing one sees on leaving the Dominican headquarters in Rome, an insult of now more than three centuries' standing!

This third phase of satire can often feature a verbal exuberance to embody and reinforce its stripping away of customary, dignified associations with the human. The prophecy of Isaiah affords one such instance, a passage Frye himself cites for this words-gone-mad quality not uncommon in satire. Isaiah 3: 16–25 begins with a ridiculing catalog of the demeanor, appearance, and even the strutting of the stately matrons of Jerusalem with a detail of ornamental dress and accoutrements that would be so heavy as to weigh down these fashionably minded women. In the day of the Lord, Isaiah, however, warns, all this finery will be taken away. What will be left is a nakedness, the state of the slave. The married women of Jerusalem shall be transformed not by the vanity of insouciant ornamentation but by the humiliation of slavery and exile. Jeremiah pictures the unfaithful Israel as "a she-camel, twisting and turning as she runs, rushing alone into the wilderness, snuffing the wind in her lust;

who can restrain her in her heat?" (Jeremiah 2: 23–4). She is the contemptible streetwalker, oblivious to the despite she occasions in those who witness her behavior (Jeremiah 4: 30). Such images take ordinarily respected subjects and present them in humiliating pictures, images of nakedness, as in Isaiah, or images of contemptible hypersexuality, as in Jeremiah.

In the prophets, dissatisfactions with the prophetic life itself can themselves be the target of demeaning presentation. Jeremiah often complains of the hardship of a prophet's life and sounds like a second Jonah, seeking to cast off the burden of God's call. In one instance, Jeremiah accuses Yahweh of having tricked him: "O Lord, thou hast duped me, and I have been thy dupe; thou has outwitted me and hast prevailed. I have been a laughing-stock all the day long, everyone mocks me" (Jeremiah 20: 7). The prophet presents himself here as the victim of a confidence game, left only with the mocking laughter of others after the deception has been revealed. If the language is sexual, as has been suggested, and Jeremiah is seduced into prophecy, then he becomes in a shocking image the sexual victim of Yahweh's enticement left to experience the mocking of others in his abandoned situation. Whatever dignity might ordinarily be associated with prophecy, the picture of the prophet conned or seduced is hardly respectable.

The ironic parallel to satire of the high norm, third-phase satire, is the irony of the nightmare, where human life is presented as a prison, a madhouse, an inexplicable confinement without the hope of release. Such a picture emerges in the apocalyptic triumph of the forces of cultural disorder in Alexander Pope's *Dunciad*, in Kurt Vonnegut's *Mother Night*, or in George Orwell's *Nineteen Eighty-Four*, terrifying destinies that have no end or end in suicide. What if Yahweh announces that He will no longer be? The terrifying and religiously numbing answer to this question is the prophecy of Hosea, studded with unintelligible language (for reasons of personal safety?) and frequently and pervasively reversing or parodying earlier biblical texts. Hosea's recapitulation of Israel's history is not a reassuring courtship by Yahweh but a record of infidelity and even the ritual murder of children. Hosea is replete with unpleasant and seamy reversals of Yahweh's earlier courtship of Israel, of the covenant assurances predicated of Abraham and Moses, and a stunning reversal of the bedrock assurance of old: "you are not my people, and I will not be your God" (Hosea 1: 9). The *I am* of Exodus becomes the *I am not* of Hosea. For its contemporaries, this statement must have been the height of blasphemous parody and flippancy, but it is Hosea's picture of the void and, in its power, anticipates a twentieth century of Beckett and Sartre. In ancient biblical satire, Hosea is probably the most completely and searingly ironic text. In *Satire and the Hebrew Prophets*, I commented:

> The Book of Hosea thus satisfies Frye's requirements for irony of the void, with its view of human life as largely unrelieved bondage, its parody of religious symbols, its disturbing note of being watched constantly by a hostile eye, its abundance of sinister parental or authority figures, its revelation of a demonic epiphany. In Hosea, this irony finds expression repeatedly in the reversal of the past language of assurance... Yahweh's

People are no longer his (1: 9); Israel returns to Egypt and to the wilderness, hungry, not fed (5: 10), thirsty, not slaked (2: 5), wandering, not settled (9: 17), deprived of children, not spared the last and worst of the plagues that humbled Egypt (9: 16). These, after all, are Israelites slaughtering their own children in fertility rites. Yahweh reverses himself indeed. The Psalmist surely speaks perceptively when he sings: "He that dwelleth in heaven shall laugh them to scorn; the LORD shall hold them in derision." (1992: 116)

Acknowledgment

Some material in this chapter substantially expands earlier discussions in my critical study, *Satire and the Hebrew Prophets* (Louisville: Westminster/John Knox Press, 1992).

References and Further Reading

Alter, Robert (1981) *The Art of Biblical Narrative*. New York: Basic Books.

—— (1985) *The Art of Biblical Poetry*. New York: Basic Books.

Eagleton, Terry (1983) *Literary Theory: An Introduction*. Oxford: Blackwell.

Elliott, Robert C. (1966) *The Power of Satire: Magic, Ritual, Art*. Princeton, NJ: Princeton University Press.

Frye, Northrop (1944) The nature of satire. *University of Toronto Quarterly* 14, 75–89.

—— (1968) *Anatomy of Criticism: Four Essays*. New York: Atheneum.

—— (1982) *The Great Code: The Bible and Literature*. New York: Harcourt Brace Jovanovich.

—— (1990) *Words with Power: Being a Second Study of the Bible and Literature*. San Diego: Harcourt Brace Jovanovich.

Jemielity, Thomas (1992) *Satire and the Hebrew Prophets*. Louisville: Westminster/John Knox Press.

Rosenheim, Jr, Edward W. (1963) *Swift and the Satirist's Art*. Chicago: University of Chicago Press.

Sandmel, Samuel (ed.) (1976) *The New English Bible with the Apocrypha*. Oxford Study Edition. New York: Oxford University Press. (Except for the citations from the King James or Authorized Version, all citations are from this translation.)

Van Doren, Mark and Samuel, Maurice (1975) *The Book of Praise: Dialogues on the Psalms*, ed. Edith Samuel. New York: John Day.

2
Defining the Art of Blame: Classical Satire
Catherine Keane

Many ancient Greek and Roman literary works, bearing a range of generic labels, contain hints of what a modern audience would call satire. Thus, a chapter on classical satire might cover a huge quantity and variety of material. The opposite tack would be to cover the very narrow range of authors named by the Roman rhetorician Quintilian, who, in the late first century CE, declared satire to be "entirely Roman" (*tota nostra*, *The Education of the Orator* 10.1.93). His pronouncement limits satire to the handful of verse authors who, as a result, came to comprise the ancient canon in the eyes of most scholars. This exclusive group consists of four writers – Lucilius, Horace, Persius, and Juvenal – who worked between the second century BCE and the generation following Quintilian's own. But even their distinctive art is the product of centuries of experimentation by Greek and Roman authors, who articulated key satiric concerns, dilemmas, and strategies. Accordingly, the present chapter will avoid the two extremes of classification, and present a diachronic story of satire's origins.

We may begin by cracking open the restricted definition of satire to find a more expansive and theoretical model lurking within. In claiming satire as a Roman invention, Quintilian relied on a formalist notion of genre shared by many ancient critics. Technical criteria, such as performance context, metrical form, style, and subject matter, underlie ancient generic classification. On these formal grounds, and by their own account, the Roman satirists certainly constitute a unique literary tradition. They wrote poems in dactylic hexameter varying in length from fifty to several hundred lines. These were collected in books, and recited to or read privately by educated members of society. Their poems typically feature a first-person speaker who mocks aspects of contemporary morality and social life. By defining satire with these criteria, we may also more precisely categorize the other ancient genres that mock contemporary society or individuals, such as iambic poetry, comic drama, and the mixed-prose-and-verse works that later came to be called Menippean satire. The latter group of texts is characterized not by a consistent agenda of social criticism, but by its distinctive narrative structure and themes (Relihan 1993); hence the significant role of Menippean satire in Bakhtin's account of the Western narrative tradition (see chapter 7).

Even a focused analysis of Roman verse satire, however, would reveal deficiencies in the formalist approach. The genre's name (*satura*, "stuffed") warns that its own nature cannot be summarized in a simple formula. Its purported founder Lucilius, whose work survives only in fragments, evidently treated a wide range of topics, used many different rhetorical tones, and even varied his metrical scheme. In addition to this variety, a number of interesting paradoxes marks the genre's formal makeup. These can point the way to a more theoretical conception of satire. While satire is a polished poetic and textual work, its other common name *sermo* ("chat") suggests informality and intimacy between author and reader. Even the most elaborate rhetorical techniques (such as the outbursts of Juvenal's angry narrator) are designed to convey emotional authenticity. Satire's metrical form also contains an intriguing paradox: hexameter is the traditional meter of ancient epic, antiquity's most elevated genre which was used to treat mythological and historical subjects such as the destruction of Troy or the rise of Rome. The everyday life and folly of Roman people, even when serious moral themes are being invoked, hardly seems suited to the grand meter of epic.

More puzzles emerge when we consider two theoretical elements: the genre's perceived social function, and the self-presentation of its author figure. The satiric poets profess to be responding to immediate, contemporary social problems; Juvenal is most emphatic on this point ("when was the crop of vices richer [than now?]," *Satires* 1.87). Yet much of satire's subject matter is very conventional, echoing the moral themes and illustrations that street-philosophers of the Greco-Roman world used in their diatribes: the corrupting influence of wealth, the dangers of ambition, and the impact of parents' behavior on children. In terms of political alignment, the genre alternates between an oppositional and a conservative, masculine stance; it condemns tyranny and social inequality, but also lashes out against foreign influences on Roman culture, class mobility, and sexual deviance. Both attitudes are seen throughout Roman humor (Richlin 1992), but their combination in a diatribe-style satire can create the impression that the speaker holds inconsistent viewpoints on social and moral issues. In other ways, too, the position of the speaking satirist appears rather inconsistent. He traditionally presses the point that he is composing his verbal attacks in a treacherous legal, social, and political climate. Yet his poetry – including the poems that explicitly discuss and defend his work – exhibits his learning and his social stability. Every formal aspect of the genre paints the satirist as an insider, despite his cultivation of an outsider's image.

These generic features, though strange and contradictory, are deliberately cultivated, and point to defining episodes in satire's historical formation. Prototypes of the Roman satirist figure contribute important techniques to the evolving art of blame, demonstrating that the satirist must oscillate between aggressive and vulnerable stances, that reiteration of shared values in mockery can be more successful than defiance, that calculated self-referential talk can be employed to manipulate the audience, and that indirection and allusion can speak as loudly as direct criticism. These lessons are learned and absorbed into satire as the occasion and purpose of literary abuse change. To "define" literally means to mark out limits (*fines*), and the story of satire's encounters with limits begins in the earliest Greek literature.

Competing Approaches to Blame: The Lessons of a Myth

The first practitioner of mocking abuse in Greek literature is a fictional character, but his experience is illuminating. In Book 2 of Homer's *Iliad,* the dispirited Greek army is gathering for an assembly when the soldier Thersites interrupts to rebuke Agamemnon, the leader of the forces (211–42). This man's low status is only one of his disadvantages: Thersites is also ugly, a poor orator, and a reputed clown – always saying "whatever he thought would get a laugh from the Argives" (215–16). But he is also bold enough to denounce Agamemnon for using the army's labor to pile up his own wealth. When the powerful Achilles delivers a similar attack in Book 1, he is left free to withdraw from the war, but the lowly Thersites meets a very different fate. He earns a prompt lecture and a beating from Agamemnon's right-hand man Odysseus, followed by mockery from the assembled soldiers, who forget their own troubles ("though they were grieved," 270) to laugh at Thersites' bloodied head.

While this scene has particular resonance within the sociopolitical world and plot of the *Iliad* (Thalmann 1988), it is also paradigmatic for literary mockery by authors in other genres, in that it illustrates two approaches to mockery that generate quite different results. Thersites' attack and his pose are often seen in later Greek and Roman "blame" genres. He focuses on his target's greed, a moral theme also taken up in Hellenistic diatribe and Roman verse satire. He also delivers a sideswipe at the soldiers who allow themselves to be exploited ("You women, not men, of Achaia!" 235); it is typical of later satire, too, to cast blame on more than one party. Even Thersites' simian appearance prefigures that of other agents of mockery and exposure in Greek literature (Lowry 1991). Homer's characterization of Thersites as an irrepressible joker brings to mind the portrait of the buffoon in the ancient rhetorical treatises that advocate a more selective and refined style of humor (Grant 1924: 26–8, 91–6). Thersites' approach is spontaneous, oppositional, and enhanced by his ridiculous appearance and lowly status.

But Thersites quickly learns that there is more than one way of practicing humorous abuse when he becomes a target himself. Odysseus employs mockery to reinforce the established social order. He declares Thersites unfit to criticize "the shepherd of the people" (254) – a sentiment duly echoed by the watching soldiers – and then seals his criticism with physical punishment. His response to Thersites is a violent precursor of the Freudian "tendentious" joke in which hostility is sublimated through humor (Freud 1960: 171–93). Odysseus converts the soldiers' resentment toward their leaders into laughter at a weaker figure. This exploitative strategy makes Odysseus the more successful entertainer, notwithstanding Thersites' reputation as a joker.

Both the successful and the unsuccessful styles of abuse showcased here are echoed in later satiric literature and generate its definitive tensions. While the two modes clash in the Homeric episode, they are gradually interwoven in the ancient comic and satiric tradition, a phenomenon that reflects their respective utility. The ridiculous and vulnerable image of the oppositional speaker has a double edge, for such a figure, having no reputation to lose, may more freely communicate biting criticisms of powerful individuals. Many authors adopt a stance that is more degraded than authoritative, as if borrowing the paradoxical license of "the basest man before Ilion" (216). But the conservative, manipulative approach of Odysseus also has its value, allowing satiric authors to establish their audiences' loyalty and to cultivate their latent desire to strike out – if only metaphorically – at already marginalized groups. Manipulative rhetoric also becomes an important tool for authorial self-presentation, in that authors find ways of asserting control over their reception. As Odysseus prescribes the proper response to Thersites' attack in his own counter-attack, so too comic and satiric texts can plant interpretive standards in their audiences' minds.

Most important, while the exchange between Thersites and Odysseus illustrates the different options open to the practitioner of mockery, it also shows the costs of each method: retaliatory attack and loss of support in the first case, and the suppression of truly critical, perspective-transforming speech in the second. When the two approaches are yoked in ancient poetry of abuse (iambic poetry, Old Comedy, Roman satire), the result is not a smoothly harmonized formula. Rather, satiric literature frequently dramatizes the author's vacillation between priorities. The art of blame risks seeming partisan and dangerous if it is too unbridled and fierce; on the other hand, retreat, refinement, or alignment with traditional authority can dilute its critical power (cf. Rosen and Baines 2002: 126–7). In the reception history of satire, much of the modern scholarly debate concerning satiric literature has been shaped by readers' different conceptions about the true priorities of the criticizing figure (Griffin 1994: 6–34). The uncertainty stems largely from the ambivalence of the ancient authors themselves.

Striking the Pose: The Iambographers

Thersites' heirs in literary history are the authors of iambic poetry – historical characters working in a literate culture, but endowed with a kind of mythic status in the Greco-Roman tradition. Iambography, personal abuse in verse, was one of the poetic genres practiced in the *poleis* (city-states) of the Aegean region in the seventh and sixth centuries BCE. Although their work survives only in fragments, Archilochos and Hipponax were celebrated throughout antiquity as the masters and symbols of the iambic genre. Their style ranges from riddling and oblique to bluntly obscene.

The iambographers combine the aggression of Thersites with the status and the coercive abusive strategy of Odysseus. Archilochos' attacks on a man named Lykambes, and Hipponax's abuse of Boupalos and Athenis, were famous in antiquity not just for their display of poetic skill, but for their savagery, which allegedly drove the victims to suicide. The extraordinary similarity between these two stories makes them more than a little suspect. But they reflect a superstition that abusive words can have the effect of real violence (a theme in the satiric tradition; Elliott 1960).

Despite their deadly image, however, the iambic performers also cast themselves as victims. The two poets' ancient biographies tell us that the two men were responding to wrongs suffered. Archilochos, it is said, was punishing Lykambes for withdrawing an offer of his daughter's hand in marriage. Many Archilochean fragments that seem concerned with the story conjure an outraged and helpless speaker (frs 172–4, 191, 193 West; cf. 118 West). The likelihood that the tale was invented or fictionalized (the girl has the suspiciously appropriate name of Neoboule, "New Plan") only confirms the idea that iambic attack hinges on the performer's own role as victim. Hipponax, for his part, was supposedly retaliating against Boupalos and Athenis, sculptors who humiliated him with an unflattering likeness. His image is even more wretched than that of Archilochos, though he cultivates it less in attacks on his targets (where he plays the scrappy brawler; frs 120–21 West) than in his laments about his humiliating poverty, as in fr. 34 West:

> [Hermes], you have not yet given me a thick cloak
> to be a guard against cold in winter,
> nor have you covered my feet in thick
> overshoes, to stop the chilblains from breaking out.

Hipponax's is an underdog pose, enhanced in this fragment by a physical sketch of the poet shivering, afflicted, and railing against the neglectful god of prosperity. It is tempting to imagine lost poems in which the poet deliberately styles himself as a Thersites-like character, even drawing attention to his own ugliness (said to be the catalyst for the mocking sculpture; Pliny the Elder, *Natural History* 36.11).

Compelling as these accounts are, however, they are almost certainly fictional. Ancient literary biographies tend to be constructed from "evidence" in the authors' work (Lefkowitz 1981), and even the qualities shared by the iambographers' personae are really poetic fictions. Iambography is an art, not the authentic self-expression of angry underdogs. It probably derived from bawdy verses recited at fertility rituals, but in the late Archaic and Classical periods it was (like drama and choral lyric) performed before the entire community for aesthetic evaluation as well as religious celebration. It is possible that the poets first showcased their work at the symposium, that institution so central to elite male socialization and cultural education, where other types of lyric poetry, treating social, political, and personal subjects, were performed. Here especially, they would have been surrounded by sympathetic listeners of similar social position. Even in public festival settings, however, the iambographer would have been granted a special status as one of the poetic authorities of the *polis*. His revenge, like his coarse or bitter persona (Latin for "mask"), was a performance.

The iambic poets thus appear less vulnerable than Thersites, who finds that his spontaneous and direct criticisms are no match for the assembly's fear of and loyalty to their leaders. The iambographer, in a festival or sympotic context, is insulated – and not just by the license granted by that context, but also by his choice of safe targets. Archilochos does not attack the social and political system itself, but focuses on a private family; the daughter (or daughters, as some fragments suggest) makes an easy target for attacks on personal virtue. The iambic poem of Semonides likening women to different animal species, an early example of misogynistic comic discourse, provides an apt comparison. Likewise, Hipponax's Boupalos is no Agamemnon. His name in Greek sounds like "bull-phallus," and the poet may have exploited this similarity so as to conjure a crude picture of his target (Rosen 1988a). Since Hipponax's own authorial image is far from aristocratic, this is not a case of a principled victim framing his enemy as a scoundrel; instead, Hipponax brings his target down to his own crude level.

Advisors to the City: The Authority of Comic Drama

A similarly aggressive authorial image in a different formal framework is seen in Greek comic drama of the late fifth and early fourth centuries BCE. Termed "Old Comedy," this genre is now represented by eleven surviving plays of Aristophanes and numerous fragments. The comedies produced at two annual Athenian festivals for Dionysos may be seen as the dramatic descendents of iambic poetry. Though we may dismiss Aristotle's assertion that iambic and comic authors have similar dispositions (*Poetics* 1449a2–4), there are clearly stylistic and programmatic connections between the genres (Rosen 1988b).

The setting of comic performance gave authors festival license like that exploited by the iambographers, though comedy had more ways of using it. The genre has a famously diverse and specialized lexicon of obscenities, and performances featured a padded costume with a prominent phallus – a vehicle for casual visual jokes that also contributed to an overall bawdiness. In this way comedy, like iambography, mimics certain Greek fertility rituals, where the more mundane aspects of the cycle of birth and death were celebrated. The same rituals also included exchanges of verbal abuse, another feature of comedy. Aristophanes' plays abound with invective against individuals both prominent and ordinary, which was a regular feature of choral interludes. In addition, many plots revolve around ridiculous figures who are either caricatures or allegorical versions of historical personages, such as Sokrates in *Clouds*, or the tanner-politician in *Knights*, who clearly stands for a frequent butt of Aristophanes, the demagogue Kleon.

Iambic poetry addresses private disputes, but the comic poet makes the *polis* itself his principal subject. This too reflects comedy's festival license, as the Athenians who filled the theater seats (possibly of both sexes, and certainly of all walks of life) would be watching themselves and their civic institutions mocked on stage. The law court, the assembly, education, religion, theater itself — none is spared, although the more powerful members of society tend to act as the blocking characters, and the average types as the protagonists, who set out on unlikely missions to change their world.

While this pattern justifies the enduring image of Old Comedy as the quintessential literary product of democratic Athens, the genre does not exactly make pure heroes out of ordinary people. Rather, the constant spotlight on low-status stock characters enables the development of a distinct comic discourse about ordinary human weaknesses and vices, a major element of all later satire. To take an example, the main butts in *Lysistrata* are the male warmongers in charge of the *polis,* whose policies are dragging on the Peloponnesian War. But the ordinary women who dominate the play, while heroic and good-hearted, also have their inconsistencies, appetites, fears, and treacherous leanings. The scenes in which the women panic at the prospect of an oath of chastity, and later attempt to escape to their husbands' beds on various false pretexts, are show-stealing comic episodes. Ultimately, the women win their suit for peace, but they are still subject to stereotyping mockery that elaborates on the "typical feminine" qualities excoriated by authors from Semonides to Juvenal. The Athenian people may have enjoyed watching ordinary bumpkins and housewives doggedly pursuing their missions, but they were also served up plenty of generic jokes aimed at those same heroes and heroines.

The comic theater taught the *polis* to laugh at itself. This laughter certainly did not have purely derogatory purposes; the theatrical exposure of Athens, person by person and institution by institution, may have helped the citizenry cultivate essential political "reading" skills (Slater 2002). Appropriately, Athenian playwrights were called teachers, *didaskaloi* — a label derived from their task of training the chorus, but evidently invested with broader meaning as well. Comic poets did not only fulfill this role from behind the scenes, but advertised it aggressively during the course of the play and for a specific purpose. All authors at the festivals were competing for prizes, but in comedy, where the dramatic illusion was frequently broken, this agonistic scenario was a foregrounded motif. This is especially characteristic of the *parabasis* (choral "digression"), where the poet asks for the judges' support and addresses political topics related to the play. A passage from the *parabasis* of *Acharnians,* another brilliant anti-war play, exemplifies Aristophanes' method of self-promotion (643–58):

> So now when the subject allies bring you tribute
> they'll come eager to see the best poet there is,
> the one who has dared to utter just things before the Athenians.
> So far has the glory of his daring traveled,
> that when the Persian king was questioning the Spartan
>   ambassadors

> he asked them first which side in the war was stronger in its navy,
> and then which side this poet mocked the most.
> For he said that these people would be made much better
> and would be victorious in the war from having him as an advisor.
> This is why the Spartans are asking you for peace
> and for Aigina back; it's not that they care about that island,
> but they want to claim this poet for themselves.
> But I say, don't ever let him go, for his comedies speak justice,
> and he says he'll teach you lots of good things, so you'll fare well;
> he'll neither flatter nor bribe nor trick you,
> nor machinate nor sprinkle you with praise, but teach you what's best.

This passage defines and justifies the comic poet's role as *didaskalos* ("he'll teach you lots of good things"), and its manipulative tactics are reminiscent of the prescriptive speech of Odysseus. The chorus promotes its creator the playwright as the "best poet" (*ton poiētēn ton ariston*), as if pushing his case before the judges of the theatrical competition. But this boast blurs into a claim of Aristophanes' strategic political value to the city (the Aigina joke is taken to mean that the poet owned property there). This significance of comedy is hinted at in the earlier complaint that Aristophanes has been "maligned by his enemies before the fickle Athenians, with the charge that he mocks the city and insults the people" (630–1). The description suggests that the context of the poet's work and reception is the *polis* as a political community, not merely as a collective judge of dramatic artistry. In Aristophanes' defense, then, the chorus invests him with heroic qualities – "so far has the glory [*kleos,* an important term in Homer] of his daring traveled" – and with the virtues of a moral leader: "the one who has dared to utter just things." These roles are connected specifically to his comic abuse of the *polis*, as implied in the absurd anecdote about the Persian king. All the poetic genres at the festivals helped to celebrate the city of Athens as a symbol of artistic, political, and military greatness; this passage goes even further, contending that the poet's comic abuse itself makes him a national treasure requiring protection.

Acharnians won first prize at the Lenaia festival in January 425 BCE, defeating entries by Aristophanes' two most formidable rivals, Eupolis and Kratinos. Perhaps this means that this *parabasis* convinced the judges that Aristophanes was the "best poet." But, Slater's view of comic reception (2002) notwithstanding, the passage in itself can prove nothing. What we may say with certainty is that it manipulatively promotes the crucial message that comedy can make citizens smarter. This looks like a challenge to viewers and readers to identify themselves as either gullible or astute: they may choose which poet is best, but, like the Greek soldiers observing Odysseus, they have had the terms for that interpretation imposed on them by the text. By inviting his judges to ponder the question of his qualifications, Aristophanes may have surreptitiously drawn them and subsequent readers into making a much more fundamental and important assumption: that comedy itself is valuable to the city. In other words, while it is a boon to win the battle, namely the dramatic competition, the poet's rhetoric is also geared toward winning a war: a positive, compliant reception for his genre.

As the *parabasis*, the political fantasy plots, and the element of abuse dropped out of later Greek comedy, the self-promotional tactics just outlined also disappeared. But they found a new context in the comic drama of second-century Rome. The balance of irreverence and conservatism that typifies Roman comedy's portrayal of domestic life (McCarthy 2000) prefigures the complex sociopolitical orientation of satire. But Roman comedy also contributes to satire's self-referential discourse, by adopting and nuancing the convention of the besieged and heroic author figure. Particularly belligerent and manipulative is the method of the playwright Terence, who is in other respects viewed as a genteel foil to his chaotic predecessor Plautus. Terence cultivates the theme of his plight as author in his prologues, where an actor routinely complains about the poet's critical public. The most famous example, the prologue of *The Mother-in-law*, refers to two previous attempts to stage the play; evidently, the rival attractions of tightrope walkers, boxers, and gladiators distracted the audiences irreparably. The poet now puts the fate of his beleaguered play in the hands of his audience (28–32, 43–8):

> Now hear what I ask of you, for my sake and with equanimity.
> I again present to you *The Mother-in-law*, which I have never been
> allowed to act in silence: so did misfortune beset it.
> Your good judgment, if it will come to aid my hard work,
> will lighten that misfortune...
> Today there's no hubbub; we have leisure and quiet.
> I've been given an opportunity to act the play; you've been given
> the power to grace this theatrical festival.
> Don't allow the fate of this dramatic art to fall
> into the hands of a few; see to it that your authority
> is the supporter and assistant of my own.

Like Aristophanes, Terence cultivates the image of a mistreated artist, suggests that appreciating his work requires serious thought, and solemnly asks for a hearing. The last lines propose that poet and spectators have a symbiotic relationship: the spectators' authority as critics bolsters Terence's as playwright. This is a tendentious gesture, regardless of the education and critical skills undoubtedly possessed by some of Terence's spectators. For in ascribing the same "power" to all present, the poet promotes the idea that comic spectatorship has certain requirements. His audience is presented with the same diagnostic choice that Aristophanes gives his in the *parabasis*: prove yourselves either competent critics or ungrateful, unperceptive fools. In Aristophanes, this rhetoric of inclusion and exclusion is used to convince the spectators that comic abuse is not just legitimate but beneficial. In the tamer comedy of Terence, the author's manipulation of his audience may instead be seen as an attempt to cultivate the image of comedy as an art that carries more meaning than meets the eye. And in their analogous self-defenses (*apologiae*), the Roman verse satirists draw on both examples in claiming unpopularity and a positive social mission. Not just their own authorial images, but the status and reception of their genre, are at stake. Arguably, satire's most salient effect is not actually to punish its targets or change its audience's views, but simply to convince that audience that the genre performs an important function in society (Keane 2002).

A Changed Scene

Although it borrows from many literary traditions, Roman satire is most frequently compared to Old Comedy. It is another definitive paradox of satire that the so-called "entirely Roman" genre is viewed as a descendent of the genre that died with Classical Athens. The late antique grammarian Diomedes describes Roman satire as a kind of poetry "composed for the purpose of carping at human vices in the manner of Old Comedy" (*ad carpenda hominum vitia archaeae comoediae charactere compositum*, Ars Grammatica III, Kiel I: 485). The obvious basis for the comparison is the two genres' shared agenda of invective and criticism, to which Horace points in his assessment of Lucilius (*Sermones* 1.4.1–5). Horace also expresses admiration for the controlled variation in tone exhibited by the comic poets (1.10.16–17). Persius echoes Horace when he declares that readers of Old Comedy will like his poetry too (*Satires* 1.123–5).

But these tantalizing comparisons steer around the fact that the art of blame encountered new limitations in the Roman period. The production contexts of Old Comedy and Roman satire – perhaps the most important factor in determining the genres' respective functions – could not have been more different. Old Comedy, superseded by the "New" genre that Aristotle and the Romans so admired, became forever associated with a particular place and time: the powerful and radically democratic Athens of the late fifth century. Political, topical, abusive Old Comedy projected an image of – and for – that version of Athens which filled the theater seats. Aristophanes and his fellow poets pressed the connection between Athens' political and military greatness, on the one hand, and its fostering of the institution of comedy, on the other hand. Such an art form could not be reproduced in an Athens under drastically different circumstances, or in a non-democratic society; as the image in Persius' first *Satire* indicates, Old Comedy became a fossil, something to be read as part of literary and rhetorical study rather than staged.

In contrast, satire was from the beginning a written text – an intricate and allusive one, aimed at Rome's relatively small and elite reading culture, and created and disseminated through the support of private patrons. Even when satirists wrote about the most ordinary human appetites, frustrations, and daily rituals, they were engaging a readership familiar with literature, rhetoric, and philosophy, all of which play roles in the satiric representation of the world. The private experience of such readers would have been very different from that of Athenian spectators, a diverse group who were nevertheless getting the message during the festival that they all belonged in the *polis*. The typical reader of satire would have come from the upper crust of Roman society, a highly stratified sociopolitical system in both the Republican and Imperial periods.

In sum, there are many things that Old Comedy could do that Roman satire could not. Satire could not put the *polis* on stage for the *polis*, for it lacked both a *polis* and a stage. Although individuals were frequently lampooned on stage in mimes and other comic pieces in the Republic, that practice was also theoretically restricted by libel laws. Literary satire, then, was not produced within an institutional framework like the dramatic festivals that permitted critical portrayals of society and politics. The production of satiric verse could not be valorized as a heroic performance of civic duty. Romans prized the freedom of speech (*libertas*) associated with the Republic, but the satirists claim to be targets of resentment and suspicion nevertheless (Horace 1.4 and 2.1; Persius 1; Juvenal 1). The genre thus operates with an awareness of limitations – on the power of words, on the influence wielded by the mocking figure, and on the topics that may be safely addressed.

This is not to say that satiric poetry stood out among Roman genres in being bounded by restrictions of form and decorum. Nor should we take too seriously the satirists' claims that their work was rewarded with social ostracism and legal threats. Rather, limitation is a programmatic theme for the poets of satire. Like their predecessors in the art of blame, the satirists write the problems of reception into their performances and thus into their generic theory. The alleged dangers of satire-writing are better understood as a fiction cultivated about the genre (analogous to the claims made in comic *parabases* and prologues) by authors who were well-connected enough to be insulated from real threats. According to Horace, writing in the turbulent thirties BCE, Lucilius in the previous century was free to attack prominent living politicians, but specifically the enemies of his own patrons (2.1.65–8), which hardly makes satire seem a daring endeavor. The ancient biography of Persius mentions that editors emended one suggestive line after the poet's death in 62 CE because it could have been construed as an attack on Nero; if the story is true, it seems a special case, a precaution taken during the emperor's most paranoid years. We are also told that the octogenarian Juvenal was punished for his lampoons with a military post in Egypt, but this story has been dismissed as a fabrication based on Juvenal's scorn for Egyptians. Overall, the staged dialogues between the satirists and invented interlocutors about the risks of satirizing are so conventional and at times exaggerated (for example, Juvenal's envisioning of his own grisly execution, 1.155–7) that we must view them as examples of the self-promoting rhetoric also cultivated by the Old Comic poets.

The real restrictions placed on satire have as much to do with formal requirements and with the expectations of Rome's reading culture as with any real dangers involved in practicing social criticism in literary form. This effectively means that what would be restrictions on a genre aimed at "carping at human vices" before a broad public are actually, in a literary genre practiced and enjoyed within an educated and status-conscious community, opportunities for developing new tools for the art of mockery.

Although the satirists claim at times simply to be describing the world around them, their art reflects a complex blending of conventions from literature, philosophy, and rhetoric. It is no surprise that the genre first took shape during the second century BCE when Rome's empire was expanding, and wealthy Romans were becoming fascinated with the products and traditions now available to them. The "stuffed" genre mimics the culture's consuming passion, as well as the moral discourse that developed around the issue of consumption (Gowers 1993). Like the Romans learning to enjoy the fruits of empire, satire seems to absorb, admire, probe, and re-enact everything around it – the grand vision and stylistic register of epic and tragedy, the low and vulgar world of comedy and mime, the institutions both native and foreign that together made up Roman culture (rhetoric, law, spectacle, patronage, religion, gastronomy). If Quintilian's characterization of satire as "entirely Roman" derives from criteria other than the formal ones already noted, one underlying idea might be that satire looks undeniably like a product of Roman culture in its drive to appropriate, mimic, and adjudicate. This is one way of describing satire's allusive, representational, and critical strategies – a description which appropriately jumbles them together in a rather anarchic manner, resistant to formalist analysis.

Disguises and Alter Egos

In addition to lacking the festival license of the Old Comic poets, the Roman satirists have no cast of characters or chorus to use as mouthpieces for social criticism. Instead, they write largely in the first person in the manner of the iambographers, and cultivate the impression that they are simply responding to what they see around them. The inaugural utterance of each poet's oeuvre frames the satirist as an observer of social behavior, whose commentary is an almost involuntary reaction: Horace asks his patron Maecenas why no one is content with his own lot (1.1.1–3) and later claims to gather his satiric material while ambling around Rome (1.4.133–9), Persius bursts out laughing at the human capacity for delusion (1.1–12), and Juvenal presents his first poem as an act of revenge against those who aggravate him (especially other writers; 1.1–18). All of these scenarios of reaction are artificially constructed, but their rhetorical purpose is to create an image of satire's subject matter as contemporary social behavior, and of the satirist as observer and commentator.

This is artifice, not autobiography. Like other authors, satirists cultivate personae, using models and techniques that advertise their genre's imitative nature. The satiric persona is fashioned from the conventions of drama, especially the predictable stock characters of comedy, and of rhetoric. The later Roman satirists had at their disposal a particularly Roman rhetorical mode: declamation, the art of constructing speeches for hypothetical contexts. By the early first century CE, declamatory exercises were a core part of Roman secondary education; students composed speeches offering advice to past political figures (*suasoriae*) and arguing the two sides of a legal conflict (*controversiae*). All educated Roman men thus knew the strategies for arguing a given viewpoint, conjuring emotions so as to be more persuasive, and constructing a persona appropriate to the occasion. Satirists put these techniques to work, contriving a variety of masks and rhetorical approaches. For the most part, the speaker in Horace's *Sermones* is characterized by a mild and self-mocking pose. On the other end of the emotional spectrum, Juvenal's early *Satires* are delivered by an angry persona, who communicates in frequent exclamations, rhetorical questions, and overgeneralizations about the degraded state of society.

The satirists' ancient readers would have recognized rhetorical techniques, but we are less sure about how that obvious artificiality affected the perception of satire's aims. When it is clear that a satirist is appropriating rhetorical and poetic tools, his moral commentary begins to appear disingenuous, an observation that forms a refrain in Anderson's (1982) influential essays on the satiric persona. It can sometimes seem as though satire's rhetorical component overwhelms its moral content, making a mockery of moralistic discourse itself. But rhetoric is only the organizing structure of a complex performance. Since persona-based readings opened Roman satire to more in-depth literary study, scholars have devised new critical approaches to the content of satiric diatribe and its cultural entanglements, and consequently to satiric theory itself (for example, Richlin 1992: 164–209; Gowers 1993: 109–219; Henderson 1999: 173–273).

Regarding the persona itself, scholars now recognize that the satiric poets are not restricted to trotting out stock masks, but use many different techniques to cultivate the dramatic potential of satire and to establish the perspectives of speaking characters. A few poems illustrate the flexibility and depth of the constructed author figure and the implications of that figure's attitudes for satiric theory. Some satires are dramatic dialogues in which the poet is only an invisible orchestrator of the interaction. For example, Persius' fourth *Satire* resembles a play or philosophical dialogue, and the poet announces at the outset that the two speaking characters represent the Athenians Sokrates and Alkibiades. But a more common use of the satiric persona is as a first-person voice that holds the floor, diatribe-style, throughout a poem.

Persius' *Satires* are intriguing cases: most conjure an intimacy between speaker and reader, but the speaker's personality is elusive and mutable. Persius seems distanced and cynical at one moment, and earnest at another. These shifts are not haphazard, however. Persius poses as a mischievous boy in his first *Satire*, metaphorically describing his work as a desecration of society's sacred places ("this place is holy; piss elsewhere," says his imaginary critic; 113–14), but in *Satires* 5, he speaks as a learned Stoic now engaging his own teacher, Cornutus, in discussion. By the sixth and last poem in the book, it appears that the poet has been constructing a pseudo-autobiography. In the epistolary *Satires* 6, Persius addresses a friend from a coastal retreat, declaring his intention to enjoy his estate. This persona derives from a common satiric subject, the industry of legacy-hunting (for example, Horace 2.5; Juvenal 12). Rather than discussing the topic from an objective position, Persius innovatively plays the part of the highly courted estate-owner repelling his potential heirs. The pose also serves to link the poem's content with the external reality of the poet's career and reception, since the speaker's desirable legacy may be seen as a metaphor for the poet's work (Henderson 1999: 241–2; Freudenburg 2001: 195–208). Persius' chosen persona, appropriate to the book's final poem, does not simply represent a discrete and artificial performance, but the final stage of a larger narrative that has both an organic feel and meta-literary resonance.

Other cases of impersonation do not require character-drawing skills, but simply plant the satirist in an alien body, as in Horace 1.8. Horace speaks as a statue of Priapus, the boundary-making god who watched over private property. In other examples of Roman Priapic poetry, the god stands watch in a garden and drives intruders away with a sexual threat. In this case, Priapus' image and strategy are especially comical: he manages to scare off the witches in his garden with a loud fart. This act of impersonation benefits Horace by allowing him access to a restricted area, while the reader knows not to equate him with the crude god. In his thick, wooden, and ultimately damaged disguise, Horace appears to exploit the freedom of the ugly Thersites without putting his real status at risk.

But some suggestive connections between Priapus and the Horace of the *Sermones* imply that the satiric persona, even one as alien as this, should not simply be viewed as a distancing device. The setting of the poem is a garden newly established by Maecenas, the patron who has recently taken the real Horace under his wing. Horace-as-Priapus, privileged by his residence in the garden and charged with protecting its privacy, metaphorically re-enacts the more concrete account of the poet's social and economic ascent presented in 1.6. He also faces the consequences of that ascent in the witches' invasion, which parallels the poet's confrontation in 1.9 with an outsider eager for an introduction. All three poems reflect Horace's protective attitude toward Maecenas' group, and thematize the poet's own insecurity and vulnerability (Henderson 1999: 202–27). Thus the mask of Priapus is really a variation on the autobiographical mode prevalent in the *Sermones*, one that represents the poet's position in ways that Horace's own body cannot. And an exposed body brings with it the vulnerability of the traditional satirist figure. The poem concludes with the statue's heroic self-mutilation – "I burst my fig-wood buttocks apart" (47) – recalling the violent end of the Thersites episode. Like past satirist figures, Horace-Priapus is as vulnerable as the targets at whom he aims.

Satiric alter egos may convey emotional as well as physical vulnerability. Juvenal begins his fourth book of *Satires* with an admiring portrait of Demokritos, the atomist philosopher famous for his attitude of detached amusement (10.28–53). This represents a departure from Juvenal's earlier angry persona and so seems to signal a major shift in his satiric approach (Bellandi 1980: 66–101). The book's remaining two poems situate the poet in a domestic retreat, where he expresses his preference for the simple and virtuous life – evidence, perhaps, of his new detached perspective (Braund 1988: 184–9). But a more dynamic reading of the book and a closer comparison of satirist with alter ego produces a different impression of Juvenal's emotional state. Demokritos is a difficult model for the satirist to emulate, to judge from the fact that, while the laughing philosopher is positioned right in the streets of Rome, Juvenal himself goes on to contemplate the urban scene from a safe distance indoors. His choice, compared with Demokritos' ability to look upon Rome's mad scene and not be shaken, looks a bit like a pre-emptive withdrawal. The pose of the philosopher is not equivalent to Juvenal's own persona, but serves as a model that illuminates subtle shifts in the satirist's attitude.

Between Trauma and Trivia

The dramatic elements of satire – personae, stock scenes and moral exempla, diction appropriate to comedy or tragedy – would have entertained the genre's learned ancient audience. But the irony and indirection enabled by such devices are also elements of satire's critical agenda. Claims about the risks entailed in writing satire should be viewed not as realities being documented, but as programmatic fictions, a vital part of the satiric art and authorial image.

The Roman satirists avoid confronting power directly in the manner of Thersites and the Old Comic poets. Historical and political characters certainly make convenient moral exempla: the impetuous Alkibiades is a suitable target for a lecture on self-awareness (Persius 4), and the fates of Sejanus, Demosthenes, Cicero, and Hannibal all attest the dangers of ambition (Juvenal 10). But there is a difference between utilitarian equation of historical characters with certain flaws and criticism of the powerful or contemplation of traumatic historical events. The legendary direct method of Lucilius is a model that his successors ostentatiously decline to follow. Instead, they devise subtle satiric strategies that underscore their claims about the volatile and repressive environment of the principate (Freudenburg 2001). Juvenal is most melodramatic on this point, promising his critical interlocutor that he will restrict his attacks to persons already dead (1.170–1).

In his fourth *Satire*, Juvenal launches such an attack on the late emperor Domitian. But this poem lacks Lucilian vehemence: besides being an already-vilified figure from the past, and therefore hardly a risky satiric subject, Domitian is here portrayed engaging in a trivial "crime," an emergency council meeting concerning the proper cooking and presentation of an enormous fish. The episode certainly affords the satirist an opportunity to illustrate Domitian's major offenses along the way: each member of the council has a story attached to him that attests Domitian's cruelty, capriciousness, and demand for extraordinary honors. The poem's mock-epic tone and imagery underscore these characteristics. But the parenthetical references to the greater outrages of Domitian's reign highlight the gap between the most terrible stories associated with the emperor and Juvenal's present choice of narrative topic.

The poem illustrates the difficult choices that the satirist himself faces in approaching his subject. Each character who attends Domitian is visibly influenced by the oppressive atmosphere. The fisherman who brings his offering plays the humble worshipper; the virtuous nobles in the council tremble and hide their fear and painful losses. Their calculated performance, and their failure to express opposition or outrage, mirror the satirist's own indirection and his focus on "trivia" (*nugae*, 150; Sweet 1979). But another possible approach is hinted at in the allusion, at the poem's ending, to Domitian's eventual assassination (153–4). Significantly, the motley group of conspirators who overcame the emperor (Juvenal calls them "workmen," *cerdones*) are not the same men as the degraded nobles shown in the fish episode. The poem thus dramatizes two very different responses to Domitian, arising from different groups: the silent suffering and caution of those who possess status, and the violent revenge exacted by those who lack it. The reader is prompted to consider the question of which group Juvenal, or Juvenal's satire, most resembles (cf. Freudenburg 2001: 264–77 on other such cases). This question, rather than its indeterminate answer, defines the satirist figure, who perennially navigates between excessive caution and excessive defiance.

Horace 1.7 also summons up a violent moment in history that contrasts with the poem's trivial main subject, a verbal squabble before the judge Brutus in the province of Asia. The dramatic date is 43 or 42 BCE, between the assassination of Julius Caesar (led by Brutus himself) and the resulting military conflict that would ultimately secure the position of Octavian, later the emperor Augustus, as Caesar's political heir. The poem ends with a surprising pun referring to the assassination. The litigant Persius turns to the judge for help in silencing his opponent, who is named Rex ("King"): "Brutus, I beg you – you're accustomed to dispatching kings – why don't you cut this Rex's throat? Believe me, this is a job for you" (33–5).

Like Juvenal's fish tale, this poem positions satire's agenda between direct confrontation with the painful past and entertaining focus on minor conflicts – the first being too dangerous, and the latter perplexingly insignificant. Scholars long blamed Horace's raw youth for the mediocrity of the concluding pun, combined with the inflammatory label of "king" for the dictator Caesar and the crass reference to the murder that incited so much bloodshed. But more recent readings (for example, Henderson 1998: 73–107) have seen serious historical commentary in the poet's strange juxtaposition of past and present circumstances, serious and trivial conflicts, and strategies of physical and verbal aggression. In the first century BCE, the Roman state was torn apart repeatedly by civil war, as Horace knew well (he had fought briefly on the assassins' side in the aftermath of 44), and the twin goals of Augustan ideology would be to cover over these wounds and to present the new state as a restored Republic, not a monarchy. The punning close of *Sermones* 1.7 could be seen as working in Augustus' favor, discharging the suggestive joke in a safe context as if to preclude further rumblings from more threatening parties. But the joke also revives the brutal memory to leave it hanging unresolved, unprocessed by judge and readers alike. In this sense, the poem acts out the reverse of the Augustan healing process, even as it simultaneously admits a conservative reading.

Horace 1.7 and Juvenal 4 demonstrate and explore satire's limitations in the political realm. Both examples suggest that the poets avoid performing the task that Thersites and the Old Comic playwrights undertook – the direct criticism of powerful individuals and the sociopolitical system that they exploit. Just as personae, alter egos, and dramatic speakers give the satirists protection and special access to forbidden places, their indirection in dealing with power and politics is a kind of self-insulation. But these gestures of avoidance, displacement, and metaphorizing draw attention to themselves, expressing the enduring dilemma of the genre. Satire operates in the shadow of real power and violence, represented by the silent presence of Domitian and Brutus.

A Composite Art

The satirists' indirect handling of dangerous topics contrasts with their perfection of a discourse about the garden-variety vices, excesses, and dilemmas of ordinary people. Juvenal calls human "prayers, fears, anger, pleasures, joys, and goings-on" the "fodder" (*farrago*) of his book (1.85–6). The metaphor of consumption is appropriate to the "stuffed" genre, which absorbs not only a great range of material, but discourses that are the usual vehicles for that material. While Juvenal's tag is directed at his own work, it also aptly describes the tradition that he is now joining, inviting new appreciation of satire's inherent variety.

The satirists depict themselves as surrounded by other poets and poetry, which become part of their own genre's identity. Each poet positions himself in a landscape that teems with literary activity, in which he risks being criticized, drowned out, or ignored. Horace concludes his first satiric performance by comparing himself, in mock self-deprecation, to a long-winded diatribist (1.1.120–1), and complains of being challenged to extemporizing contests by rivals (1.4.13–21). In their own programmatic poems, both Persius and Juvenal deride Rome's frequent poetry recitals, and champion satire as a much-needed alternative. These gestures to the contemporary poetry industry set up a spectrum of literary foils for satire: sloppy compositions rattled off for show, pompous epic, trite tragedy, frivolous elegy. But these foils also become a crucial part of the genre that mocks them, both because their status as foils makes them necessary to satire's definition, and because the satirists often appropriate their respective stylistic conventions. The line between parody and assimilation blurs; satire makes other literature into *farrago*.

This strategy may be observed in earlier satiric authors such as Aristophanes, who frequently parodies tragic diction, and Hipponax, who curses an enemy in mock-epic language ("Muse, tell me of son-of-Eurymedon, the sea-swallower," fr. 128 West). Even Homer's Thersites is a kind of belated imitator, as he echoes some of Achilles' criticisms in Book 1 of the *Iliad*, but is only given the opportunity to utter them at the assembly in Book 2. Interestingly, Homer seems to have trouble characterizing Thersites' speaking style – the man is "disordered in his words" (*ametroepēs*, 212), but also a "clear speaker" (*ligus agorētēs*, 246). The double-edged portrayal may suggest that Thersites' individual style does not yet have a name, or a place, in the epic world. Thersites' position as a latecomer who uses what tools he can find to launch his attack makes him a useful paradigm for the satirist figure.

But the Roman satirists have more resources to exploit. Roman poetry in general is known for its intricate intertextuality, but satire is especially voracious in its quotation and imitation of other genres and texts. Even the most banal satiric topics may be approached through imitation of other literary treatments. Horace's poem on sexual behavior (1.2) is a good example; its scenes of erotic misadventure resemble stock comic scenes more than ordinary reality. Even the direct speech in the poem has a literary flavor: for example, one man justifies his misbehavior by citing an erotic epigram of the Greek poet Kallimachos (105–9):

> [The adulterer] sings "the hunter pursues
> a hare in the deep snow, but refuses to touch one placed
> before him," adding "my love is like this; for it flies past
> what is lying in the open, and tries to catch what flees."

Horace mocks the man for linking his experience with an idealized poetic world: "Do you hope that with neat little verses like these, the suffering and storms and heavy anxiety can be driven from your breast?" (110–11). The poet counters with the sentiment of another Greek poet, Philodemos, who rejects unavailable women in favor of "the kind who neither costs a lot nor delays when she's sent for" (122). Thus Horace pits one poetic world against another as he strings together his "chat." His juxtapositions and distortions appear inept at times, but this all helps to construct his self-mocking persona (Freudenburg 1993), and can have the ironic effect of making his satiric world look more authentic. The simplicity of Horace's "pedestrian muse" (*musa pedestris*, 2.6.17) is deceptive.

Satire often sheds new light on the literary discourses that it appropriates by twisting a single word or juxtaposing incongruous images or terms (techniques catalogued in Schmitz 2000). But as with rhetoric, it would be reductive to interpret the poet's aim as pure parody. The surface implication of terms such as "mock-epic" and "mock-tragic" notwithstanding, satiric imitation is both ambivalent and creative. A passage that was long read simply as derisive parody, Juvenal's epic pastiche at the opening of *Satires* 1 is more fruitfully interpreted as a self-conscious and competitive performance, which assimilates the satirist to the poets whom he mocks (Henderson 1999: 249–73). In other words, Juvenal deliberately presents himself to the reader as a belated author. Once we begin to entertain the possibility that this is a purposeful strategy rather than simply a reflection of the satirists' urge to demonstrate their learning or reject all other literary discourses, we may better appreciate the complexity and subtlety of their imitative methods. Imitation is Persius' *modus operandi*, but his technique consists of creative interrogation of source texts, rather than simple extraction of useful nuggets (Hooley 1997). A famous passage from Juvenal's bombastic satire on wives sums up the double-sided relationship between satire and its model genres. The poet imagines his reader complaining that his shocking anecdotes smack of Greek tragedy, but points out that his subject is more serious because it is not fiction ("I wish I were making this up," 6.638). While this punch-line deems tragedy inadequate as a model for satire, Juvenal first milks the relationship for all it is worth, even figuring his imitation as a pretentious disguise: "my satire [is] putting on the high tragic boot" (*altum satura sumente coturnum*, 6.634).

Even when satirists do not overtly label their imitations as such, they draw heavily on other literary traditions to portray human experiences and dilemmas. Persius probes the thoughts of people engaged in sacrifice and prayer (the first of the quintessential human activities in Juvenal's list at 1.85–6) in a way that represents routine activities as grand dramas (2.44–51):

> Hoping to pile up wealth by slaughtering an ox, you summon
> Mercury with its liver: "Make my household prosper,
> give me cattle and offspring for my flocks!" How, wretch,
> when so many of your heifers' entrails are melting away in the flames?
> Still he goes on striving for success with organs and
> rich cakes: "now my farm is growing, now the sheepfold grows;
> it's going to come to me, it's happening now!" – until, dejected
>   and hopeless,
> one penny sighs vainly in the bottom of the jar.

This scene resembles a miniature tragedy. As Persius shifts from direct address to the third person, the poem's reader becomes something like a spectator watching a character walk ignorantly into disaster. The theme of unsuccessful sacrifice is typical of tragedy; here, also in tragic fashion, the man's delusion intensifies along with his expenditures (he utters the word *iam*, "now," five times in two lines). Like Agave in Euripides' *Bacchae*, who ecstatically waves her son's severed head in the belief that she has killed a lion, this man's ignorance of his own loss creates dramatic irony.

At the same time, Persius knows how to deflate a tragic mood, as indicated by the comic personification of the lone penny in the final line of the vignette. This move forecasts Persius' overt dismissal of overblown poetic diction, the "lumps of solid poetry" (5.5) that he claims have no value for his own intimate address to Cornutus. There, the satirist describes his technique not as the presentation of essentially grand "lumps," but as "sharp joining" (*iunctura acris*, 14) of words and ideas. This strange phrase, a surprising re-formulation of the "ingenious joining" that Horace admires in a poet (*callida iunctura*, Ars Poetica 47–8), aptly describes Persius' difficult, intricate style, his special contribution to the genre. The resultant shifts in tone are also "sharp": the reader of the passage on sacrifice is carried from the level of plain speech up to the intense mood of tragedy, and then is suddenly denied the clarity of a tragic conclusion when faced with the ridiculous final image.

From Myth to Text

Persius' tag *iunctura acris*, a jarring phrase to describe the jarring use of words, has broader application than its immediate context. The imitative strategies seen throughout Roman satire, its combinations of language and imagery from other genres to treat the stuff of everyday life, are also examples of "sharp joining." Satire performs its most memorable work in its unexpected fusions of images, ideas, and language that do not seem naturally related. The finished picture, the representational tapestry of satire, is marked by seams, gaps, and jolting shifts, which are too numerous and prominent to be easily smoothed over in the reading. Rather, the often difficult process of reading and interpretation that satire invites is part of the genre's work.

The genre's "sharp joinings" also bear witness to the diachronic process of satire's evolution, its navigation of a changing context. They are vestiges of the unacceptable aggression that is tamed and re-styled in the mythic account of mockery. Odysseus manages to dispel the danger posed by Thersites' words by re-directing attention from the target of abuse to the agent, making his style and image objects of mockery. This sacrifice of the original satirist figure to scrutiny and ridicule becomes the sanctioned mode of abuse in the Homeric community. In the subsequent tradition, the satirists perform the roles of Thersites and Odysseus at once. Because words cannot do literal harm or enact immediate change, and because abusive words aimed directly at a target bring risks both to the abuser and to his community, satire finds ways of re-enacting its primordial ferocity on a safer, textual level. The satiric text itself is as much a recipient of "abuse" – here of a metaphorical and verbal nature – as it is a tool for attacking objects in the external world.

The story of satire's evolution has adaptation, loss, and creative parasitism as its dominant themes. Perhaps the extensive and creative cultivation of these themes by the Roman satirists is what gives their genre the look of an unprecedented creation, born from specific historical conditions. In a fundamental sense, all satire is a product of its immediate circumstances. Yet in every context the genre is energized, and its literary achievement inspired, by the memory of a lost potency.

References and Further Reading

Anderson, William S. (1982) *Essays in Roman Satire*. Princeton, NJ: Princeton University Press.

Bellandi, Franco (1980) *Etica diatribica e protesta sociale nelle Satire di Giovenale*. Bologna: Pàtron.

Braund, Susan H. (1988) *Beyond Anger: A Study of Juvenal's Third Book of Satires*. Cambridge: Cambridge University Press.

Elliott, Robert C. (1960) *The Power of Satire: Magic, Ritual, Art*. Princeton, NJ: Princeton University Press.

Freud, Sigmund (1960) *Jokes and their Relation to the Unconscious*, trans. and ed. James Strachey. New York: W. W. Norton.

Freudenburg, Kirk (1993) *The Walking Muse: Horace on the Theory of Satire*. Princeton, NJ: Princeton University Press.

——(2001) *Satires of Rome: Threatening Poses from Lucilius to Juvenal*. Cambridge: Cambridge University Press.

Gowers, Emily (1993) *The Loaded Table: Representations of Food in Roman Literature*. Oxford: Oxford University Press.

Grant, Mary A. (1924) *The Ancient Rhetorical Theories of the Laughable: The Greek Rhetoricians and Cicero*. Madison: University of Wisconsin.

Griffin, Dustin (1994) *Satire: A Critical Reintroduction*. Lexington: University Press of Kentucky.

Henderson, John (1998) *Fighting for Rome: Poets and Caesars, History, and Civil War.* Cambridge: Cambridge University Press.

—— (1999) *Writing down Rome: Satire, Comedy, and Other Offences in Latin Poetry.* Oxford: Oxford University Press.

Hooley, Daniel M. (1997) *The Knotted Thong: Structures of Mimesis in Persius.* Ann Arbor: University of Michigan Press.

Keane, Catherine (2002) The critical contexts of satiric discourse. *Classical and Modern Literature* 22.2, 7–31.

—— (2006) *Figuring Genre in Roman Satire.* Oxford: Oxford University Press.

Kiel, Heinrich (1857) *Grammatici Latini*, vol. I. Leipzig: Teubner (reprinted Hildesheim: Olms, 1962).

Lefkowitz, Mary R. (1981) *The Lives of the Greek Poets.* London: Duckworth.

Lowry, Eddie R. (1991) *Thersites: A Study in Comic Shame.* New York: Garland.

McCarthy, Kathleen (2000) *Slaves, Masters, and the Art of Authority in Plautine Comedy.* Princeton, NJ: Princeton University Press.

Relihan, Joel C. (1993) *Ancient Menippean Satire.* Baltimore, MD: The Johns Hopkins University Press.

Richlin, Amy (1992) *The Garden of Priapus: Sexuality and Aggression in Roman Humor*, rev. edn. New York: Oxford University Press.

Rosen, Ralph M. (1988a) Hipponax, Boupalos, and the conventions of the *psogos*. *Transactions of the American Philological Association* 118, 29–41.

—— (1988b) *Old Comedy and the Iambographic Tradition.* Atlanta: Scholars Press.

—— and Baines, Victoria (2002) "I am whatever you say I am...": satiric program in Juvenal and Eminem. *Classical and Modern Literature* 22.2, 103–27.

Schmitz, Christine (2000) *Das Satirische in Juvenals Satiren.* Berlin: De Gruyter.

Slater, Niall W. (2002) *Spectator Politics: Metatheatre and Performance in Aristophanes.* Philadelphia: University of Pennsylvania Press.

Sweet, David R. (1979) Juvenal's *Satire* 4: poetic uses of indirection. *California Studies in Classical Antiquity* 12, 283–303.

Thalmann, William G. (1988) Thersites: comedy, scapegoats, and heroic ideology in the *Iliad*. *Transactions of the American Philological Association* 118, 1–18.

West, M. (1989) *Iambi et elegi Graeci ante Alexandrum cantati*, vol. I. New York: Oxford University Press.

3
Medieval Satire
Laura Kendrick

The two greatest late-medieval English writers, Geoffrey Chaucer and William Langland, were both superb satirists, even though the tone and technique of their satires could hardly be more different. Neither of these men wrote an entire work that we might call a satire, largely because satire was not a genre for them, but a mode of writing. The satire in Chaucer's *Canterbury Tales* occurs mainly in the "General Prologue" as well as in certain tales, such as the Summoner's and Friar's, and in Langland's *Piers Plowman* the satire occurs mainly in the prologue and the first five sections featuring the personified Meed (Lady Lucre) and her prospective marriage to Falsehood. The most famous passage of satire against preaching friars in the Middle Ages surges up unexpectedly in Jean de Meun's section of the *Roman de la rose* (*Romance of the Rose*) in the self-revealing monologue of False Seeming (Faux Semblant) or hypocrisy personified (Lecoy 1966: 83–114). In short, most medieval satire is episodic and appears within works such as romances, fables, sermons, visions, songs, or other medieval genres. Even works that are almost exclusively devoted to satire go under other generic labels, such as the fourteenth-century French "romance," the *Roman de Fauvel*, an allegorical narrative by Gervais du Bus about how the different ranks of society curry the horse Fauvel, that is, curry favor (Långfors 1919).

Differences between Medieval and Classical Satire

Only in relatively short Latin poems did writers use the term *satire* as a generic label. Walter of Châtillon, a twelfth-century cleric, is something of an exception in calling several of his Latin poems *satires* and citing Juvenal and Horace by name (Strecker 1929: 63, 70, 75, 86). When a medieval Latin writer called his work a satire, he did so to situate it with respect to classical satire, often to distinguish it from irate or anger-provoking satire of the Juvenalian sort: *"Scribo novam satyram, sed sic ne seminet iram"* ("I write a new satire, yet let it not on that account sow anger"). With this phrase,

John of Garland opened his thirteenth-century collection of moral maxims, *Morale scolarium* (Kindermann 1978: 4); half a century later, an anonymous Latin poet repeated this line verbatim to identify his own equally preachy text (Wright 1839: 160). Most medieval works containing satire were and still are known under other labels, and even those explicitly identified as satires by their writers may seem more like sermons to modern readers. Because it does not conform very closely to the models of classical satire, medieval satire can be difficult to recognize.

John Peter has argued that the "vast medieval literature of reproof... commonly included under satire, is much better left distinct" and is more accurately categorized as "complaint" (1956: 3). Peter's definition of satire is classical, based mainly on the models of Horace and Juvenal. The subject matter of satire is the speaker's criticism of immorality or vice in those around him in his society. However, the content alone is not enough to define satire in Peter's view, for its critical manner or technique is essential. The speaker must be personalized; his individual subjectivity foregrounded; and his criticism must focus on particulars, on named individuals and concrete situations described in detail. The person(s) criticized must be different from the speaker's audience (who do not feel targeted themselves). The speaker's tone "tends to be scornful, often reflecting only a token desire for reform" (1956: 10). On these grounds, Peter judges that Chaucer is the sole medieval English writer who can be called a satirist.

As Peter points out, the medieval literature of reproof tends to be impersonal, generalizing, abstract, and often allegorical; it is addressed to an audience that may feel guilty of the behavior being criticized; and its chief purpose is to correct vice, not merely to denounce it. Like most attempts to bring out contrasts, Peter's characterizations of the medieval literature of reproof do not always hold true in specific instances; yet, on the whole, his distinctions between classical satire and medieval are useful, although his conclusion – that satire hardly existed in the Middle Ages – is a minority view.

Medieval satire differs from classical satire, inevitably, to the extent that medieval societies (agrarian and feudal, but increasingly commercial) and their values (Catholic) differed from those of the classical world. Even when a medieval writer sets his Latin poetry squarely within the classical tradition by ending every strophe with an authoritative line quoted from a classical author or satirist, as does the anonymous thirteenth-century author of a poem beginning "*Quam sit lata scelerum et quam longa tela*" ("How wide and how long is the web of crimes"; Wright 1839: 27–38), the satire proceeds from medieval assumptions concerning good Christian behavior; it criticizes different targets or categories of people, in this case the venality of the clergy, from the papal curia down through parish priests, and the rapacity of the laity, from princes and their courts down through lawyers and burghers. The poem ends by combining classical philosophical considerations on moderation with Christian exhortations to "treasure up" charitable actions for the good of one's soul after death. In short, medieval Latin satirists deliberately adapted the classical tradition to their own concerns.

Medieval teachers who have left commentaries on classical satire or on the art of writing poetry stress the corrective intention behind satire's criticism of vices. They choose to understand satire as a fundamentally charitable act motivated by concern for one's neighbor rather than a desire to do him harm. John of Garland in his *Poetria*, for example, contrasts invective, motivated by bad intentions, with reproof or satire (*reprehensio sive satira*) which narrates bad deeds to correct them (Kindermann 1978: 56). From late classical etymologizing associations of satires (Latin *satura*) with the adjective meaning "full" (*satur*), medieval scholars developed the idea of an abundance that involved variety or diversity; this notion is summarized, for example, in Vincent of Beauvais' thirteenth-century *Speculum doctrinale*, where he points out that satire is copious and sates the appetite because it speaks of several different things (Kindermann 1978: 31, 36). The classical satirical medley of themes was turned by medieval satirists into a more deliberately comprehensive criticism covering the vices of the different estates of society in hierarchical order. In the fullest versions, everyone was served, whether cleric or layman, high or low. Medieval poets developed this new, totalizing kind of satire of the vices of society out of their particular understanding of definitions of classical satire. As opposed to the rhetoric teacher and theorist John of Garland, most medieval satirists did not proclaim themselves to be writing "new satire"; they simply did it. It is up to us to perceive their innovations.

Latin Satire of Ecclesiastical Venality and Greed

The obvious place to begin is with the critical themes of medieval satire; that is, the ideals it is based upon and the types of misbehavior it castigates for flouting these ideals. One of the earliest surviving Latin satires, the prose *Tractatus Garciae* (*Little Tract of Garcia*), was written in 1099 or shortly afterwards by a canon of Toledo who had accompanied his archbishop, intent on becoming legate of Aquitaine, to the papal curia in Rome. *Garcia* is probably an assumed name, and the archbishop of Toledo's identity is veiled by substituting the name *Grimoard* for *Bernard*. The inflated account of the archbishhop's "epic" quest for office, in which bribes of gold and silver are euphemistically called relics of the martyred saints Rufinus (ruddy gold) and Albinus (white silver), announces what will turn out to be the main theme of Latin satire for the entire Middle Ages: the greed or avarice of the clergy, and especially of those at the head of the Catholic Church, the pope and his curia, those who are expected to set a virtuous example but, instead, through simony (bribe-taking), corrupt the entire body of Christian society. In passages such as the following homily, which begins in hyperbole ("*O quam preciosi martires Albinus atque Rufinus*") and ends in obvious parody of Christ's teachings (Luke 11: 9–10), the miraculous intercessory powers of Gold and Silver are praised exuberantly:

> O how precious are the martyrs Gold and Silver! How much to be proclaimed! How greatly to be praised! Sinners who possess their relics are perpetually justified, made fit

for heaven from being earthly, turned from impiety to innocence. We have seen, we have seen simoniac bishops, sacrilegious, and dissipators of their churches, come to the pope, cleansed with the apostolic blessing on account of these martyrs' relics, no longer enmeshed in crime, not retaining any of their old blame, return home new and as if reborn... Come, come, simoniac archbishops, bishops, archdeacons, abbots, deacons and priors, offer the Roman pontiff the two martyrs through whom is granted entry into the Roman Church... Ask therefore through Silver, and you shall receive, seek through Gold and you shall find, knock through either martyr and it shall be opened unto you. For everyone that asketh through Silver receiveth, and he that seeketh through Gold findeth, and to him that knocketh through either martyr, it shall be opened. (Thomson 1973: 19–21)

In the mouth of Cardinal Gregory of Pavia, this praise of the power of money to purify sinners and to buy offices for them in the Church can only be understood as highly ironic because it so clearly contradicts the teachings of Christ, even as it parodies the outward forms (the words and syntax) of those teachings.

Criticism of the ecclesiastical elite for insisting on pecuniary penance and for selling what cannot be sold – divine forgiveness, grace, justice, or any decision that was God's to make – is a theme that runs through Latin satire from the beginning to the end of the Middle Ages. The sale of God's grace, figured as the prostitution for money of the "Bride of Christ" (the Church), is the object of Walter of Châtillon's satire in a short poem, full of untranslatable Latin wordplay, beginning "*Licet eger cum egrotis*" ("Let me, though ill among the ill"):

> The clergy's state has fallen so low
> The Bride of Christ is put to sale,
> From generous sunk to general;
> What reverence then can laymen show?
>   Altars are at auction,
>   The eucharist bartered;
>   But grace is useless
>   Bought and sold.
>   (Whicher 1949: 132)

Spiritual, anti-materialistic Christian ideals lie behind such criticism; for example, the idea that only inner change (repentance for sin) can bring divine forgiveness. Secular justice had long depended on pecuniary punishments for crimes or the substitution of money for corporal – even capital – punishment, as is attested by the Old English word *wergild* (literally, "man price"). It was this practice of making amends with money that Langland attacked in *Piers Plowman* through the character of Reason, who argues, against the lawyers Wit and Wisdom, that it is a corruption of secular justice for the wrongdoer to get off by paying, without showing any humility or contrition (Bennett 1972: 34–5; passus 4, lines 113–42). The medieval papacy's extension of this secular practice to the realm of the spirit was criticized as a money-making ploy inspired by avarice. In order to be absolved of his sins, and thus avoid divine punishment in hell for them, the sinner could suffer instead "in his pocketbook" by giving the required sum to an officer of the Church. Likewise, the papacy sold what could not be sold when, in return for money (bribes), it granted benefices (offices in the Church) and favorable judicial decisions in its court of appeals.

John Yunck has argued that Latin satire on the theme of ecclesiastical venality, a common concern in the twelfth and thirteenth centuries, expressed the fear of conservative clergymen in the face of a developing commercial economy based on money payments rather than traditional loyalties and duties (1963: 112–14). The reforming papacy's attempts to increase the powers of the Church required additional revenues beyond its customary feudal and agrarian ones, which it sought to raise by trying to "tax" or require payment for services that had traditionally been "gratuities." The criticism of papal venality stuck, as is demonstrated by the many different versions from the thirteenth century through the Renaissance of a witty collection (*cento*) of Latin sayings imitating the vocabulary and syntax of teachings from the Gospels, a parodic text which came to be known as the "Money Gospel" or "Gospel of Silver Mark" ("*Evangelium secundum marcas argenti*"). The setting of this satire is the papal curia, where the pope instructs his cardinals in a doctrine of avarice (instead of the doctrine of charity preached in the Gospels). The papal version of the Beatitudes (Matthew 5: 3), for example, is a total inversion of Christian ethics: "Blessed are the rich, for they shall be satisfied. Blessed are they that have, for they shall not be empty-handed. Blessed are they that have money, for theirs is the curia of Rome..." (Bayless 1999: 330–1). By blatantly imitating the outward forms of familiar Latin biblical and liturgical texts, but replacing their idealizing spiritual message with a grossly materialistic one, such parody served to point medieval satire.

Satire in Latin on the theme of ecclesiastical venality or greed was written by clerics for clerics, for internal consumption, so to speak, because very few laymen could understand Latin. This helps to explain why mockery of the higher clergy by the lower was tolerated, especially at celebrations of a Saturnalian type such as the Feast of Fools or the Feast of the Ass, when the hierarchy was deliberately turned upside down, so that a canon who called himself *Garcia*, for example, could invent with impunity the most damning praise of his archbishop's physique (voiced through the mouth of a cardinal): "He was fat, oily, refined, rotund, heavy, ponderous, weighty, massive, cyclopean, a giant in body, broad-chested, deep-bellied, fat-buttocked, his eyes set wide apart, with a jutting forehead, a ferocious countenance, commanding of respect, with a good shock of hair and a bull-neck" (Thomson 1973: 39).

Latin satire seems to have arisen in the twelfth century in the scholarly environment of the revived cathedral schools and developing universities (Thomson 1978: 76). Walter of Châtillon, for example, was a teacher in the cathedral school at Laon and then a canon of Reims cathedral before holding office in the chancery of Henry II of England under Thomas Beckett and then returning to France to teach. The composition of satire in Latin verse and prose appears to have been the special province of the lesser clergy: canons or beneficed cathedral clergy, men "frustrated on their way up" (Thomson 1978: 80); and also of wandering clerics with an education but no permanent office whatsoever, marginal men dependent on the charity or hospitality of their superiors. Two of the most famous of these satirical have-nots, who wrote in the self-mocking persona of sinner all too prone to drink and dice, went under the epithets of Primas and Archpoet, names which proclaim their superiority as artists. Most, however, remained anonymous, and their Latin verse was sometimes attributed to "Golias," the generic persona of the wandering cleric who specialized in self-derision as well as derision of ecclesiastical rulers.

One widely appreciated Latin verse satire, if we judge from the relatively large number of 68 surviving manuscript copies, was known as the *Apocalypsis Goliae* (*Apocalypse of Golias*) or the *Apocalypsis Goliae episcopi*, which suggests a festive reversal, with Golias in the temporary role of bishop (Wright 1841: 1–20, 271–92, for a Latin text and two Renaissance English translations). The satire is comprehensive in the new medieval way, for it covers in descending order all ecclesiastical office-holders or secular clergy, from the pope down to priests' vicars, and it ends with a section on the regular clergy (abbots and monks). Furthermore, the *Apocalypse of Golias* moves from classical authorities to biblical ones. The visionary experience of the first-person speaker begins under the guidance of Pythagoras, who shows him various classical authors, but the scene abruptly changes to a parody of Saint John's *Apocalypse*, with an angel as guide and interpreter. The angel discloses the contents of a book with seven seals, one ostentatiously closing each of its seven sections devoted to description of the greedy actions of different officers of the church.

Predatory officials of the secular and regular clergy were often represented figuratively in medieval Latin satire as rapacious beasts, especially wolves (in stark contrast with the biblical ideal of the "Good Shepherd" protecting the Christian flock). The mid-twelfth-century beast epic known as *Ysengrimus* after the name of its chief character, the wolf, is an allegory about the worst sorts of human behavior. The vicious exploits of the predators, chiefly Ysengrimus and his arch-rival Renard the fox, are narrated in numerous episodes and voiced, often by the beasts themselves, in a sententious, rhetorical style, "with endlessly inventive streams of verbiage" that point the contrast between fine words and foul deeds (Mann 1987: 59). Book five of *Ysengrimus* offers highly ironic instances of predatory beasts which look to bishops for instruction in rapacity. After relaxing his grip on the cock in order to taunt his pursuers and defend his honor, Renard launches into a "savage castigat[ion] of his teeth for having foolishly opened," a tirade that offers a new twist on Latin venality satire by praising the predatory expertise of the Bishop of Tournai as an example to be imitated:

You're teeth? You bite a cock? Shall I allow your sort to disgrace my mouth any further? Gaping open, not being clamped shut, relaxing, not gripping, is what you're expert at – now you can gape as much as you want! ... So far you've not been put through the school that teaches biting... What use to me is the nobility that doesn't take away hunger? Money advances wretches, money eclipses a man's grandfathers ... In pursuit of this virtue, Rome is outstripped by Tournai, the city blessed with Bishop Anselm. This good shepherd of Tournai himself shears off the fleeces from sheep and goats alike down to the living flesh. If only he were one of my teeth! He'd give his brothers a lesson in biting. He prowls around the churches as a hungry lion does the sheepfold, leaving only what he can't find ... It's as if he bristles with as many robbers as he has teeth, and he doesn't allow the shorn fleeces to grow again; he gets in first, and would take, if he could, more than he finds – what a pity that he *can't* take more than he finds! He is sorry that he can't alter the limit to taking, and is sure that this is the only thing wrong with plunder ... You should imitate the excellent behaviour of this bishop, who devours like Satan and holds like Hell. (Mann 1987: 425–7)

Later in book five, attracted by Renard's account of the monks' copious diet there, Ysengrimus becomes a monk in the monastery of Blandinium. After a drunken bout in the monks' wine cellar, Ysengrimus justifies his greedy guzzling by arguing that he was merely demonstrating that he has the qualities necessary to be a bishop:

I, hoping to become a high priest of these rituals, am giving an advance demonstration of my zeal: I devour, plunder, swallow. I have accomplished the work of numberless days in a single heroic act, in emptying all the vessels of their gushing wine. Rumour usually travels far and fast once some notable subject-matter has set it going. Therefore I wanted to commit an outstanding deed, desirous of making my greed known at once, so that if any bishop is perhaps to be got rid of because his ravages are too restricted, I might fitly be appointed in his place. (Mann 1987: 473)

Ysengrimus judges that monks elected as bishops make far more thorough and efficient predators than do bishops drawn from the secular clergy, who "don't gulp down everything, but sip in half-mouthfuls," whereas a monk elected bishop will "leave nothing" but "first gobble, then scrape, and finally lick" (Mann 1987: 471–3). Speeches such as these in book five, in which Renard and Ysengrimus specifically compare their own behavior to that of the rulers of the Church, serve to explain the allegory and to remind us that the actions of the different beasts, as they prey upon, trick, or torment one another, have referents in the human world, even if no specific individual is targeted.

Extension of the Themes and Targets of Latin Satire

Nigel Longchamp, also known as Nigel Wireker, a Benedictine monk of the priory of Christchurch, Canterbury, composed in Latin verse, around 1180, another such allegorical beast epic: the quest of Burnel the ass for a longer tail to match his long ears. As Nigel himself explained in an epilogue, Burnel's frustrated ambitions should serve as a *Speculum stultorum* (*Mirror for Fools*) in which his clerical audience might recognize its own foolish penchants mocked and reproved:

Nigel...would have the adventure of Burnel be an example to all, and recommends the reader to ponder the inward rather than the outward significance of the tale, so that he can avoid such dangers in his own case. For there are some who spend nights and days in ambitious projects, the only result of which is sudden and disastrous failure. None can strive against Nature or the lot that is appointed for him. Let Burnel be a witness, who for all his foolish strivings yet in the end remained what he was in the first. (Mozley 1963: 133)

Burnel the ass is a figure for any ambitious cleric who wants to become bishop or abbot. After Burnel loses most of his natural tail to the vicious dogs of Cistercian monks, he decides to seek honors (promotion) through learning – a sort of symbolic tail – and he travels to Paris to join the English nation of scholars, partly for their reputation as liberal spenders on food and drink, but also because of a popular slander that accused all English men (and women) of having hidden tails:

> So with the English would he comrade be,
> And live like them in their own company;
> Which he desires the more for having heard
> In public talk of them a random word;
> Company alters manners, and if so
> Could not their company make something grow?
> Nature to them past nature has been kind,
> Why not to him – in front or else behind?
> (Mozley 1963: 51)

In spite of his years of study, Burnel, a native Italian ass, is unable to learn so much as a word of French. Hence his ambitions turn religious: he decides to found a new religious order by taking the "best" (most comfortable) features from the rules of existing orders – from the Templars their right to fine horses, from the Cistercians their right to go without breeches, and so on – in order to create a supremely "easy" rule of conduct, which may well have inspired a thirteenth-century Anglo-Norman poem known as the "Ordre de Bel-Eyse" ("Order of Fair Ease") that ironically praises monastic luxury in the same way, beginning with the Abbey of Sempringham, where monks and nuns live in close proximity (Wright 1839: 137–48).

The *Speculum stultorum* is a compendium of medieval satirical themes and techniques, a collection enabled by the episodic form of the quest narrative. After deciding to found his new monastic order, Burnel suddenly breaks out into a long lament on the corruption of the rulers of the Christian world: first the papacy and curia, then secular princes, then bishops, finally abbots and priors. The topics and images of this monologue are those of medieval venality satire. The papal curia is described as a gaping maw, which evokes medieval representations of the mouth of hell; bishops are ravening wolves; abbots and priors wallow in the sins of the flesh they have promised to renounce, returning to their sins like dogs to their own vomit. Some of Nigel's most innovative touches occur in his description of the worldliness of bishops: the luxury of the bishop's court and table, with its silver and gold vessels when pewter is used on the altar; the bishop's frequent hunting parties and greater concern for a wounded dog or injured falcon than for the loss of a cleric; and the possession of some bishoprics by mere babies, for whom the benefices have been bought:

> Boys we have seen, who've not yet grown a beard,
> Pastors of churches, even to sees preferred.
> Of such a one, when once a king essayed
> To make him prelate, 'twas in answer said:
> "A prelate? but we cannot yet make out
> Whether 'tis boy or girl; there's still a doubt."
> (Mozley 1963: 94)

Even though Nigel writes in Latin, he includes secular princes in his criticism, calling them robbers, not rulers; he adapts to secular courts familiar themes and techniques from satire of the papal curia's venality. Chief of these is the litany-like celebration of the different ways in which gifts get what the giver wants from the prince and his court (that is, bribes corrupt law and justice):

> Gifts can excite or smooth a monarch's frown,
> Gifts can bring peace and then again bring war,
> ...
> Gifts flout decrees and break established rules
> And tear ancestral rights up from the root.
> Gifts lend a charm to great men's wicked ways,
> And screen ill deeds that they may more abound.
> (Mozley 1963: 88)

The venality of ecclesiastical courts was the target of other Latin satirical litanies listing the exploits of *Nummus* (Money); for example, the many-versioned lyric beginning "*Manus ferens munera / pium facit impium*" (The hand that holds a heavy purse / makes right of wrong, better of worse; Whicher 1949: 146–7). By applying the same technique of ironic celebration to the venality of secular princes and their courts, Nigel's *Speculum stultorum* paves the way for Langland's satire, in *Piers Plowman*, of the effects of Meed on both secular and ecclesiastical justice, and he foreshadows vernacular lyric litanies of the fourteenth and fifteenth centuries that ironically praise the powers of Dan Denier (the French personification of money) and the English Sir Penny (Wright 1841: 357–61):

> Peny is an hardy knyght,
> Peny is mekyl of myght,
> Peny of wrong he makyt ryght
> In every cuntre quer he goo.

> Thow I have a man I-slawe
> & forfetyd the kynges lawe,
> I xal fyndyn a man of lawe
> Wyl takyn myn peny & let me goo.
> (Robbins 1952: 50, first two stanzas)

Partisan Motivations of Satire in Latin and the Vernaculars

Rivalry between the secular clergy and the monastic orders (or regulars) seems to have stimulated much twelfth-century Latin satire. In his *De nugis curialium* (*Courtiers' Trifles*), written in prose while he was a royal clerk serving Henry II, Walter Map took the secular clergy's side and explained how they were being dispossessed by the regulars. For example, knights who had the right to bestow benefices were granting these in perpetuity to the new order of the Hospitallers:

> They increase ever, and we decrease. The livelihood of the altar, given us at first by God, was afterwards continued to us by the patriarchs. We do not succeed to our father's heritage. We may not trade, we can beg. Yet this modesty forbids, reverence avoids... What support, then, is there for us, and whence? The regulars possess almost all altars... (Brooke and Mynors 1983: 71)

The Cistercians had other methods of reducing the number of benefices available to secular clerics: "Because their rule does not allow them to govern parishioners, they proceed to raze villages, they overthrow churches, and turn out parishoners, not scrupling to cast down the altars and level everything before the ploughshare..." (Brooke and Mynors 1983: 93).

Walter emphasizes his satire of Cistercian greed with biblical parody. But instead of citing only the textual travesty (which he attributes to the Cistercians) and expecting his audience to compare this mentally with the biblical original, he makes the comparisons himself by first citing the text of Christ's teachings and then the Cistercian travesty of it:

> Our God is not as their god; our God is the God of Abraham, Isaac and Jacob, and no new god; but indeed theirs is a new one. Our God says: "Whoso leaveth not all things for my sake is not worthy of me." Theirs says: "Whoso gaineth not all things for his own sake, is not worthy of me."...Says ours: "Blessed is he that considereth the poor and needy." Says theirs: "Blessed is he that maketh any poor and needy."...Says ours: "No man can serve God and Mammon." Says theirs: "No man can serve God without Mammon." (Brooke and Mynors 1983: 93)

Like the *Apocalypse of Golias*, which was often attributed to Walter Map, the *De nugis curialium* veers from satirical allegory based on classical models to satire based on the Bible. It begins by explaining the similarities between Henry II's court and the classical hell with its different punishments (Sisyphus and his rock, Ixion and his wheel, and so forth), but it quickly turns to satire of the regular orders that relies on biblical authority. By calling the secular clergy Egyptians (outsiders) and the regular clergy Hebrews (God's chosen people), he keeps up a sort of intermittent allegory that heightens the irony of his critique. Yet in the end he takes care to deny any partisan motivation; his intention is not to denigrate enemies but to correct sinners for their own good: "The Hebrews have already scented out this book, and call me a persecutor of religion. It is faults that I reprove, not a way of life – false professors, not a well-ruled Order" (Brooke and Mynors 1983: 111).

Although time and new contexts have erased the real-life referents of many figurative or generalizing allusions, medieval satire was often partisan and polemical; its criticism was aimed at opponents of the poet's partisan group (or of his patron) not merely to correct their faults, but to denigrate them personally, thus reducing their prestige and power. When satirists began to use the vernacular to attack papal political and fiscal policy, for example, they were using words as instruments of persuasion addressed to a lay audience potentially much broader than the clerical audience of Latin satire. Such is the case, for example, with Walter von der Vogelweide's German lyric beginning "*Ahî wie kristenlîche nû der bâbest lachet*," written in 1213 after the Pope had crusade offering boxes set out:

> Ah, how like a Christian laughs the Pope at last,
> as he tells his Italians, "I've finally got them finessed."
> He never should have thought what he says there to their graces.
> He says, "I've got two Germans under one crown,
> let them wreck their nation and burn it up and bring it down –
> in the meantime we fill up the cases.
> I've driven them like cows to my collection box – all their stuff is mine,
> their German silver rides in my Italian chest.
> Eat chicken, priests, drink wine,
> and let the lay Germans get skinny and fast."
>
> (Goldin 1973: 107)

This self-congratulatory monologue voiced by a triumphantly devious and avaricious Pope is, in effect, a devastating satire of papal policy intended for the ears of the German laymen who suffer from it.

In the medieval Occitan vernacular from the end of the twelfth century through the thirteenth, verse criticism and satire usually took the form of the *sirventes* (which reused the melodies of love songs or *canso* and imitated their metrical and rhyme schemes). Peire Cardenal, a petty noble who lived through the Albigensian Crusade and Inquisition that accompanied the Northern French conquest of the South, wrote a great many *sirventes* satirizing the hypocrisy and avarice of the clergy, especially the preaching friars (who carried out the Inquisition and preached to the populace in the vernacular). The first strophe of one such *sirventes*, written sometime after 1229 against the Jacobins (Dominicans), "*Ab votz d'angel, lengu'esperta, non bleza*," is one long sentence – a syntactical tour de force – praising their polished performances:

> With the voice of an angel, expert tongue not lisping,
> with subtle words, smoother than English cloth,
> well placed, well said, without repetition,
> better listened to, without coughing, than learned,
> with laments, with sobs, showing the way
> of Jesus Christ that each should
> follow, as He was willing to follow it for us,
> they go preaching how we might see God.

If there was any doubt about the ironic intention behind such hyperbolic praise, the next strophe makes the hypocrisy of the preaching friars perfectly clear by completing praise of their fine preaching with praise of their fine cuisine. The Occitan speaker concludes facetiously: "If by fine living, dressing, eating, and sleeping / one wins God, then they may well win Him" (Lavaud 1957: 160; my translation). The troubadour is an advocate of the old secular culture of the South against the new one encouraged by the Pope and the French monarchy, who founded and supported the friars to preach to the people and control their faith in their own language.

The Parisian poet who called himself *Rutebeuf* (a rustic-sounding persona) satirized the monastic orders, especially the preaching friars, and King Louis IX for blindly supporting them and letting them control the kingdom to the detriment of his traditional noble allies and of others (including poets like himself) who depended on the king's patronage. In an allegorical poem entitled "*Renart le bestourné*" ("Renard in Reverse"), Rutebeuf parodied the beast epic of Renard the Fox (the *Roman de Renard*, a vernacular continuation of the Latin *Ysengrimus*) in order to mock Louis IX's new custom of eating in private, thus reducing expenses on food and entertainment. Rutebeuf presents Noble the lion (Louis IX) as a naïve dupe, who "believes his salvation depends on Renart" (the friars). So that the king will know what is being said about him "throughout the town," Rutebeuf claims to report the conversation of two village women, who judge that the kingdom is going to the dogs, so to speak: "Sir Noble separates himself / from the animals, / who cannot stick their heads / into his house / on festive occasions or holidays, / for no other reason / but that he fears rising / costs." The ignoble advisors with whom the king surrounds himself are responsible for the institution of such vile customs: "They don't like noise or disorder / or loud talking. / When Sir Noble eats, / everyone leaves the pasture. / No one remains. / Soon we won't even know where he's staying" (Zink 1989: 254–8; my translation).

In his partisan verse, Rutebeuf draws upon the entire repertoire of Latin venality satire criticizing the religious orders and the papacy, and he adds some contemporary twists. For example, in the context of a crusade exhortation, he criticizes the mendicants' ambitious building programs financed by legacies gained from abuse of their inquisitorial powers (that is, from taking bribes to protect heretics and usurers):

> What has become of the money
> the Jacobins and Minorite friars
> received as legacies

> from heretics they certified to be faithful Christians
> and from hoary old usurers
> who died suddenly
> and also from clerics?
> They have tons of it;
> God's army could have been supported by it.
> But they use it otherwise,
> for their great building projects,
> while God remains naked overseas.
>
> (Zink 1989: 362; my translation)

As well as including the Beguines in poems entirely devoted to satire of the different religious orders ("*Les ordres de Paris*" and "*La chanson des ordres*"), Rutebeuf devotes to this feminine order favored by Louis IX a two-strophe lyric, the very brevity of which contributes to its satirical point:

> Whatever a Beguine may say,
> take it for the best.
> All is religious
> that one sees in her life.
> Her speech is prophetic;
> if she smiles, it's to be sociable;
> if she weeps, it's out of devotion;
> if she sleeps, she's in religious ecstasy;
> if she dreams, it's a vision;
> if she lies, don't believe her.

After considering how Beguines change their vocation to marry, Rutebeuf concludes the second and final strophe with tongue in cheek, "Never say anything but good of them: otherwise the king won't tolerate it" (Zink 1989: 240; my translation). Rutebeuf's satire of the Beguines prefigures Chaucer's technique of ironic praise in his description of the Prioress and of other pilgrims in *The Canterbury Tales*. It is as if Chaucer had taken to heart Rutebeuf's advice never to say anything bad about a woman in religious orders, but to put a Christian interpretation on worldly behavior. Thus, for example, Chaucer attributes to "charity," "conscience," and "tender-heartedness" the Prioress's tears over the whipping of one of her pet dogs, fed on roasted meat, milk, and fine white bread (Benson 1987: 25–6, lines 118–62).

Vernacular Estates Satire

Rutebeuf, like Chaucer, may have found the example for such ironic praise in the work of one of the earliest vernacular estates satirists, the Recluse of Molliens, as he called himself, author of the *Roman de Carité* (*Romance of Charity*), a late twelfth-century allegorical quest for Charity. Although the virtue he seeks is nowhere to be found, the Recluse professes to admire the new rules monks have invented so as not to interfere with their practice of courtesy:

> I don't reprove them in the least
> for their suave courtesy.
> They have established very pretty rules,
> these new Benedicts and Augustines.
> One of the new rules is worth nine of the old.
> (Van Hamel 1974: 78)

Nor was Rutebeuf the first to extend satire of the vices of society beyond the ecclesiastical orders and secular princes to the lower orders of the laity ("*De l'estat du monde*," Zink 1989: 78–87). Vernacular satire of the estates grew ever more comprehensive and analytic from its first appearance in the last quarter of the twelfth century in the *Livre des manières* (*Book of Behaviors*) of Etienne de Fougères, Bishop of Rennes and former chaplain to Henry II, who treated the clergy as part of a more comprehensive scheme: the king, the clergy, knights, peasants, burghers, and women.

One of the best and most thorough of these estates satires is an anonymous English poem from the early fourteenth century, beginning "Whii werre and wrake in londe and manslauht is i-come" (Wright 1839: 323–45). The first-person speaker attributes the evil times (famine, disease, and war) to the avarice and pride of all orders of society, the clergy first (papal curia, archbishops, and bishops, parsons, abbots, and priors, the four orders of friars, officials and deans, physicians) and then the laity (earls, barons, knights, squires, justices, sheriffs, mayors, bailiffs, beadles, attorneys, merchants, craftsmen). Vivid descriptive sketches present vice in action: for example, the physician (perhaps a friar) examining the urine of a sick man, deceiving the man's wife about the gravity of his case to extract money for noxious medicines, and ordering a delicious French menu (capon and beef roast) for himself, of which the hungry sick man gets only the broth:

> And yit ther is another craft that toucheth the clergie,
> That ben thise false fisiciens that helpen men to die;
> He wole wagge his urine in a vessel of glaz,
> And swereth that he is sekere than evere yit he was, and sein,
> "Dame, for faute of helpe, thin housebond is neih slain."
>
> ...
>
> He doth the wif sethe a chapoun and piece beof,
> Ne tit the gode man noht therof, be him nevere so leof;
> The best he piketh up himself, and maketh his mawe tought;
> And geveth the gode man soupe, the lene broth that nis noht for seke;
> That so serveth eny man, Godes curs in his cheke!
> (Wright 1839: 333–4)

We are not far here from the satirical details of Chaucer's "Summoner's Tale," wherein a friar comes to inquire about the husband's health (medical advice and legacy-hunting go together) and orders himself a fine dinner at the sick man's expense, all the while hypocritically professing to be satisfied with very little:

> "Now, dame," quod he, "now *je vous dy sanz doute*,
> Have I nat of a capon but the lyvere,
> And of youre softe breed nat but a shyvere,
> And after that a rosted pigges heed –
> But that I nolde no beest for me were deed –
> Thanne hadde I with yow hoomly suffisaunce.
> I am a man of litel sustenaunce,
> My spirit hath his fostrying in the Bible.
> The body is ay so redy and penyble
> To wake, that my stomak is destroyed."
> (Benson 1987: 130–1, lines 1838–47)

In this estates satire, description of the physician's deceit produces a lively sketch, one in a long series. Chaucer, on the other hand, motivates the plot of his satirical *fabliau* by using similar details to show the friar's hypocrisy and greed, which will lead him to grope for a hidden purse under the sick man's buttocks and receive a fart in the face.

Although he organized his "General Prologue" to *The Canterbury Tales* according to the general principle of estates satire (with each estate now represented by an individual pilgrim), he left out the clerical and secular elites (whose participation in a pilgrimage and story-telling contest with common folk would be unbelievable), and he did not respect the usual division between clergy and laity or the hierarchy within each order. Langland, likewise, in the several versions of estates satire that occur in the course of *Piers Plowman,* tended to mix clergy and laity and to treat the different estates and occupations in different and more random order than was conventional. In his opening description of fourteenth-century society and its flaws, he works from the bottom up, beginning with plowmen and ending with the papal curia and the king (Bennett 1972: 1–4). Later, when Conscience refuses to marry Meed because she has corrupted so many estates and occupational groups, he lists these helter-skelter, beginning with wives and widows (who "learn lechery" to obtain gifts), the king's father (Edward II, who was "felled" through false promises), popes ("poisoned" by bribery), monks, minstrels, lepers, jurors, summoners, sheriffs, and others (Bennett 1972: 24–5; passus 3, lines 119–68).

Whereas medieval estates satire deliberately avoided individualizing criticism, Chaucer returned to the classical technique of satirizing representative individuals, albeit fictive ones. Langland also personified and individualized the estates or occupations prone to certain vices, but only the lowest occupations and to a far lesser extent than Chaucer. For example, in *Piers Plowman* the confession and acting out of the deadly sin of Gluttony occurs in the tavern, where Glutton has much company: Cesse the shoemaker, Watte the warren keeper, Hikke the coachman, Hugh the needle pedlar, Clarice of Cokkeslane (a prostitute), Dawe the ditchdigger, and others (Bennett 1972: 46–8; passus 5, lines 304–41). All these individuals, whose names identify them with their occupational groups, are implicated in the sin of gluttony.

More often than was customary in estates satire, Chaucer relied on ironic praise to express criticism. He even went so far as to break conventions by sincerely praising some pilgrims: the Knight, the Parson, and the Plowman. These entirely positive portraits may provide a standard against which to judge other behaviors. Chaucer's contemporary, John Gower, in his sermonizing *Mirour de l'Omme* (*Mirror of Mankind*), explicitly contrasted good behavior with bad for each estate (Wilson 1992). In his revised version of estates satire, Chaucer intermingled the truly praiseworthy examples of three pilgrims (representing the three orders of those who fight, pray, and work) with many more dubiously praiseworthy ones. For instance, Chaucer approves the Summoner, whose job is to summon people to ecclesiastical court for their sins, for his goodness in overlooking misconduct for small bribes:

> A bettre felawe sholde men noght fynde.
> He wolde suffre for a quart of wyn
> A good felawe to have his concubyn
> A twelf month, and excuse hym atte fulle.
> (Benson 1987: 53, lines 648–51)

In the allegory of Langland's *Piers Plowman*, summoners are clearly denigrated as "vice-ridden" when they are saddled like horses to carry Simony to court; by their bribe-taking, they support Simony, not God (Bennett 1972: 18; passus 2, line 169). When Chaucer praises a pilgrim character for the very actions and attitudes that are usually the targets of criticism for his estate or profession, it is not difficult to perceive the irony.

Jill Mann has argued that Chaucer's originality as a satirist is to show us the pilgrims from their own point of view (through the narrative technique today called internal focalization) and thus to complicate or circumvent moral judgment of them (Mann 1973: 20, 27). But if there is no moral judgment, there is no satire. We have seen in earlier medieval satire many examples of smug self-revelation of misconduct when vice is dramatized and personified vices or vice-ridden characters speak. The most famous of these is the monologue of False Seeming in the *Romance of the Rose*, which Chaucer imitates in the prologues of his self-revealing Pardoner and Wife of Bath, who congratulate themselves on their vices: avarice, in the case of the Pardoner, and, in the case of the Wife, all the flaws traditionally attributed to women in antimatrimonial satire (meant, from Saint Jerome on, to dissuade Christian clerics from marrying). Even though they praise themselves for their successful ploys, we do not miss the irony of the Pardoner's preaching against avarice to rake in greater donations for himself or the irony of the dominating Wife's brow-beating of her husbands by accusing them with, and citing extensively, their own antimatrimonial sayings and readings from a "book of wikked wyves" (Benson 1987: 114; l. 685).

If Chaucer's technique of letting these pilgrims speak for themselves does not necessarily lead us to withhold moral judgment on them, neither does his use of internal focalization in the "General Prologue" portraits. It is hard to agree with the praise or approval of Chaucer's narrator when it seems to reflect the pilgrim character's self-congratulation or self-justification for misconduct conventionally associated with his estate or profession, as is the case, for example, with the worldly Monk who refuses the cloistered life of prayer, study, and manual labor:

> And I seyde his opinion was good.
> What sholde he studie and make hymselven wood,
> Upon a book in cloystre alwey to poure,
> Or swynken with his handes, and laboure,
> As Austyn bit? How shal the world be served?
> Lat Austyn have his swynk to him reserved!
> (Benson 1987: 26, lines 183–8)

Compared to the heavily exaggerated satirical praise of the worldly ecclesiastic in the *Little Tract of Garcia* (quoted above, "He was fat, oily, refined..."), Chaucer is delicate in praising the Monk for being a "manly man, to been an abbot able" and for being so fat that his skin shines:

> His heed was balled, that shoon as any glas,
> And eek his face, as he hadde been enoynt.
> He was a lord ful fat and in good poynt.
> (Benson 1987: 26, lines 198–200)

Yet every detail evokes a vice, even the fat monk's oily shine. If the Archbishop of Toledo's oiliness suggests his readiness to "grease palms" (give bribes), so might Chaucer's monk's – either to give them (for attaining higher office) or to take them (in his role as "outrider" or supervisor of monastic interests in the community). Chaucer's smiling satire is the tip of the iceberg of the medieval satirical tradition. To understand and appreciate his subtle ironies, one needs to know that often ponderous tradition.

References and Further Reading

Bayless, Martha (1999) *Parody in the Middle Ages: The Latin Tradition*. Ann Arbor: University of Michigan Press.

Bennett, J. A. W. (ed.) (1972) *Piers Plowman: The Prologue and Passus I–VII of the B Text* [by William Langland]. Oxford: Clarendon.

Benson, Larry D. (ed.) (1987) *The Riverside Chaucer*, 3rd edn. Boston: Houghton Mifflin.

Brooke, C. N. L. and Mynors, R. A. B. (eds) (1983) *De nugis curialium / Courtiers' Trifles* [by Walter Map], trans. M. R. James, rev. edn. Oxford: Clarendon (first published 1914).

Goldin, Frederick (trans.) (1973) *German and Italian Lyrics of the Middle Ages: Original Texts, with Translations and Introductions*. New York: Anchor.

Kendrick, Laura (1983) Medieval satire. In W. T. H. Jackson and George Stade (eds), *European Writers: The Middle Ages and the Renaissance*, pp. 337–75. New York: Scribner's Sons.

Kindermann, Udo (1978) *Satyra: Die Theorie der Satire im Mittellateinischen. Vorstudie zu einer Gattungsgeschichte* [*Satyra: The Medieval Latin Theory of Satire. Preliminary Study for the History of a Genre*]. Nuremberg: Hans Carl.

Långfors, Arthur (ed.) (1919) *Le Roman de Fauvel* [by Gervais du Bus]. Paris: Firmin-Didot.

Lavaud, René (ed.) (1957) *Poésies complètes du troubadour Peire Cardenal (1180–1278)*. Toulouse: Privat.

Lecoy, Félix (ed.) (1966) *Le Roman de la rose* [by Jean de Meun], vol. 2. Paris: Champion.

Mann, Jill (1973) *Chaucer and Medieval Estates Satire: The Literature of Social Classes and the General Prologue to The Canterbury Tales*. Cambridge: Cambridge University Press.

—— (1987) *Ysengrimus: Text with Translation, Commentary and Introduction*. Leiden: Brill.

Mozley, J. H. (trans.) (1963) *A Mirror for Fools: The Book of Burnel the Ass* [by Nigel Longchamp]. Notre Dame: University of Notre Dame Press.

Peter, John (1956) *Complaint and Satire in Early English Literature*. Oxford: Clarendon Press.

Robbins, Rossell Hope (ed.) (1952) *Secular Lyrics of the 14th and 15th Centuries*. Oxford. Clarendon Press.

Strecker, Karl (ed.) (1929) *Moralische-satirische Gedichte Walters von Châtillon* [*Moral-satirical Poems of Walter of Châtillon*]. Heidelberg: Carl Winter.

Thomson, Rodney M. (ed. and trans.) (1973) *Tractatus Garciae* [*Little Tract of Garcia*]. Textus Minores 46. Leiden: Brill.

—— (1978) The origins of Latin satire in twelfth-century Europe. *Mittellateinisches Jahrbuch* 13, 73–83.

Van Hamel, A. G. (ed.) (1974) *Li Romans de Carité ... du Renclus de Moiliens* [*The Romance of Charity ... by the Recluse of Molliens*]. Geneva: Slatkine (first published 1885).

Whicher, George F. (ed. and trans.) (1949) *The Goliard Poets: Medieval Latin Songs and Satires*. New York: New Directions.

Wilson, William Burton (trans.) (1992) *Mirour de l'Omme* [*The Mirror of Mankind* by John Gower]. East Lansing: Colleagues Press.

Wright, Thomas (ed. and trans.) (1839) *Political Songs of England from the Reign of John to that of Edward II*. London: Camden Society. (Reprinted with introduction by Peter Coss. Cambridge: Cambridge University Press, 1996.)

—— (1841) *The Latin Poems Commonly Attributed to Walter Mapes*. London: Camden Society.

Yunck, John A. (1963) *The Lineage of Lady Meed: The Development of Medieval Venality Satire*. Notre Dame: University of Notre Dame Press.

Zink, Michel (ed.) (1989) *Rutebeuf: Oeuvres complètes*, vol. 1. Paris: Bordas.

4
Rabelais and French Renaissance Satire
Edwin M. Duval

The early French Renaissance witnessed a great flowering of satirical writing in which traditional comic mechanisms of farce, fabliau, and mock Arthurian epic were combined with newly rediscovered modes of classical irony to produce some of the most brilliant and influential works of prose satire in Western literature. The undisputed master and model of this new kind of satirical literature was François Rabelais (1483?–1553), a Franciscan and Benedictine monk, who left the orders to become a doctor of medicine and an accomplished scholar of Greek medicine, Roman law, the Greek New Testament, and classical literature. Rabelais' works, collectively known as *Gargantua and Pantagruel*, combine the most exquisite classical learning and the most indecorous popular humor, the ideals of pre-Reformation evangelism and the disreputable pranks of rascals, "high sacraments and horrific mysteries concerning our religion as well as political and domestic government" (*Gargantua* prologue) expressed in what Mikhail Bakhtin euphemistically referred to as the "language of the marketplace."

A Renaissance of Menippean Satire

To appreciate the originality and importance of Rabelais' satire, it is essential to consider the intellectual climate in which it originated. During the reign of Francis I (1515–47), a cataclysmic culture war broke out in France as a new generation of scholars, inspired by Italian and northern humanists and devoted to the study of classical and biblical antiquity, challenged the institutions of medieval learning based on the authority of tradition and syllogistic logic. King Francis himself entered the fray in 1530 by sponsoring, over the strenuous objections of the reactionary University of Paris, independent professors of classical Latin, Greek, and Hebrew, the "three languages" of humanism that afford direct access to the original sources of Western culture, uncontaminated by the "gothic" corruptions of the Middle Ages.

This "Renaissance," as it is known today, contributed to the transformation of European satirical writing in two related ways: it found an irresistible new object of satire in the medieval ideologies and institutions it opposed, and it discovered powerful new techniques and forms of satire in the classical literature it promoted. Among the many works rediscovered and widely disseminated as a result of the return to cultural origins were the satirical dialogues and essays of the second-century Greek writer Lucian of Samosata, the philosophical dialogues of Plato, and the Greek New Testament. From these works a new generation of writers learned the lost art of irony – the falsely naïve and subtly mocking questions of Plato's Socrates and of Lucian's Menippus, the parodic antics and insolent quips of the cynic philosopher Diogenes, and the paradoxical sayings and sly evasions of Jesus (for example, Matthew 22: 15–22 and John 8: 2–11) – as well as some new ironic forms of satire. One of these is the *paradoxical encomium*, which subjects a banal or baneful object (for example, baldness or the plague) to ironic hyperbolic praise. Another is something we might call the *discrediting representative*, which allows an ideology or institution to be undermined from within by one of its own proponents, either as a willing witness who testifies to the crimes of his own brethren or, more ironically, as an unworthy spokesman who unwittingly reveals through his own speech the defects of the point of view he defends. Through a combination of these techniques, a spokesman could be made, ironically and very effectively, to condemn both himself and the very things he admires through his own comical illogic and paradoxical praise.

All of these techniques were exploited during the second decade of the sixteenth century in highly influential Latin works by northern humanists. The best known of these are Erasmus' *Praise of Folly* (1511), a virtuoso piece of demonstrative rhetoric in which the allegorical figure of Folly praises herself as the greatest boon to humankind and indirectly condemns various beliefs and practices by claiming them as her own inventions; Thomas More's *Utopia* (1516), in which the narrator Raphael Hythlodaeus ("nonsense-peddler") describes in admiring detail the society of an anti-Europe called "Nowhere," indirectly indicting the political and economic institutions of England and France; and Ulrich von Hutten's *Epistles of Obscure Men* (1517), a fictional exchange of letters attributed to living enemies of humanism, written in comically wretched Latin and revealing the vanity and stupidity of their presumed authors.

In French vernacular literature, meanwhile, the traditional forms of popular satire we usually associate with the late Middle Ages not only survived but flourished well into the second half of the century. Chief among these were morality plays, in which allegorical figures, representing everything from human vices and social classes to religious practices and royal policies, played out a satirical struggle between good and bad; carnival plays, in which a war between *Charnage* (meat-eating) and *Carême* (Lent) ended in an equitable division of the liturgical calendar between fat days and lean days; farces, in which individual transgressions against societal norms of behavior were ridiculed and punished; and the more recent *sotties*, or fools' plays, in which political and religious polemics were waged behind the mask of universal folly. A particularly noteworthy example of the latter is Pierre Gringore's famous *Jeu du Prince des Sots et la Mère Sotte* (1513), a piece of Mardi Gras royal propaganda that defends the interests of the French king Louis XII (the "Prince of Fools") against the growing temporal power of the Holy Roman Catholic Church (the "Foolish Mother" or "Mother Fool") under Pope Julius II.

The genius of Rabelais was to fuse the erudite humanist satire of an Erasmus with the popular medieval satire of a Gringore to produce vernacular works of extraordinary comic effect and polemical force. The satire of these works can be said to be "Menippean" in the loose, non-technical sense that it is generically hybrid and stylistically mixed, combining the incompatible registers and genres of high and low culture in fantastical comic fictions and freewheeling, antinormative, even subversive criticism. (For a good general characterization of Menippean satire, see Relihan 1993: 34–6.) More specifically, Rabelais' satire can be said to be Lucianic in its bemused but profound skepticism regarding all metaphysical speculation, including theology. But unlike classical Menippean or even Lucianic satire, Rabelais' work – and Renaissance satire generally – is almost never neutral, detached, or cynical. On the contrary, it tends to be highly *engagé*, ideological, and even idealistic, arising from a firm commitment to positive values contrary to the negative values it mocks. Its objects are not character types or social mores, but ideologies, institutions, and practices antithetical to those of the humanist avant-garde: the antiquated curriculum and teaching methods of the medieval university; scholastic theology as it was practiced by the reactionary Sorbonne; monasticism, pilgrimages, and the cult of saints; an unjust legal system based on medieval glosses to Roman law; the secular power of the papacy based on canon law; the scourges of imperialistic war and tyranny; and behind all of these, the arrogance of power, privilege, and wealth.

Satire in the Works of Rabelais

Rabelais' literary career may usefully be divided into two distinct periods: the early Lyonese period illustrated by *Pantagruel* (1532) and its more elaborate "prequel" *Gargantua* (1534?), and the late Parisian period illustrated by two sequels to *Pantagruel*: *Le Tiers livre de Pantagruel* (*Third Book*, 1546) and *Le Quart livre de Pantagruel* (*Fourth Book*, 1548 and 1552). The two books of the early period are small popular chapbooks printed in gothic type, published under the anagrammatic pseudonym "Alcofribas Nasier" and intended for sale at the international commercial fairs of Lyon. Their plots are strictly parallel, each narrating with truculent verve the miraculous birth, uncouth childhood, civilizing education, and military triumph of a popular giant hero. Both heroes are recalled from their studies abroad to defend their fathers' realm against an invasion by a neighboring king. The two books of the late period were published in Paris under Rabelais' own name and printed in humanistic Roman type. Clearly intended for a more elite audience, they are more complex in structure, elevated in tone, and erudite in their cultural references. The *Third Book* narrates the fruitless attempts of Pantagruel's companion Panurge to make up his mind whether or not to marry, while the *Fourth* narrates a sea voyage in search of an imaginary "Temple of the Holy Bottle," which Panurge foolishly believes will provide the definitive answer he vainly seeks. Rather than burlesque heroic narratives inspired by late medieval epics, these later books are open-ended quests inspired by Plato's *Apology of Socrates*, and by the *Odyssey* and Lucian's *True Story*. A *Fifth Book of Pantagruel*, published in 1564, some eleven years after Rabelais' death, completes the voyage of the *Fourth*, but is almost certainly a spurious concoction of abandoned drafts by Rabelais and later interpolations by other hands.

In all four books the basic narrative structure serves as a framework for more or less discrete episodes of satire. The object and nature of this satire, however, shifts noticeably from book to book. In the first two, late medieval literary form and popular culture are adopted as vehicles for anti-medieval, pro-humanistic satire. In the last two, a more humanistic form and network of cultural references are adopted as vehicles for a satire of ideological obstinacy and intransigence that humanism has proved powerless to correct.

The Early Works

Rabelais' first work in the vernacular, *Pantagruel*, is the most schematic in its satire of medieval institutions and in its corresponding promotion of Renaissance humanism as the remedy to all the ills of the world. A frequent device of this satire is the simple juxtaposition of opposites, in which the negative representation of something bad is followed by the favorable representation of a positive counterpart. The chapters devoted to Pantagruel's education (chs 6–8) are a good example of this device. The young hero begins his studies at each of the ten universities of France, only to be discouraged by the incompetence, squalor, boredom, and sloth he finds there. The desultory narrative of his tour of universities is complemented by a long and disorderly catalog of books in one of the most famous scholastic libraries of Europe: books bearing parodic titles such as "*Ars honeste petandi in societate* [*The Art of Farting Decently in Public*], per M. Ortuinum" and "Beda, *De optimitate triparum* [*On the Excellence of Tripe*]," Ortuinus and Beda being real-life adversaries of Erasmus. These disjointed satirical chapters representing the futility and inanity of medieval learning are immediately followed by a beautifully composed, eloquent letter in which the hero's father evokes a marvelous rebirth of learning and exhorts his son to master all the newly revived languages of antiquity and the newly restored disciplines of humanistic studies (ch. 8). In form and style as well as in content, the letter stands in stark contrast to the preceding chapters, thus focusing the satire of medieval learning and anchoring it in an opposing, positive ideal. That the positive term trumps the negative is shown unambiguously two chapters later when Pantagruel, having now mastered the entire humanistic curriculum outlined by his father, utterly confounds the representatives of the medieval university in a public defense of 9,764 theses in all disciplines, and uses his knowledge of Roman law and classical moral philosophy to arrive at a miraculously equitable judgment in a legal dispute so complex (and so comically incomprehensible) that it has driven the greatest legal scholars of the old school to despair (chs 10–14).

Another common satirical device in *Pantagruel* is comic inversion. After condemning imperialistic wars and the abuse of power in the person of the usurping king Anarche ("without legitimate authority to rule"), the narrative takes us to Hades to witness the punishment of Anarche's predecessors in crime – famous epic heroes, roman emperors, kings, and popes – all of whom are forced to practice abject menial occupations, while the poor and dispossessed of this world (beggars and philosophers) lord it over them (ch. 30). The episode is inspired directly by Lucian's satirical dialogue *Menippus*, but differs from its model in one significant respect: Lucian's uniform leveling of all estates has here become a systematic inversion of high and low estates. In this way, Rabelais transforms the disillusioned cynicism of true Menippean satire into a comically optimistic representation of the kingdom of heaven as defined by Jesus himself, in which "the last will be first, and the first last" (Matthew 20: 16) and in which "every one who exalts himself will be humbled, and he who humbles himself will be exalted" (Luke 14: 11 and 18: 14). The satire of contemporary European wars of aggression is thus grounded in the suggestion that imperialism is the polar opposite of the reign of Christ.

A similar function is performed throughout *Pantagruel* by the most ambiguous character of the work, Pantagruel's epic companion Panurge ("crafty, cunning, knavish"), a prankster with the experience and wiles of Odysseus and the scatological rascality of Tyl Eulenspiegel. Panurge's role is to humiliate all who exalt themselves above their fellow human beings: a haughty, gorgeously dressed lady whom he publicly reduces to the state of a bitch in heat with the aid of a pack of rutting dogs; an arrogant English alchemist and astrologer, Thaumaste ("marvel"), whose pretensions to arcane and forbidden knowledge he confounds and ridicules with obscene gestures in a mock-serious debate by signs; and the defeated King Anarche, whom he transforms into a street peddler and marries to an old whore. In all such unsavory pranks, Panurge is the agent of a universally debunking satire that complements the more refined and focused satire of the humanist hero Pantagruel. It is important to note, however, that the satirical debunking of social, intellectual, and political pretension by Panurge does not come into conflict with the promotion of vast humanistic learning by Pantagruel. On the contrary, it helps to highlight the role of humanism as the agent of universal peace and justice. This is particularly evident in the crucial distinction Rabelais draws between curious investigations into things that transcend natural human ken, which he presents as a sacrilege and a sin (punished by Panurge in the person of Thaumaste), and an encyclopedic knowledge of all things human, which he presents as a gift of God (incarnate in the person of Pantagruel). Rabelais' Lucianic skepticism regarding all forms of metaphysics, from astrology to scholastic theology, is very far removed from a Menippean subversion of all values and ideologies. It is an integral part of a coherent satirical defense of classical and Christian humanism against its multifarious adversaries.

Gargantua, published a mere two years after *Pantagruel*, is in some ways an elaborate rewriting of the earlier work, but which greatly increases the force and focus of its satire. Anti-scholastic satire is far more developed here, and more narrowly directed against the reactionary Faculty of Theology at the University of Paris (the Sorbonne). The attack begins with the familiar technique of juxtaposed opposites. The young hero is instructed for more than fifty-five years by two successive "doctors in theology," using outmoded manuals of grammar and dialectic. At the end of this scholastic marathon, Gargantua has learned nothing more than to recite the alphabet backwards (ch. 14). By contrast, a twelve-year-old page named Eudemon ("fortunate"), who has been instructed by humanists, is able to extemporize an eloquent Ciceronian oration in praise of the doltish Gargantua, who bursts into tears for shame (ch. 15). A similar juxtaposition shows that under the old regime of his scholastic preceptors, Gargantua would waste his entire day sleeping, eating, drinking, playing idle games, reciting canonical hours, and attending Mass (chs 21–2), while under the new regime of his humanist preceptor Ponocrates ("force of hard work"), he makes use of every waking minute in a disciplined regimen of study, observation, discussion, diet, exercise, spontaneous prayer, and Bible readings (chs 23–4).

The most effective technique for anti-scholastic satire in *Gargantua*, however, is the discrediting representative. When Gargantua removes the great bells of the cathedral of Notre Dame to use them as ornaments for his enormous horse, the Faculty of Theology dispatches its most distinguished senior theologian to persuade the hero to return the property of the Church. As its finest representative it chooses Janotus de Bragmardo, a comic caricature of squalor, selfishness, vanity, and self-blind stupidity. In an incoherent concatenation of absurd arguments, parodic syllogisms ("*Omnis clocha clochabilis, in clocherio clochando, clochans clochative...*"), and misapplied, self-incriminating biblical quotations, punctuated by inelegant throat clearings ("*Hen, hasch, ehasch, grenhenhasch!*") and patches of wretchedly incorrect Latin ("*Ego occidi unum porcum, et ego habet bon vino*"), Janotus brilliantly but unwittingly exposes the ignorance and incompetence of the most powerful institution of medieval learning (chs 18–20).

Political satire, which was merely suggested in *Pantagruel* through the one-dimensional King Anarche, is elaborated at great length in *Gargantua* through the fully developed character of Picrochole, whose name ("bitter bile") defines him in medico-psychological terms as being of choleric or bilious temperament. On the pretext of a petty squabble among peasants, Picrochole flies into a towering rage and launches a full-scale military assault against the kingdom of his peaceful neighbor, King Grandgousier. As his undisciplined armies destroy and pillage everything in their path, Picrochole and his counselors concoct (in an episode inspired by Lucian's dialogue *The Ship*) a delusional plan for the conquest of the entire world (ch. 33). The satire of these chapters is clearly directed against Renaissance aspirations to universal empire, and against the Holy Roman Emperor Charles V in particular. Through the familiar technique of juxtaposed opposites, the good king

Grandgousier is presented in point-for-point opposition to Picrochole. He reacts to news of his neighbor's depredations with humble evangelical prayers to God, diplomatic protestations of friendship to Picrochole, and even exorbitant reparations for any harm he may unwittingly have done. This stark contrast between a mad, bellicose tyrant and a pious, pacifist Christian prince is systematically elaborated throughout the second half of the work. But in a novel twist, this opposition is not resolved in favor of its positive term. Picrochole's alienation from God and reason is so absolute that even Grandgousier's comically exaggerated attempts at pacification fail. The mordant satire of imperialists and tyrants is thus no longer complemented by the simple triumph of an ideal Christian prince, but by a gentler counter-satire of the idealistic Erasmian notion that pure evil can be overcome by pure goodness alone. Here we see the first signs in Rabelais of what will become an increasingly complex and nuanced satirical vision of the world.

An important new target of satire in *Gargantua* is monasticism. Dissolute and hypocritical monks had been frequent butts of medieval satire, and Rabelais continues this tradition by representing monasteries as havens of ignorance, drunkenness, and debauchery. But it is the institution of monasticism itself that Rabelais attacks with special vigor, representing the sixth sacrament of the medieval Church as the very antithesis of Christianity as instituted by Jesus and Paul. The anti-monastic satire of *Gargantua* begins in chapter 27 with the sudden and unexpected entrance of the most colorful character of the book, Friar John. As Picrochole's marauding soldiers attack and pillage the Abbey of Seuilly, the terrified and stammering monks attempt to defend their vineyards (and thus their precious wine) with comically ineffectual liturgical prayers and processions. In direct opposition to these "typical" monks, Friar John instantly springs into action, cursing, threatening, and single-handedly massacring the enemy using only his frock as armor and the staff of a processional cross as his weapon. The implications of this opposition are spelled out explicitly several chapters later when Gargantua and his companions praise Friar John for his active heroism and condemn the other monks for living a life of useless idleness. Gargantua goes so far as to assert that the whole world shuns monks because they "eat the shit of the world, that is its sins." To Grandgousier's orthodox objection that monks "pray for us," Gargantua replies that in mechanically reciting canonical hours at the sound of a bell without understanding the meaning of the words they utter, monks do not pray to God but mock him. Friar John is good precisely because he is the polar opposite of all other monks.

But Friar John is more complex than this simple opposition would suggest. On the one hand, he appears to be an anti-monk, an extreme practitioner of the active, rather than the contemplative life. By his own account (chs 39–41), he is never idle: even during prayers he keeps himself busy making crossbow strings and bolts and fashioning traps to hunt rabbits. On the other hand, he loves wine, women, and dirty jokes just as much as the next monk; he knows his breviary inside out and is a prodigiously rapid reciter of masses and hours; he is proud of his total ignorance of classical languages and humanistic learning; and he insists that his monastic frock is endowed with magical powers that protect him against harm and augment his sexual potency. Both an anti-monk and a super-monk, Friar John is a profoundly ambiguous figure. And yet he is embraced without reserve by Gargantua and his companions. He is in fact the most engaging character of the book. This, together with the fact that Friar John eventually emerges as the true hero of the Picrocholine war, suggests that while monasticism is an unredeemable evil in *Gargantua*, humanism is not the only redeeming good. Joy, hilarity, and human companionship are the true positive counterparts to the various evils satirized in *Gargantua*. Humanistic learning and pious evangelism, while positive values, are no longer sufficient or even necessary means to that end.

The subtlest form of anti-monastic satire in *Gargantua* is contained in a comic inversion in the final episode of the book. Here Gargantua founds a new monastic order at Thelema which is antithetical to all existing orders: no walls will segregate monks from the world; no bells will call them to mandatory prayers throughout the day; no dress code will require a religious habit; no dietary code will forbid certain foods on certain days; the sexes will not be segregated; and so on. In short, this is to be a perfect anti-monastery in which the Benedictine Rule is turned completely on its head: in place of chastity, the freedom to marry; in place of poverty, wealth; in place of obedience, the freedom to live however one pleases. The fundamental principle of absolute freedom is enshrined in the very name of the abbey (*thelema* being Greek for "what you will" or "as you like it") and in a single rule, which is in fact a non-rule: *"fay ce que vouldras"* ("do as you will").

The logic behind this satirical inversion of monasticism, like that of Hades in *Pantagruel*, is evangelical. Erasmus, following Saint Paul, had defined Christianity in terms of love and freedom: as a liberation from the Law of the Old Testament (because the single commandment of love fulfills the entire Law) and from the myriad regulations of Judaism (because circumcision, dietary and vestimentary restrictions, ritual acts, and prayers no longer count for anything following the redemption of humanity through Christ's sacrifice). Seen from this perspective, monasticism appears to be the very antithesis of Christianity: a return to pre-Christian servitude under the Law. The anti-monasticism of Thelema is thus the antithesis of an antithesis: a true Christian community arrived at indirectly, and ironically, through the utopian inversion of a profoundly anti-Christian institution. This explains why the absolute freedom of Thelema results not in anarchy, Hobbesian individualism, or orgiastic licentiousness, but in a decorous and paradoxically conformist society. Freed from the servitude of laws and constraints, the Thelemites spontaneously wish to do whatever pleases their fellows. Unlike monks, they live in true Christian love and harmony.

Yet another dimension to this complex anti-monastic satire may be seen in the fact that the buildings of Thelema are described in terms that recall the chateaux of the Loire valley, while the dress, activities, and general comportment of the Thelemites are those of idealized courtiers at the court of Francis I. In this way, Rabelais' satire suggests that the opposite of monasticism is not only an ideal Christian community, but an ideal royal court like the very one the king himself was then fashioning for himself. Subtly but unmistakably, Rabelais' satire maneuvers the King of France into his own corner in his battle against the dark forces of medieval reaction.

The Late Works

The *Third Book of Pantagruel* is by far the most learned and the least satirical of all Rabelais' books. The focus here is no longer on ideologies and institutions, but on Panurge's egotistical quest for domestic security – that is, the benefits of marriage without the danger of being cuckolded, beaten, and robbed by his future wife. Although Panurge's paralysis of the will is shown in an entirely negative light, there appears to be no particular satirical intention behind his fruitless quest, except to the extent that his inability to act on his wishes is linked to a new superstitious reverence for monasticism and other forms of Catholic orthodoxy, for which he is duly ridiculed. The trickster of *Pantagruel* has here become the victim of his own mystifications, and the principal object of Rabelais' anti-monastic satire.

At the same time, Panurge's quest serves as the vehicle for discrete episodes satirizing unreasonable claims to knowledge, especially arcane knowledge of the kind condemned in *Pantagruel*. Pantagruel, now a perfect Socratic ironist, pretends to share Panurge's curiosity and to lead him on a quest for an answer that he knows cannot be found except in the quester himself. The quest includes recourse to various popular methods of divination (Virgilian lots, dreams, and so on), all of which demonstrate in comic fashion that the future can never be known. This anti-gnostic satire is most vigorous in Panurge's consultation with Her Trippa, an expert in all forms of "scientific" prognostication (astrology, chiromancy, geomancy), whose name recalls the historical magus Cornelius Agrippa of Nettesheim. Her Trippa claims to know all past and future events, including Panurge's future cuckoldry, but is ignorant of the single fact that concerns him most – namely, that he himself is a notorious cuckold whose wife's promiscuity is known to all but him. Her Trippa thus embodies the absurdity of curious inquisitions into things above and beyond human ken, as opposed to an earth-bound, Socratic knowledge of one's self and one's own affairs.

Panurge also consults representatives of the legitimate professions: theology (Hippothadée), medicine (Rondibilis), law (Bridoye), and philosophy (Trouillogan). These vivid characters are treated with varying degrees of sympathy and amused detachment, some satirically. Trouillogan, for example, is a Pyrrhonian skeptic so noncommittal that he avoids answering even the most straightforward questions of fact. Judge Bridoye is a learned fool who can quote all of civil and canon law by heart but misunderstands and misapplies every law he quotes, interpreting each with a myopic comic literalism. Rather than a systematic satire of the professions, these episodes offer a more general critique of self-satisfied expertise. The point seems to be that learning and knowledge are something entirely different from wisdom and self-knowledge, and that no external authority, no matter how legitimate, can sanction a personal decision whose consequences affect no one but the one who must decide.

Whereas the ostentatiously popular *Pantagruel* presented humanist learning as the sole means to a new age of peace and justice, the ostentatiously learned *Third Book* suggests that learning is neither necessary nor even very helpful in the pursuit of personal happiness.

With the *Fourth Book* Rabelais returned to the purely political and religious satire of the first two books, but developed a new resource for his satire with the systematic use of allegory. Here an open-ended sea voyage, modeled on Lucian's burlesque *True History*, takes Pantagruel and his companions to a series of allegorical islands and adventures at sea, each representing one of the extreme ideological forces at work in mid-century Europe. Written as the Council of Trent was hammering out precise formulations of Christian doctrine, thus hardening the opposition between Catholic orthodoxy and various reformed heterodoxies and preparing the way for the armed conflict of the Wars of Religion, the *Fourth Book* offers a sustained and bitter attack against doctrinal intransigence of all kinds, and against Rome and the papacy in particular.

The attack begins with the Council of Trent itself, as an encounter with a ship of monks en route to the "Council of Chesil" ("fool" or "idiot" in Hebrew) to "scrutinize the articles of faith against the new heretics" (ch. 18) coincides with a violent sea storm in which the Pantagruelians nearly perish. This obviously allegorical storm (inspired in part by Erasmus' dialogue, *The Shipwreck*) in turn provides the occasion for a biting satire of Catholic superstitions: a terrified Panurge makes insincere vows to the Virgin and all the saints, while begging Friar John to hear his confession and administer extreme unction (two of the sacraments maintained by the Council of Trent but rejected by all reformed churches). Friar John, meanwhile, true to his role as the anti-monk of Seuilly, curses and swears by all the devils, berates Panurge for his idleness, and relies exclusively on his own heroic efforts to save the ship. Pantagruel, representing an evangelical golden mean between superstition and incredulity, faith and works, places his salvation in God's hands with an evangelical prayer while at the same time holding the ship's mast in place (chs 18–24).

The fierce antagonism between Catholics and Protestants, now made irreconcilable by the intervention of the Council of Trent, is represented in degraded form through an ingenious elaboration of the traditional Mardi Gras battle between Lent and meat-eating (chs 29–32 and 35–42). "Quaresmeprenant" (Lent, or Ash Wednesday) is a grotesque monster and a humorless killjoy "abounding in pardons, indulgences, and solemn masses" – which is to say, "a good Catholic and of great piety" (ch. 29). The "Andouilles" (sausages, which are of course forbidden during Lent), worshipers of a flying, multi-colored, mustard-dispensing pig that is the "Idea of Mardi Gras," are treacherous firebrands who attack Pantagruel as an enemy because they do not immediately recognize him as a friend. The identification of "*saulcisses*" (sausages) as the "*Souisses*" (Swiss), and an allusion to a standoff between Charles V and Swiss Calvinists, suggest that these Andouilles, "fuller of shit than of gall," are Protestants. In the harsh satire of Rabelais' last book, ridicule has lost its optimistic good humor, and the juxtaposition of opposites no longer serves to promote a positive value by ridiculing its negative counterpart: both sides of an unbridgeable confessional divide are irredeemably condemned as hellish creatures of a nightmare.

Because unchecked power remained in the hands of the Church, however, the harshest treatment is reserved for Rome. In a more realistic pairing of antagonistic islands, the Popefigs, once merry mockers of the Pope, are now a defeated and humiliated people forced to perform Catholic rites in their own devastated land (ch. 45). Their triumphant enemies, the Papimaniacs, on the other hand, are satirized at great length as idolaters who worship the Pope instead of God or Christ, referring to him as "the One Who Is" and "God on earth," and awaiting his arrival as that of "the Messiah, so long awaited by the Jews" (chs 48–54). But the real target of this satire is the temporal power of the Pope, authorized by the later books of canon law known as the Decretals. The case against the Decretals is made in part through a brilliant combination of the discrediting representative and the paradoxical encomium: the Papimaniacs' bishop, Homenaz (Big Oaf), delivers an ecstatic, bibulous harangue, extolling the miraculous powers of the "holy Decretals," which displace the Bible as God's divine revelation to man, a gift from heaven like the "law given to the Jews by Moses, written by the very fingers of God." On this sacred book depend the salvation of all souls and a return to a Golden Age of universal peace and brotherly love – except, of course, for "heretics," whom the pope-god is authorized to destroy in body and soul by means of war, torture, and excommunication. Pantagruel and his companions contribute to the irony of this paradoxical encomium with testimonials of their own about counter-miracles: from bodily ailments, including hemorrhoids, caused by physical contact with the pages of the Decretals, to the occult power of the Decretals to draw immense quantities of gold from France to Rome – an obvious critique of ecclesiastical taxes and indulgences by which the papacy filled its own coffers, thus allowing the Pope to subsidize the forces of reaction (monasteries and scholastic universities) and to wage war against legitimate Christian princes.

A final piece of anti-Catholic satire is contained in the episode of Messere Gaster, or Master Belly (chs 57–62), in which materialistic idolaters literally "worship the belly as their god" (Philippians 3: 19 and Romans 16: 17–18). These worshipers consist of two groups – Engastrimyths (ventriloquists) and Gastrolaters (idolaters of the belly) – in whom we easily recognize Catholic priests and monks, and in whose sacrifices we easily see a grotesque parody of the Catholic mass (chs 58–60). Here, as elsewhere in the *Fourth Book*, Rabelais adopts the gratuitous Alice-in-Wonderland zaniness of Lucian's *True History* as the vehicle for a focused polemic against the formalism and materialism of the Catholic Eucharist, as opposed to the purely spiritual communion favored by Erasmian evangelical Christianity.

The posthumous *Fifth Book*, though of doubtful authorship, contains a few satirical episodes worthy of Rabelais. The *Ile Sonante* (Ringing Island), for example, continues the indictment of monasticism by describing a hierarchized clergy of caged birds whose sole purpose in life is to sing whenever the island's ubiquitous and deafening bells sound. And the episode of the *Chats-fourrez* (Furred Cats) extends the satire of a corrupt and venal legal system begun in the *Fourth Book* with the episode of the

Chicqanous (Chicaners, chs 12–16). The question of authorship aside, the publication of this continuation in 1564 indicates that Rabelais' particular brand of Menippean, Lucianic satire retained its power well beyond Rabelais' own lifetime.

A Renaissance of Verse Satire

In order to understand the evolution of French satire after Rabelais, we must turn to another front in the culture wars engendered by Renaissance humanism, and to a completely different tradition of ancient satire. In the late 1540s a second generation of Renaissance poets known as the "Pléiade," inspired by the literary works of antiquity recently rediscovered by humanist scholars, undertook a radical transformation of French literature based on a return to the lost traditions of Greek and Latin poetry. Their program, spelled out by Joachim Du Bellay (1522–60) in his *Défense et illustration de la langue française* (1549), called for a wholesale rejection of the traditional genres and forms of medieval French literature and the creation of a completely new kind of poetry, modeled directly on classical exemplars like the odes of Pindar and Horace and the elegies of Ovid, Tibullus, and Propertius. Among the genres recommended for imitation and transposition into French was verse satire, that characteristically Roman invention perfected by Horace, Persius, and Juvenal.

Du Bellay and his collaborators correctly viewed Roman satire as something entirely distinct in both form and content from the Greek satirical tradition represented by Lucian and adapted to French by Rabelais. Rather than a literary *mode* appropriate to many different kinds of prose writing (mock heroic narratives, monologues, dialogues, and so on), it is a poetic *genre* in its own right. Its targets, moreover, are not political and religious ideologies and institutions, but social mores, personal habits, and character types. A satire (as opposed to satirical writing) was defined by Du Bellay and others, following Martial (*Epigrams* 10.33.9–10), as a moral poem that castigates individual vices and foibles, while sparing the individuals themselves ("*parcere personis, dicere de vitiis*").

In practice, Renaissance verse satires could be decorous and urbane in the manner of Horace or harsh and acerbic in the manner of Juvenal, and could easily slip into scurrilous *ad hominem* attacks in the manner of the epigrammatists Catullus and Martial. A frequent object of this new kind of satire was the ugly, vicious old woman. Though a staple of medieval literature from Jean de Meun's *Roman de la rose* to François Villon's *Testament*, the theme survived and flourished in the humanistic poetry of the Renaissance thanks to obscene invectives against sexually insatiable and repellent hags in Horace (*Epodes* 8 and 12) and against old procuresses in Ovid (*Amores* 1.8) and Propertius (*Elegies* 4.5). An even more common object of French satire of this Roman type was the affected, over-refined manners and hypocritical behavior attributed to Italians and to courtiers. This theme also had a long history in France, but took on a new life with the rising influence of Castiglione's *Corteggiano* (1528) and

Machiavelli's *Il Principe* (1532), and with the increasing power of the Florentine Catherine de Medici as Queen (1547–59) and Regent (1559–89) of France. Underlying this abundant anti-Italian and "anti-aulic" literature is a constant moral preoccupation with the difference between being (*être*) and appearing (*paraître*) – that is, between authenticity and artifice or hypocrisy.

Du Bellay himself was the first and greatest writer of French satires of the Roman type, producing discursive poems that would serve as models well into the seventeenth century – portraits of old procuresses from "*L'Antérotique de la vieille et de la jeune amye*" (1549) to "*La vieille courtisanne*" (1558) and portraits of the ignorant courtier such as the famous "*Poète courtisan*" (1559). Du Bellay's most sustained and original experiment in Roman satire is to be found in a sonnet sequence, *Les Regrets* (1558), which evokes the poet's changing circumstances and emotional states during a four-year stay in Rome. The satiric aspect of this work is revealed in the second sonnet of the sequence through clear textual echoes of satires by Horace and Persius, and of Horace's remarks on satire in the *Ars poetica*. Even more explicit is sonnet 62, where Du Bellay invokes Horace and quotes Persius to define his own work as a satire. Sonnets 63–127 are indeed concise satires of a vast range of Roman types and customs, from pedants to pederasts, from supercilious courtiers to over-priced courtesans, from the scheming intrigues of the Roman curia to the excesses of Roman carnival, culminating in a series of scurrilous libels against Popes Julius III, Marcel II, and Paul IV. Sonnets 128–38 offer satirical vignettes of the cities through which the poet travels on his way home to France, and sonnets 139–51 assail the ignorance of French courtiers who understand nothing of serious poetry like Du Bellay's.

Other members of the Pléiade followed Du Bellay in writing occasional verse satires, but the genre was in fact too humble and too topical to be of great interest to poets whose ambition was to promote French as a language of high culture by creating timeless works of literature. Only in the less ambitious period following the Wars of Religion did verse satire become a favored genre in France, especially among so-called "libertine" poets of the early seventeenth century. In 1608, Mathurin Régnier published the first single-volume collection of verse satires under the generic title *Satires*, thus setting a precedent that would be followed in the neo-classical age by Nicolas Boileau.

New Directions in Late Renaissance Satire

During the Wars of Religion (1562–98), the separate traditions of Greek (Menippean) and Roman (verse) satire, revived by Rabelais and Du Bellay respectively, were modified and frequently combined in novel ways to serve the various agendas of this contentious and violent period of French history. The merging of traditions is observable not only in form and style but also in content as well, as Protestant polemics against the Roman Church added a political and ideological dimension to the purely moral satire against Italians and courtiers.

An example of this development is the *Deux dialogues du nouveau langage français italianisé* (1578) by the Protestant printer and lexicographer Henri Estienne (1531–98). This work takes the form of a Lucianic dialogue (and is in fact modeled in its opening pages on Lucian's *Charon*) but develops a traditional theme of verse satire (and alludes directly to Horace and Juvenal) by satirizing the affectation of Italian expressions and fashions at the notoriously mannered and effeminate court of King Henry III. The conversation between Philausone, an occasionally ridiculous representative of the offending practice, and Celtophile, an innocent purist who has just returned from a long absence and is astounded to learn from his interlocutor how French courtiers now speak, dress, and behave, allows for occasional caricatures and ironies in the best tradition of Menippean satire. A richer example of the same tendency is the *Aventures du baron Faeneste* (1617–30) by the militant Protestant Agrippa d'Aubigné (1552–1630). This set of four prose dialogues opposes a sincere French nobleman Enay ("To Be") and an absurd would-be courtier Faeneste ("To Appear") whose swaggering bravado and obsession with courtly manners is constantly undercut by Enay's ironic observations and by his own poverty, cowardice, and ridiculous provincial accent. D'Aubigné gave an even more polemical edge to this satire in the second book of his historical epic, *Les Tragiques* (begun in 1577, first published in 1616), which represents the French court under Catherine de Medici as a Sodom and Gomorrah of androgyny and perversion from which Truth has been banished by fear and flattery, and which portrays Catherine's three sons (Charles IX, Henry III, and Francis of Alençon) as incarnations of moral and sexual depravity. A similar view of the court is offered in Artus Thomas' *L'Ile des Hermaphrodites* (1605), a falsely naïve description of the customs and laws of a morally and sexually degenerate anti-Utopia.

Even more common in this period was a more overtly ideological strain of satire produced by partisans of all factions in the Wars of Religion: Catholics, Huguenots, and "Politiques" (moderate Catholic defenders of the French monarchy against the extremist agendas and foreign alliances of the two other factions). In addition to the thousands of pamphlets, libels, and pasquinades collected by Pierre de L'Estoile in his *Journals* (1574–1611), the wars produced some highly original experiments in literary satire. Henri Estienne's *Apologie pour Hérodote* (1566) is a long treatise whose ostensible purpose is to defend the integrity of the Greek historian Herodotus by demonstrating that the famously implausible beliefs and practices he reports are in fact less absurd or scandalous than modern beliefs and practices, which we have seen with our own eyes. The entire argument is a pretext for documenting at great length, through pungent anecdotes and proverbs, the crimes and sins of the Catholic clergy (lecherousness, drunkenness, larceny, murder) and the manifold errors of Catholic doctrine, including the sale of indulgences and the primitive practice of "theophagy" (the Catholic Eucharist). Although the themes are Rabelais', Rabelaisian humor and inventiveness are entirely absent from this sober and dour work.

Another example is d'Aubigné's *Confession du sieur de Sancy* (written 1597–1617), a treatise-apologia written in the name of an actual convert to Catholicism, which suggests an intimate connection between politically motivated conversions and the most contested articles of Catholic doctrine, and condemns both by means of arguments that prove the opposite of what they appear to intend. But the best-known and most successful satire of this kind is the *Satyre Ménippée* (1594), a collective work published anonymously by a group of "Politiques" to ridicule and discredit the meeting of the Estates General assembled in Paris in 1593 by the ultra-Catholic League for the purpose of electing a Catholic king to displace the legitimate but Protestant successor to the throne, Henri de Navarre (Henry IV). Under the guise of a report to good Catholics concerning the proceedings of the Estates, the work skewers the agenda and the motives of the League through devastating caricatures. Following a fantastical chapter on "Spanish Catholicon," a miraculous panacea hawked in the streets of Paris by two foreign-born "charlatans" of the League, the *Satyre* presents a series of self-incriminating and mutually incriminating "harangues" in which the principal players of the assembly reveal their cynicism and hypocrisy, their ruthless indifference to the suffering of loyal Frenchmen, and their treasonous allegiance to Philip II of Spain. Throughout the work we recognize the characteristic techniques of Menippean satire perfected by Rabelais, including the paradoxical encomium and the discrediting representative. The best of the "haranguers" are in fact worthy successors to Rabelais' Janotus de Bragmardo and Homenaz, and the entire work is a worthy successor to *Gargantua* and the *Fourth Book*. In true Rabelaisian fashion, the last harangue by a "Politique" provides a positive counterpart to all the satirical harangues that precede it: a powerful, completely un-ironic indictment of the crimes of the League and a stirring defense of Henri de Navarre's virtue and legitimacy.

The Renaissance tradition of religious satire survived into the seventeenth century in Blaise Pascal's anti-Jesuit *Provinciales* (1657), while Rabelais' distinctive influence can still be felt in Cyrano de Bergerac's dangerously subversive and atheistic *L'autre monde, ou voyage dans la lune* (written in the 1640s and published posthumously in 1657). But the fertile Renaissance age of satire may be said to end in the age of absolutism, not only with the canonization of verse satire as a neoclassical genre in Boileau's *Satires* (1666), but also with the emergence of three entirely new genres in which the satirical mode found a natural place: the realist comic novel inaugurated by Charles Sorel's *Histoire comique de Francion* (1623), the comedies of Molière, and the lapidary writing of fabulists and moralists like La Fontaine, La Rochefoucauld, and La Bruyère.

References and Further Reading

Bailbé, Jacques (1964) Le thème de la vieille femme dans la poésie satirique du XVIe et du début du XVIIe siècles. *Bibliothèque d'Humanisme et Renaissance* 26, 98–119.

Bakhtin, Mikhail (1968) *Rabelais and his World*, trans. Hélène Iswolsky. Bloomington, IN: Indiana University Press.

Blanchard, Scott W. (1995) *Scholars' Bedlam: Menippean Satire in the Renaissance*. Lewisburg: Bucknell University Press.

Colie, Rosalie L. (1966) *Paradoxia Epidemica: The Renaissance Tradition of Paradox*. Princeton, NJ: Princeton University Press.

De Smet, Ingrid A. R. (1996) *Menippean Satire and the Republic of Letters, 1581–1655*. Travaux du Grand Siècle 2. Geneva: Droz.

Marsh, David (1998) *Lucian among the Latins: Humor and Humanism in the Early Renaissance*. Ann Arbor: University of Michigan Press.

Mayer, C-A. (1984) *Lucien de Samosate et la Renaissance française*. La Renaissance Française 3. Geneva: Slatkine.

Relihan, Joel C. (1993) *Ancient Menippean Satire*. Baltimore, MD: The Johns Hopkins University Press.

Salmon, J. H. M. (1987) French satire in the late sixteenth century. In *Renaissance and Revolt: Essays in the Intellectual and Social History of Early Modern France*, pp. 73–97. Cambridge: Cambridge University Press.

Screech, Michael Andrew (1979) *Rabelais*. Ithaca, NY: Cornell University Press.

Smith, Pauline M. (1966) *The Anti-courtier Trend in Sixteenth-century French Literature*. THR 84. Geneva: Droz.

Tomarkan, Annette H. (1990) *The Smile of Truth: The French Satirical Eulogy and its Antecedents*. Princeton, NJ: Princeton University Press.

5
Satire of the Spanish Golden Age
Alberta Gatti

In the sixteenth and the seventeenth centuries, spanning the Renaissance and Baroque periods, Spanish writers produced an unparalleled quantity and quality of literature. From the popular to the learned, lyric, pastoral, epic, religious, and satiric poetry flourished with works by Garcilaso de la Vega (1501?–36), Fray Luis de León (1527–91), San Juan de la Cruz (1542–91), Luis de Góngora (1561–1627), Lope de Vega (1562–1635), and Francisco de Quevedo (1580–1645). The art of playwriting was renewed by Lope de Vega, who, in the spirit of the new age, created the national theater. Calderón de la Barca (1600–80), author of the philosophical comedy *La vida es sueño* (Life is a Dream), followed. Prose evolved from the early work of Ricardo de Rojas, *La Celestina* (1499), which contained the seeds of a layered fiction, to the creation of the picaresque novel, with the publication of *Lazarillo de Tormes* (1554) – and culminated with what is considered the first modern novel, Cervantes' masterpiece *Don Quijote de la Mancha* (the first part was published in 1605 and the second in 1615).

Language, literature, and empire had begun to evolve in synchronism. In 1492, the humanist Antonio de Nebrija (1444–1522) presented his grammar of Castilian to Queen Isabella, which was the first grammatical compilation of a modern European language. The queen inquired about its usefulness, and the Bishop of Ávila, representing Nebrija, responded with "language is the perfect instrument of empire" (*"siempre la lengua fue compañera del imperio"*). The Castilian language was about to rise to the occasion, paralleling with its vitality that of the Catholic monarchs. And, even later, as the Spanish empire began its decline, the Castilian language would continue to mature in the hands of superb writers.

Throughout the period, known as the Golden Age, satiric elements were frequently present in otherwise non-satirical works. Authors tended to combine parody, humor, and the depiction of the low and creatural with direct criticism of particular targets. At the same time, most major writers, especially during the seventeenth century, wrote satiric works of outstanding quality under a broad conception of satire, from moralistic works to the invective, considered negatively but practiced nonetheless, and ranging through a form of satire that relied heavily on humor and integrated many of the oxymoronic elements of the Menippea. For our purposes here, although it could equally be differentiated by its stylistic qualities or by its diverse satiric topics, satiric production in the Golden Age may be placed into three groups following a chronological division: the first group coincides with the apogee of the Spanish empire during the first half of the sixteenth century and the Spanish Renaissance; the second with the time of transition between centuries and artistic movements; and the third with the Baroque period, a time of crisis for Spanish society.

The Early Sixteenth Century and the Spanish Renaissance

Ferdinand of Aragón and Isabella of Castile set in motion an aggressive campaign to consolidate power and expand their territory by conquering Granada, and ending eight centuries of Arabic presence in the peninsula, and by financing Columbus' voyages. This expansion would be furthered through carefully calibrated matrimonial arrangements, resulting in a Spanish king, Charles V, in control of a vast empire conceived as both territorial and spiritual. Following Ferdinand and Isabella's religious plan as protectors of Catholicism, which included the creation of the Holy Tribunal of the Inquisition (1478) and the expulsion of the Jews (1492) and the Muslims (1502), Charles V became the political head of Christianity and was crowned Holy Roman Emperor in 1519.

Between 1527 and 1532, the works of Erasmus (1466–1536) were widely read and discussed in Spain. Earlier in this period, various policies of religious reform had established a climate favorable for Erasmus, and interest in his works would be sustained by the imperial court of Charles V (1515–56), which was populated with ardent followers of the Rotterdam scholar. The aspects of Erasmus' doctrine that attracted Spaniards were both religious and political. Erasmus' conception of essential Christianity, his criticism of the emphasis on heavy ceremonial elements, and his preaching of the indiscriminate love of Christ appealed to many Spaniards who were descendants of *conversos* (converted Jews and Muslims) and as such were treated as "secondhand Christians." At the same time, the main political topic of the sixteenth century was religion, and Charles V's court used Erasmus' ideas to formulate the notion of an empire that was the tool for Christian spiritual unity.

The interest in Erasmus' works coincided with the rediscovery of the Syrian Lucian of Samosata (second century AD). Spanish readers of the sixteenth century regarded Lucian as a moral philosopher, and several of his texts were used for educational purposes. This serious view of Lucian, however, did not prevent writers from imitating his more playful Menippean style in both satires and non-satiric texts – employing a style characterized by a combination of realistic and even naturalistic elements with fantastic ones, a particular perspectivism, experimentation with different mental states, the mixing of various literary forms (verse, prose, and dialogue), and diverse stylistic tones. Some of these elements, one could argue, were already present in medieval literature, but it is the combination of all of them that gave texts that oxymoronic quality so characteristic of the Menippea. Thus, the combined influence of Erasmus and Lucian can be seen in a number of dialogues with satiric elements – *Diálogo de las cosas ocurridas en Roma* (The Sack of Rome, 1527) by Alfonso de Valdés, *La lozana andaluza* (Portrait of Lozana, 1528) by Francisco Delicado, and *Viaje de Turquía* (Voyage to Turkey, 1553), attributed to Cristóbal de Villalón – and in two full-fledged satiric dialogues – *Diálogo de Mercurio y Carón* (Dialogue of Mercury and Charon, 1528?) by Alfonso de Valdés and *El Crótalon* (Castanets, 1553), attributed to Cristóbal de Villalón.

In a Christian spin on the mythological world, the *Diálogo de Mercurio y Carón* situates the two main characters, Mercury and Charon, at the entrances of both Hell and Paradise, where they interview the souls in passing while discussing the politics of the day. Charon is desolate. The wars in Europe have brought so many souls for him to transport that he has invested all he had in a scow. Recently, though, he has heard that peace has been signed in Spain and, with that, his bankruptcy declared. Mercury, however, brings good news: the kings of France and England have challenged the emperor and conflict is certain to arise again. Mercury's historical speech is clear-cut political propaganda in defense of Charles V's imperial policies, and Charon listens while sustaining the story's humorous vein by becoming entangled in the contradiction between his personal interest (war) and the serious objectives of the political propaganda (supposedly peace). This political exposition is interrupted by souls asking for passage to the world of the dead. Most of these souls are condemned, having been accused of hypocrisy, superstition, and the practice of empty rites. Some of the souls took this wrong way of life quite by ignorance, as, for instance, the chancellor to a "very powerful king" who has been taught that by following all the formal requirements of his religion (baptism, confirmation, observation of official church holidays, pilgrimages, and so on) his soul would be saved. But most of the condemned souls are well aware that they have lived a dual life, not acting as true Christians and building a façade of Christian rituals.

Although the political propaganda in Valdés's *Diálogo de Mercurio y Carón* defends imperial policies, the dialogue with the souls becomes a satirical text in taking aim at all kinds of authority, specifically that of the Church. To counterbalance such a display of sinners, later in the book the doctrine of the good Christian is clearly presented in long responses from the souls who go to Heaven. But in a subtle move, Valdés will not let go of his deep criticism. While the presence of the good Christians unnerves Charon ("If many more like this one arise among Christians, they can whip me for a vagabond"; Valdés 1986: 158), Mercury is quick to assure him that for each good Christian, there are many more souls that are lost.

The other satirical dialogue of the period, *El Crótalon*, presents a more subtle doctrinal influence of Erasmus and a more evident influence of Lucian. Some passages have a great similitude with Lucianic texts, which is often recognized by the author. One morning, the Cock speaks to his master, the poor shoemaker Miçilo. After recovering from the shock of a talking animal, Miçilo listens to the Cock's stories of his past lives. Its soul has transmigrated for centuries, incarnating in sublime and low characters: "Before I became a cock, I was transformed into a wide range of animals and people among which I have been a frog, a low but popular man, and a king" (*"Primero que viniesse a ser gallo fue transformado en otras diversidades de animales y gentes, entre las cuales he sido rana, y hombre bajo popular y rey"*; my translation). The subject of persuasion, so central to satire itself, is discussed often by the two interlocutors, since the Cock is obliged to give a convincing spin to his unlikely transformations. Our feathered storyteller tells realistic stories alongside fantastic ones, causing Miçilo to react with awe and mistrust but piquing his desire to hear more.

El Crótalon lampoons classical satirical targets, such as the vices of gluttony, homosexuality, and vagrancy; religious figures (Erasmus' views resound here, as well as criticism of church officials present in medieval Spanish literature); a variety of occupations – theologians, philosophers, and soldiers; the Inquisition, war, and, of course, women. Only friendship is treated in a positive way. Political discussion, so central to Valdés' *Diálogo*, is present only once in a very ambiguous praising of Charles V. The satire is wrapped up by a final negative view of humanity delivered by Miçilo's neighbor, Demophón, at the closing of the dialogue. Yet, in spite of so much apparent attack, the mechanism used to expose it counteracts its force. The Cock, being both the sinner and the judge, cannot avoid being sympathetic to his "former selves," delivering criticism but at the same time presenting a compassionate view of us, poor, misguided human beings.

In both dialogues, the laudatory messages of the "good Christian," delivered by Mercury and by Demophón, are each shaded by the ambiguous voices of Charon and of the Cock. As a result of this combination of perspectives, the texts become a mixture of Menippean and formal satire. One salient characteristic of these early works is the open discussion of religious issues and a very explicit criticism of religious authorities from the friar to the influential prelate. This satiric directness will contrast with the remainder of the satiric production of the Golden Age, which is marked by a need to avoid censorship.

Period of Transition from the Sixteenth to the Seventeenth Century

The ideas of Erasmus and his followers will succumb to the religious suspicion that was generated by the Counter-Reformation which immersed Spain in a repressive climate marked by religious prosecution, censorship, and isolation from Europe. In fact, the first decree issued by Philip II (1556–98) forbade Spaniards to study outside the kingdom. In this atmosphere of suspicion, constant warring, in order to sustain Spain's supremacy in Europe, together with poor economic policies, would gradually submerge the peninsula into social and economic crises. Miguel de Cervantes' life and work straddled the two eras of Spain's fortune. He participated as a brave soldier in the great triumph of the Spanish Armada, the *Armada invencible*, against the Turks at Lepanto in

1571, and he witnessed the defeat of the same Armada by England in 1588. He will be a man of the Renaissance, but he will also be a man of the new Baroque period, a time of the "conflictive" society, as designated by Antonio Maravall (1986).

In several texts Cervantes both elaborates on his ideas on satire and practices satire. Besides concrete satiric works such as his *Viaje del Parnaso* (Voyage in Parnassus, 1614) and his *Entremeses* (Interludes, 1615), Cervantes' most read, admired, and influential work, *Don Quijote de la Mancha*, has an undeniable kinship with satire. Or, more accurately, it is satiric works, especially those of the Menippean kind, that have a kinship to the evolving novelistic form found in *Don Quijote* (as noted by Mikhail Bakhtin). Satiric elements, which are found in precursors such as *La Celestina* and the picaresque novel, are evident in *Don Quijote*, specifically in Cervantes' use of parody, humor, irony, and dialogue. Undeniably, the novel is a comic parody. In its plot, characters, and linguistic style, it parodies the novels of chivalry, as well as other literary forms, such as epic poetry and pastoral novels. And, it is filled with humor. In the myriad of possible readings and the multiplicity of interpretations the text stimulates, there is one element that all readers of the novel experience: laughter. An anecdote asserts that King Philip III, upon seeing a man with a book in his hand laughing effusively, said: "Either he is mad or he is reading the *Quijote*." Our author also exploits masterfully the comic effect of irony intertwined with humor. Cervantes, as noted by E. C. Riley (1992), has a unique ironic voice that allows him simultaneously to criticize and sympathize. In *Don Quijote*, irony is used on many levels. The narrator possesses an ironic voice, yet also creates irony by stratifying into layers the voices of the different storytellers, primarily those of the "author" Benengeli and the narrator "Cervantes." Lastly, dialogue is made a constitutive part of the action and used (as in the Menippea) as an exploration of truth, a process not requiring a definite conclusion.

Cervantes' ideas about satire coincide with those of contemporary theorists, such as López Pinciano (*Filosofía Antigua poética* [The Philosophia Antigua Poetica], 1596), Francisco Cascales (*Tablas poéticas* [Poetic Tables], 1617), and Cristóbal Suárez de Figueroa (*El pasajero* [The Passenger], 1617). These humanists agree on the existence of two forms of satire: one that conducts a direct and personal attack (lampoon, usually connected to the Greek satire), and another that reproves vices with a moralizing objective (called "*sátira latina*"). Pinciano recognizes that the direct attack is reprehensible but that this kind of satire is the one that the public enjoys. In *Don Quijote*, in a conversation between Don Quijote and a *hidalgo* whose son is a poet, our *caballero* praises poetry but warns about keeping her "within her proper bounds and not let[ing] her run off into clumsy satires or icy-cold sonnets" ("*hala de tener, el que la tuviere, a raya, no dejándola correr en torpes sátiras ni en desalmados sonetos*"). Later, Don Quijote recommends: "Reprimand your son, your grace, should he pen satirical verses impugning other people's honor...but if his satires are such as Horace wrote, attacking vice in general as elegantly as Horace attacked it, then praise him" ("*Riña vuestra merced a vuestro hijo si hiciere sátiras que perjudiquen las honras ajenas...pero si hiciere sermones al modo de Horacio, donde reprehenda los vicios en general, como tan elegantemente él lo hizo, alábele*"; Cervantes 1999: vol. 2, ch. 16). According to these ideas, Cervantes' critical voice is a benign one, in maintaining the appropriate decorum and elegance and avoiding the invective. One exception, though, should be noted. A topic that touches a nerve with Cervantes and unleashes his indignation is the apocryphal second part of the *Quijote* written by the Aragonese Avellaneda. Avellaneda's book becomes part of a vision experienced by a damsel pretending to be in love with Don Quijote. In it, she witnesses a strange ball game between devils using books as balls when they come across the apocryphal *Quijote*:

> One of the devils said to another: "Hey, what book is that?" And the second devil answered: "That's the so-called second part of Don Quijote de la Mancha's history, not written by Sidi-Hamid, the original author, but by some Aragonese fellow"... "Get it out of here," said the first devil, "and throw it down into the very deepest pit of Hell: I don't ever want to see it again." "Is it really that bad?" asked the second devil. "It's so bad," the first one said, "that even if I myself tried to write a worse one, I couldn't do it." (Cervantes 1999: vol. 2, ch. 70)

Cervantes' satiric epic *Viaje del Parnaso* also combines the practice of satire with a discussion on satire. The practice, as in *Don Quijote*, employs parody extensively. The whole poem, in which Cervantes' character is hired by Mercury to help protect Mount Parnassus from an imminent invasion of bad poets, is a parody of *Viaggio in Parnassus* by the Italian Cesare Caporali (1582). The evaluation of poets is a parody of encomiastic catalogs, and the encounter between good and bad poets in the battlefield parodies epic poetry. At the conclusion of the *Viaje*, Cervantes attaches "Privileges, Orders and Regulations, Which Apollo Sends to the Spanish Poets," which is a parody of legal ordinances. In addition to parody, Cervantes employs a myriad of satiric weapons: humor and irony in a Menippean-inspired context of fantasy and realism, dialogue, and a variety of forms (poetry, prose, and epistle). The combination of these elements results in a rendering of several perspectives, if not in plain ambiguity. For example, during the battle of good against bad poets, it becomes impossible to distinguish who is who: "So mingled all, that none exist who can / Discern what is evil, or what is good" (*"Tan mezclados están, que no hay quien pueda / discernir cuál es malo o cuál es bueno"*; Cervantes 1870: 7.292–3).

The concept appearing in *Don Quijote* of the existence of two kinds of satire dependent on the ability and good judgment of the satirist is repeated in the *Viaje*: "Verses to make doth indignation move, / Should the indignant wight be somewhat wild, / The verses will partake of the perverse" (*"Suele la indignación componer versos, / Pero si el indignado es algún tonto, / Ellos tendrán su todo de perversos,"* 4.1–3). The *Viaje* also stresses the magical power of satire to hurt physically. Satirical poet Juan de Ochoa can cause the death of his satiric victim: "Of this youth in his praise I do allege / He can accelerate, and death impose / Upon an enemy by his discourse" (*"Deste varón en su alabanza digo / que puede acelerar y dar la muerte / Con su claro discurso al enemigo,"* 2.10–12). Similar lines are used to describe Quevedo's satiric power (2.306–12), and in the battle of poets, the satiric books are the most lethal of weapons.

Cervantes also wrote satire in his *entremeses*, another genre born during the Golden Age at a time when there was great demand for theater pieces. Luis Quiñones de Benavente (1600–50) is credited with giving the genre its definite form: a light, comical, sometimes burlesque, interlude with the objective of entertaining the audience between acts of a longer theatrical representation. The characters are usually taken from folklore, such as the old husband married to the very young girl, and the old woman versed in all kinds of remedies and superstitious practices. They are almost puppets in order to avoid any identification with the public: the objective is to laugh at them shamelessly. The plot typically revolves around a trick, played on an unsuspecting victim, in which the deceiver always triumphs. The pieces close on a festive note with music and dance that sometimes contradict the message delivered through the satirical attack. Benavente's *El Martinillo*, for example, is a variation on the medieval *danzas de la muerte* (dances of death). In this case, the condemned are not passing to the world of the dead but end up in a mad house, and the final message is *"vivir y beber"* (live and drink).

This light burlesque form becomes less innocent in Cervantes' hand. He writes his *entremeses* in prose, giving them a more realistic tone. His characters, although still taken from the bag of stereotypes, and still the objects of a joke, have a certain humanity that sets them apart from the traditional puppet-like characters of the *entremés*, which is achieved by Cervantes' particular ironic voice. Cervantes also directs his criticism at social obsessions of the time, as in the case of *El retablo de las maravillas* (The Marvellous Puppet Show, 1615) which elaborates on a medieval folkloric tale (later popularized as "The Emperor's New Clothes"). In Cervantes' version, two *autores*, play authors as well as directors, offer the distinguished and very gullible authorities of a small town to stage a play that can only be seen by those who are "old Christians," that is, those whose blood has not been "tainted" by Jewish or Arab ancestry. The idea of purity of blood, *limpieza de sangre*, was one of the obsessions of the Golden Age repeatedly found in literature. With the aid of a musician to create an ambience, the *autores* describe to their audience what they are supposed to see: mythological figures, the Jordan River, rats, lions, and bulls. The audience at first follows the "representation" by commenting on what they "see." But soon they begin participating in the creation of the invisible play (the women try to get splashed by the Jordan River, or jump on the chairs to avoid the mice), creating layers of authorship. Cervantes chooses not to reveal the deception to his characters who, at the end of the play, do not realize that they have been deceived. As in *Don Quijote* and in the *Viaje*, Cervantes' *entremeses* offer a sympathetic view of the satiric victim.

The Baroque Period

While Cervantes advises against personal attacks, the great masters of Spanish Baroque satire do not feel compelled to follow his guidance. Poetry and prose become the battlefield of stylistic innovation, as when, earlier, Garcilaso had introduced the

Italian sonnet during the Renaissance and many had accused him of corrupting Spanish poetry by employing foreign forms; Cristóbal de Castillejo (c.1492–1550), in fact, had compared the Italian form to Luther's Protestantism, finding it worthy of denunciation to the Inquisition. At the center of the new battle are two styles, *conceptismo* and *culteranismo*, and three writers, Don Luis de Góngora (1561–1627), Lope Félix de Vega Carpio (1562–1635), and Francisco de Quevedo (c.1580–1645).

Don Luis de Góngora was born in Córdoba of a noble family, lived in Madrid, and returned to Córdoba to die, when his arch-enemy, Francisco de Quevedo, demonstrating that poetic rivalry is a serious matter, bought the property where the sick Cordoban lived and evicted him. Góngora represents the culmination of a style that can be called truly Baroque yet with roots in the Renaissance poetry of Hernando de Herrera (1534–97). Following Dámaso Alonso, who actually designates *culteranismo* as *gongorismo*, the opposition between this style and the one practiced by Quevedo (*conceptismo*) resides in the fact that *culteranismo* appeals to the senses, focusing on the elaboration of expression, while *conceptismo* appeals to the intellect, focusing on the elaboration of meaning.

For Góngora, poetry in its elemental form presupposes the creation of something beautiful. The way in which Góngora achieves this objective is what generated such a stir. He writes an aristocratic poetry replete with Latin syntax and vocabulary. His extreme hyperbatons, together with symmetry, correlation (taken from Petrarch), and contrasting images, produce a very difficult poetic language. And it is common to find humor in Góngora's poems in general. Notwithstanding, he cultivated the satiric vein and created some of the outstanding satiric poems of the Golden Age. His satiric sonnets and the lighter satiric *letrillas* (a popular form often put to music, divided into stanzas, and closed by a refrain that repeats the main idea of the poem) attack the court, historic events and places, as well as popular and burlesque subjects in order to criticize pretension and hypocrisy.

Góngora's satiric masterpiece is a longer poem in the learned vein, which tells the story of Pyramus and Thisbe ("*Fábula de Píramo y Tisbe*"). Besides its parodic and burlesque intent, this is a meta-fictional text in which Góngora reflects on his *gongorismo* and the criticism it provoked. For instance, Pyramus finds Thisbe's cape stained with blood and believes that his lover has been killed by a lion. In describing her arms ("*miembros*") as imagined by Pyramus, Góngora lets us have a glimpse at the process of the selection of adjectives. The options are a widely used word, "*divinos*," or the obscure Latinism "*ebúrneos*" (whose verbal obscurity is lost in the translation to "ivory"): "*Esparcidos imagina / por el fragoso arcabuco / (¿ebúrneos diré, o divinos?/ Divinos, digo, y ebúrneos)*" ("He imagines, scattered / through the rough thicket, / [Shall I say they were ivory or divine? / I say they were divine and ivory]"; Garrison 1994). Góngora pretends to be indecisive about describing her arms as "*ebúrneos*," while he has just thrown to us, without any hesitation, the equally arcane phrase "*fragoso arcabuco*" ("the rough thicket").

Some critics maintain that the *Fábula* entails a self-mockery of *culteranismo*, while others find in it a confirmation of the style. Probably both things are present. What is true is that Góngora uses full-blown *gongorismo* put to the service of comic effect. As in Góngora's satiric sonnets, beauty is never sacrificed, and although the effect is comical and satirical, the images are never grotesque. A perfect example is the description of Thisbe, as also noted by the poem's editor David Garrison (1994): *"Las pechugas, si huvo Phénix, / suias son; si no lo huvo, / de los jardines de Venus / pomos eran no maduros"* ("Her breasts, if there was a Phoenix, / are those of that bird; if there wasn't, / then they were unripe apples / from the gardens of Venus"). The logical formula, asserting A, if not B (*"si la huvo"* / *"si no la huvo"*), a trademark of the *gongorismo*, is used here to compare Thisbe's chest (*"Las pechugas"*) with that of the Phoenix and with unripe apples from Venus' garden. Góngora gives not one but two metaphors. The overall description is parodic and is comic; its humor centers on the word *"pechuga,"* which turns young Thisbe into an animal, but the artful metaphor and the elaborated sound, full of alliteration, elevate the image. The topic may be laughable but the description is pure beauty.

Góngora's intricate style is contrasted sharply with the *estilo llano* (plain style) of his rival Lope de Vega, who is compared to an ignorant duck in the satiric sonnet *"A los apasionados por Lope de Vega"* ("To Lope de Vega's Followers"), while Góngora himself appears as a swan. This expressed dislike of Lope, in portraying him as the commoner bird, was probably fomented by jealousy toward the prolific author, who had achieved great fame with his *comedias* and was also a successful prose and poetry writer. At any rate, the dislike was mutual, and poetry was the weapon used to voice it.

Toward the end of his life, Lope published his satiric poetry under the title *Rimas humanas y divinas del Licenciado Tomé de Burguillos* (Rhymes Human and Divine of the Licentiate Tomé de Burguillos, 1634). The work is a parody of Renaissance poetry and its conventions. According to one of his editors, Lope writes the "anti-Canzoniere," mocking all the topics of Renaissance poetry: the poet himself, the object of love, the language, and the commonplaces of Renaissance description. Burguillos, the lover, is actually a poor priest, while Juana, the object of his passion, is a laundress, who is described as surrounded by white laundry suds. Satire is also directed toward Góngora's difficult style. In the sonnet *"El laurel de Apolo"* ("Apollo's Laurel"), Lope imagines Garcilaso and his poet-friend Boscán looking for an inn to spend the night, when an innkeeper, using the *gongorista* language, informs them that she has no available rooms and so it will be better for them to leave: *"– Que afecten paso, / que obstenta limbos el mentido ocaso / y el sol despingue la porción rosada"* ("Effect retreat, / while dusk obstends its aforementioned limbos / and the sun distills its pink particulate"; Vega 1634, trans. Alix Ingber). The two poets, confused and unable to decipher what she says, believe they have left Castile by mistake and entered a foreign land.

Literary parody is also the main topic of the mock-epic poem closing Burguillos' book, *La gatomaquia*, which portrays a love triangle among three cats: Marramaquiz, Zapaquilda, and Micifuf. Lope identifies in the text several parodic models for his burlesque epic, the *Iliad* being one of them, as Zapaquilda is compared to Helen and Marramaquiz, who will be defeated, is called "Trojan cat" (*"gato troyano"*). But the main parody, and the most successful one, is, again, the parody of styles, the styles of

Renaissance poetry and *culteranismo*. In one case, Zapaquilda is serenaded with a poem composed by Micifuf using the fashionable style of the *culteranos*. The composer himself does not understand what he has composed: "*y así, llegando del balcón enfrente de Zapaquilda bella, / cantaron un romance que por Ella / compuso Micifuf, poeta al uso,/ que él tampoco entendió lo que compuso*" ("Getting to Zapaquilda's balcony they sang a song composed in her name by Micifuf, fashionable poet, who could not understand what he himself had composed"; my translation).

Besides parody, Lope achieves a comic effect by first drawing readers into the beauty of the verse then striking them with the burlesque that comprises the true intent of the poem. We hear, for example, Marramaquiz's voice complaining to Zapaquilda of her unfaithful preference for the new cat on the block. He reminds her of the freezing nights he spent outside her house, covered with frost like a soldier. The verses, beautiful and deeply felt, echo one of Lope's best religious sonnets in which Jesus waits outside Lope's door, night after night, covered in dew. But the next reproach brings us to the reality of burlesque when Marramaquiz reminds his lover that he has entered every kitchen in town to bring her food. He uses the word *garrafiñar* (to grab with claws), an unusual but very specific verb that brings us immediately to the reality of the text: it is a cat talking to another cat. The verb shifts the poem to the names of foods that Marramaquiz stole for his "lady," a gradual lowering of tone that begins with fish and birds ("*peces y aves*"), descending to pastry, and winding up with sausage ("*¡Qué pastel no te truje, qué salchicha!*").

The third poet, Francisco de Quevedo represents the epitome of the satiric production of the Golden Age. He wrote extensively, practicing many genres and literary modes: short stories, the picaresque novel, poetry, moral, satiric, lyrical, and philosophical literature. His satire portrays human absurdity skillfully painted with words. More universal in scope than that of the Erasmian period, and detached from targets with a clear tie to a socio-historical epoch, Quevedo's satire becomes a criticism of everybody and everything: women of all social strata, particularly old women; tavern keepers, who are accused of adding water to the wine they sell; pastry sellers, who fill their pastries with meat from domestic animals and even with human remains; lawyers, doctors, magistrates, judges, notaries, and tailors. The victims are prototypical characters many times condemned for "false sins" as ugliness or old age.

The emphasis, however, is not on theme or target but on style. Quevedo writes within the tradition of *agudeza* and *concepto* cultivated by most writers at the end of the sixteenth century and throughout the seventeenth century. His contemporary, Baltasar Gracián (*Agudeza y arte de ingenio* [The Mind's Wit and Art], 1648) defines *agudeza* as a "conceptual artifice" consisting of "an exquisite concordance, of a harmonic correlation between two or three recognizable extremes, expressed by an act of intellect" (my translation). A *concepto* (conceit) is "the intellectual act [*acto del entendimiento*] that extracts the correspondence that exists between things." The more extreme the difference between the compared terms, the harder the mind must work to interpret the *concepto*. Quevedo exercised these intellectual games both in his poetry and prose, whatever the topic or the tone, and exploited their humoristic potential in his satire.

In *A un hombre de una gran nariz* (To a Man with a Big Nose), Quevedo's inverted figure creates a man attached to a nose, who becomes an *"alquitara medio viva"* (a nearly-living still) by the association of the nose and still through the fact that both "distill." In the *Carta de Escarramán a la Méndez* (Letter from Escarramán to La Méndez), a poem mocking the underworld, Escarramán says he is in jail because *"unos alfileres vivos / Me prendieron sin pensar"* ("a group of living pins caught me without warning"; my translation). Although lost in the English translation, the word play presents officers of justice who are turned into "live pins" as a result of the double meaning of the verb *prender*, meaning both "to seize" and "to pin."

Many times Quevedo concatenates conceits, generating a seemingly endless parade of human absurdity. The octosyllabic song to the River Manzanares (*"Describe al río Manzanares, cuando concurren en él en el verano a bañarse en él"*) begins as a satire directed to the river. After devoting several stanzas to create images to scorn the river, the true target of this satire appears to be its visitors, all sorts of them. An old mistress is undressing herself *"ab initio"* believing the Manzanares will be as the Jordan River to her "centuries" (*"Agora está una Dueña / desnudando el ab initio, / haciéndoles encreyentes / que es el Jordán a sus siglos"*); a lawyer is tucking in his incredibly long beard to avoid catching waste with it (*"El barbón y los bigotes / se enfalda un jurisperito, / por no sacarlos después / con cazcarrias en racimo"*); old women, ugly women, mangy students, murderous doctors, and more. The heavy emphasis on physicality and decay makes the images hilarious and grotesque, forging a disproportion between the satiric motive (the river and its visitors) and its description.

The same combined use of *conceptismo*, the grotesque, and the proliferation of images flourishes in Quevedo's satiric prose. An early collection of satires, *Obras festivas* (Festive Works), is followed by two major works, *Sueños* (Dreams or Visions) and *Discursos* (Discourses), deservingly considered as the epitome of narrative satire of the Spanish Golden Age. The five *Sueños*, composed early in Quevedo's life though not published until much later, are *El sueño del Juicio Final* (The Dream of the Last Judgment, 1607), *El alguacil endemoniado* (The Bedeviled Constable, also from 1607), *El sueño del infierno* (The Vision of Hell, 1608), *El mundo por de dentro* (The World Inside Out, 1612), and *El sueño de la muerte* (The Dream of Death, 1621–2). The two *Discursos* are *Discurso de todos los diablos o el infierno enmendado* (Hell Reformed, 1621) and *La Fortuna con seso y la hora de todos* (The Hour of All Men and Fortune in her Wits, written in 1636 but published in 1650). This last discourse is considered Quevedo's best.

In his satiric narrative, Quevedo revives the medieval association between satire and visions. The narrator finds himself in the midst of improbable places and companions: at the moment of the final judgment, or on the road to Hell, or with a possessed constable. The use of fantastic trips, combined with his criticism of a myriad of professions and human types, resembles Lucian's works. But Lucian exploits dialogue as a satiric medium of intermingling views and perspectives that concurrently progress his story. On the other hand, Quevedo advances his satirical anecdote though a narrator/witness, who creates scenes where characters perform a brief and complete theatrical act, for it is the physical action of sinners that condemns them in Quevedo's literature. In *El sueño del Juicio Final*, a parade of satiric victims march to their Last Judgment. An innkeeper, tailors, and highwaymen play out three brief scenes completed by an "army" of characters resulting in an accumulation of people and scenes, which are expressed with absolute economy:

> An innkeeper, in an agony of fear and anxiety, was in such extremities that drops of sweat fell from him at every step, and I noticed one of the devils say to him: "Good, get rid of your sweat now, and you won't be trying to sell it to us for wine later on." One of the tailors, a small round-faced individual with an unkempt beard and a body even worse made up, repeated over and over again: "But what did I ever steal – I, who was always almost dying of hunger?" Whereupon, seeing that he denied being a thief, his fellows set upon him saying that he was a disgrace to the trade.
>
> While thus engaged, they happened upon a gathering of highwaymen and footpads, proceeding very warily and taking good care to keep clear of one another. The devils took charge of them in a trice, maintaining that they could well be accommodated together with the rest, seeing that robbers and domestic cats sometimes do. There was an altercation among them, one lot regarding it as an affront to be in the company of the other, but finally they arrived together in the valley. Hard on the heels of this throng marched the army of the mad, flanked by four battalions made up of poets, musicians, lovers and duelists.... (Quevedo 1989: 45)

Physicality is central to Quevedo's satire as a form of criticism. In placing the human body at the center of his scenes, his vignettes incorporate grotesque and even eschatological undertones. Many times body parts take on a life of their own, fracturing the totality of the body into a caricatured distortion:

> The next thing I noticed was that some souls, in fear and revulsion, were refusing to wear their former bodies. Some were missing an arm or one eye, and I could not help but be amused at the very diversity of shapes and countenances while being forced to wonder by what providence it was, given that all the bodily remains were so mixed one with another, that no-one put on an arm or a leg belonging to his neighbor. (Quevedo 1989: 41)

The overarching theme of Quevedo's satire is hypocrisy. He delights in unmasking characters and behaviors in order to discover "reality" behind "appearances." In his vision *World Inside Out*, Desengaño (Undeceiver) takes "Quevedo" to a main street where he will be able to see "the real world." "Quevedo" inquires for the name of that street, and the answer is: "Its name... is Hypocrisy, a street that both begins and ends in the world, and there is scarcely anyone who doesn't have, if not a house, then at least rooms or temporary lodgings along the length of it" ("*Llámase... Hipocresía. Calle que empieza en el mundo y se acabará con él, y no hay nadie casi que no tenga, si no una casa, un cuarto o un aposento en Ella*"; Quevedo 1989: 189). *La hora de todos* unleashes the ultimate mechanism used to reveal hypocrisy. Fortune, under order of the gods degraded into underworld figures (perhaps a reference to the political degradation of Philip IV's government), will give to everyone what everyone deserves on a certain day at a certain time. When "Hour" (Hora) appears, in a cinematic move, she turns the scene inside out in order to let truth appear:

> Judges were sitting on a bench deciding a case. One of them merely out of ill nature was projecting how he might sentence both parties. Another, being a downright ignoramus and understanding nothing of the matter, was resolved to give his opinion, as all blockheads do, as a thoughtless venture... Another, a learned and upright judge, sat mutely like a cipher next to the last who was corrupted with bribes... but at the very instant of giving judgment, Hour captivates them, and instead of saying, "The court is of the opinion that such a one is cast and condemned," they said, "The court does award that ourselves be damned, and accordingly we are damned"... In a moment their gowns were converted into snake-skins, and they falling together by the ears soon stripped one another's faces, everyone carrying away his neighbor's beard to show that their judgment lay in their fingers and not in their heads. (Quevedo 1977: 301–2)

One interesting feature of Quevedo's satire is his placement of the didactic or moralistic message in the mouth of devils. In the *Vision of the Catchpole Caught*, the Catchpole is mercilessly criticized by the devil that possesses him; in the *Vision of Hell*, devils point to all the vices of humanity with a condemning tone of "moral superiority." The satirist realizes that this strange tactic requires an explanation, which he offers in the prologue or at the end of a particular dream: "And so I now pray that Your Excellency will pay special heed to what has been written without troubling yourself about the author. For it is recorded that Herod himself prophesied, and streams of water are known to issue from the mouth of a stone serpent" ("*Vuestra excelencia con curiosa atención mire esto y no mire quien lo dijo: que Herodes profetizó y por la boca de una sierpe de piedra sale un caño de agua,*" *El alguacil endemoniado*; Quevedo 1989: 89). But, even this kind of explanation cannot erase the "atmosphere of infernal continuity" ("*atmósfera de continuidad infernal*"; Lida 1981: 187) found in Quevedo's satire. The combined effect of these moralizing devils together with the overwhelmingly elaborated images that often take over the critical aspect of the satire, making the style call attention to itself rather than to the corrective element, make it difficult to extract a clear satiric message. Quevedo tends to despise the world rather than portray ways of improving it.

Quevedo's style was imitated in a number of satiric works. Probably the most accomplished of them is Luis Vélez de Guevara's *El diablo cojuelo* (The Devil upon Two Sticks, 1641). With an entertaining and sometimes brilliant style, Guevara incorporates the fantastic world of Menippea to show us a familiar place, Madrid, from an unfamiliar perspective. Similar to Quevedo, the condemned are the ones who moralize, creating the satiric voice of a sinner who, paradoxically, points his finger at all kinds of sins. Another one of Quevedo's imitators is Francisco Santos, who wrote at the end of the Golden Age. His narrations follow Quevedo's *Visions*, but they are, nonetheless, quite different from the model, mainly because of a strong moralizing message. Formally he writes the quintessential *satura lanx*, for his works are a protean mix of narrative, dialogue, and verse, with elements of the picaresque novel and *costumbrismo* (literature portraying life and prevalent customs). While some works, such as *Verdad en el potro y el Cid resucitado* (Truth under Fire and the Cid Resurrected, 1671), handle the mix with cohesiveness, this is not always the case. In *Rey Gallo y discursos de la Hormiga* (King Cock and Parliament of the Ant, 1671), for instance, the narration interrupts the dialogue in unusual places, obstructing the fluency. This responds, it seems, to the urge to ensure that readers will extract the correct moralizing message.

References and Further Reading

Abellán, José Luis (1982) *El erasmismo español* [Spanish Erasmism]. Madrid: Espasa-Calpe.

Alonso, Dámaso (1960) *Estudios y ensayos gongorinos* [Studies and Essays on Góngora]. Madrid: Gredos.

Arellano Ayuso, Ignacio (1984) *Poesía satírico-burlesca de Quevedo: estudio y anotación filológica de los sonetos* [Satirical-Burlesque Poetry by Quevedo: Study and Philological Notation of the Sonnets]. Pamplona: Ediciones Universidad de Navarra.

Bataillon, Marcel (1950) *Erasmo y España: estudios sobre la historia espiritual del siglo XVI* [Erasmus and Spain: Studies on the Spiritual History of the Sixteenth Century]. México: Fondo de Cultura Económica.

Cervantes Saavedra, Miguel de (1870) *Voyage to Parnassus*, trans. Gordon Willoughby James Gyll. London: A. Murray.

——(1999) *Don Quijote*, trans. Burton Raffael. New York: Norton.

Close, Anthony (2000) *Cervantes and the Comic Mind of his Age*. Oxford: Oxford University Press.

Elliott, J. H. (1990) *Imperial Spain 1469–1716*. London: Penguin (originally published in 1963).

Etreros, Mercedes (1983) *La sátira política en el siglo XVI* [Political Satire in the Sixteenth Century]. Madrid: Fundación Universitaria Española.

Garrison, David (1994) *Góngora and the "Pyramus and Thisbe" Myth from Ovid to Shakespeare*. Newark: Juan de la Cuesta.

Iffland, James (1978–82) *Quevedo and the Grotesque*, 2 vols. London: Tamesis Books.

Lida, Raimundo (1981) *Prosas de Quevedo* [Quevedo's Prose]. Barcelona: Crítica.

Lokos, Ellen D. (1991) *The Solitary Journey: Cervantes' Voyage to Parnassus*. New York: Peter Lang.

Maravall, José Antonio (1986) *Culture of the Baroque: Analysis of a Historical Structure*, trans. Terry Cochran. Minneapolis, MN: University of Minnesota Press (originally published in 1975).

Nolting-Hauff, Ilse (1974) *Visión satírica y agudeza en los "Sueños" de Quevedo* [Satiric Vision and Witticism in Quevedo's "Dreams"], trans. Ana Pérez de Linares. Madrid: Gredos (originally published in 1968).

Peale, George C. (1977) *La anatomía de* El diablo cojuelo: *deslindes del género anatomístico* [Anatomy of "El Diablo cojuelo": Demarcation of the Anatomistic Genre]. Valencia: Artes Gráficas Soler.

Pérez Lasheras, Antonio (1994) *Fustigat Mores: hacia el concepto de la sátira en el siglo XVII* [Fustigat Mores: Towards the Concept of Satire in the Seventeenth Century]. Zaragoza: Universidad de Zaragoza.

Quevedo, Francisco de (1977) *Choice of Humorous and Satirical Works*, trans. Roger L'Estrange, John Stevens, et al. Westport, CT: Hyperion.

——(1989) *Dreams and Discourses*, trans. R. K. Britton. Warminster: Aris and Phillips.

Riley, E. C. (1992) *Cervantes's Theory of the Novel*. Delaware: Juan de la Cuesta (originally published in 1962).

Scholberg, Kenneth R. (1979) *Algunos aspectos de la sátira del siglo XVI* [Aspects of Sixteenth-century Satire]. Berne: Peter Lang.

Valdés, Alfonso de (1986) *Dialogue of Mercury and Charon*, trans. Joseph V. Ricapito. Bloomington, IN: Indiana University Press.

Vega, Lope de (1634) "El laurel de Apolo" ["Apollo's Laurel"]. In *Rimas humanas y divinas del Licenciado Tomé de Burguillos*, trans. Alix Ingber (1995). Available at http://sonnets.spanish.sbc.edu

Vives Coll, Antonio (1959) *Luciano de Samosata en España (1500–1700)* [Lucian of Samosata in Spain (1500–1700)]. Valladolid: Seber Cuesta.

Zappala, Michael O. (1990) *Lucian of Samosata in the Two Hesperias: An Essay in Literary and Cultural Translation*. Maryland: Scripta Humanistica.

6
Verse Satire in the English Renaissance
Ejner J. Jensen

Any just account of the verse satire of the English Renaissance is likely to seem diffuse and multi-faceted, wide-ranging and selectively focused, engaged with the theory of satire but persuaded by its practice, and fundamentally uncertain about whether satire ought to be considered "a kind of writing" or "a way of writing" (Spacks 1968: 15). Renaissance satire is in almost every important dimension an epitome of the period in which it came to life; nearly every cliché that defines the period is applicable to its satire. Native elements and elements of a classical revival have joint shares in its origins and growth; it offers here and there claims of innovation even as it acknowledges its debts to the past. Over a period of some one hundred and fifty years – from John Skelton to Andrew Marvell – Renaissance satire reflects the defining features of its time. It exhibits nearly everywhere a delight in energy and play, a fondness for discovery, a fecund linguistic imagination, and unchecked pleasure in showing off. In an increasingly urban world, the satirists of the sixteenth and early seventeenth centuries respond by exploiting the city as the site of dramatic action and the field of poetic competition.

George Puttenham, in *The Arte of English Poesie* (1589), wrote of a "kind of Poet, who intended to taxe the common abuses and vice of the people in rough and bitter speaches, and their invectives were called *Satyres*, and them selves *Satyriques*"; and he went on to name "*Lucilius, Juvenall*, and *Persius* among the Latines" as writers of such works (1936: 26). Puttenham, whose compendious work provides helpful insight into Renaissance ideas about genre, later provides a fuller account of "*Satyre*," which he calls "the first and most bitter invective against vice and vicious men." He goes on to describe an elaborate theatrical fiction in which writers for the stage:

> to make their admonitions and reproofs seeme graver and of more efficacie... made wise as if the gods of the woods, whom they called *Satyres* or *Silvanes*, would appeare and

recite those verses of rebuke, whereas in deede they were but disguised persons under the shape of *Satyres*, as who would say these terrene and base gods, being conversant with mans affairs, and spiers out of all their secret faults: had some great care over man. (1936: 31)

Thus, satire, in Puttenham's view, has a clear social purpose. Though harsh in design and delivery, it grows out of a concern for its audience: the satirist has "some great care over man."

The Role of Satire

This self-assured account of satire and its creators is less than the full story. Throughout the Renaissance, ideas about satire and the satirist's role were anything but clear. An index to this uncertainty appears in a poem by Thomas Drant published as a preface to his translation of the *Satires* of Horace (1566). There, satire is connected variously to a sharp instrument; to Satyrus, the "rude, / Uncivile god" of the wood; to "waspishe Saturne," for a "Satyrist must be a waspe in moode"; and to "satura," with the implication of full or stuffed, a kind of abundant medley (7, 13, 19–20). While each of these connections remains in some sort viable, they are not finely distinguished and no one of them gains absolute dominance. Drant's own definition of satire at the beginning of the poem establishes one important line of definition: "A satyre is a tarte, and carping kinde of verse, / An instrument to pynche the prankes of men" (1–2). The notion of satire as "instrumental" takes a variety of forms. Satirists elevate purpose over aesthetic concerns as they set about their tasks of exposure and correction. John Skelton has his Colin Clout offer the assurance that

>...though my rhyme be raggéd
>Tattered and jaggéd,
>Rudely rain-beaten,
>Rusty and moth-eaten,
>If ye take well therewith
>It hath in it some pith.
>(53–8)

Satire for Everard Guilpin, as he describes it in his "Satyre Preludium" (*Skialetheia*, 1598) is "the Strappado, rack and some such paine / To base lewd vice" (82–3), its "scourge" and "*Tamberlaine.*" Joseph Hall's *Virgidemiarum* (1597–8; i.e., a bundle of rods) announces by its title how the poet wishes his work to be understood, and John Marston insists nearly everywhere that deliberate roughness in style and vocabulary is the means to achieving satiric purposes.

Again and again, the major satirists of the Renaissance make clear that the corrective impulse in their verse takes precedence over other concerns related to poetic design or style; or, to put it another way, that the style appropriate to satire sets it apart from other kinds of poetry. "The sowrest Stoicke," says Guilpin, or "The stricktest (*Plato*) that for virtues health: / Will banish poets forth his commonwealth" would give satire pride of place over "the whynyng love-song" ("Satyre Preludium," 102–8). Thus Marston calls on a surprising Muse – Reproof – as he begins the third of his *Certaine Satyres* (1598): "Now grim *Reprofe*, swel in my rough-hew'd rime, / That thou maist vex the guilty of our time" (1–2).

This choice of matter over manner, the idea that the aims of satire determine its style and commit its practitioners to roughness in language and acerbity in tone, shaped the argument and provided the title for the most influential single critical work on Renaissance satire, Alvin Kernan's *The Cankered Muse: Satire of the English Renaissance* (1959). In Kernan's view, the key marker of satire in the early modern period appears in the kind of self-description one sees in Hall:

> The *Satyre* should be like the *Porcupine*
> That shoots sharpe quills out in each angry line,
> And wounds the blushing cheeke, and fiery eye,
> Of him that hears and readeth guiltily.
> (*Virgidemiarum* 3.1–4)

This is the persona adopted by William Rankins when he defines his preoccupation – "I am a Satyre savage is my sport" – and the style appropriate to it – "my immelodious song" (*Seven Satyres* 1598, 1.40–1). Such a poet requires his own symbols of office; his "browes are Satyre-like betwist, / With wormwood garland, not with laurel crowne" (2. 36–7). Marston cuts a similar figure when he promises to "snarle at those, which do the world beguile / With masked showes" and urges such dissimulators to "tremble at a barking Satyrist" ("The Authour in Praise of his Precedent Poem" 1598, lines 44–6). Even today, nearly a half-century after its publication, Kernan's argument enjoys widespread acceptance. Yet, its emphasis on the persona of the satirist, a figure whose origin can be traced back through Drant to early grammarians like Donatus and to the great Roman satirists (especially Juvenal), does not fully take into account the range of achievements of poets from Skelton and Sir Thomas Wyatt to John Donne, Marston, and Andrew Marvell; nor does it provide a comprehensive view of the literary pleasures these works provide to readers in our time.

The Satiric Epigram

Any discussion of the persona of the satirist and the proclivity of that figure for describing his work in terms related to biting, pricking, stinging, stabbing, and other acts that involve witty aggression carried out by sharp verbal instruments will likely lead us to think of the epigram, a form related to satire but not coterminous with it. The epigram, a kind of poem most fully developed in antiquity by the Roman poet Martial (c.38–104 CE), is generally quite brief and in English often uses verse forms – quatrains and couplets in tetrameter – that themselves contribute to the witty incisiveness of the poems. Some of the Renaissance verse satirists, Everard Guilpin and William Goddard, for example, published epigrams along with their satires. Ben Jonson, in some ways a born satirist and the creator of satiric masterpieces for the stage in *Volpone* (1606) and *The Alchemist* (1610), is a surpassingly skillful epigrammatist. For most of these writers, their debt to Martial is apparent in both the manner and the matter of their verse. Often what makes the epigram effective is a kind of laconic delivery, punctuated explosively by a surprising turn and conclusion. Thus Martial writes of the futile antagonism of a fellow writer: "Cinna attacks me, calls me dirt? / Let him. Who isn't read, can't hurt" (3.9). Robert Herrick writes of one Rook, who "sells feathers, yet he still doth crie / Fie on this pride, this Female vanitie. / Thus, though the Rooke do's raile against the sin, / He loves the gain that vanity brings in" (1963: 163).

Another significant feature of the Renaissance epigram, and one that had also marked many of Martial's verses, is a kind of self-delighted bawdiness. We see this, for example, in Goddard's Epigram 98 from *A Neaste of Waspes* (1615). Hartes-head's wife has died, and the speaker urges him to create an appropriate memorial in a gravestone for her:

> Therefore Hartes-head, t'eternize her good name
> Laie o'er her one, write this upon the same
> > Here lies one dead under this marble stone
> > Which when she liv'd laye under more then one.
> Uppon her stone write this: yet dost thou heare
> At name of stone she'll rise againe I feare.

But the epigram, finally, stands in relation to fully developed satire as a sketch does to a painting or a bright fragment of a tune to a fully developed musical composition. While the writer of epigrams exhibits his talent by employing hit-and-run tactics, sharp jabs, and stinging verbal slaps, the satirist relies on a strategy that unfolds over time and makes greater use of detailed observation and extended analysis. The major Renaissance verse satirists manage this sort of extended verbal attack again and again with power and wit.

Satiric Complexity: Skelton and Wyatt

We can understand what the Renaissance satirists do and what they do for us by considering one of the commonplaces of satire criticism, the notion that Horace and Juvenal, the two great Roman satirists, represent two radically different ways of writing satire and that the writers who follow them in writing satire can be evaluated primarily and most usefully in terms of how "Horatian" or "Juvenalian" they are in their practices and point of view. Put in its starkest form, this opposition regards Horace as urbane, finely nuanced, engaging, detached, thoughtful, and amused.

Juvenal, on the other hand, emerges from the comparison labeled as harsh, acerbic, contentious, vituperative, and lacking in control. While one can imagine a satirist located clearly on one side or the other of this opposition, it seems unnecessary to insist on the absoluteness of such a division; in fact, most satirists range over the whole spectrum from "Horatian" to "Juvenalian" in their attitudes toward their subjects, their language, their style, and their tone. Moreover, the stances suggested by this common division present a false binary, leaving no room for the many complexities that arise from the mixture of subjects, styles, attitudes, and formal arrangements that go into the creation of a particular verse satire.

At the very beginning of the sixteenth century, the poems of John Skelton illustrate the difficulty of confining Renaissance satire within narrow theoretical boundaries. The epigraph to "Colin Clout" (1521–2), from Psalms 94, is lofty and portentous: "Who will rise up with me against evil-doers? Or who will stand up with me against the workers of iniquity? No one, O Lord!" Yet the speaker of the poem, humble and unassuming, presents himself as a simple man who, "As I go about, / And wandering as I walk, / I hear the people talk" (288–90). That talk reflects a world in which, Colin says, "as far as I can see / It is wrong with each degree" (59–60). The laity find fault with the church at every level, from the humblest priest to the highest church authority; and those in ecclesiastical positions are equally inclined to "grudge and complain / Upon the temporal men" (64–5). As he presents this contentious society, Skelton moves through a lengthy catalogue of abuses, citing churchmen whose whole energy is devoted to self-promotion, who lack learning, who fail (out of sloth, but more especially out of ignorance) to write sermons, who buy and sell church offices. But the laity is not without fault, and Skelton assembles as well an imposing list of their misbehaviors, most of which involve inappropriate opposition to the teachings and authority of the church.

The stakes in "Colin Clout" are considerable; they involve the common weal in the most comprehensive sense. But in no way is the speaker of the poem constrained by the weightiness of his subject or any narrow conception of decorum that it might impose. Hurtling through his examples, in a verse form (called "Skeltonics") of the poet's own devising, Colin employs neologisms, nonsense syllables, Latin, punchy monosyllables, and self-consciously showy sesquipedalian words, all of which lend his verse enormous energy. His language can be homespun –

> He chides and he chatters,
> He prates and he patters
> He clitters and he clatters
> He meddles and he smatters
> He gloses and he flatters
> (21–5)

– or deliberately Latinate –

> Some make epilogation
> Of high predestination;

> And of recidivation
> They make interpretation.
> (521–4)

At times, Colin makes his point through broad comedy, as when he charges that priests simply ignore church rules:

> in holy Lenten season
> Ye will neither beans ne peason
> But ye look to be let loose
> To a pig or to a goose.
> (212–15)

At other times, he speaks with intense bitterness of the disparity between the luxurious life of the higher clergy and the abject poverty of their flock: "Their mules gold do eat, / Their neighbours die for meat" (321–2). And Colin strikes yet another note. For all his flamboyance, for all his willingness to call attention to his own performance, he can adopt as well a voice of calm reasonableness:

> ...take no disdain
> At my style rude and plain;
> For I rebuke no man
> That virtuous is: why then
> Wreak ye your anger on me?
> For those that virtuous be
> Have no cause to say
> That I speak out of the way.
> (1089–96)

This is a recurrent argument in the rhetoric of satire: if you, reader, are guiltless then my words don't apply to you. By objecting to what I write, you only succeed in calling attention to your faults. This mild advice is a wonderful comic trap. Today, after Joseph Heller, we would call it a Catch-22. Like so much of what Skelton does, it underscores the pleasure he takes in adopting the satirist's role.

Pleasure is less evident in "Why Come Ye Not to Court?" (1522), a daring attack on Thomas Cardinal Wolsey in which Skelton strikes with unrelenting anger at Wolsey's arrogance, cupidity, intellectual limitations, and "greasy genealogy" (492). Wolsey, Lord Chancellor to Henry the Eighth and Archbishop of York, held extraordinary power in both church and state. He was a skillful and unscrupulous political maneuverer who was widely disliked. In every sphere, Skelton finds the Cardinal lacking; he is, the poet argues, marked by "Presumption and vainglory, / Envy, wrath, and lechery, / Couvetise and gluttony, / Slothful to do good, / Now franticke, now stark wood" (374–8). In "Why Come Ye Not to Court?" Skelton writes without the protection of a mask; no Colin Clout reports what he has overheard on his journeying.

Instead, the poet himself describes the excesses of Wolsey and notes the taints and traits of character that ought to disqualify him from public office. Some might wonder, Skelton writes, what led him "Thus boldly for to bark" (1206); and his answer is that of his forerunner Juvenal: *"Quia difficile est / Satiram non scribere"* ("Because it's difficult not to write satire," 1216–17).

That response very nearly defines the kind of satire we call Juvenalian. It is the explanation of one whose rage at the world has reached the point of exploding; who can see nothing around him but excess, corruption, and endless venality; and who must give public voice to his anger. Again, the other pole of such a satiric voice is one influenced by Horace: private, quiet, gently persuasive. Such a voice is that of Sir Thomas Wyatt (1503–42). In his first satire, "Mine Own John Poyntz" (1557), Wyatt borrows heavily from Horace for both the style and content of his argument. Nothing could be more relaxed than its opening or more remote from the staccato urgency of Skelton's verse. His *terza rima* stanzas, used in all three of his satires, lend themselves through enjambment to the leisurely development of thought. The first sentence of this first satire continues through twelve full lines. In its argument, "Mine Own John Poyntz" sets out Wyatt's reasons for rejecting court life and choosing instead to abide comfortably "in Kent and Christendom / Among the Muses where I read and rhyme" (100–1). Here Wyatt invokes one of the commonest strategies of satire, opposing the hazards and demands of court life to the life of pastoral content.

Wyatt's speaker patiently explains to Poyntz how unfitted he is for court life. He cannot practice cruelty, nor flatter, nor ignore malfeasance, nor countenance deceit, nor play the toady. He lacks the eloquence that could "make the crow singing as the swan" or "Praise Sir Thopas for a noble tale, / And scorn the story that the knight told" (50–1). With each example of his incapacity for the court life, Wyatt's speaker exposes another of its evils, until by the end of the poem the reader feels with him a deep sense of relief at escaping from a world in which duplicity and abject flattery are keys to survival. Wyatt's other satires are equally indebted to Horace and, like the first, exhibit the steady moral earnestness permitted to those who take the long view.

But the long view is not often available to the satirist; he is more likely to be governed by a felt need for immediacy, either because the objects of his satire affect him so powerfully or because he adopts a rhetorical strategy that requires an especially vivid and confrontational presentation of his evidence. In Renaissance verse satire, the instrument for carrying out that strategy was predominantly the decasyllabic couplet, though some writers employed six- or seven-line stanzas. But the couplet was the form employed by many of the satirists of the 1590s, and it served them well. Earlier writers used other forms, though with mixed success. Thomas Drant, for example, presenting Horace's *Satires* 2.1 in jog-trot fourteeners, misses the tone of his original. When Drant has the Roman poet object to Trebatius that he is not suited to write of battles and heroes – "Not every man . . . / The puissant Percy plucked from horse, / praiseworthy can display" (29, 33–4) – one is likely to assent, for the overbearing alliteration and forced rhyme of Drant's chosen form seems as unsuited to military subjects as to the critical purposes of satire. George Gascoigne, in *The Steele Glass* (1576), finds rhyme inadequate to his high purpose and uses "rhymeless verse" to attack the "forte of fame" ("The Author to the Reader"). But most readers are likely to find Gascoigne's satire flaccid and repetitious, a long, almost undifferentiated catalogue of complaints rather than a lively and pointed satire.

Satire in the Late 1590s

After Skelton and Wyatt, with the possible exception of Edmund Spenser, whose "Mother Hubbard's Tale" (1591) offers telling indictments of the court system drawn in part from the poet's own experience, English verse satire has no very strong presence until the latter part of the 1590s. This decade witnessed the circulation in manuscript of John Donne's satires and the publication of works by, among others, Joseph Hall, John Marston, Thomas Lodge, Everard Guilpin, William Rankins, and the author of *Micro-Cynicon, or Six Snarling Satyres* (1599), who is probably someone other than Thomas Middleton, to whom they are often attributed. This remarkable outbreak of satiric writing came to a close at the decade's end when in 1599 the Archbishop of Canterbury, John Whitgift, and the Bishop of London, Richard Bancroft, "issued to the master and wardens of the Stationers' Company [the guild responsible for licensing and printing books] a ban prohibiting the further publication of certain works, and providing for the destruction of such copies as already existed" (McCabe 1981: 188). Among those works called in, the order specified the following:

> Satyres tearmed Halls Satyres, viz Virgidemiarum,
> Or his tootheles or bitinge Satyres/
> Pigmalion with certaine other Satyres/
> The scourge of villanye/
> The Shadowe of truthe in Epigrams and Satyres/
> Snarlinge Satyres –

That is, all the satiric works of Hall and Marston, Guilpin's *Skialetheia*, and *Micro-Cynicon* (McCabe 1981: 188).

This extraordinary political act presents students of Renaissance literature with a curious double-edged historical problem. What led the authorities to ban these satirical works, and what in the first place led to the striking and prolific emergence of satire during the last decade of the sixteenth century? One explanation of the ban has to do with the incendiary potential of satire, its capacity for personal abuse. Here the notion is simply that attacks on individuals need to be controlled as a means of assuring civic order. Another view suggests that the method of satiric attack was the key issue and the bishops had pornography and obscenity in their sights rather than satire itself as a literary kind. Still another view is that of Richard McCabe, who believes that "the new writers were beginning to realize the full potential of their medium as a vehicle for social complaint" and that "the authorities of the day were more concerned with bringing the press into line than protecting public morality" (1981: 191, 193).

Thus, the first question – what brought an end to the satire of the 1590s? – has a clear answer in the action of the church authorities, and a set of likely secondary answers, the most persuasive of which has to do with the need on the part of the government to assert control over an important source of public opinion. The second question – why the remarkable efflorescence of satire in this period? – seems harder to answer. Satire was not, of course, the sole literary genre to appear so abundantly and with such force at the close of the century. The sonnet – in sequences by Sidney, Daniel, Drayton, Spenser, Shakespeare, and others – earned great favor but also less favorable attention, including mockery by certain of the satirists. Hall, in *Virgidemiarum* 6.1, writes of one misguided poet who praises his beloved's teeth, which

> ...might likened bee
> To two fayre rankes of pales of ivory,
> To fence in sure the wild beast of her tongue
> From eyther going farre, or going wrong.
> (283–6)

The erotic epyllion, of which Marston's *The Metamorphosis of Pygmalion's Image* (1598) is either a prime example or a misunderstood parody, also enjoyed a significant vogue. Both Marlowe and Shakespeare contributed to its popularity. And, of course, the drama in its many forms, perhaps especially the history play, also flourished in the last years of the reign of Queen Elizabeth I.

In general, these developments can be attributed to the ongoing emergence of London as a great urban center and to the growing presence in the city of significant numbers of young men down from the university, some of whom, like Marston, took up residence at the Inns of Court, and many of whom saw in literature a means of attracting public attention. Among the literary kinds available to such writers, satire offered a number of attractive features. It encouraged imitation of classical models, so a young writer could exploit his knowledge of Horace and Juvenal while addressing the features of contemporary life that made it "difficult *not* to write satire." It afforded a nearly limitless range of subjects: following Juvenal, English satirists of the 1590s could claim that "all the doings of mankind, their vows, their fears, their angers and their pleasures, their joys and goings to and fro, shall form the motley subject of my page" (1.85–6). But while the form provided well-established precedent, it also encouraged innovation and experimentation. Thus Hall's challenge to his peers – "I first adventure: follow me who list, / And be the second English Satyrist" (1 Prologue, 3–4) – though an inaccurate boast, is at the same time an invitation to become a literary pioneer.

The trail-blazing spirit Hall embodies and welcomes in this invitation contributes to many of the central features of Renaissance verse satire: its often breathless energy, its chest-thumping assertiveness, vivid language and situations, impatience with decorum, and a sense of being on display. Among the prose writers of the period, Thomas Nashe represents these characteristics in a most striking fashion. Over a period of some years, Nashe and a pedantic figure named Gabriel Harvey engaged in a public controversy that continued through a number of publications. In *Have with You to Saffron-Walden* (1596), Nashe has the ingenious notion of pretending to have discovered a letter sent by Harvey's tutor to the young man's father. In the passage that follows, the writer of the letter reports on Harvey's first happy discovery of the Latin word "ergo," or "therefore":

> *upon his first manumission in the mysterie of Logique, because he observ'd* Ergo *was the deadly clap of the peece, or driv'n home stab of the Syllogisme, hee accustomed to make it the Faburden to anie thing hee spake; As, if anie of his companions complained hee was hungrie, hee would straight conclude* Ergo *you must goe to dinner; or if the clocke had stroke or bell towld,* Ergo *you must goe to such a Lecture; or if anie stranger said he came to seeke such a one, and desir'd him he would shew him which was his chamber he would forthwith come upon him with* Ergo *he must go up such a paire of staires: whereupon (for a great while) he was cald nothing but* Gabriell Ergo *up and downe the Colledge.* (Nashe 1958: 66–7)

The exuberance – the sheer fun – of this passage drives it from beginning to end, and each repetition of "ergo" leads us to imagine what other uses of this remarkably useful word Harvey might discover. Nashe, meanwhile, shares in our delight as he rolls out each new example.

We witness similar passages from the verse satirists. Like a child who looks around before each utterance to make certain that he or she has an attentive audience, the personae of these poems often seem to perform only after having signaled, explicitly or otherwise, "Watch me." Satire was, in other words, a congenial and capacious literary vehicle with an appeal to young writers on the make. But those young writers needed appropriate subject matter and a receptive audience. The conditions of English life at the close of the Elizabethan age furnished the first of these; an ever-expanding print culture and its ability to attract consumers to its products furnished the second.

Themes in Verse Satire

One recurring theme in Renaissance satire is the morally corrosive nature of life at court, where suitors and hangers-on make themselves look foolish in the effort to ingratiate themselves and to earn or keep a place. One sees this in Wyatt, who describes how the effort to please requires a willed commitment to falsehood in claiming, for example, that "he is rude that cannot lie and feign, / The lecher a lover, and tyranny / To be the right of a prince's reign" ("Mine Own John Poyntz," 73–5). This focus on court life continues in the major figures of the 1590s, where Thomas Lodge, in Satire 2 of *A Fig for Momus* (1595) writes of court flattery, declaring that

> He is a gallant fit to serve my Lord
> Which claws and soothes him up at every word,
> That cries, when his lame poesie he heares,
> "'Tis rare (my Lord) 'twill pass the nicest eares."
> (7–10)

Donne, too, takes up this theme, describing, in his fourth satire, an encounter with a court bore, whose endless supply of gossip and inane chatter leads the speaker-satirist to "whisper, 'God! / How have I sinned, that thy wraths furious rod, / This fellow chuseth me?'" (49–51). William Goddard, a less notable figure than Lodge or Donne, attracts considerable attention with his title alone, *A Mastif Whelp with other ruff-Island-lik currs fetcht from amongst the Antipedes: which both bite and bark at the fantasticall humorists and abusers of the time* (1599). The effectiveness of Goddard's satires, though, derives in large measure from the persona he adopts, that of a rough, blunt soldier, addressing his poems to friends back in London and residents at the Inns of Court. In a brief how-to manual addressed to one such friend, he writes about the demeaning requirements for success at court:

> *Dartus*, if thou'dst a Courtier learne to be,
> Then take a glasse, that book shall straight teach thee.
> Look in thy glasse, and frowne, or skowle, or smile
> And shalt see one doo soe an other while,
> Laugh thou, ther's one will laugh: shedd thou a teare
> A tear ther's one will shedd; I dust thou heare?
> Thy bodie bow, gape, winke, or nodd thy pate,
> Do what thou wilt, ther's one will imitate.
> *To great men (if thou wilt a Courtier bee)*
> *Thou must doe, as thy shadowe dus to thee.*
>
> (Satire 74)

These brief passages suggest something about the remarkable liveliness of satire in the 1590s. In the passage from "Mine Own John Poyntz," Wyatt makes his argument through a generalization and supporting examples: you are considered unacceptable at court if you cannot traffic in falsehood, calling lechery by the name of love, for example, or tyranny the lawful practice of a ruler. Moving to Lodge and Donne, one sees a shift to a more fully dramatic presentation. We have characters in action, something like stage directions that allow us to witness their movements and gestures, and an authentic voice. While Goddard does not quite achieve the level of Donne and Lodge, he does deliver a satiric attack animated by creative energy and a consistent voice.

The dramatic vividness seen in the passages from Lodge and Donne seems most pronounced in the satirists' creation of London itself – the rough-and-tumble of the city, its noise and confusion, its abundance of comic types and satiric targets. Guilpin, in a satire indebted to Horace (*Satires* 1.10), Juvenal (*Satires* 3), and Donne (Satire 1), sets out the satirist's perception of the city:

> ... whose gall is't that would not overflow,
> To meet in every street where he shall goe,
> With folly maskt in divers semblances?
> The Cittie is the mappe of vanities,

> The marte of fooles, the *Magazin* of gulles,
> The painted shop of Antickes.
>
> (5.63–8)

Guilpin offers a catalogue of the city's parade of "apes," stopping just short of giving his figures full dramatic life. This wide-ranging vision does, however, present us with a lively pageant of city types, including, among others, the bully-soldier, the malcontent, the parasite, the Inns-of-Court man, and others. Donne, in the poem Guilpin levies on here, has a tighter focus in a satire whose comedy depends on the behavior of a single bore imposing his ceaseless idiocy on the reluctant poet-scholar whom he draws into the life of the metropolis.

While the court and the city offered theaters for the display of comic figures and their various excesses and affectations, the country provided a very different setting, one in which long-standing values and social relationships were being eroded. Throughout the sixteenth century, cultivable land was increasingly being subjected to enclosure, a practice that involved the fencing off of land for raising sheep, the displacement of farm laborers, and the abandonment of a system of dependency of the sort idealized in a poem like Ben Jonson's "To Penshurst" (1616). The pastoral ideal celebrated in that poem reflects a mutuality of support in which "all come in . . . / And no one empty-handed, to salute/ Thy lord and lady" and the estate's "liberal board doth flow/ With all that hospitality doth know" (48–50, 59–60). The full, even overflowing, tables of the great house stand here as an emblem of the abundance made possible by this society, whose dependent members also bestow gifts.

Hall, in *Virgidemiarum* 5.2, draws a picture of the decay of hospitality that is as dark and leaden as Jonson's view of Penshurst is bright and buoyant. He announces his theme in an unequivocal opening – "Housekeeping's dead" – and reinforces it with passages of unrelenting somberness:

> Look to the towred chymneis which should bee
> The wind-pipes of good hospitalitie,
> Through which it breatheth to the open ayre,
> Betokening life and liberall welfaire,
> Lo, there th'unthankfull swallow takes her rest,
> And fills the Tonuell with her circled nest,
> Nor half that smoke from all his chymneis goes
> Which one Tabacco-pipe drives through his nose.
>
> (67–74)

Donne offers yet another perspective on this aspect of social upheaval when he remarks on the press of citizens to the court. Those who have abandoned the country spend beyond their means to prepare themselves for the court scene. Thus, when they arrive at their second stop (after earlier activity at "the Mues, / Baloune, Tennis, Dyet, or the stewes"), "As fresh, and sweet their Apparrells be, as bee / The fields they sold to buy them" (4.175–6, 180–1).

A Spectrum of Styles: Marston, Hall, and Donne

If the verse satirists of the 1590s followed Juvenal in taking "whatever men do" as their subject field, they were equally open to the use of diverse styles in writing about these varied displays of folly, as can be seen in three poems by Marston, Hall, and Donne on the subject of religion. In Satire 2 of *The Scourge of Villanie* (1598), Marston warms to the task of exposing religious malpractice with a rhetorical question: "What dry braine melts not sharp mustard rime / To purge the snottery of our slimie time?" (70–1). Outrage and outrageous means of expressing it are staples of Marston's work as a satirist. Here he turns his over-heated language on communion practices, deriding equally those who in their "frenzie.../ Adore wheat dough, as real deitie" (83–4) and "lewd Precisians. / Who scorning Church rites, take the simbole up / As slovenly as carelesse Courtiers slup / Their mutton gruel" (93–6). Marston attacks not only the Catholic Church and the doctrine of transubstantiation, but the lax observance of communion at the Universities.

Hall, too, in Satire 4.7 of *Virgidemiarum*, begins with a rhetorical question, designed to enlist the reader's support for his attack on Catholicism: "Who say's these Romish Pageants bene too hy / To be the scorne of sportfull Poesy?" Invoking the authority of the past as a foundation for his argument, Hall imagines how Juvenal would respond to the misuse and displacement of Roman symbols of authority, how "his enraged Ghost would stamp and stare / That *Caesars* throne is turn'd to *Peters* chayre" (1–2, 11–12), or how he would recoil in disgust

> To see an old shorne *Lozell* perched hy
> Crossing beneath a golden *Canopy*,
> The whiles a thousand hairlesse crownes crouch low
> To kiss the precious case of his proud Toe.
> (13–16)

Into a poem of seventy-four lines, Hall packs an astounding arsenal of anti-Catholic propaganda. He writes of a corrupt church hierarchy establishing houses of prostitution, of children branded by searing irons at baptism, of wealthy men buried in the habit of St Francis to improve the odds of their being accepted into heaven. In his account, symbols of authority become signs of evil: "th'horned Miter, and the bloudy hat." He lists the "shameless Legends" designed to seduce a credulous public, repeats the story of the female Father of the Church, Pope Joan, and reserves his final derisive observation for the "new Calendere / Pestred with mungrel Saints, and reliques dere" (71–2).

Throughout this attack, Hall's tone works chiefly with notes of intellectual pity and contempt, not surprising attitudes for someone trained in Puritan traditions at Emmanuel College, Cambridge, and destined to become an Anglican divine. Yet this attack, like Marston's in *The Scourge of Villanie* 2, may have helped to generate the response from ecclesiastical authorities that led to the ban on satires in 1599. As several critics have pointed out, an attack on the Catholic Mass almost necessarily raised questions about the English church's eucharistic observances, and in a time of uncertainty about the Queen's successor (a constant worry from the time she ascended the throne, and one exacerbated as she reached forty years in power) satire directed at the church must have seemed especially disruptive.

In raising (and answering) their questions about church practices, Marston and Hall adopt an aggressive, even vituperative, tone. Donne's "Satire 3" (1633), the most familiar of his satires, takes a wholly different approach. Donne, too, begins his poem in the interrogative mood. Four questions over fifteen lines prepare the reader for a discussion of religion that is remarkable for its range, depth, and intellectual engagement. In this poem, there is little of the rage and impatience we associate with Juvenal. Instead, Donne's speaker sets out an intellectual problem and pursues it by rational means: asking insightful questions, bringing wide learning to bear on the effort to answer them, and creating comparisons and analogies that challenge our usual habits of thought. In other words, Donne the satirist creates rhetorical effects like those created by Donne the elegist and Donne the writer of the Holy Sonnets. Thus in devoting the central portion of his poem to the irrationality of religious choices, he argues that men choose their religion as they choose their mistresses – for reasons that seem misguided, or perverse, or founded on unthinking prejudice. "Carelesse Phrygius doth abhorre / All, because all cannot be good, as one / Knowing some women whores, dares marry none," while "Gracchus loves all as one," imagining that "As women do in divers countries goe / In divers habits, yet are still one kinde, / So doth, so is Religion" (62–4, 65–8). Canvassing all the grounds for allying oneself with a church, Donne in his poem reflects a struggle that shaped his own life, and his earnestness leads him to assert that "in strange way / To stand inquiring right, is not to stray; / To sleepe, or runne wrong, is" (77–9).

Nonetheless, he argues, one must at last take action that will lead to a decision; and he solidifies that argument with one of the most frequently quoted passages from the whole canon of Renaissance satire:

> On a huge hill,
> Cragged, and steep, Truth stands, and he that will
> Reach her, about must, and about must goe;
> And what th'hill's suddenness resists, winne so;
> Yet strive so, that before age, deaths twilight,
> Thy Soule rest, for none can worke in that night.
> (79–84)

Donne's powerful figure for the hard access to religious truth stands quite apart, in its solemnity and earnestness, from Hall's derisive abuse of Catholic beliefs and practices or Marston's apoplectic sputtering as he complains that "mart is made of faire Religion" (*The Scourge of Villanie* 2.73). Here, in the three leading verse satirists of the time, one can witness something of the rich variety in style and attitude that characterizes Renaissance satire. One can see as well how far removed from that of our own age is the early modern sense of poetry's function. For the writers of the sixteenth and seventeenth centuries, rhetoric and poetry were near allied; it was no surprise, indeed it was expected, that poets would address the major social and political issues of the time. Nor was it a surprise that the authorities of church and state should want to set boundaries to the forms and directness of that writing.

Seventeenth-century Verse Satire

After the startling outburst of satiric writing in the 1590s, satire in verse suffers a period of relative insignificance. Some critics have argued that the prohibitions of 1599 forced satirists to find another venue for their aggressive arguments and that the comical satires of Ben Jonson, John Marston, and even William Shakespeare reflect an effort to find an outlet for the critical and reforming arguments put forward earlier in poems indebted to Horace and Juvenal. But verse satire did not entirely die out. Samuel Rowlands's *The Letting of Humour's Blood in the Head-Vein* was ordered to be called in just two weeks after its publication in 1600, but as Richard McCabe reports, "the work was reissued in 1603, 1607, 1611, and 1613, the 1607 edition appearing under a new title" (1981: 191). Over the next decades, the works of Nicholas Breton (*No Whippinge, nor trippinge: but a kinde friendly Snippinge*, 1601), R.C. (*The Time's Whistle*, 1615), John Taylor (*The Nipping and snipping of Abuses*, 1614), Henry Fitzgeffrey (*Satyres and Satiricall Epigrams*, 1617), Henry Hutton (*Follies Anatomie*, 1619), Richard Brathwait (*Natures Embassie. Divine and Morall Satyres*, 1621), and the prolific George Wither (*Abuses Stript and Whipt*, 1613) kept satire, if only intermittently, available for public consumption, though for their pains these writers were generally ignored or, in the case of Taylor and Wither, widely subjected to mockery.

It seems unfortunate to close this account of Renaissance verse satire, at its best so wonderfully vital and inventive, on such a diminished note. Perhaps a slight adjustment to the public record will permit a more emphatic conclusion. Andrew Marvell wrote, in 1651, a poem entitled "Flecknoe, an Irish Priest in Rome," which remained unpublished until 1681, well outside the chronological limits of this discussion. If we accept the date of composition, however, the poem stands as a useful point of connection between the satire of the Renaissance and that of the Restoration. Richard Flecknoe, a figure noted for his eccentricities and his pretensions, is the subject here of a lengthy and detailed satiric portrait of the kind developed later with such skill in the satires of Dryden and those of Pope. At the same time, Marvell's handling of Flecknoe reminds us of the way in which Donne brings to life and makes palpable the annoying persistence of the busybody of "Satire 1" and the court monster of "Satire 4" (1633).

The speaker in Marvell's poem, like the scholar in Donne's first satire, is a bit world-weary. His cynicism is leavened, though, by the wit that punctuates his observations, wit often dropped in by means of a parenthetical afterthought. Thus Marvell begins his poem in the most casual fashion –

> Obliged by frequent visits of this man,
> Whom as priest, poet, and musician,

> I for some branch of Melchizidek took,
> (Though he derives himself from my Lord Brooke)
> I sought his lodging
>
> (1–5)

– but in the process strikes with twin satiric barbs, one related to his own supposed recognition of a high lineage for Flecknoe, the other an apparently straightforward acceptance of the priest-poet's own claim to a distinguished ancestry. What the speaker discovers once he locates the lodging is a minuscule room; what he experiences is a "martyrdom" so excruciating that he wishes only for someone who might record his suffering for posterity and "assure / The future ages how I did endure" (29–30). The place itself is a perfect site for torture; penned in, the speaker is first subjected to a harsh and high-decibel recital of his host's "hideous verse" (20). When that ends, Flecknoe assaults him with his lute, played to a surprising accompaniment:

> ... while he with his gouty fingers crawls
> Over the lute, his murm'ring belly calls
> Whose hungry guts to the same straitness twined
> In echo to the trembling strings repined.
>
> (41–4)

As the poem's events unfold – a new visitor to Flecknoe's apartment, dinner for three as the young man joins them, an ignorant mangling of Flecknoe's poems by the newcomer even as he praises them – Marvell makes use of slapstick comedy as well as nicely calibrated wit. Thus, in a poem whose strokes are alternately subtle and bold, Marvell recalls the best of the verse satires of the 1590s. At the same time, he looks forward to a poem like Dryden's "MacFlecknoe" (1682), in which the poet satirizes the playwright Thomas Shadwell as the "son" of Flecknoe, whose literary output included a play entitled *Love's Kingdom*. In Dryden's poem, the crowd assembled for MacFlecknoe's coronation offers an ironic evaluation of the English Priest's achievement: "Beyond love's Kingdom let him stretch his Pen; / He paus'd, and all the people cry'd *Amen*" (143–4).

Marvell's poem can stand usefully as the end point of Renaissance verse satire and as an indicator of what lies ahead in the English satiric tradition. It carries forward a remarkable legacy of energy and inventiveness, sharp observation and sly judgment, an inheritance of wit. Recognizing that legacy involves a significant reassessment of the progress of satire in the English literary tradition. While the satiric poetry of the Restoration and the early eighteenth century undoubtedly sets the standard for achievement in this field, verse satire did not have to await an Augustan Age to establish itself in England. As with so many of the writers responsible for what is great and lasting in the unfolding of literary history in England, from the writers of the sonnet sequences to the playwrights who created landmark compositions for the stage, Renaissance verse satirists located models in the past, domesticated and modified them to their own purposes, and created a form both varied and subtle, powerful and direct.

References and Further Reading

Alden, Raymond MacDonald (1899) *The Rise of Formal Satire in England under Classical Influence*. Philadelphia: University of Pennsylvania Press.

Caputi, Anthony (1961) *John Marston, Satirist*. Ithaca, NY: Cornell University Press.

Gransden, K. W. (ed.) (1970) *Tudor Verse Satire*. London: Athlone Press.

Griffin, Dustin (1994) *Satire: A Critical Reintroduction*. Lexington: University Press of Kentucky.

Herrick, Robert (1963) *The Poetical Works of Robert Herrick*, ed. L. C. Martin. Oxford: Clarendon Press.

Hester, Thomas (1982) *Kinde Pitty and Brave Spleen: John Donne's Satyres*. Durham: Duke University Press.

Jensen, Ejner J. (1972) The wit of renaissance satire. *Philological Quarterly* 51, 394–409.

Kernan, Alvin (1959) *The Cankered Muse: Satire of the English Renaissance*. New Haven, CT: Yale University Press.

—— (1965) *The Plot of Satire*. New Haven, CT: Yale University Press.

McCabe, Richard A. (1981) Elizabethan satire and the bishops' ban of 1599. *The Yearbook of English Studies* 11, 188–93.

—— (1982) *Joseph Hall: A Study in Satire and Meditation*. Oxford: Clarendon Press.

McRae, Andrew (2004) *Literature, Satire, and the Early Stuart State*. Cambridge: Cambridge University Press.

Nashe, Thomas (rpt. 1958) *The Works of Thomas Nashe*, 5 vols, edited by Ronald B. McKerrow and F. P. Wilson. Oxford: Blackwell.

Peter, John (1956) *Complaint and Satire in Early English Literature*. Oxford: Clarendon Press.

Powers, Doris C. (1971) *English Formal Satire: Elizabethan to Augustan*. The Hague: Mouton.

Puttenham, George (1936) *The Arte of English Poesie*, ed. Gladys Doidge Willcock and Alice Walker. Cambridge: Cambridge University Press.

Randolph, Mary Clare (1942) The structural design of formal verse satire. *Philological Quarterly* 21, 368–84.

Rawson, Claude (1984) *English Satire and the Satiric Tradition*. Oxford: Blackwell.

Rhodes, Neil (1992) *The Power of Eloquence and English Renaissance Literature*. New York: St Martin's Press.

Selden, Raman (1978) *English Verse Satire, 1590–1765*. London: George Allen and Unwin.

Spacks, Patricia Meyer (1968) Some reflections on satire. *Genre* 1, 13–20.

Wheeler, Angela J. (1992) *English Verse Satire from Donne to Dryden: Imitation of Classical Models*. Heidelberg: Carl Winter.

7
Renaissance Prose Satire: Italy and England
W. Scott Blanchard

While many of the critical judgments expressed in Jacob Burckhardt's *The Civilization of the Renaissance in Italy* (1958) have not survived in the more rigorous and specialized environment for scholarship of the past several decades, at least one of his observations seems to have remained uncontested: that the Italian Renaissance witnessed the birth of a distinctly modern spirit of "wit and satire" (Burckhardt 1958: 1.163–82). The production of satirical writing in Italy from roughly the middle of the fifteenth century onwards attests to its popularity in increasingly literate urban milieux, where literature that focused on the contemporary scene (as all satire does) probably held the same level of interest for the consuming public that modern journalism holds today. The use of satire as a genre for the expression of social dissensus and, perhaps most interestingly, its potential as a form of writing that could be flexible, experimental, and even avant-garde, made it an especially appealing form for those who appreciated strong opinions, whether progressive or reactionary, and who found those opinions more easily digestible when spiced with humor, ridicule, or even abuse.

And while another of Burckhardt's observations – his thesis concerning the birth of "the individual" in the Italian Renaissance – has been repudiated by many recent historians of culture, we would do well to observe that the flourishing of satire in this period was marked by an unmistakable tendency for satirical writing, and its close cousin, invective, to become highly personal. Whatever the status of the early modern "individual" – whether as a socially constructed subject, as a grandiose, entrepreneurial or self-fashioned ego, or as a self-effaced member of a residual, medieval corporate sodality – the early modern self could clearly be the *object* of attack, lending at least a measure of credence to Burckhardt's famous thesis about Renaissance individualism. The resolutely public nature of all satirical writing throughout history and the deeply public dimension of civic life in the Italian city-states of the Renaissance allowed for an especially fertile growth of satire, while Italy's cultural and literary leadership in fifteenth- and sixteenth-century Europe assured that the lead of its finest authors would be followed in northern European countries. Finally, the cultural project of Renaissance humanism in the larger European context guaranteed that classical authors, whether writers of verse, prose, or a mixture of the two, could provide models for both imitation and innovative transformation by authors in both neo-Latin and the vernacular.

In this chapter, we shall trace in a broad manner developments in several kinds of satirical prose writing in both Italy and England, leaving aside for the most part Italian authors who wrote verse satire in either neo-Latin or the vernacular and English writers of verse satire. Our focus shall remain on three distinct kinds of satirical writing: academic satires, whose roots are to be found in the oratorical tradition; fictive satires, either modeled on the Hellenistic author Lucian of Samosata, and often cast in the form of a dialogue, or on the Roman author Seneca's lampoon known as the *Apocolocyntosis*, which took the form of a dream vision; and hybrid satirical forms, such as mock learned symposia, encyclopedic literary "anatomies," and other expansive forms of satire that emerged in the later Renaissance and that may be more profitably viewed as a product of the Renaissance itself rather than from a perspective that would emphasize the classical models (such as the *Noctes Atticae* of Aulus Gellius) from which they swerved so greatly in their creative scope and linguistic plenitude. In this latter group we encounter discussions, sometimes in dialogue form, that survey a topic or field of learning with the purpose of undermining intellectual credibility, philosophical certainty, or political legitimacy and that invariably convey a profoundly ironic sensibility.

A great number of Renaissance prose satires have been classified as "Menippean" satires by a variety of scholars, implying with that term that the satire is of an intellectual, academic, or cerebral nature, in contrast to satires that expose vices that are non-intellectual in nature and that tend to be the domain of verse satirists. Satire of the Menippean kind originated in the classical world in the works of the ancient Cynics, who composed diatribes, mock symposia, and satirical eulogies praising unworthy subjects or topics; most of these are now lost, but we can gather from other evidence that this tradition of satire had as its object of attack the pretenses and vanity of both professional philosophers and rhetoricians, the two most authoritative intellectual practitioners of the classical world. The satirist Lucian is our best witness to that tradition, and in his work the ancient Cynics Menippus and Diogenes of Sinope often make guest appearances. But for our purposes we shall confine our discussion to a more descriptive overview of prose satire in the Italian and English Renaissance, letting readers judge for themselves whether or not specific satires contain sufficient exposure of philosophical pretense or debunking of intellectual claims of authoritative certainty to warrant the adjective "Menippean" (Kirk 1980; Relihan 1993; Blanchard 1995; De Smet 1996).

Satire of all forms in the European Renaissance was composed with classical models in mind, though the rage for imitation in the fifteenth and sixteenth centuries did not necessarily involve the same classical authors as it would for writers of the Augustan age in England or for the French *philosophes*. Lucian, Seneca, Apuleius, and Petronius carried at least as much authority for writers of the early Renaissance as Horace and Juvenal would for later writers working the deeper veins of satire, and it may be worthwhile to note at least briefly some of the theoretical treatments of satire among Italian humanists, though their commentaries are not as theoretically sophisticated as we might wish. Throughout the period, the term "satire" was confused with the biologically hybrid figure of the "satyr," even though Renaissance humanists knew next to nothing about the Greek satyr plays. But such confusion allowed Renaissance authors to associate satirical writing with theatrical buffoonery, and some humanist authors imagined that the satyr figure's abuse and mockery provided an important classical warrant for an author's freedom to criticize individuals and institutions, a festive license to undermine the more official and respectable opinions of the literary or political status quo.

Renaissance humanists also lacked a clear understanding of fictional discourse in general, so that works like Apuleius' *The Metamorphosis* (which modern scholars would classify as a romance that contains moments of satirical expression) were largely misunderstood by authors of the period. The humanists mostly relied on rather brief statements about satire in the Roman authors Quintilian and Varro (the latter as quoted in Cicero's *Academica*) for their theoretical understanding of the genre, gleaning from them only that more conventional Roman verse satire was a Roman invention and that Menippean satire mixed prose and verse, while displaying a more scattered canvas of topics and a paradoxical mixture of audience response in the reception of its "serio-comic" messages. It was perhaps the very paucity of theoretical comment on satire in antiquity that enabled Renaissance humanists to take prose satire in such a bewildering variety of directions, and more than one modern scholar has traced the development of modern, "novelistic" forms of discourse to Renaissance satire, while others have found in the satirical effusions of the period elements that would later reach expressive maturity as journalistic exposé and pornography (Rhodes 1980; Bakhtin 1984; Moulton 2000). However we judge the importance of Renaissance satire for the understanding of the cultural phenomenon of the Renaissance, there is little doubt that the satirical imagination of Renaissance authors had an enormous influence on later developments in modern European literature.

Satirical Encomia and their Academic Contexts

In the classical tradition of oratory, one of the rhetorical forms used in public speaking was the epideictic oration, distinguished from the two other forms of rhetoric used for academic, political, or forensic purposes ("judicial" and "deliberative" rhetoric). Epideictic oratory survives today in the form of commencement addresses and serves a largely ritual function, at its worst devolving into a litany of empty platitudes and cheap bromides, and at its best engendering a measure of collective pride in civic or community achievement or commending a particular individual for his or her talents or virtues. The epideictic oration or encomium served the function of "praise," the morally superior if not the most interesting half of the classical "praise and blame" dyad that was the traditional province of verse satire as defined by the Romans. These oratorical exercises in demonstrating the praiseworthiness of an individual, an institution, or a particular topic or field of study were especially prevalent in academic contexts in the Renaissance, and a special oration of this kind was the humanistic *praelectio*, an inaugural lecture usually delivered on the first day of classes at an Italian university or *studium*; its purpose was to give a broad overview of a particular field of study, to enumerate the best authors within that field, and to prepare the students for the intellectual feast that lay ahead of them in the work of the particular author or authors to be studied. In non-satirical examples of this type of oration, we encounter a variety of classical authors or subjects that are praised, varying from orations on the great value and utility of historical authors to the special aesthetic merits as well as the vast knowledge to be found in an author like Homer. The grandiose claims made for these praiseworthy subjects and subject matters, as well as the often self-promoting dimension of the speech in boosting the lecturer's own public reputation for learning and eloquence, made this rhetorical form ripe for parody and satirical treatment, since vanity and intellectual pride were so prevalent in the genre.

In a moment we shall turn to the best-known example of this form of satire, Erasmus' *The Praise of Folly* (*Moriae Encomium*), but first we need to appreciate the Italian traditions that lie behind it. The earliest example of this form is to be found in the work of the comic playwright Ugo Pisani, who parodied the academic exercise known as the scholastic *repetitio*, a sort of qualifying exam pronounced by students as they progressed to laureation for the baccalaureate degree, in a comedy entitled *Repetitio Magistri Zanini Coqui* (The Recitation of Master Zanino the Cook). Rather than enumerating or anatomizing a field of learning like ethics, in which the seven virtues and the seven vices might receive eloquent and expansive elaboration in a display of the student's exhaustive learning, Pisani has his actors in this skit (perhaps actually performed at the University of Pavia in the 1430s) discourse at length upon the virtues of cookery. Here we encounter a strategy typical of satirical writing, the debasement of the intellect and its pretensions at the hands of a human body whose material and biological needs burst forth into comic expression at the expense of the vaunting human intellect (Bakhtin 1968). Thematically, the work illustrates the universal nature of human stupidity, drawing its authority from the biblical diagnosis of human folly in Ecclesiastes: "Infinite are the kinds of fools" (Viti 1982: 98). Pisani's skit is not an oration *per se*, but more of a dramatic form subsuming a number of comic speeches whose *mise-en-scène* is clearly the academic world with its oratorical rituals. Here we might note that this neo-Latin drama is written in a language that is far from classical in its idiom and vocabulary, reminding us that satire always found itself ranked in both antiquity and the Renaissance along with comedy as the lowest (that is, the most debased) of literary forms, and consequently one which allowed for the greatest freedom of speech and linguistic diversity, since canons of decorum constrained it least of all other genres of writing. Pisani's work provides an interesting and useful transition from the goliardic traditions of medieval culture, where satire tended to center on clerical culture and its institutions, to the more philologically various, philosophically adventurous, and worldly productions of Renaissance academic satire.

The mock encomium was at its most popular in the academic scene of the 1490s in Italy, but an earlier, important example can be found in the *Encomion S. Thomae* (*The Praise of St Thomas Aquinas*) of the brilliant and innovative humanist Lorenzo Valla. Written to celebrate St Thomas's birthday at an assembly of Dominicans in Rome in 1457, Valla's work opens with praise for the encyclopedic learning of the famous saint, but ends by mocking the excessive ratiocination and complexity of his highly technical philosophy. In this lecture, Valla accomplishes nothing less than a thorough discrediting of scholasticism's overly determined systematization, appealing at the lecture's close to the simple and elegant expressions of St Paul and his sage advice to "Beware [the] philosophy and vain deceit" (Colossians 2: 8) that students might encounter in the cumbersome instruments of late medieval dialectic. St Thomas's praise, envisioned as a Roman triumphal procession including most of the worthies of the early Christian tradition, ends with Aquinas taking up the rear, clashing together cacophonous musical cymbals (noisemakers, really) as he forms the end of this procession of intellectual and religious worthies. Valla, in this instance, chooses satire for its capacity to destabilize traditional or official status or rank, and where his audience may have expected praise, he delivers blame. We might acknowledge, furthermore, that Valla's send-up of the revered saint conveys alongside its personal abuse a quite serious message, registering the cultural friction that the humanist movement could still encounter in its struggles to unseat medieval scholasticism as a dominant mode of thought and style of expression (Valla 1982; Camporeale 1976). The more serious aim of undercutting the intellectual or academic status quo lies beneath Erasmus' better-known effort in this rhetorical form of satire in *The Praise of Folly*, reminding us that satire can often serve destructive as well as constructive purposes. And Valla's use of a mock procession or "triumph" would have imitators in the English Augustan age in the works of Dryden and Pope.

The Florentine humanist Angelo Poliziano took the humanist inaugural lecture or *praelectio* in new directions on at least two occasions, composing in the early 1490s two satirical neo-Latin orations that were entitled *Lamia* (The Witch) and *Panepistemon* (All Knowledge; Poliziano 1972; Wesseling 1986). The latter satire purports to survey all forms of human knowledge and the professions associated with them, becoming a comic encyclopedia of human types, an early witness to what the critical anatomist Northrop Frye called satire of "social roles and professions" that tends to destabilize hierarchy and status in order to perceive a rather *lumpen* humanity as enjoying, at the very least, a kind of democracy of delusional tendencies and folly (Frye 1957: 308–12). The *Lamia*, however, is a more accomplished satirical effort, and through inserting a folk belief drawn from popular culture into a lecture purporting to introduce the high-minded study of Aristotle's difficult logical work, the *Prior Analytics*, Poliziano achieves a level of ironic discourse capable of challenging philosophy's claims of truth by exposing those claims as merely highbrow fables produced by a class of intellectuals largely unaware of their own propensity for folly and self-delusion: philosophy transmogrified into old wives' tales. His satires, as well as another of a similar nature by the Bolognese humanist Codro Urceo, are crucial antecedents to Erasmus' experiment in the satirical academic *laus* or *praelectio*, *The Praise of Folly* (Blanchard 1990). Satirical eulogies would have a long afterlife in late Renaissance culture, producing in France, England, and the Low Countries numerous examples of rhetoric used for ironic purposes to unsettle common-sense valuations of human experience (Tomarken 1990).

While a literary creation as rich and ironic as Erasmus' *The Praise of Folly* cannot easily be contained within the category of "academic satire," much less even within the broader category of "satire" itself, it is important to recognize that Erasmus at least began the construction of his inimitable work with the traditions of academic satire in mind. Composed in England in Latin in the first decade of the sixteenth century, the *Moriae Encomium*, whose title puns on the name of the book's dedicatee, Sir Thomas More, is the most fully developed example of the epideictic mock oration. Erasmus gave to the speaker of his poem the gender of a woman and the allegorical label "Stultitia," most accurately translated as "stupidity" but usually rendered with the more fluid and evocative English term "folly." While the work is carried out with a graceful levity of style, its message forces readers to question the very boundaries that separate the comic from the serious, engaging them in what an anthropologist might term a sort of "deep play" with their common sense and with the conventions that human beings often accept so uncritically. Erasmus followed the prejudices of his age in endowing the figure of Stultitia with a female gender in order to highlight her "irrational" qualities, but he also thereby linked "folly" to a putatively primordial (or at least pre-patriarchal) archaic *festivitas*, a sort of Renaissance version of the pleasure principle, an experience of the sacred that inhabits the imaginary spaces of myth or the provisional stagings of the theater, spaces where the ludic dimension of human beings can become a primary rather than a secondary feature of their ontology.

The trope of the world as a theater, used to great effect by Alberti (see below), is a central trope throughout *The Praise of Folly*, as Erasmus recognizes that the human need for ritual play-acting, while ostensibly a foolish and even childlike facet of human culture, may constitute the most human (and humane) of behaviors. Rather than succumbing to a despairing vision of human beings as delusional in their pursuit of illusions (or, in the manner of Aretino, accepting the universal dissimulation and insincerity of human beings as a misanthropic given), Erasmus chooses to view the human attachment to illusions as not merely a necessary ethical stance for the healthy pursuit of pleasure but even as a constitutive feature of human desire itself. Linking "folly" or "stultitia" to Plato's theories of divine madness, Erasmus is at the same time able to enlist the theology of St Paul in his argument, particularly in the first letter to the Corinthians, where the Christian in pursuit of higher truths is asked to set aside the "wisdom of the world" and replace it with "the foolishness of God" (1 Corinthians 1: 20–5), contemplating those non-rational features of Christian doctrine most conducive to faith. In Erasmus' work, folly or "stultitia" as a term becomes so overloaded as a signifier as to become a virtual synonym for the human condition, a strategy that in many ways looks back to the biblical use of the term "vanity" for a similar purpose in Ecclesiastes, while it looks forward to the similarly manic polysemy of Robert Burton's term "melancholy"; all are terms that come to mean everything – or nothing at all – and that thereby voice a radical skepticism concerning the capacity of humans to place any meaningful definitions upon their experiences of the world.

Erasmus' work was probably meant to blend two genres that had come to be used for satire: the satirical academic oration and the mock learned compendium, where a single term or category becomes a pretext for an encyclopedic survey of the concept's pervasive influence in human affairs. This latter strategy was probably learned from Juvenal's pursuit of the topic of vanity in his tenth satire, but would have a long life in the later history of satire, and for Erasmus it allowed him virtually to ransack the classical and Christian traditions for examples of foolish behavior. At the same time, Erasmus did not spare himself from attacking some of the specific vices of his age – such as excessive religious superstition, which had also been mocked by Alberti – and especially vices of an intellectual nature. There is much topical satire of professional academics and other influential social types (courtiers, princes, and ecclesiastics), targets that Erasmus also took aim at in his *Colloquies* and in many of his more developed *Adagia*. Both the overly determined ratiocinations of scholastic theology and the rhetorical excesses of Renaissance humanism come in for a good deal of ridicule by Erasmus, reminding us that Erasmus' critical spirit was generous enough to allow for some deprecatory self-reference. And paradox is everywhere apparent in Erasmus' work, a rhetorical strategy that not only allowed for the discovery of a wide variety of "wise fools" who had fully appreciated and lived their theatrical roles in the comedy of humanity, but also for the debunking of self-fashioned Stoics who had not. For Erasmus, the fashionable Stoicism of many Renaissance thinkers amounts to a denial of the roles of passion and pleasure in human affairs; in *The Praise of Folly* such killjoys appear as pretentious wise men looking all the more foolish for their self-vaunting (and self-loving) poses of superiority and this-worldly transcendence.

Erasmus' analysis of the ubiquity of folly reaches a level of high seriousness in the closing pages of his oration, where a distinctly Christian folly is celebrated as a kind of divine ecstasy allowing the individual to dissolve his or her identity in an experience of the sacred, thereby melding Platonic frenzy with Pauline mysticism. What emerges so forcefully from a reading of Erasmus' work is a recognition that would have a wide resonance in Renaissance literature as a whole, though it may be difficult to trace it directly in later borrowings: the acknowledgment that human beings are the stuff of artifice, that creative play and play-acting are the essence of the human spirit, or – to historicize this observation more completely – at least were central features of the Renaissance's fluid and metamorphic notion of human identity in the fifteenth and sixteenth centuries. Put more simply, the "essence" of being human is not to have an essence. Erasmus might have endorsed such a self-canceling formulation with an ironic, seriocomic smile. And while not as cynical by temperament as other satirists, Erasmus was capable of acknowledging that the human love of role-playing could at times provoke a response of pathos rather than laughter: "The mind of man is so constructed that it is taken far more with disguises than realities" (Erasmus 1969: 63). It is in such uncompromisingly honest and self-critical formulations as this that we find ourselves reaching to the very bedrock of the satiric mind.

Fictive Satires

If the social context of the mock encomium or *praelectio* is resolutely academic, fictional satires in the Renaissance are shaped against a background that often reflects the dominant social realities of the period, a world of courts and princes, of courtiers who are often literary artists or intellectuals *manqués*, and of deceit, duplicity, and verbal aggression that we can only expect to flow from such an anxious and politically unstable milieu. The mock fictional allegory of the Renaissance polymath Leon Battista Alberti entitled *Momus* is a work unique for its time (c.1450) that combines satire of intellectual pretentiousness, especially of philosophers, with a scathing analysis of the life of courtiers (Alberti 2003b). The work is best described as a satirical allegory presided over by the scabrous and irreducibly plural figure of Momus, the Greek god of criticism, and its point may have been to satirize directly the efforts of Pope Nicholas V to renovate the city of Rome in the mid-fifteenth century, but its satire is broad enough in scope to amount to a deeper investigation of the sources of human folly in envy, competitiveness, and self-interest, all values likely to be found in abundance in Renaissance courts. Alberti situates much of his critique in the behaviors of the classical gods, who are all depicted as quite human in their motivations and whose influence on humanity is therefore to make the earthly world a reflection of their own foolish and vain interests. As they compete for human attention, the gods clearly become allegorical figures for human leadership in society, where rulers are influenced by sycophancy rather than wisdom, and where the considered policies of responsible humanist intellectuals, who write volumes expected to serve as authoritative "mirrors" or manuals for princes, go largely unread and unconsulted. Alberti's satire is loosely constructed and somewhat episodic, but it is clear that he intended to satirize both courtiers and philosophers, both the active, civic dimension of life in Renaissance culture and its more contemplative dimensions. The work is clearly Lucianic in inspiration.

Announcing at the opening of the third book of his work that he intended to treat "serious and weighty matters" with "many jokes and laughter" (Alberti 2003b: 199), Alberti's seriocomic work probably reflected some of his disaffection with his own culture, for he had been raised in a family exiled from Florence during his youth, just as Momus, banished from Mount Olympus as a punishment for his misbehaviors and sentenced to live (and cause trouble) among the world of mortals, leads an exilic existence. Alberti was himself dependent on a world of patronage and politics for his livelihood as an artist, author, and intellectual, and the work betrays his cynical cast of mind. As we shall see, Alberti's work established an important, indeed dominant, topic for later satirists in its analysis of the vicissitudes of courtiers in a culture that valued intellectuals for speaking or writing what their patrons wanted to hear or read rather than what their consciences might have led them to express. Satire, in the hands of a figure like Alberti, could become an important antidote to – or at least consolation for – the co-opted roles of intellectuals in their troubled and compromised relations with the powerful elites of Renaissance Italy. Alberti also composed a number of other satirical works, such as the shorter satirical vignettes (sometimes termed "apologues" and vaguely Aesopian in nature) and Lucianic dialogues known as the *Intercenales* (Dinner Pieces), and he was deeply influenced by the derisive treatment of religious belief and philosophical pretense in Lucian (Alberti 1987, 2003a; Marsh, 1995).

Alberti's Lucianic satires, though they are less strictly imitative than those of some of his followers, helped to legitimize this kind of "fictional" satirical writing in the early Renaissance, and we have other neo-Latin examples of Lucianic satire by later humanists like Giovanni Pontano, Caelio Calcagnini, and others. But the dialogue form was taken to new and much bolder heights in the work of one of the most notorious authors of the Italian Renaissance, Pietro Aretino. Styled by Ariosto the "scourge of princes" (*il flagello dei principi*) and styling himself a "secretary of the world," Aretino's vernacular satire is notable for its direct, aggressive attacks, unparalleled in their audacity, on powerful individuals and institutions, for its anatomization of the insincere and duplicitous life of the courtier class, and for its shameless treatment of human morality, including sexuality (Innamorati 1962; Larivaille 1997; Waddington 2003). Aretino eventually resided in Venice after fruitless efforts to secure papal patronage in Rome, and from the protection of his Venetian *palazzo* wrote with a freedom that was unrivaled in its time, incurring there the reputation of an author and publicist that was feared by the greatest princes of Europe and using the very active Venetian market in printed books to his own economic advantage. Perhaps his most influential work was a series of six dialogues entitled *Ragionamenti* (Arguments or Dialogues; also known as the *Sei Giornate*, or Six Days), a work in which Aretino established his extreme form of satire as a kind of "anti-literature," a form of writing that refuses to acknowledge any norms of human behavior or ideals of conduct, reflecting on the human condition from the ground zero of prostitutes, bawds, and thieves and rejecting the idealizations of the Petrarchism so much then in vogue (Innamorati 1962: 93). From this perspective, Aretino can perhaps lay claim to being the first "slum realist" and journalist of Western culture.

In the *Ragionamenti* we can detect influences from Boccaccio and other earlier Italian *novellieri* who often based their stories on anecdotes about practical jokes (*beffe*), or who targeted religious personnel for their satires, but Aretino's world is somehow darker, more deeply compromised in its moral dimensions, more sadistic in its grim, shameless humor. Aretino focused especially on courtiers, women, and both male and female members of religious orders in his work, discovering in all of these walks of life, both high and low, a kind of universal law of nature: "Everything in this world goes hand in hand with deception" (Aretino 1994: 127). It is the satirist's task, then, to expose the vices of a world so construed, and if it is hard to imagine how an author at times so obscene (more than one student of his work has applied to him the adjective "pornographic") could have perceived himself as a moral reformer, we should remind ourselves that ethical consistency and integrity are distinctly modern, not Renaissance, virtues, and that the satirist can often hide behind a persona or behind his characters while still claiming moral rectitude as an author. In the male betrayers of Aretino's *Ragionamenti*, as well as in the conniving females of the tales of the first three days that center on the lives of nuns, wives, and whores, we are close to the rogues and prostitutes that people the early European novel and the world of picaresque fiction. Aretino's work would find a special appeal among Elizabethan authors writing for popular audiences, such as Thomas Nashe (Rhodes 1980; Moulton 2000). Aretino's refusal to be contained – both in terms of subject matter and style – reflects his own grandiose image of himself as a "secretary of the world," but also makes an important claim about the freedom of the satiric author. It is arguable that a figure like Aretino represents one of the first economically self-sufficient authors in Western culture (even if his patrons often were compelled to support him through a system that amounted to extortion by the "divine" Aretino), but it is just as important to recognize that it is in the genre of satire that we see the emergence of the clearest conception of "the author" as an oppositional figure capable of conducting autonomous critique of the dominant institutions and values of his society. As has been recently argued, Aretino's later reputation as an "erotic" author should not allow us to miss the clearly political dimension of his career as an author, since his work bears more resemblance to the world of Renaissance satire than to the modern genre of pornography (Moulton 2000).

Aretino's lead was followed by a number of authors who came to be known as *poligrafi* and who continued to pursue a vigorous critique of Italian civilization in the more crisis-laden context of the Counter-Reformation of the sixteenth century. Authors such as Anton Francesco Doni, Nicolò Franco, and Ortensio Lando earned the name of *poligrafi* for their capacity to write in a variety of genres but also for the perception that they were writing for profit, without any concern for truth or out of any sense of commitment to a specific set of values. Though not as brilliant or provocative as other satirists, these authors nevertheless figure importantly in the history of the emergence of the modern author and in the growth of oppositional discourses in the West. While they may have written with economic profit in mind and were most certainly a product of the sixteenth-century Venetian book market, their satirical works challenged Italian institutions and made bridges to the spirit of religious reform in northern European authors like Erasmus and Sir Thomas More (Grendler 1969). Writing from an Italy that was now in a declining phase of the Renaissance, all of these writers attacked what they perceived to be the pedantry of humanistic learning and encouraged a religious reform not much different from that advocated by intellectuals in northern Europe – a Christianity purged of courtly wealth and the complex, ecclesiastical accretions of more recent centuries. Doni imitated More's *Utopia* in a utopian work of his own, the *I Mondi* of 1552, while Lando made More's work available in an Italian translation of 1548. Eventually, conditions of censorship in post-Tridentine Italy made it difficult for such authors of satire to enjoy the freedom that Venice had afforded them in the mid-sixteenth century under the lead of Aretino, while literary academies placed aesthetic constraints on the kind of literature deemed decorous and worthy of print, of which satire was the least acceptable kind.

Next to the French writer Rabelais, probably no satiric author of the Renaissance influenced the later history of literary forms more than did Sir Thomas More, whose *Utopia*, composed in Latin in 1516, continues to shape the Western literary imagination; it is a palpable influence on such modern works as *Brave New World* (1932) and *Nineteen Eighty-Four* (1949), and it had an enormous influence on the production of literature in seventeenth-century England. More's work is in many ways, however, far less straightforward than the works of his later imitators, in part because More's work blended more direct social criticisms of his contemporary world (Book 1) with a fictional travel narrative to the New World habitus of the island kingdom of Utopia (which can mean both No-place and Happy Place) in Book 2. Furthermore, in the likable, cosmopolitan figure of Raphael Hythlodaeus, the traveler whose reports from Utopia are conveyed in Book 2 – a figure modeled on Lucian's Menippus and one whose witty retorts recall the sharp tongue of the ancient Cynic Diogenes – More placed opinions that clearly ran counter to his own beliefs, especially in the areas of religion and religious tolerance.

The multiple frames of *Utopia* and the ironic possibilities on which More capitalized continue to baffle his ablest critics. When we consider, for example, that the European Reformation had opened up a virtual Pandora's box of alternative or counter-cultural perspectives in its appeals for greater religious tolerance and for a more primitive Christianity rooted in the original texts of the New Testament, how do we then take Raphael's energetic endorsement of a society that has abandoned the institution of private property and that has virtually eliminated money as a feature of its culture, Utopian innovations that are obviously counter-cultural in the extreme, knowing as we do that More in his later life persecuted Lutheran heretics and remained an orthodox Catholic until the moment of his martyrdom? More's *Utopia*, from the perspective of satire, is perhaps best understood as a work that served the purpose of opening up new perspectives on human institutions and that began to unpack the concept of "custom" in a manner that anticipates the later work of Montaigne, rather than being construed as pursuing a particular ideological or religious agenda. In this respect, *Utopia* registers with a ludic profundity, not found in most authors who responded to the discovery of the New World, and with a disquieting wonder at the presence of previously unthought – or at least neglected – concepts of human social organization and control, for More ventures well beyond the experimental notions found in Lucian or Plato's *Republic*, using the iconoclastic Raphael as a sounding-board for sometimes radical and disturbing ideas.

More's work, which begins as a dialogue, opens with the standard litany of satiric complaints concerning social abuses, some of which were part of the native tradition of satire in Langland and in More's contemporary, John Skelton: the lassitude of the entrenched nobility and their neglect of their customary functions and obligations; the social dislocation and economic turmoil caused by land enclosures; the intransigence of the European powers in their attempts to secure peace; and the ineffectual role of courtiers and advisers to provide "mirrors" for their princes that might assist in ameliorating the social and political conditions of England. Renaissance humanism, insofar as it may have dreamed of a more enlightened role for intellectuals in their service as secretaries and advisers to princes, has failed: "There's no room at court for philosophy" (More 1961: 63). Unlike Alberti, however, who similarly lamented the impossibility of transforming society through the cultivation of philosopher-kings, More's work provokes a far more optimistic and constructive reaction when we are introduced to the Utopians, for it is in Book 2 that More re-created, in the spirit of the classical philosophical dialogue, a conversation that would focus on the great desideratum of ethical philosophy in the ancient world by engaging in an unvarnished investigation of the nature of human happiness.

The alternative world of Utopia turns out to be, perhaps like satire itself (in the word's primary etymological sense of *satura*), a medley or mixed bag of blessings and curses. Certainly, many of its features would appeal to progressive-minded readers today and would have been perceived as literally revolutionary to its Renaissance readership. Utopian society as a whole is oriented toward the public interest (*publicum commodum*) rather than dominated by self-interest; in this sense it is a literal *res publica* or republic where the distribution of resources is equitable and where private property as an institution is disallowed. Utopia does not represent an utterly classless society, however, since More's narrator Raphael indicates that a small intelligentsia of well-educated intellectual workers supply political leadership, while an even smaller number of priests maintain religious institutions (and there *is* religious pluralism in Utopia). The great number of ordinary citizens, however, labor for the common good, and because wealth does not accumulate, the average workday is only six hours in length, allowing for ample leisure time for citizens to pursue learning in their spare time. (Karl Marx in *The German Ideology* was no doubt influenced by More's average Utopian, for under communism, we are to be persuaded, comrades will of course labor, but there will be ample time to hunt and fish while also studying dialectical and historical materialism in leisure time.) Philosophically, the Utopians are Epicureans in their understanding that pleasure is the highest good and that "cultivat[ing] the mind" is the "secret of a happy life" (with a hint of Stoicism in their recognition that nature alone will teach them what they need, as opposed to what they desire; More 1961: 79, 92 ff). Perhaps the most innovative elements of Utopian civilization lie in its recognition that the pursuit of wealth and the establishment of structures of social differentiation based on invidious distinction are all what we would today call "learned behaviors": if children are not introduced to such notions, or are taught to scorn gold and silver by having their chamber pots made of precious metals, a vast array of social evils will forthwith vanish. More here presents his readers at times with a topsy-turvy world (*le monde renversé*), a technique to be found in Lucian but one also characteristic of key New Testament texts celebrating poverty at the expense of wealth, or socially "low" occupations at the expense of powerful elites. Such rhetorical strategies, which were a staple of the discourse of the ancient Cynics, are here used to challenge the reader to think of cultural alternatives that are indeed both emancipatory and mind-expanding.

But few readers will find that all is well in Utopia, for life there often has a troubling habit of betraying its citizens into conformity, reminding us what we might become if we all, in the words of the modern critic Theodor Adorno, were forced to lead "administered lives." Utopia's penal code is harsh, and its political institutions operate in order to establish an extreme degree of conformity; slavery is a practice that, while reserved for criminals, also relies on convicts from other societies, so that we are not far removed from the practices of slavery in the emerging, imperial phases of Western civilization. Human sexuality is treated in a disturbing manner as well, with grooms and brides forced to strip naked before wedlock to ensure physical compatibility. Freedom, at least by twenty-first-century standards, is largely absent in Utopia. And More's work appears to have some contradictions as well: while we are told that the Utopians have made their society so efficient that the need for human labor is minimized in order to maximize the pursuit of pleasure, we are also told that the work ethic is vigorous, even ascetic in its underlying motivations, in a major religious sect that practices celibacy; while in another dominant sect that allows marriage, "procreation is a duty" and pleasure is allowed "so long as it doesn't interfere with work" (More 1961: 123). As a whole, More's *Utopia* is a challenging satire that balances its attack on contemporary abuses with innovative suggestions for constructive reform; though not without its imaginative excesses, it is a work that was imitated widely in Italy and in More's native England and that represents a major contribution to the emerging fictional discourses of Western literature.

Hybrid Satiric Forms: Learned Compendia, Anatomies, and Encyclopedic Forms

Renaissance reading habits encouraged the practice of keeping commonplace books, and the paucity of dictionaries and reference works – though such tools were beginning to emerge – meant that authors might have a broad if somewhat disparate variety of sources ready to hand as they composed their works. Coupled with the vast enterprise of Renaissance humanism itself – the recovery of the entire extant textual tradition of the classical world of learning – such practices of reading and writing in the early modern period necessarily reflected, at least to some degree, what was clearly a somewhat unmanageable explosion of information in Renaissance culture, perhaps rivaled only by our own society's struggle with computerization, specialization, and information overload. By the later Renaissance, humanistic authors found their learned volumes swelling to encyclopedic dimensions as the sheer volume of sources expanded in both number and, thanks to the invention of printing, availability. While learned compendia and swollen textual commentaries of a scholarly nature began to appear in late fifteenth-century Italy, produced by such authors as Angelo Poliziano and Niccolò Perotti, and while Erasmus carried out a nearly endless task in compiling his *Adagia* in the following generation, the impact of Renaissance encyclopedism on satire was a late development of the Renaissance, leaving its mark on a number of English authors whose works are clearly satirical but defy easy classification.

The term "anatomy" was used by a number of Elizabethan and Jacobean authors to describe works that, while clearly satirical, exhibit great variety in their organization (or conscious disorganization). Prose satire of this period generally takes the form of an anatomy, a term that implied a dissection or analysis – often prolix in the extreme, and critical in intention – of a concept, of a particular social type, or of a social totality. The anatomy form often absorbed other forms of satire into it, so we must apply the term loosely. For example, in Thomas Dekker's *The Guls Horne-booke* (1609), the author asks his reader to consider his work as a sort of "how-to" manual on becoming a courtier, clearly intending to parody the vogue for behavioral manuals for would-be courtiers in the manner of Castiglione or Guazzo, but the organization of the work and its satirical messages have the feel of an "anatomy" or analysis of a social type, even though we can detect traces of other satirical traditions like the mock encomium in Dekker's inserted "praise of sleep." Similarly, Thomas Lodge's *Catharos: Diogenes in his Singularitie* of 1591, subtitled *A Nettle for Nice Noses*, starts out in the manner of a fictive Lucianic dialogue set in Athens, but ends up as a complaint over the many forms of "newfanglenes" in early modern London. Lodge's character of Diogenes complains that "the World runnes all a masking ... so many bad men thrive by countenance" (Lodge 1883: 2.5), but this universal diagnosis eventually gives way to an analysis that focuses on the dissolute nature of London's intellectuals, who have forsworn their social and political responsibilities. Satire in the late Elizabethan age is often the province of disaffected intellectuals, upstart journalistic entrepreneurs, or a mixture of the two. In another work, *Wits Miserie, and the Worlds Madnesse* (1596), Lodge recurred to a more traditional scheme of organization by providing an anatomy of the abuses of his age that relied on the structuring principle of the seven deadly sins, blending religious homily, personification allegory, and social satire into a withering indictment of his age's faults.

More creative in their efforts were the Elizabethan satirists Sir John Harington and Thomas Nashe. Harington's *A New Discourse of a Stale Subject, Called the Metamorphosis of Ajax* (1596) takes the mock encomium in praise of an unworthy subject or topic – in this case, his invention of a modern, sanitary "jakes" – in the direction of digressive and encyclopedic plenitude, for the work eventually becomes an *omnium gatherum*, a compendium of mock learning stuffed with references to human excrement and the technologies that surround it, all erudition drawn from a host of classical and patristic sources. Harington's point may have been not to have had one, but clearly his work reflects at least obliquely on the silliness of the humanist enterprise, since he trots out scores of learned references and allusions for the most vulgar (and least edifying) of purposes. His prose often strays far from its putative topic in a work that he himself terms "fantasticall," scurrilous, and "satyricall," written on the "basest, barrennest, and most witlesse subject" (Harington 1962: 181 ff). But there is, perhaps, a larger purpose at work here: by elaborating on his topic, he hopes thereby also to be spying on the "privie faults" of his age in a more serious manner than his wit and bad puns might indicate, summarized in his conclusion that "the world is so full of dissimulation, and hypocrisie" (1962: 183, 220). Harington's work has multiple, heterogeneous parts and was clearly not meant as an oratorical exercise, persuading us to consider it as a mock compendium rather than a mock encomium. His *Apologie* for the work follows upon *An Anatomie of the Metamorphosed Ajax*; in the latter we are treated to actual schematic diagrams of the author's invention, provided by his servant, while the former section anticipates his future readers' objections and contains a dream/vision in which Harington imagines himself arraigned before a court on charges of causing public scandal with the publication of his work. Formally, therefore, the work weaves together many of the threads of Renaissance satire and is laced with an ample amount of proverbial wisdom set alongside its more rarefied classical gleanings, conflating lowbrow or "homely" matter with highbrow window dressing. And while there is some topical satire of specific abuses (monopolies, religious fanaticism, malcontents, courtly pretension), and some carefully concealed allusions to specific persons, his work is a Rabelaisian *jeu d'esprit* that satisfies mostly by its sheer nuttiness, written from within a culture that Harington himself acknowledged to be "so toying" (1962: 212).

The richly varied works of Thomas Nashe, who proudly assumed the role of an "English Aretine" in his more licentious moments, can only be treated here with a few gestures indicating the magnitude of his satirical achievement. In addition to being one of the finest practitioners of literary invective (against rival authors Robert Greene and Gabriel Harvey) of the Elizabethan age, Nashe composed a work of fiction, *The Unfortunate Traveller* (1594), a satirical play featuring the court fool Will Summers, several treatises of satiric exposé (including *The Anatomy of Absurdity*, 1589, which focuses on the conditions of self-promoting intellectuals in the late sixteenth century), a famously bawdy poem that has come to be known as *The Choice of Valentines* (date unknown) and his masterwork, *Lenten Stuff* (1599). In all of these works, Nashe reveals himself to be a daring, opinionated personality whose verbal and rhetorical energies are unleashed on nearly every page that he wrote. His coining of neologisms bears comparison to Shakespeare's, and his style, at times approaching an almost macaronic linguistic plenitude that blurs the distinction between oral and written discourse and that even employs typographic effects for humorous purposes, would make him a touchstone for later writers like Sterne and Joyce.

Nashe's most accomplished work, *Lenten Stuff*, is rooted in the tradition of the mock encomium, since its title page informs the reader that the work contains a "new play never played before" concerning the "praise of the RED HERRING" (Nashe 1958:

3.147). The reader never of course encounters this "play," though there is much praise given *inter alia* for the humble fish that is a staple source of food for the citizens of Yarmouth, a coastal town to which Nashe exiled himself after being implicated in the writing of a scurrilous play (now lost) entitled *The Isle of Dogs* (1587). Nashe's strategy is similar to Harington's, in that the work's ostensive subject matter, apparently trivial, conceals or deflects some of the power of his satire's more pointed political and social commentary. While Nashe encourages his readers to ignore any "deep politic state meaning" (3.214) that they might discover in his text, *Lenten Stuff*'s strategy is to contrast methodically the virtues of the marginal, distinctly un-cosmopolitan town of Yarmouth with the novelties, both social and political, of England's cultural center, London, and to employ a number of "red herrings," or diversionary strategies, in order to camouflage his more subversive remarks. Nashe in fact claimed that the citizens of Yarmouth praised the red herring as a source of "freedoms and immunities" (3.187) from the English crown's centralizing, authoritarian tendencies, and likewise Nashe paradoxically used the period of his Lenten penance for his civil misdemeanors to voice in a distinctly carnivalized language his anger and frustration at the authorities' employment of a politically motivated *ragione di stato* against his authorial freedoms.

Interlarding his work with a good deal of copious "stuff" drawn from both the learned traditions of European humanism and the more local and popular legends of English folklore, Nashe perfected in his work the art of the digression, allowing his work to stray into all manner of topics and to enlist a host of satirical methods. A long section pillories the rage for mythological "minor" epics like Marlowe's *Hero and Leander* (1592?, pub. 1598), thereby serving the purpose of literary criticism before the age of formal literary reviews, while scattered throughout the work are passages that are more directly topical and expose the vices of courtiers, the decline of hospitality, and the pretenses of humanist rhetoric. On the one hand, Nashe certainly displays some sentiments that encourage us to see him as a "social conservative," especially in his reaction to the cultural and economic changes that seem to be violently overtaking his native England. On the other hand, Nashe also uses his satire to deplore the grasping, manipulating behaviors of his culture's leaders, adopting the persona of an outspoken, upstart urban author who is among the most alienated of England's intellectuals. His satire falls on nearly all of the social types that appear on his canvas: courtiers, lawyers, nobles, the landed gentry, and even – though more obliquely – the monarch herself. By mixing up the commonplace valuations by which his society conferred distinction on its subjects and institutions, by making great things out of small and small things out of great, Nashe's literary masterpiece is in its own way one of the most radical, and certainly the most innovative, works of literature that the Elizabethan age produced.

If Nashe is to be acknowledged as the most experimental, avant-garde author of the English Renaissance, then Robert Burton deserves recognition as the most congenial, albeit compulsive, satiric personality of the period. Here we only have space to acknowledge the satiric moorings of his splendid, polymathic tome, *The Anatomy of*

Melancholy (completed in 1632). Burton acknowledged that in his work he was relying on all of the traditions of satire that had preceded him, for his satiric persona of "Democritus Junior" informs his readers that he is familiar with "the Varronists and Lucianists of our time, satirists, epigrammatists, comedians, apologists, etc." (Burton 1977: 343). Yet, at the same time, Burton's irenic temperament compelled him to voice a claim not often heard from other Renaissance authors of satire: his work was written not to harm others but to cure the human race of its universal affliction of melancholy, and while he might have to "tax vice" in order to effect this cure, his motives were entirely directed toward the interests of his neighbors.

Burton's work shares with Erasmus' a sensibility that is profoundly Christian, despite the manic classical erudition displayed in his work. And while there is certainly a healthy dose of bawdiness of the "material bodily lower stratum" kind in his work, *The Anatomy of Melancholy*, composed at a time when religious enthusiasms were beginning to show their froth, uses humor to dispel the humors of his age, which were running in the directions of extremism, dogmatism, and sectarianism. Ostensibly organizing his work according to the chief types of melancholy – love melancholy and religious melancholy – Burton nevertheless freely digressed on all manner of subjects: his famous "Digression of Air" surveys the cultural landscape from an aerial perspective, a technique borrowed from Lucian, while the digressive section on the "Miseries of Scholars" picks up on a theme dear to the Italian humanists, whose breadth of learning only Burton and a few others in England had ever rivaled. Alone among satirists, Burton seems to have a therapist's touch: his satirical lash is made of velvet, and there is nothing of the angry young man about him at all. We can understand his choice of satire as a form best if we imagine his composition of the work constituting for himself a form of cure for what Pope termed "this long disease, my life." Where other writers of satire often only allude to the medical possibilities that lie latent in the form – a talking or writing cure *avant la lettre* – Burton seems more explicit: if the psychological condition of melancholy amounts to defining "the character of mortality," then his own efforts at writing about it have been undertaken so as to make "an antidote" from a significant cause of the disease in excessive study (1977: 144, 21).

Burton's work asks us, wisely, to consider both intelligence and emotion in his "anatomical" diagnosis of the human condition, and to understand the profoundly interconnected nature of these human faculties of the mind, as of our bodily organs, in order to appreciate the tenuous hold that human beings have on their sanity. More recreative than engaged, and more palliative than aggressive, Burton's authorial sensibility shows more charity toward its objects than most satirists. Although cultural and intellectual historians have legitimate reasons for thinking that civilizations in their waning phases produce art that is decadent or somehow ignoble, Burton's work defies that judgment, for his is a book that recovers wisdom from the vast scrapheap of humanistic learning that ironically underwrites his enterprise, composed during what is most certainly the "autumn" of the European Renaissance.

While it has become commonplace to cast satirists in the role of social conservatives, such a judgment of the satirical author may conceal some important cultural functions that satire could serve in early modern Europe (Kernan 1959). Certainly many satirists could attack the novelties of their contemporary world as innovations that they felt were debasing their civilization, but it may be anachronistic to assume that "progressive" and "conservative" agendas were as mutually exclusive in the Renaissance as they seem to be in the modern world. The satiric author's capacity to expose abuse, to smoke out hypocrisy, and to unmask the most egregious forms of dissimulation and deceit bears witness to a social function for satire that is an important development in the growth of critically reflective, open societies. Satiric authors in both Italy and England, while working under varying degrees of social and political constraint, were heirs to a classical tradition of Cynicism that had prized freedom of speech ("the most beautiful thing in the world," according to the Cynic Diogenes) and to traditions of both Roman and medieval satire, both of which lent to this form of writing an aggression, a *chutzpah*, that could be just as congenial to the aesthetic innovator as it might be to the social reactionary. It is not therefore surprising that the emerging, modern (and "liberal") cultural practices of journalism and fictional narrative would find their most immediate pedigrees in the traditions of Renaissance satire; nor is it surprising that satire would achieve such preeminence as a literary form in subsequent phases of intellectual and literary history – the English Augustan age and the European Enlightenment.

As a genre whose claims of freedom allowed for both literary and cultural experimentation, satire in its Renaissance incarnations resists easy definitions, especially when we consider its prose or prosimetric variants, and it harbored sensibilities that could be comic and serious, charitable and destructive, detached and engaged – sometimes all in the same breath. The practice of satire in the period compels us to repudiate the attempts of modern critics to define satire as either progressive or conservative, or to define (and confine) it by appealing to one literary system or another. As a form that often attacked systematic or reductive thinking itself, satire urges us to withhold judgment and rather attend to "whatever men do," as Juvenal so bluntly expressed his intentions in writing satire. No better evidence for the recreative and restorative powers of satire can be found than in its insistent claim to pursue truth – and sanity – in a world characterized by unstable – indeed, impersonated – identities and by labile structures of social distinction. We should not be surprised to find that some of the finest minds of the Renaissance found sanctuary from their crowded, confused worlds, and from their own overstuffed minds, in the open spaces of satiric discourse.

REFERENCES AND FURTHER READING

Alberti, Leon Battista (1987) *Dinner Pieces*, trans. David Marsh. Binghamton: Medieval and Renaissance Texts and Studies.

——(2003a) *Intercenales*, ed. and trans. Franco Bacchelli and Luca D'Ascia. Bologna: Pendragon.

—— (2003b) *Momus*, ed. Virginia Brown and Sarah Knight; trans. Sarah Knight. Cambridge, MA: Harvard University Press.

Aretino, Pietro (1994) *Aretino's Dialogues*, trans. Raymond Rosenthal. New York: Marsilio.

Bakhtin, Mikhail (1968) *Rabelais and his World*, trans. Hélène Iswolsky. Cambridge, MA: MIT Press.

—— (1984) *Problems in Dostoevsky's Poetics*, ed. and trans. Caryl Emerson. Minneapolis, MN: University of Minnesota Press.

Blanchard, W. Scott (1990) O Miseri Philologi: Codro Urceo's satire on professionalism and its context. *Journal of Medieval and Renaissance Studies* 20, 91–122.

—— (1995) *Scholars' Bedlam: Menippean Satire in the Renaissance*. Lewisburg: Bucknell University Press.

Burckhardt, Jacob (1958) *The Civilization of the Renaissance in Italy*, 2 vols, trans. S. G. C. Middlemore. New York: Harper and Row.

Burton, Robert (1977) *The Anatomy of Melancholy*, ed. Holbrook Jackson. New York: Vintage.

Camporeale, Salvatore (1976) Lorenzo Valla tra Medioevo e Rinascimento: *Encomion S. Thomae*, 1457. *Memorie Domenicane* n.s. 7, 11–148.

De Smet, Ingrid (1996) *Menippean Satire and the Republic of Letters, 1581–1655*. Geneva: Librairie Droz.

Erasmus, Desiderius (1969) *The Praise of Folly*, trans. Hoyt Hudson. Princeton, NJ: Princeton University Press.

Frye, Northrop (1957) *Anatomy of Criticism*. Princeton, NJ: Princeton University Press.

Grendler, Paul F. (1969) *Critics of the Italian World, 1530–60: Anton Francesco Doni, Nicolò Franco, and Ortensio Lando*. Madison: University of Wisconsin Press.

Harington, Sir John (1962) *A New Discourse of a Stale Subject, Called the Metamorphosis of Ajax*, ed. Elizabeth Donno. New York: Columbia University Press.

Innamorati, Giuliano (1962) Aretino, Pietro. *Dizionario biografico degli italiani* 4, 89–104. Rome: Istituto della Enciclopedica Italiana.

Kernan, Alvin (1959) *The Cankered Muse: Satire of the English Renaissance*. New Haven, CT: Yale University Press.

Kirk, Eugene (1980) *Menippean Satire: An Annotated Catalogue of Texts and Criticism*. New York: Garland.

Larivaille, Paul (1997) *Pietro Aretino*. Rome: Salerno.

Lodge, Thomas (1883) *The Complete Works of Thomas Lodge*, 4 vols, ed. Edmund Gosse. Glasgow: Hunterian Club.

Marsh, David (1995) *Lucian among the Latins*. Ann Arbor: University of Michigan Press.

Moulton, Ian Frederick (2000) *Before Pornography: Erotic Writing in Early Modern England*. Oxford: Oxford University Press.

More, Sir Thomas (1961) *Utopia*, trans. Paul Turner. Harmondsworth: Penguin.

Nashe, Thomas (1958) *The Works of Thomas Nashe*, 5 vols, ed. R. B. McKerrow. Oxford: Oxford University Press.

Poliziano, Angelo (1972) *Opera Omnia*, 3 vols, ed. Ida Maier. Turin: Bottega d'Erasmo.

Relihan, Joel (1993) *Ancient Menippean Satire*. Baltimore, MD: The Johns Hopkins University Press.

Rhodes, Neil (1980) *Elizabethan Grotesque*. London: Routledge and Kegan Paul.

Tomarken, Annette (1990) *The Smile of Truth: The Satirical Eulogy in France*. Princeton, NJ: Princeton University Press.

Valla, Lorenzo (1982) *Opera Omnia*, 2 vols, ed. Eugenio Garin. Turin: Bottega d'Erasmo.

Viti, Paolo (1982) *Due Commedie Umanistiche Pavesi*. Padua: Editrice Antenore.

Waddington, Raymond (2003) *Aretino's Satyr: Sexuality, Satire, and Self-projection in Sixteenth Century Literature and Art*. Toronto: University of Toronto Press.

Wesseling, Ari (1986) *Lamia: Praelectio in Priora Aristotelis Analytica*. Leiden: Brill.

Part II
Restoration and Eighteenth-century England and France

Part II

8
Satire in Seventeenth- and Eighteenth-century France
Russell Goulbourne

Writing in 1668, Nicolas Boileau offers a usefully pithy definition of satire in his ninth *Satire*. The poem takes the form of a dialogue between the poet and his mind about the merits of satire. The poet ironically takes his mind to task for writing such bold satires, echoing and comically undermining the views of his critics. The poet's mind puts forward what we might reasonably take as Boileau's own defense of satire:

> Satire, fertile in lessons and novelties,
> Alone unites the pleasing and the instructive,
> And, with each perfect line of common-sense verse,
> Releases minds from the errors of their times.
> (267–70)

Satire has a significant and seemingly immediate social function: it alone fulfills the Horatian precept of offering both entertainment and enlightenment. But perhaps more importantly still, satire also has an important aesthetic function: it is the site of generic, stylistic, and thematic innovation and exploration, a fruitful meeting-place of tradition and experimentation, of ancient models and contemporary concerns. The fertile originality of satire makes any generalizations difficult. But this is precisely what makes French satire in the seventeenth and eighteenth centuries so interesting. Tracing its history involves charting the satirists' negotiation of several interconnected relationships: between past and present, between constraint and freedom, and between the impulse to ridicule and the claim to reform.

The Seventeenth Century

Of course, when Boileau refers to satire, he means the formal genre in alexandrines (the French equivalent of the Latin hexameter), inspired by the examples of Horace,

Juvenal, and Persius. Satire in this strict sense only really developed in France at the very beginning of the seventeenth century: for most of the preceding century, in the works of Rabelais, Ronsard, and d'Aubigné for example, satire was a tone rather than a genre. But the rediscovery of Aristotle's *Poetics* and the growing influence of Stoic philosophy at the end of the sixteenth century favored a revival of interest in the ancient satirists: comparisons between Horace, Juvenal, and Persius soon became a fashionable critical exercise.

Horace was favored by many literary theorists and practicing writers alike, including Jean Vauquelin de la Fresnaye, Desmarets de Saint-Sorlin, and René Rapin, who saw in him the prototype of the civilized, worldly *honnête homme* in vogue in the second half of the seventeenth century: his conversational *sermones* were the very model of witty *badinage* (Marmier 1962: 123–43, 305–7). Others, by contrast, such as Isaac Casaubon and Isaac de La Grange, who published substantial commentaries on Juvenal in 1605 and 1614 respectively, and Nicolas Rigault, whose major edition of Juvenal appeared in 1616, criticized Horace for simply writing gently mocking *sermones* that focus only on the folly of human behavior, whereas Juvenal wrote powerfully indignant satires targeting the villainy of criminals. Precisely those qualities that had made sixteenth-century writers place Juvenal beneath Horace – his sometimes shockingly aggressive manner and his frequent contraventions of good taste – were those, perhaps paradoxically, that many in the seemingly civilized seventeenth century prized above all. Indeed, Juvenal's posthumous success was perhaps never greater than in the seventeenth century (Debailly 1995a).

Crucially, however, the ancient satirists were usually read in expurgated editions and translations, with the harshest and most obscene sections carefully excised. Jérôme Tarteron, for example, in his 1689 translation of Persius and Juvenal, proudly reduces Juvenal's sixth satire, on women, by about a fifth; and Guillaume de Silvecane dedicates his 1690 translation of Horace, Juvenal, and Persius to Louis XIV, assuring the king in his preface that, thanks to the translator's art, the ancient satirists have been "reprimanded" and now speak "the chaste language of the French muses" (Abramovici 2003: 59). The ancient satirists were thus assimilated in seventeenth-century France into an intricate network of aesthetic codes and moral norms. And in this way, the debate about the relative merits of Horace and Juvenal in particular came to shape the development of French verse satire at the time; for French verse satire defines itself with explicit reference to earlier models: the difference is essentially between a playful conception of satire and a more serious, indignant one.

The twin influences of Horace and Juvenal can be seen in the work of Mathurin Régnier, who played a crucial role in establishing regular verse satire in seventeenth-century France. He wrote seventeen satires, the first thirteen of which were published between 1608 and 1612; the last four were published posthumously (1613, 1652). In them, he satirizes contemporary manners, literature, pedants, religious hypocrisy, worthless nobility, the corruption of women, and the affectation of courtiers and pedants. But if he satirizes seemingly contemporary vices, he is also explicitly aware of a literary tradition. In *Satire* 1, for example, he claims to be imitating the Roman satirists in writing for the good of the state (lines 105–8), and in *Satire* 14, he explicitly presents himself as a follower of Horace (lines 101–5). It is true that the form of Régnier's satires suggests the influence of Horace's artful artlessness. But in *Satire* 2 he claims to prefer Juvenal's spirit of freedom to Horace's excessive discretion (line 16), and he even goes so far as to preface the first edition of his *Satires* with Juvenal's exclamation: "*Difficile est saturam non scribere*" (*Satires* 1.30). He certainly shares Juvenal's indignation at the spectacle of moral corruption all around him, and he is not afraid to infringe the niceties of literary taste to make his satirical point. In *Satire* 2, for example, Régnier echoes Juvenal ("*facit indignatio versum*," *Satires* 1.79) when he playfully posits an organic link between his indignation and his instinct to write satire:

> Like a whore, I have difficulty keeping quiet,
> I simply have to have my say however I can,
> And anger is often the source of good verse.
> (96–8)

The satirist knows that he is right: his moral outrage becomes a redoubtable weapon.

In both his choice of subject and his conception of satire, Régnier anticipated, but was overshadowed by, Boileau, who was undoubtedly the most important verse satirist in seventeenth-century France. Boileau wrote his first seven satires between 1657 and 1665 and published them in 1666, prefaced by a *Discours au roi*. They were an immediate success, and two years later, in 1668, he published a new edition of the satires, with two new poems and an important *Discours sur la satire*. He added a tenth and eleventh satire to his collection in 1694 and 1701 respectively, but he failed to secure publication in his lifetime of his twelfth and final satire, an attack on Jesuit casuistry, which only appeared in 1716, five years after his death.

Boileau may seem to be the Horace of seventeenth-century France, writing satires as well as epistles (1674, 1683) and an *Art poétique* (1674). There are clear echoes of Horace in many of his poems: for instance, *Satire* 3, about a ridiculous dinner party, recalls Horace's *Satires* 2.8; *Satire* 4, on human folly and self-delusion, is indebted to Horace's *Satires* 2.3; and *Satire* 7, in which the poet engages in extended self-assessment, recalls Horace's *Satires* 2.1 (Marmier 1962: 273–90). The influence of Juvenal, however, seems to have been even stronger (Colton 1987). Boileau's discussion of ancient satire in the second canto of the *Art poétique* (lines 147–67) tellingly devotes two lines to Persius, four lines each to Lucilius and Horace, and eleven to Juvenal; and in *Satire* 7, he expresses a preference for Juvenal's "biting pen" as it pours forth "floods of bile and bitterness" (77–8).

Juvenal's influence on Boileau can be seen in terms of subject matter, techniques, and, more broadly, a shared conception of satire. Boileau's *Satires* 1 and 6, on the discomforts of living in Paris, both echo Juvenal's *Satire* 3 on the grievances of the worthy poor; the major source for *Satire* 5, on worthless nobles, seems to be Juvenal's *Satire* 8; and *Satire* 10, on women, can be read as an imitation of Juvenal's *Satire* 6. More importantly still,

Boileau's satirical stance could also be said to be characteristically Juvenalian. He sets himself up as a kind of epic hero, the I-persona who ridicules vice and denounces decadence, the last remaining guardian of truth and enemy of humbug. In *Satire 7*, for example, like Juvenal before him, he presents satire as an irresistible moral imperative (lines 49–56, 89–90); and in the *Discours au roi*, he compares writing satire to fighting wars (lines 67–70). Donning a mask of authority in order to lend weight and seriousness to his attacks and judgments, he presents himself as the defender of virtue and reason. The satirist is thus endowed with an important social and literary role in Louis XIV's kingdom and in the Republic of Letters more broadly: the satirist arms himself with common sense in the fight against folly.

Closely associated with this is Boileau's epic conception of satire, which is also influenced by Juvenal. Anticipating Dryden's theories in his "Discourse Concerning the Original and Progress of Satire" (1693), Boileau's originality lies in his attempt to give satire a role and a prestige equivalent in the literary hierarchy to that of epic poetry (Debailly 1995b). Epic was at the very top of that hierarchy, and satire was in some senses its direct counterpart and mirror-image: the high is brought low as noble values are debased and the intrepid hero of epic becomes the cowardly fool of satire. Influenced by the trenchant fervor of Juvenal, Boileau takes satire seriously, and he wants his readers to do the same. When he says, in *Satire 9*, that satire "alone unites the pleasing and the instructive," he is implicitly elevating it from its lowly status to a position of complete superiority. For Boileau, the translator of pseudo-Longinus' *Traité du sublime* (1674, though begun as early as 1663), bitterness and anger can and should reach the heights of the sublime, as they do in Juvenal, whom Boileau praises in the second canto of the *Art poétique* for his "sublime beauties" and "writings full of fire" (160, 167). Indeed, in some senses Boileau's translation of pseudo-Longinus can be seen as the *ars poetica* that informs his satirical poetry. The definition of the sublime in the *Traité du sublime* closely parallels Boileau's definition of satire: like satire, the sublime derives some of its ability to "ravish" and "transport" the reader from its capacity to "*tell the truth*" (ch. 1), such is its "noble fury" and "wholly divine fire and vigor" (ch. 6). If the *Traité du sublime* can be read as an enquiry into literary excellence, it also parallels the *Satires*, in which Boileau denounces all forms of literary mediocrity.

Boileau extends the scope of French satire, which had traditionally been limited to questions of morality, by dealing with bad works of literature and their writers. He presses satire into the service of literary criticism, just as he writes literary criticism that is satirical: even his *Art poétique* can be seen as a satirical entertainment as much as a poetic statement of literary theory. A satirical vision runs through much of Boileau's poetry, and the object on which it most frequently focuses is literature. This is most evident in *Satires* 2, 3, and 9. *Satire 2*, for instance, on the pains of writing poetry, is peppered with satirical references to rhymesters and hack poets, including Michel de Pure, who had made the mistake of penning a satirical attack on Boileau a few years earlier, and Georges de Scudéry, whose prolificacy Boileau denounces wittily with the bold metaphor of monthly childbirth (lines 77–8).

If Boileau echoes Juvenal in satirizing writers, he also echoes him in choosing to call those writers by name. If the satirist's job is to denounce, it follows, for Boileau, that he must name names, as he boldly affirms in *Satire* 1 (lines 51–2). Attacking people by name had been relatively common in epigrammatic writing, but Boileau was innovative, and caused a scandal, by introducing the technique into the genre of regular verse satire. In the *Discours sur la satire*, Boileau defends his practice by making an eloquent appeal to the ancient example of Juvenal, alluding in particular to his *Satires* 1 and 3. However, as original as the prevalence of literary concerns in Boileau's *Satires* may be, it is possible that his most daring feature could also be his least endearing one, certainly as far as posterity is concerned. For satire is most likely to stand the test of time when its target is some aspect of human behavior in general, not a particular named individual, let alone a long forgotten seventeenth-century hack writer.

But, Boileau does not only denounce. Like Horace ("*ridendo dicere verum*," *Satires* 1.24), he also integrates laughter into his definition of satire: laughter and truth-telling form a powerful duo. In the *Discours sur la satire*, he argues that satirical laughter is to do with exposing vice-ridden individuals to public ridicule and ritual humiliation. Public scorn is the key to satire's corrective function: satirical laughter strips vice of its mask of virtue and thereby ensures the effectiveness of the criticism. So we find Boileau arousing laughter in a theatrical way, creating contrasting characters, characters who make fools of themselves and also poke fun at each other, as in *Satire* 3. To this extent at least, Boileau's satire is not limited by his practice of naming names: he also succeeds in creating characters who are social types, examples of a humanity that is more general.

Between the end of Régnier's career as a satirist and the start of Boileau's, there was an important political upheaval that had major implications for writers too: the period of civil insurrection during the minority of Louis XIV, known as the Fronde (1648–53). The courts of appeal (the *parlements*) and the high nobility formed a shaky alliance in opposition to the centralizing policies of the king's first minister, the Italian-born Cardinal Mazarin. The revival of interest in the Latin satirical poets seems to have coincided with the Fronde: troubled times were fertile ground for polemical literature. Formal verse satire became one of the great literary genres of the Fronde, though there was also a vogue for ephemeral satirical writing of all kinds. Echoing the attacks by both Catholics and Protestants on Henri III in the 1580s, writers in the Fronde used a combination of religious, political, and sexual themes in their attacks on Mazarin (Merrick 1994; Carrier 1996: 255–95, 361–418). Some of these so-called *mazarinades* follow Régnier's example and use the consecrated forms of formal verse satire to express their subversive views. Paul Scarron used not alexandrines, but nearly four hundred octosyllables in his famous poem *Mazarinade* (1651), in which he launched a frenetic attack on Mazarin's alleged homosexuality:

> Constable with a rod of Sodom,
> Exploiting the kingdom left and right,
> Buggering bugger, buggered bugger,

> And bugger in the highest degree,
> Bugger this way and bugger that way,
> Bugger in large and small size,
> Bugger sodomizing the state,
> And bugger of the highest carat.
>   (349–56)

Diverse forms of satirical prose also developed during the Fronde, such as mock wills, including one published in June 1652 in which Mazarin is made to bequeath to the king "all the hospitals founded by him in France, which have no income, and of which there are more than 30,000, on the condition that His Majesty looks after the feeding and care of the poor souls therein"; and mock catechisms, including a parody of the creed, written in 1652, in which the believer satirically declares of Mazarin: "He has ascended the throne and is seated at the right hand of an almighty King; from thence he shall come to persecute the living and the dead." Sex, politics, and religion were all within the satirists' scope.

This satirical freedom unleashed during the Fronde paved the way for the satirists of the second half of the seventeenth century and the eighteenth century. Moreover, the Fronde led to the concentration of power in the absolute monarch, Louis XIV, and this in turn gave the satirist more freedom than before to mock those elites whose power base had been undermined. As Montesquieu was to suggest in 1748, in his *De l'Esprit des lois* (12.13), satire can thrive in a monarchical system, whereas the diffusion of power in an aristocratic system puts too many individuals in a position to suppress subversive voices. If satire as a formal verse genre, despite (or perhaps because of) Boileau's success, gradually lost ground in the second half of the seventeenth century, satire as a manner did not. Instead, it became an important ingredient in genres as diverse as comedies, novels, fables, "characters," and polemical letters.

Seventeenth-century comic theater is predominated by Molière. Recent criticism has tended to play down the satirical element in his theater, but satire is an integral part of many of his plays. He satirizes *marquis*, *précieuses*, pedants, tyrannical parents, cuckolds, religious hypocrites, misanthropists, social climbers, misers, courtiers, hypochondriacs, doctors, masters and servants, peasants, merchants, lawyers, hack writers, and many more: his satirical gaze is seemingly all-embracing. His satirized characters have both universal and particular characteristics: he echoes Juvenal and Boileau in satirizing recognizable contemporary figures and figures holding specifically seventeenth-century attitudes, but his satire always transcends time and space: Molière's topicality is not the same as Boileau's, for it does not rely in the same way on naming names. Like Boileau, however, Molière makes laughter central to his enterprise. The key to his comedies is ridicule. Or rather, Molière's particular skill is his blend of normality and exaggeration, representation and ridicule.

Before Molière, verse comedy for the public stage in seventeenth-century France had set itself the aim of offering, in Pierre Corneille's words, "the depiction of the conversation of decent folk" (*Examen* of *Mélite* [1629], 1660). This view had a long heritage: the Ciceronian definition of comedy as *imitatio vitae, speculum consuetudinis* (the imitation of life, the mirror of customs), held great sway in the first part of the seventeenth century. By contrast, Molière sought to combine social observation with satirical laughter. His characters are at once lifelike and laughable, recognizable and ridiculous: Molière depicts ordinary people with some character weakness or comic obsession, which he ruthlessly ridicules. In *La Critique de l'Ecole des femmes* (1663), Dorante, whom we might see as Molière's mouthpiece on these questions, declares that the aim of the comic dramatist is to "deal, as is befitting, with mankind's ridiculousness and to offer a pleasing representation on the stage of the failings of all people" (scene 6). Molière's aim seems to have been to depict satirically the faults of his day: making audiences laugh aloud at their own society was his lasting contribution to French comedy.

But the distance between satirizing humankind and correcting it is large. Molière has often been portrayed, misleadingly, as a castigator of wrong, a corrector of the moral failings of his contemporaries. At the very beginning of the first petition that Molière addressed to Louis XIV in 1664 when *Tartuffe* was first banned, the dramatist makes a clear connection between comedy and moral correction: "Since the role of comedy is to correct people at the same time as entertaining them, I thought that, in my position, the best thing I could do was to attack my century's vices by portraying them in a ridiculous light." Of course, Molière is trying to persuade the king to allow his play to be performed in public, and in an age when the theater was regarded with mistrust by the Church, what better rhetorical strategy could there be for a compromised comic dramatist than to proclaim his play's moral worth? But what this petition also makes clear is that the vaunted moral purpose of comedy comes not from preaching, but from exposing the absurdity of certain attitudes or forms of behavior: "An effective way of attacking vice is to expose it to public ridicule." Nothing is more stinging than ridicule. The ridicule of pretence, falsehood, exaggeration, self-centeredness, and gullibility is the key to the representation, in *Tartuffe*, of both the religious hypocrite himself and his "victims," namely Orgon and his mother, Mme Pernelle. In the comic context, Molière's characters are examined not against a standard of absolute moral worth, but against a standard of normality: the satirical perspective is comic, not moral or didactic.

The importance of satire in Molière's theater is reflected by the fact that, from as early as *L'Ecole des femmes* (1662), if not earlier, Molière could be said to be reflecting self-consciously and ironically in his comedies on the nature and function of comedy and of the role of the satirist in particular. The ridiculous cuckold Arnolphe reserves the right, he proudly declares, to satirize his peers (1.1.43–4), but he does not realize that he too is an object of satire. Hence, the warning given to him by his friend Chrysalde that he who laughs at others has to fear being laughed at in his turn (1.1.45–6). Arnolphe does not learn his lesson and ends up being punished by being driven out. His lack of self-awareness characterizes many of Molière's other protagonists too; and a number of Molière's plays can be read as reflections on the limits of satire, even as expressions of a more general distrust in the seventeenth century of the satirist's capacity for moral correction.

The turning point in Molière's career, from what might be termed "corrective" to "compromise" comedy (Defaux 1980), seems to be the crisis of *Tartuffe*, which was twice banned as a result of the intervention of the ecclesiastical authorities for its supposedly aggressive attitude to Christianity as a whole (the version we have today is the third and final version, performed with great success in 1669, five years after the first version). In this context, *Dom Juan* (1665) and *Le Misanthrope* (1666) represent Molière's reassessment of his role as a corrector of society. Some critics see *Dom Juan* as a kind of morality play, the philandering protagonist receiving his just deserts at the end as he is dragged down into the flames of hell. But Molière unsettles such moral and satirical certainties by showing the central character to be both good and bad: he is a mischievous philanderer, but he is a likeable trickster too, a deft role-player who cleverly exploits social and religious codes and conventions for his own ends. And, in fact, what sends Dom Juan to his apparent doom is not his lust, polygamy, or blasphemy, but his religious hypocrisy: he pretends to his father to have become a good, pious Christian (5.1). The moral-cum-satirical lesson of the play, if there is one, is that religious hypocrites, like both those represented in and those who objected to *Tartuffe*, are the only ones who deserve the fires of hell.

In *Le Misanthrope* (1666), a comedy of aristocratic misbehavior that Voltaire would describe in his *Vie de Molière* (1733) as "a wiser and more refined satire than those of Horace and Boileau," the eponymous Alceste offers a seemingly comprehensive attack on contemporary social vices: echoing Boileau's *Satire* 1, he satirizes empty social conventions and the calculating duplicity of social behavior; and anticipating Boileau's *Satire* 9, he cannot tolerate bad writing. But Alceste is also a ridiculous, old-fashioned figure who tries to assert his authority by criticizing and humiliating others, and actually finds himself marginalized by his ill temper and anger, highlighted theatrically by his physical isolation on stage. Alceste becomes the butt of much laughter: the satirist is satirized. Echoing Chrysalde's words in *L'Ecole des femmes* and Boileau's strictures in *Satire* 4, also published in 1666, on the folly of those who try to judge others, Alceste's stance of moral and specifically satirical superiority becomes laughable. As his friend Philinte points out to him in the first scene: "It's utter folly, folly of the highest order, / To want to try to correct everyone else's ways" (157–8). The play works as a kind of aesthetic self-critique: *Le Misanthrope* calls into question the satirical dramatist's supposed aim to "correct people at the same time as entertaining them."

Subsequently, in *Le Bourgeois Gentilhomme* (1670), the characters are seen accommodating themselves to the central character's folly rather than rejecting it, as in earlier comedies. And likewise in *Le Malade imaginaire* (1673), Molière uses all the old devices of corrective comedy, but the play ends with the triumph of folly and laughter. Argan, the eponymous hypochondriac, is an obsessed fool, like Orgon, but obsessed with his body rather than his soul. But whereas Orgon is cured of his obsession with Tartuffe, Argan is not cured of his obsession with medicine. The characters decide in the end to defer to his fantasies, and the play ends with a burlesque musical ceremony as Argan is supposedly instated as a doctor. Molière the satirist seems to be alive above all to the carnival of life, to society's rich fabric, into which all individuals have to be woven.

Outside the comic theater, satire also thrives in other, apparently less significant genres. It flourishes in the new genre of the novel, particularly the comic novels of Sorel, Scarron (*Le Roman comique*, 1651–7), and Furetière (*Le Roman bourgeois*, 1666), which satirize both the contemporary world and the conventions of heroic and romantic fiction. For example, Sorel's *Histoire comique de Francion* (1623–33) includes unsparing satire of a number of corrupt professional types, including doctors, who are ridiculed for their jargon; grotesque pedants, the satire of whom echoes Rabelais's satire of academics in *Gargantua* (1534–5); and lawyers, whom Francion's father denounces as "those damned people who simply live off other people's misfortunes." Echoing the author's claim in the preface to the novel that his aim is to "show men the vices to which they unwittingly fall victim," Francion, the hero of the novel, sets himself up, albeit problematically, as a satirical observer of humankind, a kind of moral policeman: even as a child, he says, "I had some kind of instinct that drove me to hate the shoddy deeds, stupid words and dim-witted ways of my schoolfriends." The hero of a comic novel paves the way for Boileau's stance in his *Satires*.

In contrast to the, at times, disorientatingly mundane world of the comic novel, fantasy and defamiliarization are the keys to the satirical method of La Fontaine's *Fables*. La Fontaine sets up tellingly satirical comparisons between men and animals. He published his twelve books of fables between 1668 and 1694, and many of them are based on ancient models, namely Aesop and Phaedrus. But these ancient texts become the pretext for strikingly modern – and satirical – tales. La Fontaine uses distancing techniques to make his satire all the more subtle and potentially subversive: he writes about animals in order to tell truths about humans, as he makes clear in the liminal poem addressed to the king's son, to whom he dedicates the first six books: "I use animals to teach men." In this fantasy world of talking beasts, humankind is satirically reduced to its basest form, as lions rule by dint of sheer force: anticipating Orwell's *Animal Farm*, the allegory serves as a vehicle for criticism and comment. The fables paint a satirical picture of human nature in general: "These fables," La Fontaine says in the preface to the first collection, "are a painting in which each of us is depicted."

That said, La Fontaine often leaves it up to the reader to spot the resemblance and make the satirical point. "*Les Animaux malades de la peste*" (7.1) is a good example of this kind of indirect satire, in this case of court society: ravaged by the plague, the community of animals resorts instinctively to a combination of cowardly and self-serving obedience to the lion (referred to as "the king"), on the one hand, and, on the other, cruelty to the simple, honest donkey. Similarly, "*Les Obsèques de la lionne*" (8.14), about the death of the wife of another ruling lion, this time referred to as "a prince," shows how death has become an empty social ritual, with the other animals, referred to as "courtiers," eager to be seen aping the king's grief in a show of flattery. Similarly, there is satire of human self-regard and greed, as in "*Le Cerf malade*" (12.6), about a stag who suffers all the more when seemingly concerned friends eat him out of house and home; satire of the justice system, as in *"Les Frelons et les mouches à miel"* (1.21), about a ridiculously interminable dispute between hornets and bees over the ownership of honey; and satire of the Church, as in *"Le Rat qui s'est retiré du monde"* (7.3), in which the rat is a "devout character" who withdraws from the world and into a piece of delicious Dutch cheese.

La Fontaine, however, does sometimes explicitly point up the satirical moral, as in *"La Grenouille qui se veut faire aussi grosse que le bœuf"* (1.3), where the frog's fatal attempt to blow itself up to the size of an ox is explicitly compared to the pomposity of bourgeois would-be gentlemen; and in *"Le Serpent et la lime"* (5.16), where the snake's folly in chewing on steel is explicitly compared to the bitterness of hack writers who take pleasure in criticizing other writers' work. But sometimes even the explicit satirical lesson is left open to question, as in *"Le Loup et l'agneau"* (1.10): does the wolf's decision to kill the lamb really confirm that "might is right"? La Fontaine the satirist is alive, above all, to the ridiculousness, illogicality, and injustice of life.

Like La Fontaine, La Bruyère also defines his position as a satirist in relation to ancient authority. He published only one book, *Les Caractères*, the first edition of which, published in 1688, was presented as a translation of Theophrastus together with *Les Caractères ou les mœurs de ce siècle*. La Bruyère had in reality begun his own text several years earlier: translating Theophrastus was an ancient pretext for his own modern text. Between 1688 and 1694, no fewer than eight editions of *Les Caractères* appeared, each bigger than the one before: in 1688 the text consisted of 440 "remarks"; by 1694 the number of these had risen to 1,120. These remarks, which take the form of maxims, portraits, dialogues, reflections, enigmas, and short essays, are divided into sixteen thematic chapters, though the divisions between these are not watertight.

La Bruyère works at the interface of satire and moral philosophy, at once an observer and a critic, both a *moraliste*, in the sense of an author of reflections on human nature and society, and the heir of Juvenal, Horace, and Boileau. The *moraliste* seems to come to the fore in the opening remark of chapter 11, *"De l'Homme,"* where he diagnoses humankind's problem: human nature is resolutely fixed in its wickedness, harshness, ingratitude, injustice, and self-obsession. And, moreover, La Bruyère argues, like Molière's Philinte, it is pointless to try to do anything about it. Remark 14 in the same chapter goes further still, explicitly calling into question satire altogether, for a "thoroughly uncivilized man" will not even recognize himself in the satirical portrait: "It is like hurling insults at a deaf man." Seemingly like Molière, La Bruyère is skeptical about the capacity of one human being to reveal the truth to another. Instead of a conventionally satirical stance, La Bruyère adopts that of an amused observer of society.

La Bruyère's position is more nuanced, however, for in remark 34 in the first chapter, *"Des ouvrages de l'esprit,"* he implicitly sets himself up as a philosopher, not in the modern sense (he has no coherent system, as the fragmentary nature of his text suggests), but almost in the eighteenth-century sense of the term: he is a reforming writer, questioning appearances and established traditions, "searching out vice and ridiculousness" in order to improve people. As he observes in remark 68 of the same chapter: "If there is ridiculousness, it must be seen, brought out gracefully and in a way which is both pleasing and instructive." The language of exposing folly to the light of reason echoes Boileau; the twin aims of pleasure and instruction are distinctively Horatian. La Bruyère is both a *moraliste* and a satirist.

As a satirical observer, La Bruyère offers a pessimistic view of society: people are vain (3.8, 71), greedy (6.13, 40), and unfaithful (3.67, 73); money corrupts but brings worldly success (6.7, 36, 58); society neglects the poor (6.18, 47); the court is a place of hypocrisy, misery, and self-interest (8.8, 63; 13.21); justice is rare (14.41, 43); religion is abused by spiritual directors and hypocrites (3.44–5); people are driven by appearances, not reality (3.46; 8.99). La Bruyère adopts a daringly critical approach toward man in society and the way in which different strata of society operate and interrelate. He offers his readers serious food for thought on a range of social and moral issues, inviting them to reflect on how things might be improved. He excels at leaving his own views unstated, preferring instead to describe features of behavior or appearance in an enumerative style from which readers make their own deductions.

La Bruyère's stance, moreover, is ambivalent. He longs for justice and sympathy for the downtrodden, for example, as in remark 26 of "*Des Biens de fortune*," where, seemingly anticipating Voltaire, he indignantly attacks the shameful wealth of the Church when compared to the poverty of the people, a criticism he repeats elsewhere in this chapter (6.47, 58). But this attitude sits ill with his affirmation in the final chapter, "*Des Esprits forts*," that God sanctions the current social order (16.48): he tellingly offers an idealistic vision of current society working well, even though most of his text shows that it does not.

This tension in La Bruyère's work underlies his emphasis, in the first chapter, on the limits of satire in seventeenth-century France: "A man born a Christian and a Frenchman finds himself constrained in satire; the big subjects are forbidden" (1.65). Perhaps there is a tinge of regret here. But there is also a clever satirical point: La Bruyère is perhaps saying less about the limits imposed on the satirist and more about the vast expanses of wickedness that stretch beyond the satirist's reach.

And those vast expanses certainly did not go unexplored, as the *mazarinades* and Molière's *Tartuffe* demonstrate. But Molière's satirical daring was anticipated, surprisingly perhaps, by Pascal's as early as 1656, three years after the end of the Fronde. Pascal's impetus in writing his polemical *Lettres provinciales* was not political, however, but religious. The seventeenth century saw a lengthy dispute within the Catholic Church between Jesuits (members of the Society of Jesus) and Jansenists (followers of the doctrine of Cornelius Jansen, a Flemish theologian who defended the teachings of St Augustine). The unbending Augustinianism of the Jansenists set them at odds with the less rigid doctrines of the Jesuits, who were powerful in France, not least because they acted as spiritual confessors to the king.

Pascal began his *Lettres provinciales* in 1656, at the height of the quarrel between the Jesuits and the Jansenists, in order to defend the latter. They were published anonymously, eighteen appearing at regular intervals between January 1656 and

March 1657; they were published as a composite volume for the first time in 1657. Of the eighteen letters, the first three and last two focus on the contemporary theological controversy over the roles of divine grace and free will, the Jansenists arguing for the former, the Jesuits for the latter; while letters 4 to 16, first satirically and then more openly, attack the Jesuits, initially for their spiritual and moral laxity, and then for their alleged defamation of the unnamed author of the *Lettres provinciales*, for after the appearance of the third letter, the Jesuits started writing their own polemical counter-attacks, to which the speaker in the later letters responds.

Pascal writes not as a theologian, but as a man of the world. Letters 1–10 stage the interaction between the mock-naïve writer of the letters, which are addressed to a provincial friend, a reasonable Jansenist, and some foolish Jesuits. If Pascal wrote the *Lettres provinciales* to defend Jansenism against the Jesuits, his main weapon was satirical attack. He is at his most sharply satirical in letters 4–10 as he sets his sights on the Jesuits and their lax moral principles. In letter 4, for example, the reader, implicitly invited to share the letter-writer's stance of seemingly innocent ignorance and open-minded curiosity, is drawn into laughing at the irascible and verbose Jesuit, whose replies to the letter-writer's questions exploring the differences between traditional doctrine and Jansenist teaching contrast tellingly with those of the clear-headed, sensible Jansenist. Using the tried-and-tested satirical technique of mockery through reduction (*reductio ad absurdum*), Pascal presents the arguments against Jansenists as hollow and contradictory. Like a comic dramatist, Pascal makes the Jesuits condemn themselves out of their own mouths: what they say, and how they say it, makes them appear narrow-minded, stubbornly obscure, and utterly ridiculous. Manipulating the characters like puppets, Pascal succeeds in turning dry, dusty theological disputes into hard-hitting, entertaining satire.

Pascal's satirical method was to prove influential. His ability to make things look ridiculous by reducing them to their bare essentials, combined, crucially, with his use of a mock-naïve, questioning outsider-figure, influenced the well-known satirists of the eighteenth century. Voltaire, for instance, would describe Pascal, in chapter 37 of his *Siècle de Louis XIV* (1751), as the first of the French satirists, and the *Lettres provinciales* as "a model of eloquence and humor," adding that "Molière's best comedies do not have as much wit as the first few of the *Lettres provinciales*." But the irony of Pascal's influence on the eighteenth century is this: whereas Pascal sought to use satire in order to bring readers back to what he saw as Christian orthodoxy, the eighteenth-century satirists would use his methods in order to point readers forward to a future unfettered by religious dogma and to question the principle of an established order.

The Eighteenth Century

The eighteenth century was the satirical century *par excellence*. The ancient satirists were still widely read, edited, and commented upon. Diderot, for example, admired Juvenal, who came into vogue in the second half of the eighteenth century, with the search for a less refined, more immediate art that was deemed to be closer, at least in aesthetic terms, to the growing bourgeois public. He also read Persius, correcting the abbé Le Monnier's translation of the *Satires* in 1771 and subsequently writing a *Satire contre le luxe à la manière de Perse*, first published (posthumously) in 1798. And he was greatly influenced by Horace too, translating *Satires* 1.1 and writing an imitation of *Satires* 1.6. Boileau, too, had his fair share of defenders and detractors in the eighteenth century (Miller 1942). However, attempts to write formal verse satire in the period were limited. Instead, satire found its voice in many different kinds of writing, including comic drama, travel literature, philosophical fiction, and personal polemic. And more importantly still, the eighteenth century broadened its satirical focus from ridiculing human foibles to denouncing humankind's capacity for cruelty and injustice. The Enlightenment satirists targeted social problems, religious intolerance, and political abuse. Believing that society was free to work out its own destiny through tolerance and the community spirit, the eighteenth-century satirists were not interested in exploring human psychology in the same way as their seventeenth-century forebears; rather, they concentrated on human needs. They championed freedom, not least freedom of thought, and they often did so satirically.

Satire found a home in the theater in this stage-struck age. Satirical theater in the Molièresque model persisted throughout the century, from Lesage's *Turcaret* (1709), which provoked a scandal because of its biting satire of a corrupt tax farmer at a time of poverty and suffering in France, via Destouches's *Le Glorieux* (1732), about a poor but obsessively rank-conscious noble, to Voltaire's *Le Dépositaire* (1772), which echoes Molière's *Tartuffe*. Like their seventeenth-century models, such plays focus on character types who are satirized for their absurd unwillingness to change their foolish ways.

Marivaux's characters, by contrast, are not immobile in this way. Rather, their significance lies in their changeability; and this is the key to the satirical element in his theater too. He wrote more than thirty comedies, some for the French actors, the rest for the Italian. Most of his characters are stock types drawn from the Italian theater, and for that reason, it could be argued, they do not invite the satirical, topical readings that other eighteenth-century texts encourage. But abstraction does not preclude satire; rather, it can veil it artfully. *La Double Inconstance*, for example, first performed at the Comédie-Italienne in 1723, is Marivaux's first play to contain elements of social criticism: it satirizes court morals by playing on the contrast between the authentic simplicity of the rustic existence enjoyed by Arlequin and Silvia, and the sometimes cynical tricks of the aristocratic world, represented by the Prince, who has fallen in love with Silvia and is determined to possess her, and the scheming Flaminia, who plays on Silvia's vanity to make her abandon Arlequin in favor of the Prince. As in La Fontaine's *Fables*, the powerful oppress the weak. But this is not the stuff of revolution, for the play ends with two seemingly happy marriages: the Prince wins Silvia, and Arlequin is consoled by marriage to Flaminia.

Again like La Fontaine, Marivaux also produces a satirical unsettling of certainties through the distancing techniques of fantasy and allegory. *L'Ile des esclaves* (1725), for example, written for the Italian actors, is a satirical allegory in which masters and servants change places when they are shipwrecked on an island. The master and mistress are forced to listen to satirical portraits of themselves: as in Boileau, correction comes through ridicule. The play offers a satirical analysis of institutionalized social structures. But Marivaux, again, is no revolutionary: everything turns out well in the end, as the servants take pity on their masters and the social order is reinstituted, though attitudes within it, the dramatic action suggests, have been changed forever – and for the better.

After Marivaux, the eighteenth century's most enduring dramatist was Beaumarchais. Figaro, his indefatigable trouble-maker, offers a number of stingingly satirical one-liners in *Le Barbier de Séville* (1775), including "Great people treat the rest of us well enough when they're not actually doing us any harm" and "Given the virtues required of servants, does your Lordship know many masters who would make a half-decent valet?" (1.2). The dramatic action also gives scope for satire of medicine (2.13) and the legal profession (4.8). But, like Marivaux's Arlequin, Figaro is no revolutionary: his satirical jibes do not coalesce into a rounded philosophical stance. In their context, they are witty rejoinders, satirical insights, but nothing more. The comic structure of *Le Barbier de Séville* is conventional: a servant and his aristocratic master join forces to outwit Bartholo, a bumbling bourgeois conservative, and win the girl. Figaro's social satire is limited in scope.

Can the same be said of the sequel, *Le Mariage de Figaro* (1784)? The revolutionary potential of the play is partly veiled, as in Marivaux, by the setting: Almaviva is a Spanish *corregidor*, not a French aristocrat; like *Le Barbier*, *Le Mariage* exudes an air of cheerful unreality. Yet, the play bristles with satirical jibes: there is some conventional satire of the legal system in act 3, but more importantly there is an attack on social inequalities and a critique of noble pretensions as Almaviva tries to claim his feudal right to sleep with Figaro's fiancée, Suzanne. But throughout, the context is comic: justice is denounced as arbitrary, but only when Figaro faces the grotesque prospect of being forced to marry his own mother; Almaviva abuses his privilege not for political ends, but for his own sexual gratification; and the servant Figaro may go against his master Almaviva, but the same social divide is breached by the women, the Countess and Suzanne, who join forces in outwitting the Count, who ends the play by coming to his senses. As in Marivaux's island comedies, after all the topsy-turvy events, order is restored. Marivaux and Beaumarchais are not revolutionaries; their plays are not political manifestos. Like Molière, they knew that it is comedy's job to be against things, not for them.

This critical, even anti-didactic, strategy was central to the new spirit of intellectual inquiry that characterized the eighteenth century. For this was a period preoccupied with breaking out of traditional systems of thought and thinking empirically, thinking differently, and even thinking as "the Other." This in turn led to the adoption of a very particular satirical device in the period: that of ironical false naïvety, or what has been termed "polemical stupidity" (Howells 2002), the starting-point for which, as we have already seen, was Pascal's *Lettres provinciales*. This stance is often adopted in different kinds of travel literature, or texts that illustrate "satiric nationalism" (Knight 2004: 50–80). The figure of the philosophical traveler offered an ideal literary vehicle for the satirical spirit of the Enlightenment: fictional visitors could interrogate France and its customs, making the familiar appear strange and exposing the humbug of the humdrum; and, conversely, the French visitor abroad could also challenge and even ridicule national preconceptions through a process of critical comparison.

Montesquieu's *Lettres persanes* (1721) is widely acknowledged to be the first masterpiece of the French eighteenth century; it is also the century's first great satirical text. Montesquieu apes Pascal both in his use of the fragmentary epistolary form and in his polemical use of mock-naïve characters who are pressed into the service of satirical defamiliarization. Montesquieu invites French readers to imagine their own country as alien. In the *Lettres persanes*, published anonymously and presented, with mock disingenuousness, as a genuine correspondence dating from 1712 to 1720, two Persians, Usbek and Rica, travel to France and comment on French customs in letters addressed to friends back home. Their status as outsiders gives them the privilege of commenting afresh on old customs and conventions: Usbek observes with Juvenalian indignation, Rica with Horatian amusement. In letter 1, Usbek, like Pascal's inquisitive letter-writer, makes it clear that he and Rica have come in search of knowledge; and from letter 8 it emerges that Usbek fell foul of the Persian authorities for telling the truth and that he has been exiled for being, in effect, a satirist: "As soon as I experienced vice, I took my distance from it; but then I went back to it in order to unmask it." The satire takes in both a wide range of social types and professions, from women (letters 52, 56, 99, 110) to obsequious courtiers (letter 124), as well as, albeit euphemistically, specific individuals, including Louis XIV and the Pope: the king is presented as a "great magician" who makes his subjects believe whatever he wants, while the Pope is "a more powerful magician still," who makes people believe that "three are one, that the bread they eat is not bread or that the wine they drink is not wine" (letter 24). Like the protagonist of Pascal's *Lettres provinciales*, Montesquieu's Persians foreground what strikes them as odd, and often this is the language, absurdity, and corruption of the Church, including the easy morality of the Jesuits (letter 57) and the Catholic laws against divorce (letter 116) and in favor of celibacy (letter 117). The outside perspective offered by the Persians constitutes a form of satirical demystification that is more far-reaching and subversive than that ever envisaged by Pascal.

The satire is not all one-sided in the *Lettres persanes*, and in this way it gains added force. Montesquieu does not simply praise Persia in order to attack France. Rather, both countries are presented as equally flawed, with the result that, for instance, French monarchy is presented as being hardly different from Persian despotism (letters 18, 103). So it is not a case of Persians being right and Europeans wrong, or vice versa: the truth of this satire is more fluid. This tension is embodied in Usbek himself, who is at once an apparently enlightened and inquisitive outside observer and a Persian despot who responds tyrannically when his wives back in Persia launch a revolt in the harem (letters 20, 21). Endowed with satirical acumen, Usbek sees faults in others, but not always in himself. In this way, Montesquieu's text becomes in part at least a self-conscious reflection on satire: the satirical voice is exposed as flawed and limited by dint of being rooted in his own customs and values. Like Molière's Alceste, the vehicle of the satire becomes its target.

Montesquieu's fictional Persians soon became the model of the philosophical traveler, influencing, for instance, Goldsmith's Chinese visitor to England in *The Citizen of the World* (1762). In France, they provided the model for Zilia, the Peruvian heroine of Françoise de Graffigny's best-selling *Lettres d'une Péruvienne* (1752). Abducted from the Temple of the Sun first by marauding Spaniards, then by equally savage Frenchmen, Zilia is taken to France by boat, which she refers to unknowingly as "a floating house," and set up in Paris by her besotted French captor, Déterville. Once there, she becomes a resistance heroine, pursuing a developmental quest of her own design, and learning French in order to be able to understand and, crucially, to comment satirically on the foreign culture in which she finds herself. Writing to her lover back in Peru, she focuses in particular on the superficiality of French manners as well as on the Church. Such satirical insights may seem banal, but Graffigny's originality is to present a satirist who is a woman and whose satire is specifically feminine, even feminist: where Montesquieu's cultural outsiders satirize women for their coquetry, Graffigny's Zilia goes beneath the surfaces to offer a far-reaching satirical critique of the social and political structures in France that subordinate women (letter 34), a structural device which Diderot would develop in his novel *La Religieuse* (begun in 1760, but not published until 1796), the heroine-narrator of which is an outsider within her own country, literally a novice, a young girl forced to become a nun against her will, whose passionate appeal for freedom constitutes a powerful satire not just of ecclesiastical corruption, but also of all forms of misused power and authority.

Diderot also offers an important illustration of the satirical counterpart to accounts of foreign travelers in France, namely accounts of the French traveling abroad. The French began to discover the outside world in the late seventeenth century, thanks in part to the Jesuit missionaries, and this historical reality became a fictional tool for satirists. Exploring the Other became a way of challenging one's own received ideas and assumptions; writing about foreign lands became a way of telling some satirical home-truths.

In 1771, the explorer Bougainville published his *Voyage autour du monde*, including an account of his visit to the idyllic island of Tahiti. The following year, Diderot wrote his *Supplément au Voyage de Bougainville*, complete with an epigraph from Horace. Actual travel becomes the springboard for an imagined journey. This fictitious addition to an existing work presents what is supposedly a hitherto unpublished part of Bougainville's *Voyage*; in reality, Diderot is exploiting the now familiar technique of the innocent eye for satirical effect. The *Supplément* has at its heart a conversation between Orou, a Tahitian elder, and the French chaplain, a conversation which provides Diderot with a satirical foil against which European practices can be made to appear absurd. Orou greets the chaplain in the traditional manner and invites him to sleep with one of his daughters. The chaplain's confusion is comic: the satire is in part anti-clerical. Where Orou represents natural morality, the chaplain represents Christian morality in all its anti-social muddle and illogical inconsistency. However, as in the *Lettres persanes*, the satire in the *Supplément* is slippery. The text may offer a powerful critique of French colonizers who have corrupted Tahiti with modern notions of property and propriety, but the very faults diagnosed in the French infect the Tahitians too. We see this most clearly when Orou, by offering them to the chaplain, objectifies his daughters and uses them as a form of social and sexual currency with which he hopes to improve the Tahitian stock. The ambiguity of the satire makes it all the more far-reaching: Tahiti is not simply conceived as a model for France; rather, Diderot seems to call into question all globalizing codes of behavior.

The eighteenth-century writer who seems to have made the greatest and most complex use of the satirical technique of "polemical stupidity," often associated with travel, is Voltaire. Voltaire made his name as a social, political, religious, and literary critic with his *Lettres philosophiques* (1734). Not for nothing does the very form of Voltaire's text echo that of both the *Lettres persanes* and the *Lettres provinciales*. The *Lettres philosophiques* are a kind of philosophical and satirical travelogue: an inquisitive Frenchman travels to England and writes letters about his experiences there, much as Voltaire himself did during his exile in the 1720s. In letter 1, for example, the Frenchman converses with an English Quaker: the latter's disarmingly frank and unfussy attitude becomes a satirical indictment of the Frenchman's convention-bound behavior, with the result that, in the course of their reported conversation, bowing is satirically defamiliarized in the same way as Roman Catholic dogma, particularly baptism, both being emptied of all meaning and exposed as hollow shams.

This first letter sets the tone for the rest of the text, which offers, to a large extent, an idealized picture of England as a haven of open-mindedness and tolerance in order satirically to expose faults in France: the social, scientific, and intellectual accomplishments of the English become a stick with which to beat French limitations. England's good example explicitly or implicitly satirizes France: English clerics behave better than their French counterparts (letter 5); different sects trade peacefully and profitably in the Royal Exchange (letter 6); civil wars in England aim at liberty, unlike in France (letter 8); England encourages business, France aristocracy (letter 10); the English inoculate against smallpox, the French do not (letter 11); Locke thinks critically, Descartes metaphysically (letter 13); gentlemen practice letters in England, but not in France (letter 20); and England celebrates and commemorates its great actors and actresses, whereas in France they are excommunicated (letter 23).

But at other points in the text, French sophistication becomes the basis for judging the crudities of the English. Sometimes England is criticized, and France is praised: Anglicanism is worryingly dominant (letters 4 and 5); English theater is inferior to French (letter 18); and the French have institutions to encourage the arts, unlike the English (letter 23). The satire is double-edged, which is perhaps unsurprising in a text that was published first in England and in English (*Letters Concerning the English*

Nation, 1733): the dual readership creates multiple ironies. But more importantly still, this complex satirical structure suggests that Voltaire wants the reader to think critically and to draw conclusions accordingly. In letter 8, for example, comparing the legal condemnation of Charles I in England with the fanatical assassination of Henri IV in France, the narrator addresses the reader directly: "Weigh up these events and make a judgement." Voltaire's satire, no doubt on account of the perils of censorship, leaves some things unsaid and accords a central role to the active reader.

This satirical use of travel, ironical false naïvety, and defamiliarization is also the structuring principle of many of Voltaire's well-known *contes philosophiques*, or short stories, from *Le Monde comme il va* via *Zadig*, *Micromégas*, and *Candide* to *L'Ingénu*. Voltaire's *contes* have an important satirical function: they debunk narrow-minded systems of thought by ridiculing spurious reasoning and exposing received ideas as irrational and absurd, and they thereby encourage the reader to become in turn a satirist, one who through determined dissent casts off masks and sees things as they really are (Pearson 1993).

Travel plays a crucial role in this satirical project, as the outsider protagonist sets off in search of knowledge and, all too often, happiness, only to be confronted by the satirical contrast between illusion and reality. In *Le Monde comme il va* (1748), for example, Babouc, the naïve hero and alien observer in the mold of Montesquieu's Persians, travels to Persepolis, which is a thinly veiled allegory of Paris, and comments demystifyingly on religion and politics. The title itself sums up what all satire may be said to be about.

An Oriental voyage of reason also allows for satirical comments on national customs and religious rituals in *Zadig* (1748). The virtuous hero endures a series of misadventures, naïvely calling into question along the way the injustices of the justice system, the corruption at the heart of courtly society, and such traditions as Arabian widows burning themselves on their late husbands' pyres, leaving their jewelry behind to be snapped up by the priests. To the merchant Sétoc's fearful question, "Which of us will dare to change a time-honoured law?" Zadig replies: "Reason is older still" (ch. 11).

Two journeys combine to satirical effect in *Micromégas* (1751): one terrestrial, the other intergalactic. Voltaire deftly blends fact and Lucianic fantasy: French scholars on a polar expedition, not unlike that organized by the scientist Maupertuis in 1737, are confronted by a traveler eight leagues tall from Sirius who has come to inspect the earth. Like *Gulliver's Travels*, this story satirically cuts down to size all human pretensions to grandeur. The intergalactic voyager is at once horrified by humankind's potential for folly (particularly ridiculous are the philosophers' pointless squabbles over the nature of the human soul) and admiring of its capacity for scientific endeavor and empirical investigation.

This satirical preference for practicality over metaphysics recurs most notably in *Candide* (1759), which, with its biting philosophical, social, and political satire, is probably the best and certainly the most famous example of a trend running throughout Voltaire's fiction. It demonstrates how Voltaire is able to combine satire of the particular with satire of the general. The story offers a memorably bitter satire of Leibnizian Optimism, exemplified by Pangloss's obsessive and irrational belief that "all is for the best in the best of all possible worlds": at every turn his empty reasoning is belied by the horrors of reality. Unlike Pangloss, the appropriately named eponymous hero goes through life with his eyes wide open: traveling from Westphalia via Portugal to Paraguay and then back again to Europe, and experiencing no little suffering too, helps to convince him that Pangloss's philosophical system, like any philosophy that deals with philosophizing rather than practical reality, is woefully inadequate.

Like the *Lettres persanes* and the *Lettres d'une Péruvienne*, Voltaire's *L'Ingénu* (1767) also uses the device of a traveler to France for satirical ends. The Huron's penetrating naïvety is Voltaire's sharpest satirical tool: the outsider who views things under a new light, exposing what appears to be normal as bizarre and irrational. The questioning hero is endowed, according to the narrator in chapter 14, with the ability to "see things for what they are, whereas the ideas fed to us as children make us see things for the rest of our lives as they are not," echoing Voltaire's *Dictionnaire philosophique* article "*Enthousiasme*" (1764), according to which "reason involves always seeing things for what they really are." There is satire in *L'Ingénu* of Catholic doctrine and practices through the Ingénu's naïve comments on baptism and marriage; there is satire of religious corruption, as the Huron's beloved Mlle de Saint-Yves is bullied into granting a priest sexual favors in the hope of securing her lover's release from prison; there is political satire, when the Huron is summarily imprisoned without knowing why; and there is abundant social satire, including provincial prejudices, immoral courtiers, and the venality of public offices. The *conte* is set in 1689, in the final phase of Louis XIV's reign and just four years after the Revocation of the Edict of Nantes, which put an end to the tolerance that the Protestants in France had enjoyed since 1598; but the satirical insights say just as much, if not more, about 1767, the year of the *conte*'s publication, when Voltaire was preoccupied above all with political and religious injustice and prejudice, illustrated by the infamous Calas affair.

It is clear why Voltaire towers over the eighteenth century as the supreme satirist. But it is nevertheless surprising, given his frequently reiterated concerns about satire, and personal satire in particular. Voltaire spoke for many of his contemporaries, friends and foes alike, when he criticized Boileau's *Satires* for being both ephemeral and the products of personal spite and malevolence. In his *Discours de réception à l'Académie française* (1746), for example, he argues that "satire dies along with its victims," and in his short story *Aventure de la mémoire* (1773), he even expresses moral and philosophical doubts, calling into question the idea that one human being can correct another through mockery and ridicule.

Nowhere is Voltaire's fundamental ambivalence toward satire better displayed than in his *Mémoire sur la satire* (1739), a quirky history of satire from Boileau to Desfontaines, in which he denounces the practice of naming names, but then proceeds to do so himself. It was, significantly, when he wrote a personal satire that Voltaire first came to the attention of the public and the authorities: his brief *Regnante puero*

(1717) is a satirical attack on the personal immorality of the then Regent of France, Philippe d'Orléans, which earned its author a stay in the Bastille. But this was not Voltaire's first personal satire: one of his earliest works, *Le Bourbier* (1714), written when he was only 20, is a verse satire in which he attacks Houdar de La Motte, a member of the Académie Française and more than twenty years his senior, for not supporting his entry in the recent poetry competition; and in *La Crépinade* (1736), another verse satire, he launches a sustained and brilliantly witty attack on the successful lyric poet Jean-Baptiste Rousseau, a sometime friend and later sworn enemy. Like Boileau, Voltaire uses satire as a form of literary criticism.

More importantly than literary satire, Voltaire, in common with many of his contemporaries, used personal satire as a weapon in the ongoing struggle of the freethinking *philosophes* against the forces of conservatism. These personal satires are intimately linked with the satire of intolerance and injustice in the works already considered. The late 1750s and the 1760s, in particular, are a crucial period for the *philosophes*, both as they face attacks from their enemies (the condemnation of the *Encyclopédie* by the Parlement de Paris in 1758, for example) and as they are confronted with more evidence of moral and physical evil, such as the Lisbon earthquake and the Seven Years' War. Satire of particular philosophical enemies goes hand in hand with broader satire of obscurantism and outmoded systems of thought.

Two of the most notorious enemies of the *philosophes* were Charles Palissot and Elie-Catherine Fréron. Palissot's 1755 comedy *Le Cercle ou les Originaux* included a satirical portrait of Jean-Jacques Rousseau, living out his call for a return to nature by crawling around the stage on all fours, munching a lettuce. Five years later, in May 1760, his controversial comedy *Les Philosophes* was first staged at the Comédie-Française. Palissot ridiculed Diderot, presenting him, via the Latinized anagram "Dortidius," as pompous and wicked. Voltaire responded with his satirical comedy *L'Ecossaise*, first performed in July 1760, in which he satirizes Fréron, the staunchly Catholic and monarchist journalist and general thorn in the side of the *philosophes*, under the thin but meaningful guise of "Frélon" (recalling the French word for hornet), a ridiculously envious hack writer.

Diderot's response to Palissot was to start writing his dialogue *Le Neveu de Rameau*, though the text was not published until the nineteenth century. In *Le Neveu de Rameau*, which Diderot subtitled "*Satire seconde*" (the first being an Horatian reflection on the variability of human life written in 1773–4) and in which he quotes Horace's first book of *Satires* three times, the uninhibited and unorthodox bohemian hero, the nephew of the famous composer Jean-Philippe Rameau, referred to as "Lui," apes the position of the outsider familiar from travel writing and, in conversation with "Moi," mercilessly unmasks social man, satirizing the seamier sides of Parisian "polite" society, where elegance barely conceals malevolence. The text can be read, in part at least, as a satire of the enemies of the *philosophes*. In a text where "Moi" has tentatively been identified with the author himself, Diderot's satirical sleight of hand is to place what we might assume to be his own criticisms in the mouth of "Lui," who is a distinctly Juvenalian character. And like that other Juvenalian satirist, Boileau, "Lui" engages in specifically literary satire, presenting the enemies of the *philosophes* as unsuccessful hack writers gathered at the home of the fatuous tax-farmer Bertin: "Never have you seen gathered together in one place so many sorry, cantankerous, wicked and incensed animals."

But "Lui" is an unorthodox satirist, for he at once stands outside the group he satirizes and seemingly longs to be a part of it: his desire to conform, more or less involuntarily, itself functions as a satirical image of the collectivity in all its crass turpitude. In that sense, Diderot's satirical insights are less about the enemies of the *philosophes* and more about the human condition in general. His satire is disturbingly paradoxical as, even more radically than in earlier writers, the satirist is satirized. But this is perhaps fitting in a text that is itself a generic hybrid, a satire in the sense of a *satura*, a mixture of registers, tones, themes, and forms.

Though Diderot's *Le Neveu de Rameau* may superficially echo Montesquieu's *Lettres persanes* in its use of a quasi-outside figure as a satirical voice, the distance separating the form, nature, and ramifications of their satire, at opposite ends of the century, is large. Satire evolves dramatically in the course of the eighteenth century and by comparison with the previous century. By the end of the eighteenth century, it has become a polymorphous and proteiform genre. In an age when thought and its diverse forms of expression were closely policed, irony and the art of understatement became essential tools in the satirist's arsenal. Nevertheless, the shackles by which many seventeenth-century satirists felt bound were gradually shaken off, and satire became increasingly partisan, philosophical, and even political. And this process of self-liberation would reach its dramatic climax with the Revolution of 1789, which ushered in not only a new political regime, but also a whole new phase in the history of satire.

References and Further Reading

Abramovici, Jean-Christophe (2003) *Obscénité et classicisme*. Paris: Presses Universitaires de France.

Berk, Philip R. (1984) La Bruyère and Juvenal. *Classical and Modern Literature* 4, 131–41.

Bourguinat, Elisabeth (1998) *Le Siècle du persiflage, 1734–1789*. Paris: Presses Universitaires de France.

Bury, Emmanuel (1995) Fortunes et infortunes des satiriques latins de la mort de Régnier à la publication des premières satires de Boileau. *Littératures Classiques* 24, 49–63.

Carrier, Hubert (1996) *Les Muses guerrières: les mazarinades et la vie littéraire au milieu du XVIIe siècle*. Paris: Klincksieck.

Colton, Robert E. (1987) *Juvenal and Boileau: A Study of Literary Influence*. Hildesheim: Georg Olms.

Corum, Robert T. (1998) *Reading Boileau: An Integrative Study of the Early Satires*. West Lafayette: Purdue University Press.

Dalnekoff, Donna I. (1973) A familiar stranger: the outsider of eighteenth-century satire. *Neophilologus* 57, 121–34.

Debailly, Pascal (1995a) Juvénal en France au XVIe et au XVIIe siècle. *Littératures Classiques* 24, 29–47.

——(1995b) *Epos* et *satura*: Calliope et le masque de Thalie. *Littératures Classiques* 24, 147–66.

Defaux, Gérard (1980) *Molière ou les métamorphoses du comique*. Lexington: French Forum.

Duval, Sophie and Martinez, Marc (2000) *La Satire: littératures française et anglaise*. Paris: Armand Colin.

Gunny, Ahmad (1977) Critical writings on satire in the seventeenth century. *Comparison* 6, 29–56.

—— (1978) Pour une théorie de la satire au 18ème siècle. *Dix-huitième Siècle* 10, 345–61.

Howarth, W. D. (1995) *Beaumarchais and the Theatre*. London: Routledge.

Howells, Robin (2002) *Playing Simplicity: Polemical Stupidity in the Writing of the French Enlightenment*. Bern: Peter Lang.

Knight, Charles A. (2004) *The Literature of Satire*. Cambridge: Cambridge University Press.

Marmier, Jean (1962) *Horace en France au dix-septième siècle*. Paris: Presses Universitaires de France.

Merrick, Jeffrey (1994) The cardinal and the queen: sexual and political disorders in the Mazarinades. *French Historical Studies* 18, 667–99.

Miller, John R. (1942) *Boileau en France au dix-huitième siècle*. Baltimore, MD: The Johns Hopkins University Press.

Norman, Larry F. (1999) *The Public Mirror: Molière and the Social Commerce of Depiction*. Chicago: University of Chicago Press.

Parish, Richard (1989) *Pascal's "Lettres provinciales": A Study in Polemic*. Oxford: Clarendon Press.

Pearson, Roger (1993) *The Fables of Reason: A Study of Voltaire's "Contes philosophiques."* Oxford: Clarendon Press.

Pocock, Gordon (1980) *Boileau and the Nature of Neo-classicism*. Cambridge: Cambridge University Press.

Strien-Bourmer, Petra (1992) *Mathurin Régnier und die Verssatire seit der Pléiade*. Paris: Biblio 17.

9
Dramatic Satire in the Restoration and Eighteenth Century
Jean I. Marsden

Dramatic satire has existed almost as long as drama itself, with the great Greek playwright Aristophanes famed for his barbed attacks on the political and literary figures of fifth-century BCE Athens. But never has it appeared in so many forms or found as enthusiastic an audience as in Restoration and eighteenth-century England. While John Gay's masterpiece *The Beggar's Opera* (1728) famously set records for the length of its run, audiences also flocked to plays as diverse as raucous Restoration comedies ridiculing sexual hypocrisy, Henry Fielding's mock puppet show exposing the politics of the London theater world, and Samuel Foote's lampoons of Methodist preachers and popular orators. Almost as soon as the theaters reopened in 1660, following the restoration of Charles II to the monarchy, playwrights began using the stage as a means of articulating their response to the social, political, and literary issues of their times. And drama provided a unique venue for voicing these concerns.

Although Restoration and eighteenth-century writers felt strongly that drama should correct human folly through ridicule, detailing how such a task was accomplished is difficult. Even today, scholars have found understanding the workings of dramatic satire a challenge, largely because drama, unlike other forms of satire, necessarily involves performance. Designed to be staged rather than read, dramatic satire's impact goes beyond mere words, combining visual and aural, as well as verbal elements of ridicule. In "Comedy, Satire, or Farce?," Deborah C. Payne (1995) explains that because drama lacks a narrative voice to establish authority, distinguishing between what is satiric and what is merely comic can be almost impossible. By contrast, J. Douglas Canfield (1997) expands the boundaries of the genre, seeing satiric possibilities in a wide range of dramas, from comedy to tragedy.

Given the difficulties inherent in defining dramatic satire, it might be more useful to consider satire on the stage as existing along a spectrum rather than as a single specific category. At one end of the spectrum, one could place the more generalized satire of social follies or vices, while at the other end would be the very specific "travesty" or lampoon, which ridicules a specific person or literary work. In between lies the "burlesque," a play related directly to literary or artistic issues in which these issues are parodied for a critical purpose. In Restoration and eighteenth-century drama, such burlesques most frequently parodied other dramatic works, often in the form of a mock play. Because it is difficult to sustain the specific parody of a burlesque or lampoon at length, most of these satires are short plays of one, two, or three acts and were staged as afterpieces rather than as the theater's main attraction. In these works, plot becomes a secondary consideration as dramatists focus on political, social, or literary commentary. By contrast, plays that incorporate more generalized social satire were more likely to be full-length, main pieces.

English dramatic satire did not simply begin with the return of Charles II. Satiric elements can be traced in numerous Renaissance dramas, such as Shakespeare's mock tragedy of Pyramus and Thisbe in *A Midsummer Night's Dream*, Francis Beaumont's *Knight of the Burning Pestle* (1607), and the social commentary of the so-called "city" comedies in the early seventeenth century. Most famous, however, are the great satiric comedies of Ben Jonson in which characters with a strong controlling passion or "humor" become the object of ridicule. In plays such as *Volpone* (1606), Jonson uses a dominant trait (here, avarice) as a means to mock a vice. It was Jonson's brilliant mockery that resonated most strongly with Restoration playwrights and audiences; while most other forms of Renaissance dramatic satire fell out of favor during the Restoration, Jonson's plays enjoyed steady popularity.

Yet, perhaps the strongest influence on Restoration dramatic satire came not from England's own past but from across the Channel. The great French dramatist Molière (Jean Baptiste Poquelin, 1622–73), author of more than twenty plays and sketches, profoundly influenced the comic drama of the entire Restoration and eighteenth century. Like Jonson's characters of humors, his satiric portraits, such as Tartuffe, the religious hypocrite (*Tartuffe*, 1664), and Harpagon, the miser (*The Miser*, 1668), often focus on specific vices, yet his representations are more biting and sardonic. Like the French audiences who flocked to his plays, Molière's English contemporaries were delighted by his ability to delineate the follies of his society, and in the years following the Restoration, dozens of playwrights translated, adapted, or imitated almost every play Molière wrote. A century after his death, the influence of Molière was still pervasive, with later dramatists copying earlier English writers who in turn mimicked Molière. By making Molière "English," using his style of biting wit and distinctive characterization within their own social setting, playwrights found a new and potent mode of satire, whether they adapted a specific drama or simply used the French playwright as a model.

Restoration Satiric Comedies

It is appropriate that one of the first new plays staged in 1660 was John Tatham's *The Rump; or, The Mirrour of the Late Times*, a satirical look at the waning days of the

Commonwealth. The play's title refers to the "Rump" Parliament, the last remnant of the Long Parliament of the Interregnum. Tatham, who also wrote pageants for the Mayor of London, brings the broad comedy of the streets into his lampoons of leading political figures of the Commonwealth and their wives, depicting them as crass upstarts obsessed with the trappings of power (Lady Lampert and Mrs Cromwell, for example, argue vehemently over who gets to be called "Her Highness"). The play ends with the members of the "Rump" turned out into the streets as the citizens of London celebrate by roasting rumps of mutton.

As theater became more established in the 1670s and 1680s, few plays utilized the overtly partisan techniques found in *The Rump*. Probably most familiar to the occasional reader of Restoration drama is the more traditional comedy of wit in which couples spar before joining hands (and estates). Nonetheless, Restoration playwrights incorporated large doses of satire within this familiar structure of marriage and social renewal, ridiculing everything from the overly Frenchified mannerisms of the aristocracy to the crass materialism of the rising merchant class or "citizens." In *The Man of Mode* (1676), George Etherege creates the memorable figure of Sir Fopling Flutter, whose excessive vanity, extreme wardrobe, and elevation of all things French mark him as the satiric butt whose behavior the audience should shun. So undiscriminating is Sir Fopling that he even changes the name of his footman because the man's English name is simply too "barbarous" (3.3.287). Sir Fopling and his descendants became popular figures upon the Restoration and eighteenth-century stage, their effeminate appearance even more than their words becoming a satiric shorthand for the anti-British qualities a playwright wished to attack.

In addition to social criticism, a strong thread of political satire runs through much of the drama of the Restoration. Both Whig and Tory playwrights used the public stage as a venue for expressing their views, sometimes so overtly that their plays were censored. Using a series of superannuated, foolish aldermen as her satiric butts, Aphra Behn attacks Whig politicians and their supporters in plays such as *The Roundheads* (1681) and *The Lucky Chance; or, An Alderman's Bargain* (1686). Whig playwrights, such as Thomas Shadwell, on the other hand, represented the pro-royalist aristocracy as little more than a bunch of carousing hoodlums, trampling on the rights of true Englishmen and women. Yet the most arresting political satire of the age appeared not in a comedy but in a tragedy, Thomas Otway's masterpiece, *Venice Preserv'd; or, a Plot Discovered* (1682). Against the backdrop of a corrupt senate and equally corrupt plot to overthrow it, Otway placed the figure of Antonio, a thinly veiled portrait of the Earl of Shaftesbury, a leading Whig and supporter of the Duke of Monmouth's rebellion against Charles II. Antonio, a leading senator, memorably appears as a perverse masochist speaking in baby talk, barking like a dog, cowering on the ground and kissing the toes of the courtesan Aquilina. Antonio's depravity becomes only the most vivid indicator of the depravity of the entire political system of Venice, a popular model for Whig politicians. Yet, the men who plot against Antonio and his fellow senators seem little better, their corruption also represented through sexual deviance as one lead conspirator attempts to rape the play's heroine. In the end, Otway provides no clean tragic conclusion, only a picture of a society both morally and politically bankrupt.

Otway avoids closure in order to articulate the point of his satire, a move paralleled in some satiric comedies. While plays such as *The Man of Mode* stay within the traditional formula of marriage and comic completion, in other plays the satiric impulse breaks away from this pattern. One such play is William Wycherley's *The Country Wife* (1675). Here the marriage plot is noticeably marginalized, and any resolution it might provide is distinctly overshadowed by the main action of the play. Instead, the play focuses on the exploits of the aptly named Horner, a rake whose goal in life is to sleep with as many women as possible. In order to outwit the husbands of willing women, including the title character, he claims to be impotent, a ploy that succeeds admirably. In the process, Wycherley ridicules the hypocrisy of his society, as the ladies of fashion care more about their reputation than their honor, while the country wife of the title needs only a little more experience before she cuckolds her husband, who cannot distinguish between the naïveté born of ignorance and true virtue. Despite the famous china scene, in which Horner has a tryst with one lady (under the guise of buying china) while her husband waits outside the bedroom door, the play ends with vice unpunished. Horner's scheme remains unexposed, and Wycherley's sardonic portrait of sexual mores refuses the comforting illusion of justice served, thus implying that society shares these failings. Wycherley's last play, *The Plain Dealer* (1676) expands this critique, exploring double-dealing on all levels of society. In this frequently bitter comedy, Wycherley uses Manly, the plain dealer of the play's title, to point out the endemic falsity of English society, from the superficial niceties of court behavior to the lip service accorded friendship, even using the play as a means to mock the women who complained about the indecency of *The Country Wife*. While the play ends with the betrothal of Manly to the faithful Fidelia, their union represents a retreat from society, not a communal regeneration.

As with Wycherley, comic formulas often come second to social and political satire in the works of Thomas Shadwell. Famously remembered today as the object of Dryden's ridicule in "MacFlecknoe," during his lifetime Shadwell was a leading dramatist. Styling himself a "son of Ben [Jonson]," Shadwell used exaggerated characters of humors, such as upper-class dilettantes infatuated with new discoveries in science (*The Virtuoso*, 1676) and miserly husbands (*The Woman Captain*, 1679/80), in order to ridicule the excesses of his age, especially those of upper-class Tories. A staunch Whig, Shadwell larded his plays with political satire. One of his most enduringly popular plays, *The Lancashire Witches and Tegue o Divelly the Irish Priest* (1681/2), written during the turmoil surrounding the Exclusion Crisis, takes aim at Tories and Catholics (linked together in Whig rhetoric) through the figure of Tegue o Divelly, a foolish priest who embodies the stereotypical traits that would characterize the Irish on stage for centuries to come. The witches of the title terrorize Tegue and the characters who espouse Tory views and whose superstitious beliefs link them to Tegue's Catholicism and, by extension, to absolutist rule rather than English "liberty." The broad visual humor of Shadwell's mockery provides a useful example of the crucial role that performance plays in understanding how dramatic satire operates; Shadwell demonstrates the folly of his satiric characters not through language but through their actions, through the servile fear of his Tory fools or the ridiculous experiments of his pompous scientists. When studied as text, the visual impact is lost.

The Rehearsal and Other Plays about the Theater

The most influential and long-lived of Restoration satiric dramas is George Villiers, Duke of Buckingham's burlesque, *The Rehearsal* (1671/2). Buckingham's only original drama, it ridicules the serious drama of the Restoration, in particular the heroic drama popularized by playwrights such as Dryden and Sir Robert Howard. These plays, written in rhyme, featured larger than life characters, exotic settings, and extravagant and often improbable plot lines. Buckingham's play, written at the height of the heroic drama's popularity, hilariously mimics the absurdity of these plays and may even have helped turn the tide against the production of more such plays. *The Rehearsal*, as its title suggests, is set during a supposed rehearsal. The play includes a frame in which two sensible men converse with a playwright about his play as well as the rehearsal itself. The playwright, Bayes, is a thinly veiled representation of Dryden, then Poet Laureate as well as the foremost writer of heroic dramas. The satire operates on two distinct levels: one, the play-within-a-play, which is patently absurd; and two, the frame with its mockery of Dryden. As he demonstrates the "beauties" of his play, Bayes reveals the extent to which he strains for novelty while slavishly imitating others. At the same time, the two gentlemen articulate the follies of the supposed play, thus making Buckingham's argument clear to the larger audience in the theater, a characteristic typical of subsequent "rehearsal" plays.

Absurdities mount as the rehearsal progresses. Bayes's play includes two kings, two usurpers, a romantic hero, Prince Prettyman, and a strutting warrior named Drawcansir based clearly on the hero of Dryden's *Conquest of Granada*. It includes a visitation from Pallas with her lance filled with wine, as well as a dance between the Earth, the Moon, and the Sun rendered ridiculous by the low language in which the heavenly bodies speak. The dance is followed immediately by a battle in which Drawcansir kills everyone on both sides. At this point, the gentlemen escape, and the rehearsal (and *The Rehearsal*) ends in a shambles. As the epilogue explains, "The Play is at an end, but where's the Plot? / That circumstance our Poet *Bayes* forgot."

Often, Buckingham directly parodies lines from actual plays, as, for example:

Drawcansir: He that dares drink, and for that drink dares dye,
        And, knowing this, dares yet drink on, am I.   (4.1.222–3)

The lines imitate those of Dryden's own Almanzor in the two parts of *The Conquest of Granada* (1670, 1671), a man torn, repeatedly, by the competing claims of love and honor.

> He who dares love; and for that love must dy,
> And, knowing this, dares yet love on, am I.
> (4.3.157–8)

While knowledge of the plays on which Buckingham's parody is based certainly enhances reading and viewing of the satire, it is by no means necessary. The play's ridicule of overblown writing, formulaic and frequently nonsensical plotting, and novelty for the sake of novelty enabled it to retain its viability on the stage long after the specific objects of its satire had vanished.

While *The Rehearsal* was not the first satiric drama directly mocking the theater, it was certainly the most influential. Numerous playwrights after Buckingham employed not only the technique of burlesquing popular drama but even made use of the rehearsal frame, which had enabled Buckingham to satirize both Dryden and heroic drama; many such plays blatantly attempt to cash in on the popularity of *The Rehearsal* by alluding to it in their titles. Among these purported sequels were plays such as the anonymous *The Female Wits; Or, The Triumvirate of Poets at Rehearsal* (1696/1704), which uses the device of the rehearsal as a means of attacking three women writers, Catherine Trotter, Mary Pix, and especially Delarivier Manley. Other writers dropped the rehearsal format and simply created burlesques that directly parodied dramatic trends, often focusing their energies on a specific play. Thomas Duffett, for example, penned three such burlesques, each ridiculing a single play: *The Empress of Morocco* (1673), mocking Elkanah Settle's play of the same name; *The Mock-Tempest* (1674, Shadwell's spectacle-laden adaptation of *The Tempest*); and *Psyche Debauch'd* (1675, Shadwell's *Psyche*). Later writers such as Gay, Fielding, and Sheridan would make use of the play-within-a-play both to ridicule the drama of their own age and, especially in the case of Fielding, to attack larger literary and political issues. The form that Buckingham employed so trenchantly is still an effective vehicle for satirizing literary and even cinematic clichés and conventions, as seen in films such as *The Player* (1992), where director Robert Altman uses the filming of a clichéd Hollywood blockbuster both to mock the film industry and demonstrate the moral degeneration of his main character.

John Gay, Satire, and the Theater

If Buckingham was responsible for the most influential dramatic satire of the later seventeenth century, playwright and poet John Gay was, without doubt, the source of the most memorable satiric drama of the eighteenth century and perhaps of all English theater history. Of his twelve dramatic works, over half are satiric, including his three best-known plays, *The What d'ye Call It* (1715), *Three Hours after Marriage* (written with Pope and Arbuthnot, 1717), and his greatest triumph, *The Beggar's Opera* (1728). Both *The What d'ye Call It* and *The Beggar's Opera* held the stage for the eighteenth century and beyond, although their modes of using satire differ. Like *The Rehearsal*, *The What d'ye Call It* uses a play-within-a-play in order to burlesque contemporary theater practice. In this case, the object of Gay's satire is the contemporary vogue for pathetic tragedy and for overly sentimental drama in general. Gay included an elaborate, mock-serious preface with the published version of the play, outlining the structural niceties of his play and defending it against supposed scholarly critics. Placing his earthy burlesque in the context of the finest works of the contemporary stage, he reduces these serious works to the level of his "tragi-comi-pastoral farce":

> *The Judicious Reader will easily perceive, that the Unities are kept as in the most perfect Pieces, that the Scenes are unbroken, and Poetical Justice strictly observ'd; the Ghost of the* Embryo *and the* Parish-Girl *are entire new Characters. I might enlarge further upon the Conduct of the particular Scenes, and of the Piece in general, but shall only say, that the Success this piece has met with upon the Stage, gives encouragement to our Dramatick Writers to follow its Model; and evidently demonstrates that this sort of* Drama *is no less fit for the Theatre than those they have succeeded in.*

Gay peoples his play with country villagers, but, unlike the peasants of contemporary pastoral, these characters steal hens, lust after each other, and worry about press gangs. Using the elevated emotions of the tragic stage, Gay ridicules popular tragedies such as Ambrose Phillips's *The Distrest Mother* (1712); the contrast between his characters' overstated emotions and the play's mundane events exposes the convention of pathos as an empty cliché. The emotional breakdown of Timothy Peascod, a countryman condemned to death for running away from a press gang, provides an especially ludicrous example of this technique. Handed a "good book" to read, he finds the contents overwhelming:

>   Lend me thy handkercher— *The Pilgrim's Pro—*
>   *{Reads and weeps*
>   (I cannot see for Tears) *Pro— Progress—* Oh!
>   *The Pilgrim's Progress— Eighth— Edi— ti— on*
>   *Lon— don— Prin— ted— for— Ni— cho— las Bod— ding— ton:*
>   *With new Ad— di— tions never made before.*
>   Oh! 'tis so moving, I can read no more.
>   (2.1.24–9)

While, overall, the aim of *The What d'ye Call It* is general satire rather than specific mockery, Gay occasionally parodies specific passages from popular plays as when the heroine Kitty goes mad after the departure of her lover in a rant easily recognizable as based on Belvidera's famous mad scene in *Venice Preserv'd*:

> *Belvidera*: Murmuring streams, soft shades, and springing flowers
> Lutes, laurels, seas of milk, and ships of amber;   (5.2.290–1)
>
> *Kitty*: Bagpipes in butter, flocks in fleecy fountains,
> Churns, sheep-hooks, seas of milk, and honey mountains.   (2.8.82–5)

Laughable in their own right, these passages also suggest that the form that they mimic so carefully is itself ridiculous.

Gay's next play, written in collaboration with Pope and Arbuthnot, never achieved the popular success of *The What d'ye Call It*. *Three Hours after Marriage* does not burlesque a distinct dramatic trend, but satirizes specific eighteenth-century literary figures, such as the critic John Dennis and the playwright/actor Colley Cibber. The play was staged briefly and not revived. Over a decade later, Gay produced his most popular play, *The Beggar's Opera*, a work that not only established a new record for popularity, but also was the progenitor of an entirely new form of drama, the ballad opera. Like *The What d'ye Call It*, *The Beggar's Opera* burlesques a popular dramatic form, in this case the wildly successful Italian opera. *The Beggar's Opera* takes the plot conventions of opera and sets them not among the heroes and heroines of legend but among London low life. Gay's "hero," Macheath, is no Xerxes or Aeneas but a highwayman who cavorts with whores, steals purses, and ultimately runs into difficulties because he claims to have married two women. One wife, Polly Peachum, is the daughter of an informant; the other, Lucy Lockit, of a prison warden. Rather than elaborate arias, Gay has his characters sing songs set to popular ballads, often expressed in distinctly earthy language. (To the tune of "Oh London is a fine town," Polly's mother sings: "Our *Polly* is a sad Slut! Nor heeds why we have taught her" [1.8.1–7], and Macheath concludes the play by singing – to the tune of "Lumps of Pudding" – "thus I stand like the Turk with his doxies around" [3.17.12–20].) The play gets its title from its supposed author, a beggar, who, like the speaker in the Preface to *The What d'ye Call It*, claims to be abiding by strict dramatic rules. As the play draws to a close, Macheath is to be executed, but one of the players objects, "for an Opera must end happily" (3.16.9). The beggar agrees: "Your Objection, Sir, is very just; and is easily remov'd. For you must allow, that in this kind of Drama, 'tis no matter how absurdly things are brought about. – So, you Rabble there – run and cry a Reprieve – let the Prisoner be brought back to his Wives in Triumph" (3.16.11–15).

But *The Beggar's Opera* is more than simply a burlesque of an overblown art form. On a deeper level, Gay uses his tale of beggars and thieves to point to the similarities between low life and high life: the world of politics and high society is just as corrupt as the world of Newgate prison. The play's first air sounds this theme as Peachum sings:

> Through all the Employments of Life
>   Each Neighbor abuses his Brother;
> Whore and Rogue they call Husband and Wife:
>   All Professions be-rogue one another.
> The Priest calls the Lawyer a Cheat,
>   The Lawyer be-knaves the Divine,
> And the Statesman, because he's so great,
>   Thinks his Trade as honest as mine.
>   (1.1.1–8)

The politician is as much of a scoundrel as the highwayman, and, while Gay stresses the general applicability of this idea, *The Beggar's Opera* also directly satirizes the government of prime minister Robert Walpole. Gay uses nicknames for Walpole in a list of criminals, and Macheath is sometimes seen as a veiled reference to the "great man" himself. Trying to recapture the success of *The Beggar's Opera*, Gay wrote a sequel, *Polly*, that more explicitly attacked Walpole, but Walpole had the play banned, and *The Beggar's Opera* was the last of Gay's works to reach the stage in his lifetime.

Henry Fielding

Just as *The Rehearsal* spawned a host of imitations, so too did *The Beggar's Opera*. Most simply made use of the new genre, but others found, as Gay had, that ballad opera provided a ready medium for satire. One such playwright was Henry Fielding, today known best as a novelist, but also one of the leading playwrights of the mid-eighteenth century. George Bernard Shaw even claimed that Fielding was "the greatest practising dramatist, with the single exception of Shakespeare, produced by England between the Middle Ages and the nineteenth century" (1970: 19–20). Somewhat less hyperbolic is Robert D. Hume's assessment that "no other English playwright of the eighteenth century was so dominant in his own time, so frequently successful, or so well paid for his efforts" (1988: 256). In a ten-year span between 1728 and 1737, when his career in theater was cut short by the Licensing Act, Fielding wrote twenty-seven plays, almost all satires. Fielding's earliest successes were burlesques that satirized contemporary drama. In his later plays, he expanded his range into topical social and political satire. In the process, he created some of the most original and experimental plays of the century.

Fielding clearly saw satiric drama as his natural métier, adapting two plays from Molière and even attempting some full-length social satires. The greatest triumphs in the first half of his dramatic career were short burlesques and afterpieces. In his first major success, *The Author's Farce, and the Pleasures of the Town* (1730), Fielding used the familiar play-within-a-play format to structure his satire, but with a difference: here the play staged is not a rehearsal but an actual performance. Within the frame, he depicts the story of a poor playwright, Luckless, in love with his landlady's daughter but unable to pay the rent. Not only did this frame allow Fielding to introduce his burlesque of the current taste for novelty in the theater above all else, but it also provided a venue for deriding the politics of the London theater world by including figures such as Marplay, a wickedly funny representation of Colley Cibber, then an influential manager at Drury Lane theater, and in a subsequent revision of the play (1734), he added the figure of Marplay junior, a lampoon of Cibber's actor son Theophilus. As his name suggests, Marplay does his best to alter Luckless's play for the worse, an allusion to Cibber's well-known propensity for adapting other playwrights, including Shakespeare and Molière. Where Fielding's play breaks new ground is in its version of the play-within-a-play. In this case, the play is a puppet show, *The Pleasures of the Town*, performed not by puppets but by living actors. *The Pleasures of the Town* features puppet characters, such as Punch and Joan (Judy), along with more allegorical figures, such as Signor Opera and Sir Farcical Comic. *The Author's Farce* concludes with a series of wild coincidences as

Fielding breaks down the barrier between representation and "reality": at the conclusion of the puppet show, Luckless is revealed to be King of Bantam, his beloved Harriot, the Princess of Old Bentford and sister to the puppet Punch. The absurdities pile up as Fielding mocks the providential endings common in comedies such as Richard Steele's *The Conscious Lovers* (1722).

Fielding's next play, *Tom Thumb* (1730), was written shortly after *The Author's Farce* and even presented with it as an afterpiece. Fielding solemnly declares his farce "a Tragedy," and brilliantly ridicules the excesses of heroic tragedies by making his hero a midget (played by a young girl). This literal mock heroic is made all the more ridiculous by Fielding's skillful use of bathos, in the manner described by Pope in *Peri Bathous; or, The Art of Sinking in Poetry* (1728). Fielding's bathos uses elaborate similes to link high to low and thus achieve the "sinking" of bathos, as when the king says to his daughter, "A Country Dance of Joys is in your Face, / Your Eyes spit Fire, your Cheeks grow red as Beef" (2.4.23–4). A more extended example appears when the king ordains the marriage of Tom Thumb and his beloved Huncamunca:

> Long may ye live, and love, and propagate,
> 'Till the whole Land be peopled with *Tom Thumb*s.
> So when the *Cheshire*-Cheese a Maggot breeds,
> Another and another still succeeds;
> By thousands and ten thousands they encrease,
> Till one continu'd Maggot fills the rotten Cheese.
> (2.8.26–31)

The comparison is in itself ludicrous, but through it Fielding also mocks the elevated language of the tragic stage; in many cases, his examples of bathos are drawn directly from plays his audience would have recognized.

The absurd catastrophe, featuring the ghost of Tom Thumb (who has been eaten by a cow) and the death of all the characters, ridicules the bloody conventions of English tragedy:

Ghost of Tom Thumb *rises.*

Ghost:	Tom Thumb I am – but am not eke alive.	
	My Body's in the Cow, my Ghost is here.	
Grizzle:	Thanks, O ye Stars, my Vengeance is restor'd	
	Nor shalt thou fly me – for I'll kill thy Ghost.	[*Kills the Ghost*
Huncamunca:	O barbarous Deed! – I will revenge him so.	[*Kills* Grizzle
Doodle:	Ha! *Grizzle* kill'd – then Murtheress beware.	[*Kills* Hunca.
Queen:	O wretch! – have at thee.	[*Kills* Doodle
Noodle:	And have at thee too.	[*Kills the* Queen
Cleora:	Thou'st kill'd the Queen.	[*Kills* Noodle
Mustacha:	And hast kill'd my Lover.	[*Kills* Cleora
King:	Ha! Murtheress vile, take that.	[*Kills* Mustacha
	And take thou this.	[*Kills himself, and falls*

As he had with *The Author's Farce*, Fielding later revised *Tom Thumb* as *The Tragedy of Tragedies; or, The Life and Death of Tom Thumb the Great* (1731), a work designed more for reading than for performance. In *The Tragedy of Tragedies*, Fielding provides his play with an elaborate scholarly apparatus in the style of Pope's *Dunciad*. A third burlesque, *The Covent-Garden Tragedy* (1732), also mocks contemporary tragedy, but failed after a single performance when audiences objected to its setting within a brothel.

Later in his career, Fielding's dramatic satire becomes more overtly political, ultimately, like Gay, attacking Walpole and his government. His next great success, *Pasquin: A Dramatic Satire on the Times* (1736), contains the rehearsal of not one but two plays, one a comedy and one a tragedy. But, in this case, Fielding expands his satiric vision to include both the literary world of the theater and the broader scope of electoral politics and corruption. The first play rehearsed, *The Election*, a comedy, attacks abuses of the electoral system by showing both sides as equally corrupt. In the second rehearsal, Fielding returns to ridiculing the world of London theater. He saved his most direct political salvos for *The Historical Register for the Year 1736* (1737) and *Eurydice Hissed; or, A Word to the Wise* performed in tandem and published together. Both plays mock Walpole, representing him in a variety of different guises. Where *The Historical Register* is another rehearsal play and *Eurydice Hissed* depicts poets and playwrights, Fielding explicitly states that this time the literary setting depicts the world of politics, as his playwright Medley explains in *The Historical Register*: "you may remember I told you before my rehearsal that there was a strict resemblance between the states political and theatrical. There is a ministry in the latter as well as in the former, and I believe as weak a ministry as any poor kingdom could boast of" (2.289–92). *Eurydice Hissed* builds upon this parallel, with the failed playwright Pillage identified as "a very Great Man," the phrase popularly attached to Walpole by his political opponents, and as a master of a playhouse and a poet – albeit one whose play is hissed.

Fielding was not alone in using the stage to take aim at Walpole, but he was certainly the most successful. The debate incited by *The Historical Register* and *Eurydice Hissed* spilled into partisan newspapers, and the ultimate official response to the attacks on Walpole's ministry was to reshape completely the world of London theater. In 1737, Parliament passed an act requiring all new plays and all adaptations of old plays to be licensed by the Lord Chamberlain and limiting the theaters in London to those with official patents, thus putting Fielding's company out of business. Under these restrictive conditions, political satire was severely curtailed, and for the remainder of the eighteenth century, most dramatic satire took the safer form of general social satire.

Sheridan, Garrick, and the Later Eighteenth Century

With theater restricted to two playhouses and the threat of censorship imposed on all plays, the number of new plays staged in London plummeted after the Licensing Act, and few of those plays staged shared Fielding's wildly inventive wit. The effect of the

Licensing Act on English drama was momentous, as playwrights not only had fewer venues for their plays, but faced very real limits on the content of their writing. Any dramatic work that attacked the government could be banned, thus limiting the reach of political and even personal satire. As a result, playwrights with satiric interests turned away from contemporary politics, and drama instead focused increasingly on the foibles of the Beau Monde. In the years after 1737, dramatic satire followed the pattern of drama in general in being genteel rather than biting and using humor rather than invective.

One exception to the trend of genteel social satire was actor-playwright Samuel Foote. Called "The English Aristophanes," a sobriquet in which he took great pride, Foote wrote nearly two dozen plays, most of which were satires. As an actor, Foote was known for his ability to mimic public figures familiar to his audiences, and he brought this quality into his written works as well. The objects of his wit were specific people not general failings, and he used his own talents as an impersonator to make his lampoons effective. His most popular – and controversial – work, *The Minor* (1760), demonstrates these qualities. Like so many other satiric plays, *The Minor* makes use of the structuring device of a play in rehearsal, but here the play rehearsed is not a burlesque of other dramatic works – rather, it itself contains the meat of Foote's satire, in this case directed against Methodism and, in particular, one of the most popular Methodist preachers of the day, George Whitehead. While Squintum (Whitehead) never appears in the play, Foote's satire on the hypocrisy of evangelical religion appears in the character of Mrs Cole, a bawd who professes to be "saved." Through his ridicule of famous actors, wealthy nabobs, and notable bankrupts, Foote connected laughable characters and recognizable public figures in order to satirize general vices.

David Garrick, the eighteenth-century's greatest actor and a popular dramatist in his own right, stands in contrast to Foote, both as an actor and as a satirist. Famed not for impersonating specific figures when on the stage but for "representing Nature," Garrick applied this standard to his own writing, producing a series of afterpieces and interludes filled with recognizable social types whose follies provide both the plays' comedy and their satiric edge. In the popular *Lethe; or, Esop in the Shades: A Dramatic Satire*, for example, Garrick not only created satiric butts representing contemporary vices but even altered his play to adapt to changes in the society around him. *Lethe* was first staged in 1740, before Garrick made his debut as an actor, and it continued to be performed long after his retirement from the stage. The action, what there is of it, is framed by a conversation between Charon and Aesop as they watch a series of mortals who come to drink the waters of Lethe and forget their woes, which turn out to be all of their own making. The characters are all recognizable social types: a drunken man, a fine gentleman, a failed poet, and a lady of fashion. Over the years, Garrick updated his cast of characters, expanding the role of the lady of fashion, removing an attorney, and making the characterization of his fine gentleman more current. At the end, Aesop delivers the play's moral:

Now, mortals, attend! I have perceived from your examinations, that you have mistaken the effect of your distempers for the cause. You would willingly be relieved from the many things which interfere with your passions and affectations, while your vices, from which all your cares and misfortunes arise, are totally forgotten and neglected. Then follow me and drink to the forgetfulness of vice.
'Tis vice alone disturbs the human breast;
Care dies with guilt; be virtuous and be blest.   (817–25)

In all, Garrick wrote more than twenty original plays, at least half of which can be considered satiric. Aiming for the instruction of his audience, Garrick presented them with exaggerated pictures of their own foibles, adding moral tags to point the cure for folly. Compared to the harsher tactics of satirists such as Wycherley, Gay, and Fielding, Garrick's emphasis on gentle correction exemplifies many of the qualities of dramatic satire after the Licensing Act.

Richard Brinsley Sheridan, perhaps the best-known dramatist of the later eighteenth century, also incorporated social satire into several of his comedies. *The School for Scandal* (1777/80), for example, mocks gossipmongers as well as the "man of sentiment" found in the "weeping" or sentimental comedies popular in the second half of the century. While Sheridan included satiric figures and plot lines in plays such as *The School for Scandal*, his most extended satiric drama was also his last original play, *The Critic; or, A Tragedy Rehearsed* (1779/81). As the title announces, Sheridan's satire follows the lead of Buckingham's *Rehearsal*, with the final two acts centered around the rehearsal of an (inevitably) awful tragedy. Unlike *The Rehearsal* or other burlesques such as *Tom Thumb*, *The Critic* does not parody specific plays or even a distinct literary trend. Rather, it ridicules bad writing in general through the character of Mr Puff, the play's author, who supports himself by writing overblown descriptions or "puffs." Like his puffs, his play is both verbose and absurd. So prolix is this tragedy, we are told, that the actors have cut away most of it, including an entire scene describing the horse and side-saddle of Queen Elizabeth – who never appears but is "talked of forever" (2.2.489), a wryly appropriate description of Mr Puff's mode of writing. What remains in rehearsal allows Sheridan, a theater manager as well as a playwright, to take aim at clichés in both writing and acting. The literary satire is most cutting in the play's opening act, as Sheridan takes aim at contemporary playwright Richard Cumberland, depicting his rival as Sir Fretful Plagiary, whose name epitomizes his character.

A Shadow is Cast

With political figures and administrations off limits, playwrights of the later eighteenth century focused their energies on satirizing general trends in literature or in society. When their portraits became more specific, as in the case of Foote's lampoons or Sheridan's Sir Fretful, these figures remained comfortably outside the political realm that the Licensing Act had made untouchable. The Act remained in effect until 1843 with censorship in effect by the Lord Chamberlain until 1968; during the intervening decades, satiric drama could not overstep the bounds declared permissible by subsequent governments. With the advent of the nineteenth century, indecency, as well as potential sedition, was deemed intolerable, and satire on the stage lost much of its bite.

If the end of the eighteenth century might be said to usher in a dark age for dramatic satire, it may be in part because the works that appeared in the previous century and a half were among the finest in the genre that the English stage has ever known. From the first days of the Restoration, dramatists recognized the potential that the stage offered for social, political, and literary commentary. Even more notable than the volume of satire that followed the reopening of the theaters, however, was its sheer originality and verve, as playwrights experimented not only with standard components, such as character and plot, but with the very form of drama itself. It was an age of invention, wit, and often caustic humor.

Because the stage utilizes visual and aural as well as verbal components, drama represents perhaps the most ephemeral of satires; just as we can never quite recapture the nuances of a specific performance or of a specific actor's intonation, we can never entirely appreciate the details of these satires in their original form. Yet, the element of performance can also keep them alive, allowing new generations of performers to inflect these works with their own observations on the world around them, imbuing the works of Wycherley and Buckingham, of Gay and of Sheridan, with fresh meaning.

References and Further Reading

Canfield, J. D. (1997) *Tricksters and Estates: On the Ideology of Restoration Comedy*. Lexington: University Press of Kentucky.

—— and Payne, D. C. (eds) (1995) *Cultural Readings of Restoration and Eighteenth-century Theater*. Athens: University of Georgia Press.

Freeman, L. A. (2002) *Character's Theater: Genre and Identity on the Eighteenth-century English Stage*. Philadelphia: University of Pennsylvania Press.

Gill, J. E. (ed.) (1995) *Cutting Edges: Postmodern Critical Essays on Eighteenth-century Satire*. Knoxville: University of Tennessee Press.

Hume, R. D. (1988) *Henry Fielding and the London Theatre, 1728–1737*. Oxford: Clarendon Press.

Kern, J. (1976) *Dramatic Satire in the Age of Walpole, 1720–1750*. Ames: Iowa State University Press.

Kernan, A. (1959) *The Cankered Muse: Satire of the English Renaissance*. New Haven, CT: Yale University Press.

Lewis, P. (1987) *Fielding's Burlesque Drama: Its Place in the Tradition*. Edinburgh: Edinburgh University Press.

Loftis, J. (1963) *The Politics of Drama in Augustan England*. Oxford: Clarendon Press.

—— (1977) *Sheridan and the Drama of Georgian England*. Cambridge, MA: Harvard University Press.

Munns, J. (1995) *Restoration Politics and Drama: The Plays of Thomas Otway, 1675–1683*. Newark: Delaware University Press.

Payne, D. C. (1995) Comedy, satire or farce? Or the generic difficulties of Restoration dramatic satire. In J. E. Gill (ed.), *Cutting Edges: Postmodern Critical*

Essays on Eighteenth-century Satire, pp. 1–22. Knoxville: University of Tennessee Press.

Shaw, G. B. (1970) Mainly about myself. In *Plays Unpleasant*, pp. 11–34. London: The Bodley Head.

Smith, D. F. (1936) *Plays about the Theater in England from* The Rehearsal *in 1671 to the Licensing Act in 1737 or, the Self-conscious Stage and its Burlesque and Satirical Reflections in the Age of Criticism*. London: Oxford University Press.

10
Dryden and Restoration Satire
Dustin Griffin

John Dryden (1631–1700) has long been regarded as the greatest of the Restoration satirists. His "Absalom and Achitophel" (1681) and "MacFlecknoe" (1682), routinely regarded as the best satires of the period, and commonly anthologized, are often the only Restoration satires that non-specialists know. But in fact Dryden was not primarily a satirist. In the eyes of his contemporaries, he was primarily a dramatist and poet laureate (who discharged those duties in both historical poems and panegyrics), and latterly a translator of Virgil, as well as of the Roman satirists Juvenal and Persius. His work in satire, apart from his translations, consists only of three poems: the aforementioned "Absalom and Achitophel" and "MacFlecknoe," along with "The Medall" (1682). And Dryden took steps to de-emphasize his association with satire as a literary kind. "MacFlecknoe" was first published anonymously, and not claimed by Dryden for perhaps six years. Although "MacFlecknoe" and "The Medall" were identified on their title pages as "Satyr," "Absalom and Achitophel" was called simply "A Poem." Dryden was perhaps being disingenuous, and scholars often cite his own words that "Satire will have room, where e'er I write" ("To Kneller," line 94).

But it remains true that satire constitutes but a small part of Dryden's canon, and that (for his contemporaries, if not for present-day readers) he was not the leading satirist of the day. In the 1660s, that title would probably have gone to Samuel Butler, author of the famous *Hudibras*, or to Andrew Marvell (for his "Last Instructions to a Painter"), in the 1670s to John Wilmot, Earl of Rochester, for his court satires, and to John Oldham for his *Satyrs on the Jesuits*. If one looked around for satire after Rochester's death in 1680 and Oldham's death in 1683 (Marvell had died in 1678 and Butler in 1680), one might have had to settle on another court poet, Charles Sackville, Earl of Dorset. It was to Dorset, indeed, that Dryden in 1693 dedicated his "Discourse Concerning the Original and Progress of Satire," prefaced to his translation of Juvenal and Persius. In the "Discourse," Dryden declares that Dorset is "the first of the Age" in satire (1974: 12), perhaps not merely as a piece of dedicatory flattery.

It might be argued, however, that Dryden's own massive "Discourse" clearly established his credentials as the chief judge of satire. Indeed, his essay became, and has remained, the pre-eminent theoretical document in the history of English satire. Dryden's theory and practice, it is commonly said, both defined and elevated satire as a literary kind, and significantly influenced the greatest poetic satirist in the next age, Alexander Pope, as well as most subsequent theorizing of the form. On the strength of the "Discourse" alone, Dryden should perhaps, so some would say, be restored to his throne as the leading satirist of the Restoration period. But what most strikes the reader who works through the long, rambling, digressive "Discourse" is that, in Dryden's view, the satire of his own age largely fails to meet the standards he wishes to set for both stylistic refinement and moral design. Whether we regard Dryden as essentially right, or whether we think he either misunderstands or misrepresents his contemporaries in satire, this chapter on the satiric writing of his age should perhaps be entitled "Dryden *versus* Restoration Satire." The first step in understanding the satire of the period is to make sure that we are not unwitting captives of Dryden's own persuasive view of the topic.

Dryden, we should remember, was writing at a time when satiric theory was still being actively debated: was satire, as some scholars argued, a form of drama, or a poem? Did it originate in the shaggy rough music of the *satyr*, or in the *lanx satura* (an overflowing plate – full of miscellaneous choice bits)? Was its style appropriately chatty and sly, or declamatory and majestic? Was the satirist essentially a bitter mocker or a high-minded moralist? And Dryden entered these debates not as an objective analyst but as a participant, with his own opinions and preferences. One of his favorite metaphors for the development of satire from its pre-classical origins was an agricultural one: originally a form of "natural" speech, coarse and harsh, satire, as Dryden sees it, ripens over time into "better fruit," into an art, and it is that process of refinement that he wants to promote in modern English satire. His review of the "original and progress" of satire leads ultimately to his instructions for "how a Modern satire shou'd be made" (1974: 78). By "Modern satire" he means neither "lampoon" (an attack against a "particular Person," and for that reason "a dangerous sort of Weapon, and for the most part Unlawful") nor a "Varronian" satire, a tradition which for Dryden seems to involve narrative in which serious matters are "mingl'd with Pleasantries" and "sprinkled with a kind of mirth, and gayety" (1974: 47) – he cites as examples Spenser's "Mother Hubbard's Tale," Butler's *Hudibras*, and his own "MacFlecknoe" and "Absalom and Achitophel." "Modern satire" in Dryden's "Discourse" means essentially what later critics called "formal verse satire," the kind of poem written by Persius and Juvenal. From their example, Dryden derives some "rules": that satire "ought to treat of one Subject; to be confin'd to one particular Theme; or, at least, to one principally"; that the satirist ought to construct an essentially binary design: he is "bound, and that *ex Officio*, to give his Reader some one Precept of Moral Virtue; and to caution him against some one particular Vice or Folly" (1974: 80). Dryden's theory is not only polemical; it is unmistakably prescriptive. Critics have from time to time tried to apply it retrospectively – and without much success – to the satires that Dryden himself and his contemporaries wrote.

It is also helpful to remember that Dryden's "Discourse" (1693) was written shortly after collections of contemporary satiric "Poems on Affairs of State" began appearing – and implicitly, one might argue, in response to them. These collections were poems, composed over the previous thirty-five years, that had largely circulated in manuscript. It was only after the Revolution of 1688 that these satires, most of them claiming to expose the folly, deceit, or corruption in and around the courts of the Stuart monarchs, Charles II (1660–85) and his Roman Catholic brother James II (1685–8), could be safely printed – as they were in 1689. Dryden, as an apologist for both Charles and James and a recent convert to the Roman Catholic Church, would have had a political motive for seeking to dismiss the importance of poems that promised to reveal the truth about "Popery and Tyranny" at the English court. So it is perhaps not surprising that, without referring to the collections of "state poems" by title or noting their political content, he dismissed them as coarse and dull lampoons that violated "Decency" and essentially attacked private persons (1974: 60). At least six such collections were published in 1689. Despite Dryden's dismissal of their importance, they continued to find readers, and further editions ("corrected and much enlarged"), containing poems by or attributed to Rochester, Buckingham, Marvell, Dorset, Dryden himself, and others, were published from 1697 to 1705.

Dryden's "Discourse" in effect sought to efface the memory of the "state poems" and to redirect the attention of English readers and would-be satirists to the Roman tradition of Persius, Juvenal, and Horace, to which he devotes most of his attention. Nowhere in the "Discourse" does Dryden mention Andrew Marvell or John Oldham. Rochester is named once in passing. Butler is noticed for his "good Sense," but though Dryden declares him to be "above my Censure," he delivers some back-handed compliments: *Hudibras*, with its short tetrameter couplets and "double rhymes" (i.e., feminine rhymes), "gives us a Boyish kind of Pleasure," a kind of "unseasonable Delight, when we know he cou'd have given us a better, and more solid" (1974: 80). Dryden may have thought it "unseasonable," but *Hudibras* continued to delight English readers for generations. Any account of Restoration satire that gives short shrift to Butler is an unbalanced one.

Fifty years ago, a respected survey of "Augustan satire" could treat the Restoration period by discussing only Dryden and Butler. In the intervening decades, other satirists of the period have regained critical visibility. The publication of the multi-volume Yale edition of *Poems on Affairs of State* (Lord 1963–75) made available, in well-edited and annotated versions, the "state poems" that Dryden regarded so imperiously. New scholarly editions of the complete poems of Rochester (from Vieth's edition in 1968 to Love's in 1999), Marvell (from Donno's 1972 edition to Nigel Smith's in 2003), and Oldham (1987) have recognized their inclusion in the ranks of Restoration satirists. But the canon of Restoration satire remains fairly small. The writers of the state poems, with the exception of Marvell, Waller, Rochester, and Dorset, still (thirty years after the completion of the Yale edition) receive little close critical attention, and even less classroom time. As a result, the range and vigor of Restoration satire are not fully recognized. Satiric writers of the 1660s of some real ability, such as Robert Wild and John Cleveland, have yet to be properly rediscovered.

Furthermore, most readers of "Restoration satire" continue to assume that satire somehow appeared out of thin air at the Restoration in 1660. Even those familiar with such Renaissance satirical writers as John Donne, Ben Jonson, John Marston, and Joseph Hall commonly regard Restoration satire as a new beginning. Underlying this view is an assumption that the culture of England had significantly changed, whether because the returning exiled courtiers brought with them from France a taste for French neo-classical satire, or because the nation at large reveled triumphantly (and mockingly) at the overthrow of the Puritan spoilsports and king-killers, or because of a large-scale turning away (prompted by the bitter experience of civil war) from heroic conceptions of life toward a more skeptical and even cynical outlook, reflected, for example, in the mid-century popularity in both France and England of "travesties" of Virgil's revered *Aeneid* by Paul Scarron (*Le Virgile Travesti*, 1648–62) and Charles Cotton (*Scarronides, or, Virgile Travestie*, 1664). Despite the efforts of such scholars as C. V. Wedgwood (1960) and Margaret Doody (1985), readers and even teachers of Restoration satire fail to recognize that the several decades prior to the Restoration witnessed an outburst of satire in both prose and verse, in high forms and low, that helped fuel and shape the continuing appearance of satire after the Restoration itself. Political controversy raged in the pages of the *Mercurius Pragmaticus* (pro-Royalist) and *Mercurius Britannicus* (pro-Parliament) newsletters. Comic ballads, drinking songs, and satiric parodies, collected in such volumes as *Rump: Or an Exact Collection of the Choycest Poems and Songs relating to the Late Times* (1662), were probably spawned in taverns, army camps, and booksellers' shops. Most of the poems that survive in print are Royalist in sympathy, but manuscript collections show that the Parliamentarians were not behindhand in the production of popular satire. More high-minded ecclesiastical controversialists challenged each other in what Milton called "the wars of truth," publishing "animadversions" (point-for-point refutations, usually accompanied by scathing and sardonic rhetoric and grim joking) on each other's pamphlets. As scholars today turn increasingly to popular literature (if only to reach a better understanding of the relationship between "high" and "low" culture), this Civil-War era satire in verse and prose will begin to take its place in our sense of the period.

English satirists did not wait for the return of Charles II. In the month before his arrival in May 1660, Londoners in large numbers were reading Robert Wild's *Iter Boreale*, published in late April, a long, rollicking verse chronicle (407 lines) of the march by General Monck from Scotland to London in the winter of 1659–60 to expel the Rump Parliament and clear the way for the king's return. The poem, which laughs at the defeated Puritans, was apparently so popular that (according to Dryden) it was being read "in the midst of Change-time" – that is, it kept Londoners from attending to business. It deserves to be read in conjunction with such contemporary writings as Milton's last-gasp *Readie and Easie Way to Establish a Commonwealth* (March 1660), which angrily urged his back-sliding contemporaries not to return to the "Egypt" of monarchy, and Dryden's panegyrical "Astraea Redux" (June 1660), which celebrated Charles's return. But it is still commonly agreed that the first great satire to emerge after the Restoration was Samuel Butler's *Hudibras*, which began appearing in December 1662.

Samuel Butler

Hudibras was more ambitious than any satiric poem that had appeared in English. It was nothing less than a full-scale parody of chivalric romance: Sir Hudibras is a burlesque version of a Spenserian knight on adventures to right the wrongs of the world. The first part (1662), in three cantos, runs to nearly 3,500 lines, the second part (1663), in three cantos, another 3,000 lines, and the third part (1677) more than 4,800. Added together, that makes a poem longer than *Paradise Lost* (1667), another modern "heroic" poem (not coincidentally) from the same decade. Butler's knight was formed, Johnson argued, on the model of Cervantes' great Quixote (still a relatively new figure in the European imagination less than fifty years after the publication of *Don Quixote* in 1605 and 1615), ridiculous to all except himself and his squire. It was an ingenious means of mocking the reform projects of the Puritans, solemnly determined as they were to new-model not only the government, the church, and the army, but the culture itself. Hudibras, as Johnson says, "is a Presbyterian justice, who, in the confidence of legal authority and the rage of zealous ignorance, ranges the country to repress superstition and correct abuses, accompanied by an Independent [i.e., a smaller Protestant sect] Clerk, disputatious and obstinate, with whom he often debates, but never conquers him" (1905: 1.210). Most readers of Cervantes conclude that he has a deep fondness for his hero; nobody ever suspected Butler of such fondness.

The poem was hugely enjoyed in its own day for its ridicule of the defeated Puritans and Parliamentarians, but perhaps equally for what Johnson called its "inexhaustible wit." Many of its mocking couplets entered the language as proverbial sayings. Butler's form – the short tetrameter couplet, with comic double rhymes – no doubt helped to make his lines memorable. Some of their impact is probably due to the fact that Butler manages to be both completely colloquial in the diction, syntax, and word order, and yet metronomically regular in his iambic meter, idiomatic and formal at the same time. Although Dryden tried to establish the five-foot couplet as the standard measure for English satire, Butler's "Hudibrastics" remained an alternative tradition, whose greatest exemplar was Jonathan Swift. Dryden aimed for "majesty" and "stateliness," and Butler (and his descendants) aimed, as Johnson noted, for the "quick, spritely, and colloquial."

Despite their partisan bias, Butler's first readers could not have missed the acerbic and leveling wit that reduces virtually all human endeavor (not just that of the Puritans) to self-gratification, hypocrisy, and self-deception. In this respect, *Hudibras* is perhaps a sign of the general post-Renaissance disenchantment of the world, the increasing sense that what was once regarded as noble or spiritual, an immaterial essence (an idea of government, or the church, or love) is in fact material at bottom – prompted by a Hobbesian human appetite for power or food. Hudibras, even on horseback, keeps plenty of victuals close at hand, and often seems mere matter in motion. Nobody in the world of Hudibras seems exempt from Butler's skeptical eye. It has proved notoriously difficult for critics to infer a set of normative standards by which Butler measures and judges the world.

The three parts of *Hudibras* were published over a period of more than fifteen years, but the poem was never completed. Hudibras would no doubt have been sent on more adventures, but, as Johnson saw, "the action could not have been one; there could only have been a succession of incidents, each of which might have happened without the rest, and which could not at all cooperate to any single conclusion" (1905: 1.211). In this respect, Butler's poem differs sharply from Dryden's narrative satires, "MacFlecknoe" and "Absalom and Achitophel," each of which consists of a single Aristotelian "action." But it raises the question of whether a satire might achieve what Dryden called "unity of Design" by some means other than a single narrative "action." Johnson also thought Butler's poem too tied to its historical moment, its satire founded too narrowly on the peculiar manners of the "ancient Puritans" (rather than on more broadly human vanities and foibles). But in light of the argument, in some modern theory, that satire always requires an attack on "historical particulars," *Hudibras* is a good case to test Johnson's claim that the best satire (indeed, the best poetry) is not wholly tied to its historical moment.

In the early 1670s Butler also wrote a number of shorter verse satires, including "The Elephant in the Moon" and "Satire upon the Royal Society," not published until 1759. In addition, he composed more than two hundred prose "characters," sketches of familiar moral or psychological types ("A Glutton," "A Melancholy Man," "The Perfidious Man"), professional types ("An Empiric," "A Shopkeeper," "An Astrologer"), or historical characters ("A Duke of Bucks"). Here Butler was working in an established literary tradition, descending from the classical writer, Theophrastus. His Renaissance predecessors include the satirist Joseph Hall, Sir Thomas Overbury, and John Earle; his contemporaries, the satirist John Cleveland and the butt of Dryden's satire, Richard Flecknoe. Virtually all of Butler's characters are satirical; most are fairly brief (a paragraph in length), but a few much longer. Some critics have noticed resemblances between the squire Ralpho and such characters as "An Hermetic Philosopher," "A Quaker," and "An Hypocritical Nonconformist." The brief and incisive character sketch was to play a prominent part in the satire of Dryden, Pope, and Johnson. Butler's "A Duke of Bucks" has demonstrable affinities with the famous portrait of "Zimri" (based on the Duke of Buckingham) in "Absalom and Achitophel."

Butler also composed a number of prose "observations," compiled in his notebooks perhaps for possible use in later writings, but not published until after his death. Some of these "observations" may provide clues to the tart sensibility that underpinned Butler's view of his contemporaries. "This Age," he wrote, "will serve to make a very pretty Farce for the Next, if it have any Witt at all to make Use of it" (1979: 3). They may also suggest his conception of satire, and hint that the relationship between Butler and his chivalric mock-hero was complicated. "A Satyr," he wrote, "is a kind of Knight Errant that go's upon Adventures to Relieve the Distressed Damsel Virtue, and redeeme Honour out of Inchanted Castles, And opprest Truth, and Reason out of the Captivity of Gyants and Magitians: and though his meaning be very honest, yet some believe he is no wiser then those wandring Heros usd to be, though his Performances and Atchievments be ever so Renownd and Heroicall" (1979: 215).

Andrew Marvell

Andrew Marvell (1621–78) is still chiefly known (except to specialists) as the last of what T. S. Eliot taught us to call the seventeenth-century "metaphysical poets." In his own day he was recognized not as a writer of delicate lyrics (they remained unpublished until after his death), but as a public writer – panegyrist of Oliver Cromwell, staunch proponent of Parliamentary interests, relentless critic of the corrupt circle of advisers around the king, and defender of toleration for nonconformists. In his "Discourse," Dryden ignored Marvell's contributions to poetic satire, though he clearly knew Marvell's prose satire, *The Rehearsal Transpros'd* (1672). Dryden probably dismissed Marvell because of his ecclesiastical politics, his defense of nonconformists (which made him the modern equivalent of the Elizabethan Martin Mar-Prelate, a "Presbyterian Scribler, who sanctify'd Libels and Scurrility to the use of the Good Old Cause," Dryden 1972: 106), and what he regarded as overheated warnings of the "Growth of Popery." But Marvell's satires figured prominently in the volumes of "poems on affairs of state" published in the 1690s, and in recent years critics, emphasizing the intertwining of literature and politics in the late seventeenth century, have made Marvell the central spokesman for the parliamentary opposition to the court of Charles II.

Marvell's satires are somewhat forbidding to new readers for several reasons:

1 *Prodigious length*: his best satiric poem, "Last Instructions to a Painter" (1667), runs to nearly a thousand lines, and *The Rehearsal Transpros'd* (in modern editions) more than 300 pages.
2 *Apparent formlessness*: his best verse satire is organized not as a narrative (like Dryden's "Absalom" or Butler's *Hudibras*), but as a loose set of "instructions," resolving into a series of distinct but unrelated scenes. Dryden says nothing at all of the "painter poems" of the 1660s, no doubt regarding them as coarse and formless.
3 *Topical density* of writings designed essentially for well-informed insiders: Marvell's poems require substantial footnoting to identify the people and events in his references and allusions; his prose requires that we, following Marvell, pay constant attention to the verbal details of his adversary's arguments.

4 *Satiric style*: modern readers accustomed to Marvell's finely tuned lyrics may be put off by the calculated coarseness, in tone and in metrical movement, of the verse satire; although Marvell's first readers, including the king, reportedly found his prose "answer" to Parker to be highly droll and "merry," many readers today will be puzzled by the shifting back and forth from "jest" to "earnest" argument.

The prose satires will perhaps remain of interest only to specialists, but "Last Instructions" deserves attention from a wider range of readers as a strenuous, ambitious, and sometimes brilliant poem that replies with devastating effectiveness to contemporary panegyrics on Charles II and his court. It conducts its satire as if bearing in mind the traditions of *satura* – the well-filled dish or satiric miscellany – and the rough and ill-mannered *satyr*. Furthermore, like three other major poems of the 1660s, Butler's *Hudibras*, Dryden's *Annus Mirabilis* (1667), and Milton's *Paradise Lost*, it mounts a new kind of self-consciously epic narrative (Marvell calls his poem a "great work," line 945) and (like Butler's and Milton's poems) a critique of traditional military heroism.

Marvell's poem is most obviously an answer to the famous "Instructions to a Painter" (1665) by Edmund Waller, a poem designed to celebrate a key English naval victory in the so-called Second Dutch War. Waller's poem takes the form of a set of "instructions" to a court painter "for the drawing of the posture and progress of his Majesty's Forces at Sea... together with the Victory Obtained over the Dutch, June 3, 1665." Ostensibly an account of what a painting should portray ("First draw the sea... But, nearer home, thy pencil use once more / And place our navy by the Holland shore"), the poem shifts into disguised present-tense narrative ("Against him first Opdam his squadron leads... And now our royal Admiral success / With all the marks of victory, does bless"). Contemporary readers accepted Waller's convention, but did not accept his carefully tailored account of a battle that in fact concluded with the escape of the Dutch fleet. Waller's poem was quickly greeted by a satirical "Second Advice to a Painter" (1665), which drew attention to embarrassing facts that Waller had discreetly omitted, and went on to note other English naval failures, and a "Third Advice to a Painter" (1666), which extended the critique of what the court preferred to think of as glorious victories. Although authorship of these two replies to Waller has been long disputed, the consensus today is that Marvell is the author of both. Scholars have never doubted that Marvell was the author of the most effective reply to Waller, the "Last Instructions to a Painter" (1667).

But Marvell's most comprehensive satire perhaps more significantly replies to a comprehensive panegyric on the king, "Annus Mirabilis," published in early 1667 by his poet laureate. Dryden's poem celebrates 1666, a "Year of Wonders" (the Dutch war, the great plague, and the Fire of London); Marvell's poem surveys a year (roughly from November 1666 to September 1667) of "monsters" in parliamentary and military affairs (the Excise Bill, which the court party was trying to push through the Commons; a "Patent" granted by the king's chief minister to the monopolistic Canary Company; and the burning of the English fleet in the Medway by the Dutch).

Dryden's reveals a country in which disaster produces a spirit of self-sacrifice and national unity; Marvell's a country in which self-interest and division rule, as courtiers and politicians loot the treasury. Dryden's is a king who seeks to "supply" the fire's survivors; Marvell's is a king who strategizes to gain his own parliamentary "supply." Dryden has a "suffering servant" (the king, who prays that God "On me alone thy just displeasure lay, / But take thy judgments from this mourning Land," 1059–60); Marvell has a scapegoat (the hapless Peter Pett, the Navy Commissioner who takes the blame for the government's failure in the Dutch war). In Dryden's "Annus Mirabilis," the fire that consumed nearly a third of the City of London is imagined as a sexual ravisher (stanzas 221–2); Marvell's "Last Instructions" begins with the prodigious sexual appetites of the king's courtiers and ends with a scene in which the king himself (like Ixion chasing Juno) makes an attempt to ravish what turns out to be an airy "vision" of England: it is as if the king were attempting to gratify his obsessive sexual desires on the very body of the nation. Critics debate the political position that the poem adopts. In the closing address to the king, Marvell professes to speak for the loyal opposition, a band of "country" parliamentarians who blame the king's corrupt ministers but stand ready to advise him. Some critics take Marvell at his word; others conclude that, under cover of a professed loyalty, Marvell locates the source of the country's corruption in the king himself.

In addition to "Last Instructions," Marvell wrote a number of other verse satires, two on fellow poets, "Flecknoe, an English Priest at Rome" (c.1646) and "Tom May's Death" (written 1650), and at least two on current international politics, "The Character of Holland" (1650) and "The Loyal Scot" (c.1667–73), the latter a spin-off from "Last Instructions." Although none of these poems rises to the level of "Last Instructions," and none has attracted much critical attention, the poem on "Flecknoe" is a very readable early instance of satire on a notoriously bad poet, and thus a forerunner of Dryden's "MacFlecknoe" and Pope's *Dunciad* (1728, 1743).

In the 1670s, Marvell turned his hand to ecclesiastical politics, publishing polemical replies to Bishop Samuel Parker's assertion of royal absolutism in matters of religion (*The Rehearsal Transpros'd*, 1672; the *Second Part*, 1673), Francis Turner's attack on the mild-mannered Bishop of Hereford (*Mr Smirke: Or, The Divine in Mode*, 1676), and a summary *Account of the Growth of Popery and Arbitrary Government in England* (1678), an indictment of what he – and many Protestant Englishmen of the day – regarded as the danger that underlay all other crises of the 1670s. In all but the last of these pamphlets, Marvell deploys drollery and ridicule to advance his polemical purpose: to destroy the credibility of his adversary. Some modern readers will be puzzled by the pleasantry, but Marvell was working within a well-established contemporary convention, going back through Milton's Smectymnuan pamphlets of the 1640s to "Martin Marprelate," that licensed the use of satire in religious polemic. Indeed, Marvell can claim to be doing nothing more than his opponent, Parker, who had himself defended "the Lawfulness and Expedience of Railing" (line 75) and the use of "smart and twingeing Satyrs" (quoted in Patterson 1978: 187) in the service of ecclesiastical argument. But Marvell's satire is more genial than Milton's grim, harsh laughter, and his self-conscious defense of using invective against a churchman has persuaded some readers that he himself had some misgivings about mixing satire and ecclesiastical matters.

The title of Marvell's *Rehearsal Transpros'd* suggests that he will appropriate Buckingham's witty mockery of Dryden (as "Bayes") in *The Rehearsal*, recently produced and published, to make fun of a new "Bayes the Second" (as Marvell calls Parker), who resembles the first in his "expressions...humour...contempt and quarreling of all others." Just as Buckingham's Bayes is ready to turn stolen prose into verse ("transversing") or verse into prose ("transprosing"), so the second Bayes misappropriates the Bible – "transproses" it – to concoct what Marvell insists on calling "plays" (fictions of royal sovereignty in matters of religion). *Mr Smirke* likewise takes its title from the contemporary stage: Smirke, a name that would ring in his readers' ears, is a standard Restoration "wouldwit," drawn from Etherege's *The Man of Mode* (1676); Marvell's Mr Smirke, "the Divine in Mode," like his namesake, tries to be wittily severe but succeeds only in displaying his witlessness.

Given their intense topicality, their status as "serious" polemic, and their mixture of point-for-point straightforward refutation (the classic form of the "animadversion") and cheerful fantasy, Marvell's prose satires raise anew an old question about the location of the frontier between satire (based, most theorists argue, on some kind of "fiction") and polemical rhetoric (based, fundamentally, on "fact"). Literary historians will remind us that Marvell's prose pamphlets are precisely what the seventeenth century regarded as great satire; some theorists will insist that "satire" need not be based on a "fiction"; others will argue that satire is a mode rather than a genre, and that Marvell was simply deploying modal satire for essentially polemical purposes. Readers, like Warren Chernaik, wanting satire to "break free from the pressure of sordid fact" (1983: 203), will probably concede that Marvell's tract is only intermittently satiric. Swift's *A Tale of a Tub* (written, so he claimed, in 1694) makes a good case for comparison. Swift admired *The Rehearsal Transpros'd*: "We still read *Marvel's* Answer to Parker with Pleasure, tho' the Book it answers be sunk long ago" (Swift 1958: 10). The "Apology" (1710) offers the *Tub* as a straightforward contribution to ecclesiastical controversy, and insists that his rhetorical purpose is simply to celebrate the Church of England as the most perfect in both doctrine and discipline. But regardless of his claim, readers ever since have been skeptical.

John Wilmot, Earl of Rochester

Whether he is writing verse "instructions" or witty prose polemic, Marvell subordinates his satire to his political objective as a member of the parliamentary opposition to the king's party and spokesman for toleration. By contrast, the young courtier John Wilmot, Earl of Rochester (1647–80), Marvell's junior by more than twenty-five years, was ready to turn any serious matter of church and state politics to jest, and to apply his skeptical wit to sexual and literary politics and to a Butler-like mockery of pretension of all kinds. Dryden, who had dedicated his life to writing, regarded Rochester as merely a man "of pleasant Conversation" with "a trifling kind of fancy, perhaps helped out by some smattering of Latin," witty in his way but "not qualified to decide sovereignly concerning poetry" (Preface to *All for Love*, 1678). But Dryden had a number of reasons for dismissing Rochester, who had once served as his patron and had then allied himself with a rival literary faction. He was also replying to Rochester's "Allusion to Horace" (1675), which attempted to define the difference between a poet (i.e., Dryden) who wrote to please the rabble in the playhouse and a poet (i.e., Rochester) who wrote to please himself and a few discerning judges. A generation later, Pope was intrigued with Rochester, and though he pretended to dismiss him (along with Dorset and the rest) as "holiday writers – as gentlemen that diverted themselves now and then with poetry, rather than as poets," he was clearly attracted to the idea of aristocratic ease and graceful negligence. Rochester was something of a model for the young Pope, though he discreetly dropped the insolence, libertinism, and impiety.

In his 1693 "Discourse" on satire, Dryden dismissed Rochester with a sneering witticism, as if he were one of the ephemeral court wits whose works were already forgotten. In fact, Rochester's poems had been recently republished by Dryden's own publisher, Jacob Tonson, in 1691 in a handsome edition, complete with an admiring preface (written by Thomas Rymer) that implicitly claimed a place for him as one of the standard English poets. But it was probably more than rivalry that led Dryden to pass over Rochester's claims as a satirist. Rochester's satiric poems did not fit within Dryden's definition of how a "Modern satire" should be made.

A number of Rochester's satires seem indifferent to conventional moral considerations. Several are lampoons – personal attacks on named contemporaries (the Earl of Mulgrave and Sir Carr Scroope). This was in fact a common form in the period, which perhaps suggests why Dryden felt the need to outlaw it in his "Discourse." It is difficult to show that the lampoonist endorses any particular "Precept of Moral Virtue" or cautions against "some one particular Vice or Folly." Although lampoons at first glance appear to be little more than coarse abuse designed to belittle or even (metaphorically) to "kill" their victim, they are, as further inspection shows, highly conventional poems, many of them drawing on a common repertoire of insults (often directed at the victim's alleged lack of satiric or sexual potency). One might regard a skilled lampoon, in turn, as a competitive display of the satirist's own potency.

Other Rochester poems take the related form of a vehement and extended curse (that sometimes reflects unflatteringly on the ranting speaker) as in "A Ramble in St James's Park" (where a disappointed lecher denounces a courtesan who has taken up other clients for the night) and "The Imperfect Enjoyment" (where an aroused lover denounced his own member for failing him in the crisis). Before concluding that the foul-mouthed poet is filled with murderous rage or frustration and self-mockery (or even self-loathing), we should consider the curse as a kind of deliberately over-the-top rhetorical display. Still other Rochester satires consist of the impudent and witty display of blatant immorality, or attitudes (for example, toward the conduct of love affairs, toward the writing of poetry) conventionally regarded as offensive or unapproved, as in "The Disabled Debauchee," "A Very Heroical Epistle," and "An Epistolary Essay." When an old debauched rake muses on the "important mischief" to which he will inspire his younger colleagues, when an imperious lover waves off the complaints of an abandoned woman, and when a swaggering poet declares that "I'd fart just as I write, for my own ease," one doubts that the satirist aims only to draw forth the reader's moral censure of the speaker.

Many of Rochester's poems do invite moral judgment – indeed, their speakers make moral or philosophical judgments (about the proper use of "right reason," for example), and invite us to share them, as in the "Letter from Artemiza in the Towne to Chloe in the Country" or the famous "Satyre against Reason and Mankind." But Rochester, having laid down a philosophical principle ("Thoughts are given for Actions government, / Where Action ceases, Thought's impertinent"), is rarely content to leave the matter there. He engages his readers in the complexities and ambiguities of his topic, pushes the envelope of conventional thought to explore paradox: perhaps it really *would* be better to be an animal than a man; perhaps it is *indeed* folly to behave morally in an immoral world; given the way of the world, perhaps it *does* make more sense for a woman to take brainless studs as lovers than to risk loving a man of wit. Sometimes Rochester's satires seem to hover on the boundary between rhetorical performance and cynical nihilism. "Upon Nothing" might be regarded as a kind of bravura feat – a "paradoxical encomium" that utters (in trenchant triplets of mounting intensity) what can be said, against all received wisdom, in praise of emptiness or nothingness. But the poem is clearly more than a display of Rochester's witty rhetorical skill: its withering and undiscriminating satire leaves nothing untouched, from "king's promises" to "whore's vows."

Rochester's satire, unlike (say) Marvell's or Dryden's, has seemed to some critics to be almost apolitical, either because it laughs at the empty posturing of politicians or darkly dismisses statecraft as mere lies, treachery, and self-serving. But in recent years critics have increasingly argued for a political dimension to Rochester's satire. His poems make clear that the court of Charles II is riven with factional infighting (Rochester himself was aligned with the Duke of Buckingham, his enemy Mulgrave with the Duke of York), and that political success was often measured by one's personal access to the king. (Rochester himself, a royal favorite, had unusually privileged access to the king – and notoriously lost it from time to time by overstepping the bounds and offending the monarch.) Rochester's sometimes pornographic satires portray even more luridly than Marvell's the prevailing atmosphere of sexual profligacy and rampant carnal appetite at the court. In the famous "scepter lampoon" ("In the Isle of Brittain"), Charles is even more sexually obsessed than in Marvell's "Last Instructions" (where the king mistakes a vision of "England, or the Peace" for a fleshly presence):

> Peace was his Aime, his gentleness was such
> And Love, he lov'd, for he lov'd Fucking much,

> Nor was his high desire above his Strength:
> His Scepter and his Prick were of a length,
> And she may sway the one who plays with t'other
> Which makes him little wiser then his Brother.
> (A8–A13)

This is not simply ribaldry among rakes. Many contemporaries in Parliament suspected that a series of powerful women – the royal whores – had some dangerous control over Charles, if only because, enamored of his mistresses, he "attends more to his pleasures than to royal business" (as John Aubrey observed) and was only too ready to grant favors in return for theirs. Most of the king's mistresses (all but the actress Nell Gwyn) were given titles: the Countess of Castlemain, the Duchess of Cleveland, the Duchess of Portsmouth, the Duchess of Mazarin. They were also provided with large pensions and gifts, a significant drain on the treasury at a time when the monarchy had trouble paying its bills. They were said to exercise influence on royal appointments, and to have intrigued in support of the French and Roman Catholic interests. The sexually besotted king was denounced as a slave to his own lust, and thus in contemporary parlance "effeminate." These charges are not surprisingly found in poems by the king's political enemies, but also in poems by his royalist allies.

The political purpose and effect of such satires from the king's friends has been debated. It seems unlikely that Rochester, an apparently committed royalist, could have sought to undermine or limit the king's authority, or to force him to yield to the desires of a nascent political opposition in parliament. And yet the effect of his satires and lampoons on the king and his mistresses might well have been to corroborate the fears and suspicions of the king's enemies. Harold Love suggests that Rochester's overt purpose is not to subvert the court or to promote a party. It is rather to warn the king and his ministers that they should never "place any excessive trust in the power promised by legitimating fictions," and should remember that their authority rested on "ingeniously figured lies" (1998: 176). But the poems, Love suggests, also served to solidify bonds between members of a ruling elite, who share worldly skepticism, even cynicism, about monarchical politics, and implicitly sneer at the credulous world outside the court circle, who still believe in the "fictions."

The "politics" of Rochester's obscene satires probably extends beyond the political world of the court to the realm of what we now call "gender politics." He commonly imagines sexual relations in terms of power: his Bajazet dreams of a sultan's world in which "Each Man's thy slave, and Womankind's thy whore" ("A Very Heroical Epistle"). The power wielded by the royal mistresses can be seen as a highly visible instance of the power of the female body, which in turn provokes male anxiety about an omnivorous female sexuality: the Duchess of Cleveland, says one of Rochester's obscene satires, has "swallowed more pricks than the ocean has sand." Fear of female power might well have prompted male fantasies about female independence. It is worth noting that one of Rochester's satiric ballads, "Signior Dildo," imagines women making do without the sexual services of men. The pornographic play, *Sodom, or the Quintessence of Debauchery*, possibly written by

Rochester, imagines a world in which men satisfy their sexual needs without women. But some critics have argued that even these pornographic pieces also engage court politics: that "Signior Dildo" carries an anti-Yorkist bias (Signior Dildo having arrived in England as part of the entourage of the Duke of York's Catholic wife-to-be), that *Sodom* targets, among other things, "the infinite venality of courtiers" (1999: 497).

John Oldham

Pornographic satire in the Restoration does not always carry a political resonance. Rochester's younger contemporary and admirer John Oldham (1653–83) is the author of "Sardanapalus," a lurid mock-Pindaric ode about the final hours of the notoriously priapic last king of Assyria, who allegedly planned his own death *in flagrante delicto*. Although some have suggested that even this poem is a political attack on the sexually obsessed Charles, darkly warning of his tendencies toward popery and tyranny, most scholars find little more than gross obscenity and a choreographed orgiastic extravaganza. Oldham, whose short career was intertwined with that of Rochester (Rochester promoted and inspired Oldham's work, Oldham published a pastoral elegy on Rochester in 1680), carved out a distinctive satiric style. Rochester is more subtle and slippery in his tone than Oldham, who tends to adopt a single note and embellish it.

Best known for his *Satyrs on the Jesuits* (1679), Oldham's satiric style was not one that Dryden highly valued. In his famous elegiac tribute "To the Memory of Mr Oldham" (1684), Dryden noted that "Knaves and Fools we both abhorr'd alike: / To the same Goal did both our Studies drive, / The last set out the soonest did arrive" (6–8). That is, although he was younger and still unpublished when Dryden began circulating "MacFlecknoe" (c.1676), Oldham was the first to publish satire: *Satyrs on the Jesuits* appeared in a pirated edition in 1679 and an official edition in January 1681, "Absalom and Achitophel" not until November 1681 and "MacFlecknoe" not until 1682. Dryden also thinks of Oldham as working within the same satiric tradition (though less refined and polished – Dryden excuses in Oldham "the harsh cadence of a rugged line"). Dryden in effect tries to accommodate Oldham to his own model of satire. But Oldham seems to have been aiming at different effects.

In Johnson's view, Oldham shared with Rochester the honor of being the first to write what came to be called "imitations" – "in which the ancients are familiarised, by adapting their sentiments to *modern* topics, by making Horace say of Shakespeare what he originally said of Ennius" (1905: 2.192). Johnson implicitly regards Oldham, who imitated both Horace and Juvenal, as a model for Pope's imitations of Horace in the 1730s. *Satyrs on the Jesuits* (1679) might also be regarded as "imitations" of Juvenal. In the "Prologue," Oldham advertises that he adopts a self-consciously Juvenalian stance: "Who can longer hold? ... Indignation can create a muse" (alluding to Juvenal's famous *"indignatio facit versum"*). There are some suggestions that Oldham also draws on the vaunting defiance of Milton's Satan: "Henceforth an endless war / I and my muse with them and theirs declare" (32–3). Oldham's satirist defines himself not as a *vir bonus* or moralist, but as an inflamed and vengeful punisher: "I with utmost spite and vengeance [will never] cease / To prosecute and plague their cursed race" with "my rank envenom'd spleen...my stabbing pen...red hot with vengeance" (49–50, 57–8, 61).

Oldham is clearly *performing* a Juvenalian role in the "Prologue." Rather than continuing in this vein, he ostensibly withdraws, yielding the stage to the Jesuit enemy, who in turn performs the role of conscious conspiratorial villain, reveling in wickedness accomplished or still to be done. The first, third, and fourth of the satires take the form of monologues by leading Jesuit conspirators, Father Garnett (executed for his role in the Gunpowder Plot of 1605) and St Ignatius Loyola himself (founder of the order). One might regard these "Satyrs" as imitations in another sense – impersonations, what a dramatic speaker might say on a particular occasion.

The premise of the poem – its point of departure – is that Jesuits are the mortal enemies of the English Protestant succession. What keeps a reader engaged is not the old news of Roman Catholic plots, but the breathtaking impudence and outrageousness of Jesuits who boast with delight, and in detail, about every crime of which they have been accused by Protestant tradition. In "Satire I" (modeled, as Oldham notes, on a speech by Sulla's ghost in Jonson's *Catiline*, 1611), the ghost of Father Garnett appears to celebrate the deeds of "cruelty" and "wickedness" wrought by the plotters of 1605 and to urge on the plotters of 1679. In "Satire III" (modeled on a sixteenth-century Latin satire against the Franciscans), a dying Loyola provides "instructions" to his followers. And in "Satire IV," a wooden image of Loyola confidently reports on the ruses and schemes by which Jesuits have swindled credulous papist believers. Only in the second satire does the satirist speak in his own voice, though before turning to address Loyola and his followers he imagines what would be said by "some rev'rend villain" (lines 127–56) and by Garnett (lines 172–82).

The primary thrust of the satires is unmistakable – they are plainly written "against the Jesuits," and directed to a Protestant audience ready to suspect the papists of any crime in the alleged "Popish Plot" to overthrow the king. But the secondary effects are oblique. Oldham also implicitly invites his readers to take some pleasure both in the hyperbolic rhetoric he uses to denounce the Jesuits, and the hyperbolic villainy to which his Jesuits themselves confess. He shares with Dryden ("MacFlecknoe") and Rochester ("The Disabled Debauchee," "A Very Heroical Epistle," "An Epistolary Essay") satiric gratification in putting self-justifying words into the mouths of speakers who violate conventional standards. Perhaps too he invites his readers to see the Jesuits in the context of Restoration court politics, where intrigue, hypocrisy, and treachery are assumed to be commonplace, and where the mysteries of all statecraft whatsoever are, as Rochester's satires claim, cheats and lies.

Oldham's other satires might likewise be best understood as rhetorical "performances" of two related kinds in which Rochester excelled: the "mock encomium" (extravagant praise of something conventionally regarded as undeserving), and what Puttenham called the "dira" (violent "imprecation" or vehement curse). Examples of the former kind include his "Dithyrambique on Drinking" – in which a rakish drunkard declares "It is resolv'd; I will drink on and dy" – and "Sardanapalus" – rapturous praise of the old fornicator (though Oldham transforms the historical king, a voluptuary who allegedly dressed as a woman and preferred the company of his eunuchs, into a prodigious sexual athlete with a passing resemblance to Charles II). Examples of the latter include the "Satyr upon a Woman, who by her Falshood and Scorn was the Death of my Friend," "Upon a Bookseller, that expos'd him by Printing a Piece of his grosly mangled, and faulty," and "Upon the Author of the Play call'd Sodom." In each the satirist strings together a series of denunciations rhetorically suited to the target announced in the title. All of these poems show some kinship with dramatic utterance, as if Oldham had designed speeches to be delivered from an imagined stage – and in particular the Restoration stage of the 1670s, on which wicked villains and audacious heroes ranted extravagantly in contemporary heroic plays. The printed version of "Dithyrambique" is subtitled "The Drunkards Speech in a Mask," and is provided at the end with the equivalent of a stage direction: "Tries to go off, but tumbles down, and falls asleep." (In the manuscript version the poem is "Suppos'd to be Spoken by Rochester at the Guinny-Club," and the stage direction simply reads "Exit reeling.") The more famous "Satyr Against Vertue," which Oldham's modern editor calls an inverted version of the mock encomium, is (in the words of the subtitle) "Suppos'd to be spoken by a Court-Hector at Breaking of the Dial in Privy-Garden" (i.e., Rochester again, on the occasion of one of his infamous drunken exploits). Admired by Pope as one of Oldham's "most Remarkable Works," this poem has occasioned some debate among modern critics attempting to determine whether Oldham is satirizing or celebrating his Rochesterian court hector. It is more useful to think of the poem as a modernization and free adaptation of Juvenal's declaration in his first satire (deployed by Oldham as his epigraph) that in dissolute Rome anybody who wants to advance must commit some bold crime. No doubt Oldham (and his first readers) were fascinated (and made somewhat ambivalent) by the spectacle of rakish mayhem at Charles' royal court. But the primary appeal of the satire is not to the reader's moral sense. As with some of Rochester's poems, we may go astray if we try to determine whether Oldham "really means" what he says, or is perhaps "merely satirizing" his dramatic speaker. Oldham pleases by means of what is understood as rhetorical performance – satire as display of the satirist's (and the author's) skill in witty denunciation and cheeky impudence.

Perhaps "imitation" is the key to Oldham's satire. Oldham typically speaks not in his "own" voice, but sets out to "imitate" or to "impersonate" a Juvenalian declaimer, a Jesuit conspirator, a Rochesterian rake. In another set of satires, Oldham adopts the role of distressed poet ("A Satyr address'd to a Friend," "Spenser's Ghost," "Letter from the Country to a Friend in Town"). Some critics have suggested that this role is closest to Oldham himself, but it may simply be another rhetorical pose.

John Dryden

Each of the period's major satirists – Butler, Marvell, Rochester, and Oldham – ought to be viewed in relation to the critical and theoretical pronouncements of Dryden, unquestionably the greatest writer of the period. It is fitting to conclude this survey with a brief consideration of Dryden's own satires, all published within twelve months of each other in 1681–2. Two of them might be regarded as demonstrations that Dryden, when he wanted, could write like his fellow satirists. The third suggests what Dryden meant when he argued, in the "Discourse," that satire is closely allied to epic.

"MacFlecknoe," an elegant lampoon on the rival (and very popularly successful) playwright, Thomas Shadwell, was probably written about 1676 but not published until 1682. Its occasion is usually thought to have been the ongoing public dispute between Dryden and Shadwell concerning the best way to emulate the nature of Ben Jonson's stage comedy. In his "Discourse," Dryden conceded that there might be two justifiable reasons for writing otherwise unlawful lampoons: "Revenge, when we have been affronted in the same Nature, or have been any ways notoriously abus'd, and can make our selves no other Reparation," and "to make examples of vicious Men" (1974: 59–60). That Shadwell's offense against Dryden amounted (even in his own mind) to notorious abuse or to vicious conduct seems unlikely. In any case, Dryden magisterially disposed of Shadwell by reducing him to "Sh—," son not to Ben Jonson but the laughably bad poet, Richard Flecknoe (whom Marvell had lampooned some thirty years earlier). Dryden deploys several of the familiar insults conventionally found in Restoration lampoons: the hapless victim is said to lack potency, both as a satirist ("thy inoffensive Satyrs never bite") and as a progenitor ("Pangs without birth, and fruitless industry"); and is gross of both body ("A Tun of Man in thy Large bulk is writ") and mind (he is by nature "dull" and sluggish). But, as critics have long observed, in Dryden's hands abusive lampoon is transmuted into something almost genial. The abuse, disguised as compliment, is placed in the mouth of "Father Flecknoe," who utters what is in effect a paradoxical encomium in praise of the writer who, of all his sons, "stands confirm'd in full stupidity." Flecknoe's speech, furthermore, is set within a narrative frame, so that the poem becomes a parodic version of an inauguration ceremony. And Thomas Shadwell himself is virtually re-created as the blissfully dull "Sh—," less an historical figure than a comic creation. Pope, in his much longer satire on literary dullness, acknowledged that he learned much by emulating Dryden's poem.

"MacFlecknoe," like other Restoration lampoons, seems clearly designed to display Dryden's own skill. Yet what Dryden wields is not the blunt club but the rapier, as if to suggest that his poem is the best proof that he, rather than Shadwell, understands the nature of true wit. It also suggests that Dryden may have had another target in mind: the Earl of Rochester, who had, some few months before "MacFlecknoe" was written, laughed at Dryden in the "Allusion to Horace" (1675) as a crowd-pleaser with a dull "lumpish fancy," a wouldwit who clumsily imitated the conversation of gentlemen, and whose short and portly body earned him the nickname of "Poet Squab." In the same poem, Rochester had suggested that a good writer ought to imitate Jonson, that Dryden found Jonson "dull," and that Shadwell, by contrast, was one of the few modern wits who have managed to write "true comedy." One might well read "MacFlecknoe" as Dryden's indirect reply to Rochester by means of an attack on Shadwell, a Rochester protegé and proxy. The insults Dryden had received are here flung back: it is Shadwell who is dull and lumpish in both body and mind. But Dryden's manner matches the cool elegance and calculated rudeness of Rochester's couplets. Although Shadwell was Dryden's social and professional equal, Dryden's satire labels him as an inferior, demonstrating that he could appropriate the manner and style of a gentleman-writer if and when he chose. That may explain why he chose to keep "MacFlecknoe" unprinted, and to let it circulate, like the writings of a court wit, in manuscript.

"MacFlecknoe" and "Absalom and Achitophel" are often bracketed as Dryden's two "mock-heroic poems." Both infuse the spirit of wit into lofty and resounding heroic couplets, but the former might better be regarded as a mock encomium and the latter as a witty historical poem. It is only intermittently "satiric" in any conventional sense, primarily in the character sketches of the principal members of the opposition to King David (Charles II): Absalom (Duke of Monmouth, illegitimate son of the king), Achitophel (Earl of Shaftesbury), and Zimri (Duke of Buckingham), leaders of the opposition, Shimei (Slingsby Bethel, sheriff of London), and Corah (Titus Oates, the leading witness to the alleged "Popish Plot"). Dryden himself thought the character of Zimri (not unlike Butler's character of "A Duke of Bucks") one of his best pieces of "fine Raillery," "nice" and "delicate" in its satire, a "Jest" which succeeded in making Buckingham look "ridiculous": he declared that it was "worth the whole Poem" (1974: 71). If the ordinary lampoon is like "the slovenly Butchering of a Man," Dryden says, his satiric characters are like the work of an expert hangman, Jack Ketch, who knew how "to make a Malefactor die sweetly" (1974: 71). When Dryden contributed two satiric characters to Nahum Tate's "Second Part of Absalom and Achitophel" (November 1682), he reverted to the butchery of the conventional lampoon. His Og (Elkanah Settle) is a blundering poet, whose "invective muse" calls you "Rogue" and "Rascal" with no more wit than a parrot. Dryden responds with his own invective: though a defender of the king's enemies, "This Animal's below committing Treason" (line 434). His Doeg (Shadwell again) is "A Monstrous mass of foul corrupted matter" (line 464). Dryden could use a blunt instrument when he chose. (In his final years, he composed a crude lampoon on his bookseller, Jacob Tonson, apparently as a means of compelling him to meet contractual obligations.)

But in "Absalom and Achitophel" the members of the king's party are exempted from satire. David himself is treated with bemused irony, especially in the poem's famous opening paragraph, where Dryden converts the familiar satiric picture of a sex-crazed monarch into an image of divinely endorsed procreative power. There is no denying that the poem is pervasively witty, so much so that one suspects Dryden's real model to be Ovid (famous for treating everything with wit), whose epistles Dryden had just translated in 1680. ("Absalom and Achitophel" was to be reprinted in a 1684 volume of *Miscellany Poems* that included Ovid's elegies, one of them translated by Dryden himself.) Dryden never acknowledged the debt to Ovid, though in his discussion of the historical poem in the account of "Annus Mirabilis" he spends as much time on Ovid as he does on Virgil. When, in the "Discourse" on satire, Dryden himself suggested that his "Absalom" might be regarded as "Varronian" satire, he was probably thinking of its serious mirth.

Among the serious matters Dryden takes up in the poem are the gravest political questions of the day: on what grounds might one mount a defense of the king's prior conduct? And who is to succeed him? Dryden finesses the second question by declaring only that the illegitimate Monmouth cannot succeed. His answer to the former question has been much debated. It used to be claimed that Dryden invited his readers to regard David/Charles as a divinely ordained monarch, whose conduct was not to be challenged by mere men, or that Dryden takes a pragmatist's view of David as a skillful politician, a shrewd manager of men, the right man for troubled times. More recent critics have suggested that Dryden presents a dangerously indulgent king who needs to be urged to take a firm stand against his enemies – among them his favorite (bastard) son.

"The Medall" (March 1682) takes up the same political crisis a few months later. In the interim, Shaftesbury had appeared to triumph, a London grand jury packed with sympathizers having refused to indict him for treason, and the Whigs having struck a medal to celebrate his release. Dryden's response is in effect to rewrite the grand jury's opinion and to produce what he plainly calls a "Satyre against Sedition." The style of Dryden's satire is correspondingly severe, bitter invective rather than fine raillery, much more like Oldham's angry curses than Dryden's other satiric poems. Indeed, the poem might be regarded as an extended curse, directed at the City of London ("How shall I praise or curse to thy desert!" (line 169), the two London sheriffs ("Those let me curse," line 187), and Shaftesbury himself ("What curses on thy blasted Name will fall!" line 260). The choice of topics is prompted by the scenes that appear on the medal – Shaftesbury's head in profile on one side, a panorama of the City of London on the other – Dryden, perhaps bearing in mind the "instructions to a painter" convention, reviling what the Whiggish engraver has represented.

Some critics, observing the sharp change in satiric style and tone, and the prophecy of impending chaos at the close of the poem, draw the conclusion that Dryden as satirist has lost his poise and urbanity, presumably because of a loss of confidence in the political wisdom of the nation and its prospects for stability. But in fact by the time "The Medall" appeared, the king's party knew that Shaftesbury's power had been broken and that the crisis had passed. The anger and dire warnings are calculated, and an indication that Dryden, when he chooses, is the master of several different satiric styles. His own "Discourse" on satire is no better guide to his own writings than it is to the variety of satire produced in the Restoration.

References and Further Reading

Butler, Samuel (1967) *Hudibras*, ed. John Wilders. Oxford: Clarendon Press.

—— (1970) *Characters*, ed. Charles Daves. Cleveland: Press of Case Western Reserve University.

—— (1979) *Prose Observations*, ed. Hugh De Quehen. Oxford: Clarendon Press.

Chernaik, Warren L. (1983) *The Poet's Time: Politics and Religion in the Work of Andrew Marvell*. Cambridge: Cambridge University Press.

Doody, Margaret (1985) *The Daring Muse: Augustan Poetry Reconsidered*. Cambridge: Cambridge University Press.

Dorset, Charles Sackville, Earl of (1979) *The Poems of Charles Sackville, Sixth Earl of Dorset*, ed. Brice Harris. New York: Garland.

Dryden, John (1972) *The Works of John Dryden, Vol. II: Poems 1681–1684*, ed. H. T. Swedenberg, Jr and Vinton A. Dearing. Berkeley, CA: University of California Press.

—— (1974) *The Works of John Dryden, Vol. IV: Poems 1693–1696*, ed. A. B. Chambers, William Frost, and Vinton A. Dearing. Berkeley, CA: University of California Press.

Griffin, Dustin (1974) *Satires against Man: The Poems of Rochester*. Berkeley, CA: University of California Press.

—— (1994) *Satire: A Critical Re-introduction*. Lexington: University Press of Kentucky.

Hume, Robert (2005) "Satire" in the reign of Charles II. *Modern Philology* 102.2, 332–71.

Jack, Ian (1952) *Augustan Satire: Intention and Idiom in English Poetry, 1660–1750*. Oxford: Clarendon Press.

Johnson, Samuel (1905) *Lives of the English Poets*, 3 vols, ed. G. B. Hill. Oxford: Clarendon Press.

Lord, George (ed.) (1963–75) *Poems on Affairs of State: Augustan Satirical Verse, 1660–1714*, 7 vols. New Haven, CT: Yale University Press.

Love, Harold (1998) *The Culture and Commerce of Texts: Scribal Publication in Seventeenth-century England*. Amherst: University of Massachusetts Press (originally published as *Scribal Publication in Seventeenth-century England*. Oxford: Clarendon Press, 1993).

—— (2004) *English Clandestine Satire, 1660–1702*. Oxford: Oxford University Press.

McKeon, Michael (1998) What were poems on affairs of state? *1660–1850* 4, 363–82.

Marvell, Andrew (1971) *The Rehearsal Transpros'd, and The Rehearsal Transpros'd, The Second Part*, ed. D. I. B. Smith. Oxford: Clarendon Press.

—— (1972) *Andrew Marvell: The Complete Poems*, ed. E. S. Donno. Harmondsworth: Penguin.

—— (2003a) *The Poems of Andrew Marvell*, ed. Nigel Smith. London: Pearson Longman.

—— (2003b) *The Prose Works of Andrew Marvell*, 2 vols, ed. Martin Dzelzainis and Annabel Patterson. New Haven, CT: Yale University Press.

Milton, John (1953) *Complete Prose Works of John Milton*, vol. 1, ed. Don M. Wolfe. New Haven, CT: Yale University Press.

Oldham, John (1987) *The Poems of John Oldham*, ed. Harold Brooks. Oxford: Clarendon Press.

Patterson, Annabel (1978) *Marvell and the Civic Crown*. Princeton, NJ: Princeton University Press.

Rochester, John Wilmot, Earl of (1968) *The Complete Poems of John Wilmot, Earl of Rochester*, ed. David M. Vieth. New Haven, CT: Yale University Press.

—— (1999) *The Works of John Wilmot, Earl of Rochester*, ed. Harold Love. Oxford: Oxford University Press.

Selden, Raman (1984) Oldham, Pope, and Restoration satire. In Claude Rawson (ed.), *English Satire and the Satiric Tradition*, pp. 109–26. Oxford: Blackwell.

Spence, Joseph (1966) *Observations, Anecdotes, and Characters of Books and Men*, 2 vols, ed. James M. Osborn. Oxford: Clarendon Press.

Spurr, John (2000) *England in the 1670s: "This Masquerading Age."* Oxford: Blackwell.

Swift, Jonathan (1958) *A Tale of a Tub*, ed. C. Guthkelch and D. Nichol Smith, 2nd edn. Oxford: Clarendon Press.

Trickett, Rachel (1967) *The Honest Muse: A Study in Augustan Verse*. Oxford: Clarendon Press.

Vieth, David M. (1963) *Attribution in Restoration Poetry: A Study of Rochester's "Poems" of 1680*. New Haven, CT: Yale University Press.

Wedgwood, C. V. (1960) *Poetry and Politics under the Stuarts*. Cambridge: Cambridge University Press.

Zwicker, Steven (1993) *Lines of Authority: Politics and English Literary Culture, 1649–1689*. Ithaca, NY: Cornell University Press.

11
Jonathan Swift
Frank Boyle

What higher accolade can a reviewer pay to a contemporary satirist than to call his or her work *Swiftian*? The term is often employed in reviews of Martin Amis's novels, for example, and is not infrequently used to describe the work of certain decidedly non-mainstream filmmakers. And yet, unlike most terms meant to draw a comparison with some great master of a form, the laurel, *Swiftian*, signals not only surpassing satiric achievement, but something less evidently complimentary. A review that describes a novel or a film as a laugh-out-loud-satire on sex, politics, religion, business, or the like expects to attract a willing audience, but the review that draws a comparison with Swift signals that a work is no mere send up of its subject. Its greater substance brings a graver sort of humor, comic levity mixed up with, if not giving way to, both weight and darkness. *Swiftian* signals not only a serious use of humor, but also something deeply unsavory: the gastronomical adjective ideally suited to the author who imagined, in *A Modest Proposal* (1729), commercially slaughtered Irish infants being *"Stewed, Roasted, Baked,* or *Boiled"* and served up in a fricassee or ragout. If the label *Swiftian* identifies a novelist or filmmaker as a satiric genius, it also suggests that this is not the sort of genius one would be pleased to be introduced to at a potluck dinner.

Calling a work *Swiftian* will make us look at once admiringly and warily on the author/creator, and this comes directly from the long history of how readers have approached Swift's own satires. It is rare, if not unknown, for even the most naïve of readers to attribute Iago's ideas to Shakespeare, but something like this has been a common – at times pervasive – practice of readers of Swift from naïve to professional. So insistent is the conflation of Swift and his works that the critical success of the term the "intentional fallacy" – the principle that, because no reader can recover what was in an artist's mind at the time of composition, a work of art must necessarily be considered on its own terms – did little to slow such reading of Swift's works. Student readers still regularly interchange Swift for Gulliver in their discussion of the *Travels*, even as they recognize that Gulliver is a character Swift has created. And professional readers become more nuanced, often discovering places in Swift's fiction where Swift dropped his fictional cover and revealed his "true" position, in effect making Swift's fictions elaborate illustrations of, or disguises for, more straightforward religious, political, or philosophical ideas.

Our contemporary term *Swiftian* means funny, dark, cruel, unsavory, insightful, revealing, mean, biting, ironic, difficult, brilliant. A *Swiftian* work should leave you exhilarated and aghast at the same time. You have been moved to look at the world or yourself in some new and unexpected way, but, rather than new horizons, you have discovered some new shocking depth to your own sense of reality. The challenge of reading Swift's work is first, and maybe last, to our own assumptions. If we can say the creator of some darkly humorous film or of *A Modest Proposal* is "sick," or "warped," or if we are able to employ a label from our arsenal of terms for mental illness – the satirist is obsessed, or fixated, paranoid, or a sociopath – we add a layer of defense between us and works we find disturbingly engaging. In this chapter I will try to demonstrate how the conflation of satiric author and satiric work is a way into the unsettling insights of the texts, rather than a means of defense, or distance or domestication. Satirist and satiric narrator are in relation as actual readers are in relation to fictional readers figured in the satires, the argument being that, properly read, the most *Swiftian* of satiric characteristics is when a work allows no one, neither satirist nor reader, a safe place beyond the often violent implications of the satire.

It must be acknowledged that Swift criticism is replete with reflections on the difficulties of reading Swift's works. It is almost ritualistic in the criticism to point out that Swift mocked critical enterprises analogous in discomforting ways to nearly every professional reading of his work. While critics may be motivated in such reflections by humility and respect, observations on the difficulty and indeterminacy of elucidating Swift's satires can be intimidating to those new to the critical study of Swift's work. But both new and long-time students of Swift do well to remember that critics, at their best, open paths to great works of art, that many paths may lead to the same destination, and that the work, to the extent that it is great, will not ultimately be contained by our attempts to map it. Above all, a reader new to the serious study of Swift's work will do well to recognize that Swift himself was extremely playful: he loved puns and pranks, mocked himself, his loved ones, and his benefactors, usually in rhyme, throughout his life, and his signature character, Gulliver, is one that the vast majority of readers are first introduced to as children's play. This invitation to set aside critical intimidation and start playing must come with a typically *Swiftian* caveat: as he said, "Most kinds of diversion in men, children, and other animals, are an imitation of fighting."

Swift wrote a wide variety of satiric works; in fact, a satiric vein runs throughout most of Swift's writing, including even the intimate, such as the poems Swift composed for Stella (Esther Johnson) each year on her birthday. Much can be learned about satire from studying all the forms Swift employed, but it will be challenge enough in the limited space of this chapter to identify common characteristics of satire in Swift's major works. His best known, *The Travels into Several Remote Nations*

(1726), now commonly referred to as *Gulliver's Travels*, is a work that draws upon a hugely popular form at the time, the travel account, as well as techniques associated with the novel, emerging at the time in its English form. It is the work's narrative characteristics — much of it can be read as a fabulous adventure story — that account for its continuing popular success. The next best known of Swift's works is *A Modest Proposal*. Often anthologized and unforgettable, it is among the greatest short masterpieces in the English language. After these two works, a general audience knows of other works by Swift by accidents of education or special interest: a student learns of a poem by Swift for a standardized test, or a student of Irish history discovers Swift's many works written in the Irish interest. Strikingly, a work that many critics consider Swift's most impressive, *A Tale of a Tub* (1704), is largely unknown to a general audience. Here, I will focus at some length on *A Modest Proposal* to identify characteristics of Swift's satire that will be useful to readings of the popular *Travels* as well as to the brilliant but difficult *Tale*.

A Modest Proposal

Swift's last great satire, *A Modest Proposal*, is not only an accessible work, it is an object lesson in how satire works. The *Proposal* is a pamphlet, purportedly by a projector — a scientifically minded person interested in progress — offering a solution to the effects of rampant poverty in Ireland. The projector enumerates the problem, particularly in terms of population, and then uses the high birth rate as a central factor in his proposed solution. Much of the rest of the short pamphlet is a defense against various objections that might be raised to the proposal. The twist in this otherwise apparently reasonable tract is that the proposal is to raise, slaughter, and cannibalize Irish infants to improve the economy and reduce the population.

Some of the features that I will identify in discussing the *Proposal* that will be useful for discussing the *Travels* and *A Tale* are as follows. The satire is created within a specific historical context. The satire approaches the reality of the context as discourse, usually positioning itself at or just beyond the limits of the historical discourse, often extending the rhetoric in a way that calls into question the stability and even the reality of the non-fictional discourse. Swift's prose satires feature central characters who are only knowable to readers from what can be gleaned or inferred from their first-person testimonials. These characters seem always to be drawn in some sense from some composite of the biographical author and — we infer this from negotiating the irony of the satires — from all that he reviles. These first-person speakers establish relationships in the texts with readers they imagine. Swift's speakers in the *Proposal*, the *Travels*, and *A Tale*, each reveal himself, by avowal or inadvertently, to be mad, and the relationships these speakers establish with their readers, provide the basis for haunting satiric challenges to the sanity of readers.

I will always remember the reaction of a first-year college student to reading the *Proposal*. He observed, with what appeared a guarded admiration, that "in those days, when they had a problem, they didn't pussy-foot around." He had reasoned that the harsh times of the early eighteenth century meant people were open to addressing problems in ways we (more recent readers) would find unacceptable. In other words, he assumed the *Proposal* was a straightforward document in the debate of the issues of its historical moment. His more sophisticated classmates – those who knew to equate Swift's name with satire – laughed at this student's failure to negotiate irony and felt themselves in-the-know with the professor and, ultimately, with the great satirist. Ironically, this student was in one very important sense closer to the meaning of the *Proposal* than were his classmates who ridiculed him for thinking the work was "serious."

Those who are introduced to Swift's *Proposal* together with related documents of the period, as in *The Longman Anthology of British Literature*, recognize that Swift's piece is an extension of the discourse on the Irish situation of his time rather than a wicked fantasy concocted for shock value. In fact, readers of William Petty's *Political Arithmetic* (1691), a foundational work in the history of modern economics, recognize that proposals for dealing with Irish "savages" in systemic and inhumane ways had been part of the discourse among the English and the Anglo-Irish for nearly half a century when the *Modest Proposal* appeared. For example, one of the shocking aspects of Swift's *Proposal* is the way in which his speaker dispassionately tallies the number of Irish people to estimate the number of women who "are breeders" and so to figure how many children will be available for his scheme (*Prose Works* 12.110). In *Political Arithmetic*, Petty had systematically counted the Irish with a particular focus on the numbers of "teeming women," the percentage of those who were married, and the birth rate ("a child every two years and a half") in connection with his own scheme for removing most of the Irish from Ireland (Sherman 1999: 2458). Read in its historical context, the humor of Swift's *Proposal* is created out of the stuff of a non-fictional discourse well known to his readers, a discourse that had deadly serious consequences for the Irish of Swift's day. The outrageousness of the *Proposal* is arresting, immediate, and easy to spot, but one important step in understanding this work, and each of Swift's major satires, is recognizing the relationships between the satiric discourse and the historical discourse in which it participates.

Reading the satire in its historical context is a step to understanding rather than a key to it. Swift's satires, like other important works of literature, are made of the stuff of the author's world but manage to speak to readers in their often distant places and times. The native Irish were subjects of a political discourse in which they were regularly figured as sub-human. This rhetoric allowed political decisions that systematically stripped the Irish of even the basic means of subsistence. The closest thing to a key to Swift's *Proposal* is recognizing that it is, in context, modest. That is, in relation to a system in which poverty, and consequent indigence, disease, starvation, and unlawfulness are the givens, the proposal to organize the "savages" on a model of animal husbandry is a logical, even a measured, next step. The human taboo against cannibalism makes the proposal shocking to readers of any time or place, but Swift's proposal is built on the idea that the taboo has been rendered largely meaningless in practice. In rhetoric and in political and economic practice, the native Irish have already been reduced to sub-human status. This proposal is modest in that it merely aims to acknowledge, clean up, and organize what we might describe, with a Swiftian phrase of our own time, the facts on the ground.

Discussion of *A Modest Proposal* invariably considers the speaker's claim that the slaughtered Irish infants will be food "very *proper for Landlords*; who, as they have already devoured most of the Parents, seem to have the best Title to the Children" (*Prose Works* 12.112). Critics have called the technique Swift uses here, literalizing the metaphor. Thinking through the common metaphoric description of landlords devouring their tenants, the satirist develops a proposal for systematic cannibalism. A less strict understanding of the critical term applies to the work as a whole. The relentless description of the Irish as "savages" gives rise to a proposal in which the ultimate marker of savagery, that is, cannibalism, will be used to domesticate (hence, civilize) the Irish. Swift's satire, and presumably all satire, is fundamentally rhetorical. The clichéd hyperbole of a landlord devouring his tenants is re-energized, not only by the image of the landlord being served a steaming dish of freshly carved infant flesh but by the argument in the *Proposal* that the suffering of the tenants is such that they would embrace the cannibalistic solution over the unbearable, morbid economic trap they find themselves in. Similarly, the *Proposal* exposes the way in which the epithet "savages" has allowed the ascendant class to treat the native Irish as sub-human without actually making them non-human: no one will really be comfortable eating the flesh of these beings who have in every other respect been treated worse than animals. The work then reveals itself as satire at the level of rhetoric.

Everything I have said about the *Proposal* so far suggests a fairly clear line between monstrous English policies and the oppressed native Irish. One may further this reading by noticing that the metaphor of devouring is extended to the English nation as a whole: "*I could name a Country, which would be glad to eat up our whole Nation*" (*Prose Works* 12.117). But other aspects of the *Proposal* add unsettling complications to this simple Irish/English formulation. A passage that should receive at least as much attention as those concerning rapacious landlords is the following: "As to our City of *Dublin*, Shambles may be appointed for this Purpose in the most convenient Parts of it; and Butchers we may be assured will not be wanting; although I rather recommend buying the Children alive and dressing them hot from the Knife, as we do *roasting Pigs*" (*Prose Works* 12.112–13). The shocking brutality of the end of this sentence can obscure what is at its center. The Irish will be the butchers of their own children. If the intent of this piece is to expose the way in which the English are oppressing the Irish, why would the satirist represent the Irish as willing participants in the dismemberment of their own children? Perhaps this says more about Swift's speaker than about the Irish themselves? This explanation might work if the speaker were English, but he tells us in a chillingly brilliant final paragraph that his own children are grown and his wife past childbearing so that he can in no way profit from his proposal. In other words, he confirms what is apparent throughout: he is Irish. His own children, were he to have any of appropriate age, could be subject to the terms of the *Proposal*. With the policies of the English a given, the Irish are imagined in the *Proposal* conceiving and executing their own final solution.

How to understand the role of the speaker is one of the great puzzles of this work and raises a question central to reading all of Swift's satire. First, it is clear that the speaker is in important respects a character invented for a particular role. The few biographical details he gives us – he is married and has had children – definitively distinguish him from the biographical Swift, who was, by all mainstream accounts, always unmarried and without offspring. But the impulse of readers to align Swift's characters with Swift himself goes beyond the simplistic inclination to line up any first-person narrator with the work's author. This impulse helps explain why, rather than referring to the Proposer, or the Hack of *A Tale of a Tub*, or Gulliver, as characters as we do when speaking of drama or novels, an important trend in Swift criticism has been to discuss how Swift speaks through a persona or mask. The term *persona* helped readers avoid the mistake of directly attributing the words of Swift's various speakers to Swift himself, formalizing the need for at least a double reading of the text.

Claude Rawson, one of the most important Swift critics of our time, has argued that persona criticism went too far, treating Swift's first-person speakers "as if they were autonomous creations analogous to the characters of a novel or play" (2000: 250). Rather than too far, it is my own sense that this is precisely the direction in which we as readers should head, acknowledging the usefulness of the term *persona* and leaving it behind. It makes sense to speak of a persona when Horace adopts a mask for part or all of a satire, but leaves the reader with little doubt about the author's moral point. The term is similarly useful in considering much of Swift's poetry, when, for example, in his Market Hill poems, he adopts a variety of masks but never leaves the reader with any doubt about his esteem for his hosts. In the major satires, including *A Modest Proposal*, the characters Swift creates are too complex to be called masks.

A part of the critical inclination to call Swift's characters masks is the recognition that Swift's speakers seem, in sometimes disturbing ways, to be drawn from Swift's own life. Swift's speaker in *A Modest Proposal* is a Dubliner, is evidently highly educated, clearly distinguishes himself from the native, largely Roman Catholic, population, has a clear sense of responsibility about the social ills that plague Ireland, despises absentee landlords, blames the English for unjust policies, implicates the Irish as participants in their own degradation, is one who has thought at length about the economic underpinnings of the Irish situation, and who has made various proposals for improvement that have been ignored, and, not least, is a writer with a clear and direct style who is able to draw visually arresting images with his words. Each of these things can be said of both the speaker and of Swift himself. (For a discussion of Swift's proposals, see Ferguson 1995.)

That we can draw correspondences between a character and its creator should not in itself lead us to conclude that the character is a mask for the author. In fact, many of the richest characters in fiction and drama have just such correspondences. Here, I am not thinking of thinly disguised autobiographical novels, but of complex links, which we could invoke from the usual sources when discussing Swift – Sterne, Joyce,

Beckett, Roth — but which I will illustrate by invoking that moment when a reader notices that Milton's Satan is using the revolutionary vocabulary against God that Milton himself had employed in his political writings against the monarchy. In a manner not wholly dissimilar to Milton's relationship with his Satan, Swift has created a character he disdains — Swift is not endorsing stewing Irish children any more than Milton is advocating war against God — and yet who, largely because he is created out of the predicament Swift lived everyday, is anything but a mask that can be lifted to reveal some clear moral truth.

Just as we will go on debating the meaning of Milton's representation of Satan, so Swift's Satan — a systematizer of human slaughter — is not reducible to a technique that can be figured out and fixed. Just as we are certain Milton would have us contemplate his Satan in the context of timeless human questions about good and evil, so Swift has given us a character born of the horrifying ironies of Swift's own life and times, and embodying an evil arguably more terrifying than the intentional evil of ego-wounded Lucifer. Swift's monster is a man convinced of his own good intentions, empowered by a scientific (economics) vocabulary and logic that allows him to think of human beings and human lives as so many numbers that can be arranged and figured. One benefit of his program that the speaker twice points to is that it would greatly lessen "the Number of *Papists* among us" (*Prose Works* 12.112), advocating what we would now term ethnic cleansing. If Swift had chosen a strawman for his speaker — an English visitor, for example, who offered the same solution to Ireland's ills — much of our reading so far would remain the same and the condemnation of the English might be even more explicitly drawn. But by creating his speaker out of his own endlessly frustrating engagement with poverty — economic, political, and cultural — in Ireland, Swift managed, not only to represent his sense of the complexities of the English/Irish situation, but to imagine a time when evil would come packaged, not as Satan or Iago, villains, however tortured, of choice, but as an enlightened program of human advancement. Satan, for many in the contemporary world, has become a philosophical abstraction — a metaphor, but monsters who advocate genocidal "solutions," often in the name of advancing civilization, often following efficient economic models, are anything but an abstraction.

Ultimately more important than the historical and biographical context of *A Modest Proposal* is the relationship between the satire and the reader. The thing that makes the *Proposal* a work of unending interest to readers is not what it says about Ireland and England in the eighteenth century, but what it says about a reader's own world. One necessarily enters the world of the *Modest Proposal* with the somewhat pompous but sympathetic speaker. He decries the poverty and suffering he sees, and believes that society should reward whoever (himself, of course) can correct the situation. Rather than wallowing in the sentimental, the speaker shows his attractive modernism by undertaking an accounting of the situation: images of the poor beggar mother with her brood give way swiftly to population figures and estimates of necessary resources. This is so universally the approach to social and economic ills in modern cultures that it is hard to imagine the reader who would not travel alongside the speaker, despite his quirks, right up to the point where he reveals his scheme. Moving then as quickly as possible from the speaker, readers will move to a place of solidarity with the poor Irish victims.

An historical approach can leave some readers stuck at this point, but the reader who continues to travel through the work finds that this, too, is an untenable position either because the suffering is unimaginable or because the vile charge of complicity – butchers will not be wanting – rings true in a way that cannot be countenanced. At the point a reader realizes his or her distance, however much abstract sympathy is retained for the victims, the experience of *A Modest Proposal* actually becomes more uncomfortable. For each of us lives in a world where economic and political suffering, including genocidal suffering, exists. Where in the template of the *Proposal* am I? Some of us will, miserably, find ourselves absentee landlords, individuals concerned with our own economic and social comfort with only passing involvement with the policies paid for by our taxes or the specific consequences of our investments. Where should I be? If the satire offers an answer, it must be to return us to the speaker, an individual concerned enough to crunch the numbers, put pen to paper, risk the calumny of critics of his work, and one whose efforts are not determined by his own financial interest. He is a monster to be sure, but a monster who, by comparison with everyone else on the satiric landscape, deserves the statue he asks for at the outset of his pamphlet.

Space here will not allow a full examination of each of Swift's major works, but a schematic look at *A Tale of a Tub* and the *Travels* will demonstrate how many of the features we have identified in *A Modest Proposal* are constants of Swift's satire.

A Tale of a Tub

While Swift's reputation today rests largely on his *Travels*, the work that put him in the center of the literary world of his day was *A Tale of a Tub*. Samuel Johnson, who was unimpressed with Gulliver, seemed to harbor some doubts that Swift was really the author of so great a work of genius as *A Tale*. Late in life, Swift himself commented on the genius of his early work with wonder. And though there has never been a poll, I suspect that among readers who have spent years studying Swift's works, few would disagree that, judged on the basis of dazzling literary brilliance, *A Tale* is Swift's greatest work. If this is so, why is *A Tale* not a work that every educated reader knows? The answer is rather straightforward and related to the first feature I have identified for reading Swift's satires. Like *A Modest Proposal*, *A Tale* is written in the context of an important historical discourse, one that, while infinitely fascinating, is also infinitely complex. Educated readers will recognize the historical moment broadly construed as the point in European intellectual history when traditional, primarily scripturally based learning was challenged by new methodological approaches, particularly those associated with what was referred to at the time as the New Philosophy, and which we now call the New Science, or just science. The problem is that even those who know this intellectual history well can be flummoxed by Swift's *Tale*, which is told by an avowed madman, and which pits theologies against theologies, supposedly rational discourses against representations of reason, and in which the only triumphant value (at a surface level) is madness itself.

In 1610, John Donne could already write that "New Philosophy calls all in doubt," and this was before the full impact of Descartes, or Bacon, Hobbes, Spinoza, Locke, Boyle, Newton, and the Puritan Revolution, each of which, together with Luther, Calvin, and the Reformation and Counter-Reformation generally, play important roles in the context of *A Tale*. Indeed, Swift seems to have somehow taken in and madly re-presented the intellectual world of late seventeenth-century Europe, and, as if this were not complex enough, he does so often via the voices, not directly of the great figures themselves but of what might be called, in the language of the *Tale*, their lackeys. These lackeys include not only hack writers like the *Tale*'s speaker, who need to absorb enough of the intellectual zeitgeist to ensure their works will sell, but also include figures like William Wotton and Richard Bentley, contemporaries and arguably rivals of Swift. Surely not hack writers, these men were respectable Anglican intellectuals, who were working to translate the difficult and often distant ideas associated with the Royal Society, England's most important scientific institution, into what they clearly expected would become the intellectual mainstream. It is some measure of the complexity of the background of *A Tale* that it figures a world in which science and religion, far from being at war with one another, are merging into a single messianic phenomenon. Wotton and Bentley are represented as lackeys, working to turn the "divine" work of great men like Isaac Newton and Robert Boyle into a doctrine that transforms the New Philosophy into – what Wotton is singled out in *A Tale* as particularly qualified to establish – a "new Religion" (Swift 1958: 169).

Rather than further emphasizing the contextual complexities of *A Tale*, I would observe that the *Tale* is approachable by the satiric pattern I have outlined from *A Modest Proposal*. Recognizing that the text is written in the context of great European revolutions, in politics, in religion, and in learning, a reader will note that the center of the speaker's treatise is a doctrine of revolutions. The seemingly limitless historical context of *A Tale* is, at least ostensibly, organized by the speaker himself, who clearly – in fact, as clear as anything in *A Tale* – assigns himself the role of tracing the etiology of revolutions in human culture. As in *A Modest Proposal*, *A Tale* features a first-person narrator who is mad – in this case avowedly so and proud of it. The case for connecting the speaker with Swift rests not on specific biographical details, but on the fact that Swift was so successful in inhabiting the discourse he parodied that his work was mistaken as the most notorious of a genre of scandalous texts that appeared after the Licensing Act had been allowed to lapse in 1695 (see Boyle 2000: 149–52). Just as Swift is able to extend the discourse of projects for reform of the Irish situation to the breaking point because he knew the discourse so well, so with *A Tale*, Swift was able to take the frenzied freethinking discourse of his time to a place where it explicitly trumpeted its own madness while being mistaken, at least by some important readers, as a discourse in, rather than against, the genre it parodied.

We think generally of parody in terms of specific and identifiable subjects. (For a discussion of parody across Swift's satires, see Suarez 2003: 116–27.) The view that *A Tale* may parody a pantheon of major thinkers from Descartes to Newton, as well as, perhaps, dozens of lesser lights, with no one from either group holding the stage exclusively for long, challenges conventional notions of parody. The multiplicity of potential parodic targets can make it difficult to discuss specific instances of caricature. Hobbes and his *Leviathan* are invoked by name in the *Tale*, and various Hobbesian concepts can be found throughout the text. But when the *Leviathan* is mentioned, it is in the context of the "Grandees" of church and state appropriating the metaphor of "the tub" from whaling to divert the effects of the *Leviathan* (Swift 1958: 39–41). Who is being caricatured? Hobbes, for his own use of the biblical metaphor? The leaders of church and state, for taking to water with Hobbes in an attempt to divert and co-opt the dangerous forces unleashed by the *Leviathan*? Or the "unquiet Spirits" who are either the dangerous followers of Hobbes or, if adequately paid by the established powers, as the Hack claims to be, instruments of the status quo? The obvious answer – that *A Tale* puts all of these things in satiric play – helps to illustrate why at least conventional uses of the term *parody* rarely describe what happens in Swift's major satires.

Rather than caricature, Swift more often draws his satiric figures such that they resemble, not an exaggerated version of themselves, but a version of their antithesis, of the thing they have most defined themselves against. So in the present instance, the figures of church and state are represented commissioning the scandalous text, *A Tale*, for their own Hobbesian ends; the unquiet spirits are represented as revolutionary in direct relation to their financial self-interest; and the great authoritarian, Hobbes, is shown as an unwitting instrument of a kind of economic democracy where power is maintained through the skillful use of capital. Just as *A Modest Proposal* draws the sympathetic modern reformer as the most savage of human destroyers, so *A Tale* is replete with figures who end up as the image of their supposed opposite. If this is parody, it is a kind of Derridean parody, by which Swift's satires collapse identity, so that the satiric target becomes, as in the ultimate classical tragedy, *Oedipus*, the one thing you are most sure you are not, the one thing you have most defined yourself against.

What is said for the figures in the satiric text may ultimately be the position of the reader. Unlike *A Modest Proposal*, where a reader may quickly run out of textual refuges and so be forced into an examination of individual correspondences with the text, *A Tale* is a universe in which a reader may choose never to stop seeking new satiric frontiers. But, all seeking in *A Tale* leads to intellectual precipices. The experience of making almost any positivist argument in reading *A Tale* leads a reader to a place like that of a cartoon character who is running for a time on air before consciousness of the absurdity of the position sends him hurtling into the abyss. While such moments might occur at almost any moment in a reader's contemplation of the text, they are in effect staged in *A Tale* and in the *Travels* when Swift's speakers turn to address the reader directly.

Direct address of the reader happens at key moments throughout *A Tale*, from the end of the preface to the final paragraphs, figuring the text as an extended conversation between the Hack and a reader. Here we can instance the address of the reader at the end of the "Digression on Madness," where the Hack does not so much admit as claim that he himself belongs in the pantheon of madmen he has been discussing:

> I my self, the Author of these momentous Truths, am a Person whose Imaginations are hard-mouth'd, and exceedingly disposed to run away with his Reason, which I have observed from long Experience to be a very light Rider, and easily shook off... which, perhaps the gentle, courteous, and candid Reader, brimful of that *Modern* Charity and Tenderness usually annexed to his Office, will be very hardly persuaded to believe. (Swift 1958: 180)

Just as the satiric follow-through in *A Modest Proposal* figures the reader as one whose concern at the end of the proposal will be economic, the modern reader at the end of this digression is one who is figured as so convinced of the clear sense of the Hack's many demonstrations of his theory of madness that he will be reluctant to accept the Hack's avowal of madness.

On an immediate level, neither of these representations of the reader is true. No reader, I think, reaches the end of the *Proposal* concerned about corrupt financial motives behind this reasonable scheme, and no reader of the digression will need much persuasion that the Hack is mad. But the satiric figuring of the reader defies the reader to deny the truth of the apparently false constructions. In the intellectual world of the Hack's system of vapors, men whose madness should be apparent from the grandiosity of their "universal" systems become the deities of the modern "Empire of Reason" (Swift 1958: 167). Descartes learns in a dream of his destiny to set all human knowledge on a new course, one in which certainty is built on doubt about all things. Newton offers no less than a "System of the World," acknowledging in the preface to the *Principia* (1687) that he hopes his mechanical explanation may serve not only in demonstrations of the existence of God, but also to explain all "the rest of the phenomena of Nature." In short, the reader at the end of the "Digression on Madness" is positioned as one who so regularly accepts universal systems from men who could easily be accounted mad that he has little standing to dismiss the theory of madness by an avowed madman. That the meta-theory the Hack offers is a system of the mind – a psychology – derived from the study of types of madness that he traces to sexual desire and anal fixation will give pause to any reader inclined to dismiss lightly the Hack's representation of the predispositions of candid modern readers.

Gulliver's Travels

As with *A Tale*, *The Travels into Several Remote Nations* offers open-ended possibilities for the study of contexts. Because much of the satire, particularly of the first two voyages, is political, readers have regularly traced analogies between the text and the politics of Swift's historical period. With rare exception, however, tracing these analogies much beyond the notes in a good edition creates myopic readings in which the local and temporal possibilities of the text obscure the remarkable portrayal of political cultures that might be found at almost any time or in any place. One discourse in which the *Travels* participates (and that has received a good deal of critical attention but may never receive enough) is that of travel itself. Because Europe was still "discovering" parts of the world, because travel accounts were increasingly important to commercial and political interests, and because travel narratives were often entertaining as they employed techniques of narration that would become the tools of modern novelists, the literature of travel became the popular literature of the early modern period. The overlapping of prose fiction and travel narratives can be traced to ancient times, but in the decade before Swift's *Travels* stands the startlingly successful example of Defoe's *Robinson Crusoe*. Just as the *Modest Proposal* participated in the discourse on Ireland as a colonial project, and *A Tale* participated in the revolutionary thinking of modern freethinkers, so the *Travels* must be understood in the context of the discourse of travel and discovery. Lemuel Gulliver travels via modern metaphors of discovery through realms political, scientific, and philosophical, all the while unwittingly reprising the figure of modern travelers in one of Swift's earliest poems, who

> [search] contentedly the whole world round,
> To make some great discovery,
>   And scorn it when 'tis found.
>   ("Ode to the Athenian Society," 142–4)

The novelistic realism that makes Gulliver such a success with readers at all levels disguises the nearly allegorical features of Gulliver's biography. The reader who carefully works with the few dates Gulliver provides will note that Gulliver is born in 1660, the year of the Restoration of Charles II, and he sets sail on the voyages he recounts in the *Travels* in 1699 on the eve of the eighteenth century. In the intervening years he is buffeted by the changing "fortunes" of a world in transition. (For a full chronology, see Boyle 2000: 29–31.) Reverses in his father's "fortune" force Lemuel to leave off studies at Emmanuel College, Cambridge, where he would have been trained for the clergy, and take up medical training as an apprentice to a surgeon, all the while applying himself to "learning Navigation, and Other parts of the Mathematics" because he "always believed it would be some time or other my Fortune" to travel (*Prose Works* 11.19). As fortune would have it, Gulliver is also able to continue his medical studies at the University at Leiden, which was recognized in the 1680s, when Gulliver is in attendance, as "the undisputed center – in our modern sense – for the study of the *sciences of man*: not merely man medically considered, but man in his crucial posture as an anatomical, physiological, and chemical animal" (Rousseau 1989: 199). While each of these details of Gulliver's biography adds to the novelistic realism of the account, they also signal Gulliver's role as a representative modern.

Born in a sense out of the compromises that ended the Puritan revolution, Gulliver is driven by fortune, which pointedly comes to mean money, from the traditions of landed wealth and religious training to the secular, specifically scientific and mechanistic, study of man and to the historical and symbolic opposite of landed wealth, to a fortune dependent on travel into remote nations. At the outset of his *Travels*, Gulliver sets sail into the eighteenth century because he is a character created to embody a man embarking on the modern world.

Commentators have often noted Gulliver's lack of interest in religion, and some have attributed this to Swift having been chastised for his history of Christianity in *A Tale of a Tub*. In fact, Gulliver is nothing if not a messianic traveler. His utopian expectations in his travels seem to increase with successive disappointments (discoveries scorned when found) until the ultimate disappointment for a traveling physician – as even immortality (among the Struldbrugs) offers no cure for the human condition – gives way to a mad determination to find utopia even if it means humanity itself must be exterminated to obtain it. That Gulliver expects his travel account will reform all human vices within six months of publication underscores the sense in which he sees his text as announcing a doctrine with transformative powers beyond any known sacred text. Gulliver is the representative modern traveler who has left behind the religious messianism of the Puritans (its capital in the Leiden of *A Tale*'s mad Jack Calvin) only unknowingly to rediscover it in the ostensibly secular enterprise (centered again in Leiden) of the new science of man.

Like Gulliver, Swift was born into the Restoration, dependent on the generosity of relatives to finance his education, and introduced (at Trinity College Dublin, not Leiden) to new rational and scientific methodologies. Unlike Gulliver, Swift pursued his Masters of Divinity and made his living in the church, but Swift seems to have followed this course only after having failed to be set on a secular career by his benefactor, Sir William Temple. I am being only partially facetious in pointing out that Swift, like Gulliver, is best known for a book of travel into several remote nations, and there is no denying that many of the political features of the nations Gulliver "discovers" are observable in political worlds in which Swift spent much of his life as a participant. The point of drawing these forced correspondences is not to suggest that Gulliver is modeled on Swift, but that Gulliver, like Swift's other first-person narrators, is a character created very much out of Swift's own world and, as such, able to represent the complexities of that world.

The large concerns of the *Travels* are reinforced at every turn by the implication of the reader being in untenable situations analogous to those we have observed in *A Modest Proposal* and *A Tale*. In this most novelistic of Swift's satires, readers are able to travel along for a while, imagining themselves in the wondrous, trying, often terrifying, predicaments of Gulliver's adventure. Read as a novel, the *Travels* seems satiric because Gulliver so often ends up in ridiculous and embarrassing situations, and because the work is populated by bad institutions, individuals, and ideas, and the good that Gulliver encounters is most often misunderstood or disparaged by him or those in charge of the cultures he visits. But it is the relationship between fictional author and fictional reader – the reader figured by direct address – that moves an actual reader from novelistic identification to satiric mortification. A reader may identify with Gulliver pinned down on the beach, may feel the slight weight of Lilliputian bodies on his torso, and may be thrilled to have found a way to communicate peacefully with the people of this diminutive nation. Though not what we generally expect from an adventure story, Gulliver's relation of the circumstances of urinating for the first time in Lilliput passes as a humorous and realistic detail. But when Gulliver launches into a vigorous defense of the circumstances of first defecating in Lilliput, the reader is not, I think, crouching with Gulliver at the full length of his chain, but looking on reluctantly from a distance.

Gulliver seems to understand this, appealing to "the candid Reader" for "some allowance, after he hath maturely and impartially considered my Case." When Gulliver tells us he is dwelling "so long" on these circumstances to answer "some of my Maligners" who have questioned his character "in Point of Cleanliness," the distance from which many a reader has observed him is clinical: Gulliver – and often the diagnosis is extended to Swift – has a fixation on his bodily excretions and is paranoid. But the satire has here taken the reader to a place of identification beyond what even the novel might effect. Maturely and impartially considered, each reader lives, along with Gulliver, "between Urgency and Shame," as the necessities of our bodies are in tension with idealized (cleanly) images of self. And no small part of this tension is a conversation in our heads (Aristotle calls shame the "imagination of a disgrace") with maligners who would take note of the unpleasant effects of our bodily excretions. While a novelistic rendering of this episode (but when do people defecate in "realistic" novels?) would invite sympathetic identification with Gulliver's embarrassment, the satire uses the direct address of the reader to provoke identification with Gulliver's defensiveness. We work to distance ourselves from Gulliver as he works to distance himself from his bodily exigencies. But maturely and impartially considered, these circumstances that "at first Sight may appear not very momentous" are no less momentous in our daily constructions of self than is Gulliver's "uneasy Load" monumentally "disburthened" in the Lilliputian context (*Prose Works* 11.29; for a discussion of Swift's satire and the novel, see Seidel 1996; for further readings of the defecation scene in Lilliput, see Rawson 1973 and Boyle 2000: 31–4).

Swift's Reader

One cannot work successfully with Swift's satire without getting dirty. Like Gulliver's attempt to demonstrate his prowess in Brobdingnag by vaulting cow dung, a successful engagement with the satires can be one that leaves the reader "filthily bemired" (*Prose Works* 11.124). This is one important aspect of the pattern of the major satires that creates a discourse with reality, and particularly the parts of reality that we are conditioned to avoid contemplating. The historical and biographical features are hurdles for new readers, who need to know enough to be able to see that the satires participate in a context that has passed as reality. The historical and biographical can be traps for those who know the most about Swift and his works, invitations to historicize and so localize satiric assaults to the context they draw upon. Swift's first-person narrators are characters, not masks, developed out of the (nearly) imponderable ironies of lived experience – a young man of meager means born into a century of revolutions, political, religious, social, and philosophical, in which only ultimate designs and universal treatises have currency; a doctor, a student of man, who sets sail into an Enlightenment world governed by the expectation that man is an improvable animal, that some cure for a diseased world must be possible; an Anglo-Irish man with a conscience, who will craft a way forward out of a calculated assessment of the motivating interests of each side of his hyphenated identity.

Swift's characters are not drawn to be immediately mimetic – to give an impression of a particular life – but to engage or provoke a conversation, rather than an identification, with a reader usually figured as candid or gentle or impartial in the texts. This conversation itself is in a sense mimetic, an imitation of the thoughts each of us has in response to ironies of lived experience, but which we, like the characters we love in conventional novels, smooth out into orderly, cleanly narratives of self. The direct addresses to the reader in Swift's text invite us to demonstrate our superior, usually moral, prowess – I would never offer the king of Brobdingnag the formula for gunpowder as Gulliver does – only to leave us intellectually bemired, when we realize that even the most absurd propositions of Swift's speakers – happiness is the perpetual possession of being well deceived; or, systematically cannibalizing Irish infants will be good for the Irish – are more intellectually coherent, more true to the deep ironies of reality, than are our usual positions, crafted out of denials of the body, denials of self-interest, denials of the overwhelming evidence that humans are more fundamentally Yahoos than Houyhnhnms.

When we call the work of a contemporary artist *Swiftian*, we signal surpassing satiric achievement and something else, something that, like infant flesh, will not go down easily, will never be swallowed whole. We have reason to look askance at people who want to dwell on things that the rest of us are invested in deeming "not very momentous," who make their art out of a recognition of the ironies of lived experience, and who make us laugh as much from discomfort as surprise. It might make a Swift critic sound important to say the model of satire that Swift offers is inimitable, that no later satirist deserves the encomium. But whatever self-evident truth there may be to that claim, the emphasis here is very nearly the opposite. Each of us as reader is invited to participate in the production of Swift's satire – for they are designed for such participation. The truths they produce are neither universal nor sacred, but rigorously contingent – the truths that we come to when the satire has led us to recognize through the laughter that our greatest hopes and achievements, as well as our most deeply criminal designs, are mediated by this and every mortal moment of experience, lived between urgency and shame.

References and Further Reading

Boyle, Frank T. (2000) *Swift as Nemesis: Modernity and its Satirist*. Stanford: Stanford University Press.

Craven, Kenneth (1992) *Jonathan Swift and the Millennium of Madness*. Leiden: Brill.

Ehrenpreis, Irvin (1962–83) *Swift: The Man, his Work, and the Age*. Vol. 1: *Mr Swift and his Contemporaries* (1962); Vol. 2: *Dr Swift* (1967); Vol. 3: *Dean Swift* (1983). London: Methuen.

Elliott, Robert C. (1982) *The Literary Persona*. Chicago: University of Chicago Press.

Ferguson, Oliver W. (1995) The last proposals. In Claude Rawson (ed.), *Jonathan Swift: A Collection of Critical Essays*, pp. 280–90. Englewood Cliffs, NJ: Prentice Hall.

Rawson, Claude (1973) *Gulliver and the Gentle Reader: Studies in Swift and our Time*. London: Routledge.

——(2000) Jonathan Swift, *A Tale of a Tub*. In David Womersley (ed.), *A Companion to Literature from Milton to Blake*, pp. 244–52. Oxford: Blackwell.

——(2002) *God, Gulliver and Genocide: Barbarism and the European Imagination, 1492–1945*. Oxford: Oxford University Press.

Rosenheim, Edward W. (1963) *Swift and the Satirist's Art*. Chicago: University of Chicago Press.

Rousseau, G. S. (1989) Science and medicine at Leiden. In Robert Maccubbin and Martha Hamilton-Phillips (eds), *The Age of William III and Mary II*, pp. 198–201. Williamsburg: The College of William and Mary.

Seidel, Michael (1996) *Gulliver's Travels* and the contracts of fiction. In John Richetti (ed.), *The Cambridge Companion to the Eighteenth Century Novel*, pp. 72–89. Cambridge: Cambridge University Press.

Sherman, Stuart (ed.) (1999) The Restoration and the eighteenth century. In David Damrosch (ed.), *The Longman Anthology of British Literature*, vol. 1, pp. 1979–2874. New York: Longman.

Suarez SJ, Michael (2003) Swift's satire and parody. In Christopher Fox (ed.), *The Cambridge Companion to Jonathan Swift*, pp. 112–27. Cambridge: Cambridge University Press.

Swift, Jonathan (1939–74) *Prose Works*, 16 vols, ed. Herbert Davis et al. Oxford: Blackwell.

——(1958) *A Tale of a Tub*, ed. A. C. Guthkelch and D. Nichol Smith, 2nd edn. Oxford: Clarendon Press.

——(1983) *Complete Poems*, ed. Pat Rogers. New Haven, CT: Yale University Press.

12
Pope and Augustan Verse Satire
Ruben Quintero

An Augustan Age

By the end of the seventeenth century, English satire has rooted itself as a native tradition. Authors of the next fifty years, publishing from Samuel Garth's *The Dispensary* (1699–1718) to Samuel Johnson's "The Vanity of Human Wishes" (1749), create another Augustan Age, for this period rivals imperial Rome in its elevation of satiric poetry into a national idiom. Almost every poet of the period seems to have written something satirical, and as Clark Lecturer James Sutherland once said, "By the middle of the eighteenth century satire had become a literary habit" (1958: 68). Published anonymously or pseudonymously, satire, from squib to cosmic mock epic, becomes a popular art of public redress. Its tone may vary from coarse and quibbling to high-minded and preachy. Its critical method may be dialectical, oppositional, or reductive. Whatever its form, satire weathers, shapes, and projects public ideals of civic virtue – the desired – by artistic inquiry and challenge, outrage and censure, or castigation of the undesirable. This rain of satiric discourse refracts for all to see an idealized but tested and tangible moral universe, as does the dream within the dream in Bunyan's *The Pilgrim's Progress* (1678). What becomes identifiably "Augustan" within this spectrum of satiric imagination is that alluring rainbow of attainable excellence perceived by a people with a heightening sense of national identification.

In this period, satire will range well beyond the rhetorical confinement of political and religious dogma. Earlier, in 1688, a powerful, reactionary, anti-Catholic alliance, comprised of formerly opposed ideological camps, had forced the departure of the Stuart king, James II, and placed on the throne Protestant monarchs, William III and Mary. In sum, the concerted determination of these otherwise quarrelsome Protestant factions to maintain a Protestant throne, a corollary loosening of governmental strictures against the more extreme Protestant dissenters, the more than symbolic Union of 1707 with Scotland that created "Great Britain," and the ever-pressing, costly sacrifices of the War of the Spanish Succession (1702–13) had shifted political interests closer to a common center and nourished an incipient nationalism. Moreover, following Queen Anne's death (1714), Whigs will control parliament for many years under the ministry of Robert Walpole (1721–42), yet will be kept nervous and vigilant by a tireless and vocal Tory opposition. A rhetorical result of these conditions will be that satirists will explore new subtleties in cautious masking and become more deliberately indirect and artful. And, when the speaker is a directly moralizing satirist, the poem will defensively assume a tone of apology or, as in the poetic epistles of Edward Young (1683–1765) or Alexander Pope (1688–1744), may feature on balance more praise of exemplary character, past or present, than the contrary censure of contemporary misconduct. Furthermore, satiric discourse, in both prose and poetry, generally will assume a high-minded critical role for its attentive readers, especially for middle-class readers consciously fashioning a social identity within a rapidly advancing metropolitan society cultivating new standards of taste.

This half-century, ruled by four monarchs (William III, Anne, and Georges I and II), lacks some fundamental components of the now mythic Augustan Age. There is no protective, overarching literary patron such as Caesar Augustus, nor is there a *Pax Romana*, an undistracted quiescence of empire, for England does have its wars and fearful invasions, and bustling, gritty mercantile London, though nearing 700,000 inhabitants and once called "Londinium Augusta," is really no majestic Rome. But for English literate culture, there is an Augustan shifting of gears, perhaps more conceptual than actual, for a modern print world has emerged. The sustentative patronage of book buyers will serve collectively as an author's modern Maecenas and foster individual talent of all sorts across classes. As had the ticket-buying audience in English theater for over a century, common readers will soon liberate writers from the selective and also the restrictive favors of wealthy peer patrons and will determine the fortune of authors. There is a market for poetry, especially for satire, and the professional writer will become a reality during this period, the premier example being Alexander Pope, a modern Horace in his poetic achievement, but one who earns and cherishes a financial and a political independence free of feudal patronage: "Oh let me live my own! and die so!" ("Epistle to Dr Arbuthnot," 1735, 261).

In retrospect, Pope could not have been born at a better time. In 1709, the year of Pope's first published poetry, "for the Encouragement of learned Men to write and compose useful books" parliament passes an act that will become the basis of modern copyright law (8 Anne cap. 19), establishing an author's right to intellectual property and engendering the profession of writing (or scribbling). A modern print culture is evolving rapidly with an eager readership, and a new cultural aristocracy will be ascending through publication, as wit and poetical talent become market commodities and verse satire thrives (Quintero 2001: 288–90). In the openly prosperous publishing world of an urbanized London, poverty for a writer equates to failure and lack of talent, though an ambitious as yet anonymous Samuel Johnson (1709–84) will challenge the circularity of this false social logic in his imitation of Juvenal's *Satire 3*:

> This mournful Truth is ev'ry where confest,
> *Slow rises Worth, by Poverty deprest*:
> But here more slow, where all are Slaves to Gold,
> Where Looks are Merchandise, and Smiles are sold,
> Where won by Bribes, by Flatteries implor'd,
> The Groom retails the Favours of his Lord.
> ("London," 1738, 176–81)

Though the ascent may be difficult, a person of humble origin with talent and some luck can make it in the metropolis and remain true to himself. With interested readers and market success, an individual writer can emerge from anonymity and achieve a liberating celebrity, as does Johnson.

Danger lurks in writing satire, as always, for there are legislated boundaries to what may be said. After the Restoration of 1660, chastised by a memory of bloody civil war, two decades of corrosive factionalism, and the traumatic regicide of Charles I (1649), England prefers reform to revolt. As one might expect, the volatile coupling of a zealous spirit of reformation with undeterred political or religious partisan interests further produces a great amount of satire, while a corollary governmental fear of political instability results in periodic institutional efforts to control dissent. Parliament seeks to prevent incendiary publication by passing the Licensing Act of 1662, a governmental censorship that will formally end in 1695. Regulation of imprints, another kind of official control but enforced after publication, will be established by an ordinance of the Stationers' Company (1681), and the financial restraints imposed by the Stamp Act of 1712 will further inhibit satiric voices during this period (Foxon 1991: 1ff). These laws, by requiring imprints on publications, can hold accountable for libel or seditious expression "publishers" (persons who sold books for booksellers), "booksellers" (like publishers of today, persons who often held copyright and managed the production of books), printers (persons who printed for booksellers or, in the case of Pope, sometimes for authors), and authors, if known. The satirist's art thus will remain a risky business of toeing the line of legality, as evident in these remarks by William Blackstone (1723–80) on "libels that disrupt the public peace," in his influential *Commentaries on the Laws of England* (1765–9):

> The liberty of the press is indeed essential to the nature of a free state: but this consists in laying no *previous* restraints upon publications, and not in freedom from censure for criminal matter when published. Every freeman has an undoubted right to say what sentiments he pleases before the public: to forbid this, is to destroy the freedom of the press: but if he publishes what is improper, mischievous, or illegal, he must take the consequence of his own temerity. (Book 4, ch. 11, s. 13)

Thus, beyond freedom from government censorship after 1695, when the Licensing Act lapses, there is no unrestricted freedom of expression. And, moreover, on the stage, censorship of plays in royal theaters will be instituted with the Licensing Act of 1737, a parliamentary statute pushed by first minister Robert Walpole, who was provoked by satiric attacks on the corruptions of his Whig administration, especially those made by Henry Fielding (1707–54) in his *Pasquin* (1736) and *The Historical Register for 1736* (1737). Fielding perforce abandons playwriting and turns his talents to prose fiction, but he remains a master satirist of other subjects, as seen in his anonymous *Shamela* (1741), a satiric travesty of Samuel Richardson's *Pamela, or Virtue Rewarded* (1740), which ridicules Richardson's first novel for treating virginity as a commodity for obtaining marriage. By recognizing how easily one might be accused of seditious libel during this time, we might increase our appreciation of the moral integrity and the personal courage of such commonly misunderstood political satirists as Daniel Defoe (1660–1731) and Jonathan Swift (1667–1745), who at personal peril used satire as a populist tool for challenging questionable political policies and promoting social justice.

Satire is a rhetorical art that must toy with convention and audience expectation for advantage, and, thereby, the early eighteenth century becomes an especially innovative time for satire in both prose and poetry, as satiric authors openly experiment within all genres for more effective ways to instruct savvy readers about folly and human nature. When normative values are not clearly understood, satiric art will be loud, divisive, and combative, for it is only upon accepted values that recognition of the ridiculous is premised. We cannot know what is absurd unless we know, or believe we know, what is, or would be, reasonable, and this period developed a firm sense of what it considered ethically reasonable. It is this common ground of perceived understanding that makes the eighteenth century one of the richest periods of satire in any language and allows for interesting and unexpected expansions of the generic envelope. In this chapter, I will focus selectively and, perforce, briefly on several works of period satirists in order to sketch out a few of the developments in satire. Key authors in verse satire are Samuel Garth (1661–1719), Daniel Defoe, Matthew Prior (1664–1721), Bernard Mandeville (c.1670–1733), Jonathan Swift, Edward Young, John Gay (1685–1732), and Alexander Pope. I will also discuss contributions of the Scriblerus Club, a group of authors who established an open bridge for innovation across poetry and prose. The satiric milieu of the period was catalytic for such talents. Pope, setting aside his collaborative works as a Scriblerian author, as a poet attains such a high-water mark in the quality and the scope of his verse satire that one may justifiably wonder if such individual achievement – and, with his contemporaries, such collective achievement – in satire will ever be repeated within another span of a half-century.

Verse satire, notwithstanding the death of Pope in 1744, will continue to thrive after mid-century and even into the first quarter of the nineteenth century, as seen, in the brilliantly wry works of George Crabbe (1754–1832) and George Gordon, Lord Byron (1788–1824). At the same time, novelists, such as Fielding and Tobias Smollett (1721–71), will generate a new satirical rhetoric by expropriating many literary strategies from traditional satiric poetry. Indeed, much of the finest satire that follows will be found nestled within the modern novel, a more accessible didactic vehicle, which will captivate and instruct a broader audience by requiring of its reader less classical learning than its poetical counterpart. The loose and baggy novel, which at its most banal invites propaganda and social polemic, at its best delivers its critique through masterful satire and allows for a new rhetoric, as seen in the second half of the century, through a more subjectively expressed admixture of satiric appeals, of pity alternating with indignation, for a new kind of reader – men and women of feeling.

The Scriblerus Club and Scriblerian Satire

In a literary period so unapologetically intertextual, inventive cross-fertilization occurs among authors not only within satiric poetry, but also across generic borders, and the Scriblerus Club is the greatest of such progenitive influences. The original aim of the club, first conceived by Pope and Swift as a collaborative project to produce a journal mocking false learning, which would be edited by an editorial dunce-persona Martinus Scriblerus, changed as "the group found itself embarked on a program not merely of ridiculing the follies of party writers, critics, editors, and commentators but of satirizing all follies among men of learning, whether philosophers or artists, antiquarians or travelers, teachers or poets, lawyers or dancing masters" (Kerby-Miller 1950: 29). Winnowed by Tory sympathies, the club's membership became Pope, Swift, Gay, the queen's physician Dr John Arbuthnot (1667–1735), the erudite and short-lived Irish poet Thomas Parnell (1679–1718), and the Tory minister Robert Harley, 1st Earl of Oxford (1661–1724), more of a political luminary and prospective patron in the club than authorial contributor. As a club, members met in London as often as they could in 1713 and 1714, but over the next decades after the death of Queen Anne, which ended the Tory administration and caused Arbuthnot and Harley to leave the capital city altogether, there was infrequent collaboration between members. For more about this remarkable assemblage of great wits, see Charles Kerby-Miller's *The Memoirs of the Extraordinary Life, Works, and Discoveries of Martinus Scriblerus* (1950), which provides, as much as scattered evidence permits, a background history of how the club came to be created, its activities, and those works historically linked to the club.

Scriblerian satire functions as a loose generic category. Arbuthnot, with Swift's private encouragement and usual "hints," had published the popular *John Bull* pamphlets (1712), satirizing the politics of the war with France through the risible personification of national characters. So effectively did he capture an archetypal caricature that Arbuthnot's forthright John Bull to this day functions as a national icon, similar to the bearded American counterpart of Uncle Sam. Though written before the club formed, because of its laughing chemistry, humanely comic (Arbuthnot) but also politically pointed (Swift), one is tempted to call the *John Bull* pamphlets "Scriblerian." In the decades after the club had formally dissolved, similarly collaborative writings and mutually inspired satiric creations will continue to be produced by original club authors and merit a place in the Scriblerian oeuvre. Thus, the Scriblerus Club has given us a name for a type of satire, but one that is not so easy to define outside a direct or a self-proclaimed association to the eponymous character Scriblerus or the individual Scriblerian authors. Calling to mind familiar generic features of Menippean, or Varronian, satire, Scriblerian satire often uses irony and parody within a generically mixed form or across genres to mock the "learned" fool but also attack many other subjects. As a shared multipurpose satiric vehicle associated by name, we are reminded of goliardic satire of the twelfth and thirteenth centuries, comprised of works separately composed by different anonymous authors under the same nom de plume of the fictional Bishop Golias.

Misunderstanding and ludicrous misinformation are regular fodder for Scriblerian satires. "The twisting of facts to suit one's own system or ends, the prideful display of knowledge for its own sake, the lack of charity, the anger and the pettiness," as Christopher Fox observes, "all are central motifs of the *'Polemical* Arts' in *The Memoirs of Martinus Scriblerus*," which stands as the mock-biographical centerpiece of the club (Fox 1988: 90). Beyond simply earmarking "authentic" Scriblerian works, the name "Scriblerian satire" may be instructively applied to other satiric works inscribed by them. For mockery of misdirected erudition or modernist positivism, Scriblerian satire will employ a liberating mask that can be many faces of folly – an ambitious and vain editor, a laughable or an irascible speaker, or a mentally unbalanced autobiographical author – all of whom are ironically transparent to the reader, as was the original Martinus Scriblerus.

Martinus Scriblerus' scholarly fascination with oddities and monstrosities, whether conceptual or concrete, is often the source of generic parody, absurd behavior, and the deflation of bathos. In *The Memoirs of Martinus Scriblerus* (1741), there are two biographically connected parodies that provide us with an illustration of this kind of Scriblerian satire (Kerby-Miller 1950: chs 14–15). The chapter episode entitled "The Double Mistress," probably composed in 1717, burlesques Scriblerus' love affair and taboo marriage to a Siamese twin in the melodramatic style of a tawdry heroic romance – in a style "*so singularly different from the rest, that it is hard to conceive by whom it was penn'd*" (Kerby-Miller 1950: 143). Scriblerus and a three-foot, raree-show "black prince" have each married one of the beautiful Siamese-twin sisters, Lindamira and Indamora, who, unfortunately for all, share only one set of loins and one pudendum. A mock-courtroom drama of hair-splitting legal arguments for and against the validity of each marriage ensues. The final result is a legal dissolution of both marriages, thus ending the high jinks. Prior to composing "The Double Mistress" episode of the *Memoirs*, in the farce *Three Hours after Marriage* (1717), Gay, with Arbuthnot and Pope, had created another absurd marriage, more recognizable as that of the foolish old-man lover (the *senex amans*) of Roman comedy but with a Scriblerian type of cuckold, Dr Fossile, a physician and an antiquarian pedant. Mechanically adhering to the three unities of neoclassical drama, the farce remains another satire on false learning and folly's wit, comprised of three acts of exaggerated language and action, with foolish cuckolding characters in various disguises, the zaniest being the grotesque costumes of a mummy and a crocodile/alligator.

Pope and Arbuthnot produce a poetical treatise for composing mediocre poetry in the wildly funny *Peri Bathous, or the Art of Sinking in Poetry* (1728), in which Scriblerus functions as a modernist persona in a parody of Longinus' classical treatise for achieving the lofty style of sublime poetry, *Peri hupsous* (*On the Sublime*; circa first century AD). The Greek word *hupsous* is ambivalent and can suggest the elevation of sublimity as well as the depth of profundity, but Scriblerus applies a confused metaphorical logic in advocating *bathos* or sinking in poetry as a form of profundity for a complementary appreciation of the neglected mass of modern poetry considered mediocre or tasteless according to classical standards. Thus, Scriblerus immerses his readers in the muddy modern deeps of bad poetry by inventing a new rhetoric with ludicrous categories illustrated by flawed poetry. Twisting the ideas of Longinus, Scriblerus expresses a notion that we are all born poets capable of bathos and satirically anticipates the child-is-father-to-the-man idea of Wordsworth's Romanticism:

> The Taste of the Bathos is implanted by Nature itself in the soul of man; till, perverted by custom or example, he is taught, or rather compell'd, to relish the Sublime. Accordingly, we see the unprejudiced minds of Children delight only in such productions, and in such images, as our true modern writers set before them. I have observ'd how fast the general Taste is returning to this first Simplicity and Innocence: and if the intent of all Poetry be to divert and instruct, certainly that kind that diverts and instructs the *greatest number* is to be preferr'd. Let us look round among the Admirers of Poetry, we shall find those who have a taste of the Sublime to be very few; but the Profound strikes universally, and is adapted to every capacity. (Pope 1986: 188)

Pope published *Peri Bathous* in the Pope–Swift *Miscellanies* (1728) in place of the original three-book *Dunciad* (1728), with Tibbald as the hero. *The Dunciad* would be printed individually and anonymously that year, probably to stir up published critical reactions, which would be incorporated in the subsequent variorum version of 1729, edited by Scriblerus.

Spiritual children of Scriblerus' topsy-turvy worldview are Swift's *Gulliver's Travels* (1726, 1735), a faux-travel book, describing four voyages similar to those planned by Scriblerus in chapter 16 of the *Memoirs* (1742); Gay's ballad-opera *The Beggar's Opera* (1728), which, two centuries later, will be the imitative model for Bertolt Brecht's satire of a rogue world of capitalist corruption, *The Threepenny Opera* (1928); and Pope's mock-epic *The Dunciad* (1728–43), whose lasting wit and relevance may be as much a result of the pertinacity of literary dullness as of Pope's genius. In these three major works, serious in intent, a somewhat obtuse or intellectually crack-brained Scriblerian editor/author/speaker will naïvely use radical juxtaposition that provokes humor, evincing some form of bathos, diminution, ironic undercutting, or puncturing disclosure: Gulliver, physically out of place, is either a giant, a tiny *lusus naturae* (freak of nature), or an anomalous Yahoo; the dark lyrics of the *demi-monde* in *The Beggar's Opera* are sung as popular airs; the *Dunciad* poet champions an unheroic drama of cultural eclipse in an epic manner; and Scriblerus himself, with the seriousness of a classical or biblical scholar, edits, over time, a gathering bricolage of critical commentary that almost buries the *Dunciad* poem in the final four-book version (1743).

Scriblerian satire may also include such comic farces as *The What d'ye Call It* (1715) by Gay and *The Author's Farce* and *The Life and Death of Tom Thumb the Great* (both in 1730) by Henry Fielding; the entertaining, meta-novelistic, fictional autobiography *The Life and Opinions of Tristram Shandy* (1760–67) by Laurence Sterne (1713–68), indebted somewhat to the *Memoirs of Scriblerus* and satirically ridiculing Locke's epistemology; and satiric verses, such as *The Rosciad* (1761), mocking stage players of the day, by Charles Churchill (1731–64), to name only a few obvious examples. Closely fitting the Scriblerian mold in the twentieth century, for all of their marvelous uniqueness, are Vladimir Nabokov's *Pale Fire* (1962) and Herbert Lindenberger's *Saul's Fall* (1979). The protean style of Scriblerian works cannot be generically pinned down, for all of these works seem ambiguously playful, and as Patricia Carr Brückmann asserts, "Nothing ends. Everything goes on. Ovidian flux is a major part of their universe" (1997: 134).

A Satiric Idiom

In Shakespeare's day, even a penny groundling at the Globe could probably follow most of the fast-paced wit on stage – and, of course, without footnotes or time for critical reflection. Spectators did not need a liberal arts education to understand a popular art that had become social currency, and such a fluency in understanding dramatic performances must have encouraged the high achievement of Elizabethan and Jacobean dramatists. Similarly in Pope's day existed a satiric idiom that fostered some of the best satire written in any language. Augustan readers could recognize imitation, allusion, parody, mock-forms, multiple-edged irony, and masked indirection as the way of the world in satire, even if partisan wits or alleged fools, for being satiric targets, might willfully ignore the literary playfulness of disjunctive levels of meaning, the display of mock-epic buffoonery at their expense, or the situational irony that unmasked their kind of presumed hypocrisy. It was no coincidence that Pope, hands down the best poet, was also the most favored poet of his day. High culture and popular taste were still convivial in the matter of poetry and certainly bedmates when it came to verse satire.

Augustan readers had a humanistic cast of mind. For them, literature was held accountable. It should be instructive, memorable, communal, and morally responsible, and it should play a civilizing role in improving fallible individual behavior and, thereby, society. And poetry was considered a storehouse of acquired wisdom and a cultural beacon for contemporary judgment. With humanity serving as the common denominator, past and present life was melded, and thusly was poetry a living tradition. Classical reading shaped readers' expectations, and literary subjects would be on ordinary commonplaces, on traditional moral subjects fashioned anew in contemporary dress. In Pope's familiar words:

> *True Wit* is *Nature* to Advantage drest,
> What oft was *Thought*, but ne'er so well *Exprest*,
> *Something*, whose Truth convinc'd at Sight we find,
> That gives us back the Image of our Mind.
> (*An Essay on Criticism*, 1711, 297–300)

A poet's genius for poetic art would be found in the craft, not in the novelty of the subject, and never at the expense of craft. Even in the matter of invention, pioneering poets, giants like Homer or Pindar, were revered for discovering or composing – but not conjuring out of nothing – a sublime conception. Not curiosity of subject, but novelty of treatment – including, the deftness of measure, the propriety of diction, the witty uses of figuration, and the arrangement of thought or image – was the key element on which a writer was judged. Lucidity and propriety were discriminatory bases for judging poetry. Thus, mediocre poets were scorned for recognizably inferior craft, and superior poets were valued as cultural heroes. Such an almost adulatory perspective on poetry differs from our own of indifference. Our stock of contemporary poetry has hit bottom. Too many modern poets, most stridently in the past several decades, have cultivated a fetish for inventive novelty at the expense of any formal craft, and this has significantly undermined poetical standards of taste. Without any reliable critical discrimination common to all readers, poetry has relinquished an important position in our culture. An almost total absence of a satiric idiom and a prevalence of subjective aesthetic criteria may be why poetry no longer serves us as cultural ballast. We have a better sense of what makes a good movie than a good poem.

The Augustans had a firm and a satirical sense of their world and of their poetry. They viewed the Genesis drama of man's disobedience – the Fall – as a satiric, not a tragic, scene of human blindness, making us victim to the knavish wiles of Satan. We are fallible beings, foolish and sometimes devilish, and subject always to committing folly and to the temptation of our vanity. There was, of course, a competing Pelagian perspective evolving along with European Enlightenment thought that viewed our intrinsic human nature in positive terms (for example, in the writing of Anthony Ashley Cooper, 3rd Earl of Shaftesbury), and this optimism later in the century would variously fuel revolutionary ideas of government and a new literary aesthetic in Romanticism. But, as the saying goes, history does not turn at right angles. The dominant conception at this time, it seems fair to say, was of a risible creature, most effectively captured by Pope, in his otherwise philosophical poem *An Essay on Man* (1733–4):

> Plac'd on this isthmus of a middle state,
> A being darkly wise and rudely great:
> With too much knowledge for the Sceptic side,
> With too much weakness for the Stoic's pride,
> He hangs between; in doubt to act, or rest,
> In doubt to deem himself a God, or Beast;
> In doubt his Mind or Body to prefer,

>
> Born but to die, and reas'ning but to err;
> Alike in ignorance, his reason such,
> Whether he thinks too little, or too much:
> Chaos of Thought and Passion, all confus'd;
> Still by himself abus'd, or disabus'd;
> Created half to rise, and half to fall;
> Great lord of all things, yet a prey to all;
> Sole judge of Truth, in endless Error hurl'd:
> The glory, jest, and riddle of the world!
>
> (Ep. 2.3–18)

This satiric picture of fragile and equivocal humankind invites humility and a compliant understanding that God has designed a world beyond our comprehension. The moral criticism is trite but not the exceptional eloquence that Pope has applied to a contemporary view of humankind.

Three decades before, offering something of a bookend to Pope's description, and with a different kind of poetical energy and purpose, Defoe gives us a congruent view of human nature in his satiric poem "The Dyet of Poland, A Satyr" (1705). As Frank H. Ellis states, "what Poland meant to Defoe was a country divided and almost destroyed by party conflict," and the poem is intended as an "analogy between Poland and England – or a cautionary tale about succession to the throne and foreign invasion" (Ellis 1975: 72). For Defoe, unjustifiable pride is the vice of the (English) people in this satiric tableau that seemingly augurs the transcending perspective of Pope in *An Essay on Man*:

> A mighty Nation throngs the groaning Land,
> Rude as the Climate, num'rous as the Sand:
> Uncommon monstrous *Vertues* they possess,
> Strange odd preposterous *Polish* Qualities;
> Mysterious Contraries they reconcile,
> The *Pleasing Frown* and the *Destroying Smile*;
> Precisely gay, and most absurdly grave,
> Most *humbly high*, and *barbarously brave*;
> *Debauch'dly Civil* and *Prophanely Good*,
> And fill'd with *Gen'rous* brave *Ingratitude*,
> By *Bounty disoblig'd*, by Hatred *won*,
> Bold in their Danger, Cowards when 'tis gone;
> To their own Ruin they're the only Tools,
> Wary of Knaves, and eas'ly chous'd by *Fools*;
> *Profoundly empty*, yet *declar'dly wise*,
> And fond of blind Impossibilities;
> *Swell'd with Conceit*, they boast of all they do,
> First praise themselves, then think that Praise their Due:
> So fond of flatt'ring Words, so vain in Pride,
> The World *Mocks* them, and they the World *Deride*;
> Value themselves upon their Nations Merit,

> In Spight of all the Vices they inherit;
> So wedded to the Country where they dwell,
> They think that's Heav'n, and all the World's a Hell.
>   (15–38)

This commonly accepted view of a lapsable (as well as corrigible) human nature will function as the idiomatic basis, the ground zero, for censure and praise in verse satire of the period. Furthermore, paradigms for reinforcing this view will be derived again and again from the stuff of generational experiences. Pat Rogers shares this position in his book study of Grub Street subculture, which "sought to show how the Augustan satirists built upon the facts of contemporary life":

> Firstly, that the recollection of disasters of a generation before still operated powerfully in people's minds at the opening of the eighteenth century. Secondly, that the characteristic idiom of Augustan satire (whether the actual vocabulary, at a local level, or the wider rhetorical and fictional resources used) makes use of this residual memory, though often at a subliminal level. And thirdly, that the images centrally derived from the historical events (plague/epidemic/burning etc.) were peculiarly suited to the things these satirists actually wanted to say – peculiarly effective weapons for exposing the kind of danger they saw in the contemporary world. (Rogers 1972: 98)

Thus, the imaginative domain of verse satirists is contoured by a legacy of nightmarish memories collectively shared with their readers (the Civil War, the plague of 1665, the fire of London, the Glorious Revolution, the War of the Spanish Succession, the War of Jenkins' Ear, and so on). Their empirical imagination moves inductively, from lived experience (either through the "residual" past or present) to practicing idea. In this sense, tested truth and authenticity must underlie Augustan satiric verse.

How the Augustan social imagination is formed, in being so much influenced by a literary exchange of satirical coinage, may also shed light on our own moment. Ironically, over the past centuries, as communication technology has penetrated communities, assisted the growth of nationalisms, and, most recently, seeded corporate transnationalism, it has also reduced the world of our collective imagination through conceptual homogenizing (i.e., though numerically there are more of us, there are fewer of us who really think differently). Perhaps, as Marshall McLuhan once prophesized, our globe is becoming a village, but a wired one, as being "on line" approximates to getting "in line." More and more, so seems the trajectory of our microchip progress, we are being left a Hobson's choice, where even the writer's imagination may be experiencing containment within a virtual text, a product of the world-wide web, which is itself another's product. And, our universities as institutions cannot exclude themselves from this envelopment if a society does not insist on such a separation. Indeed, it seems the tow of an impressionable, biotic cultural memory – media-nourished daily by bromidic tropes originally sourced from actual events, disasters, or conditions that we all progressively *feel* we know first-hand but have really only learned through second-hand and continual repetition – has torn away our anchor. In a so-called "post 9/11 world" (an assumption, perhaps, as yet insufficiently challenged and rationally understood), we may be drowning for being entangled within a network of reductive and imbricated, and maybe meaningless, metaphors – of collapse, crisis, war, terror, with their equally neutered counterparts of building, continuity, peace, democracy, and such – while floating on a sea of sentiments and impassioned opinion. Consider this as a hypothesis: the generations of Swift and Pope may have experienced more national traumas and wars than us, and their deeply felt satire may be more clairvoyant than we have thought. These writers seem to possess a seriousness that most of ours lack. In a scene worthy of *The Dunciad* or of the science-fiction film *Invasion of the Body Snatchers* (1956), a mutant-Orwellian global-speak may be leaving each of us tongue-tied. If so, asking why is a first step toward a renewed satirical understanding.

Some Developments in Augustan Verse Satire

Verse satire of the period extends well beyond the distinguishing structural design of the formal verse satire developed by the classical Roman poets. As Mary Claire Randolph noted:

> Ranking English men of letters... even in England's greatest age of satire, wrote very few original formal verse satires. Dryden himself wrote none; Swift, Gay, Addison and Steele, and Arbuthnot wrote none; only Edward Young and Alexander Pope, in company with a few of the lesser poets, wrote any formal verse satires that could be properly termed original. Add to these the five formal *Satyres* of John Donne, and one has England's chief original contributions to the genre. (Randolph 1971: 183)

Though it might seem otherwise, this paucity of "original" *formal* verse satire results from both a high regard for the classical genre and a concomitant spirit of inventive transgression among Augustan satirists, for whom satire and its poetical form had more than mere aesthetic value.

It almost seems that Augustan classicism and Protestantism amicably joined in viewing as divine or Edenic attributes of perfection (and, thereby, of moral good) such features of classical beauty as concordance, harmony, unity, symmetry, and proportion. For them, these qualities, when naturally suggested and not forcibly imposed, variously made a beautiful garden, as well as a beautiful poem. On the other hand, a suggestion of ugliness, monstrosity, deformity, oddity, and the like (to which may be added cacophony or noise) could readily invoke ideas of corruption, error, or immorality. This objective sense of a golden world, reflected either naturally or unnaturally in their brazen one (as a world of harmonious discord), tooled readers for recognition of authorial intention in satirical poetry. And, perhaps, here I should note that contrary developments in aesthetics and an increasing reliance on subjectivity will soon place classical beauty, for many, on a second tier beneath a reconceived idea of the sublime originally put forth by Longinus in *Peri hupsous*. Augustan ideas of beauty, as well as of imperfection, will be challenged by such trends in the sister arts as, for example, the picturesque and the Gothic, offshoots of the ascendant interest in the sublime; but, again, the transformational force of these aesthetic shifts will gain competitive prominence later in the century and be embraced by Romantic poets. In any case, generic conformity during the first half-century was surely something Augustans understood and valued. Thus, in the matter of verse satire, in which poets have license for generic play, the poetry of classical satirists served as a comparative basis for innovation.

Edward Young's highly successful volume of seven satiric epistles, *Love of Fame, the Universal Passion* (1728), comprised of poems individually published from 1725 to 1728, are original contributions to the classical genre of formal verse satire and precede Pope's more exceptional *Epistles to Several Persons* (1731–5), also known as the *Moral Essays*, comprised of four poetic epistles (addressed to Cobham, a Lady, Bathurst, and Burlington). Randolph describes the classical design of this kind of satiric poetry:

> The formal verse satire, as composed by Lucilius, Horace, Persius, and Juvenal, was evidently bi-partite in structure, that is, some specific vice or folly, selected for attack, was turned about on all its sides in Part A (if one may arbitrarily call it so) in something of the way premises are turned about in the octave of a sonnet; and its opposing virtue was recommended in Part B. (1971: 172)

Young's satires are worthy efforts, though weakened by excessive poetical praise of patrons, and his popular epistles, it seems, encouraged Pope to the poetical form. But if Young's satiric epistles are fine chalk drawings, Pope's are color portraits. Pope's epistles carry the classical form to new heights, profiting from Young's first and commendable efforts. Moreover, Young's poetry was not Pope's only instructive model, for in his use of character portraits, Pope owes much to his master Dryden, who, as Randolph points out, never wrote an original in the form.

Another point to be made in the matter of Pope's innovation is that within each of his satiric epistles, Pope allows us a comparative utopian glimpse through the illustration of exemplary character and the declaration of laudable precepts – as, for example, in his "Epistle to Burlington" (1731):

> To build, to plant, whatever you intend,
> To rear the Column, or the Arch to bend,
> To swell the Terras, or to sink the Grot;
> In all, let Nature never be forgot.
> (47–50)

Such normative grounding effected by the poet's direct statement of *what ought to be the case* might be found throughout Pope's non-Scriblerian verse satires, all of which employ an ultimately reasonable and reliable poet persona, such as found in his *Epistles to Several Persons* and *Imitations of Horace* (1733–8). This strategy of evaluative comparison through direct assertion of the poet persona also structures *An Essay on Criticism*, a poem that, on balance, is not a satire, though it includes satiric verses. Pope's *Essay* follows in the spirit of Horace's epistle to the Pisones, *The Art of Poetry*, and positions antitheses that allow the poet persona opportunities for denunciatory satire, as with its classical predecessor. In Pope's Scriblerian poetry, however, the poetic speaker is not to be trusted as a spokesman for Pope, a distancing of the historical author that tinges any moral teaching with subversive irony. This seems rather clear in the *Dunciad* poem, but a foggier example may be Clarissa's moralizing speech in *The Rape of the Lock* (1714), which, for its being expressed by a character within the poetic drama, is tainted by her previous actions (her assistance of the Baron in his snipping of Belinda's lock) and, thereby, is shaded by her hypocrisy.

And finally, let us note how the poet's direct expression of values, such as in Pope's *Epistles*, effectively educates and shapes his readers, which establishes the background of the poetical canvas against which Pope can dramatically foreground an undressing of diseased character and a display of flawed behavior. Morally focused, the finely discriminated details of the poem are infused with satiric meaning. In his "Epistle to Burlington," Pope's deftness at juxtaposition of the commendable and the censurable may be seen in his poetic description of Timon's Villa, which gives the lie to the precept – "let Nature never be forgot" (50) – expressed in the paragraph above. Timon is a wealthy aristocrat with abominable taste, who demonstrates how elements of classical beauty applied disproportionately (Timon's vain effort at being like God) produce the grotesquely ludicrous. Timon's unnatural estate and garden represent, by implication, his own character, immoral for being so wasteful and, thereby, irresponsible for doing no good:

> At Timon's Villa let us pass a day,
> Where all cry out, "What sums are thrown away!"
> So proud, so grand, of that stupendous air,
> Soft and Agreeable come never there.
> Greatness, with Timon, dwells in such a draught
> As brings all Brobdignag [sic] before your thought.
>   (99–104)

Timon vulgarly makes his building, his pond, his parterre, and everything, in fact, too big. For that, he becomes as "a puny insect, shiv'ring at a breeze" with "huge heaps of littleness around!" (108–9). So, tons of marble lie everywhere – "a labour'd Quarry above ground"; and his gardens have little variety – "No pleasing Intricacies intervene, / No artful wildness to perfect the scene" (115–16). Thus, "The suff'ring eye inverted Nature sees, / Trees cut to Statues, Statues thick as trees . . . " (119–20). He also owns heaps of old books valued for their bindings and their imprints, "but they are Wood" to him (138). The poet persona will then have dinner within the villa. But "Is this a dinner? this a Genial room?" he asks; "No, 'tis a Temple, and a Hecatomb" (155–6). And thus, we progress to the poet's convincingly justified scorn: "I curse such lavish cost, and little skill, / And swear no Day was ever past so ill" (167–8). Pope is the greatest satirical poet of the language, and his satiric ingenuity can only be touched on in this chapter. Paul Baines's *The Complete Critical Guide to Alexander Pope* (2000) offers an excellent starting place for more complete study of this extraordinary poet.

Another development in verse satire is the painter poem. The painter poem begins with Edmund Waller's "Instructions to a Painter" (1665), a panegyric to the then recent achievements of the English navy. Andrew Marvell anonymously responds to Waller's poem with the satire of his own painter poems "Second Advice" and "Third Advice to a Painter" (both published in 1666), which instead portray an English navy of misjudgment, mismanagement, and corruption. Marvell's poems shift their satire away from the direct denunciation of the poet persona of formal verse satire; as George deF. Lord notes, "In painter poems the satirist adopts the mask of the patriotic ironist who in turn engages a painter to depict the satirical scene" (1963: lii). Marvell's poems function as speaking pictures (literally Horace's *ut pictura poesis*). In Marvell's "Third Advice," for example, the poetic speaker has the painter draw the Duchess of Albermarle, who then comes to life and speaks for much of the remainder of the poem, serving the satirist's purpose through ironic indirection, as she displays at first-hand her coarseness and foolishness. The satiric messages of these poems are conveyed less flatly and more seductively than the "bi-partite" structure that formal verse satire affords, as Marvell's iconic imagery allegorically generates a three-dimensional manifold of meaning.

Looking now at an anonymous satirical painter poem "Advice to a Painter" (1697; Ellis 1970: 12–25), one of many satiric painter poems that follow Marvell's example, we find a dark painting of unregenerate court corruption. This is not the place for an involved discussion of the implied politics of the poem, but we can immediately note that the poet must not be happy with the vain, indifferent conduct of an absolutist monarch (King William III), who presumably is the "Hero" flanked by two corrupt allegorical figures, the "Priest" and the "Lawyer," themselves representing England's church and law:

> First Draw the Hero seated on the Throne,
> Spite of all Laws, himself observing none;
> Let *English* rights all gasping round him lie,
> And native Freedom thrown neglected by:
> On either hand the Priest and Lawyer set,
> Two fit Supporters of the Monarch's Seat.
> There in greasy Rotchet cloth'd, describe
> The bulky Oracle of the Preaching Tribe;
> That solid necessary Tool of State,
> Profoundly Dull, Divinely Obstinate.
> Here in polluted Robes just reeking, draw
> Th'Adulterous Moderator of the Law;
> Whose wrinkled Cheeks and sallow Looks proclaim,
> The ill Effects of his distemper'd Flame.
> (15–28)

Stupid and stubborn, the law has been corrupted by his slutty lover, the church, and they have displaced and toppled English civil rights and "native Freedom." Politically, England has been leveled to a lawless place of gross power.

Compare these lines near the opening of Pope's "New Dunciad" (1742), later book four of his final version of *The Dunciad* (1743). Whereas Waller's poet would have brought his foolish dramatic speaker to life *within* the generic painter poem, Pope gives that role to the *Dunciad* poet himself, a persona transparently naïve and dramatically ironic, who describes the grisly and violent events. Note also how Pope has changed the scale from national to global allegory in suggesting the end of all liberal arts and civilization as known:

> She mounts the Throne: her head a Cloud conceal'd,
> In broad Effulgence all below reveal'd,
> ('Tis thus aspiring Dulness ever shines)
> Soft on her lap her Laureat son reclines.
> Beneath her foot-stool, *Science* groans in Chains,
> And *Wit* dreads Exile, Penalties and Pains,
> There foam's rebellious *Logic*, gagg'd and bound,
> There, stript, fair *Rhet'ric* languished on the ground;
> His blunted Arms by *Sophistry* are born,
> And shameless *Billingsgate* her Robes adorn.
> *Morality*, by her false Guardians drawn,
> *Chicane* in Furs, and *Casuistry* in Lawn,
> Gasps, as they straiten at each end the cord,
> And dies, when Dulness gives her Page the word.
> Mad *Mathesis* alone was unconfin'd,
> Too mad for more material chains to bind,
> Now to pure Space lifts her extatic stare,
> Now running round the Circle finds it square.
>   (4.17–34)

Pope's personification of a "Mad *Mathesis*," who goes "unconfin'd," satirizes more than any excesses of particular contemporaries in mathematical or abstract reasoning, of individuals whose absurd conclusions probably only his scientific friend Dr Arbuthnot could have recognized (Pope 1963: 343n31). Pope's poetical tableau shows us a world that has unleashed a destructive freethinking divorced from reason and tradition. More than English rights and freedom are lost in this scene, as all of the personified tools for truth and good conduct have been vanquished or enchained. Horrendous though it be, this is satiric wit for Pope's Augustan reader. For readers of a more frightful and less humorous age, with a perpetual-crisis mania, such as ours seems at times, the devastating sweep of Pope's satire, even if projected indirectly through his *Dunciad* poet, might suggest, not a retributive Nemesis that a sagacious satiric reader might perceive as a lesson from which to learn, but a complete, unmitigated disaster, an inverted, annihilating apocalypse without redemption. Though time may transform the idiomatic basis for reading a satire, the satirical imagination, for its being based on reason and logic, may keep us from being surprised, even if it cannot from being shocked.

This satiric Augustan posture toward detached, systematic, and abstract thinking – or of metaphysical speculation, as when Pope warns, "Know then thyself, presume not God to scan; / The proper study of Mankind is Man" (*An Essay on Man*, Ep. 2.102) – will be taken up later in the century by Edmund Burke (1729–97) in his contemporary analysis of recent events of the French Revolution. In his *Reflections on the Revolution in France* (1790), written primarily as a book-length epistle, but containing diatribe as well as satiric narrative, Burke decries that, for the cause of liberty, the French revolutionaries have chosen the mad alternative of the abstract thinker, and they have run amok:

> I flatter myself that I love a manly, moral, regulated liberty as well as any gentleman of that society... But I cannot stand forward, and give praise or blame to any thing which relates to human actions, and human concerns, on a simple view of the object, as it stands stripped of every relation, in all the nakedness and solitude of metaphysical abstraction. (1968: 90)

Burke's severe criticism of the revolution will spark a major public controversy, and Joseph Priestley (1733–1804), famed chemist and dissenting clergyman, will publish an epistolary rebuttal, *Letters to the Right Honourable Edmund Burke* (1791). Significant to our concerns in this chapter, Priestley uses two epigraphs for his *Letters* drawn from Burke's own words in his *Reflections*, and one of them tellingly reads: "Steady independent minds, when they have an object of so serious a concern to mankind, as GOVERNMENT, under their contemplation, will disdain to assume the part of *satirists* and *declaimers*" (Priestley 1791: title page). Priestley is sometimes sarcastic, often sermonic, but not satirical. By the end of the century, it appears that the idiom has notably changed, for the satirist by then seems to have lost a cast of seriousness and, thus also, an advantageous rhetorical effectiveness in public forums.

At the beginning of the century, however, good government was often the serious subject of satire, even if it was sometimes treated with a playful spirit, as in Bernard Mandeville's ironic and darkly amusing "The Grumbling Hive: Or Knaves *turn'd Honest*" (1705). The poem presents a satiric reversal of the view that a selfish human nature can be socially destructive. Published again in 1714, in *The Fable of the Bees: Or, Private Vices, Publick Benefits*, the poem is glossed by ironic textual commentary (twenty-two "Remarks") and by a further explanatory essay, "An Enquiry into the Origin of Moral Virtue," which begins with a premise that reflects back onto the portrayal of human nature in the poem: "All untaught Animals are only solicitous of pleasing themselves, and naturally follow the bent of their own Inclinations, without considering the good or harm that from their being pleased will accrue to others" (Mandeville 1924: 1.41). The "main Design of the Fable," according to Mandeville in his Preface to the poem (1714), "is to shew the Impossibility of enjoying all the most elegant Comforts of Life that are to be met with in an industrious, wealthy and powerful Nation, and at the same time be bless'd with all the Virtue and Innocence that can be wish'd for in a Golden Age." That is, we cannot have our cake (i.e., be virtuous) and eat it too (i.e., be prosperous), and thus Mandeville intends "to expose the Unreasonableness and Folly of those, that desirous of being opulent and flourishing People, and wonderfully greedy after all the Benefits they can receive as such, are yet always murmuring at and exclaiming against those Vices and Inconveniences" (Mandeville 1924: 1.6–7).

In the fable of the poem, bees represent human behavior: "These Insects liv'd like Men, and all / Our Actions they perform'd in small" (13–14); the bee society prospers, though all of its professions are corrupted with knavish ambitions: "Thus every Part was full of Vice, / Yet the whole Mass a Paradise" (155–6); and those at the bottom of the social scale benefit most:

> Thus Vice nurs'd Ingenuity,
> Which join'd with Time and Industry,
> Had carry'd Life's Conveniencies,
> It's real Pleasures, Comforts, Ease,
> To such a Height, the very Poor
> Liv'd better than the Rich before,
> And nothing could be added more.
> (197–203)

A self-destructive desire for virtue becomes the vanity of human wishes: "Good Gods, Had we but Honesty!" (225); Jove hears and angrily gives them their wish: "But *Jove* with Indignation mov'd, / At last in Anger swore, *He'd rid / The bawling Hive of Fraud*; and did" (229–31); and their prosperity vanishes.

The thesis of Mandeville's poem – "*Private Vices, Publick Benefits*" – provoked many of his readers, and his later prose "Remarks" about the poem, for their recalcitrant irony, rather than assuaging criticism, generated even more adverse comment. Richard I. Cook, who rightly calls Mandeville a satiric gadfly, remarks: "No English author since Thomas Hobbes had touched so raw a nerve, and men who agreed in almost nothing else became united in their condemnation of Mandeville. Even Swift, who in *Gulliver's Travels* set out deliberately to vex the world, met with less widespread indignation than Mandeville, who ostensibly sought only to divert it" (1974: 117).

Mandeville's satirical audacity in provocatively stripping away illusion may have provided an indirect model for the Scriblerians, though one can only speculate about the creative catalysis of any of their works. The market logic and materialism of Gay's *The Beggar's Opera* do echo that of Mandeville's poem, and Macheath is called to mind in Mandeville's "Remark (T)": "What our common Rogues when they are going to be hanged chiefly complain of, as the Cause of their untimely End, is, next to the neglect of the Sabbath, their having kept Company with ill Women, meaning Whores; and I don't question, but that among the lesser Villains many venture their Necks to indulge and satisfy their low Amours" (Mandeville 1924: 1.224).

Swift, though for the most part a deeply serious prose satirist, in his verse satires does share with Mandeville the zestful spirit of a satiric gadfly. Swift's verse satires, something of an anti-poetry in doing away with any affectation of poetry as a higher discourse, gives us a gross realism that violently unmasks any idealizing fancies. In "A Description of a City Shower" (1710), for example, burlesquing language describes how a personified "Sable Cloud a-thwart the Welkin" (14) swills and then vomits like a drunk and washes the all-too-common daily life of the city with torrents of water. The poem concludes with a triplet, including an alexandrine in the final line, formally suggesting as it describes the convergence of a city's offal from a flash flood:

> Sweepings from Butchers Stalls, Dung, Guts, and Blood,
> Drown'd puppies, stinking Sprats, all drench'd in mud,
> Dead Cats and Turnip-Tops come rumbling down the
>   Flood.
>   (61–3)

Elsewhere, Swift, with shocking detail, literally undresses fabricated female beauty in order to mock the female idolatry of surface-thinking men in his scatological poems "The Lady's Dressing Room" (1732), and "A Beautiful Young Nymph Going to Bed," "Strephon and Chloe," and "Cassinus and Peter," published two years later (1734). His finest satiric poem is "Verses on the Death of Dr Swift, D.S.P.D." (1731, 1733), a self-mocking *jeu d'esprit* that was "Occasioned by Reading a Maxim in Rochefoucault," which is translated as an epigraph: "In the Adversity of our best Friends, we find something that doth not displease us." Swift's autobiographical persona imagines his own death, and we listen to "one quite indiff'rent in the Cause" (305) give us (presumably in retrospect) an apologia for Swift's life explaining his various deeds. In one place, he defends Swift's satire:

> Perhaps I may allow, the Dean
> Had too much Satyr in his Vein;
> And seem'd determin'd not to starve it,
> Because no Age could more deserve it.
> Yet, Malice never was his Aim;
> He lash'd the Vice but spar'd the Name.
> No Individual could resent,
> Where Thousands equally were meant.
> His Satyr points at no Defect,
> But what all Mortals may correct.
>   (455–64)

That Swift eschewed personal attack and aimed at a satire that was so universalizing may be why biographical critics have mistakenly scorned Swift for misanthropy. Time and scholarship have given the lie to this perspective, as we have become more understanding of his satirical strategies. We might remember also that, significantly for the history of satire, Swift dissuaded the younger Pope from descending to literary dueling and mere lampoonery. Pope, who was mercilessly attacked throughout his career, had cause for lashing back at individuals, but the older Swift would caution Pope against it, as he does in a letter of autumn 1716: "And who are all these enemies you hint at? I can only think of Curl, Gildon, Squire Burnet, Blackmore, and a few others whose fame I have forgot: Tools in my opinion as necessary for a good writer, as pen, ink, and paper. And besides, I would fain know whether every Draper does not shew you three or four damned pieces of stuff to set off his good one?" (Pope 1956: 1.358–9).

One of the most prolific of verse satirists during the first decade is Daniel Defoe. He was a capable poet, though he lacked the classical training that might have made him a greater poet. Superbly gifted, which readers may know only from his novels, he was also exceptionally innovative in verse satire. He established his poetical fame with *The True-Born Englishman* (1701), in which he challenged a national prejudice against William III's Dutch origins and satirized English xenophobia and aristocratic pride of pedigree: "We have been *Europe*'s Sink, *the Jakes* where she / Voids all her Offal Out-cast Progeny" (249–50). Defoe's more important verse satires can be found in two volumes of *Poems of Affairs of State*, with helpful editorial commentary by Frank H. Ellis (Ellis 1970, 1975). Defoe was a brilliant writing machine. Three of his verse satires, for example, published in 1706 and excluded by Ellis from his volume, totaled 9,940 lines (Ellis 1975: xxxvi).

Garth's ingenuity in revising his mock-heroic *Dispensary*, Prior's delicate poetical mastery in, for example, "The Country Mouse and the City Mouse" (1687) and in his satirical masterpieces about domestic life, such as "Jinny the Just" and "An Epitaph" (1718) to name only two, and Gay's comical satire, as in such poems as his blank-verse burlesque *Wine* (1708), his mock pastorals *The Shepherd's Week* (1714), and his mock-heroic *Trivia, or The Art of Walking the Streets of London* (1716), must be given proper light elsewhere. Much more remains to be said about satirical poetry in this fecund period.

References and Further Reading

Baines, Paul (2000) *The Complete Critical Guide to Alexander Pope*. London: Routledge.

Brückmann, Patricia Carr (1997) *A Manner of Correspondence: A Study of the Scriblerus Club*. Montreal: McGill-Queen's University Press.

Bullitt, John M. (1953) *Jonathan Swift and the Anatomy of Satire: A Study of Satiric Technique*. Cambridge. MA: Harvard University Press.

Burke, Edmund (1968) *Reflections on the Revolution in France and on the Proceedings in Certain Societies in London Relative to that Event* [1790], ed. Conor Cruise O'Brien. New York: Penguin.

Cook, Richard I. (1974) *Bernard Mandeville*. Boston: Twayne.

——(1980) *Samuel Garth*. Boston: Twayne.

Ellis, Frank H. (ed.) (1970) *Poems on Affairs of State: Augustan Satirical Verse, 1660–1714, vol. 6: 1697–1704*. New Haven, CT: Yale University Press.

——(ed.) (1975) *Poems on Affairs of State: Augustan Satirical Verse, 1660–1714, vol. 7: 1704–1714*. New Haven, CT: Yale University Press.

Fox, Christopher (1988) *Locke and the Scriblerians: Identity and Consciousness in Early Eighteenth-century Britain*. Berkeley, CA: University of California Press.

Foxon, David (1991) *Pope and the Early Eighteenth-century Book Trade*, ed. James McLaverty. Oxford: Clarendon Press.

Kerby-Miller, Charles (ed.) (1950) *The Memoirs of the Extraordinary Life, Works, and Discoveries of Martinus Scriblerus*. Oxford: Oxford University Press.

Lord, George deF. (ed.) (1963) *Poems on Affairs of State: Augustan Satirical Verse, 1660–1714, vol. 1: 1660–1678*. New Haven, CT: Yale University Press.

Mandeville, Bernard (1924) *The Fable of the Bees: Or, Private Vices, Publick Benefits*, 2 vols, ed. F. B. Kaye. Oxford: Clarendon Press.

Maresca, Thomas E. (1966) *Pope's Horatian Poems*. Columbus: Ohio State University Press.

Pope, Alexander (1956) *The Correspondence of Alexander Pope*, 5 vols, ed. George Sherburn. Oxford: Clarendon Press.

—— (1963) *The Dunciad*, vol. 5, ed. James Sutherland. Twickenham Edition of the Poems of Alexander Pope. London: Methuen (originally published in 1943).

—— (1986) *The Prose Works of Alexander Pope, vol. 2: The Major Works, 1725–1744*, ed. Rosemary Cowler. Hamden, CT: Archon Books.

Priestley, Joseph (1791) *Letters to the Right Honourable Edmund Burke, Occasioned by his Reflections on the Revolution in France, etc. The third edition, corrected*. Birmingham: Thomas Pearson.

Quintero, Ruben (2001) "Serious and merry by turns": The Pope–Swift *Miscellanies*. In *From Letter to Publication: Studies on Correspondence and the History of the Book. SVEC* 10: 287–95. Oxford: Voltaire Foundation.

Randolph, Mary Claire (1971) The structural design of the formal verse satire. In Ronald Paulson (ed.), *Satire: Modern Essays in Criticism*, pp. 171–89. Englewood Cliffs, NJ: Prentice-Hall (originally published in *Philological Quarterly* 21 [1942]: 368–84).

Rogers, Pat (1972) *Grub Street: Studies in a Subculture*. London: Methuen.

Rogers, Robert W. (1955) *The Major Satires of Alexander Pope*. Urbana: University of Illinois Press.

Sitter, John E. (1971) *The Poetry of Pope's Dunciad*. Minneapolis, MN: University of Minnesota Press.

Sutherland, James (1958) *English Satire*. Cambridge: Cambridge University Press.

Weinbrot, Howard D. (1969) *The Formal Strain: Studies in Augustan Imitation and Satire*. Chicago: University of Chicago Press.

Williams, Aubrey L. (1955) *Pope's Dunciad: A Study of its Meaning*. London: Methuen.

13
Satiric Spirits of the Later Eighteenth Century: Johnson to Crabbe

James Engell

Following the death of Alexander Pope, English satiric poetry shifts away from *formal* verse satire. The satiric spirit emerges in a broader literature of cultural comment, social protest, and private disaffection. Rage and raillery are increasingly replaced by reflective anger, alienation, and even a satiric nostalgia that decries the loss of a simpler, more virtuous life. Some objects of this new, mixed satire still appear in satiric portraits. However, the targets now include larger, more intractable, anonymous forces: government policies and bureaucracies, a growing gap between the rich and poor, attitudes toward rural poverty, enclosures (the agribusiness of that age), abuses and crimes committed by the professional class, incipient industrialization that dehumanizes workers, the evils of globalization (economic exploitation and slavery), and the self-reinforcing hypocrisy of institutions that resist reforms because their first goal is to enlarge their own corporate power.

If the satire of this half-century seems diffuse, it is in part because no canonical writer, with the possible exception of Charles Churchill, represents it. It acts on a broadened stage of cultural and social uncertainty. It addresses a world recognizably modern. Imitation of classical models falls off. Fixation on court and crown does not disappear but does decrease. It is hard for formal satire, a classical genre, to deal with *accelerating* change and volatility. For the first time in history, writers now employ that adjective to characterize the pace of change.

During this time, England fought three major, protracted wars, ruthlessly suppressed a violent internal rebellion, lost thirteen North American colonies, established control by force of arms over much of the Indian subcontinent, experienced the rise of a powerful, new religious movement in Methodism, suffered anti-Catholic riots in the capital, debated the abolition of the slave trade and slavery, dealt with the mental instability of its long-reigning monarch, reorganized land and agricultural policies, and began to develop a modern industrial base, the first nation to do so. The middle class grew in numbers and wealth, literacy rose markedly, and disposable incomes established a consumer economy of increased physical as well as social mobility.

A decline in formal satire is what one might expect after *The Dunciad* (1743), perhaps the greatest verse satire in English, yet also a critique of modern life in general. Part of Book 4 Pope had originally planned as a poem on education. But if Book 4 is the last complete poem Pope published, he had foreseen in the *Epilogue to the Satires* (1738) the closure of his own art: "So – Satire is no more – I feel it die" (83). The judgment is universally accepted – and repeated without reflection – that satiric poetry of the second half of the eighteenth century declines in power, quality, and prevalence from the height it reached in the Restoration and Augustan Age. To take a common ploy of criticism and to invert this collective opinion of previous studies would be too easy and misleading. Yet, well-worn narratives of literary history are rarely questioned. As a consequence, the unique, arresting, and varied satiric voices that speak after 1750 frequently get no hearing at all.

This chapter advances several arguments:

1. Verse satire after 1750 is astonishingly varied. It defies labels or characterizations. Its practitioners include imitators of Pope, among them Johnson and, surprisingly, Smollett, Smart, Crabbe (directly in his early verse), and Chatterton. John Wilkes, Richard Owen Cambridge, and David Garrick also try to follow in Pope's footsteps, each wearing a somewhat different, though smaller, shoe. The "angry young men" – Charles Churchill, Robert Lloyd, and (no relation) Evan Lloyd – forge a direct, biting satire. Christopher Anstey is comic and flip, light yet clever. John Wolcot ("Peter Pindar") writes satire late in the century that vacillates between Juvenalian anger and comic attack. Goldsmith mixes sentiment and sympathy with satiric comment. Cowper's meditative realism includes strong satiric moments; Crabbe's direct realism hones a satiric edge. William Gifford, Mary Alcock, the Anti-Jacobins, and others pick up satire in part to hold back the tide of sentiment. This remarkable variety may be interpreted as a sign of vitality or as an indicator that verse satire is under pressure to keep pace with social changes and conditions that it can no longer pretend to control. Both interpretations would be right.

2. Reasons for the decline in formal verse satire are several and complex.

3. The strong and lasting influence of Pope remains. As with any great model, especially one so recent, his ghost at times inspires, at other times suffocates; while many imitate, none duplicate, yet one or two of the imitations excel, especially Johnson's "London" (1738) and a poem of genuine political influence written by the Connecticut Wits, *The Anarchiad* (1786–7).

4. In the 1750s and 1760s a group of friends – Churchill, Evan Lloyd, Robert Lloyd, and their compatriot John Wilkes – prosecute verse satires with zest and success;

yet Churchill dies at thirty-three, Robert Lloyd at thirty-one, and Evan Lloyd barely past forty. The new satiric chapter they are writing is cut short.

5 As changes in social, political, economic, and class conditions gain momentum, as Great Britain becomes more firmly and rapidly connected by transportation and print culture, and as (often unregulated) markets spread their power, verse satire shifts its center away from "town names," London, Grub Street, and literary spats. The entire country and overall state of society come more clearly into view. Verse satire still carries personal invective, but it often contributes to a reflective literature of social protest. Its poets enjoy scant political influence. In several instances born in rural poverty or provincial obscurity, they may find their subjects there. It is with these poets – Goldsmith, Cowper, Crabbe, Burns – that we also get some of the best poetry of the 1770s and 1780s. Their satiric objects include enclosure, the sentimentalizing of poverty, religious establishments, mass fashion, consumerism, the knowledge explosion, luxury, cultural decline, and national decadence.

The Fate of Formal Verse Satire, Johnson, and Pope's Imitators

Reasons for the decline in *formal* verse satire are several and may be summarized briefly. First, although rarely stated as a reason, the later eighteenth century simply lacked a satirist as commanding in power and scope as Dryden, or as consummate in skill and variety as Pope. If we put these two earlier writers out of mind, we would be hard pressed to speak of a decline in satire of any kind – formal or informal. (Yet that cannot be done, and its impossibility only proves how deeply one or two authors can dictate the grounds of any literary canon, history, or period.) Second, *any* poet faced a devaluation of Augustan wit. Beginning in the 1740s, Joseph and Thomas Warton, and later Richard Hurd and others, degraded wit and satire as inherently lesser forms of poetry and aesthetic sensibility. The social and literary exclusivity of wit was diluted by new tastes and a broader reading public. Critics noted this as early as the 1730s. Third, the imitators of Pope – no matter how talented – failed to blend, mix, and balance their models as he had. They tended to be excessively Juvenalian (Churchill) or Horatian, but not the ever-shifting combination that Pope made his own. Fourth, imitation itself came under fire, and imitation was a center pillar of satire, especially formal verse satire (the Roman models were Horace, Juvenal, and Persius). Johnson warned others – and himself – that "No man ever yet became great by imitation" (*Rambler* no. 154). Edward Young's *Conjectures on Original Composition* (1759) demoted imitation, yet Johnson felt surprised that Young would "receive as novelties what he thought very common maxims" (Boswell 1950: 5.269). Fifth, it may be that Pope, drawing on several models, so perfected a particular kind of satire, that *any* attempt to follow could not improve. Johnson stated that "New sentiments and new images others may produce, but to attempt any further improvement of versification will be dangerous" (1905: 3.251). Sixth, there was an uneasy sense, reflected in criticism and verse, that satire vents anger and disapproval but rarely corrects vice or folly. To the reader of "Absalom and Achitophel," Dryden says that satire aims for "the amendment of vices by *correction*." But what it criticized in the later eighteenth century often seemed too distant or too deeply rooted to flinch, let alone reform. Ridicule and rage brought few results. Seventh, the epic, epistle, and dramatic tragedy, genres supporting the art of Dryden and Pope, were giving way to other forms. Smollett's novels, and Austen's, drew from verse satires by Anstey and Crabbe. Mary Alcock satirized in verse the formulaic romances that swept the 1790s. And, finally, while some poets mixed sympathy and sentiment with satire, the rising influence of moral benevolists, the theory of sympathy as innate, and the cult of sensibility all discouraged or rejected satire.

Pope proved a daunting, often crushing model. When T. S. Eliot included lines imitating Pope in a draft of *The Waste Land* (1922), Ezra Pound advised, "Pope has done this so well that you cannot do it better; and if you mean this as a burlesque, you had better suppress it, for you cannot parody Pope unless you can write better verse than Pope – and you can't" (Pound 1928: introduction). It has often proved more fruitful to follow not the literary parent but a grand- or great-grandparent. After 1750, this meant Milton or Spenser. In the later 1700s, Pope's successful imitators turned his style and techniques to venture away from formal verse satire. Erasmus Darwin, who influenced all the canonical romantic poets, and George Crabbe are exemplary.

The most talented imitators of Pope also soon gave up imitating him. Johnson, Byron, and Crabbe, who retained strengths from Pope throughout their work, nevertheless ceased close imitation early in their careers. Johnson's "London" imitates Juvenal's third *Satire* and also follows Pope. It ranks among the finest examples of each kind of imitation in English. "London" appeared anonymously and was instantly well received. Many thought Pope the author. Pope praised the poem and declared that its author "will soon be déterré." In Johnson's London,

> Here Malice, Rapine, Accident, conspire,
> And now a Rabble rages, now a Fire;
> Their Ambush here relentless Ruffians lay,
> And here the fell Attorney prowls for Prey;
> Here falling Houses thunder on your Head,
> And here a female Atheist talks you dead.
> (13–18)

The poem attacks corruption, Walpole's government, and even (as Pope had in his "Epistle to Bathurst," 1733) the king. Lines near the end cast aspersion on George II's habit of sailing in the "tempting spring" to meet his continental mistress, and the line "To rig another Convoy for the K—g" invokes the sexual innuendo of "rig" and "riggish." Yet, for all the skill in "London," the poem is cast in a mold. We hear echoes of Pope's phrases, rhythms, and style. And it is significant that this excellent poem produced in his manner appears six years *before* Pope passes away. Johnson himself, still in his late twenties, would never again imitate so directly.

"The Vanity of Human Wishes" (1749), the first work Johnson published under his own name, imitates Juvenal's tenth *Satire* and owes a debt to Pope too. But here Johnson emulates rather than imitates. Critics have debated whether the poem qualifies as satire and, if so, what kind. It is hard to regard a poem as satirical when its author once suddenly "burst into a passion of tears" reading aloud a passage that describes an aspiring scholar at Oxford:

> When first the College Rolls receive his Name,
> The young Enthusiast quits his Ease for Fame;
> Through all his Veins the Fever of Renown
> Burns from the strong Contagion of the Gown;
> O'er *Bodley's* Dome his future Labours spread,
> And *Bacon's* Mansion trembles o'er his Head;
> Are these thy Views? proceed, illustrious Youth,
> And Virtue guard thee to the Throne of Truth,
> Yet should thy Soul indulge the gen'rous Heat,
> Till captive Science yields her last Retreat;
> Should Reason guide thee with her brightest Ray,
> And pour on misty Doubt resistless Day;
> Should no false Kindness lure to loose Delight,
> Nor Praise relax, nor Difficulty fright;
> Should tempting Novelty thy Cell refrain,
> And Sloth effuse her opiate Fumes in vain;
> Should Beauty blunt on Fops her fatal Dart,
> Nor claim the Triumph of a letter'd Heart;
> Should no disease thy torpid Veins invade,
> Nor Melancholy's Phantoms haunt thy Shade;
> Yet hope not Life from Grief or Danger free,
> Nor think the Doom of Man revers'd for thee:
> Deign on the passing World to turn thine Eyes,
> And pause awhile from Letters to be wise;
> There mark what Ills the Scholar's Life assail,
> Toil, Envy, Want, the Patron, and the Jail.
> (135–60)

Johnson himself had felt something like this at Oxford, where he had hoped to gain renown by his Latin version of Pope's *Messiah*, but was forced to leave for lack of money. Sir Walter Scott, who regarded the early eighteenth century as "the Golden Age of English Satire," stated that "The Vanity" "has often extracted tears from those whose eyes wander dry over pages professedly sentimental" (Scott 1834: 3.264). These are tears for a larger sense of human limitation.

Certainly, though, a satiric impulse exposes the repeated fantasies of world domination pursued by conquerors such as Xerxes and Charles XII; the same impulse highlights the ironic fate of Wolsey, a Lord Chancellor but accused by his king of high treason, and of Laud, head of both church and Oxford, but executed. Johnson also deplores the prevalence of greed. The poem is Juvenalian, yet Juvenal tempered and toned down, then magnificently broadened and transformed. Its sense of tragedy, more medieval than Aristotelian, recalls "The Monk's Tale" in Chaucer. Johnson crosscuts between types ("the hireling judge," "the needy traveler," "the suppliant") and historical figures. Near the end, rather than follow Juvenal's spleen and Stoicism, he provides a religious, though not specifically Christian, consolation. Yet, even the virtuous and benevolent person cannot escape life's ills. And religion itself is not immune from the self-undercutting and destructive potential of whatever human beings desire. Even faith is subject to "The secret Ambush of a specious Pray'r" (354).

"The Vanity" encompasses almost all forms that explicitly moral writing can take: aphorism, exemplum, portrait, historical commentary, charitable understanding, psychological insight, religious meditation, and satire. If the types and historical personages portrayed and mentioned, powerfully, in passing ("Hear *Lydiat*'s life and *Galileo*'s end") present object lessons and reminders, as Charles XII does, "To point a Moral or adorn a Tale" (222), then the poem is also about its own author, once the "young enthusiast," and also about every reader. Johnson includes in his large arch of consideration the most basic of human instincts and drives: "Where then shall Hope and Fear their Objects find?" (343). Superbly equipped to prosecute satire, gifted with wit, blessed with compression of language, possessing minute knowledge of historical particulars, quick with a sense of reductionism, and angered by a strong moral sense outraged, Johnson nevertheless muzzles any snarling instinct to degrade. Instead, he turns the poem to a form of wisdom literature. Yet, the darker ground of satire remains. Later in life, on the tour to the Hebrides, Johnson, when pressed, claimed that man was not "naturally good." "No," he told Lady MacLeod, "no more than a wolf." She replied in an undertone, "This is worse than Swift." A tendency to Swiftian excess Johnson holds in check in "The Vanity" and, as so often when power is held in check (as Coleridge says meter holds passion in check to strengthen it), such power appears all the stronger. Johnson also holds it in check to remind us how, once unleashed, it can come back, like a boomerang, to hunt its master. There is a self-warning in this profound moral stance, and Johnson selects a great soldier and statesman to illustrate how life, in the end, may treat the most esteemed and accomplished of men ("From *Marlb'rough*'s Eyes the Streams of Dotage flow") or the greatest of satirists ("And *Swift* expires a Driv'ler and a Show") (315–16).

Tobias Smollett's "Advice" (1746) and "Reproof" (1747) are surprisingly good formal verse satires for such a youthful endeavor (Smollett was in his early twenties). But leaning heavily on Pope and Juvenal, Smollett wisely drops his ambition in this line. So does Christopher Smart, who in 1752 starts the *Hilliad*, a poem projected in six books. Fortunately, he completes only one. Wordsworth reworks Juvenal's eighth satire in 1795 (in the political atmosphere of the 1790s Juvenal is revived), but that early foray into formal satire remains his only one. All these accomplished writers test Popian imitation but then turn elsewhere.

Richard Owen Cambridge's *Scribleriad* (1752) once commanded space in textbooks and anthologies but the winds of time have rightly winnowed it out. It should not be confused with the *Scribleriad* of 1742, shorter and anonymous, written to defend Pope. Both poems engage in literary vituperation and combat, a topic of waning interest, though revived in the 1790s. David Garrick's *Fribbleriad* (1760?) joins a quarrel in the theater world and is mildly amusing (not as funny as Garrick's farce *The Lying Valet*, 1742) but seems trivial next to its models, Pope and Milton.

A special word might be said about John Wilkes and Thomas Potter. Their infamous and omnibus parody of several poems by Pope – the *Essay on Man*, "Universal Prayer," "The Dying Christian to His Soul," and also the ancient hymn "Veni Creator" – is *An Essay on Woman* (1763). This bawdy work is, for the most part, apparently lost. Out of more than a thousand lines, only about 250, retained by the crown and privately printed in order to prosecute Wilkes, remain. The poem is misogynist or, more broadly, comically pornographic, not so much attacking women as describing – and celebrating – women (and men) as sex objects free from the trammels of law and restraint. Potter and Wilkes employ slang and lewd lingo inventively. The sexual transgressions are between consenting adults. Wilkes' burlesque, funny to compare with Pope's originals, went too far, however, and when "The Maid's Prayer" (after "Veni Creator") likens "pego" (the penis) and its testicles to the Trinity, we are pretty much at the mock-heroic (and blasphemous) height of a certain brand of patriarchy. Yet Wilkes was in public life unprejudiced. He attacked government corruption, he helped end general arrest warrants, and he kept his finger on the pulse of public opinion. He deeply influenced American jurisprudence. So highly regarded was he in North America that a major settlement on the Susquehanna, Wilkes-Barre, was named to honor him.

The imitation of Pope that carried greatest political weight in the eighteenth century helped muster support for the federal constitution of the United States. Written by Joel Barlow, David Humphreys (aide and friend of George Washington), John Trumbull, and Lemuel Hopkins (known collectively as the Connecticut Wits), *The Anarchiad* appeared in serial form in a Connecticut newspaper from October 1786 through September 1787. Many newspapers and printers in the fledgling republic, invited to pirate the work, did so. The climactic number of the poem appeared during the tense period of negotiation that produced the "Connecticut Compromise" – one legislative chamber apportioned by population, but the second, the Senate, with two members from each state. While the authors of the poem were not constitutional delegates, they were members of the influential Connecticut state society of the Cincinnati. Humphreys attended the national meeting of the Cincinnati in May 1787 and accompanied Washington there. (Jefferson and others were deeply suspicious of the Cincinnati.) *The Anarchiad*, tremendously popular, proved the most famous political satire in America. It urged a strong federal constitution against the claims of states, claims to avoid federal taxation and to print separate currencies. In Massachusetts, Shays's Rebellion, an armed and violent movement, had alarmed pro-federalists that the new union could easily fall apart, prey to internecine wrangling and ad hoc militias.

While the versification of *The Anarchiad* lacks Pope's finish, the Connecticut Wits do well enough. Having studied Pope at Yale, they follow the general outline of

The Dunciad but turn the enemy into the chaos of political disunion and the hero, now a genuine one, into Washington. At first, some thought the poem was modeled on *The Rolliad* (1784) attributed to Fox, Sheridan, and their circle. But Pope is clearly the inspiration in design and ornament:

> Behold the reign of anarchy, begun,
> And half the business of confusion done
> From hell's dark caverns discord sounds alarms,
> Blows her loud trump, and calls my Shays to arms.

The central plea of the young nation becomes clear:

> Each requisition wastes in fleeting air,
> And not one State regards the powerless prayer.
> . . .
> On you she calls! attend the warning cry:
> YE LIVE UNITED, OR DIVIDED DIE!

The idea that several ex-colonial poets took strength from Pope to fashion a poem that would promote the passage of a strong federal constitution in Philadelphia may seem strange, yet it reflects how satire and political engagement of real impact could still go hand in hand.

The Angry Young Men of the '50s and '60s – and Anstey

A trio of writers hoped to inherit Pope's mantle but naturally rebelled against it too. They could be called Britain's "angry young men" of the 1750s and 1760s. Charles Churchill, Robert Lloyd, and Evan Lloyd produced heavy, thumping verse. If Dryden had spoken of "the fineness of a stroke that separates the head from the body, and leaves it standing in its place," such a stroke required a sharp saber. Churchill handled a club or, to use his phrase, a "mighty Flail." His satire returns to insult, curse, and to list-making of enemies and their faults. Churchill writes with little design and seldom with correction:

> Had I the pow'r, I could not have the time,
> Whilst spirits flow, and Life is in her prime,
> Without a sin 'gainst Pleasure, to design
> A plan, to methodize each thought, each line
> Highly to finish, and make ev'ry grace,
> In itself charming, take new charms from place.
> Nothing of Books, and little known of men,
> When the mad fit comes on, I seize the pen,
> Rough as they run, the rapid thoughts set down,

>   Rough as they run, discharge them on the Town,
>   Hence rude, unfinish'd brats, before their time,
>   Are born into this idle world of rime,
>   And the poor *slattern* MUSE is brought to bed
>   With all her imperfections on her head.
>   (*Gotham*, 2.165–78)

Strangely – but from a psychological point of view understandable – there must be found some ground on which to rebel. Churchill blamed Pope's craft for being good too consistently and claimed his "excellence, unvaried, tedious grows." He complained, "Verses must run, to charm a modern ear, / From all harsh, rugged interruptions clear" (*Apology*, 340–1). But in returning to what Dryden had heard in John Oldham's youthful satire, "the harsh cadence of a rugged line" (16), Churchill failed to achieve the blending of tones and sources that had shaped Pope's verse into such a strong alloy.

Nevertheless, Churchill remains a premier satirist. If his forceful lines do not pierce or explode, then like heavy cannon balls they knock down by massy weight. They are hard to aim, but Churchill seems not to care:

>   But now, *Decorum* lost, I stand
>   *Bemus'd*, a Pencil in my hand,
>   And, dead to ev'ry sense of shame,
>   Careless of Safety and of Fame,
>   The names of Scoundrels minute down,
>   And Libel more than half the Town.
>   (*The Ghost*, 4.727–32)

Churchill attended Westminster School near where his father, a clergyman, taught school. His own teacher, Pierson Lloyd, father of Robert, a schoolmate and close friend, guided the young Churchill, who then attended St John's College, Cambridge. But at eighteen Churchill married and ended his days at university. Churchill's kindly father housed the couple and trained his son for the church. In his early twenties Churchill practiced as an ordained deacon; then for two years, now a priest, acted as his father's curate in Rainham. At twenty-seven he was elected to succeed his father as lecturer of St John's, Westminster. But with two children, a spousal budget he could not check, and his own inclination for town entertainments, he fell into serious debt. The man who rescued and preserved him from prison was Pierson Lloyd, his old schoolmaster.

Churchill turned to verse. "The Bard" (1760), a Hudibrastic poem, never left manuscript. "The Conclave" (1760) so libeled the dean and chapter of Westminster that its publisher dared not sell it. (Satires against the clergy, lawyers, and doctors were increasingly common, but this one went too far.) Then, selecting a subject less close to home but clearly in his ken, Churchill with his own funds published anonymously a satire on the contemporary stage, *The Rosciad* (1761). Its title comes from the legendary Roman actor Roscius. The poem proved a hit, a bestseller. Churchill paid his debts, gave an allowance to his estranged wife, and set out on a second career with confidence and bristle. His old friend Robert Lloyd, who had attended Trinity College, Cambridge, and then followed his father Pierson as an usher at Westminster, now fell in again with Churchill. Lloyd's friendship with the man two years his senior led – as if by baleful magnetic attraction – to loss of employment. Lloyd's own literary endeavors were relatively weak. He was imprisoned for debt. Churchill, loyal, visited him and paid him a weekly allowance but could not extricate Robert in the way that Robert's own father had saved Churchill.

Churchill also befriended Wilkes and wrote much of the prose in *The North Briton*. When Wilkes and several dozen others were arrested on a general warrant after publication of *The North Briton* no. 45 (1763), Wilkes saved Churchill by calling him "Mr Thompson" in front of the arresting officer, thus giving Churchill time to escape. Churchill returned to verse satire with political ends. *The Prophecy of Famine* (1763), probably his best satire, excoriates Bute and the Scots.

For twenty months, until November 1764, Churchill traveled and poured out vitriol on political and social targets. He wrote poetry that is not satiric, too, including *Gotham*, which Cowper praised. While on his way to see the exiled Wilkes in Paris, Churchill died in Boulogne of a sudden fever. He was thirty-three. His poetic career had lasted little more than three years. Barely a month after Churchill died, Robert Lloyd, still in prison, passed away at thirty-one.

If any writer promised to continue Churchill's legacy it was Evan Lloyd. Educated at Cambridge (Jesus College) like Churchill and Robert Lloyd, Evan Lloyd took orders, also like Churchill, and in 1762 accepted a living in Wales. There, a neighboring squire ignited Lloyd's ire. Lloyd wrote *The Methodist* (1766), a sharp, inventive satire, so sharp it landed Lloyd, found guilty of libel, as an inmate in the King's Bench Prison. There he, too, grew friends with Wilkes, now returned from France and a fellow prisoner.

The Methodist, in octosyllabic couplets, reminds one of Swift's versification, Pope's more extreme anger, and Dryden's disdain for democratic religion and democratic politics. Its storyline recalls *Paradise Lost*. All the ethical and literary anchors for Lloyd's attack come from previous generations. This poem of a thousand lines demolishes a man portrayed as self-righteous, enthusiastical, lecherous, and hypocritical. Methodism as a whole is the target, too. We can recall that John Wesley was accused of seducing young girls and of accepting improper payment – accused, in short, of every transgression that televangelists face today. In the 1760s and 1770s Methodism came under strong attack. Its growing popularity, its appeal to the poorer classes, including laborers and farm workers, its massive open-air meetings, its moving sermons and oratory, its suggestion that social and economic ills are a product of social and class structures rather than of personal failures – all this made Methodism a nexus of volatile national conditions undergoing rapid change. Methodism suffered, too, for its rebuke to the Anglican establishment. Wesley questioned the smug assumption that people who are poor are "poor only because they are idle"

(*Journal*, February 8, 1753). Implicitly, he criticized the Church of England for ignoring its own doctrines.

So, Lloyd, an articulate but one-dimensional cultural conservative, goes after his neighboring squire and after Methodism in general.

> As well the *Muse* might one of these
> *Poets' Impossibilities*
> Assay to do, and speed as well,
> As if She should attempt to tell
> The *Names* and *Characters* of *all*
> That on the Name of *Satan* call,
> That preach, and lie, and whine, and cant,
> Soldiers for *Hell's Church Militant*;
> And use the Head, the Heart, the Hand,
> To spread *its Doctrines* thro' the Land.

Yet, at bottom, *The Methodist* is more than a poem against one man or one sect. It is a poem about cultural decline, the decay of beauty, virtue, political stability, social order, and true religion. Lloyd fears decadence in all its modish disguises. He fires a salvo in the growing culture wars of the later eighteenth century: "*Cities* and *Empires* will decay, / And to *Corruption* fall a prey!" Reason, royalty, and politics all fall under Lloyd's scourge: "Thus let us turn where'er we will, / Each *Machiavel's* a *Changeling* still." Lloyd cannot stand the idea that the working classes could interpret their own religion or control their own government. *The Methodist* is Evan Lloyd's best effort. In two earlier satires, *The Powers of the Pen* (1766) and *The Curate* (1766), he had styled himself a devotee of Churchill, pursued literary disputes, and depicted his own life as a minister, essentially concluding that he alone followed the golden rule. After *The Methodist*, Lloyd wrote *Conversation* (1767), which follows Pope's pentameter couplets. As others had started their careers by imitating Pope but then shrewdly turned to other opportunities, Lloyd effectively closed his by a retrograde move.

Even as Evan Lloyd ran from the social flux, cultural instability, and religious innovation of the 1760s, Christopher Anstey seemed almost to revel in them. *The New Bath Guide* (1766) both delights in and punctures the consumerism, professionalism, quackery, fashion, fads, pretension, and celebrityhood of that center of the *bon ton*. Curiously, this satire seems to wish that its objects would *not* reform or desist. *The New Bath Guide* criticizes yet feels weirdly comfortable with them, much in the way glossy magazines or television programs criticize yet also titillate as they feed rather than suppress the appetite for glitz and gossip. (Anstey was so attracted to Bath that he moved there as one of the first residents of the Crescent. Imagine Pope settling in Timon's Villa!) In paradoxical fashion, *The New Bath Guide* virtually promotes what it satirizes (one exception is Methodism). What better way to guarantee a continued readership and never-ending subject matter? Of course, Anstey isn't afraid to poke and prod. There are palpable hits. A young lady greets one of the physicians who will treat her for *wind*:

> "Good Doctor, I'm your's – 'tis a fine Day for walking –
> "Sad News in the Papers – G-d knows who's to blame –
> "The Colonies seem to be all in a Flame –
> "This Stamp-Act, no doubt, might be good for the Crown –"
>
> (Letter 4, 16–19)

The doctors, indeed, are more concerned with politics than her health:

> So thus they brush'd off, each his cane at his Nose,
> When JENNY came in, who had heard all their Prose:
> I'll teach them, says she, at their next Consultation,
> To come and take Fees for the Good of the Nation.
>
> (Letter 4, 44–7)

Part of the buzz is that one is flattered by being so important that one could be taken advantage of:

> I'm sure I have travell'd our Country all o'er
> And ne'er was so civilly treated before:
> Would you think, my dear Mother, (without the least Hint
> That we all should be glad of appearing in Print)
> The News-Writers here were so kind as to give all
> The World an Account of our happy Arrival? –
> You scarce can imagine what Numbers I've met
> (Tho' to me they are perfectly Strangers as yet)
> Who all with Address and Civility came,
> And seem'd vastly proud of SUBSCRIBING our Name.
>
> (Letter 7, 14–23)

There are brief lessons in economics:

> From the earliest Ages, dear Mother, till now,
> All Statesmen and great Politicians allow
> That nothing advances the Good of a Nation,
> Like giving all Money a free Circulation...
>
> (Letter 8, 1–4)

> "Circulation of Cash – Circulation decay'd –
> "Is at once the Destruction and Ruin of Trade; –
> "Circulation – I say – Circulation it is,
> "Gives Life to Commercial Countries like this...
>
> (Letter 8, 13–16)

Approved ways to stimulate the consumer economy include gambling and lotteries:

> And *Gaming*, no doubt, is of infinite use
> That same Circulation of Cash to produce;

> What true public-spirited People are here
> Who for that very Purpose come every Year!
> (Letter 8, 23–6)

The rising young men, very clever, inherit no titles:

> 'Tis your Men of fine Heads, and of nice Calculations
> That afford so much Service to Administrations,
> Who by frequent Experience know how to devize
> The speediest Methods of raising Supplies.
> 'Tis such Men as these, Men of Honour and Worth,
> That challenge Respect from all Persons of Birth,
> And is it not right they should all be carest
> When they're all so polite and so very well drest;
> When they circulate freely the Money they've won,
> And wear a lac'd Coat, tho' their Fathers wore none?
> (Letter 8, 37–46)

Satirizing that fashionable, ineluctable quality of literature and character then known as *spirit*, Anstey portrays his rising young women as shopping till they drop:

> What makes KITTY SPICER, and little Miss SAGO
> To Auctions and Milliners Shops ev'ry Day go;
> What makes them to vie with each other and quarrel
> Which spends the most Money for splendid Apparel?
> Why *Spirit* – to shew they have much better Sense
> Than their Fathers, who rais'd it by Shillings and Pence.
> (Letter 10, 19–24)

His titty-*tum* titty-*tum* anapests ferment the lines into a quaffing wine rather than a fine vintage. It was enormously popular. *The New Bath Guide* is a short comic epistolary novel in verse, revealing hypocrisy and vanity, those two species of the genus ridiculous (or affectation) that Fielding identified in his Preface to *Joseph Andrews* (1742). With Anstey, satire and social commentary morph into the novelistic. Smollett drew elements of *Humphry Clinker* (1771) from *The New Bath Guide*.

The Satire of Social Critique and Outraged Sentiment

It is hard to think first of Cowper, Goldsmith, Burns, or perhaps even Crabbe, as satirists. In collections of satiric poetry, only Goldsmith's *Retaliation* (1774) and Burns' "Holy Willie's Prayer" (1808) or "Epitaph on Holy Willie" are liable to appear. These poems are satires, whole and entire. Yet, as a literary mode, satire can surface in almost any genre. Excellent satire appears in poems that in their entirety are not overtly satiric. *The Deserted Village* (1770), *The Task* (1785), *The Parish Register* (1807) – all set in the country by those who knew the country – they oppose the spread of corruption, the rise of luxury, and the decline of simpler virtues. In the case of Crabbe, we see folly and hypocrisy as much in the village or on the farm as in the city. Goldsmith, Cowper, and Crabbe, sense the growing interdependence of city, country, and colony; luxury in the metropolis may rest on rural poverty; rural poverty can decline into hopelessness and famine; and wage and chattel slavery cast a shadow over all.

If passages in Cowper's *Task*, Goldsmith's *Deserted Village*, and Crabbe's many works lack the "spice of malignity" that Wordsworth deemed the core of satire, we can approach that core from another angle. A critique that exposes harmful social conditions, questionable economic transactions, and corrupt political practices may be regarded as satiric. A critique that ridicules those practices even while eliciting sympathy for their victims, or for those whose weaknesses render them unable to overcome the harsh conditions perpetuated by those policies, may be regarded as satiric. A critique that aims to alter the moral compass of the reader, arouse social indignation, and heighten political consciousness – this represents a new satiric spirit. This spirit may mix attack with meditation, nostalgia, even elegy. David Fairer (2004) speaks of the genre of "sentimental satire." It is not in the spirit of Horace or Persius or Juvenal, nor that of Dryden or Pope. It is modern and postclassical. It constitutes a literature of dissent. It may use sentiment, but may also eschew or even satirize sentimentality, as Goldsmith does Cumberland's sentimental comedies, or as Crabbe does Goldsmith's own emotional tone in *The Deserted Village*.

Goldsmith wrote *Retaliation* from what Johnson once called "*defensive* pride." Members of the Literary Club, among them Burke, Reynolds, and Garrick, had turned with pleasant raillery on the nature of Goldsmith's conversation. Garrick composed a mock epitaph: "Here lies Nolly Goldsmith, for shortness called Noll, / Who wrote like an angel, but talked like poor Poll." Goldsmith kept his peace, but soon responded by circulating more anapestic epitaphs. Here is Burke's:

> Here lies our good Edmund, whose genius was such,
> We scarcely can praise it, or blame it too much;
> Who, born for the Universe, narrow'd his mind,
> And to party gave up, what was meant for mankind.
> Tho' fraught with all learning, kept straining his throat,
> To persuade Tommy Townshend to lend him a vote;
> Who, too deep for his hearers, still went on refining,
> And thought of convincing, while they thought of dining;
> Tho' equal to all things, for all things unfit;
> Too nice for a statesman, too proud for a wit:
> For a patriot too cool; for a drudge, disobedient;
> And too fond of the *right* to pursue the *expedient*.
> (29–40)

Goldsmith praises Garrick ("An abridgement of all that was pleasant in man," line 94), but then strikes:

> Yet, with talents like these, and an excellent heart,
> The man had his failings, a dupe to his art;
> Like an ill-judging beauty, his colours he spread,
> And beplaistered, with rouge, his own natural red.
> On the stage he was natural, simple, affecting,
> 'Twas only that, when he was off, he was acting.
> (97–102)

Garrick's friendship is won "by finessing and trick": "He cast off his friends, as a huntsman his pack; / For he knew when he pleased he could whistle them back" (107–8). The wounds are never mortal, but Goldsmith's eye needs no pair of spectacles, green or otherwise, to aim well.

A deeper, more complex discontent pervades *The Traveller* (1766) and *The Deserted Village*. Commerce had long been regarded as the way to national wealth and international prosperity. Dryden in *Annus Mirabilis* (1667) and Pope in *Windsor Forest* (1713) confirm this attitude, with England leading a new globalization. But for Goldsmith and many of his contemporaries, there could be too much of a good thing. One couplet in *The Traveller* puts it succinctly: "Where wealth and freedom reign contentment fails, / And honour sinks where commerce long prevails" (91–2).

Goldsmith generally accepted a class system and social subordination. He thought freedom could suffer alike "The rabble's rage, and tyrant's angry steel" (*The Traveller*, 366), but he feared that the class system could too easily become stretched. As the rich engross themselves and the gap between rich and poor widens – the rich get richer, the poor get poorer – the consequences prove disastrous:

> For just experience tells in every soil,
> That those who think must govern those that toil,
> And all that freedom's highest aims can reach,
> Is but to lay proportion'd loads on each.
> Hence, should one order disproportion'd grow,
> Its double weight must ruin all below.
> (*The Traveller*, 371–6)

Six years later, *The Deserted Village* pursues this theme by attacking land enclosures and the loss of the open-field system. Economic historians judge that, over time, enclosures probably promoted general prosperity, but many small yeomen and poor farmers suffered. Goldsmith sees the slow destruction of a once strong human fabric:

> Ill fares the land, to hastening ills a prey,
> Where wealth accumulates, and men decay;

> Princes and lords may flourish, or may fade;
> A breath can make them, as a breath has made.
> But a bold peasantry, their country's pride,
> When once destroyed, can never be supplied.
> (51–6)

Like Pope (and Burke), he uses a past-present *topos* to underscore the deterioration:

> But times are altered; trade's unfeeling train
> Usurp the land, and dispossess the swain;
> Along the lawn, where scattered hamlets rose,
> Unwieldy wealth, and cumbrous pomp repose...
> (63–6)

New trophy houses and conspicuous consumption hardly help those homeless left behind. Goldsmith turns his eye to a "wretched matron, forced, in age, for bread, / To strip the brook with mantling cresses spread" (131–2). The message is clear, if only someone would listen and act (though no Man of Ross appears):

> Ye friends to truth, ye statesmen who survey
> The rich man's joys encrease, the poor's decay,
> 'Tis yours to judge, how wide the limits stand
> Between a splendid and an happy land.
> (265–8)

Global trade and the new economy were producing great wealth but also growing inequality. "Thus fares the land, by luxury betrayed," laments Goldsmith, and each common laborer in the midst of new "palaces" has not "one arm to save, / The country blooms – a garden, and a grave" (295, 301–2).

Cowper's marvelous blank verse in *The Task* (1785) pursues these themes, too. Like Goldsmith, he can paint a satiric portrait, as he does of the "macaroni parson," the fashionable William Dodd, executed for forgery (despite Johnson's efforts to secure clemency) on June 27, 1777:

> But loose in morals, and in manners vain,
> In conversation frivolous, in dress
> Extreme, at once rapacious and profuse,
> Frequent in park, with lady at his side,
> Ambling and prattling scandal as he goes
> ...
> Or will he seek to dazzle me with tropes,
> As with the di'mond on his lily hand,
> And play his brilliant parts before my eyes,
> When I am hungry for the bread of life?
> (2.378–2, 423–6)

But Cowper does not relish personal attack. When even religion proves ineffective against current ills, he doubts how effective he might be:

> Since pulpits fail, and sounding-boards reflect
> Most part an empty ineffectual sound,
> What chance that I, to fame so little known,
> Nor conversant with men or manners much,
> Should speak to purpose, or with better hope
> Crack the satyric thong?
>
> (3.21–6)

Yet he does, and adds an eloquent voice to the chorus witnessing a national "shipwreck," as he sees it, "Of honor, dignity, and fair renown!" (59). His protests are numerous. First, society has "become so candid and so fair, / So lib'ral in construction" (3.93–4) that transgressions now are safe:

> ... Well dress'd, well bred,
> Well equipaged, is ticket good enough
> To pass us readily through every door.
>
> (3.97–9)

"No. We are polish'd now," Cowper declares ironically, for this is a "good-natured age!" (4.534; 3.95).

Cowper also sees a growing chasm between rich and poor. He compares the idleness of the rich with "the cares," as well as the "vigilance, the labour, and the skill," of "the world's more num'rous half," who toil and live "by contriving delicates for you" (see 3.544–52). This split he relates to the division of city and country. One passage sums up his burden:

> The town has tinged the country. And the stain
> Appears a spot upon a vestal's robe,
> The worse for what it soils. The fashion runs
> Down into scenes still rural; but, alas!
> Scenes rarely graced with rural manners now.
>
> (4.553–7)

London – "London ingulfs them all. The shark is there" (3.816) – comes off as the center of luxury, influence peddling, politics, white-collar crime, and moral chicanery. The revolving door of "Ministerial grace" or "some private purse" (795, 797) offers backing in the form of a loan to any civil servant or member of parliament, "To be refunded duely, when his vote / Well-managed, shall have earn'd its worthy price" (3.799–800).

Yet, Cowper does not harbor fantasies that the rural poor are always virtuous, the past always preferable, and the country always a better place to live. He explicitly and intelligently denies these prejudices. He even says that "poverty, with most who whimper forth / ... is self-inflicted woe, / Th' effect of laziness or sottish waste" (4.429–31). He admits that an earlier, more virtuous time is a "Vain wish! those days were never." He declares that in thinking so "the poet's hand ... Imposed a gay delirium for a truth" (4.525–8). Still, he envies those who could favor such a dream.

Cowper protests against "Improvement too, the idol of the age" (3.764), an idea associated with Whig attitudes and commercial enterprise. In a fine passage too long to quote in full (3.746–810), he envisions the "patrimonial timber" sold off, lands "Then advertised, and auctioneer'd away" (3.752, 756). The older home, "tasteless," is knocked down for a gaudy palace, and the landscape, with great labor and "enormous cost," is transformed – by Capability Brown. Yet even this magic leaves the owner dissatisfied. It is the vanity of human wishes set among the modern aspirations of the insecurely affluent:

> He sighs, departs, and leaves the accomplished plan
> That he has touch'd, retouch'd, many a long day
> Labor'd, and many a night pursued in dreams,
> Just when it meets his hopes, and proves the heav'n
> He wanted, for a wealthier to enjoy!
> (3.785–9)

Real-estate speculation, gated communities, the razing of comfortable, modest homes for new, gargantuan "McMansions," leveraged loans, exorbitant vacation retreats occupied for but a few weeks each year, the obliteration of all natural features to "improve" them: Cowper paints every one.

He also puts his finger on two more issues that most satirists of this time target. For Cowper, they are interconnected: unethical action is becoming more corporate, consolidated in companies and groups, where personal liability is hard to pin down and harder to pursue; punishment and correction prove elusive. We have heard Cowper complain that "pulpits fail" and that a sense of shame cannot crack the "good-natured" hypocrisy of his age. He is now more explicit. Hard as it is to castigate a local oaf or officious fool, it seems impossible to change a corporate mentality that perpetrates fraud, urges its members to be "team players," vilifies whistleblowers, and throws a wall of legal protection around true culprits. This condition Cowper sees developing in his own day: "Lamented change! to which full many a cause / Invet'rate, hopeless of a cure, conspires" (4.576–7). His word "conspires" is apt, for it suggests how corporate conduct can deteriorate into self-protection, and how executive conduct can enrich itself at the expense of honest business:

> And burghers, men immaculate perhaps,
> In all their private functions, once combined
> Become a loathsome body, only fit
> For dissolution, hurtful to the main.

> Hence merchants, unimpeachable of sin
> Against the charities of domestic life,
> Incorporated, seem at once to lose
> Their nature; and, disclaiming all regard
> For mercy and the common rights of man,
> Build factories with blood, conducting trade
> At the sword's point, and dying the white robe
> Of innocent commercial justice red.
>   (4.672–83)

Cowper's sadness here is not unrelated to Britain's foreign policy, her wars of interest not protection, and her chartered companies:

> Is India free? and does she wear her plumed
> And jewelled turban with a smile of peace,
> Or do we grind her still?
>   (4.28–30)

Crabbe and Burns

Crabbe, more conventionally regarded as a satirist than Goldsmith or Cowper, does not indulge in accusations of general decline and decay. More intimately acquainted with rural penury (though Goldsmith knew it too), Crabbe spent his youth where he was born, the small village of Aldeburgh, Suffolk. There his apprenticeship to a surgeon proved unsuccessful. Later, in London, he studied for orders and was ordained. Burke encouraged his literary efforts, as did Johnson, and Burke helped secure a place for him in the church. Crabbe's poetry won a strong early reputation: *The Library* (1781), *The Village* (1783), and *The Newspaper* (1785), with the middle work a great success. He wrote at least three novels, and more verses, all tossed in the flames with the assistance of his young sons. Between 1785 and 1807, until he was fifty-three, Crabbe attended to his pastoral care and family. He published nothing. Then, *The Parish Register* (1807), *The Borough* (1810), *Tales in Verse* (1812), and *Tales of the Hall* (1819) further secured his reputation, at that time ranked with Scott's. Jane Austen remarked that she would not mind being known as Mrs George Crabbe.

Crabbe satirizes some denizens of the village, and some whose marriages or deaths are recorded in *The Parish Register*. He also satirizes, indirectly through his strong realism and irony, any sentimentalizing of rural life. He has no truck with pastoral conventions; *The Village* verges on a sober parody of Goldsmith's *Deserted Village*. So, Crabbe blends a critique of what appears to be innate human folly and depravation with an indictment of harsh social and economic conditions that catalyze human weaknesses into misery. To this he adds absolute distrust of the sentimental or Gothic and, joining other satirists of different stripes (Anstey, Cowper, Burns,

Evan Lloyd), a tart rendering of the professional class, especially of doctors and ministers, whose care often becomes abuse.

There are hints that Crabbe sees a change for the worse in national conditions, but the focus remains local. "I sought the simple life that Nature yields," he confesses, but finds that "Rapine and Wrong and Fear usurp'd her place." He instances how shore folk lure ships to destruction: "Theirs, or the ocean's, miserable prey" (*The Village*, 1.110–11, 118). Crabbe is clear that a rift separates poor laborers and spoiled consumers. He deprecates that rift, especially when the lives of impoverished farmers or miners are romanticized. Their work is killing not healthy, painful not pleasant. Yet he adds this jab: "Then own that labour may as fatal be / To these thy slaves, as thine excess to thee" (*The Village*, 1.152–3).

For the sick soul there is little succor anywhere: "The rich disdain him; nay, the poor disdain" (1.195). In the end, Crabbe *protests* the human condition, especially when found in penury, but what he *satirizes* are the ways in which we delude ourselves in thinking about that condition, and how we comfort ourselves with imagined palliatives that actually deepen suffering. In the parish poorhouse:

> Here, sorrowing, they each kindred sorrow scan,
> And the cold charities of man to man:
> Whose laws indeed for ruin'd age provide,
> And strong compulsion plucks the scrap from pride;
> But still that scrap is bought with many a sigh,
> And pride embitters what it can't deny.
> (*The Village* 1.244–9)

Meanwhile, Crabbe does not spare those who are fortunate yet self-indulgent:

> Say ye, oppress'd by some fantastic woes,
> Some jarring nerve that baffles your repose;
> Who press the downy couch, while slaves advance
> With timid eye, to read the distant glance;
> Who with sad prayers the weary doctor tease,
> To name the nameless ever-new disease;
> Who with mock patience dire complaints endure,
> Which real pain and that alone can cure;
> How would ye bear in real pain to lie,
> Despised, neglected, left alone to die?
> (*The Village*, 1.250–9)

As Swift had satirized abuses of those most valued of human accomplishments and practices, religion and learning, Crabbe joins others to attack the inefficacy, hypocrisy, and corruption of doctors and clergy. Have we heard of self-important physicians interrupting patients, lacking empathy, and prescribing needless medicines or procedures? If treatment is reckless, how likely is prosecution? All this is familiar to Crabbe:

> Anon, a figure enters, quaintly neat,
> All pride and business, bustle and conceit;
> With looks unalter'd by these scenes of woe,
> With speed that, entering, speaks his haste to go,
> He bids the gazing throng around him fly,
> And carries fate and physic in his eye:
> A potent quack, long versed in human ills,
> Who first insults the victim whom he kills;
> Whose murd'rous hand a drowsy Bench protect,
> And whose most tender mercy is neglect.
> (*The Village*, 1.276–85)

Goldsmith's minister in *The Deserted Village* was "passing rich with forty pounds a year," a line Crabbe quotes ironically to introduce his version of the country parson:

> A jovial youth, who thinks his Sunday's task
> As much as God or man can fairly ask;
> ...
> A sportsman keen, he shoots through half the day,
> And, skill'd at whist, devotes the night to play.
> (*The Village*, 1.306–7, 312–13)

When a poor man dies and even the village children suspend their sport to mourn the friend who made them bows and balls, bats and wickets:

> The busy priest, detain'd by weightier care,
> Defers his duty till the day of prayer;
> And, waiting long, the crowd retire distress'd,
> To think a poor man's bones should lie unbless'd.
> (1.343–6)

Burns first made a name for himself not by his songs, few of which he published (they almost all appeared posthumously), but by his satires and, to some extent, his epistles. The satires were so hard on the orthodox Kirk and its self-righteous members that Burns kept several of them out of print, too. While "Address to the Deil," "The Holy Fair," and "Address to the Unco Guid" appeared in 1786 and 1787, "Holy Willie's Prayer" and "To the Rev. John M'Math" waited until 1808, twelve years after Burns died. The sting of these satires proved so sharp that they fueled attacks on Burns and prompted false stories accusing him of drunkenness and immorality. When Burns attacks the "rigidly righteous," he only wishes he could do it more keenly:

> O Pope, had I thy satire's darts
> To gie the rascals their deserts,
> I'd rip their rotten, hollow hearts,

> An' tell aloud
> Their jugglin' hocus pocus arts
> To cheat the crowd.
> ("To the Rev. John M'Math," 37–42)

The irony of "Holy Willie's Prayer," a dramatic monologue in the form of a self-indicting address to the Almighty, exposes not only the cruelty of its speaker and his sins (lack of charity, drunkenness, fornication), it also rejects the Calvinist doctrine of election and makes fun of disputes within the Presbyterian Church. In little more than a hundred lines, with medieval more than classical models, Burns fells numerous targets with gust and point.

Peter Pindar, Politics, and Personal Attack

John Wolcot, who wrote under the name "Peter Pindar," was a sometimes funny, always abusive, gossip *cum* political columnist in verse. By no means was Augustan satire dead at the end of the eighteenth century. The French Revolution and reaction against its sympathizers created a renaissance of partisan attacks, public literary brawls, and personal quarrels. Byron did not return to Pope's manner out of thin air. Wolcot came to London in 1781, accompanied by the painter John Opie, whose talent he discovered. But little seemed to make Wolcot happy. Imitating Pope's *Epilogue to the Satires*, he launched a poetic broadside against George III and the court. He also attacked the Royal Academy, the Royal Society, Pitt, Paine, and countless others. Ever the self-righteous pundit, his own personal life was a shambles. Peter Pindar's notoriety and notoriousness knew no bounds. Generally rising above the mean in comic quality, his verse is consistently mean-spirited. In his *Poetical and Congratulatory Epistle to James Boswell* (1786), he reports of Boswell's relationship to Johnson: "Yes! his broad wing had raised thee, (no bad hack) / A tom-tit, twittering on an eagle's back" (21–2).

Yet Peter Pindar was no latter-day Theban eagle himself; "no bad hack" serves as a good self-description. In 1800, William Gifford revenged himself on Wolcot, who believed (wrongly) that Gifford, editor of *The Anti-Jacobin*, had attacked him. Gifford's *Epistle to Peter Pindar* (1800) matches Wolcot in nasty personal address:

> False fugitive! back to thy vomit flee –
> Troll the lascivious song, the fulsome glee,
> Truck praise for lust, hunt infant genius down,
> Strip modest merit of its last half-crown,
> Blow from thy mildew'd lips on virtue blow,
> And blight the goodness thou can'st never know;
> 'Tis well. But why on ME?
> (29–35)

The political climate of the 1790s produced many verse satires. John Courtenay, a member of parliament who had supported Burke in the prosecution of Warren Hastings, turned against Burke's *Reflections* in *A Poetical and Philosophical Essay* (1793). Courtenay plays on the class warfare that, long simmering in England, had exploded in France:

> To Nobles, Priests, ye People bow the head,
> Tho' spurn'd by those, who by your toils are fed:
> Ye rich and great, who weep your fancy'd woes,
> Look up to Heav'n, and give your souls repose.
> (21–4)

Application

English verse satire of the latter half of the eighteenth century engages the flux and volatility of several culture wars, several actual wars, a constantly challenged political establishment, foreign entanglements, the growing influence of corporate bodies, a new economy, rapid globalization, religious ferment, and class divisions. If these conditions and the responses to them seem to foreshadow life two and a half centuries later, it is not because they have been portrayed to do so – it is because they do. Mindful of this, we can return with a renewed appreciation to read and apply those satiric spirits who first grappled not only with a deeply flawed world, but with a modern and endlessly complex one as well.

References and Further Reading

Bate, W. Jackson (1970) Johnson and satire *manqué*. In W. H. Bond (ed.), *Eighteenth-century Studies: In Honor of Donald F. Hyde*, pp. 145–60. New York: The Grolier Club.

Bentman, Raymond (ed.) (1972) *The Methodist: A Poem* [by Evan Lloyd]. Los Angeles: William Andrews Clark Memorial Library (The Augustan Reprint Society).

Bogel, Fredric V. (2001) *The Difference Satire Makes: Rhetoric and Reading from Jonson to Byron*. Ithaca, NY: Cornell University Press.

Boswell, James (1950) *Boswell's Life of Johnson Together with Boswell's Journey of a Tour to the Hebrides and Johnson's Diary of a Journey into North Wales*, ed. George Birkbeck Hill, revised and enlarged by L. F. Powell, 6 vols. Oxford: Clarendon Press.

Brunström, Conrad (2004) *William Cowper: Religion, Satire, Society*. Lewisburg: Bucknell University Press.

Carnochan, W. B. (1970) Satire, sublimity, and sentiment: theory and practice in post-Augustan satire. *Proceedings of the Modern Language Association* 85, 260–7.

Carretta, Vincent (1983) *The Snarling Muse: Verbal and Visual Political Satire from Pope to Churchill*. Philadelphia: University of Pennsylvania Press.

Cash, Arthur H. (ed.) (2000) *An Essay on Woman* [by John Wilkes and Thomas Potter]. New York: AMS Press.

Day, Martin S. (1948) Anstey and anapestic satire in the late eighteenth century. *English Literary History* 15 (2), 122–46.

Dowling, William C. (1990) *Poetry and Ideology in Revolutionary Connecticut*. Athens: University of Georgia Press.

Engell, James (1999) Pope's American constitution [on *The Anarchiad*]. In *The Committed Word: Literature and Public Values*, pp. 33–49. University Park, PA: Pennsylvania State University Press.

Fairer, David (2004) Panel paper on satire. ASECS Annual Meeting, Boston, MA, March 24–26.

Faulkner, Peter (1991) William Cowper and the poetry of empire. *Durham University Journal* 52 (2), 165–73.

Griggs, Jeanne (1997) Self-praise and the ironic personal panegyric of Peter Pindar. *Age of Johnson* 8, 223–53.

Hatch, Ronald B. (1989) Charles Churchill and the poetry of "Charter'd Freedom." *English Studies in Canada* 15 (3), 277–87.

Heringman, Noah (2004) "Peter Pindar," Joseph Banks, and the case against natural history. *The Wordsworth Circle* 35 (1), 21–30.

Jemielity, Thomas (1984) *The Vanity of Human Wishes*: satire foiled or achieved. *Essays in Literature* 11, 35–45.

Johnson, Samuel (1905) *Lives of the English Poets*, ed. George Birkbeck Hill, 3 vols. Oxford: Clarendon Press.

Kinsley, James and Boulton, James T. (eds) (1966) *English Satiric Poetry: Dryden to Byron*. London: Edward Arnold.

Lockwood, Thomas (1979) *Post-Augustan Satire: Charles Churchill and Satirical Poetry, 1750–1800*. Seattle: University of Washington Press.

New, Peter (1976) *George Crabbe's Poetry*. New York: St Martin's Press.

Noggle, James (2001) *The Skeptical Sublime: Aesthetic Ideology in Pope and the Tory Satirists*. Oxford: Oxford University Press.

Pound, Ezra (1928) *Selected Poems*, ed. T. S. Eliot. London: Faber and Gwyer.

Scott, Walter (1834) *The Prose Works of Sir Walter Scott*, 28 vols. Edinburgh: Robert Cadell.

Selden, Raman (1978) *English Verse Satire, 1590–1765*. London: Allen and Unwin.

Strachan, John (ed.) (2003) *British Satire, 1785–1840*, 5 vols. London: Pickering and Chatto.

Turner, Gavin (ed.) (1994) *The New Bath Guide* [by Christopher Anstey]. Bristol: Broadcast Books.

Venturo, David F. (1999) *Johnson the Poet: The Poetic Career of Samuel Johnson*. Newark: University of Delaware Press.

Weinbrot, Howard D. (1988) *Eighteenth-century Satire: Essays on Text and Context from Dryden to Peter Pindar*. Cambridge: Cambridge University Press.

Wilkinson, Andrew M. (1952) The decline of English verse satire in the middle years of the eighteenth century. *The Review of English Studies*, n.s. 3 (11), 222–33.

Yu, Christopher (2003) *Nothing to Admire: The Politics of Poetic Satire from Dryden to Merrill*. New York: Oxford University Press.

Zall, Paul M. (ed.) (1972) *Peter Pindar's Poems* (foreword by A. L. Rowse). Bath: Adam and Dart.

14
Restoration and Eighteenth-century Satiric Fiction
Joseph F. Bartolomeo

The same period that saw the greatest flourishing, at least in Britain, of satire also gave rise to the new genre of the novel. Questions regarding the complex interactions between the two have long occupied scholars and critics, especially in the nearly four decades since the publication of Ronald Paulson's seminal study *Satire and the Novel in Eighteenth-century England* (1967). Although it has been common to regard satire as influencing and/or eventually giving way to the novel, the influence did not flow in one direction only: the emergence of the novel also transformed the scope and character of satire, as is most evident in works like *Gulliver's Travels* (1726) and *Tristram Shandy* (1760–7). In fact, during this period, both satire as a mode and the novel as a genre remained flexible and open to considerable experimentation, allowing for a proliferation of hybrid forms. In some eighteenth-century novels, satire plays an extremely prominent role; in other novels, a marginal one. Whenever they do appear in prose fiction, satiric ends and means come into contact — which is sometimes harmonious and complementary, sometimes dissonant and contradictory — with other formal, ideological, and moral agendas.

Rabelais, Cervantes, and Swift

The two most important early modern forebears for satiric novelists of the eighteenth century, and beyond, are Rabelais and Cervantes, due both to the range of strategies and aims that inform their satire and to their innovations with narrative form. *Pantagruel* (1532) and *Gargantua* (1534), Rabelais' chronicles of the adventures of a giant and his father, have been justly celebrated for bawdy humor, but also for clever mockery of the various authorities of church and state, most notably the theologians of the Sorbonne and the medieval scholasticism that they continued to prop up in spite of the advent of humanism. For many critics, however, Rabelais' satire sometimes extends to the humanist program itself. For instance, Gargantua's famous letter detailing the education that Pantagruel should receive has been interpreted as both a sincere celebration of humanist learning and as a parody of it. Whatever his targets, Rabelais' focus on education makes his works prominent examples of Menippean satire, which usually features a series of dialogues or debates in which pedantic, professional, or literary "learning" is ridiculed through the folly of those who attempt to embody it. Menippean satire also has a loose, miscellaneous structure, which Mikhail Bakhtin (1984) highlighted in his influential study of Rabelais. While his principal focus is the "carnivalesque" nature of Rabelais' fiction, Bakhtin also analyzes its polyphonic dimensions. This mixing of modes and voices was attractive to later writers working in a genre that invited inclusiveness, and *Tristram Shandy* is only the most extreme example of a practice widespread in eighteenth-century fiction and, as Bakhtin would argue, characteristic of the novel in general.

Long-standing critical debates about the purpose and nature of Cervantes' *Don Quixote* (1605–15) and its eponymous hero center around satire. The author's prologue identifies the work as an attack on the romances of chivalry, and throughout the novel Don Quixote frequently appears ridiculous in his chivalric delusions, is punished for them, and causes harm to others – especially his "squire," Sancho Panza – because of them. As Anthony Close (1978) has demonstrated, this "hard" view of the novel began to soften during the Romantic period, leading to an interpretation of the hero as a noble idealist, opposed to and by a base reality, and of his story as a tragedy. For eighteenth-century readers, the emphasis was placed squarely on comedy and on Don Quixote as an object of satire, but many nevertheless admired certain facets of the knight's character. For eighteenth-century novelists, including several imitators – acknowledged or otherwise – of Cervantes, some of the most important debts to *Don Quixote* lay in aspects of the novel on which "hard" and "soft" interpreters could agree: that the "real" world represented by Cervantes is replete with vanity and venality; and that while the novel attacks chivalric romances, it is ambivalent about romance in general. Many of the interpolated stories include romance-derived characters that are presented sympathetically, and the Canon of Toledo, who criticizes romance, also imagines and celebrates its ideal form, which is similar to what Cervantes created in *Persiles and Sigismunda*, published posthumously in 1617.

Equally significant for Cervantes' successors was *Don Quixote*'s highly self-conscious and metafictional form, which raises pivotal questions about authorship, authority, and the status of fiction. Part 1 has two "authors," one relying on records and interviews for the "history" of Don Quixote, the other relying on an account by the Moor Cide Hamete Benengeli, itself mediated through translation. Part 2, published ten years later, begins with an attack on Alonso Fernández de Avellaneda's spurious sequel, and has the characters directly confront their notoriety as a result not only of that sequel but also of the publication of Part 1. Continuous commentary from and dialogue between the "author" and Cide Hamete, not to mention remarks from the characters themselves on how to tell the story, had a profound impact on the narrative voice and practice of Fielding, Smollett, Sterne, and other novelists.

In the eighteenth century itself, the most enduring and significant work of satiric fiction was not a novel, and in fact satirized the emerging genre. *Gulliver's Travels* (1726) resembles novels by Jonathan Swift's contemporaries (and successors), but includes among its many targets the novel and the kind of consciousness that it imagines and inscribes. J. Paul Hunter (1990) has traced numerous ways in which Swift's work parodies Daniel Defoe's phenomenally popular first novel, *Robinson Crusoe* (1719) – from the contents of Gulliver's pockets to an opening that situates him squarely in the middle of the middle class to a miserable final homecoming more like that of Defoe's real-life model, Alexander Selkirk, than the ecstatic and profitable return of Crusoe to England. More generally, Hunter persuasively casts *Gulliver's Travels* as "an accreting generic or class parody," not only of travel narratives but of other first-person fiction that stresses "the importance of the contemporary, the knowableness through personal experience of large cosmic patterns, the significance of the individual, and the imperialistic possibilities of the human mind" (1990: 69) – in other words, of the novel.

Yet the parody, in one important sense, becomes implicated in that which it rejects. Book 4, precisely where Swift is most novelistic in portraying a unified, complex experience, has occasioned the most contentious disputes about the direction and meaning of its satire. "Hard-school" critics consider Gulliver a flexible and inconsistent satiric device, whose disgust at the Yahoos and admiration/emulation of the Houyhnhnms Swift uses to articulate his satire against human depravity and irrationality. On the other side, "soft-school" readings position Gulliver as a more unified novelistic character, whose turn to pride and misanthropy renders him more the object than the agent of satire. The impasse, which has never been resolved, derives in part from habits of reading that the novel has inculcated and enshrined.

Early Women Novelists

Swift's most immediate novelistic target, Defoe, wrote accomplished satire in other genres, including the poem "The True-born Englishman" (1700) and the pamphlet *The Shortest Way with the Dissenters* (1702), but his novels did not engage with satire in any sustained, significant way. The early novelist with the most direct investment in satire was Defoe's female contemporary, the Tory propagandist Delarivier Manley, who used the form of the scandal chronicle, or *chronique scandaleuse*, to attack leading figures in court and political life. Manley's practice recalls Aphra Behn's *Love-letters between a Nobleman and his Sister* (1684–7), which connects a story of illicit love to the Duke of Monmouth's rebellions against his father, Charles II, and his uncle, James II, but while Behn draws broad analogies between personal and political corruption, Manley offers the direct and personal satire of the *roman-à-clef*. *Queen Zarah* (1705) targets Sarah Churchill, Duchess of Marlborough and confidante to Queen Anne, portraying her as an ambitious, greedy, manipulative monster, who rises to the height of power not in spite of but because of individual and systemic depravity. In the dedication of volume 2 of her best-known work, *The New Atalantis* (1709), Manley compares it directly to Menippean satire because of its loose structure and various subjects, quotes Dryden on the efficacy of scourging vice, and defends personal satire from the strictures voiced in the influential periodical *The Tatler*, even as she pretends not to engage in it! The narrative itself, a collection of self-contained stories, portraits, and comments, is organized around an allegorical framework in which Astrea, the goddess of justice, and her mother, Virtue, are given a tour of Atalantis (England) by Intelligence, so that Astrea can observe human vices in preparation for educating a future king. As Ruth Herman has noted, in this work Manley includes some Tories as well as the usual Whigs in her sights, and she combines "scandal fiction, romance, and *ad hominem* satire" (Herman 2003: 69) in order to make her political commentary entertaining and to broaden its appeal.

Eliza Haywood, whose more prolific and varied output has won her greater prominence and critical attention from scholars of early women novelists, followed Manley's model in two scandal novels in the 1720s, but her most interesting and important satiric fiction came later. In *The Adventures of Eovaai, Princess of Ijaveo* (1736), Haywood, adopting what Ros Ballaster (2000: 154) has called "the dystopic single history favored in the separate books of... *Gulliver's Travels*," narrows her focus and uses the form of oriental fiction to satirize Sir Robert Walpole, the most powerful political figure of the early eighteenth century. The plot, too complex for brief summary, parallels the abuses of power by a villainous prime minister (a fictionalized version of Walpole) with his attempts to seduce, rape, and murder the heroine. Ballaster ultimately classifies *Eovaai* as a "mock romance, the feminocentric inverse of the Scriblerian mock epic" (2000: 164), a work that both embraces and undercuts romance in the process of attacking a corrupt man and politician.

Five years after *Eovaai*, Haywood's *Anti-Pamela* (1741), published anonymously, participated in the fray over Samuel Richardson's phenomenally popular first novel. Haywood's contribution stands out in two important respects: she was the only woman writer directly involved in the "anti-Pamelist" camp, and was responding to a text that, while written in direct opposition to the kind of amatory fiction for which she had become famous, also appropriated and adapted elements from that fiction. Haywood's novel does not offer a close parody and instead selectively incorporates some key elements of *Pamela* – the pursuit of a servant girl by her master and the epistolary form – into a story about a bold and admitted manipulator of men, the aptly named Syrena Tricksy. As I have argued elsewhere (Bartolomeo 2002), the title of the novel is ambiguous, implying either that Syrena represents the polar opposite of the transparently virtuous Pamela, or that Syrena differs from Pamela only in her self-consciousness and honesty about her hypocrisy. The ambiguity surfaces again in the frank, cynical letters between Syrena and her equally venal and greedy mother, the discovery of which twice frees a man from Syrena's clutches. These letters could be contrasted with Pamela's letters and journal, which convert her master from a seducer to a repentant suitor, or could reflect what critics of Richardson saw as Pamela's dishonesty to her parents and herself about her true motives in remaining with her master, and in forgiving him so quickly after his conversion. Epistolarity is the exception rather than the rule, however: most of the novel comes through the voice of a third-person narrator who inveighs against the heroine's corruption but also allows Haywood to incorporate salacious material under the sanction of moral instruction – precisely the charge leveled at Richardson.

The Novels of Henry Fielding

The most famous riposte to *Pamela*, *Shamela* (1741), marks Henry Fielding's debut as an author of satiric fiction. Prior to this, he had already established a reputation as a satirist in other genres: his plays lampooning the Walpole government helped bring about the Licensing Act of 1737, which ended his theatrical career, and he also published satiric political journalism in *The Champion*. Fielding's parody of *Pamela* hews more closely than Haywood's to the original, and condenses it to key episodes that demonstrate that the iconic Pamela is actually a Sham-ela, who pretends to value her "vartue," which she has already surrendered to Parson Williams (Pamela's beleaguered ally in Richardson's text), in order to trap her master into marrying her. Fielding also burlesques the form of *Pamela*, replacing the commendatory letters with which Richardson had prefixed the novel with ones from "John Puff" and from the "editor" to himself, and mocking the practice of writing to the moment by having Shamela self-consciously write in the present tense as she describes her master climbing into bed with her.

Beyond its most obvious target, *Shamela* directs its satire at religious, political, and literary corruption. Parson Williams's debauched conduct and his idiosyncratic interpretation of the scriptural admonition against being overly righteous accord with his admiration of George Whitefield, the co-founder of Methodism, as Fielding attacks through Williams the new sect's emphasis on faith over works. The mock-dedication to "Miss Fanny" recalls Pope's nickname for the effeminate Lord Hervey, a symbol for Fielding as for Pope of the rot of the Walpole regime. The purported author of the dedication, and of *Shamela* itself, is one Conny Keyber, a reference both to Conyers Middleton, who dedicated his *Life of Cicero* (1741) to Hervey, and to Colley Cibber, the actor, playwright, theater manager, and "hero" of the revised *Dunciad*, whose toadying to Walpole won him an appointment as Poet Laureate, and whose autobiographical *Apology* (1740) drew Fielding's scorn for its vanity and self-promotion.

The work in Fielding's corpus that most resembles *Shamela* in its emphasis on satire over novelistic sophistication is *Jonathan Wild* (1743). Long regarded as specifically directed against Walpole, it has more recently been read as a generalized assault on the "greatness" of those who hold power, as represented by the figure of Wild, notorious in real life as a thief and informer. Fielding's principal satiric method is inversion: throughout Wild's "history," from his disreputable birth and his corrupt education to his criminal enterprises and his execution, the narrator consistently praises the hero's greatness – even, ironically enough, when he fails to be an effective criminal. Conversely, the "good" Heartfree, an honest jeweler repeatedly victimized by Wild, and his faithful wife, the object of Wild's (characteristically unsuccessful) sexual advances, are derided as weak and silly. Wild's career serves as a biting analogue for an amoral lust for power, political or otherwise. Heartfree, on the other hand, represents a positive norm, but the thinness of his characterization, often noted by critics, suggests Fielding's primary interest in attack. Mrs Heartfree disappears for much of the novel, only to return near the end with a narrative of her adventures in exotic locales, which has been criticized as unnecessary padding but also defended as a burlesque of travel books, and as an exemplum of the power of Providence.

Joseph Andrews (1742), published between *Shamela* and *Jonathan Wild*, begins in a similar parodic vein, this time based on gender inversion: the servant guarding his virtue is a man, the brother of Pamela, and the sexual aggressor his mistress. Pamela herself appears near the end of the novel as an embodiment of nouveau-riche snobbery, but by that time, parody has given way to the creation of a different kind of fictional world. Joseph's refusal of Lady Booby's advances and quick dismissal from her service leads him to the road and to a series of encounters that have a satiric edge. The famous preface, which sets forth a new and elevated conception of the novel as a "comic epic-poem in prose," does not directly invoke satire, but Fielding's identification of his subject as the "ridiculous," the sources of which are vanity and hypocrisy, leads naturally to the exposure of these vices throughout the novel.

As a major vehicle for the satire, Fielding relies, in a novel professed to be written in the manner of Cervantes, on the quixotic figure of Parson Adams, Joseph's friend and mentor. If Adams shares none of Quixote's chivalric delusions, he is equally idealistic and gullible, and therefore is preyed upon by greedy innkeepers, uncharitable clergy, a sadistic country squire, and others – all of them objects of Fielding's scorn. Yet Adams is more than a mere victim. In spite of his own vanity (about publishing his sermons) and inconsistency (he recommends stoicism to Joseph and his lover, Fanny, but immediately rejects it when he thinks his son has died), Adams's generosity and his willingness literally to fight for a good cause render him a positive norm against which the satiric targets can be measured. The titular hero, while not as eccentric or appealing as Adams, is also victimized, not only by Lady Booby but also often by many of the same characters who abuse Adams. Unlike Adams's static character, however, Joseph's develops in a number of important ways, and he grows from would-be boy toy to a serious decision-maker who protects and defends Fanny, and eventually wins her hand and discovers his true parentage, which raises his social status. The progress toward a happy ending, again with providential overtones, contributes to a move from the satiric to the comic, but satire remains an integral part of the novel.

The blending of satire and comedy also characterizes the commentary of the narrator, a more fully developed and engaging presence than any of the characters. As Simon Varey (1990) has detailed, the witty narrative voice that directly addresses the reader establishes solidarity between the author and his audience, a necessary condition for successful satire. The habitual ironic tone conveys several sharp satiric thrusts, and the narrator's claim to focus on manners instead of men, and the species instead of the individual, accords with customary satiric theory and practice. At the same time, the narrator's geniality and bemusement separate him from the harshness of Juvenalian satire, and make the comic ending, which relies on a series of unlikely developments, seem inevitable and justified.

In *Tom Jones* (1749), the narrator's prominence is even greater, especially in the introductory chapters to each of the eighteen books, in which he articulates his aims and strategies for a new genre. Paulson (1967) regards the narrator as the strongest manifestation of the influence of Lucianic satire on Fielding. Like the cynical Lucian, this ironic commentator is "the observer and questioner who probes past appearances" (1967: 138) to expose fraud and hypocrisy. Ironic exposure works in the simplest and most straightforward way with secondary characters, as the narrator quickly peels away Blifil's piety, to show his jealousy of and malice toward Tom, and Thwackum's religious scruples, to show his greed and sadism. But even minor characters who seem to be obvious targets can reveal hidden complexities. At first, Square appears nothing more than a secular counterpart to Thwackum, a philosopher whose devotion to reason is no more serious than Thwackum's to religion, a hypocrite who condemns Tom for sexual indiscretions with Molly Seagrim only to be discovered by Tom hiding in her bedroom, and a co-conspirator with Blifil and Thwackum to deceive Tom's patron, Allworthy, and turn him against the hero. Near the end of the novel, however, Square writes a deathbed letter to Allworthy, repenting his sins, praising Tom, and detailing his conversion to religious faith. Cases like this support Paulson's conclusion that irony "is transformed by Fielding from a satiric strategy to a technique for suggesting the complexity of reality and the mitigating forces that make the 'mixed' character in whom he is most interested" (1967: 141).

The most important mixed character, of course, is the hero, and as Paulson (1967) notes, the narrator's insistence on judging a character not by individual actions but by the whole of his nature and experience runs counter to the more categorical judgments demanded by satire. As it was with Adams and Joseph, the treatment of Tom by others can be used as a gauge of their worth and, therefore, as a tool of satire. When Tom is subject rather than object, however, the good nature that represents his defining characteristic moves the thrust of the novel away from satire. Even though Tom's good-hearted actions sometimes seem impulsive and self-indulgent, and need, the narrator argues, to be tempered by prudence, they deflect attention from his faults and position him as an important precursor to the benevolent heroes of novels of sensibility. The plot, too, diminishes the satiric thrust as it tends toward a celebratory comic resolution that, in spite of the narrator's explicit objections to poetic justice, perfectly punishes vice and rewards virtue, leaving Tom – like Joseph – in possession of his true identity and of a wife, but also of a status and fortune that Joseph could not even imagine.

Sophia, ultimately Tom's spouse, serves as more than the mere prop, aspiration, and reward that Fanny was to Joseph. Fielding devotes a significant portion of the novel to her story, which, as recent feminist critics have observed, portrays a bold, autonomous woman who resists parental tyranny and social pressure in the choice of a husband – at least until the end, when, conveniently enough for Fielding, her desires coincide with her father's, Tom's, and most readers'. The relative complexity of her character, like Tom's, is antithetical to satire. And the centrality of her character and of the love story contributes to the change that Paulson (1967: 153) has identified "from a concern with the public realm to a concern with the social and the private."

Fielding's final novel, *Amelia* (1751), also focuses on the domestic, but with little of the comic optimism of *Tom Jones*. Rather than a happy conclusion, marriage marks the beginning of a powerful struggle for the novel's central couple, against poverty, manipulative false friends, the husband's fecklessness and infidelity, and attempts on the wife's honor. Sensibility informs most of the novel, in the representation not, as in *Tom Jones*, of a triumphant benevolism, but of virtue in distress, as the misfortunes of Amelia and Booth seem designed to evoke the reader's sympathy and perhaps tears. The happy ending of the novel might please the most sentimental readers, but the reversal of fortune on which it depends strikes most critics as contrived and unsatisfying. Yet, sensibility need not preclude satire. For Angela Smallwood (1989), the beleaguered Amelia's impeccable performance of her wifely duties satirizes the more fashionable women in the novel who neglect them. More broadly, Simon Varey (1986) argues that Booth and Amelia suffer at the hands of others because they cannot see behind the façades erected by them, a weakness that they share with the narrator, so much less penetrating and authoritative than his counterpart in *Tom Jones*. The satire against these hypocrites is, therefore, often more implicit than in Fielding's earlier fiction.

In the famous opening scene of the novel, Fielding skewers the legal system through his portrait of the ignorant and corrupt Justice Thrasher, the first of many agents of legal cruelty to the chronically debt-ridden Booth. The military, the nobility, and the clergy come in for similar censure in the course of the novel, so much so that some critics see a fundamental divide between social satire and domestic fiction. Alternatively, the novel can be viewed, aside from the artificial happy ending, as a satiric exposure of the deleterious effects of larger social forces on sympathetic individuals. In this regard, as Varey (1986) notes, the novel resembles *Jonathan Wild*, but because the characters of Amelia and Booth are much more fully realized than the Heartfrees, there is more poignancy in and greater outrage at their plight. Fielding's increased pessimism connects *Amelia* most closely to Scriblerian gloom, as the fairy-tale ending does nothing to eliminate or even to ameliorate ubiquitous institutional corruption.

The Novels of Smollett

Although Fielding's fiction engages with satire in varied and important ways, the eighteenth-century novelist most identified – for good and ill – with satiric goals and strategies is his contemporary Tobias Smollett. Smollett's pronounced commitment to satire may help account for the recent diminution of his canonical status, given a prevailing consensus that his narratives are primarily satiric but conclude with arbitrary and therefore often jarring comic endings. Jerry Beasley, who seeks to restore Smollett's reputation as a novelist, regards the novels instead as comedies that "strain themselves over a tension created by the strong satiric impulses that drive them" (1998: 187). Both positions have merit, and both proceed from a desire to reconcile the omnipresence of satire in Smollett's fiction with his gestures toward more novelistic plotting, characterization, and closure.

The one fictional work by Smollett universally regarded as a satire but not essentially a novel is *The History and Adventures of an Atom*, published anonymously in 1769. This scatological *roman-à-clef* satirizes politicians – not only Smollett's usual targets, the Whigs, but also Tories, including William Pitt and Lord Bute – and political life during the period of the Seven Years' War. Borrowing from Charles Johnstone's *Chrysal; or, The Adventures of a Guinea* (1760), Smollett creates a non-human narrator: an atom, which had previously resided in the bodies of leading political figures, settles in the brain of Nathaniel Peacock, a London haberdasher, and gives him an account of "Japanese" history that is analogous to events in Britain. In addition to the debt to Johnstone, Robert Adams Day (1989) has traced connections between the work and satire by Rabelais, Swift, and Sterne. Smollett's genuine novels differ from this text by incorporating satire in less personal, more complex, and, for most modern readers, more appealing ways.

The opening sentence to the preface of his first novel, *Roderick Random* (1748), argues that an interesting and natural story can provide a good vehicle for satire, and the narrative that follows amply illustrates the point. The picaresque adventures of a dispossessed Scot trying to attain the gentility to which he believes himself entitled give Smollett opportunity to attack all the forces arrayed against the hero: greedy and selfish relatives; an abusive schoolmaster; corrupt employers, lawyers, and politicians; London con artists; brutal naval officers; and many more. Among Smollett's foremost tools is caricature, which he uses to paint several objects of his satire as physically, as well as morally, repulsive. Roderick himself frequently lashes out at those who have harmed him, leading Paulson (1967: 171) to characterize him as "a satiric observer who recognizes, reacts, and rebukes." More recent critics, less concerned with the satiric immediacy than with the novelistic implications of Roderick's acts of revenge, have stressed the deleterious consequences of these acts for Roderick himself, and therefore the necessity of his abandoning them. Roderick may learn to safeguard his interests, but beyond that there are few examples of personal growth or development in his character. Moreover, although Smollett explicitly invites a sympathetic response to Roderick, the hero frequently participates in the corruption that he elsewhere exposes, perhaps most notably though his "hunting" of heiresses and his sadistic behavior toward his loyal friend Strap. These complications, which make Roderick as much the object as the agent of satire, are obscured but not resolved by an ending in which he finds his long-lost father, who showers him with love and money, and marries the idealized woman – the perhaps ironically named Narcissa – whom he had long desired. The satiric narrative of a struggle for survival gives way to a comic fantasy of personal, financial, and social elevation, and the seams do show.

Peregrine Pickle (1751) resembles *Roderick Random* in its episodic structure and its happy ending, but differs significantly in the social status of the hero: Perry is born into the upper class and retains the advantages that Roderick usually lacks. Wealth provides Perry with a broader field for action, and his creator with a broader canvas for satire, perhaps most notably during the protagonist's Grand Tour, in which Smollett ridicules the vices and follies of various nationalities, especially the Dutch and the French. Even in England, Perry has access to segments of society closed off from Roderick, enabling Smollett to expand his satire of law, medicine, the theater, religion, and politics. A principal mechanism for the satire, Perry's countless practical jokes, may expose numerous frauds and quacks, but at the cost of the reader's sympathy for the hero. While Roderick's attacks on his enemies are motivated by revenge, which readers can reject but nevertheless understand, Perry's pranks seem motivated by little more than cruelty and selfishness. Although his victims often deserve what they get, it is hard to admire a character who at one point attempts to rape the woman he eventually marries. Nor does Perry's reputation benefit from his association with Cadwallader Crabtree, the supposed fortune-teller who helps him to bilk others. Beasley considers Crabtree a "sinister presence" (1998: 96) whose harsh, cynical view of the world Smollett intends to expose and renounce. Even if Smollett is more comfortable with Crabtree's misanthropy than Beasley suggests, the absence of a normative or at least sympathetic major character in the novel inevitably complicates the reader's response to the satiric strategy.

In *Ferdinand Count Fathom* (1753), Smollett makes the nominal hero unequivocally a villain, as Fielding did in *Jonathan Wild*, but he eschews Fielding's mock-panegyric irony and instead presents Fathom as a negative example whose snares the reader is taught to avoid. As in *Roderick Random*, the opening chapter places the work in the satiric tradition, and as in *Peregrine Pickle*, the novel uses a selfish and deceitful protagonist to expose medical, legal, political, and other corruption, and, as Paulson (1967) notes, the folly of those taken advantage of by Fathom. The problem, however, is that evil characters, Fathom's partners and/or competitors in crime, often see through him, while some of those whom he dupes are idealistic and benevolent, none more so than his childhood companion Renaldo and Renaldo's lover, Monimia. The story of their victimization by Fathom, their separation, Monimia's supposed death, and their surprising reunion comprises a sentimental counterpart to Fathom's story, even if their relatively pallid characters cannot compare to Fathom's flamboyant villainy. At the conclusion of the novel, they incorporate him into their plot by forgiving him after he repents his manifold offenses. The satire, while biting as ever, must compete with and is ultimately absorbed into a sentimental romance, which, along with some striking Gothic interludes, redirects the reader's interest and attention.

While *Fathom* may or may not be directly indebted to *Jonathan Wild*, Smollett's next novel, *Sir Launcelot Greaves*, published serially in 1760–1, openly acknowledges the influence of *Don Quixote*, which Smollett himself had translated. The first direct reference, however, points to the principal difference between the works, as Greaves – who, unlike Don Quixote, is young, handsome, and really a knight – self-consciously dissociates himself from the lunacy of Cervantes' hero as he defends his decision to don the armor of a knight-errant in order to combat evil. His "madness," therefore, is more limited, and Smollett later provides an explanation for it: his frustrated love for Aurelia Darnel. When he is ultimately reunited with her, he repudiates knight-errantry and returns to his rightful place as a provincial aristocrat. In his embrace of Quixote's desire to right wrongs, Greaves sometimes appears foolish, but as in the case of Cervantes' novel, the "sane" world often seems worse. Smollett trains his satire on the larger institutional forces behind the individual abuses that Greaves combats: the law, as personified by the illiterate, pretentious, and mercenary Justice Gobble; politics, as represented by an election in which both parties pursue selfish ends, while the crowd shouts down Greaves's attempt to advocate moderation; and the penal system, as reflected in the devolution of a couple inhabiting a debtor's prison and the kidnapping and entrapment of innocents, including Greaves himself and Aurelia, in an asylum for the insane. Robert Folkenflik (2002) has cast Greaves as a literal embodiment of Pope's chivalric description of himself as a satirist ("arm'd for Virtue") in *The First Epistle of the Second Book of Horace Imitated* (1737). Beasley also relates the novel to formal verse satire, finding it the closest of all Smollett's novels to the "bitterness and intolerance" of Juvenal, with a "sharper satirical edge" (1998: 161) and a more pessimistic vision than *Don Quixote*. This judgment may underestimate the force and significance of the comic scenes in the novel, but Beasley is certainly correct that the happy ending amounts, once again, to a retreat from a vicious world, and that Greaves's righting of individual wrongs leaves their root causes intact.

Smollett's final novel, *Humphry Clinker*, published shortly before his death in 1771, differs from all his previous works in its epistolary form, and the multiplicity of voices that the form allows has a profound impact on the place and character of the satire. The chief satiric voice belongs to one of the two principal correspondents, Matthew Bramble, a valetudinarian whose travels to spas and resorts occasion his invectives against the noise, dirt, and decay of cities; frivolous fashions and social customs; and the dangers of a social leveling that has resulted in the empowerment of the mob. This conservative country squire also mounts a sustained attack on the pursuit of luxury by all social classes, which he regards as a threat to civilization (Sekora 1977). As Bramble's health improves, his tone moderates somewhat, and he is less harsh in his description of Smollett's native Scotland. Even there, however, he vents his spleen against inns and innkeepers, the filth of Edinburgh, and other familiar irritants.

Bramble has often been regarded as a spokesman for Smollett, and many of his harsh criticisms correspond with views articulated by Smollett elsewhere. Yet Bramble's is not the only voice, or even the dominant one. More space is devoted to letters by his nephew, Jery Melford, an equally acute observer, but one more bemused, and often amused, than angry at what he observes, the Horatian counterpart, according to Paulson (1967), of Bramble's Juvenalian satirist. This lighter touch informs Jery's description of the Duke of Newcastle's levee, during which the glad-handing nobleman misidentifies virtually every person to whom he speaks, and his account of the assembly of hack writers entertained and often supported by a man they often abuse in print, Mr S. (for Smollett himself). Jery also describes the acts of kindness that Bramble performs quietly and under the cover of misanthropic bluster, and his mounting affection for his uncle exemplifies what Beasley calls a move "from smug detachment to sympathetic engagement" (1998: 189). Jery's sister, Lydia, adds yet another voice, that of the sentimental heroine of a romance, and while her manner and situation seem silly and excessive at times, they cannot be easily discounted, especially since the strolling player to whom Lydia is attracted turns out to be the son of a friend of Bramble, and in Bramble's view an eminently suitable husband. Her character also undergoes a change, as giddy excitement over the attraction of Bath and London gives way to a desire to retreat to the country, a position identical to Bramble's. Bramble himself is implicated in a sentimental comic plot when Humphry Clinker, whom he takes in as a servant, turns out to be his illegitimate son. Both the variety of voices and the genuine development of the characters make the multiple reconciliations and marriages and the final retreat to Brambleton Hall seem less contrived than the similar endings in Smollett's other fiction.

Satire gets the final word, however, in the two letters that conclude the novel, written by Bramble's sister, Tabitha, and her former servant, now Clinker's wife, Winifred Jenkins. The former remains unaltered, despite her (long-sought) marriage, in her selfishness, class-consciousness, and parsimony, and her malapropisms reveal the sexual preoccupations that she tries to hide beneath a veneer of propriety. The latter shares her mistress's pretensions and mangles the language even more thoroughly, and some of her errors – for instance, "mattermoney" for "matrimony" – puncture the euphoria of romance. These parting shots do not rise to the level of outrage characteristic of the rest of Smollett's fiction, but they do show his reluctance, even in his most integrated comic resolution, to abandon the mode that suffused and energized his work.

Sterne and Sentimental Fiction

Critics who debate the relative prominence of satire or comedy in Smollett's novels can at least agree that they are novels. In the case of Laurence Sterne's *Tristram Shandy* (1761–7), the place and nature of satire constitute the grounds for a fundamental debate about genre. One line of scholarship, headed by Melvyn New (1969), classifies the work as a satire on learning in the Menippean tradition, which follows in the path of Rabelais, Cervantes, Robert Burton, and the Scriblerians, especially Swift. Adherents of this view emphasize *Tristram Shandy*'s self-consciously disordered structure, its symposium scenes, which parody learned debate, and Walter Shandy's reliance on dubious authorities and confidence in his own misguided opinions, which often lead to consequences exactly the opposite of his intentions. Most significantly, his preoccupation with names and noses does not prevent, and in fact facilitates, his son's receiving the name he most detests and having his nose mangled during delivery. Behind this kind of satire, many see Sterne's commitment to fideistic skepticism, which reveals the insufficiency, self-interest, and folly of the human mind in order to stress the necessity of trust in the divine.

Until recently, most defenders of *Tristram Shandy* as a novel have exalted it as a proto-Modernist work, with little connection to the fiction of Sterne's immediate predecessors and contemporaries. Thomas Keymer (2002) offers a persuasive alternative, reading the work not only as Menippean intellectual satire, but also as a satire on the increasingly prominent genre of the novel itself, as a self-conscious metafiction that offers "parodic intensification" of narrative techniques developed by earlier eighteenth-century novelists. Contending that Sterne shared Richardson's and Fielding's interest in and concern about the "dynamics of reception and interpretation" (2002: 41), Keymer considers Tristram's "circumstantial realism" (2002: 43) a parody of Richardson's similar tactic in *Sir Charles Grandison* (1753–4), and Tristram's equation of writing with conversation an exaggeration of the apparently collaborative but ultimately coercive dialogues with readers conducted by Fielding's narrators. He also identifies precedents for Sterne's creative and unorthodox use of the conventions of print – such as black, marbled, and blank pages – not only in Scriblerian texts but in Richardson's fiction as well, and concludes that Sterne defamiliarizes these devices to expose the "shakily arcane" (2002: 74) conventions on which novels rest.

In spite of disputes about the genre of the novel, there is strong consensus that the emphasis of *Tristram Shandy* shifts, in the later volumes, from the satiric to the sentimental, with an increased focus on love (Uncle Toby's amours) and death (the reported deaths of Bobby Shandy and Le Fever and the encroachment of death on Tristram). Yet even the sentimental scenes so valued by Sterne's contemporaries can be read as simultaneously endorsing and mocking sensibility. Toby's modesty and elevated conception of love may be endearing, but he fails because he cannot acknowledge the needs of the body, as the Widow Wadman does by questioning, in a scene of hilarious misunderstanding, precisely where Toby was wounded in battle. Similarly, Toby shows tender concern for Lieutenant Le Fever, but as Max Byrd (1985) observes, Toby's denial that Le Fever will die, voiced while he marches on one foot, renders him silly as well as admirable, and Tristram's description of the death ultimately seems most concerned with its own ingenuity. On the surface, Bobby's death prompts a contrast between the pretension and distance of Walter's elaborate rhetorical response and the simple eloquence of Corporal Trim's dropping of his hat as an emblem of mortality, but, once again, Tristram draws attention to his own linguistic virtuosity, describing and replaying the gesture in several ways, and considering alternatives to it. As a result, the tears from Trim's audience may be accompanied with laughter from Sterne's.

A similar dynamic characterizes some major examples of avowed sentimental fiction that flourished in the 1760s, a pivotal decade in many accounts of a transition from an age of satire to one of sensibility. Sterne's signal contribution to the genre,

A Sentimental Journey (1768), echoes volume 7 of *Tristram Shandy* by satirizing travel books that are excessively preoccupied with listing and measuring, and it specifically attacks Smollett's nonfictional *Travels through France and Italy* (1766) for its mean-spirited, splenetic tone, ridiculing Smollett as "the learned Smelfungus." In contrast, Sterne's narrator, Parson Yorick, defines himself as a sentimental traveler and casts his travels as a series of occasions for experiencing fine feelings, which often prompt benevolent actions. Yet Yorick and the ethos he represents have both been regarded as objects of satire. Yorick often proves himself vain and self-interested, and his acts of generosity derive primarily from a desire for self-congratulation. His sentimental flights often seem exaggerated or disproportionate, especially when the catalyst is a dead ass or a caged starling. Finally, Yorick's sensibility often functions as a transparent cover for sexuality, as in his bedroom encounter with a *fille de chambre* in consecutive chapters that play on the double meaning of their titles, "The Temptation" and "The Conquest," and in the inconclusive final scene, in which the reader is left in the middle of a bedroom farce featuring Yorick, his companion – whose bed was curtained from his in accordance with a legalistic "contract" – and the *fille de chambre* who literally and figuratively comes between them. If Sterne's contemporaries tended to emphasize an uncomplicated sensibility behind the novel, more recent critics have focused on its satiric tendencies and on Sterne's bawdy humor.

The divide is even more pronounced in the case of Oliver Goldsmith's *The Vicar of Wakefield* (1766), perhaps because it lacks the titillation of Sterne's novel. For almost two centuries, Goldsmith's title character, Dr Primrose, was lauded as a loving husband and father and a simple but worthy clergyman, and readers both sympathized with the family's misfortunes and rejoiced at their reversal at the end of the novel. In the past few decades, however, the novel has usually been considered a parody of sentimentalism, and Primrose a vain, smug, and ignorant character, unable to control his family's excesses and taken advantage of by others because of his misguided confidence in his worldly acumen. To the extent that Primrose is a victim, the satire bares the malevolence of his victimizers but also his own weaknesses. The suddenness and convenience of the happy ending – brought about by a supposed poor friend of the family who reveals himself to be a benevolent *deus ex machina* – support a parodic interpretation as well. John Mullan (1988) accounts for the divergence in response by suggesting that eighteenth-century readers followed established habits and subordinated Primrose's foibles to the admirable simplicity that in some ways caused them, and concludes that if the novel was intended as a parody, it was perhaps too close to its target. For George Haggerty (1991), the novel breaks down the dichotomy between satire and sentiment, reason and emotion, as the Vicar's noble actions (saving his children from a fire and preaching in prison) redeem his character, and Goldsmith's irony licenses readers to accept the ending and to indulge otherwise unacceptable sentimental feelings. These nuanced interpretations emphasize the close and complex relationship between satire and sensibility, and the dangers of categorical approaches that segregate the two – whether in the discussion of a single novel or of the two "halves" of the eighteenth century.

Later Women Novelists

Sensibility, although frequently embraced and/or exploited by male novelists, was commonly gendered as female and considered the natural province and principal merit of women writers, who, after Richardson's and Fielding's self-conscious elevation of the novel to a position of respectability, were expected to reject the boldness and licentiousness of Behn, Manley, and Haywood, and to confine themselves to "feminine" subject matter and styles. This would seem to leave little room for satire, but some of the best women novelists managed to incorporate it into novels that both observed and transcended culturally imposed limits. Sarah Fielding's *David Simple* (1744) has been identified as a prototype of the novel of sensibility, and shares with later texts like *The Vicar of Wakefield* and Henry Mackenzie's *The Man of Feeling* (1771) a naïve hero, allowing Fielding to ridicule the more sophisticated characters who dupe and mislead him. In the early sections of the novel, David, who travels to London in search of a true friend, becomes acquainted with a series of characters – the aptly named Orgueil, Spatter, and Varnish – who unmask the hypocrisy both of the social, political, and literary worlds of London and of each other. As Sara Gadeken (2002) has pointed out, the only satirist who is not revealed to be a fraud is Cynthia, who combines a sharp mind with a good heart. Her narrative details her male relatives' disdain for her learning, her refusal to accede to her father's desire that she marry a wealthy fool, and the subsequent necessity of her becoming a "toad-eater," a companion to a wealthy, overbearing acquaintance. Through Cynthia's witty and forthright voice, Fielding criticizes the limited options for learned women (like herself), the mercenary and corrupt marriage market, and abusive social elites. Later in the novel, Cynthia offers more disinterested but no less incisive observations on London manners and mores, ascribing frivolous social pursuits to what Samuel Johnson, in imitation of Juvenal, called "the vanity of human wishes." In line with the predominance of sensibility in the novel, David marries not the clever Cynthia, but her more pathetic, emotional, and submissive friend, Camilla. Yet, through Cynthia's character, Fielding foregrounds and legitimates a female satiric voice.

Cynthia disappears for most of the sequel to the novel, *Volume the Last* (1753), as the focus shifts to the victimization of David and his family by selfish, unscrupulous characters (including Orgueil), whom the hero is too naïve and compliant to resist. The satiric voice, as Gadeken (2002) argues, is more Juvenalian in tone, but is confined almost exclusively to the narrator. As in other sentimental fiction, the emphasis on virtue in distress provokes sympathy for those who suffer and disdain for the individuals and social arrangements that cause the suffering.

Charlotte Lennox pursues a very different satiric strategy in *The Female Quixote* (1752), unique among the eighteenth-century imitations of Cervantes for having a woman as its protagonist and thus the ostensible object of satire. Arabella's immersion in seventeenth-century romances deludes her into accepting them as histories and regarding herself as an exalted heroine, the object of adoration of every man who sees her, with power to command her lovers to live or die. Henry Fielding's review of the novel in the *Covent-Garden Journal* helped establish a reading of it as a satire on implausible romances, a position supported by the behavior of the heroine that looks ridiculous to the other characters, and often to the reader. Recent feminist criticism has challenged this interpretation, contending that Lennox projects a more equivocal and often favorable attitude toward romance, which allows an otherwise constricted eighteenth-century woman to indulge a fantasy of female power. Adherents of this reading recognize but regret the necessity of "curing" Arabella, especially through a dialogue with a Johnsonian divine – in a chapter that some believe to have been written by Samuel Johnson himself.

Readers of both persuasions would agree that, as in *Don Quixote*, the more realistic world with which the deluded protagonist interacts comes in for its share of satire. Arabella pointedly criticizes the trivial pursuits engaged in, especially by women, in fashionable society. Elsewhere, she bests a foolish pedant who comes to accept her romance-derived information about ancient Greece because of his own ignorance and lack of confidence in his learning. Arabella's roles as a satiric voice and a mechanism of satire disappear in the conclusion; her marriage silences her as effectively as Don Quixote's death does him. Lennox thus bows to the familiar trajectory of domestic fiction, but not before indulging in acute, multi-dimensional, and subversive satire of society and of both romances and novels.

In *Evelina* (1778), Frances Burney integrates satire into a domestic novel of manners through a two-sided heroine and epistolary form. Evelina, who writes the bulk of the letters, combines naïveté and satiric insight in her character and correspondence. A poor, country-bred woman, ill at ease in the modish society to which she is introduced, Evelina repeatedly betrays her ignorance of social rules, thereby allowing Burney to underscore their arbitrariness and foolishness. The privacy of her letters also permits Evelina herself to engage in direct satire, with the principal targets being her affected, ignorant, and boorish grandmother, Madame Duval, and her vulgar relations the Branghtons, whose hilarious trip to the opera displays their pettiness and tastelessness. While she also ridicules the fop Lovel, her reluctance to attack other upper-class characters – including Sir Clement Willoughby, who attempts to seduce and even force himself upon her under the guise of a romantic attachment – has left both heroine and author open to the charge of snobbery.

As Evelina becomes increasingly aware of and receptive to the sincere devotion of Lord Orville, her satiric impulses, and function, diminish. Burney transfers them to the "masculine" spinster, Mrs Selwyn, who never hesitates to upbraid the manners, intelligence, and morals of the elite publicly. Evelina's disapproval of Mrs Selwyn's unfeminine boldness reflects and contributes to her evolution into a "proper" heroine, which culminates with her marriage and her silencing as a writer. Propriety may have also led Burney to displace and submerge satire, but not, significantly, to exclude it.

In her subsequent fiction, Burney uses third-person omniscient narrators, but as Julia Epstein (1989: 228) has observed, her "stylistic indirection and ambivalent authorial presence" made it difficult for earlier readers "to see her social satire as anything other or more than benignly humorous." Interpretations by Epstein and others have rectified this misapprehension by stressing Burney's trenchant social critique. In *Cecilia* (1782), the orphaned heiress's three guardians – a miser, a vain aristocrat, and a spendthrift man-about-town – have been read by Margaret Anne Doody (1988) to represent larger, coercive social patterns. Cecilia's uncle's will, which ties her inheritance to the condition that she retain her surname, constrains her autonomy, especially when she falls in love with her aristocratic guardian's son. Their eventual marriage, which comes only after considerable suffering, ultimately costs Cecilia her name and fortune, and the ostensibly happy ending cannot obscure Burney's disdain for the social and legal systems that necessitate such choices. *Camilla* (1796) details the disastrous consequences of rigid courtship, as both the heroine, at her father's insistence, and the man she loves, on his tutor's advice, refrain from revealing their feelings. The mutual reticence leads to misunderstanding, frustration, and Camilla's eventual descent into madness. Once again, the "happy" ending seems contrived, and pales before the romantic, familial, financial, and social crises that the novel depicts.

Jacobin and Anti-Jacobin Novels

Camilla was published in the middle of a decade in which, to paraphrase Juvenal, it was difficult not to write satire. In Britain, the French Revolution spurred enthusiastic applause and vehement opposition, hopes for native reform and fears of social disintegration, and many novelists directed their fiction to more openly political ends. As Gary Kelly (1976) has demonstrated in his study of the radical English Jacobin novelists, satire – often kept general, out of fear of governmental reprisals, including arrest – played a prominent role in many of their narratives. According to Kelly, Robert Bage incorporates satiric portraits and observations into all of his comic novels, but in his last novel, *Hermsprong* (1796), the satire becomes harsh, as Bage uses the title character, an outsider raised in part by American Indians, to critique political and domestic tyranny, most fully embodied by Lord Grondale, who had in fact deprived Hermsprong of his rightful inheritance. The ending, in which the virtuous characters plan to establish a utopian community in America, represents "a withdrawal from commitment to contemporary issues" (Kelly 1976: 61), a recognition that greater democracy and equality between the sexes could not emerge in a country where Jacobinism had been rejected.

Elizabeth Inchbald's *Nature and Art* (1796) shares a similar kind of ending, but precedes it by justifying its original title, "A Satire on the Times," and mounting an attack on the wastefulness, frivolity, and hypocrisy of the rich. The novel draws contrasts between two brothers and their two sons, in which one father/son pair represents the common sense that derives from nature, and the other the prejudice associated with artificiality. In *Hugh Trevor* (1794–7), Thomas Holcroft borrows significantly from *Roderick Random* to create what Kelly (1976: 147) calls a "Jacobin picaro," an impetuous but generous character who learns to balance his passions with reason. Hugh's travels provide a means for Holcroft to satirize a number of professions, vain, worldly women, religious hypocrites, and other examples of a corrupt establishment. All three of these novelists use explicit satire to offer the kind of social criticism advanced more implicitly in and through other Jacobin narratives, including the most famous of them, William Godwin's *Caleb Williams* (1794), which presents a disturbing portrait of what Godwin calls, in the rest of the title, *Things as They Are*.

Anti-Jacobin novelists opposed the French Revolution, the principles behind it, and the British apologists for both, and frequently enlisted satire to ridicule the enthusiasm and sexual licentiousness of Jacobin "philosophers" and the gullibility of their followers. Henry James Pye's novel *The Democrat* (1796) satirizes French involvement in the American fight for independence, casting the revolutionaries of either country as easily deluded fools. Also using the American setting, George Walker's *The Vagabond* (1794) and the anonymously published *Berkeley Hall* (1796) undercut the idyllic image of America conveyed in *The Emigrants* (1793), identified on the title page as the work of Gilbert Imlay but ascribed by some to his lover, Mary Wollstonecraft. This novel contrasts American freedom and innocence with European despotism and corruption, and ends with the establishment of a model society on the banks of the Ohio River. In both satiric ripostes, radical enthusiasts, often selfish in their personal conduct, find the state of nature bleak and dangerous and Americans violent and duplicitous. Many novels attack Godwin directly, including Charles Lloyd's *Edmund Oliver* (1798), which simultaneously embraces some Jacobin ideas, and Isaac D'Israeli's *Vaurien* (1797), which caricatures Godwin as "Mr Subtile." Wollstonecraft, whose radical unfinished novel *The Wrongs of Woman* was published posthumously in 1798 by her husband, Godwin, is also lampooned in *Vaurien* and in Robert Bisset's *Douglas; or, The Highlander* (1800), in which she appears both as herself and in the character of Lady Mary Manhunt. In Anti-Jacobin portraits, the personal and political reinforce each other, to devastating satiric effect.

The role of fiction like this in advancing political and ideological debate at the end of the century furnishes a final example both of the complementarity of satire and the novel, and of the benefits that each provided the other. As Paulson (1967) has concluded, satire gave eighteenth-century novelists a critical tool for analysis and a means of reconciling realism and reality. In the process, the novel absorbed and superseded "purer" forms of satire, but it also helped disseminate to a large and broad readership a satiric perspective – sometimes obvious, sometimes implicit, sometimes ambiguous – on the social, cultural, and literary worlds it described and helped constitute. This was true even after satire had apparently given way to sensibility, and would continue as the genre became institutionalized and flourished in the next century, beginning with the work of a writer extremely sensitive to the ferment of the 1790s and knowledgeable about and indebted to so many eighteenth-century predecessors, Jane Austen.

References and Further Reading

Bakhtin, M. M. (1984) *Rabelais and his World*, trans. Hélène Iswolsky. Bloomington, IN: Indiana University Press (originally published 1968).

Ballaster, Ros (2000) A gender of opposition: Eliza Haywood's scandal fiction. In Kirtsen T. Saxon and Rebecca P. Bocchicchio (eds), *The Passionate Fictions of Eliza Haywood: Essays on her Life and Works*, pp. 143–67. Lexington: University Press of Kentucky.

Bartolomeo, Joseph F. (2002) *Matched Pairs: Gender and Intertextual Dialogue in Eighteenth-century Fiction*. Newark: University of Delaware Press.

Beasley, Jerry C. (1998) *Tobias Smollett, Novelist*. Athens: University of Georgia Press.

Byrd, Max (1985) *Tristram Shandy*. London: G. Allen and Unwin.

Close, Anthony J. (1978) *The Romantic Approach to "Don Quixote": A Critical History of the Romantic Tradition in Quixote Criticism*. Cambridge: Cambridge University Press.

Day, Robert Adams (1989) Introduction to *The History and Adventures of an Atom*, by Tobias Smollett. Athens: University of Georgia Press.

Doody, Margaret Anne (1988) *Frances Burney: The Life in the Works*. New Brunswick: Rutgers University Press.

Epstein, Julia (1989) *The Iron Pen: Frances Burney and the Politics of Women's Writing*. Madison: University of Wisconsin Press.

Folkenflik, Robert (2002) Introduction to *The Life and Adventures of Sir Launcelot Greaves*, by Tobias Smollett. Athens: University of Georgia Press.

Gadeken, Sara (2002) Sarah Fielding and the salic law of wit. *Studies in English Literature* 42, 541–57.

Grenby, M. O. (2001) *The Anti-Jacobin Novel: British Conservatism and the French Revolution*. Cambridge: Cambridge University Press.

Haggerty, George E. (1991) Satire and sentiment in *The Vicar of Wakefield*. *The Eighteenth Century: Theory and Interpretation* 32, 25–38.

Herman, Ruth (2003) *The Business of a Woman: The Political Writings of Delarivier Manley*. Newark: University of Delaware Press.

Hunter, J. Paul (1990) *Gulliver's Travels* and the novel. In Frederik N. Smith (ed.), *The Genres of "Gulliver's Travels,"* pp. 56–74. Newark: University of Delaware Press.

Kelly, Gary (1976) *The English Jacobin Novel 1780–1805*. Oxford: Clarendon Press.

Keymer, Thomas (2002) *Sterne, the Moderns, and the Novel*. Oxford: Oxford University Press.

Mullan, John (1988) *Sentiment and Sociability: The Language of Feeling in the Eighteenth Century*. Oxford: Clarendon Press.

New, Melvyn (1969) *Laurence Sterne as Satirist: A Reading of "Tristram Shandy."* Gainesville: University of Florida Press.

Paulson, Ronald (1967) *Satire and the Novel in Eighteenth-century England*. New Haven, CT: Yale University Press.

Sekora, John (1977) *Luxury: The Concept in Western Thought, Eden to Smollett*. Baltimore, MD: The Johns Hopkins University Press.

Smallwood, Angela J. (1989) *Fielding and the Woman Question: The Novels of Henry Fielding and Feminist Debate, 1700–1750*. Hemel Hempstead: Harvester Wheatsheaf.

Varey, Simon (1986) *Henry Fielding*. Cambridge: Cambridge University Press.

——(1990) *"Joseph Andrews": A Satire of Modern Times*. Boston: Twayne.

15
Gendering Satire: Behn to Burney
Claudia Thomas Kairoff

"Ah, rogue! Such black eyes, such a face, such a mouth, such teeth – and so much wit!"
(Aphra Behn, *The Rover*, 1677)

"She has wit, I acknowledge, and more understanding than half her sex put together; but she keeps alive a perpetual expectation of satire, that spreads a general uneasiness among all who are in her presence." (Frances Burney, *Evelina*, 1778)

"Wit" and "satire" are not synonyms, of course, but throughout the Restoration and eighteenth century, wit conveyed through clever and strikingly phrased observations was routinely associated with satire, the genre that exposed vice for the purpose of correction. The quotations above might suggest that during the Restoration wit was considered attractive in women, but by the end of the next century, discouraged as unpleasant. In the first, Willmore, the rake-hero, extols Hellena's charms. In the second, a rakish young man describes his aversion to the heroine's chaperone. Hellena wins Willmore by assailing him with vollies, or as he says, "claw[ing him] away with broadsides," of satirical wit, while Mrs Selwyn complicates Evelina's already difficult social circumstances by alienating their acquaintances. Hellena is an adorable heroine, while Mrs Selwyn plays a minor role. A predilection for witty satire is compatible with beauty and charisma in Behn's play, while in Burney's novel, it has become a "humour," an obsession that is itself satirized.

Before addressing the cultural and literary trends that wrought the apparent change in expectations regarding women and wit, and women and satire, it is first necessary to complicate the assumption of a simple trajectory from Restoration approval to late eighteenth-century disgust. As we have learned with regard to other topics such as gender roles, social rank, and political engagement, generalizations are unwise unless heavily qualified. While preeminently a "manly" genre assuming the right to observe and criticize one's culture, one's peers, and even one's superiors, satire attracted many female writers even after its generic status declined. Women had arguably more obstacles than men to writing satiric poetry because of its association with Roman precursors, such as the satires of Horace and Juvenal, and with invective. But in drama, prose, and poetry, we find women satirists excelling in the genre that dominated literature in the Restoration and for at least half the succeeding century.

Behn's contemporary John Dryden, in the "Discourse Concerning Satire" that prefaced his translations of Juvenal in 1693, was careful to distinguish Roman satire, as a literary genre "full of pleasant Raillery, but without any mixture of obscenity," from both the rugged Greek oral tradition and the Roman festival contests that preceded it (Dryden 1974: 39). Dryden championed a pedigree for satire that began with early Roman dramatists and culminated in the masterpieces of Horace, Persius, and Juvenal. Roman satires not only "decry'd Vice, or expos'd Folly" but recommended virtue (1974: 48). But Dryden recognized that a counter-history associated the genre with actual satyrs, goatish half-beasts associated with lewd revelry. Both derivations were problematic for women writers. Certainly no lady wished to be associated with satyrs and their crude libels. On the other hand, Horace and Juvenal had censured contemporary rulers and cultural practices with an authority few, if any, women dared emulate. But when satire reigned as the literary genre of choice following the Restoration and until the mid-eighteenth century, women writers were compelled to participate in the trend. Satire enabled writers to escape prosecution for libel and sedition by granting political commentary the stature of classical rhetoric. Satire, whether of the genial Horatian or the surly Juvenalian variety, suited the era's taste for argumentation and for sheer displays of cleverness.

Women first had to contend with their almost universal lack of classical education. While male poets frequently cited, and often imitated, Latin originals, women usually had to work from English or French translations. Thus their authority was in some sense borrowed or compromised from the outset. Since "wit" also denoted intelligence, women's "witty" satirical writing might indicate borrowed intellectual acumen as well as borrowed learning. In "The Emulation" (1703), one of Behn's younger contemporaries, Sarah Fyge Egerton (1669–1722), angrily rebuked her culture for maintaining women's ignorance, while permitting "every Man [to explain] the Will of Heaven." Unable to imagine equal rights, Egerton instead envisioned turning the tables on men and establishing a "Female Reign" over "Wits Empire" (33): women will "be Wits, and then Men must be Fools" (39). In the same year, Mary, Lady Chudleigh (1656–1710) published "To the Ladies," a poem that eschews Egerton's dream of a carnivalesque reversal, but simply warns women to avoid marriage if they wish to retain any sense of themselves as autonomous, intelligent beings: "You must be proud, if you'll be wise" (24). While both poems are satirical in disclosing women's bleak cultural situation and proposing corrective alternatives, neither Egerton's nor Chudleigh's solution was practicable. Egerton's proposal was a fantasy, and few women could choose to maintain intellectual freedom through celibacy, although respected commentators such as Mary Astell (1666–1731) similarly encouraged women to avoid marriage and concentrate instead on learning. Most women writers found more practical avenues to satiric authority. The following discussion samples women's contributions in drama, poetry, and the novel, with no pretension to inclusiveness but as a guide to inspire further study.

Drama

Aphra Behn (1640–89) developed strategies that made her a strong competitor in the famously witty world of Restoration drama. She avoided the harshly cynical satire of contemporaries such as Sir George Etherege and William Wycherley, as well as much of their crude humor. Even so, as she lamented in her preface to *The Luckey Chance* (1687), her plays were sometimes accused of indecency: "they must be Criminal because a Woman's" (Behn 1996b: 215). *The Rover* (1677) provides a fine example of Behn's satirical approach. Willmore, the cavalier, is supposed to be a desirable hero: courageous and loyal to King Charles, he is also funny, sexually attractive to both Hellena and Angellica, and easygoing. Unfortunately, he drinks far too much and, under the influence of alcohol, makes stupid mistakes. Behn regales her courtly audience with a version of their own famed debauchery and its potential consequences. While no doubt intended correctively, *The Rover* ends happily, with Willmore prevented from raping Florinda, extricated from Angellica's threats, and "converted" to matrimony with Hellena. Meanwhile, Behn satirizes the Stuarts' more lukewarm supporters in Ned Blunt, the young squire whose desire for "a cheap Whore" (1.2) echoes his desire to avoid the consequences of supporting King Charles. Ned is tricked by a prostitute and dumped into the sewer, and his subsequent near-rape of Florinda seals audiences' opinion of his cowardice. Here Behn's satire is more harsh, but Ned is permitted a place in the plot's comic resolution: he apologizes to Florinda and models his new Spanish costume, "looking very ridiculously" (Behn 1996a: 519). Ned's cowardice, gullibility, and foppery contrast with Willmore's courage, wittiness, and confidence. But by making Willmore guilty of near-rape while drunk, Behn suggests to her audience that if they persist in self-indulgent, and self-destructive, behaviors, they risk becoming as despicable as those whom they consider their gulls and inferiors.

Behn's point may have been made too subtly: while modern audiences have difficulty reconciling Willmore's heroic status with his drunken sexual assaults, contemporaries found him so attractive that Behn featured him again in *The Rover, Part II* (1681), as the widowed spouse of a recently deceased Hellena. Behn was evidently more concerned with pleasing her courtly audience than chastising their failings. Her construction of Hellena's and Willmore's courtship further evinces Behn's positive approach. While deploring, no less than Egerton and Chudleigh, the double standard her society applied to men's and women's behavior, Behn created a hero who "adores" Hellena's cleverness and pronounces her wit, even more than her beauty, irresistible. Hellena refuses to compromise her virgin chastity ("[W]hat shall I get? A cradle full of noise and mischief, with a pack of repentance at my back?"; 5.1), but Behn permits her to escape her destined convent life, to claim control of her fortune, and to choose her mate, all freedoms that would have seemed controversial to contemporaries. Perhaps Behn eliminated Hellena and created La Nuche, courtesan-heroine of *The Rover, Part II*, because the notion of a lady-turned-itinerant (and married) cavalier seemed fantastic. But in *The Rover*, as in other comedies such as *The Feign'd Curtezans* (1679), *The Luckey Chance*, and *Sir Patient Fancy* (1678), Behn consistently championed strong heroines who refuse forced marriages – sometimes even after the fact – and exert considerable wit to achieve more satisfactory unions.

While satirizing Charles's allies in *The Rover*, Behn more often satirized the king's political opponents. *The Feign'd Curtezans* exposes the hypocrisy of Charles's anti-Catholic enemies through Tickletext, the amorous dissenter. *The Luckey Chance* lampoons Whig merchants in Sir Feeble Fainwould and Sir Cautious Fulbank, wealthy old cits who have lured reluctant young women into marriage. In *Sir Patient Fancy*, Lady Fancy tricks her hypochondriacal, puritanical, alderman husband out of a fortune and regains her freedom to wed young Wittmore. Each of these plays exposes Stuart opponents, while rewarding the generosity, passion, and cleverness of idealized courtiers. While Behn's touch was fairly light (her old men usually win some audience sympathy by admitting their failings), her political ideology was hardly concealed. She envisioned a world in which men and women shared equally in the pleasures of love and wit, contrasted with the bleak reality of the double standard she satirized and associated with the mercantile values of Charles's detractors.

Behn's final play, *The Widdow Ranter* (1689), appeared posthumously. Like Dryden, she wrote mainly translations and prose fiction in her latter years, as plays became subject to ever-increasing censorship and her beloved Stuarts fled to France. *The Widdow Ranter* may well have incurred censure, because it satirizes William's government in the guise of Virginia's ill-bred council. The play's tragic figure, Nathaniel Bacon, hearkens back to early Restoration love-and-honor heroes, futilely attempting to restore social order despite Indian threats and European treachery. Behn probably intended Bacon as a coda to the cavalier tradition. Her eponymous heroine, on the other hand, takes full advantage of Virginia's social chaos, donning breeches to win the man she loves by fighting with him against Bacon. If Behn imagined Bacon as the anomalous remnant of cavalier values, she may nevertheless have seen in America's colonies the promise of more egalitarian roles for women, a promise her cherished conservative political ideals had failed to support.

While Behn ended her career less sanguine about the possibility of aligning the outcomes of her satiric domestic and political plots, her immediate successors carried on her tradition. In *The Spanish Wives* (1696), Mary Pix (1666–1709) upheld Williamite anti-Catholicism; the butt of her comedy is a lustful friar. As the century ended and Restoration licentiousness was replaced at court by more restrained manners, even the dashing English colonel fails to seduce the Spanish governor's wife away from her old but indulgent husband. Pix suggests that husbands might rule their wives through trust and patience, a suggestion more like Milton's than Behn's, signaling her affinity for William and Mary's ideology. Likewise, the next significant woman playwright, Susannah Centlivre (d. 1723), espoused Whig principles in her successful comedies. Her most famous play, *A Bold Stroke for a Wife* (1718), pits yet another attractive colonel, Fainwell, against four guardians who must each consent to his marriage with Ann Lovely. Fainwell succeeds by impersonating a character appealing to each guardian in turn, including a decayed beau, a foolish virtuoso, a stockbroker. Finally, he pretends to be Simon Pure, the Quaker preacher proposed by Ann's fourth guardian, Obadiah Prim. Thanks to Ann's quick-witted charade as his convert, Fainwell succeeds despite the real Simon Pure's last-minute appearance. Centlivre's play includes even-handed satire of both Tory (ancient rake, gentleman scientist) and Whig (city merchant, dissenter). In an era characterized by harsh political divisions, this apparent fairness probably enhanced the play's appeal. However, Centlivre's personal allegiance is suggested by her choice of a military hero, reduced to half-pay after the recently concluded War of Spanish Succession. Colonel Fainwell and Ann Lovely demonstrate comparable acting ability, presaging the kind of companionate marriage emerging as the new genteel pattern.

Succeeding eighteenth-century women playwrights continued enfolding satirical social commentary within domestic comedies. As the century progressed, tastes shifted and more passive, sentimental heroines won audience favor. Women's plays followed suit; in 1779, when Frances Burney (1752–1840) showed her father and Samuel Crisp the manuscript for *The Witlings*, a satire on learned ladies, they deemed it too acidulous for production. In 1718, Ann Lovely was restricted in her activity but might still rebuke her absurd guardians quite sharply. By 1780, Hannah Cowley's *The Belle's Stratagem* features Letitia, who disguises herself as a sophisticated foreigner to counter Doricourt's distaste for "[t]he timidity of [her] English character" (Cowley 2001: 135–6). Captivated, Doricourt exults that "it is to that innate modesty, *English* husbands owe a felicity the married men of other nations are strangers to" (2001: 136). Cowley (1743–1809) satirizes women's confined role by celebrating, not an audacious heroine, but one who feigns audacity in order to attract a man worthy of conversion to more discerning taste. She also satirizes the British taste for "corrupt" European manners, cultivated on the Grand Tour, and exhorts patriotic citizens to prefer their native reticence. *The Belle's Stratagem* thus illustrates women's consistent ability to interweave political and domestic themes in their satiric plays throughout the period. Elizabeth Inchbald (1753–1821), likewise, wove social satire into her sentimental drama *Such Things Are* (1788), in a subplot involving the foppish Twineall, who gives up tattling and flattering after escaping death in the Sultan's prison. Like Cowley in *The Belle's Stratagem*, Inchbald wished to inculcate "English" plain-spokenness in an audience perhaps susceptible to "foreign" insincerity.

Poetry

Women playwrights grappled with political censorship, shifting audience tastes, and restraints on what a "female pen" might produce without compromising her reputation. Behn provided a powerful example at the Restoration's beginning, and succeeding women were left either to claim her as their model or, when the ideal of feminine behavior grew more decorous, to distance themselves through unexceptionable lives and even more unexceptionable heroines. Female poetic satirists had perhaps an even more difficult task. Some of England's most prominent playwrights had been men of middling social status like Shakespeare and Jonson, arguably lowering the barrier for ambitious women who could not claim a classical education. Poetry, on the other hand, was traditionally the pastime of gentlemen and ladies, and Latin was reserved for educated gentlemen. After Elizabeth's reign, few noble families gave their daughters a classical education. Although some families nevertheless encouraged their daughters to learn Greek and Latin, and still others indulged daughters who persisted in teaching themselves, classically trained women were rare throughout the Restoration and eighteenth century. Since the poetic satirist, more directly than the playwright, decried social abuses, women had also to adopt the pose of arbiter, a pose not always compatible with cultural ideals of feminine innocence and reticence. Given this state of affairs, it is surprising how many women elected to participate in the satiric vogue.

Behn, for example, wrote less poetic than dramatic satire. Poems such as "The Golden Age" (1684) denounce contemporary norms denying honest expressions of passion in favor of enforced "honour" (Behn 1992: 30–5). Although Behn claimed that this angrily satirical poem paraphrased a French original, it is most likely her own composition misattributed to excuse its iconoclasm. Other Restoration women likewise experimented with satiric modes. Alicia D'Anvers (fl. 1671–93) composed "Academia: Or, The Humours of The University of Oxford" (1691) in Hudibrastics (rhymed tetrameter couplets), thus tempering her satire of academic corruption with the rollicking meter and word-play of her chosen form. Another late-century poet, Elizabeth Tipper (fl. 1690s), wrote a satire against satire. "A Satyr" (1698) considers biblical precedents for using the form "to scourge the *Vice* of *Human Race*" (4) before concluding that no human can claim sufficient sanctity to justify denouncing others: "*Make me true* Christian, *tho' no* Satyrist" (45). Tipper's humility not only abjured the classical and therefore "pagan" genre but also embraced conventional feminine modesty. Anne Finch, Countess of Winchilsea (1661–1720), the most accomplished woman poet at the turn of the century, is today best known for poems such as "A Nocturnal Reverie" (1713), which inspired the Romantic generation. In addition to such meditative and lyrical verse, however, Finch adapted such forms as the fable, song, and ballad to satiric purposes. Her Hudibrastic "Tale of the Miser and the Poet" (1713), for example, allows Mammon to remain convinced of his superiority while wryly suggesting that the poet, despite his poverty, cherishes better values. Recent critical opinion has held that Finch, a maid of honor to Mary of Modena, withdrew entirely from political reflections when she and her husband went into self-exile following James II's abdication. Current scholarship modifies such an interpretation: in poems such as "The Petition for an Absolute Retreat" (1713), Finch portrays her retirement as edenic and, by implication, William and Mary's England as the fallen world, a subtle but unmistakably satiric reflection.

Lady Mary Wortley Montagu (1689–1762) struggled throughout her life to reconcile genteel decorum with her genius for satire. Her efforts sometimes failed when her privately circulated manuscripts were published without her permission. In other instances, she arranged for anonymous publication, then denied authorship. But contemporaries knew and feared her sharp wit. Her letters disclose her continual amazement at the spectacles of impropriety, foolishness, and vice provided by fashionable life. She could not resist turning many phenomena into verse. Her six "town eclogues," inspired by youthful friendship with Pope and Gay, burlesqued life among courtiers early in George I's reign. Lady Mary did not flinch even from self-exposure. She admitted that "Saturday: The Small Pox" (written 1716, published 1747), in which Flavia laments her lost beauty, expressed her own feelings of loss following the disease. The poem satirizes Flavia's trivial values ("Beauty is fled, and Dress is now no more," 54) but at the same time achieves poignancy by detailing the undeniable privileges granted beautiful young women, now forever lost. Flavia is both a figure of mockery and a melancholy reminder that ladies had few opportunities to cultivate satisfying alternatives to the pleasurable but fragile life the poem deplores.

In real life, Lady Mary had many such alternatives due to her persistent self-education, including the acquisition of Latin. Throughout her life's many vicissitudes, Lady Mary retained her penchant for skewering contemporaries and events in satirical verse. In a series of poems, she responded to Pope's characterization of her as "Sappho" in his Horatian satires. Lady Mary published only the first of her reprisals, "Verses Address'd to the Imitator of the First Satire of the Second Book of Horace" (1733). The poem appeared anonymously, and Lord Hervey, her possible collaborator, shielded her by acquiescing in claims of his authorship. The poem attacks Pope for the twisted physique that supposedly mirrors his mind and for his incapacity to emulate his Roman precursor. "*Horace* can laugh, is delicate, is clear; / You, only coarsely rail, or darkly sneer" (16–17). Lady Mary refrained from publishing her other ripostes, probably to maintain her aristocratic dignity, and thus lost her full vengeance. But her stinging rebukes reveal a propensity for angry satire, unusual among women poets of the century.

Although classically trained, Elizabeth Carter (1717–1806) produced comparatively few satires. Carter's nephew published her "only attempt at [formal] satire," a teenage version of Juvenal on the perils of Fortune, indebted in style to the satires of Edward Young (Carter 1808: 2.19–20). On the other hand, women with no Latin engaged in satire, like Carter emulating the styles of well-known contemporaries. Mary Barber (1690–1757), wife of a Dublin woollen-merchant, followed her mentor Jonathan Swift in writing amusing Hudibrastic poems on such topics as the wisdom of confining little boys in adult clothes, and the hypocrisy of rich men's claims that they lack sufficient wealth to spare for charity. Mary Chandler (1687–1745), a Bath milliner, likewise engaged in light-hearted satire but chose as her model Pope, perhaps because like him she had a crooked spine. Her poems reflect humorously on her plight as a spinster among well-meaning, match-making friends. Both Barber and Chandler wrote general satire, more concerned with praising their benefactors than criticizing antagonists. Both were probably mindful of the need to avoid invective, frequently confused with satire, and to maintain the "good humor" that writers like Pope extolled as a feminine virtue.

Other poets experimented more adventurously with satiric reflections directly modeled on those of Pope. Mary Jones (d. 1778) and Mary Leapor (1722–46) never met; Leapor was a servant in Brackley, and Jones, a clergyman's sister in Oxford. Many satires by both, however, unmistakably resemble Pope's Horatian imitations. Jones adapted Pope's Horace for poems addressed to the friends who were also her patrons. In "An Epistle to Lady Bowyer" (written 1736, published 1750), for example, Jones combines echoes of Pope's "Epistle to Burlington" (1731) and "Epistle to Dr Arbuthnot" (1735) in a poem abjuring court patronage. Like Pope defending his integrity and his profession in "Arbuthnot," Jones declares her refusal to seek courtly patrons ("For what? for whom? / To curl a favourite in a dressing-room?", 13–14). She imagines herself forced to wait among servants in hopes of securing a titled sponsor, finally departing the antechamber "Where footmen in the seat of critics sit" (83). Like Pope defending himself from Lord Hervey's and Lady Mary's slanders, Jones proclaims her honesty and her willingness to embrace frugality rather than "smile lies; eat toads, or lick the dust" (125). The poem's model is nevertheless an odd fit. While Pope rebuked numerous and usually politically motivated enemies, Jones had no apparent reason to attack the court; her best friends enjoyed close court connections. The poem seems instead based on traditional types, such as the unlearned patron Pope had mocked as Timon in "To Burlington." But despite its fictional and conventional quality, "Epistle to Lady Bowyer" is an energetic, confidently written satire.

Mary Leapor's Horatian-Popeian satires are similarly brisk and authoritative, remarkably so for a youthful cook-maid. She evidently believed that all politics are local: Leapor's satiric characters were often based on local acquaintances. "An Epistle to Artemisia" (1751), for example, describes for her patron Bridget Fremantle a procession of other possible mentors, each of whom fails to provide either constructive criticism or support. If she indeed described actual encounters, Leapor took seriously her freedom as satirist to reprove neighbors' failed support for a deserving poet. Other satires find Leapor reworking familiar themes, such as women's social constraints. "An Essay on Woman" (1751) reviews how rarely beauty, wealth, or wit ensures female happiness. Whether wise or foolish, she concludes, "Unhappy woman's but a slave at large" (60). "Man the Monarch" (1751) hypothesizes that Adam caused the original "fall" of woman into virtual servitude by denominating her "fool" (61). Rather boldly for a woman of her class, Leapor engaged satirically in sexual as well as aesthetic politics, showing keen understanding of the genre's possibilities.

Esther Lewis (*f.* 1747–89), a clergyman's daughter from Bath, revisited a subject satirized by women from Finch to Burney and beyond: women's entitlement to write and publish. In playful Hudibrastics reminiscent of Swift's "Verses on the Death of Dr Swift" (c.1731), Lewis imagined a female poet gossiped about around a tea table. (Swift imagined a similar conversation about himself in a tavern.) "A Mirror for Detractors" (1789) opens by observing that "O, she's a wit!" usually "Means self-conceit, ill-nature, pride, / And fifty hateful things beside" (13, 14–15). At about the same time, Elizabeth Hands (fl. 1789), published two poems in alexandrines imagining genteel discussion of "a Volume of Poems, by a Servant-Maid." Hands drolly exposes the pretension of dinner guests who mock her book but have little more on their minds than gossip and social rivalry. Janet Little (1759–1813), a Scottish milk-maid, composed a Hudibrastic poem in dialect "Given to a Lady Who Asked me to Write a Poem" (1792). She claims to have overheard a critic dismissing her work, but the poem implies Little's poetic descent from Pope, as well as "Swift, Thomson, Addison an' Young" (11) by way of Burns, "the glory of our nation" (26). If a "ploughman chiel" has been honored for "[sousing] his sonnets on the court" (21, 23), surely a milk-maid is welcome her "poem-books to print" (47). Like Leapor, all of these women disdained the conventions discouraging women from publishing their opinions, no matter what their social status. While humorous, their satires ask seriously: "Why is it thought in us a crime / To utter common sense in rhyme?" (Lewis 1789, "A Mirror for Detractors," 153–4).

Besides questioning constraints on their writing, women poets engaged like their male contemporaries in the great public debates of their lifetimes. An "age of sentiment" is sometimes thought to have replaced the cult of wit with cultivation of emotion, especially in women. Women indeed wrote blank verse, sonnets, elegies, and ballads that conveyed emotional responses rather than implied solutions. But women writers also satirized social and political phenomena, whether in couplets or more fashionable verse forms. "The Mouse's Petition to Doctor Priestley" (1773) by Anna Laetitia Barbauld (1743–1825) argues in whimsical form the equal entitlement to life of all created beings. Addressed to a brilliant natural philosopher, the poem subtly comments on the sense of superiority fostered by Enlightenment science. Anna Seward (1742–1809) frequently published her opinions on national issues, both literary and political. "Verses Inviting Stella to Tea on the Public Fast-Day, February 1781" comments acidly on government efforts to rally public support for its doomed war against the American colonies. Seward wonders how civilian "abstinence from beef and whist" can inspire the army to "cut provincial throats at will" (4, 8). Even Seward's Miltonic "Colebrooke Dale" (1799), a lyrical effusion, satirizes the lack of planning that allowed mines and furnaces to obliterate a valley famed for natural beauty. Seward observes that several nearby towns already deformed by industry would not suffer from further development; why then destroy a place traditionally hospitable to poetry? Modern opponents of industrial sprawl might argue in similar terms, minus Seward's lament for exiled nymphs and naiads.

Mary Alcock (c.1742–98), another Bath poet, satirized French revolutionary sentiments amidst fears that similar beliefs would sweep Britain. "Instructions, Supposed to be Written in Paris, for the Mob in England" (written c.1792, published 1799) mocks such "rights of man" as "The envied liberty to be a rogue; / The right to pay no taxes, tithes, or dues; / The liberty to do whate'er I choose" (6–8). On the other hand, "The Chimney-Sweeper's Complaint" (1799) demands social justice, implying like William Blake's similar poem that children such as the sweep, whose "feeble limbs, benumbed with cold, / Totter beneath the sack" (13–14), would be better off dead. Mary Robinson (1758–1800), known to contemporaries as much for her colorful life as for her writings, nevertheless produced poems such as "London's Summer Morning" (written 1794, published 1806), a light blank-verse satire that indicates close study of Swift's "A Description of the Morning" (1709) and Gay's *Trivia* (1716). Constructed as if a camera panned the view from the poet's window, the poem constitutes an antipastoral vision of the city, much like her predecessors' but without their hinted pathos. "January, 1795" stands in sharp contrast. Little more than a list of paired opposites, the poem details the ways in which London has become a city of violent contrasts and leaves the reader to draw a moral conclusion.

Women throughout the Restoration and eighteenth century preserved their right to participate in public religious and social debates. Pope's *Essay on Man* (1733–4), for example, drew support from Elizabeth Tollet's "The Microcosm" (1755) for its posture of humility, but was attacked by other women such as Elizabeth Carter, several of whose poems (for example, "In Diem Natalem, 1735," "On the Death of Mrs Rowe, 1739," and "To Miss D'Aeth," 1762) revise and implicitly rebuke Pope's theology. Hannah More (1745–1833) is best known for earnest religious tracts. But she rose to heights of Juvenalian fury in "Slavery, A Poem" (1788). More shared the prejudices of many contemporaries ("Strong, but luxuriant virtues, boldly shoot / From the wild vigour of a savage root," 73–4), but argued powerfully that the "White Savage!" (211) had no right to enslave millions, "O'er plundered realms to reign, detested Lord" (221). Ann Murry (c.1755–1816), a merchant's daughter, hearkened back to Gay's and Lady Mary's mock-eclogues in "The Tête à Tête, Or Fashionable Pair" (1779), a darkly satiric exchange in couplets between an earnest, sensible lady and her blustering, ultimately faithless spouse. Murry implies the benefits of companionate marriage, not to mention the wife's importance when she is more intelligent and principled than her mate, through this negative case. While women's poetic satires diminished when newer modes predominated, they never ceased, as women never ceased surveying the issues of their lifetimes with critical eyes.

The Novel

Poets inherited a privileged Latin genre; dramatists participated in a vogue for satiric commentary in comedies and even in the subplots of serious plays. As women helped develop the novel, satire was among the genres they incorporated into this new prose hybrid. Aphra Behn's prose fiction included *Love-letters between a Nobleman and his Sister* (1684–7), perhaps the first novel in English. The three-volume novel blends aspects of the French *roman-à-clef*, the English criminal narrative, and Behn's dramatic mastery in a fictionalized account of Ford, Lord Grey's seduction of, and elopement with, his sister-in-law, Henrietta Berkeley. Particularly when she began writing, Behn needed to veil her condemnation of Lord Grey and his leader, the Duke of Monmouth, in the same manner that she and her fellow playwrights routinely disguised their political opinions in domestic plots. Philander/Grey, the protagonist, reveals the hollowness of freethinking, libertine philosophy: his unfaithfulness to his wife and to Sylvia parallels Monmouth's and his followers' unfaithfulness to Charles and James. Sylvia learns from him to victimize lovers who believe that her beauty signifies innocence. At the novel's close, she continues her depredations on the Continent, perhaps representing the failure of European monarchs to support James. In her final volume, Behn cynically concludes with Philander's return to court following the failed Monmouth Rebellion: he "was at last pardoned, kiss'd the King's Hand, and came to Court in as much Splendour as ever, being very well understood by all good Men" (Behn 1993: 439). Behn's novel proved prophetic. Having turned state's witness and paying a huge fine to win his pardon from James II, Grey again betrayed his monarch and supported William of Orange in 1688. Behn's novel operates as a thoroughgoing satire of contemporary Stuart opponents, implying their corruption in both morality and philosophy.

Behn's novella *Oroonoko* (1688) commemorates the Stuarts through her eponymous protagonist, an African prince betrayed into slavery by faithless Englishmen. As in *Love-letters*, Behn satirizes the faithlessness of those who profess adherence to the concept of lawful kingship. The merchant who captures Oroonoko, for example, does so after inviting the prince to board his ship as an honored guest. When Oroonoko protests his fetters, the captain refuses to take the word of a "heathen" that he will not rebel if relieved of his chains. Incredulous, Oroonoko "replied, that He was very sorry to hear that the *Captain* pretended to the Knowledge and Worship of any *Gods*, who had taught him no better Principles" (Behn 1995: 84). Delarivier Manley (1663–1724), her most immediate female successor as novelist, learned from Behn how to craft a thoroughgoing satire of her political enemies in the guise of a scandalous narrative. As Behn had exposed the bankrupt morality of Monmouth's supporters, Manley excoriated John Churchill, Duke of Marlborough, his wife, and his fellow Whigs who had engrossed Queen Anne's confidence, enmeshing Britain in William's ill-advised continental broils. *The New Atalantis* (1709) appears to be a mixture of allegory, *roman-à-clef*, and semi-autobiographical tale in which general scandal mitigates the author's personal failings. But contemporaries quickly grasped both the pervasively anti-Whig nature of Manley's work and, thanks to separately published keys, the precise targets of her wrath. Taken together, Manley's serial tales of seduction and betrayal suggest that the same (mostly) men who destroy innocent women have perpetrated analogous crimes against the crown and people of England. *The New Atalantis* briefly landed Manley in jail for libel, but she escaped punishment by claiming at trial that the novel's sequences were simply "a few amorous Trifles" (Manley 1992: xv). Manley employed a similar approach in *Queen Zarah and the Zarasians* (1705), aimed at the Duchess of Marlborough, and other works. Although she excelled in Behn's mode of satire disguised as scandalous fiction, Manley had few successors besides Eliza Haywood (1693–1756) in her field of topical, polemical fiction. Haywood's lengthy career included *Atalantis*-like novels both attacking and supporting Manley's nemesis, the Duchess of Marlborough.

A cluster of mid-century novels, however, makes clear that although the novel evolved toward a realism primarily concerned with individual and domestic situations, social satire remained a powerful undercurrent sustaining its claim to didactic purposes. *The Adventures of David Simple* (1744–53) by Sarah Fielding (1710–68), for example, narrates the life of a naïvely honest man. How could such a person survive in modern, mercantilist Britain? Fielding's novel constitutes a thorough satire of modern life, governed in nearly every instance by greed and self-interest. After rescuing David from many dangers and settling him, blissfully married, amidst equally well-matched friends, Fielding reconsidered. In her sequel, published nine years after the initial volume, David is stripped of his little wealth, of nearly all his friends and family, and finally of his life, hounded by his pretended benefactors the Orgueils. Her bleak conclusion is that such childlike innocence would inevitably be destroyed in mid-eighteenth-century England. A modern David Simple would have to become David Skeptical, perhaps, to survive the onslaught of modern culture.

Fielding used in her novel the devices familiar to her in recent satiric drama and poetry, such as naming her characters after the traditional "types" they represented. Like her brother, Behn, Manley, Haywood, and a host of other writers, Fielding drew upon the belief in universal character types as well as in what Pope called "the Ruling Passion," the inborn drive that motivates each person's behavior throughout life. While Behn, Manley, Pope, and Henry Fielding often employed type-names to disguise satire of well-known individuals, Fielding hearkened back to a moral tradition seen often in fables, such as those by Finch, and similarly didactic texts. Her antagonists such as Mr and Mrs Orgueil thus achieve a frightening generality while also functioning as plausible, albeit predictable, characters. Eliza Haywood employed a similar technique in her best-known novel, *The History of Miss Betsy Thoughtless* (1751). Good-hearted but spoiled Betsy, despite the affectionate guardianship of Mr Goodman, involves herself in countless scrapes until finally even her chief suitor Mr Trueworth believes her compromised and marries elsewhere. Not until she has endured marriage to and separation from the petty Mr Munden, who then dies conveniently, is Betsy worthy of union with Trueworth, also providentially widowed. A veteran playwright, novelist, and journalist, Haywood surrounded Betsy with dozens of fashionable "types," most predictably imposing on her throughout her slow moral development. While Fielding detected selfishness at every level of society, Haywood focused on corruption among the gentry.

Charlotte Lennox's *The Female Quixote* (1752) also features wholesale satire of genteel English life. Lennox (1729?–1804) produced at least five other novels, but *Female Quixote* excels those due to its skillful blend of romance and satire. Arabella, the heroine, resembles Pope's Belinda and Don Quixote himself in being both attractive and ridiculous. Raised on her father's isolated estate, Arabella browses in his library with no guidance regarding the fictional nature of her late mother's cache of romances. Her education is not unlike the real self-education described by Lady Mary Wortley Montagu, although Arabella has so little contact with the world that she mistakes the romances for an image of contemporary life. Her ensuing "adventures" satirize both women's haphazard education and the foolishness of maintaining women's naïveté in a society full of potential betrayers. Arabella is not a completely "rounded" character. But the book's droll, satirical descriptions of Arabella's affected speech and imagined crises remain engaging until her predictable marriage to Mr Glanville. And although a vehicle for Lennox's satire, Arabella nudges toward plausible psychological growth when she resists the truth about romance even from an admired countess and admits its fatuity only to the clergyman who supervises her recovery from near-death after duplicating the ancient Clelia's exploits.

While Sarah Robinson Scott's *Millennium Hall* (1750) is more didactic romance than satire, the inset narratives of the Hall's residents certainly contain satiric elements. Scott (1723–95), an early feminist, established patterns such as the repeated exploitation and betrayal of women, paralleled by brutal treatment of the poor, of children, of the disabled and otherwise handicapped. The predictable nature of the ladies' histories are easily extrapolated for more general satiric purposes, exposing the continuing cruelty of men, and many women, toward the oppressed, which the ladies must band together to resist.

Muted satirical elements persist in women's novels throughout the century, particularly in minor characters who convey, as in shorthand, the authors' pejorative intentions. Such characters and their subplots support the more realistic development of a novel's major plots and characters. In Charlotte Smith's *The Old Manor House* (1793), for example, Orlando and Monimia endure many bars to their union, including Orlando's wastrel older brother Philip, miserly Mrs Rayland, her conniving housekeeper Mrs Lennard, and many others. Smith (1749–1806) masterfully builds a complex plot in which the manor house itself represents England, subject to history's ravages and encroaching modern greed. As a young man contesting his future stake in both the manor house and the "house" of England, Orlando succeeds as David Simple does not in shedding his innocence while preserving his moral claim to inheritance. Inchbald's *A Simple Story* (1791) varies the pattern of satirical minor characters. Instead, the life of youthful Miss Milner satirizes a typical spoiled coquette. Inchbald fashions her heroine in the archetypal mold of willful girls, only to break that mold by revealing the psychological drama of Miss Milner's quest for autonomy. Although the novel is ostensibly about the need for better female education, Inchbald endows each of her main characters, from haughty Lord Elmworth to docile Matilda, with poignant traits beyond their merely satiric functions.

Frances Burney was the best female novelist of the century's final quarter. She excelled in alleviating sentimental seriousness with satirical comedy. An inveterate journal-keeper and letter-writer, Burney was adept at capturing an individual's most revealing gestures and a group's characteristic speech and manners. Her minor characters seem to possess unique tics and turns of phrase, while at the same time representing an entire class. The Branghtons, Evelina's tactless, pretentious city relatives, illustrate Burney's ability. Ignorant yet bold, the Branghtons represent the smug, invidious, acquisitive aspects of mercantile manners. Their worst sin is that they do not realize how dreadful they sound and look. Since Evelina's predicament as an unacknowledged daughter requires her to behave impeccably at all times, giving no opportunity to dismiss her as less than genteel, her sojourn among the Branghtons includes many agonizing moments. Burney conveys both Evelina's dilemma and an implied correction of city manners. Besides the Branghtons, Sir Clement Willoughby and his companions, Madame Duval and Captain Mirvan, are both amusing individuals and representative satiric types. When Evelina must travel without the refined Howards, she is accompanied by Mrs Selwyn, Mr Villars's bluestocking neighbor. Wise and trustworthy, Mrs Selwyn nevertheless invites unnecessary complications due to her unpleasantly satirical tongue. Engrossed in raillery, she cannot provide Evelina the direction the young woman craves. Luckily, Mrs Selwyn's ineffectuality permits Evelina to exercise judgment and thus achieve maturity before marrying Lord Orville.

Cecilia (1782) likewise surrounds its eponymous heroine with a large group of satirical types. Cecilia begins the novel as a teenage heiress seemingly free of all constraints. The sole requirement of her late uncle's will is that her future husband must adopt her family's surname. The novel's plot steadily but irrevocably strips Cecilia of her independence, her fortune, even her reason. Her beloved's father forbids his son to change his name; the young lovers' attempt to evade the will's provision leads to disaster. Burney paints a harrowing portrait of a society so obsessed with acquisition that Cecilia herself seems no more, at times, than a bit of red meat encircled by prowling lions. Burney builds her image of modern Britain through numerous representative characters. Like Ann Lovely, Cecilia has three guardians at cross-purposes: the miserly merchant Mr Briggs, the spendthrift Mr Harrel, and the pompous Mr Delville. Because Briggs's guidance is as meager as his budget and Mr Delville holds her in contempt, Cecilia is rapidly plundered by the Harrels. A huge cast of secondary figures, ranging from Albany, the prophet of doom for a mercenary people, to the pernicious Monckton create the illusion of an oppressive world gradually claiming Cecilia until even her mind is no longer her own. Both a coming-of-age novel and a thoroughgoing satire, *Cecilia* still comments powerfully on capitalist values.

Burney continued to orchestrate various type characters in her later novels *Camilla* (1796) and *The Wanderer* (1814). As in her previous fictions, Burney's satiric types emphasize each novel's principal themes. In *Camilla*, for example, the heroine befriends a young widow, Mrs Berlinton, who resembles Lennox's Arabella in beholding life through the lenses of romantic fiction. Combined with the unwanted attentions of an officious toad-eater, Mrs Mitten, Mrs Berlinton's friendship leads Camilla into debt and disgrace. In *The Wanderer*, myriad types coalesce into a nightmarish society blocking all of Juliet's efforts to support herself. Although many are variants of traditional satiric characters, such as ill-tempered Mrs Ireton, some of Burney's supporting characters incorporate more recent trends. Miss Arbe, for example, reflects Robespierre's despotism (Burney 1991: xviii–xix); Elinor Joddrel combines Burney's impression of Mary Wollstonecraft with the self-dramatizing impulses of a sentimental heroine. Burney turns historic personages into types representing the dangerous new ideals of liberty and equality. Miss Arbe tyrannizes Juliet while claiming to help her, and Elinor embarrasses herself, her family, and the man she loves by overturning social conventions in her quest for self-fulfillment. Burney's suggestion of a world rushing headlong toward individual aggrandizement, while overlooking the oppressed, rings the truer for her invention of these modern types.

Although *The Witlings* was repressed, Burney exercised true stagecraft in her satirical use of secondary characters. To a degree unequalled until Charles Dickens, she created the impression of a world full of individuals apparently following their destinies but actually supporting her thematic purposes. Mary Wollstonecraft (1759–97) occasionally indulges in satirical wit in *A Vindication of the Rights of Woman* (1792), as when she quotes at length from conduct books only to puncture them with pithy observations. "Why are girls to be told that they resemble angels; but to sink them below women?" she inquires of a passage in Dr Fordyce's *Sermons to Young Women* (1997: 219). Wollstonecraft's novels, however, employ a more sentimental approach, although they are satirical in the broad sense of exposing for redress the wrongs of woman. Burney's younger contemporaries Jane Austen (1775–1817) and Maria Edgeworth (1768–1849) read and admired her novels. Austen's plots are sparer, her characters fewer, but she too relied on satiric types (the flirtatious soldier, the match-making mother, the obsequious clergyman, among many in *Pride and Prejudice*, 1813, alone) to create her heroines' contexts. Edgeworth wove satire into her plots and characters. Lady Delacour in *Belinda* (1811) is both a typical witty society hostess and a rounded character groping toward maturity. Harriot Freke, in the same novel, satirizes women's pursuit of rights; her notion of female equality involves adopting the coarse manners of a country squire.

Burney, Austen, and Edgeworth each negotiated her use of satire at a time when ladies were supposedly animated by sentiment. Accordingly, characters who abound in satiric wit, like Lady Delacour, must often grow beyond that propensity toward "true wit," or as Edgeworth's Belinda observes, wit refined by reason until it resembles "the refulgent moon" of "useful light" rather than "a noisy squib" or "an elegant firework" (1986: 211). Softened though it is, however, the definition of satire as a genre meant to expose vices for the purposes of correction lingers on in these novels. While women worked carefully throughout the Restoration and eighteenth century to avoid its damning association with personal invective, they maintained a strong tradition of satire, expressed usually with sparkling wit.

References and Further Reading

Alcock, Mary (1799) *Poems, etc., etc., by the Late Mrs Mary Alcock*. London: C. Dilly.

Austen, Jane (1985) *Pride and Prejudice*, ed. Tony Tanner. Harmondsworth: Penguin (originally published 1813).

Barbauld, Anna (1773) *Poems*. London: Joseph Johnson.

Barber, Mary (1734) *Poems on Several Occasions*. London: C. Rivington.

Behn, Aphra (1992) *The Works of Aphra Behn, Vol. 1: Poetry*, ed. Janet Todd. Athens: Ohio State University Press.

——(1993) *The Works of Aphra Behn, Vol. 2: Loveletters between a Nobleman and his Sister*, ed. Janet Todd. Athens: Ohio State University Press.

——(1995) *The Works of Aphra Behn, Vol. 3: The Fair Jilt and Other Stories*, ed. Janet Todd. Athens: Ohio State University Press.

—— (1996a) *The Works of Aphra Behn, Vol. 5: The Plays, 1671–1677*, ed. Janet Todd. Athens: Ohio State University Press.

—— (1996b) *The Works of Aphra Behn, Vol. 7: The Plays, 1682–1696*, ed. Janet Todd. Athens: Ohio State University Press.

Burney, Frances (1982) *Evelina*, ed. Edward A. Bloom. Oxford: Oxford University Press (originally published 1778).

—— (1983) *Camilla*, ed. Edward A. and Lillian D. Bloom. Oxford: Oxford University Press (originally published 1796).

—— (1990) *Cecilia*, ed. Margaret Doody and Peter Sabor. Oxford: Oxford University Press (originally published 1782).

—— (1991) *The Wanderer*, ed. Margaret Doody, Robert L. Mack, and Peter Sabor. Oxford: Oxford University Press (originally published 1814).

Carter, Elizabeth (1808) *Memoirs of the Life of Mrs Elizabeth Carter, with a New Edition of her Poems*, 2 vols, ed. Montagu Pennington, 2nd edn. London: F. C. and J. Rivington.

Centlivre, Susanna (1982) *The Plays of Susanna Centlivre*, 3 vols, ed. Richard C. Frushell. New York: Garland.

Chandler, Mary (1747) *The Description of Bath... with Several Other Poems*. London: H. Leake.

Chudleigh, Lady Mary (1993) *The Poems and Prose of Mary, Lady Chudleigh*, ed. Margaret J. M. Ezell. New York: Oxford University Press.

Cowley, Hannah (2001) *Eighteenth-century Women Playwrights*, vol. 5, ed. Antje Blank. London: Pickering and Chatto.

D'Anvers, Alicia (1691) *Academia: Or, The Humours of The University of Oxford*. London: Randal Taylor.

Dryden, John (1974) *The Works of John Dryden, Vol. IV: Poems 1693–1699*, ed. A. B. Chambers, William Frost, and Vinton A. Dearing. Berkeley, CA: University of California Press.

Edgeworth, Maria (1986) *Belinda*, ed. Eva Figes. London: Pandora (originally published 1811).

[Egerton], S[arah] F[yge] (1703) *Poems on Several Occasions*. London: J. Nutt.

Fielding, Sarah (1987) *The Adventures of David Simple*, ed. Malcolm Kelsall. Oxford: Oxford University Press (originally published 1744–53).

Hands, Elizabeth (1789) *The Death of Amnon... and other Poetical Pieces*. Coventry: N. Rollason.

Haywood, Eliza (1998) *The History of Miss Betsy Thoughtless*, ed. Christine Blouch. Peterborough: Broadview (originally published 1751).

Inchbald, Elizabeth (1996) *A Simple Story*, ed. Pamela Clemit. London: Penguin (originally published 1791).

—— (2001) *Eighteenth-century Women Playwrights*, vol. 6, ed. Angela J. Smallwood. London: Pickering and Chatto.

Jones, Mary (1750) *Miscellanies in Prose and Verse*. Oxford: Dodsley et al.

Leapor, Mary (1748) *Poems upon Several Occasions*. London: J. Roberts.

—— (1751) *Poems upon Several Occasions*, vol. 2. London: Samuel Richardson.

Lennox, Charlotte (1989) *The Female Quixote*, ed. Margaret Dalziel. Oxford: Oxford University Press (originally published 1752).

Lewis, Esther (1789) *Poems Moral and Entertaining*. Bath: S. Hazard.

Little, Janet (1792) *The Poetical Works of Janet Little, the Scotch Milkmaid*. Air: J. Wilson and P. Wilson.

Manley, Delarivier (1992) *The New Atalantis*, ed. Ros Ballaster. London: Penguin (originally published 1709).

Montagu, Lady Mary Wortley (1977) *Essays and Poems and Simplicity, a Comedy*, ed. Robert Halsband and Isobel Grundy. Oxford: Clarendon.

More, Hannah (1788) *Slavery, A Poem*. London: T. Cadell.

—— (1996) *Poems*, ed. Caroline Franklin. London: Routledge (originally published 1816).

Murry, Ann (1779) *Poems on Various Subjects*. London: E. and C. Dilly et al.

Pix, Mary (1982) *The Plays of Mary Pix and Catherine Trotter*, 2 vols, ed. Edna L. Steeves. New York: Garland.

Robinson, Mary (1996) *Poetical Works*, 3 vols, ed. Caroline Franklin. London: Routledge (originally published 1806).

Scott, Sarah Robinson (1999) *Millennium Hall*, ed. Gary Kelly. Peterborough: Broadview (originally published 1750).

Seward, Anna (1799) *Original Sonnets on Various Subjects; And Odes Paraphrased from Horace*. London: G. Sael.

—— (1810) *The Poetical Works of Anna Seward*, ed. Sir Walter Scott. Edinburgh: Ballantyne.

Smith, Charlotte (1989) *The Old Manor House*, ed. Anne Henry Ehrenpreis. Oxford: Oxford University Press (originally published 1793).

Tipper, Elizabeth (1698) *The Pilgrim's Viaticum*. London: J. Wilkins.

Tollet, Elizabeth (1755) *Poems on Several Occasions*, 2nd edn. London: T. Lowndes.

Winchilsea, Anne Kingsmill Finch, Countess of (1974) *The Poems of Anne Countess of Winchilsea*, ed. Myra Reynolds. New York: A.M.S. (originally published 1903).

Wollstonecraft, Mary (1997) *The Vindications: The Rights of Men, The Rights of Woman*, ed. D. L. Macdonald and Kathleen Scherf. Toronto: Broadview.

16
Pictorial Satire: From Emblem to Expression
Ronald Paulson

"The Cartoonist's Armoury": The Emblem

The question this chapter broaches is how an artist translates into images the basic situations and strategies of verbal satirists. The nucleus of pictorial satire has always been what Ernst Gombrich, in his essay "The Cartoonist's Armoury," called "the hardened metaphors of political jargon," a basic set of verbalizations upon which cartoonists draw:

> such as the summit meeting or the iron curtain; we can or cannot police the world, live under the shadow of the bomb, trim our sails to the winds of change, join hands with that group and steal a march on the other; the road ahead is arduous but the future, of course, is bright, if only we avoid the pitfalls, skirt the abyss, and stop that downward trend. (Gombrich 1963: 130)

This is, in Gombrich's words, a way of condensing "a complex idea in one striking and memorable image" and is still the primary resource of political cartoonists. We might say that Gombrich indicates the precedence of the word or the concept over the image, which merely literalizes or materializes it. Or the image forces the spectator to verbalize (in Gombrich's terms, reverbalize) itself. He is describing a form of *ekphrasis* – a poem reprised in an image or, alternatively, a picture put into words.

In the first plate of William Hogarth's *A Harlot's Progress* (1732; figure 16.1), the young country woman is related by a metonymy to the goose she brings with her in her basket: She is a goose, which equals "Winchester Goose" or whore, or a "silly goose" (proleptically, "dead as a goose"). In the second plate, her Jewish keeper is, like his monkey, "aping" London beaux; he is being "made a monkey of" by his mistress's departing lover who, by means of an optical illusion, is "stabbing him in the back" with his sword, and the antlers in the wallpaper behind his head ask to be verbalized as "cuckold." In two of James Gillray's best-known satires, Edmund Burke is "smelling out a rat" and Pitt the Younger is "a fungus on the crown" (figures 16.2 and 16.3).

While the weapons of the "cartoonist's armoury" consist of "illustrations of figures of speech" (Gombrich 1963: 132), they also – to be more historically specific – in many cases originally derived from Cesare Ripa's *Iconologia* (1593), the source book for commonly accepted imagery: the classical gods and heroes, the virtues and vices, and so on. A print like Hogarth's *The Lottery* (1724; figure 16.4) is essentially a graphic allegory. The print is datable as "early Hogarth" by the tiny figures scattered in several groups without expressive or dramatic relation to one another. Another factor, however, is the lack of any relationship but an arbitrary or conventional one between the visual images and their verbal meaning. There is nothing but the iconographic convention that links "hope" with a woman standing by an anchor or "justice" with a figure holding a scale and balance.

The emblem, best known in the collections published by Andrea Alciati (*Emblemata*, 1531), showed an image accompanied by a title above and verses below that

Figure 16.1 William Hogarth, *A Harlot's Progress*, Plate 1. Etching and engraving, 1732. Courtesy of the British Museum, London

Figure 16.2 James Gillray, *Smelling out a Rat*. Etching, 1790. Author's collection

explain the often esoteric iconography of the image. The emblem turns the classical *ekphrasis* into a puzzle to be solved. The inscription under Hogarth's *Lottery* explains: "Upon the Pedestal, National Credit [leans] on a Pillar supported by Justice. Apollo [shows] Britannia a Picture representing Earth receiving enriching showers drawn from herself (an Emblem of State Lotterys)... Before the Pedestal Suspense [is] turn'd to and fro by Hope and fear." In Hogarth's mature satires the explanatory words of the emblem (with a few exceptions) move in from the borders to infiltrate the image; verbalization spreads across a spectrum from puns and all manner of verbal play from the verbal joke (such as the goose = "Winchester Goose"; antlers = "cuckold") to words and phrases (labels) identifying the characters, present or absent ("M. H." on a trunk, "M. Hackabout" and "For my Lofing Cosen in Tems Stret in London" on pieces of paper), or explaining their actions (the clergyman's note with the address of the Bishop of London, Sir Robert Walpole's dispenser of ecclesiastical preferment, explains his ignoring of Hackabout's plight; see figure 16.1).

Hogarth's practice was to use conventional iconography sparingly and to naturalize the figures. They are embodied in contemporary characters, often recognizable likenesses, who sometimes assume or allude to the attributes of conventional and stereotypical figures: in *Harlot*, Plate 1, to an ironic "Choice of Hercules" (the girl

Figure 16.3 James Gillray, *An Excrescence; a Fungus; Alias a Toadstool upon a Dung-hill*. Etching, 1791. Author's collection

has no choice) and "Visitation," classical and Christian stereotypes. In Plate 10 of *Industry and Idleness* (1748), Francis Goodchild, as he passes judgment on Tom Idle, adopts the pose of Blind Justice. Hogarth's point is that these human beings have permitted themselves to become stereotypes, or their society has imposed these stereotypes upon them.

Figure 16.4 William Hogarth, *The Lottery*. Etching and engraving, 1724. Courtesy of the British Museum, London

Classical Models

The chief tradition of moral satire was classical, the satires of the Romans Horace and Juvenal, and in this case Juvenal, whose subject was corruption, proved for graphic satirists the richer source. Corruption for Juvenal is a falling away, decline, or reversal, most generally of the Republic into the Empire. In *Satire* 3, Rome has declined from its republican ideals into a city of foreigners; Umbricius, the last Roman, leaves Rome, now totally un-Roman, to return to the country, specifically to Cumae where Aeneas first landed and consulted the oracle, descending into the underworld to receive his vision of the Rome he will found. The visual equivalent of corruption is a simple contrast: Juvenal's eighth *Satire* begins,

> What good are the statues of heroes
> If you spent all night throwing dice, and not until daybreak
> Start for your bed, at an hour when your warrior ancestors ordered
> Camp to be moved and the march to go forward? (Juvenal 1958)

The image of Juvenal's decadent Romans was rendered pictorial by Fellini in the scene in *La Dolce Vita* (1960) where, in a Roman palazzo, contemporary Romans are passed out along a wall beneath the busts of their illustrious ancestors.

In *Satire* 3, those who have remained in Rome are victims of bad patrons, robbers, incendiaries, and murderers. Again, in *Satire* 6, Roman men have given up their traditional position in the social hierarchy and women have taken their places, have become masculine, dominating and humiliating their husbands, betraying and killing them. Juvenal enclosed in the particular situation of the corruption of an ideal the punishment of both innocent and gullible at the hands of the guilty – essentially what Hogarth materializes in the life of his Harlot in 1730s' London.

Christian Models

Trying to give a sense of what he called "the satiric scene" in verse and prose satire, Alvin Kernan turned to examples of graphic satire (Kernan 1959: 8–10). Honoré Daumier's drawing *The Incriminating Evidence* (1865–8) shows a row of grim magistrates seated under a picture of Christ on the cross; only his feet are visible – the rest is cut off by the top horizontal of Daumier's picture space. Like Juvenal's statues of Roman heroes, this picture indicates an ideal in the past, but a Christian one. It is a satire on judicial *lex talionis*, stupidity, and malice, with a bare indication of an ideal associated with forgiveness and love – but which, if we verbalize, is "dead" and "cut off."

Kernan traces the satiric "scene" back to Christian paintings, most notably North European, of Christ being mocked, flagellated, and crucified, where he is a tiny, idealized figure surrounded by – almost, in some cases, lost among – ugly, brutal, torturing, or mocking figures of Romans, soldiers, and priests. This corresponds, as Kernan suggests, to the "scene" of the Roman *satura* of Horace and Juvenal, indeed to most narrative satires as well: a great many examples of folly or knavery crowded threateningly around, crushing or drowning, a single disappearing indication of virtue, for Juvenal only a memory. It is easy to see how the Christian images of Christ mocked or whipped, surrounded and almost obliterated by evil faces, could be taken to be another version, more powerful because of its religious associations (its associations with the Incarnation and Atonement), of the Juvenalian scene. In Hogarth's *South Sea Scheme* (published at the same time as *The Lottery*), the allegorical figures of the continental Bubble prints have been Christianized – Truth is a Christ in a *flagellation* scene.

Christian iconography depicted two categories of transgressive subject matter, which were utilized by the great artists of the European Renaissance: sin and evil. Sin was based on either disobedience or offense (like Eve's and Adam's, the Original Sin) to God; the result was an abomination, the term Leviticus applied to everything from miscegenation and homosexuality to unclean objects for sacrifice or eating. Chaucer's Parson enunciated the orthodox Christian sense of sin in his sermon on the seven deadly sins: "Sin is of two kinds; it is either venial or mortal sin. Verily, when man loves any creature more than he loves Jesus Christ our Creator, then is it mortal sin. And venial sin it is if a man love Jesus Christ less than he ought." Sin involves a transaction between a human and his god, evil between humans. But evil also originates with God. The Christian interpretation of the Genesis sense of evil(s) as human *suffering*-evil (death, disease, accident) in a god-created world was the basis for our understanding of *doing*-evil as well: to do *evil* (as opposed to the god-oriented *sin*) is to make a sentient being, human or animal, suffer.

Sin was represented in medieval and Renaissance art primarily in scenes of temptation, the seven deadly sins, and hell; evil by scenes of the Passion. The first referred to God, the second to Jesus Christ. The inhabitants of hell are sinners, having found lust or avarice more important than worship of God. The imagery in Dante's *Inferno* is of punishment by God for various forms of idolatry (another name for preferring any other thing to God, such as money or fleshly love), and the evils represented in the scenes include both suffering and doing evil, the damned and their punishers either distinguished as sin and evil, or (in the case of Ugolino and Ruggieri, Satan and Judas) as equally evil.

The representations of the Passion are about evil: Jesus himself has to suffer the evils consequent upon the Original Sin (suffering of the innocent, death, and so on) in order to redeem that sin. *This*, the paintings and prints say, is what evil really looks like. With Jesus, who came to earth to redeem Adam's and our sins, evil is what the priests and soldiers do to him. The acts carried out upon him are, of course, technically examples of sin – the very sins of disobedience he is redeeming (partly why they are so appalling). But rather than being about sin, the pictorial images are about the evil imposed upon him (in the sense of the suffering he endures *as* a human): he is taking our place as sufferer for our sins, suffering evil from the doers of evil. Evil, as always, is the consequence of the concept of sin: centered on Jesus and the Passion, primarily the model of *Ecce Homo*, Flagellation, and Crucifixion scenes (as opposed to Pietas, Entombments, Resurrections, and Nativities). The form taken is of a beautiful, fragile figure surrounded by horribly ugly figures mocking and beating him.

Hogarth's first, most important, and most influential series of satiric prints was *A Harlot's Progress* (Paulson 1991, 2003). It is the Christian image of the Passion that Hogarth parodies in Plates 4 and 6 (see figures 16.5 and 16.6), where the Harlot is surrounded by mocking prison warders and by the Londoners who represent the layers of society (from clergy to magistrates) that kill her. From the religious perspective, the Harlot is a sinner, what (from Hogarth's perspective) Christ had become in order to be a human in order to redeem mankind, and so persecuted by the law and religion. She disobeys God's Commandments, *Thou shalt not worship a false god* and *Thou shalt not commit adultery*. To be a prostitute is a sin as well as legally a crime; but the Harlot's sins-crimes are victimless; she hurts no one (she steals a watch; she is shown getting but not transmitting disease), whereas the agents of society punish her with "evils" (whips, prison, disease, death), in the name of the church, law, and government. (The

Figure 16.5 William Hogarth, *A Harlot's Progress*, Plate 4 (detail), 1732. Courtesy of the British Museum, London

Figure 16.6 Albrecht Dürer, *Flagellation* (detail). Woodcut; from the Albertina Passion, c.1500. Author's collection

Bishop of London, the "Rape-Master" Colonel Charteris, and the magistrate Sir John Gonson were all supporters of, surrogates for, Sir Robert Walpole.) Hogarth juxtaposes the concepts of sin-law and evil, showing that sin is simply the name the ruling order uses to mask the evil it inflicts upon the lower orders. In fact, society punishes the Harlot for aspiring and attempting to be a "lady," that Levitical *abomination* a harlot-lady (or the Commandment about worshiping a false god).

We can draw a direct line from Bosch's and Massys's *Ecce Homo* paintings to Hogarth's *Harlot's Progress* Plate 4 – or to Plate 6, showing a room full of clergymen, mercers, whores, and bawds with a bare glimpse of the Harlot's face in her coffin, in the composition of a *Last Supper*, in which she replaces the Body and the Blood of Christ in a parodic, contemporary Eucharist – to Blake's images of Christ's Atonement recovered for religion, blood sacrifice, and orthodoxy by the church, and to James Ensor's huge painting, *Christ Entering Brussels* (1889), where a single tiny Christ is surrounded by thousands of ugly, jeering Belgians – the people whom he is redeeming, who will shortly crucify him. (Ensor also painted a version of the Daumier court scene.)

W. H. Auden wrote about such a scene in his poem "Musée des Beaux Arts" (1940), looking at Pieter Brueghel's *Fall of Icarus* as well as a *Nativity* and *Crucifixion*, but he saw the surrounding figures not as oppressors but merely as farmers continuing to plough – ordinary people carrying on their daily lives unaware, as if no tragedy, no miracle, nothing unusual had happened. ("While someone else is eating or opening a window or just walking dully along.") Two objects of satire are implied: the unaware, ignorant, and stupid; and the vicious, malicious, and cruel. An example is the first plate of the *Harlot's Progress* (figure 16.1), where the indifferent response of the clergyman (who, instead of protecting the young girl, is concerned only with his personal advancement) and the absence of the girl's "Lofing Cosen in Tems Stret" are set off against the bawd Mother Needham and the rake Colonel Francis Charteris (known as "Rape-Master of England") who are actively seducing her, the first stage in her destruction: essentially "the best lack all conviction, while the worst are full of passionate intensity" (Yeats, "Second Coming").

These examples indicate some of the subjects that pictorial satire is particularly equipped to deal with; they also suggest how the sources of graphic satire, perhaps more than of verbal, depended upon Christian iconography – not surprisingly, since graphic satire is usually thought to have originated in Western Europe with the Reformation, which coincided with the development of printing and the production and distribution of identical images in great profusion, perfect for propaganda.

In the Enlightenment – in eighteenth-century England – these images began to change and reverse their values. Iconoclasm and anti-Catholic images tended to put in question the valence of the iconography. Kernan cites, as another example of the "satiric scene," Hogarth's *Gin Lane* (1751, figure 16.7), crowded with "debris and a host of rotting things, human, animal and vegetable," with, in the far distance, an indication of the ideal in the clean, white spire of a church (Kernan 1959: 10). This would recall the apostolic church as now only a memory in Swift's *Argument against*

Figure 16.7 William Hogarth, *Gin Lane*. Etching and engraving, 1751. Courtesy of the British Museum, London

Abolishing Christianity (1711) or the surviving fragments in *Nineteen Eighty-Four* (1949) of the old nursery song, "Oranges and lemons / The Bells of St Clements." But in the 1750s the situation has become more complicated than Kernan's paradigm would suggest. Dickens was closer to the truth when, in the 1830s, he recalled the church steeple: "quite passive in the picture, it coldly surveys these things in progress under a shadow of its tower" (Dickens 1848) – although it is too far away to throw a shadow. In fact, the church steeple is not a remote ideal but represents the withdrawal of the church and its appropriation by the state. It withholds its succor from the poor of London in the foreground who now have only gin to rely upon; its cross has been replaced by a statue of the monarch (George I) and, by a typically Hogarthian trick of perspective, by the faux-cross in the foreground, the symbol of the pawnshop – as the pawnbroker has become the only civil authority in Gin Lane. The implication is that the church and crown have turned their attention elsewhere – as in the pendant, *The First Stage of Cruelty*, the arm bands ("St G.") worn by the boys show that they are the poor of St Giles Parish, but where are the governors who should be supervising them? As in *The Fall of Icarus*, the figure of the ideal is not only ignored but (to verbalize again) has "shrunk into insignificance" and "turned its back."

Narrative Satire

The most obvious way to translate a narrative satire like *Gulliver's Travels* into pictures is to employ a series of linked scenes: these have ranged from demotic fifteenth to seventeenth-century "comic strips" to Hogarth's series of six, eight, or twelve plates (Kunzle 1973). But narrative satire only secondarily tells a story; the story is an excuse (a parody of a romance plot) for a sequence of events whose true course is down Primrose Paths into ever deeper Sloughs of Despond to Apocalypse; the progression is essentially one of decline, from bad to worse; but causal, saying: if this, then this follows and this and this, the consequences piling up. The Hogarth progress (of a harlot, of a rake) is from one bad choice (or, with the Harlot, absence of choice) to ever worsening consequences, ending in prison, disease, and death.

Narrative satire was at bottom a version of *satura* or Roman formal verse satire – a spicy ragout of elements that, having no more form than that of a ragout, parasitically adapts other literary or journalistic forms, primarily those best adaptable to its aims, enumerations such as almanacs, projects, series of voyages, and the like (Swift's *Bickerstaff Papers*, 1708–9, *Gulliver's Travels*, 1726, and *Modest Proposal*, 1729). Hogarth's *Harlot's Progress* ostensibly tells a story like Bunyan's *Pilgrim's Progress* (1678), though it parodies "progress" as in fact regress. It appears to be based on the principle of crime followed by punishment, though in fact the emphasis is on the punishers rather than the punished, as in the "mourners" of Plate 6 surrounding the barely visible corpse of the Harlot.

Parody

The form of emblematic print from which Hogarth learned his trade emerged in the "Bubble" satires of circa 1719–20 that were imported from the Netherlands, along with the more sophisticated work of the Dutch artist Romeyne de Hooghe which followed his patron William of Orange to England. De Hooghe's satiric prints were grandiloquent, based on the style and compositions of North European history paintings – baroque and extravagant, imitating the works (known through engravings and woodcuts) of Goltzius, Jordaens, and Rubens. These prints, imported, copied, and adapted, were assimilated into France at the time of the Mississippi Bubble, and into England a year later with the South Sea Bubble.

In England, the greatest beneficiary was Hogarth, who cast his nets wider, gathering in echoes of specific works by Raphael and other artists of the Renaissance and Baroque. In *The Lottery* (figure 16.4), the whole composition is a parody: the money-centered society of London is again allegorized as in his Bubble models, but it is placed in a parody of Raphael's *Dispute on the Nature of the Eucharist* – the famous fresco in the Vatican Stanze, available in enough engraved and etched copies to be public fare. The demotic reality of 1720s' London is contrasted with the ideal of Raphael's history painting and its subject of the redemption of mankind. That is, the contrast (travesty) of the Holy Eucharist and the London lottery – alternate ways of getting to heaven – is, in Juvenalian terms, one the degenerate replacement for the other.

In *Hudibras and the Skimmington* (1726), the English Quixote appears in the composition of Annibale Carracci's *Procession of Bacchus and Ariadne*: Carracci's heroic lovers in Hogarth's parody are a cuckold and his wife on horseback in the English "crowd ritual" called a Charivari. These were allusions to a cultural capital shared by educated readers quite different from the verbal puns, moribund metaphors, and "illustrations of figures of speech" that came from a common stock of knowledge, immediately accessible to anyone. The most important model for Hogarth's graphic satire was literary, the satire of Dryden, Pope, and Swift, where the verbal equivalent of Juvenalian corruption was the mock heroic mode, where an elevated diction was supplemented by allusions to Rome, Augustus, and Virgil. This Hogarth translated into graphic terms through parody: a decadent contemporary situation rendered in the style, forms, and pictorial allusions of a baroque painting of heroic or sacred figures.

To emphasize the connection between law and the theology of sin, Hogarth embeds his story of the Harlot's crime and suffering of evils in images that parody paintings and prints of the Visitation, Annunciation, Flagellation, Crucifixion, and Last Supper (models as well, from Hogarth's perspective, of the fashionable baroque art that served as the basis for the academic rules of painting). The Harlot, and not Jesus, takes upon herself the sins and atones for the evils of society in 1730s' England (figures 16.1 and 16.5). Jesus is off somewhere up in heaven in the imagination of good Church of Englanders; but Hogarth's Jesus is the Jesus who defended the woman taken in adultery, attacked the moneylenders in the temple, and castigated the scribes and priests while keeping company with such as Mary Magdalen, the penitent harlot. In Matthew 23: 33, Jesus chose an adulterous woman, not a murderer or thief or rapist, to illustrate his words: "Who is without sin cast the first stone."

For the Anglican Swift, evil was the usurpation of rightful authority, as treachery, disloyalty, or betrayal of a master. Hogarth portrayed the betrayal not *of* the master but *by* the master, and *of* the servant. The mock-heroic satire in which the fishwife talks as if she is (aspires to the status of) Queen Dido he turned into travesty: Queen

Dido talks like a fishwife, exposing the reality under crowns and crosses. The biblical allusions are old and outdated customs and beliefs that cramp, discomfit, and destroy the young girl who has come to London to make her way up. They are hardly ideals from which she has fallen away. And they function in much the same way (with further complications) in *A Rake's Progress* of three years later, where Tom Rakewell is related, as imitator to imitated, to paintings of the Judgment of Paris and portraits of the Roman emperors.

Gay's *Beggar's Opera* (1728, which Hogarth painted several times) offered him the sort of satire he used in the *Harlot*: where the criminals are bad and punished, but the respectable folk (the "great") are worse and go unpunished – based on the *topos* expressed, for example, in Defoe's poem "Reformation of Manners" of 1702: "So for small crimes poor Thieves Destruction find, / And leave the Rogues of Quality behind" (ll. 180–1). While the poor rogues break the laws, the great rogues *make* the laws. The respectable folk are the effective evil that is only reflected in the more accessible (punishable) criminals/sinners such as Macheath, Jonathan Wild, and Hogarth's Harlot: thus, sin punished, evil rewarded, in this life at any rate.

Hogarth's predecessors – Dryden, Swift, and Pope – were living in a state reeling from civil war and fearful of its return; religion and politics were closely intertwined; and the model for those times was Juvenalian. Civil chaos was the evil they described, and its sources were in Puritan and Whig self-sufficiency. Hogarth came at a time when the church and state was stabilized in the long reign of the Great Man, Sir Robert Walpole; Hogarth's satire was Old Whig in that it questioned both divine and secular assumptions, but within a cover story of sin and punishment that could be taken as orthodox by *hoi poloi*.

The Rococo Style

The subject of parody – of literary works but also of art – raises the further question: what does graphic satire owe to, how does it relate to or perhaps derive from, contemporary styles of painting? If verbal satire is parasitic of contemporary literary forms (spiritual autobiography, fantastic voyages, romances), is satire not equally dependent on contemporary paintings and art styles (Baroque, Rococo, later Neoclassical, Romantic, Impressionist, Modern, Postmodern, Surreal, or Dada)? There is, I suggest, a close relationship between the graphic satire developed by Hogarth and the Rococo style that was coming into England from France just as he was emerging as an artist.

The Rococo was essentially a style of pure form, graceful, serpentine, and asymmetrical; these forms, playfully handled, represented a reduction of the grandiose Baroque forms of the seventeenth century to a smaller scale and of the Baroque (often Counter-Reformation) subjects of crucifixions, martyrdoms, and stories of religio-erotic passion to *fêtes champêtres* and *fêtes gallantes*. As a model for graphic satire, the Rococo is essentially mock-heroic, corresponding to literary works like Pope's *Rape of the Lock* (1714), which reduces the grandiloquent forms of the Baroque to their human equivalents, sets the Baroque stories of the Bible and classical myth against contemporary social reality. The Rococo echoes both the form and content of the Baroque but reduces them to smaller, more intricate and meaningful forms and a contemporary un-heroic context, which is partially defined in terms of the heroic context. In the same way, the Rococo reduces the discourse of religion and sin to practical morality: don't imitate the great, but see that they are in fact evil and punish you only for what they regard as your sin or your legal crime, which is usually concupiscence.

Hogarth had begun his career as an apprentice to a Huguenot silver engraver of Rococo patterns; then, as a painter, he followed the Rococo style and subjects of Watteau and his followers in France. Watteau was himself in England in 1719–20 and left paintings behind him – scenes involving figures from the *commedia dell'arte*. In particular, two prefigured the English Rococo that Hogarth developed: one was the *Comédiens Italiens*, which was in Dr Richard Mead's collection; the other, *L'Enseigne de Gersaint*, which was in a French collection but was reproduced by the end of the 1720s in the publication called *Le Receuil Julienne*.

Watteau's *Comédiens Italiens* (Washington, National Gallery of Art) shows the clown Pierrot, all in white, a figure of innocence, flanked by the *Commedia* troupe on a stage, posed in an *Ecce Homo* composition. Watteau has wittily reduced the scenes of Christ being mocked by the crowd, surrounded by Pharisees, priests, and Roman centurions, to a scene of actors, and in particular the simple white figure of Pierrot, facing an audience on a stage, implying an unreceptive audience. Jesus is replaced by a clown (actors were regarded by the religious as sinners, as the Pharisees regarded Jesus). Hogarth then increased the irony by turning the clown Pierrot into a harlot and showing her literally punished and killed by the forces of evil around her (her death is from the syphilis she has received from one of her clients). At the same time, he turns the purely Rococo forms – which in his *Analysis of Beauty* (1753) he would argue should lead the spectator's eye a merry chase around and through the composition – into cognitive structures: into shifting gestalts and reading structures that vary from the formal to the emblematic and the punning to the literally verbal. These forms are, in short, moving in the direction of the expressive, though still dependent on external references – to *Ecce Homo* paintings and representations of such familiar *topoi* as "The Choice of Hercules."

Hogarth's interiors follow the structure of the second Watteau painting, *L'Enseigne de Gersaint* (Berlin, Charlottenburg). The walls of Gersaint's shop are covered with pictures and the message is both satiric and programmatic. Some of these paintings, in form and content, are old and on their way out (Watteau shows a pompous portrait of Louis XIV being packed away in a box), but situated in the Rococo world of contemporary scenes, living men, and even a flea-scratching dog. From the Gersaint shop sign, Hogarth takes the contrast of nature and art, life in play with paintings or sculptures.

By way of Gersaint's shop sign, Hogarth translates Juvenal's busts into paintings hanging on the walls of his realistically depicted rooms, above the characters.

Reminders of the old Baroque style appear in these paintings, which are grim scenes not of an ideal but of evil in the past – of pain and punishment. In the first plate of *Marriage A-la-mode* (1745), Cain kills Abel, St Lawrence is martyred, Prometheus is tortured by the vulture, all in vague theological spaces, and related to the adulterous acts in the detailed perspective box scenes beneath, in which we see the bride dallying with the lawyer, the groom with his own image in the mirror, presaging the affairs they enjoy in Plates 3 and 4 with, respectively, the same lawyer and a child prostitute. The paintings are all about punishment associated with the father, the older patriarchal generation – though Hogarth shows little more sympathy with the younger generation, which simply perpetuates the tradition of the older.

The paintings are, as we have noted, stereotypes, specifically images of art that have been chosen and purchased by the characters, who thereby identify themselves – or, more often, come to imitate them, permitting their actions to be dictated from above, by the past: as if the Juvenalian busts, instead of showing a falling away of the present generation from their ancestors, had forced their outworn ideals upon the contemporary generation. (This was, in a way, Fellini's interpretation: not only degeneration, but the crushing weight of having to live up to these images kept around the palazzo as models, has led to degeneration.)

Rebellion (or disobedience) was one element of the Rococo, abomination another, both equally "sins": as Watteau shows in the shop sign, his art is *not* going to be Baroque – not about the royal figure or about martyrs and saints; it is going to be a reaction. And this is what Hogarth expresses in his turn away from religious orthodoxy as well. He represents sinning and prefers it to the idea of evil that is imposed upon sin by priests and magistrates. And he represents abomination, we have already noted, in that the Harlot's real sin in the eyes of society (versus the legal one of prostitution) is trying to pass herself off as a harlot-pseudo lady, which is a Levitical abomination.

The Rococo was the paradigmatic style of graphic satire, with its parody of the more pompous, antiquated previous "old master" style; subsequent graphic satire has tended to operate like the Rococo in its adaptation and parody of contemporary styles. Graphic satire – a term we can extend from Hogarth to Blake and to Goya's *Caprichos* – is a unique combination of high and low art, academic and demotic forms, high literature like the novel and low like the jestbook.

Caricature

A logical consequence of Rococo forms and assumptions was caricature. Caricature was an invention of the Baroque masters, in particular the Carracci and Bernini – a game they played in their spare time, by which they escaped from the rigors and portentousness of their official art. Like other forms of the Rococo, caricature began as a diversion. For with its fantastic, crude, or merely playful exaggerations, caricature represented a relaxation or escape, even a conscious rebellion, from the demands of "serious" painting, but in particular of portraiture. From this point of view, the discovery of caricature in the Baroque school of the Carracci may not only reflect the complete mastery of the techniques of realistic portraiture and hence a confidence in departures from them, but also the crushing burden of such mastery and the desire to escape from under it through release and laughter: another version of the message of Watteau's *L'Enseigne de Gersaint*. (It is no accident that some of the oldest and most durable butts of satiric caricature are the connoisseur, the antiquarian, and the art dealer.)

If the caricaturist, beginning with such high-style artists as the Carracci and Bernini (indeed, Leonardo), is an ironist, then in addition to the explicit contrast of inflation–deflation within the drawings themselves, there is an implicit contrast between the portrait caricature and the norms of formal portraiture. The formal portrait always had a tendency toward the grand and the ideal, and this was particularly the case in Hogarth's time, when caricatures were being imported by connoisseurs and cognoscenti from Italy. The connoisseur Jonathan Richardson insisted that the aim of portraiture was not to portray the sitter as he was, but to "raise the character; to divest an unbred person of his rusticity and give him something at least of a gentleman" (*Essay on the Theory of Painting*, 1715). The formal portrait, that is, portrayed the sitter as he would like to be seen – larger than life, possessing heroic stature, or at least assuming a public role.

Caricature responded to the idealization of formal portraiture by trying to cut man down to size, to remind him of his Lilliputian stature in the larger scheme of things. In this respect, it corresponded to what Watteau and Hogarth were doing to history painting, and Hogarth might have seen it as another form of his own deflationary satire, had it not entered England as a plaything of the rich, idle amateur. Caricature was, as it happened, also a way of *in*flating. As we have seen, it had remained a private entertainment for a few major artists and their friends until the beginning of the eighteenth century, at which point it began to spread throughout Europe and especially Great Britain largely through the influx of visitors to Rome and Florence on the Grand Tour, and the prints distributed in England by the entrepreneur Arthur Pond. A caricature portrait by Ghezzi, Marratti, or Internari seems to have been *de rigueur* for the young nobleman visiting Italy in the first half of the century.

The coterie appeal of caricature is obvious. Thomas Patch did all his work in Florence for a small English enclave of soldiers, diplomats, antiquaries, and dilettantes. And in his case he painted them on the scale of history paintings, as did the young Sir Joshua Reynolds himself around 1750 (*The School of Rome*, Dublin, National Gallery), placing the caricatured figures of the aristocratic young English gentlemen visiting (or lounging about) Rome in the composition of Raphael's *School of Athens*, a work generally considered the highest point of the highest genre to which an artist could aspire – just as Hogarth had, in his engraving *The Lottery* (figure 16.4), presented the contemporary English fascination with lotteries in the composition of Raphael's *Dispute on the Nature of the Eucharist*.

Reynolds' parody of Raphael's *School of Athens* may clarify the nature of the audience Hogarth addresses in his satires. The broad "popular" audience, which he certainly reached, could not be expected to recognize Reynolds' allusion any more than the allusions in *A Harlot's Progress*. Both artists were addressing, in part at least, an audience of connoisseurs, though for opposite purposes: Reynolds to attract and flatter them, Hogarth to test them and instruct them in their errors. The connoisseurs were, like it or not, an important part of the satirist's audience, as the educated had been for Swift and Pope.

In the case of the English nobility at least, we may suspect that it was motives of sophistication and exclusion that prompted their ready support for an art form which would seem at first to be an insult to the sitter. For in England of the 1750s, portraiture, once an exclusively aristocratic preserve, was now all too common. It seemed as though every sea captain, merchant, and businessman was having his portrait done, and he was coming out looking like at least an aristocrat if not a god or a hero. To the young English nobleman, the outrageous sophistication of the caricature portrait was appealing. It suggested at once a certain disdain for a tradition of portraiture which was degrading itself by its indiscriminately heroic manner, and also a kind of self-parody that was clearly beyond the understanding of the solemn, serious, and upwardly mobile merchants and captains (in fact, the subjects Hogarth made his name painting) who were far too concerned about their self-image ever to make fun of it. These young aristocrats appreciated the sophisticated paradox of the portrait caricature – which while it deflates, it also inflates. For like parody or the verbal "roast," a portrait caricature can only ridicule its subject by acknowledging and even reinforcing his celebrity. Thus, even when caricature becomes explicitly satirical, we find its victims preferring to be caricatured rather than be neglected as insignificant. This phenomenon still applies to the public figures who collect their own caricatures, however unfavorable. John Wilkes was said to have carried around Hogarth's "caricature" *John Wilkes* of 1763.

Caricature did not figure in Hogarth's satires, though his genius for catching a likeness with minimal means (as in his *John Wilkes*) could forgivably be mistaken for caricature. He set out the difference in his print of 1743, *Characters and Caricaturas* (figure 16.8) – his sense of "character" above and below at the left where he shows contrasting "characters" from Raphael's Cartoons; in the three panels on the right are caricatures by Ghezzi and a grotesque head by Leonardo. Hogarth's intention is to contrast the fluidity of the characters with the reductive shapes of the caricatures. His own satire was dramatic, based on relationships between characters set off by representations of actions in the past in the copies of art looming over the humans: art which in effect "caricatured" or made "caricatures" of the humans. Caricature for Hogarth equaled simplification and stereotype. Meaning, we have seen, was conveyed not through caricature but through metonymic relationships between a person and an animal, statue, painting, or some optical illusion, never violating probability – as his Dutch precursors often did in their more purely emblematic satires and the caricaturists did with their radical simplifications. Hogarth resented the comparisons of his work to caricature because he regarded caricature as foreign-derived, aristocratic, too easy, and altogether independent of good draughtsmanship. Perhaps most important to him, it was historically a toy of the elite young English gentlemen who brought

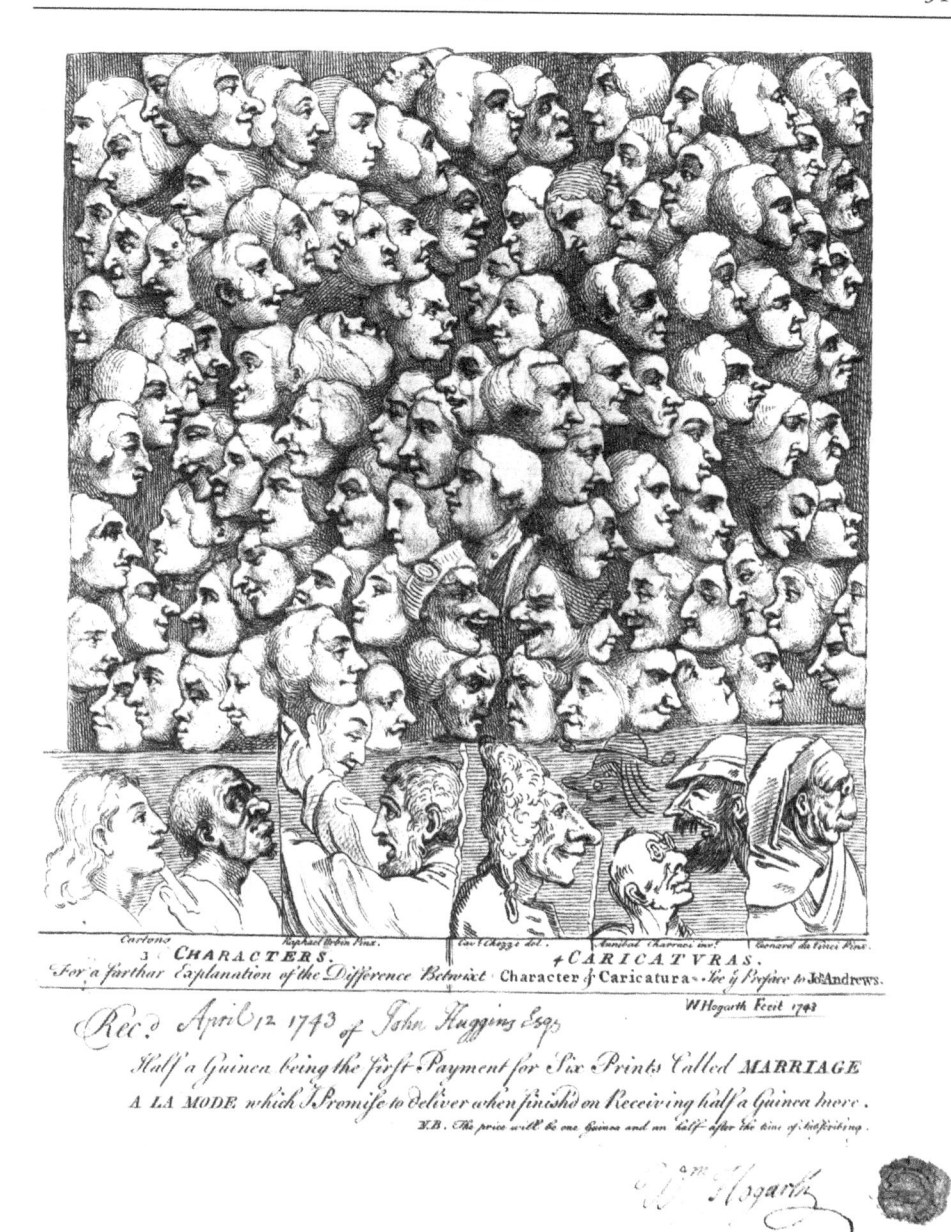

Figure 16.8 William Hogarth, *Characters and Caricaturas*. Etching, 1743. Courtesy of the British Museum, London

back caricatures of each other from Italy – and sometimes developed the knack for drawing caricatures themselves, for whom the aim was only to catch a likeness in a lucky scratch or two. After all, the facial resemblance had to be detectable by no one but the small coterie in which the caricatures were circulated.

Caricature could be regarded as either character-charged (Italian *caricare*) exaggeration or as the reduction of figure and form to its essence. Hogarth remembered "a famous Caricatura of a certain Italian Singer, that Struck at first sight, which consisted only of a Streight perpendicular Stroke with a Dot over it" (Paulson 1989: 171). He himself, in his *Analysis of Beauty* (Hogarth 1997), sought to reduce art to its essence in what he called the "serpentine line"; and early definitions of caricature, reminiscent of Hogarth's singer made of a single line and a dot, emphasized that the drawing should never take more than "three or four strokes of the pen."

In time, the term "caricature" came to refer not only to these charged likenesses but to political satires, or graphic commentaries on political events. (I should note parenthetically that "caricature" or "political satire" were the terms applied to the sort of works I discuss until the mid-nineteenth century, when the term "cartoon" was adapted from the cartoon competition for the decorations of the new Houses of Parliament. "Cartoon" had referred to the full-scale drawing or painting that was made preparatory to the execution of a fresco or tapestry.) In the mid-1750s George Townshend, one of the aristocratic young caricaturists, began caricaturing his acquaintances in the government, and thus produced the first political caricatures. Gradually two or more of these visages were related in some way, by comparison or contrast, perhaps with small vestigial bodies added and inscriptions that produced something like the old emblems. The drawings were soon being etched and sold by print sellers, and the method was then adapted by the professionals who earned a living by their pens and burins.

In the 1780s and 1790s, two English artists of genius, Thomas Rowlandson and James Gillray, developed political caricature into an art form – followed in the next generation by a third master, George Cruikshank, who carried the form through the Napoleonic period and up into the texts of Charles Dickens. Rowlandson and Gillray, in their different ways, joined caricature heads to emblematic situations and figures in the manner of Hogarth and then, satisfying decorum, caricatured the bodies as well. Whereas the heads had been merely attached previously to tiny perfunctory bodies, these artists produced bodies that went with – were extensions of – the exaggerated heads. Their experiments contributed in turn to Blake's illuminated books, which employed caricatures of George III and others, and the etchings and paintings Goya began to produce in Spain at the end of the century.

If Rowlandson expanded the faces slightly beyond Hogarth's, Gillray made them huge icons to which spindly bodies were attached. The faces are likenesses based on the exaggeration of a feature – Pitt's nose, though also his skeletal body, no longer within a convention of realism of the sort Hogarth employed; indeed, the emblematic quality is also reduced to the point of a purely expressive face and body, a simple gestalt of Pitt as a fungus or Pitt and Napoleon, two little hydrocephalic boys, gobbling a Christmas pudding which is a globe of the world they, as rulers of England and France, wish to divide (figure 16.9). At the other extreme from verbal emblems (Gombrich's "illustrations of figures of speech") is the purely graphic image that is merely a synecdoche, a part for the whole: Teddy Roosevelt's grinning teeth and FDR's cigarette holder were used as identifications by political cartoonists, but they

Figure 16.9 James Gillray, *The Plumb-pudding in Danger*. Etching, 1805. Author's Collection

also signified without verbalizing something of the political energy of the first and the jaunty assurance of the second.

As our examples suggest, there are at least two immediate differences between portrait and satiric caricature. One is that in satiric caricature the irony generated by the caricatured nature of the drawing is given a specific and controlling moral direction. But this difference in intention is achieved only by a corresponding difference in form. For as the moral point to be made becomes more specific or elaborate, an elaboration of context becomes necessary. Unlike portrait caricature, then, with its generally static figures and barely defined locale, satiric caricature typically presents a dramatic situation, however slight.

The Grotesque

The grotesque suggests caricature's most important potential, seized upon by its greatest practitioners (Goya and Daumier), who raised it to the level of high art: I mean its pushing of art to its limits and its exploration of the limits of the human. Caricature in this sense had many more antecedents than the Carracci: the fantastic forms of medieval art, the low-life drawings of the Dutch, the satiric prints of the Reformation. But perhaps the most often cited are the physiognomic studies of

Leonardo. For not only are Leonardo's grotesque faces often imitated or parodied by later caricaturists (as by Hogarth), but they also anticipate, in serious fashion, the interest in variation of form and feature, which caricature adopts more playfully.

The grotesque is the perfect vehicle for such an exploration because the grotesque itself seems fundamentally about limits and borders. Derived from the Italian *grotesco*, from grotto or cave, the grotesque at first designated an ornamental style that mixed plant, animal, and human forms into a decorative design. From the discovery of Nero's Golden House in the sixteenth century, with its elaborate decorative patterns that showed mergers of plant, animal, and human forms, and from Raphael's adaptation of these for the Vatican Loggia (reproduced and distributed widely in prints), the graphic satirist found ways to reduce humans to plant and animal forms for satiric purposes – to demonstrate the relationship between a man and an appropriate animal or plant. Though later it came to represent almost any fantastic or exaggerated form, there has always lingered over the grotesque the suggestion of a violation of integrity, a crossing of boundaries or limits that are supposed to be sacrosanct. The grotesque was, of course, in religious terms, an abomination, and so weighted down with the theological discourse of sin rather than evil. The grotesque, like caricature, is not *per se* concerned with evil actions – only with characterization. In most modern accounts, the grotesque is described as a mixed form, combining comedy and tragedy, humor and disgust, perfectly suited to satire (Harpham 1982).

The grotesque was another favored form of the Rococo artists. Hogarth used a plant pattern in the wallpaper of *Harlot* Plate 2 to suggest antlers and so "cuckold." Rowlandson, given the newer mode of caricature, carried the motif much further in faces that seem to be merging into animal or even vegetable forms – and in a series of comparative studies of human and animal faces (figure 16.10).

Satiric caricature plays with the idea of metamorphosis, particularly the kind of metamorphosis morally appropriate to the crimes one has committed. Rowlandson's caricatures in particular make the faces look as if they are metamorphosing or regressing into animals or disintegrating into some primeval substance. Gillray demonstrates a purely satiric use of the grotesque mode in his etching of William Pitt the Younger as a huge mushroom – a fungus growing parasitically on the royal crown of England. Gillray's figures change before our eyes: the effect of Lady Hamilton as Dido in *Dido in Distress* (1800) comes from both the realization that *this* is what has come of the beautiful Emma Hamilton – and that *this* Lady Hamilton and Lord Nelson is what *remains* of the great lovers Dido and Aeneas. The metamorphosis carries with its comic deflation a kind of horror at this monstrous transformation. In Gillray's satires we find politicians who are both themselves and butterflies, toadstools, bats, pigs, moneybags, dogs, and cultures.

In this regard, the world of Hogarth's satire differs dramatically from that of Rowlandson and Gillray. In the former, we are often given to understand that the figures in the center of the composition are acting *like* the dogs or other animals elsewhere in the picture or *like* the figures from myth and history whose portraits adorn the walls. Humans do sometimes behave like animals; life does sometimes

Figure 16.10 Thomas Rowlandson, *Comparative Anatomy*. Drawing, c.1800. Courtesy of the Huntington Library, Art Collections, and Botanical Gardens, San Marino, California

resemble art. But caricature has no concern for either realism or "common" sense. It presents its world in the compressed form of metaphor. In *Britannia* (1804), for instance, Gillray's Napoleon does not simply threaten death or resemble Death. He is Death. And yet he is Napoleon. Both terms of the metaphor are present at the same time that, like a metaphor, their unity is insisted upon. Visually depicted, however, the metaphor takes on the uncanny quality of a dream. And like the myths of werewolves and vampires, these metamorphoses play upon an anxiety common to all that our moral condition as beasts may begin to show itself in our very bodies.

We can see how caricature sums up one aspect of the world of satire – its relation to dream and nightmare. A fundamental characteristic of dream or nightmare is the mock-heroic and its opposite, travesty: one is always suffering from one or the other forms of paranoia, delusions of grandeur or persecution mania. One is either being raised to the skies or suffering a great fall. Appearances are torn away to reveal a squalid reality, just as pretty images are elicited to cover up base drives. Nothing is as it seems.

Both metaphor and metamorphosis are characteristic of one of the primary activities of dreamwork: condensation – Burke as spectacles-nose, TR as teeth, and FDR as a cigarette holder. Caricature is a graphic form of wit, and wit, according to Freud, is a conscious use of mainly unconscious materials. In that sense, caricature, like wit, is always playing with fire, for just beyond its playfulness are anxieties that are all too real. Portrait caricature plays with ugliness, deformity, and disfigurement. But if Gombrich and Kris (1964) are right, it was the fear of real disfigurement that prevented caricature from appearing any earlier than it did. Even now, caricature is an ambiguous form of portrayal, for there remains a latent sense of horror that we do indeed resemble our caricature, that the portrait is all too true.

Grotesque caricature stops short of the complete confrontation of self and distorted other that takes place in a real freak show. For there is still the barrier of art, the line that brilliantly catches the essence of a figure, that last bastion of witty distance between spectator and object, between man and monster. But in an age when the prevailing norms of portraiture and of history painting imposed a narrow and idealized conception of man upon its audience, caricature in general (and grotesque caricature in particular) posed the question: just how monstrous can man become and still be man? It was not a question that seemed very problematic in the civilized world of the eighteenth century. But some artists took up the gauntlet. And in retrospect we can see that caricature offered perhaps a broader, truer, and sometimes more frightening vision of humanity than any other available.

What caricature as it approaches the grotesque tries to do is to extend the kind of testing that is characteristic of all caricature and to take us to the very limit of its power as wit, to confront, if only momentarily, the hideous, and to arouse, if only in a mild form (though in Goya, not a mild form, nor often in Ralph Stedman and Gerald Scarfe), a kind of fascinated horror. I am thinking, in particular, of Goya's frontispiece to the *Caprichos* (1799), "The Dream of Reason is Monsters." In the twentieth century, the grotesque found a subset in Surrealism – in satire, the collages of John Heartfield, Hannah Hoch, and Max Ernst, or many of the early paintings of Salvador Dali.

Satire and Comedy

One distinction between satire and comedy has been made based on the matter of "historic particulars." Edward Rosenheim (1963) argued that satire must refer to historic particulars. The *Harlot's Progress* would qualify since Hogarth used likenesses and references to living contemporaries and to contemporary politics: in *Harlot*, contemporaries immediately identified Colonel Francis Charteris, Elizabeth Needham, Jack Gourlay, and Sir John Gonson. But the basic distinction seems to be not based on particular historical reference but on the presentation of an evil or folly set off against an indication of an ideal or a norm. The even balance of one against the other makes comedy; the predominance of the evil or folly has to be read as satire, even if the figures cannot be identified or are so general as to be unidentifiable.

The Rococo style was a sort of *satire on* former styles and contents of art, though it always teeters on the edge between satire and comedy, depending on the degree of judgment being passed. It is also true, however, that as Hogarth's works became less particular they shifted toward comedy. As he reduced his series from six or eight plates down to two, he turned from satire to comedy (comic contrast, juxtaposition of incongruities – or abominations, of course, from the theological point of view), and with comedy to aesthetics – beauty defined in terms of contrary forms, not necessarily ugly. Morality remained, however problematically, because Hogarth's aesthetics were constructed in opposition to the third Earl of Shaftesbury's, which simplistically, Hogarth believed, equated beauty with virtue, ugliness with evil.

In the past I have argued that Rowlandson ordinarily uses caricature less for satiric than for comic purposes – or, closely related, aesthetic purposes, exploring categories of the beautiful, novel, strange, ugly, and so on (Paulson 1972). But, as seen by V. S. Pritchett, these figures are satiric: "They are not human beings. They are lumps of animal horror or stupidity. To Rowlandson the human race are cattle or swine, a reeking fat-stock done up in ribbons or breeches, which has got into coffee houses, beds and drawing rooms" (1967: 21).

Satiric caricature requires the grotesque figure to be complemented by a normal one. In Rowlandson's case, this is a young man or woman. Caricature moves from the merely comic or ugly to satire when related to the convention that certain features – an aquiline nose, a candid or a leonine look – are noble, while a sheeplike face denotes stupidity, a foxy one slyness ("sly as a fox"). This sense of satire involves the idea of Shaftesburian aesthetics I have referred to that equates beauty with virtue, ugliness with evil. The Gombrichian conventions of "the cartoonist's armoury" would also dictate that beauty, harmony, and unity are good and that ugliness, chaos, and visual confusion are bad. Obvious graphic equivalents, these were originally part of the hierarchical theory of academic art. In the works of Hogarth and Rowlandson, however, the exemplars of beauty are seductive women, usually either disobedient daughters or unfaithful young wives.

In the *Harlot's Progress*, sin, or the illegal, is persecuted by the law (authority) and suffers evil at the hands of evil figures; sin itself is not evil – it is either innocent or – with adultery – comic and beautiful in the sense of liberating, though part of Hogarth's comedy is that of liberty trying to find outlets within his closed rooms: adultery within enclosures, possibly a visualizing of Swift's image of the vapor seeking an exit in "A Digression Concerning Madness," Section 9 of *A Tale of a Tub* first published in 1704. So the beautiful is embodied in the beautiful-but-sinning woman, usually – like Christ's woman taken in adultery – an adulteress.

The liminal area between satire and comedy lies in the subject of love, sexuality, and sin. From Watteau (and Gay's *Beggar's Opera* as well), Hogarth takes the subject of love, in the form of groups in interpersonal relationships gravitating toward desire and sexual fulfillment. To employ, beginning with the Harlot, fornication in a positive light was to satirize the most fundamental of the sins: "rebellious sexual fornication" or "religiously alienating sexual fornication" (Gaca 2003: 129–37). To set beside Jesus's defense of the woman taken in adultery, there was St Paul's use of the metaphor of fornication and adultery to describe rebellion – acts of copulation that worshiped gods other than or in addition to the only God – reinforced by Augustine's treatment of lust as the original sin due to the uncontrollable male sexual organ. From the sin of fornication as rebellion follows the seriousness of adultery, and the favorite situation of stage comedy of the old husband and the young wife or the father and daughter; the latter loves an "alien" young man and must be locked up by the father/husband, but escapes. From the *commedia dell'arte* through the Restoration comedies of fornication and adultery, the situation primarily involved the old husband cuckolded by his young wife and her young lover.

To return to the graphic tradition: Renaissance artists domesticated the sin of lust in the faces and gestures of the old men in paintings of Susannah and the Elders or in images of grotesque satyrs peering at sleeping nymphs, that is, at beautiful nude women (Tintoretto, Rubens, Watteau). Rape is implied, voyeurism shown. The pivotal case was Susannah and the Elders, where the story in the Book of Daniel tells how the elders, graduating from mere peeping-toms, threaten her with false witness unless she submits to their lust – a rape prevented when their lies are exposed by the judge Daniel. The elders peering at the nude and defenseless Susannah were another version of the mockers around Christ in *Ecce Homo* pictures. In Rococo paintings the emphasis shifted from the threat of the elders to the beauty of the woman, defined by the context of the ugly and aged men, titillatingly set off by their impotent voyeurism. The scene of a beautiful figure surrounded by ugly persecutors and mockers was a model first for religious devotion, then for one kind of satire (Juvenalian), and then a comedy of incongruous contrast – the old men and the young girl – and finally an aesthetics in which her beauty is defined in terms of their ugliness and incapacity.

In the next generation, Rowlandson develops the *Ecce Homo* scene, conflated with the *Susannah*, through the mediation of Hogarth's *Harlot*, Plate 4 and the *Analysis of Beauty* plates, into a basic composition: a mob of grotesque heads surrounding a beautiful young woman, often nude; while usually more voyeuristic and less threatening, sometimes the woman appears to be taunting these men who are obviously inadequate. When one handsome young man appears, the romantic couple sets off the old men. Rowlandson's drawings and prints endlessly elaborate this composition: the lover (Horatio Nelson) hides in an Egyptian sarcophagus, the young wife (Emma, Lady Hamilton) pressing herself into the sarcophagus to embrace her young lover, and her old and shriveled husband (the collector of antiquities, Lord Hamilton) engrossed in some art objects (figure 16.11). Or a young man poses as a cadaver, a subject for anatomical study, in order to get at the young wife into whose home he has contrived thereby to penetrate, while the old husband, the physician who has bought this body, is in fact getting out his dissecting tools – putting the young lover in imminent danger (figure 16.12). Or the lover climbs out of a trunk and is welcomed by the wife as the husband leaves, double and triple-locking the door (or the lover is climbing in a window). All have in common the handsome young lover, the beautiful young wife, and the old, ugly husband; most involve a subterfuge for getting around the jealous husband's locks and chains. The perspective is that of the young lovers, the sinners, not the gross old men.

The relation between satire, Rococo, comedy, and aesthetics is based on the situation of the old husband, young wife, young lover – the old and the new (winter and spring), in which the new is at least possibly capable of defeating the old. The latter passes beyond the conventions of satire, in which the old always defeats the young; the result is (in Northrop Frye's 1957 seasonal terms) autumnal or (in Kernan's 1959) decline.

Rhetoric

The question of how an artist translates into images the strategies of verbal satirists is complicated by the fact that most studies of verbal satire deal with rhetoric; we have dealt primarily with the ontology (*onto* = the things which exist) of satire – its subject and the formal qualities for which artists can find correspondences in other graphic works. How do we locate the rhetoric in a graphic image?

Hogarth used a neutral, reportorial style that ostensibly keeps the satirist out of the satire. The internal inscriptions, puns, and art objects act as a silent and ironic comment on the actions. Though the primary function of such contrasts is to explain the motives and actions of the owners of such self-exposing art objects, the objects become sufficiently oppressive – as in *Marriage A-la-mode*, where the past in the form of Old Master paintings presses like Fuseli's Incubus on contemporary humans – to define, limit, and stereotype them. There is the appearance of mere reportage in Goya's series of depictions of the terrors of war, mere scenes of torture, mutilation, rape, burning, and murder that have inscriptions that simply say: "Look at this," or "Can such things happen?" In Goya's *Caprichos* and *Disparates* the scenes are, like Gillray's, themselves phantasmagoric. They require no words.

Post-Hogarthian graphic satirists tend to employ the rhetoric of expressive form – Rowlandson's or Gillray's agitated style; the ballooning and shriveling figures (what we have identified as caricature) reflect something like the *saeva indignatio* (the curse, the invective) of the Juvenalian satirist, existing primarily in the line, what has been called the bite of the etcher's acid (Getlein 1964: 4). But can the graphic satirist employ the fiction of the satirist-satirized – the contamination of the satirist by his

Figure 16.11 Thomas Rowlandson, *Modern Antique.* Colored etching, 1811. Author's collection

Figure 16.12 Thomas Rowlandson, *The Anatomist*. Colored etching, c.1800. Author's collection

object, a subject popular among writers on satire since Robert C. Elliott's *Power of Satire* (1960)? There would seem to be no graphic equivalent for the satire that turns back on the satirist himself, recreating the powerful effect of Gulliver's misanthropic utterances upon his return from Houyhnhnmland. And yet if we regard the figures of Rowlandson and Gillray as hyperbolic – as rhetoric rather than reality – we might say that they may reflect more upon the artist's emotion than the subject's culpability.

One of the conventions of verbal satire (as in Horace and Juvenal, but also apparent in the Christian hell) was punishment, with the satirist the punisher. Punishment of the guilty took the form of legal-penal or of therapeutic suffering – the consequence of crime or of disease, requiring the pillory, whip, or strappado (metaphors of laceration, flogging, and so on), or the scalpel, blister, purge, and phlebotomy. The satirist's scalpel defines the distemper as it removes it. The mercury cure for the pox – which produces intense sweating and the dislodging of teeth – defines the disease through its "cure." In the case of Apuleius' Lucius, turned into an ass, punishment adjusts the appearance until it does correspond to the inner reality – body to soul. Satire externalizes internal states in crimes and follies and their consequences in suffering and punishment, to others and the self. Punishment presents the psychological inner reality of the evil action. Pritchett's description of Rowlandson's men and women implies the sort of artist who carries on this activity, through "dissection" exposing the truth of his dressed-up fops.

Edmund Burke believed that graphic images were clearer, less open to obscurity and ambiguity – therefore less effective – than words. Words offered the imagination more freedom, especially in the obscurity that Burke identified as the root of terror and the sublime. But graphic images carry one sense of indeterminacy: like Empson's ambiguous words, they invite multiple readings, offer multiple gestalts, therefore permitting the spectator to choose between readings. As Freud recognized, the meanings of images are always multivalent and, therefore, in dreams serve as a censoring mechanism, which seeks to conceal the motivating desires behind the dream. Where the possibilities for meaning are multiple, a forbidden one can easily be hidden and overlooked. The picture is *this* or *that*, an obvious metaphor or not, depending on how you choose to look at it. Censorship can be thwarted even when blasphemy is implied, as Hogarth demonstrated in *A Harlot's Progress* when he turned his Harlot into (take your choice) either a parodic Hercules in a "Choice of Hercules" or, in a second gestalt, a Virgin Mary in a "Visitation" (Paulson 2003).

Gillray implies an ambivalence toward the French Revolution when he shows Burke "Smelling out a Rat" (the Rev. Richard Price's pro-revolutionary writings), but Burke's nose and glasses make a grotesque monster looming over the helpless realistically drawn figure (no rodent) of Price: the print can be read either as against Burke or against Price, or against both. This interpretation is also possible in some of Rowlandson's rather grim later prints, such as *The Anatomist*. I am suggesting that graphic satire may have ultimately a greater potential for subversion, for "a curse on both your houses," than verbal. The comment of his caricature of Pitt-the-fungus is ambiguous in a different way: Pitt is a parasite on the crown; and the crown is a kind of rot on which fungus grows, the monarch nourishment, and lends itself to parasitism. Without the crown, identified in the caption as "a Dung-hill," there would be no fungus. Gillray has erased the conventional distinction between minister and monarch.

Napoleon and Pitt are materialized "children," their behavior "childish" (figure 16.9). It has been argued by Gombrich that the English mode of Gillray can be said, by its very over-charging, to fantasize, distance, and in effect emasculate the materials – making a Napoleon or a Pitt *less* menacing; in short, to contain them and merely amuse spectators. It is necessary to recall that Gillray and Blake – and on the continent Goya – worked during the years just before, during, and after the French Revolution, and their allegiances were shifting and at times ambiguous. Gillray was, moreover, dependent on the print sellers and party subvention. Hogarth and Blake, though at different ends of the economic spectrum, were independent artists who drew, engraved, printed, and sold their own works. The question is whether Gillray's infantilizing the dangerous, rendering Napoleon and Pitt comic, serves only the purpose of the ruling elite or of the print seller and etcher who are interested primarily in sales, or whether it expresses Gillray's deep ambivalence toward his patrons – or whether in either case it gives his audience a space in which to interpret the satire according to their own inclinations. An image can be read as either accepting both or rejecting both (as comedy or as satire).

In any case, Gillray, like Rowlandson, gives the expression priority: the shapes speak for themselves, beyond any verbalization. Gillray's drawings are to their verbal origins as Daumier's paintings of Don Quixote and Sancho Panza are to Cervantes' text. The image is in excess of the "illustrations of figures of speech," verbal text or verbalization – of, in the case of *Smelling out a Rat*, the verbal tag. The huge nose and spectacles of (essentially a synecdoche for) Burke are an objective correlative – "a set of objects, a situation, a chain of events," in T. S. Eliot's terms (referring to *Hamlet*), "expressing emotion" in excess of the words or concept for which they are to serve as a formula (Eliot, 1960:100). Hogarth sought the "complete adequacy" of the image to the concept; the images of Gillray – as in his way Rowlandson – are always "in excess of the facts as they appear," as if the emblem were (as perhaps it always was) beyond the capacity of the words attached to explain.

References and Further Reading

Atherton, Herbert M. (1974) *Political Prints in the Age of Hogarth: A Study of the Ideographic Representation of Politics*. Oxford: Clarendon Press.

Carretta, Vincent (1972) *The Snarling Muse: Verbal and Visual Political Satire from Pope to Churchill*. Philadelphia: University of Pennsylvania Press.

Dickens, Charles (1848) Review of George Cruikshank's "The Drunkard's Children: A Sequel to the Bottle." *The Examiner*, July 8.

Donald, Diane (1996) *The Age of Caricature: Satirical Prints in the Reign of George III*. New Haven, CT: Yale University Press.

Eliot, T. S. (1960) Hamlet and his problems. In *The Sacred Wood: Essays on Poetry and Criticism*. London: Methuen (originally published 1920).

Elliott, Robert C. (1960) *The Power of Satire: Magic, Ritual, Art*. Princeton, NJ: Princeton University Press.

Frye, Northrop (1957) The mythos of winter: irony and satire. In *Anatomy of Criticism: Four Essays*, pp. 223–39. Princeton, NJ: Princeton University Press.

Gaca, Kathy L. (2003) *The Making of Fornication: Eros, Ethics, and Political Reform in Greek Philosophy and Early Christianity*. Berkeley, CA: University of California Press.

George, M. Dorothy (1967) *Hogarth to Cruikshank: Social Change in Graphic Satire*. New York: Walker and Co.

Getlein, Frank (1964) *The Bite of the Print: Satire and Irony in Woodcuts, Engravings, Etchings, Lithographs and Seriographs*. London: H. Jenkins.

Gombrich, E. H. (1963) The cartoonist's armoury. In *Meditations on a Hobby Horse and Other Essays on the Theory of Art*, pp. 127–42. London: Phaidon.

—— and Kris, Ernst (1964) The principles of caricature. In Ernst Kris (ed.), *Psychoanalytic Explorations in Art*, pp. 189–203. New York: Schocken Books.

Hallett, Mark (1999) *The Spectacle of Difference: Graphic Satire in the Age of Hogarth*. New Haven, CT: Yale University Press.

Harpham, Geoffrey Galt (1982) *On the Grotesque: Strategies of Contradiction in Art and Literature*. Princeton, NJ: Princeton University Press.

Hayes, John (1972) *Rowlandson: Watercolours and Drawings*. London: Phaidon.

Hill, Draper (1963) *Mr Gillray the Caricaturist*. London: Phaidon.

Hogarth, William (1997) *The Analysis of Beauty*, ed. Ronald Paulson. New Haven, CT: Yale University Press (originally published 1753).

Juvenal (1958) *The Satires of Juvenal*, trans. Rolfe Humphries. Bloomington, IN: Indiana University Press.

Kernan, Alvin (1959) *The Cankered Muse: Satire of the English Renaissance*. New Haven, CT: Yale University Press.

Kunzle, David (1973) *The Early Comic Strip: Narrative Strips and Picture Stories in the European Broadsheet from c. 1450 to 1825*. Berkeley, CA: University of California Press.

Paulson, Ronald (1972) *Rowlandson: A New Interpretation*. London: Studio Vista.

—— (1975) *Emblem and Expression: Meaning in English Art of the Eighteenth Century*. Cambridge, MA: Harvard University Press.

—— (1983) Gillray. In *Representations of Revolution, 1789–1820*, pp. 168–214. New Haven, CT: Yale University Press.

—— (ed.) (1989) *Hogarth's Graphic Works*, 2 vols, 3rd edn. London: The Print Room.

—— (1991–3) *Hogarth*, 3 vols. New Brunswick: Rutgers University Press (originally published as *Hogarth: His Life, Art, and Times*, 2 vols, New Haven, CT: Yale University Press, 1971).

—— (2003) *Hogarth's Harlot: Sacred Parody in Enlightenment England*. Baltimore, MD: The Johns Hopkins University Press.

Pritchett, V. S. (1967) *The Living Novel*. London: Chatto and Windus.

Rosenheim, Edward W. (1963) *Swift and the Satirist's Art*. Chicago: University of Chicago Press.

Sherry, James (1976) Distance and humor: the art of Thomas Rowlandson. *Eighteenth-century Studies* 11, 457–72.

Part III
Nineteenth Century to Contemporary

17
The *Hidden* Agenda of Romantic Satire: Carlyle and Heine
Peter Brier

Huck's Problem

We begin with an excursus. In chapter 31 of *Huckleberry Finn* (1884), two-thirds of the way through the book, the appropriate spot for a climax, Huck searches his soul and decides he will go to hell after all rather than send the note to Miss Watson that would reveal the whereabouts of Jim, his friend and her escaped slave. He may be forced to live a life of everlasting shame for helping a "nigger to get his freedom," but he cannot help himself. He tries to pray, but realizes "you can't pray a lie." In one last attempt to meet the demands of what he truly believes to be his best self, he writes out the note. It makes him feel "clean of sin" and, for a moment, able to pray. He makes the mistake, however, of putting the note aside and "thinking... And went on thinking." Memories of the desperate adventures he and Jim have shared recall the affection and trust that prevails between them. He simply cannot do otherwise than tear up the note.

To this day, readers of the novel have difficulty in seeing this passage as *satirical*. Huck's struggle to overcome the conditioning of the society in which he lives, a society suffering from a deeply institutionalized racism, constitutes an intuitive kind of heroism. Indeed, as the novel winds down, by allowing Huck to sit back and let Tom Sawyer subject Jim to a series of indignities that mock the freedom he enjoyed earlier in the novel in Huck's company, Mark Twain seems to be breaking faith with his own creation by stripping Huck of the moral power he grants him in chapter 31; and unreceptive to the satirical undertone of that chapter, they find what follows – the farcical denouement of the novel – jarring.

Throughout the novel, Twain assiduously declares war on all versions of the sentimental. Think of the Grangerford feud or Miss Bott's verses; the funeral of Mary Jane's father; Colonel Sherburn's slaying of Boggs, and so on. Twain is not ridiculing the affection that Jim and Huck feel for one another; their bond humanizes both. What he is satirizing in chapter 31 is the total collapse of the Rousseauian ideal: the notion that the natural man is lord in his own house and more capable of moral action than his socially determined counterpart. Huck cannot live a lie, but he has no permeable grasp of the truth. He has revolutionary powers, but inadequate strength to challenge Tom Sawyer, the puppeteer of the *ancien régime*. As long as he and Jim were fleeing society, authenticity was in the air. But Huck cannot live up to the challenge of his own instinct for freedom. An intuitive choice is not a rational *or* an imaginative one. Huck would have us believe that he is "thinking...thinking." But what he is really doing is feeling, feeling. Twain is satirizing our sentimental error in thinking that a person whose heart is in the right place – certainly true of Huck – has earned the dignity of his own liberation when his head and imagination are still under the control of his oppressors.

But what about Huck's youth? Can we expect someone so young to rise above feelings and fears? Surely Huck's brilliant impersonations, ruses, endlessly clever strategies of survival and triumph throughout the novel preclude our believing that he is still a child? A child-man, yes, but the American Adam in full control. Twain knows that American confusion of pragmatic innovation with wisdom will tempt readers to grant Huck a moral power he himself does not presume to have. His conscience belongs to Miss Watson. For poor Huck, the cost of freedom is damnation: "All right, then, I'll go to hell." This will not make the grade. It is amusing, comical, endearing. But it merits satire.

Written in the 1880s, Twain's novel lays bare the unpleasant truth that the liberated common man of the nineteenth century falls far short of the expectations of the many revolutions waged in his name in the previous hundred years. This was an insight that fed many of Twain's later writings (for example, *What is Man*, 1906; *The Mysterious Stranger*, 1916). For all of Huck's instinctive sense of fraternity, he cannot allow himself to believe in the justice of his fellow human being's liberty and equality. He grasps the misalignment between religion and truth, but he settles for the former at its most primitive rather than pursue the latter even when his instincts seem to lead him there. In short, the century's revolutionary dedication to the "rights of man" falls so far short of the best dreams of its best minds that a rural *naïf* like Huck, bad conscience to boot, becomes its appropriate standard bearer.

Satire and the Challenge of Romantic Organicism

Incongruity is the stuff of satire, and I would suggest that satire has more to do with the literary response to the themes of liberation and revolution in the nineteenth century than we usually assume. Lyric celebration, epic dramatization, and tragic opera all come to mind more readily than satire as the typical romantic genres, particularly when it comes to emotions connected with political deliverance and social liberation. "Bliss was it in that dawn to be alive," intones Wordsworth in

The Prelude (1805), his autobiographical, lyrical, epic poem, which proffers a norm for understanding the shaping of consciousness in the age of Revolution *and* Romanticism. Humor, although omnipresent in Romanticism, is less caustic than in other periods, and we tend to associate satire with a realistic humor, indeed with realism in general, again a form not always associated with Romanticism, which thrives on fantasy and visions.

Readers of the period will disagree. What about Byron's *English Bards and Scotch Reviewers* (1809), Peacock's dialogues, Jane Austen's Mr Collins, and so on? True enough. But most of the obvious examples of Romantic satire reach back to older models of the previous century and earlier. Nevertheless, there is, of course, a satiric vein in Romanticism, a very strong one I might add, and it rises before us when we least expect it. When Blake insists that his visionary outbursts are grounded in satire, we acquiesce but are more bemused than convinced. Is the tiger finally merely the tabby cat of his famous drawing in the *Songs of Experience* (1794)? And in Shelley's *Prometheus Unbound* (1820) is there not something dangerously ludicrous in its noblest lyrical utterance: "I wish no living thing to suffer pain," an exclamation that must serve as the hinge on which the entire drama turns? Bearing in mind Shelley's doctrine of love, we may find the gentle Horatian implication strangely touching. Is the fact that we find the divine power of love ultimately comical a satirical observation at our expense? A revelation of our own spiritual awkwardness?

What I am suggesting here is that the very incongruity of our defining feelings, the contradictory emotions that feed the organic nature of the human personality, cannot help but invite the muse of satire in the very act of reaching for lyrical or dramatic transcendence. Deep into the Victorian period we hear Matthew Arnold's famous utterance: "torn between two worlds, one dead and the other powerless to be born." It is to the credit of Arnold's famous elegiac lyric, "Stanzas from the Grand Chartreuse" (1855), to which these lines provide the dramatic climax, that generations of readers have sympathized deeply with the tug of contradictory emotions they express – even though, on the face of it, the psychological and intellectual state they depict is close to farcical. Is Arnold's persona any different, finally, from Huck's? Are they not both vacillating between a religion that they no longer fully believe but which they cannot shake and a self-liberation that they are unable to bring to consummation? We think of Arnold's "Buried Life" (1852). And does this harried state not risk making them ultimately foolish – for all their appeal to our compassion or affection?

This brings us to our principal topic: the philosophical manifestos of Thomas Carlyle and Heinrich Heine, two writers juxtaposed here for their rich involvement in discovering and directing what I believe to be the satirical vein at the heart of the Romantic and Victorian sensibility. Carlyle's *Sartor Resartus* and Heine's "Religion and Philosophy in Germany" were both written in the early 1830s. Their bibliographical history is complex; they were first published, as so many important nineteenth-century works, in journals and as serial publications. The first is a philosophical *Bildungsroman* energized by a kind of international style comprised of Puritan sermonizing and Germanic syntax; the tone of the first and the lexical weight of the latter are themselves locked in a satirical struggle with each other. Carlyle himself said that he wrote *Sartor Resartus* "in a satirical frenzy." In Heine's essay, a breezy and witty anecdotal tone is held on course by a rigorously dialectical argument. Here, as well, the embracing style is satirical. After the romantic irony of his early lyricism, Heine became explicitly satirical in his poetry and prose. As with Carlyle's text, one is never quite sure whether the tone is at the service of the argument or vice versa. Although the first is a novel and the second a protracted essay, both are generically unstable – and proud of it. Both use an extravagant point of view and irony not merely to test or stretch the borders of art but to engage questions of social and cultural identity, and this constitutes the essence of their satirical force. Both are strongly cosmopolitan in spirit; Carlyle thought of himself as bringing together British and German sensibility and ideas, whereas Heine wrote his essay to explain the Germans to the French – and, in 1835, it was released in Germany but heavily censored.

The inspired cosmopolitanism of these two writers is foreshadowed, as I have already suggested, in the visionary poetry of Blake, Shelley, Keats, Hölderlin, and other Romantics. What most of these earlier figures lacked is the stomach for realism, an essential ingredient for satire. Some like Keats strained in this direction (for example, *The Fall of Hyperion*, 1819: "the poet dreams awake"), and some like Wordsworth and Goethe, as we shall see, incorporated strong doses of realism in their poetry, but in Carlyle and Heine the visionary and the satirical are crucially enjoined. Not since Pope's *Dunciad* (1743), where mock epic reached its zenith in the neoclassical period, was satire able to reach for the comic sublime. For Pope, the threatening gloom of corrupted taste and flattered stupidity seemed a cosmic threat, a terrible danger to the delicate and fragile decorum of life and art that he had championed ever since his youth. Carlyle and Heine had inherited a very different set of norms. The Rousseauian idea of the sacredness of personality, no matter how troubled or conflicted, had become deeply politicized after the French Revolution. This new idea of Man and Society demanded a vigorous imaginative and moral self-invention.

As we have seen with *Huckleberry Finn*, even by the end of the century the self-realization of the liberated man was still in its infancy. If satire could still thrive on that incongruity in 1880, it had its hands much fuller in 1830. Blake's Albion, the risen and fully integrated "New" Man of 1804 (*The Four Zoas*), is an Olympian precursor of Carlyle's "Adamite" hero in *Sartor Resartus*. Blake's mythic conception resonates with the Miltonic sublime, but Carlyle's Teufelsdröckh (devil's dung) is a tormented Puritan struggling to get out of his old "Clothes" as he aspires to intimations of transcendence that painfully push him to the trough of the "Everlasting Yea." With Heine, the satirical thrust of his historical survey of the problematic tension between spirit and sensuality in the German soul reaches its first resting place in his portrait of Luther: "How shall I describe him? He had in him something primordial, incomprehensible, miraculous, such as we find in all providential men; something naively terrible, something boorishly wise, something lofty yet circumscribed, something invincibly daemoniacal" (Heine 1959: 47). Or in an earlier passage: "This same man [Luther], who could scold like a fishwife, could also be as gentle as a sensitive maiden" (1959: 46). Horatian in its gentleness, this is nevertheless the satirical mode. And it is there because Heine, like Carlyle, had inherited the Romantic imperative at the very moment when its limitations had become obvious, when Realism's knock at the door was too loud to ignore. Satire, though shaded and often passing as irony or simple humor, empowered late Romantic writers to exalt the self in the very act of demonstrating the restrictions imposed on the self by nature and history.

Satire in Disguise

We are now ready to confront directly the theoretical heart of this discussion. It is my contention that satire is *aufgehoben* in Romanticism. *Aufgehoben* is the past participle of *Aufhebung* (which means both "to hide" and "raise"), Hegel's term for those ideas or concepts that are hidden or conserved (often in a back-paddling strategy) as the principal subject or dialectic is pursued. Think of a bas-relief in which the main subject may be foregrounded but the recessed background often pulls at our eyes. Romantic satire prefers to hide so that it can emerge suddenly or abruptly for dramatic effect. Charles Taylor, Hegel's principal interpreter to the English-speaking world, explains *Aufhebung* as that which occurs when reason and emotion transcend their differences in a *Versöhnung*, or reconciliation, whereby reason can accept its imminence in *Geist* or Spirit (Taylor 1979: 49). Often what is *aufgehoben* can re-emerge in further developments of the argument. How satire is both hidden and raised in both Carlyle and Heine – to different degrees in each – has much to do with, as stated above, the tunes called by humor and *particularly* by irony.

At the dawn of the Romantic enterprise, Friedrich Schlegel in *Athenaeum* fragment no. 116, provides a manifesto for the free-wheeling "progress" of what he conceived, as early as 1798, would be the direction of Romantic literature:

> Romantic poetry is a progressive, universal poetry. Its aim isn't merely to reunite all the separate species of poetry and put poetry in touch with philosophy and rhetoric. It tries to and should mix and fuse poetry and prose, inspiration and criticism, the poetry of art and the poetry of nature; and make poetry lively and sociable, and life and society poetical; poeticize wit and fill and saturate the forms of art with every kind of good, solid matter for instruction, and animate them with the pulsations of humor... (Schlegel 1971: 175–6)

The mixing and blending of the genres is at the heart of Romanticism. Lyric, epic, and dramatic forms interweave in Wordsworth, Goethe, Byron – to name only a few. The mixing reached its zenith in the modern novel, where it continues to whirl. Schlegel called this mixing *Verwirrung*, which can be translated as "inspirational entanglement." This kind of willful blending is captured in the English "medley" that Charles Lamb invoked to describe the comic novels of Thomas Hood in the early

1830s. Hood's combining of "farce, melodrama, pantomime, comedy, tragedy, punchery, what not" (Lamb 1935: 3.419–20) anticipated Dickens. That all of this mixing should serve a higher purpose than mere titillation had been urged by Friedrich Schiller in 1795 in his influential "Aesthetic Education of Man." Romantic *Verwirrung* would enable the arts to "instruct" mankind.

It is satire, however, that claims the honor of being the first literary genre to predicate itself on the idea of mixing literary kinds; the rustic farce scrambled dance, drama, and tale-telling in a *lanx satura* (fruit salad), from which satire derived its name. The *saturae* of Ennius and Pacuvius, "miscellaneous both in subjects and metrical forms," were medleys composed specifically for reading, not for performance. Gaius Lucilius, Horace's precursor, is recognized as the founder of literary satire. His thirty books of *Saturae*, written in various meters, handled a "great variety of topics...largely autobiographical" (Horace 1955: xiv–xv). I recall these historical details from the dawn of satire only to emphasize its open-endedness, its identification with that impulse in literary production that arises whenever literature itself is in such a state of ferment that the self-consciousness of the poet-writer or his persona moves to the center of the literary subject. I am suggesting that *ridicule*, perhaps the *sine qua non* of satire, in one form or another – benign or harsh, self-critical or hostile to the "other" – is integral to the literary act when it finds itself in an evolutionary or even revolutionary situation; when a higher "instruction" becomes imperative. Aggression and defense seem to thrive on satire, but confession also feels the need to brace itself with self-laceration to avoid sentimentality and bathos. Self-ridicule is one of the subtlest of all satirical modes. One can trace its sinuous line from Poe through Baudelaire to Dostoevsky and Eliot's Prufrock. These writers, who hover over the permutations governing the transitions from late Romanticism through Realism to Modernism often strike us as satirists incognito.

The principle of Romantic irony is another one of Friedrich Schlegel's contributions to the early theorizing of Romanticism. Rene Wellek writes that "Irony is his [Schlegel's] recognition of the fact that the world in its essence is paradoxical and that an ambivalent attitude alone can grasp its contradictory totality" (1955: 14). Critics have singled out the Romantic poet's shattering of illusion as the primary example of Romantic irony, as, for example, the narrator's intrusions in Byron's *Don Juan* (1819–24). There is more involved here than the paradox underlying the "ironic" connections between illusion and reality. The pretentious scaffolding that holds up the contractual arrangement between poet and reader is part of a satirical subtext in Romantic writings. As Wellek says, the "totality" expected from the Romantic writer is essentially "contradictory." Its organicism, according to Coleridge and August Wilhelm Schlegel (Friedrich's older brother), is based on the "reconciliation of opposites." Incongruity, as noted previously, tempts satire. Incongruity also inspires the dialectical imagination, but often the muffled laughter of satirical revelation is part of the unavoidable cost.

Goethe's *Faust* is famous for its variety of meters, tones, and forms – not to mention its juxtaposition of lyrical, tragic, and farcical scenes. The totality of its closing vision of sublimation through renunciation would ring flat if the entire drama, Parts 1 and 2 (1808/1832), had not repeatedly engaged Faust in transcendence (Gretchen, Helen) *and* satirical deflation (Auerbach's Keller, the Court of Maximilian I). The reconciliation of these opposites feeds the culminating vision. Think of that moment in Wordsworth's *Prelude* in Book Six when the poet's sublime vision of the Imagination ("in God Who is our Home") is triggered by the banal discovery that "We... had crossed the Alps without knowing it..." Wordsworth is shocked into his discovery of the full power of the Imagination by the comical realization that his senses and deductive reasoning have deluded him into thinking that the phenomenal experience of the mountain's peak was essential to the mind's excitement of being there.

Carlyle wades through the same discovery over and over in *Sartor Resartus*. Here is an early example in Chapter 9, "Adamitism":

> Consider, thou foolish Teufelsdröckh, what benefits unspeakable all ages and sexes derive from Clothes. For example, when thou thyself, a watery, pulpy, slobbery freshman and newcomer in this Planet, sattest muling and puking in thy nurse's arms; sucking thy coral, and looking forth into the world in the blankest manner, what hadst thou been without thy blankets, and bibs, and other nameless hulls? A terror to thyself and mankind!... Without Clothes, without bit or saddle, what hadst thou been... Nature is god, but she is not the best: here truly was the victory of Art over Nature. A thunderbolt indeed might have pierced thee; all short of this thou couldst defy.
>
> ... If Clothes, in these times, "so tailorise and demoralize us," have they no redeeming value; can they not be altered to serve better; must they of necessity be thrown to the dogs? The truth is, Teufelsdröckh, though a Sansculottist, is no Adamite; and much perhaps as he might wish to go forth before this degenerate age as "a Sign," would nowise wish to do it, as those old Adamites did, in a state of Nakedness. The utility of Clothes is altogether apparent to him: nay perhaps he has an insight into their more recondite, and almost mystic qualities, what we might call the omnipotent virtue of Clothes, such as was never before vouchsafed to any man. (Carlyle 1938: 58–60)

Teufelsdröckh's "puking" babe is the physical or natural man in desperate need of the new "Clothes" his transcendence-hungry mind requires. The "Symbols" of that realization, the boon the shaping Imagination provides, lie ahead. Passionately instructive, Carlyle will repeatedly shake his Professor with satirical attacks, rich in the "banter and raillery" that has characterized English satire ever since the sixteenth century, until his "Phoenix"-like imagination will finally enable him to throw off his "old clothes." The outmoded vestments of materialism and determinism, the thinking of Locke, Hartley, Hume, and Bentham must be discarded. In their place, Carlyle spreads out the alluring garb of "Novalis's mysticism, Fichte's ethical idealism, and the Spinozistic pantheism of Goethe" (Harrold in Carlyle 1938: 221).

In Heine's "Religion and Philosophy in Germany," the "medley" is comprised of almost the same ideas and philosophical schools alluded to in Carlyle. Carlyle ridicules the mentality incapable of seeing the infinite in the finite, the gospel at the heart of German Idealism. Heine mocks the self-importance of that same German Idealism for refusing to acknowledge its debt to Spinoza's pantheism. Often their arguments and language are remarkably similar:

> He [man] everywhere finds himself encompassed with Symbols... the Universe is but one vast Symbol of God; nay if thou wilt have it, what is man himself but a symbol of God; is not all that he does symbolical; a revelation to Sense of the mystic god given force that is in him... Not a Hut he builds but is the visible embodiment of a Thought; but bears visible record of invisible things; but is in the transcendental sense, symbolical as well as real. (Carlyle 1938: 220)

> Benedict Spinoza teaches: there is but one substance, which is God... Nothing but sheer unreason and malice could bestow on such a doctrine the qualification of "atheism"... Instead of saying that he denied God, one might say that he denied man. All finite things are to him but modes of the infinite substance...

> Let Schelling protest as eagerly as he may that his philosophy is something else than Spinozism, that it is rather "a living amalgam of the ideal and the real," that it is distinguishable from Spinozism "as the perfection of Greek statuary is distinguishable from the rigid Egyptian originals"; I must none the less emphatically declare that... Schelling is not to be distinguished in the slightest degree from Spinoza. He has only taken a different road to arrive at the same philosophy. (Heine 1959: 72–3)

Carlyle's Professor has to suffer anxieties of despair and disillusion before he finally comes to his transcendental vision of the interdependence of the finite and the infinite. Similarly, Heine's "Germany" stumbles through a series of religious and philosophical dips and turns in pursuit of its authentic nature – a culture in which sense and spirit are in balance. Luther had liberated religion from the weight of Catholic ritual and "tradition," but his substitution of the "letter" of the Bible for the "dogma" of the old church had merely created another tyranny over the mind that "deism" sought to correct (Heine 1959: 103). Alas, deism made the world safe for reason but kept God at a distance. When deism itself was shattered by Kant's *Critique of Pure Reason* (1781), things looked pretty grim for God's survival:

> You fancy, then, we may now go home! By my life, no! there is yet a piece to be played; after the tragedy comes the farce. Up to this point Immanuel Kant has pursued the path of inexorable philosophy; he has stormed heaven and put the whole garrison to the sword; the ontological, cosmological, and physico-theological bodyguards lie there lifeless; Deity itself, deprived of demonstration, has succumbed; there is now no All-mercifulness, no fatherly kindness, no other-world reward for renunciation in this world, the immortality of the soul lies in its last agony – you can hear its groans and death rattle; and old Lampe [Kant's faithful man servant] is standing by with his umbrella under his arm, an afflicted spectator of the scene, tears and sweat-drops of terror dropping from his countenance. Then Immanuel Kant relents and shows that he

is not merely a great philosopher but also a good man; he reflects, and half good-naturedly, half ironically, he says: "Old Lampe must have a God, otherwise the poor fellow can never be happy. Now, man ought to be happy in this world; practical reason says so; — well, I am quite willing that practical reason should also guarantee the existence of God." As the result of this argument, Kant distinguishes between the theoretical reason and the practical reason, and by means of the latter, as with a magician's wand, he revivifies deism, which theoretical reason had killed. (Heine 1959: 119)

Does philosophy simply defer to the human need for religion and give up the ghost? No, Kant's "critical spirit" was too strong to die out. "Even poetry did not escape its influence... fortunately it did not interfere in the art of cookery":

The German people is not easily set in motion; but let it be once forced into any path and it will follow it to its determination with the most dogged perseverance. Thus we exhibited our character in matters of religion, thus also we now acted in philosophy. Shall we continue to advance as consistently in politics? (Heine 1959: 121)

Before Heine attempts to answer his own question, he continues to plow his way through Fichte and Schelling in the same satirical manner that he presented Kant. In their own plodding way, the German philosophers have waged steady warfare on superstition and stifling religious tradition. Ever since Luther, the Germans have thought and fumbled their way in hopes of reaching a better and freer world. The hero of this awkward saga turns out to be Hegel, Schelling's student and Heine's own teacher. There are only a few paragraphs about him, but it is clear that Heine thinks of Hegel as the culminating philosopher of "Nature," whose dialectical powers incorporate the best of Kant's idea of reason with an historical imagination capable of bridging the gap between the phenomenal and noumenal worlds, the worlds of sense and spirit. Hegel, in other words, rediscovers Spinoza's pantheism without sacrificing the important contributions of Kant.

Political Satire: "Hidden" or "Raised?"

But what about politics? This is where the satirical vein bursts and Heine rises to a visionary prophecy that, despite its altogether different subject and intent, in its scope and "darkness" recalls Pope's triumph of Dullness in the *Dunciad*.

Christianity — and this is its fairest merit — subdued to a certain extent the brutal warrior ardor of the Germans, but it could not entirely quench it; and when the cross, that restraining talisman, falls to pieces, then will break forth again the ferocity of the old combatants, the frantic Berserker rage whereof Northern poets have said and sung so much... The old stone gods will then arise from the forgotten ruins and wipe from their eyes the dust of the centuries, and Thor with his giant hammer will arise again, and he will shatter the Gothic cathedrals... When you hear the trampling of feet and the clashing of arms... ye French, be on your guard, and see that ye mingle not in the fray going on amongst us at home in Germany. It might fare ill with you... Smile not at my counsel, at the counsel of a dreamer, who warns you against Kantians, Fichteans, Philosophers of Nature. Smile not at the fantasy of one who foresees in the region of reality the same outburst of revolution that has taken place in the region of intellect. The thought precedes the deed as the lightning the thunder. German thunder... is not very nimble, but rumbles along somewhat slowly. But come it will, and when you hear a crashing such as never before has been heard in the world's history, then know at last the German thunderbolt has fallen... There will be played in Germany a drama compared to which the French Revolution will seem but an innocent idyll. (Heine 1959: 159–60)

This passage has been interpreted as a prediction of Nazi barbarism. Heine's intention, however, was to shock the French into an awareness of the ultimate power of a culturally integrated revolutionary force, an "organic" power that had its roots in the thought, feeling, and mythology of an entire people rather than merely the rationalism of a political philosophy and the power of a strong army as was true of the French Revolution before and in its Napoleonic phase. The satire has its roots in German literary productions with which the French reading public was already familiar – the Gothic tales of Tieck and the supernatural stories of E. T. A. Hoffmann. Heine was indulging in a kind of ghoulish humor in which he was scaring the French and warning them to take the German "phenomenon" seriously. Could the clumsy German bugaboo really become a frightening monster? Here was a hot chestnut that Heine wanted to drop in their laps just to see the French jump. He wanted Germany to be taken seriously. Mme de Staël's *On Germany* (1813) had left the French with the impression that the Germans were unworldly philosophical dreamers. Did Heine believe in the extreme violence of his warning? We could just as well ask whether George Orwell would have been surprised to learn that Western society could suffer extremes of thought control without a totalitarian take over *à la* Big Brother? Or does the satirist exaggerate simply because that is what satire has to do? That Heine's exaggeration proved true – in the form of a political nightmare beyond the dark side of the Romantic or any other literary imagination – is merely one more proof that life *does* imitate art, often with consequences more stark than even Oscar Wilde could have imagined.

It is also true that *aufgehoben* in this eerie exaggeration (of what was to prove an understatement of the horror history had in store) is the relentlessly satirical perception that I suggested lies at the heart of chapter 31 in *Huckleberry Finn*: the grotesque belatedness of human emancipation. Mankind always falls short of its own ideals; the human race cannot wake to its own dream of freedom. It cannot, in the case of Germany, be expected to contain the opposites of its antinomies. It may even, as in Heine's phantasmagorical prediction, explode. There are some who would see this as tragic, but Twain's lodging of the same *truth* in his country-boy-as-man protagonist's willingness to go to hell for helping a slave gain his freedom suggests that comedy is the appropriate context – to be more specific, the comedic worlds of farce and satire. As Heine put it, "after the tragedy comes the farce" (1959: 119).

Carlyle's Professor has to experience disappointment in love to begin his tortuous climb to elementary wisdom; he is like Goethe's Werther, but instead of blowing out his brains he merely begins the basic job of filling them. It is as if Werther is forced to become the Faust of Part 2 – a telescoping of the Goethean drama of self-creation. The satire is at Teufelsdröckh's expense (for he is both anti-hero and visionary), not Goethe's, but the reader cannot escape the fact that he is being addressed (and instructed) as if he had much more in common with the Professor than with Goethe. There is also the larger joke, what I have already alluded to as the "cosmopolitan" agenda; the English reader is forced into "German" instruction – sent back to school. He must shed his insular Puritanism, avoid the desiccating rationalism of the French, and join the mainstream of European thought as expressed in Goethe and his circle. Can the English do it? Carlyle will spend his life dousing them with exhortations on the need for hero worship and the courage to accept the supervision and guidance of their superiors. There is little indication that he thought them capable of changing "Clothes" on their own. This is where he and his disciple Emerson, the prophet of "Self-Reliance," seem to part ways. Indeed, this is where Carlyle, despite his philosophical idealism, shows his deep affinity with Swift. We remember that the man who urged his readers to embrace the infinite in the finite wrote *Sartor Resartus* "in a satirical frenzy."

Heine also leaned on the "cosmopolitan" imperative for the thrust of his satire. As Carlyle used the Germans to educate the English, Heine used the Germans to educate the French – and vice versa. One would think that Carlyle should have appreciated Heine. Both were attracted to the heroic ideal, particularly when embodied in strong leaders; despite his liberalism, Heine valued autocratic politicians, like Napoleon, who embodied the people's will but discouraged a "leveling down," and Carlyle, distrustful of the mob, praised the "Captains of Industry." By the 1860s Carlyle's hopes for German literature were dashed: "All downward...a sort of Socialism rampant everywhere...[the] restorative spirit of Goethe gone." Carlyle became incensed when Heine was judged Goethe's successor in the German lyric.

> [No] new book on Goethe, but I see a great deal about a dirty, blaspheming Jew, Heinrich Heine. He has a wit of a sort, but it would be shameful to put him in front of Goethe...[who] showed us what Christianity might be without husks and cloaks that have been heaped upon it...No real religion at the present day. And the man or the nation that has no religion will come to nothing. (Wilson and MacArthur 1931: 218, 455)

Heine was more than cavalier with both Judaism and Christianity but, at various times in his life, had complimentary things to say about both of them. He was no atheist, but he flirted with blasphemy when he indulged in witticisms such as calling the Virgin Mary a "barmaid." The truth is that, aside from his anti-Semitism, what really agitated Carlyle was that Heine did not buy into the "Symbolic" contract; he never believed in the "reconciliation of opposites" – in art or life. As Ritchie Robinson has put it, "[Heine] has no last word... transcending the antinomies (e.g., the sensual and the spiritual) round which we have seen his thought restlessly circling" (1988: 101). In the narrative poem *Atta Troll* (1847), Heine adapts symbolic figures drawn from Germanic legend. Laskaro, the son of a witch, hunts down the foolish revolutionary "bears," who are limited to nineteenth-century visions of emancipation (Robinson 1988: 28). Heine's fear of communism, which toward the end of his life he thought would be the inevitable result of bourgeois corruption, led him to experiment with "Romantic" symbols that in their very atavism had the power to hold back the "leveling" juggernaut of an egalitarian social contract. Nevertheless, he was basically uncomfortable with "Romantic" visions because he saw them as rooted in medieval Catholicism and dedicated to suppressing the senses in the name of spirit.

What Carlyle seems to have forgotten is that his beloved Goethe, who was his primary model for "Christianity... without husks and cloaks," constantly undermined his own symbolic visions with satirical critique. We have already noted the connection between "incongruity" and its appeal to sublimation through dialectical and organic reconciliation *as well* as its tempting of satirical reduction. Indeed, I have suggested earlier that there is a silent contract between the two and that the latter is often *aufgehoben* in the former. In Carlyle's case, one could argue that he himself was not fully aware of the contradictions implicit in the satirical intensity with which he was advocating transcendent ideas; that his tone and anger seemed to contradict his visionary bliss. For generations this has been attributed to his dyspepsia. Yet, the stomachs of many poets growl without robbing their work of its music. The strange blend of tones and syntax, of German and English, of Puritanism and Idealism is a satirical medley in which the satirical strain is strangely absorbed (or hidden) and the transcendental vision abides. The "satirical frenzy" that Carlyle brought to *Sartor Resartus* is curiously driven to the background even as it seems to energize his search for its cure.

Unlike Carlyle, who managed to link Goethe's effortless fashioning of symbolic beauty with the German sage's ethical principle of Renunciation ("Find what thou can'st work at"), Heine was troubled by Goethe's aestheticism. "Goethe became the greatest artist in our literature," writes Heine, "and everything he wrote became a perfectly rounded work of art." This observation appears in Heine's "The Romantic School," another long essay he wrote for the French reader, also in the early 1830s. Here he contrasts Schiller with Goethe and gives Schiller the advantage. "Goethe's masterpieces... adorn our dear fatherland as beautiful statues adorn a garden, but they are, after all, statues. You can fall in love with them, but they are sterile; Goethe's works do not beget deeds as do Schiller's. A deed is the child of the word, and Goethe's beautiful words are childless" (Heine 1973: 170). In other words, Goethe's "words" do not convey the "thoughts" necessary for the evolution of *Geist* (Spirit) in History. "The thought precedes the deed as the lightning the thunder." Schiller's historical dramas make him a good Hegelian, a poet who defers to the historical principle; Goethe's sublime "reconciliations of opposites" identify him too closely with Schelling, a philosopher, says Heine, who was really a poet.

By putting "art" in its place – below history – Heine seems to be deferring to the Hegelian hierarchy, and in a sense he is. But behind his deference to Hegelian "Reason" there is more going on than a recognition of the dialectical stream of ideas. Heine flirted with many philosophical and political systems – from Saint Simonianism to republicanism, from communism to Caesarism. All his life he felt a strong attraction to Spinoza, not necessarily as a thinker to believe in but as a source for what others really believed without fully realizing it. "All our present-day philosophers, possibly without knowing it, look through glasses that Baruch Spinoza ground" (Heine 1973: 208). It is the very fluidity of thought – "Nothing is more absurd than ownership claimed for ideas" – that defines Heine's satirical project (1959: 208). He is not merely skeptical. That is the condition of the typical modern satirist, of writers like Evelyn Waugh and Aldous Huxley. Heine was too much identified with intellectual and political liberty to succumb to skepticism or its darker shadow, despair.

The belatedness of the liberated mind coming into its full legacy – Huck's dilemma – drives both Carlyle and Heine. If satire is somehow "hidden" in Carlyle, it is flamboyantly "raised" in Heine. The transcendence that Carlyle seeks is stubbornly resisted in Heine. Carlyle yearns for Resolution, and Heine soars from one resting place to the next. And yet, even he permitted himself a haunting quip as he neared death in great pain on his "mattress grave": "God will forgive me. It's his metier." Each of them is pursuing a truth beyond art, but neither could exist without the art of satire, which, in contrasting ways, is *aufgehoben* in both.

References and Further Reading

Carlyle, Thomas (1938) *Sartor Resartus: The Life and Opinions of Herr Teufelsdröckh*, ed. Charles Frederick Harrold. New York: Odyssey Press.

Heine, Heinrich (1959) *Religion and Philosophy in Germany*, trans. John Snodgrass (1882), ed. Herbert Marcuse. Boston: Beacon Press.

——(1973) *Selected Works*, trans. and ed. Helen M. Mustard. New York: Random House.

Horace (1955) *Satires, Epistles and Ars Poetica*, trans. H. Rushton Fairclough. Cambridge, MA: Harvard University Press.

Lamb, Charles (1935) Letter from Charles Lamb to Thomas Hood after October 20, 1834. In *The Letters of Charles Lamb to Which are Added Those of his Sister Mary Lamb*, 3 vols, ed. E. V. Lucas. New Haven, CT: Yale University Press.

Robinson, Ritchie (1988) *Heine*. New York: Grove Press.

Schlegel, Friedrich (1971) *Lucinde and the Fragments*, trans. Peter Firchow. Minneapolis, MN: University of Minnesota Press.

Taylor, Charles (1979) *Hegel and Modern Society*. Cambridge: Cambridge University Press.

Wellek, Rene (1955) *A History of Modern Criticism*, vol. 2. New Haven, CT: Yale University Press.

Wilson, David Alec (1931) *Carlyle to Three Score and Ten (1853–65)*. London: Routledge.

—— and MacArthur, David Wilson (1934) *Carlyle in Old Age (1865–1881)*. London: Routledge.

18
Nineteenth-century Satiric Poetry
Steven E. Jones

Satiric poetry took many forms and addressed a range of diverse topics in the nineteenth century, from popular politics, to society and manners, to emergent literary movements. Mixed forms and overlapping purposes were the rule, it must be remembered, but the topical categories just named are nevertheless convenient tools for historical analysis. It seems wise to remain skeptical about definitions of Romantic and Victorian literature, and to avoid plotting the "rise" or "fall" of any particular form of poetry over the course of the century. But it is historically the case that the relative attention of readers, reviewers, and editors, not to mention the focus of authors, fluctuated over time, such that one or another of these three strands of poetic satire – more political or more social – seems to dominate at particular cultural moments during the course of the nineteenth century.

In the early half of the century political satire was extremely prominent, given the aftermath of the French Revolution and the war against Napoleon. Popular or radical writing surged in the 1790s, but there was an answering suppression of dissent and then a wave of loyalist expressions during the war years, followed by a revivification of radicalism and the reform movement after 1815 and into the 1820s. Political verse satires by Shelley, Byron, Moore, Barbauld, Hone, and Ebenezer Elliott represent a significant cluster across the first three decades of the century, and a tradition of popular political satire developed that led directly into the Chartist verse of the latter half of the century, the work of poets such as Ernest Jones. But literary history is a long-term process that involves forgetting as well as remembering. Jones and other Chartists have been overshadowed in the anthologies and the canons they both represent and help to establish by other forms of Victorian poetry and, to an even greater degree, by the novel. Popular political satire has come to occupy a relatively marginal niche in the Victorian landscape, and this is itself an important fact of nineteenth-century literary history, of how such history was made. At the same time as the Chartists were publishing rousing political verse (including satire) in newspapers and books, the publishing world was conquered by middle-class magazines such as *Punch*, which became famous for its cartoons but printed as well a kind of light social satire (often in prose) on party politics, manners, and fashion. In the latter half of the century, this lighter social satire came to seem more generally evident than the earlier virulent forms of political satire. This does not mean that anything essential changed in the "spirit of the age" between the Romantic and Victorian periods. Instead, it points to specific changes in government and the socio-political climate, as well as changes in taste, in evaluations of what mattered and what counted, the recursive and retrospective process by which literary canons – and ideas of generic dominance – get created.

We can catch a glimpse of such forces at work in a little squib by Thomas Moore from the *Morning Chronicle* of 1840, "An Episcopal Address on Socialism." This satire, in the voice of the Tory Bishop of Exeter, mocks his aversion to radicalism (he had complained when the utopian Robert Owen was presented to the Queen):

> The Socialists were the vilest race
> That ever on earth or hell had place!
> He would not prejudice them – no! not he!
> For his soul overflowed with charity.
>
> (9–12)

A satirist and a popular poet, Moore speaks with the irreverent voice of the earlier period of his prime, the Regency. By 1840, the Bishop's fastidious piety may or may not have been more widely shared than Moore's attitude of raillery, but the record of literary history would lead one to believe so. Here we see a process of succession, as one generation's supposedly apolitical fastidiousness is being constructed at the expense of another generation's radical sympathies – the process of mutual construction revealed. The social and political threat posed by socialism and Chartism, in effect the partitioning off of radicalism from a newly constructed respectable public opinion, forms a Victorian backdrop against which to read the satires of Ernest Jones and other poets who continued nonetheless to write popular political satires.

The generation gap behind Moore's satire – Regency political conflict versus Victorian piety and propriety – can also be seen at roughly the same historical moment in an anonymous 1841 poem by Charles Dickens, the great Victorian novelist of social reform. On the occasion of the new Tory government of Robert Peel and the accompanying wave of nostalgia for the good old days, Dickens satirized claims of continuity in "The Fine Old English Gentleman. New Version. To be Said or Sung at All Conservative Dinners." (His verse form parodies a previous ballad by Henry Russell that had sentimentalized Tory country life.)

> I'll sing you a new ballad, and I'll warrant it first-rate,
> Of the days of that old gentleman who had that old estate;
> When they spent the public money at a bountiful old rate
> On ev'ry mistress, pimp, and scamp, at ev'ry noble gate,
>   In the fine old English Tory times;
>   Soon may they come again!

>   . . .
>   Those were the days for taxes, and for war's infernal din,
>   For scarcity of bread, that fine old dowagers might win;
>   For shutting men of letters up, through iron bars to grin,
>   Because they didn't think the Prince was altogether thin,
>   In the fine old English Tory times;
>   Soon may they come again!
>   (1–6, 31–6)

The phrase "shutting men of letters up" alludes to Leigh Hunt's imprisonment in 1809 for calling the Prince Regent "corpulent." Times have changed, and the new Tories are trying to revive (and revise) a past they can use. This involves revising the tone of cultural memories, inculcating a pious nostalgia in place of political conflict, and this act of forgetting is what Dickens's satire works to expose.

The conventional claim that the Victorian age was dominated by apolitical social satire should be taken with a grain of salt. It is itself a product of the social construction of Victorian culture as sober and sincere, safely apolitical, smugly bourgeois. The Dickens example also underscores the difficulty of separating social from political satire. A great deal of witty social satire was being written in the Regency and Napoleonic wars simultaneously with the most intensely Juvenalian political satire, just as militant Chartist verse was being produced in the supposedly more civil Victorian era. The sections that follow, therefore, should be understood as a matter of relative emphasis, as overlapping and interrelated pathways through the century's forms of verse satire – political, social, and literary – all of which are present to some degree at any given time (and often in various mixtures within the same poem), but each of which appears in retrospect to rise into relative prominence at its moment in the progress of the nineteenth century.

Political Satire

The Poetry of the Anti-Jacobin appeared in 1799, a collection in book form of parodic and satiric verse taken from the famous Tory weekly (1798–9) that had, under the editorship of George Canning, attempted to stem the tide of support for the French Revolution. Besides memorably funny parodies of Lake School ruralism (for example, "The Friend of Humanity and the Knife-grinder") and new-model French national hymns ("La Sainte Guillotine"), it included parodies of the general voice and tenor of liberal Enlightenment verse, such as "The Progress of Man, A Didactic Poem" – the very title of which is already ripe with satire. The verse renders absurd the airy universalisms of its targeted kind: "Ah! Who has seen the mailed lobster rise, / Clap her broad wings, and soaring claim the skies?" (44–5):

>   Nor e'er did cooling cucumbers presume
>   To flow'r like myrtle, or like violets bloom.

> – Man, only – rash, refined, presumptuous Man,
> Starts from his rank, and mars creation's plan.
> Born the free heir of nature's wide domain,
> To art's strict limits bounds his narrow'd reign;
> Resigns his native rights for meaner things,
> For Faith and Fetters – Laws, and Priests, and Kings.
> (53–60)

The culture wars that drove the *Anti-Jacobin* escalated during the war with France, though sanctions also increased for any expression of radicalism. In fact, from 1803 there was a flood of loyal, anti-French satires in the newspapers, magazines, and journals, such as a mock ode from 1804 celebrating "Bonaparte's Coronation" and addressed *"en enferis"*:

> Furies! shake the scorpion lash;
>   Imps! the song of joy begin;
> Till the roof of Hell shall clash,
>   Smitten with the gladsome din!
>   Fiends and Imps, and Daemons dance,
> Bonaparte is Lord of France! . . .
> (1–6)

Somewhat differently, "Harlequin's Invasion" (1803) imagines a grotesque Napoleon striding onto the world stage:

> No comic pantomime before
>   Could ever boast such tricks surprising:
> The hero capers Europe o'er –
>   But hush! behold the curtain rising.
>
> And, first, that little isle survey,
>   Where sleeps a peasant-boy so hearty;
> That little isle is Corsica,
>   That peasant-boy is Buonaparte.
> (1–8)

(The comic rhyme on the Emperor's name was a standard gimmick at the time.) Next Anarchy, rising from a trapdoor, urges Napoleon to invade one country after another – for twenty-six allegorical and topical stanzas.

The French had been the occasion for anxious or apocalyptic satires for some years before the beginning of the new century. An anonymous stanza looking back to the 1798 Egyptian campaign was published in *The Gentleman's Magazine* for September 1801. What could be worse for Egypt than "blains, locusts, boils, and flies, and lice," it asks? The "infernal French!" of course. Never mind that the biblical analogy oddly seems to blame Egypt ("this guilty land") for the "plague" of the French invasion.

Such mock-prophecies are at one end of the spectrum of prophetic satires; at the other end is Anna Barbauld's celebrated couplet poem, "Eighteen Hundred and Eleven."

> Still the loud death drum, thundering from afar,
> O'er the vext nations pours the storm of war:
> To the stern call still Britain bends her ear,
> Feeds the fierce strife, the alternate hope and fear;
> Bravely, though vainly, dares to strive with Fate,
> And seeks by turns to prop each sinking state.
> Colossal Power with overwhelming force
> Bears down each fort of Freedom in its course;
> Prostrate she lies beneath the Despot's sway,
> While the hushed nations curse him – and obey.
> (1–10)

The poet speaks boldly as an inspired prophetess, in a voice of righteous indignation directed to the nation as a whole, and it speaks in authoritative Augustan couplets: "And think'st thou, Britain, still to sit at ease, / An island Queen amidst thy subject seas?" Barbauld asks (39–40). Of course not: "Thou who hast shared the guilt must share the woe" (46). For 334 lines the prophetess-satirist declaims against her country's addiction to luxury and moral corruption (in part due to the slave trade) and predicts that this empire, too, shall fall, when "Genius forsakes" the British "shore" and settles instead on the land of future promise: the Americas ("Thy world, Columbus, shall be free," 334).

Barbauld's form may be Popean but the prophetic-satiric voice owes something to Juvenal and something to Jeremiah, as both were versified in Milton's sonnets ("Avenge oh Lord..."). Percy Shelley deploys a version of this same voice in his sonnet, "England in 1819." In the face of setbacks to the Reform movement, the nation seemed in that year to be trapped in a grotesque political caricature:

> An old, mad, blind, despised, and dying king, –
> Princes, the dregs of their dull race, who flow
> Through public scorn, – mud from a muddy spring, –
> Rulers who neither see, nor feel, nor know,
> But leech-like to their fainting country cling,
> Till they drop, blind in blood, without a blow...
> (1–6)

An image of the "people starved and stabbed in the untilled field" invokes the recent Peterloo Massacre, August 16, 1819, when a Reformist assembly was attacked by yeomen and soldiers on St Peter's Fields, Manchester. Outraged responses included verbal and visual satires, among them Shelley's ballad *The Mask of Anarchy*. It imagines a cartoon "masque" or triumphal procession of government figures following the goddess Anarchy, made up of the ministers Castlereagh, Eldon, and Sidmouth, wearing the allegorical masks of Murder, Fraud, and Hypocrisy. This triumph is rebuffed by a confrontation with Hope and an amorphous, luminous Shape (who may be Liberty in historical disguise). The exhortation to the people of England that follows ("Rise like lions after slumber") shifts voices and genres to reveal what might follow if the diabolical cartoon of the present were erased, offering a kind of post-satiric vision of equality and fraternity.

Shelley's *Mask* imitates the imagery and style of radical pamphlet satires such as William Hone's 1820 *Political House that Jack Built*, based on the children's rhyme and illustrated by George Cruikshank. One plate shows caricatures of magistrates and tax collectors and barristers and other officials accompanied by the verse –

> These are THE VERMIN
> That Plunder the Wealth,
> That lay in the House,
> That Jack Built

– followed on the next plate by an image of the printing press and these lines:

> This is THE THING, that, in spite of new Acts,
> And attempts to restrain it, by Soldiers or Tax,
> Will *poison* the Vermin, that plunder the Wealth
> That lay in the House,
> That Jack Built.
>   (plates 3 and 4)

The legislative Six Acts that followed Peterloo restricted assembly and expression in a way that Hone would have taken personally. He had been prosecuted for blasphemous and seditious libel in 1817 and won his case, based in part on the important argument that parody was a protected form.

Arguably the greatest verse-satirist of the century, Lord Byron also drew upon the ubiquitous pamphlets and cartoons. "The Vision of Judgment" was published in the journal *The Liberal* in 1822. It attacks Robert Southey for his bad poetry, but mostly for his bad politics as evidenced in his bad poetry, and it culminates in direct ridicule of King George III, who manages to sneak into Heaven during the uproar in response to Southey's terrible verse. Byron liked to blend satires on literary taste, society, and politics, and, whenever possible, to come as close as possible to both blasphemy *and* sedition (not to mention other forms of transgression) in the same satiric poem. The suppressed (but later pirated) Dedication to *Don Juan* is perhaps the best example, a series of 17 *ottava-rima* stanzas mixing wit with invective, punch lines with pummeling attacks. It targets the Lake School of poets, but also the hated Viscount Castlereagh, whom Byron calls a "Cold-blooded, smooth-faced, placid miscreant!" a "bungler," and a "tinkering slave-maker" (89, 105, 111). Lord Byron was writing in a brawling radical idiom, here engaging in an act of poetic downward mobility and borrowing the demotic satirical weapons used by working-class pamphleteers such as William Hone, Thomas Wooler, and William Cobbett.

These were weapons familiar to Ebenezer Elliott, who published his *Corn Law Rhymes* in 1830, a collection of sentimental rural verse, melodramatic lyrics of sensibility, as well as prophetic denunciations and satiric invectives. Elliott was a blacksmith and mechanic from a Jacobin background, and he used his identity as a working-class or "uneducated" poet to good political effect. The Corn Law of 1815 had been imposed in order to stabilize prices at the end of the Napoleonic wars. Protesters against the Corn Laws were present at Peterloo and the dispute continued into the 1840s. *Corn Law Rhymes* contains satires aimed at concrete economic targets, the material infrastructure of tariffs and other regulation, as illustrated, for example, in the popular song "The Four Dears":

> Dear Sugar, dear Tea, and dear Corn
> Conspired with dear Representation,
> To laugh worth and honor to scorn,
> And beggar the whole British nation.
> (1–4)

The pun on "dear" suggests that the high prices of commodities are directly linked to the fundamental moral values of the nation, universal human values such as "worth and honor" that the nation *should* hold as "dear."

Thomas Moore was, as we have seen, a popular satirist, though he was made famous by the series of *Irish Melodies* (1808–34). In the 1820s he also published a number of political satires on the Corn Laws and on Catholic Emancipation. Many of these satires, with a very different overall tone from Elliott's verse, were later collected in a book of 1828, *Odes upon Cash, Corn, Catholics and Other Matters*, including the meta-topical "Corn and Catholics."

> What! *still* those two infernal questions,
>   That with our meals our slumbers mix –
> That spoil our tempers and digestions –
>   Eternal Corn and Catholics!
>
> Gods! were there ever two such bores?
>   Nothing else talk'd of, night or morn –
> Nothing *in* doors, or *out* of doors,
>   But endless Catholics and Corn!
> (1–8)

This satire depends not on working-class indignation born of frustrated hopes, but on the opposite class perspective, the view from above. We see through Moore's ironic, fashionably bored speaker, just how long these issues had been on the table by 1826.

By contrast to Moore's indirect ironies, Elliott writes from a base of direct class anger, as in the didactic contrast of "How Different!"

> Poor weaver, with hopeless brow,
> And bare woe-whiten'd head;
> Thou art a pauper, all allow,
> And see thou begg'st thy bread;
> And yet thou dost not plunder slaves,
> Then tell them they are free;
> Nor hast thou join'd with tax-fed knaves,
> To corn-bill mine and me.
> (1–8)

Elliott's denunciation is simple: "yon proud pauper, dead to shame, / Is fed by mine and me" (21–2). An anonymous Chartist poem published in *The Northern Liberator*, January 18, 1840, was titled "The State Pauper's Soliloquy" and employed essentially the same charge: "Who gives us our tax-free houses fine, / And finds us wherewithal to dine, / On turtle and on Bordeaux wine? / The People."

Popular political verse was answered immediately by conservative poets, notably in a series of "March of Intellect" satires published in the 1820s. The best-known example was by Thomas Hook, published in the Tory *Blackwood's Edinburgh Magazine* for December 1825. Its basic premise is to mock lower-order pretensions to learning and the social mobility that went along with it:

> Oh! Learning's a very fine thing,
>   And also is wisdom and knowledge,
> For a man is as great as a king,
>   If he has but the airs of a college...
> (1–4)

In the stanzas that follow Hook takes on one trade association after another, beginning with the textile workers among whom violent Luddism had flourished in the previous decade:

> The WEAVER it surely becomes,
>   To talk of his web's involution,
> For doubtless the hero of thrum
>   Is a member of some institution;
> He speaks of supply and demand,
>   With the airs of a great legislator,
> And almost can tell you off-hand,
>   That the smaller is less than the greater!
> (19–26)

Other conservative satires ridiculed the tendency of radical poetry to cross over into shrill denunciation or melodramatic representations of the poor, the disenfranchised, and the working classes. Many popular satires did indeed make use of these modes.

The Chartist poet Ernest Jones, for example, was known as much for sentimental, angry, and analytical verse as for his satires. One of his best-known poems, "Song of the Low" (1852), employs ironic self-mockery to turn the tables before the fact on the would-be satirists of the poor and working classes.

> We're low – we're low – we're very, very low,
>   As low as low can be;
> The rich are high – for we make them so –
>   And a miserable lot are we!
>   And a miserable lot are we! Are we!
>   A miserable lot are we!
>
> We plow and sow – we're so very, very low,
>   That we delve in the dirty clay;
> Till we bless the plain with the golden grain,
>   And the vale with the fragrant hay.
> Our place we know – we're so very, very low,
>   'Tis down at the landlord's feet;
> We're not too low the grain to grow,
>   But too low the bread to eat.
>   We're low, we're low, etc.
>
> . . .
>
> We're low, we're low – we're very, very low –
>   And yet from our fingers glide
> The silken flow – and the robes that glow,
>   Round the limbs of the sons of pride.
> And what we get – and what we give,
>   We know – and we know our share.
> We're not too low the cloth to weave –
>   But too low the cloth to wear.
>   We're low, we're low, etc.
>
> We're low, we're low – we're very, very low,
>   And yet when the trumpets ring,
> The thrust of a poor man's arm will go
>   Through the heart of the proudest king!
> We're low, we're low – our place we know,
>   We're only the rank and the file;
> We're not too low – to kill the foe,
>   But too low to touch the spoil.
>   We're low, we're low, etc.
>   (stanzas 1–2, 4–5)

In the end, the bodily power of the "low" – the weavers' "fingers" and "poor man's arm" – is put forth in a matter of fact way that also hints at the retribution of which the "low" are potentially capable.

Social Satire

It is often difficult to disentangle political, social, and literary aspects of a satire, especially when these topics are expressed by way of coded references to social class or religion, as seen for example, in the newspaper satires by "Tabitha Bramble," a pseudonym of Mary Robinson's. As a member of the sentimental Della Cruscan school, Robinson had herself been one of the targets of the famous satires by William Gifford, the *Baviad* and *Maeviad* (1797). But she also wrote satires of her own as "Horace Juvenal" and "Tabitha Bramble." The controversy over the Della Cruscans was never merely about poetic styles; it was always political. And even where Robinson's own satires appear to be about contemporary mores, they are in context also politically charged. "The Confessor, A Sanctified Tale" (1800), an adaptation of Chaucer's "Miller's Tale," is anticlerical, licentious, and anti-authoritarian in ways that would have been politically encoded at the time.

> When SUPERSTITION ruled the land
> And Priestcraft shackled Reason,
> At GODSTOW dwelt a goodly band,
> Grey Monks they were, and but to say
> They were not always given to pray,
>   Would have been construed as Treason.
> Yet some did scoff, and some believ'd
> That sinners were themselves deceived;
> And taking Monks for more than men
> They prov'd themselves, nine out of ten,
> Mere dupes of these Old Fathers hoary...
>   (1–11)

Similarly, the numerous satiric representations of peasants and rustics during the early nineteenth century, from George Crabbe's famous satiric tales (many published as early as the 1780s, but some appearing in the first decades of the new century) to parodies of Lake School ballads, inevitably carried political meanings in the era of the French Revolution and democratic ideals. At the same time, satiric representations of court life or the upper classes were political by default.

Take, for example, Thomas Moore's very popular *Intercepted Letters; or, the Twopenny Post-Bag* (1813). Published under the name of "Thomas Brown the Younger," this collection of verse-epistles purported to be the found correspondence from a dropped post-bag, letters written by the Prince Regent, his family, and their noble acquaintances. Through this device, Moore is able to satirize the social scene as observed by the correspondents, but also the royal family and politics in general. Moore's follow-up volumes, *The Fudge Family in Paris* (1818; it mocked English tourists traveling on the Continent but also included an attack on the Viscount Castlereagh) and *The Fudges in England* (1835), used the same device, but in less tense times and with an increasingly greater admixture of social satire. The premise of the *Twopenny Post-Bag*, that we are reading someone else's mail, makes for gossipy passages such as a letter on how socially awkward it is to entertain the Prince Regent and his mistress at the same party:

> Besides, I've remark'd that (between you and I)
> The MARCHESA and he, inconvenient in more ways,
> Have taken much lately to whispering in door-ways;
> Which – consid'ring, you know, dear, the *size* of the two –
> Makes a block that one's company *cannot* get through...
> (p. 22)

In addition to the social satire in the *Twopenny Post-Bag*, there are political criticisms of the competence and morals of the royal family. Moreover, the premise of "intercepted letters" offers an implicit political satire on the reactionary culture of surveillance during the war years, as Gary Dyer has argued (in Jones 2003: 151–71).

Some Regency and Romantic period satires, however, can be described as more social than political, such as the collection of *Essays in Rhyme on Morals and Manners* by Jane Taylor (1816). In a series of brilliantly understated verses, Taylor exposes the hollow center of polite society and simultaneously encourages sympathy for the sufferings of the poor. In "Recreation" she mocks the tendency of respectable middle-class women to gossip about one another. The speaker, Miss B., and her mother arrive for tea with Mrs G., but that is merely a pretext.

> At last the tea came up, and so,
> With that, our tongues began to go.
> Now, in that house you're sure of knowing
> The smallest scrap of news that's going;
> We find it *there* the wisest way,
> To take some care of what we say.
> (19–24)

It soon becomes evident that the visitors are willing and even eager participants in the game. They are represented as "panting ... with curiosity and spleen," as they admit: "And how we did enjoy the sport!" (110–12). Then they politely leave with their "boy" – after arranging for the next week's tea.

Gossip has always been one of social satire's mainstays. Fashionable persons are the targets of Lady Anne Hamilton's *The Epics of the Ton; or, the Glories of the Great World* (1807). Published anonymously in two volumes, "The Female Book" and "The Male Book," its poems are all titled only by the semi-suppressed names (or titles) of the satirized, "M — F —" or "M — of A —," and so on.

> WHILE dull historians only sing of wars,
> Of hood-wink'd treaties hatching keen-ey'd jars;

> Of wily statesmen splitting hairs asunder,
> Of hills and orators who belch and thunder;
> Of grinding taxes, and of tott'ring thrones,
> Of him who eats up states, and picks the bones:
> Say shall the brightest glories of our age,
> Who best adorn the cut, and grace the page,
>
> Who on the top of fashion's Ida dwell,
> And gold in showers produce to either Bell;
> O say shall these, who just so bright have shone,
> Escape remembrance when they quit the Ton?
> Their laurels wither'd, and their name forgot,
> As dog on dunghill has been said to rot?
> Forbid it honour! and forbid it shame!
>
> (1–15)

Taking its cue from Pope's *Rape of the Lock* (1714), this mock-epic invocation prepares the reader to accept the name-dropping that follows in the proper spirit. The sometimes petty and sometimes vicious ridicule of the *ton*, or fashionable upper class, is thus protected by this mock-important invocation, which says in effect that the satires are a mere parlor game, a trifle, willingly subservient to more serious (though duller) politics and history.

But a fuller context reveals the political ramifications of Lady Hamilton's social satire. The first target of the "Female" volume named above is actually Mrs Fitzherbert, the notorious mistress and perhaps secret wife of the Prince Regent. She is labeled by Hamilton as one of the "r–y–l [whores]," and the larger purpose of the mock-epic is to attack the morals of the court and to defend the honor of Princess Caroline against her husband. *The Epics of the Ton* was published just after the scandalous "delicate investigation" of 1806, an attempt by the Prince to prove his wife an adulteress. All this would erupt again as the very public Queen Caroline Affair of 1820–1, in which party politics would play a central role. The courtier Lady Hamilton's early intervention on behalf of the reputation of the Princess remains, however, for the most part morally rather than politically outraged.

The mock-epic is a traditional vehicle for social satire because it opens up contrasts between the heroic past and a ludicrous present. This is one way to understand the power of Byron's *Don Juan*, an *ottava-rima* poem published in multiple canto installments between 1819 and 1824 and often called the greatest verse satire of the period – except that *Don Juan* also satirizes classical claims to heroism. (For once the mock-epic does mock the epic.) The poet himself called the poem an "Epic Satire," and in one sense this merely means *massive* satire, but in another, it means something more dialectical – a generic mix of the epic and the satiric that results in productive self-contradictions. Like the *satura* or medley of traditional verse satire, the epic is an encyclopedic form, mirroring the multiplicities of the world itself, and containing a mixture of formal styles and genres. It is also the form in which to represent a national culture or a whole society. *Don Juan* undermines its own claims to such importance, even while continuing to insist upon them. Like *Epics of the Ton*, Byron's poem gossips about high society from an insider's point of view. I have already mentioned the political satire in *Don Juan*'s suppressed Dedication, and a strain of political satire runs throughout the cantos, directed against persons as well as nations and history itself. But the political satire is often closely intertwined with a strain of social satire as well, as in the final canto's fond mockery of great-house manners among the landed aristocracy, or the justly famous passages on the fashionable life of Regency London – Byron's old milieu.

From canto 11, Juan travels in England and that section opens with his naïve picaro's view of London as seen from Primrose Hill, producing satire by immediate refutation in the reader's own commonsense experience.

> "And here," he cried, "is Freedom's chosen station;
> Here peals the people's voice, nor can entomb it
> Racks, prisons, inquisitions; resurrection
> Awaits it, each new meeting or election.
>
> 10
> "Here are chaste wives, pure lives; here people pay
> But what they please; and if that things be dear,
> 'Tis only that they love to throw away
> Their cash, to show how much they have a-year.
> Here laws are all inviolate; none lay
> Traps for the traveller; every highway's clear:
> Here" – he was interrupted by a knife,
> With, "Damn your eyes! your money or your life!"
>
> 11
> These freeborn sounds proceeded from four pads
> In ambush laid, who had perceived him loiter
> Behind his carriage; and, like handy lads,
> Had seized the lucky hour to reconnoitre,
> In which the heedless gentleman who gads
> Upon the road, unless he prove a fighter,
> May find himself within that isle of riches
> Exposed to lose his life as well as breeches.

Juan is literally mugged in the midst of reverie – but this also turns out to be an apt metaphor for what Byron does to his reader. Time and time again throughout the poem an idealization is undercut with bathetic disillusion.

A little further on in the canto, the cynicism is tempered in a celebrated *"ubi sunt"* meditation on Byron's lost social world:

76

"Where is the world?" cries Young, "at *eighty*? Where
   The world in which a man was born?" Alas!
Where is the world of *eight* years past? 'Twas there —
   I look for it — 'tis gone, a globe of glass!
Cracked, shivered, vanished, scarcely gazed on, ere
   A silent change dissolves the glittering mass.
Statesmen, chiefs, orators, queens, patriots, kings,
And dandies, all are gone on the wind's wings.

77

Where is Napoleon the Grand? God knows:
   Where little Castlereagh? The devil can tell:
Where Grattan, Curran, Sheridan, all those
   Who bound the bar or senate in their spell?
Where is the unhappy Queen, with all her woes?
   And where the Daughter, whom the Isles loved well?
Where are those martyred saints the Five per Cents?
And where — oh, where the devil are the Rents?

78

Where's Brummel? Dished. Where's Long Pole Wellesley?
   Diddled.
   Where's Whitbread? Romilly? Where's George the Third?
Where is his will? (That's not so soon unriddled.)
   And where is "Fum" the Fourth, our "royal bird"?
Gone down, it seems, to Scotland to be fiddled
   Unto by Sawney's violin, we have heard:
"Caw me, caw thee" — for six months hath been hatching
This scene of royal itch and loyal scratching.

79

Where is Lord This? And where my Lady That?
   The Honourable Mistresses and Misses?
Some laid aside like an old opera hat,
   Married, unmarried, and remarried: (this is
An evolution oft performed of late).
   Where are the Dublin shouts — and London hisses?
Where are the Grenvilles? Turned as usual. Where
My friends the Whigs? Exactly where they were.

The social world of the Regency (which in this context largely absorbs the political) has vanished like a bubble or a "globe of glass." Thus the fashionable set's claim to be "the world" (*tout le monde*) is satirized as particularly foolish, and this definitely includes Lord Byron himself, especially since his own verses reveal his continued urge to gossip about the *ton*. But as he has it elsewhere in the same canto, in the end, that "world" comes down to:

> ...the Great World, – which, being interpreted,
>   Meaneth the West or worst end of a city,
> And about twice two thousand people bred
>   By no means to be very wise or witty,
> But to sit up while others lie in bed,
>   And look down on the universe with pity...
>   (stanza 45)

Much of satire has a tendency to "look down on the universe," though not, of course, with pity. We see this condescension literalized in the concrete metaphor of one of the *Odes and Addresses to Great People* (1825) by Thomas Hood and John Hamilton Reynolds. Hood's "Ode to Mr Graham, the Aeronaut" memorializes the failed attempts at hot-air balloon flights over London in 1823 by George Graham. The rather genial speaker-satirist gets in the gondola and travels with the aeronaut, making gentle fun of the trip itself:

> Let us cast off the foolish ties
> That bind us to the earth, and rise
> And take a bird's-eye view! –
> ...
> Away! – away! – the bubble fills –
> Farewell to earth and all its hills! –
> We seem to cut the wind! –
> So high we mount, so swift we go,
> The chimney tops are far below,
> The Eagle's left behind!
>
>   4
> Ah me! My brain begins to swim! –
> The world is growing rather dim...
>   (4–6, 13–20)

In the end they land safely with a bump. Until then the device gives us a perspective from which (literally) to look down on the social life of contemporary London. The harmless folly of the balloonist is set against the myriad follies of the larger social panorama of the city itself.

The general congeniality and broad sweep across various social classes in Hood's and Reynolds' volume turned out to be prophetic of a good deal of social satire in the Victorian era. Nothing better exemplifies this genial tone than the popularity of *Punch* magazine after its first appearance in 1841. An anonymous set of "Stanzas to Pale Ale" published in the magazine sums up the general tone of many *Punch* satires: "How sweet thou art – yet bitter, too / And sparkling, like satiric fun." The editorial policy was Liberal or Radical-Reformist early on and through the 1840s and became more conservative in later decades, and there were political satires in the magazine, but a more or less comic brand of "satiric fun" remained an important element in the mix. Its visual cartoons and prose satires were more common and became better known (such as the pieces by Douglas Jerrold), but *Punch* did publish some satirical verse. Another magazine, actually entitled *Fun*, first published W. S. Gilbert's Bab Ballads (though they were later collected in book form), along with the author's illustrations, from 1866 to 1871. Resembling songs from the famous operettas (and sometimes feeding into them), these ballads contain a dose of nonsense but sometimes also darker materials.

In Gilbert's "Phrenology," Sir Herbert White calls for the arrest of an attacker only to find he has discovered a new-style policeman with more theory than common sense.

> "Observe his various bumps,
> His head as I uncover it:
> His morals lie in lumps
> All round about and over it."
> "Now take him," said SIR WHITE,
> "Or you will soon be rueing it;
> Bless me! I must be right, –
> I caught the fellow doing it!"
>
> Policeman calmly smiled,
> "Indeed you are mistaken, sir,
> You're agitated – riled –
> And very badly shaken, sir.
>
> "Sit down, and I'll explain
> My system of Phrenology...

The policeman then turns to examine the Baronet and finds that he is the true sociopath:

> "Here's Murder, Envy, Strife
> (Propensity to kill any),
> And Lies as large as life,
> And heaps of Social Villainy.
>
> "Here's Love of Bran-New Clothes,
> Embezzling – Arson – Deism –
> A taste for Slang and Oaths,
> And Fraudulent Trusteeism.
>
> "Here's Love of Groundless Charge –
> Here's Malice, too, and Trickery,
> Unusually large
> Your bump of Pocket-Pickery – "

> "Stop!" said the Bart., "my cup
> Is full – I'm worse than him in all;
> Policeman, take me up –
> No doubt I am some criminal!"
>
> That Pleeceman's scorn grew large
> (Phrenology had nettled it),
> He took that Bart. in charge –
> I don't know how they settled it.

Other ballads satirize the British clergy ("The Reverend Simon Magus" or "The Rival Curates") and religious hypocrisy ("Lost Mr Blake"). Some are more pointed in their social criticisms, such as "At a Pantomime, by a Bilious One." Here the popular theatrical entertainment becomes a vehicle for a grotesque parable of mortality, as the young enjoy the holiday pageantry and its "unaccustomed cheer." The old, however, are merely tormented, victims of a poignant Blakean Experience.

> They've seen that ghastly pantomime,
> They've felt its blighting breath,
> They know that rollicking Christmas-time
> Meant Cold and Want and Death, –
>
> Starvation – Poor Law Union fare –
> And deadly cramps and chills,
> And illness – illness everywhere,
> And crime, and Christmas bills.
>
> Those aged men so lean and wan,
> They've seen it all before,
> They know they'll see the charlatan
> But twice or three times more.
>
> And so they bear with dance and song,
> And crimson foil and green,
> They wearily sit, and grimly long
> For the Transformation Scene.

Not surprisingly (when we consider their author), the Bab Ballads with a theatrical theme are particularly effective. "Only a Dancing Girl" makes the stage a platform from which to judge social pretension. The lower-class girl hangs from her fairy's guy-wires with "fixed mechanical smile...herself, not over-clean" – in short, like the theater itself, "She acts a palpable lie." But when respectability attacks her, the author defends the tawdry thespian:

> And stately dames that bring
> Their daughters there to see,

> Pronounce the "dancing thing"
> No better than she should be,
> With her skirt at her shameful knee,
> And her painted, tainted phiz:
> Ah, matron, which of us is?
>
> (And, in sooth, it oft occurs
> That while these matrons sigh,
> Their dresses are lower than hers,
> And sometimes half as high;
> And their hair is hair they buy,
> And they use their glasses, too,
> In a way she'd blush to do.)

Taking a Dickensian turn, the ballad then shifts into a sentimental tableau of virtuous poverty.

> But change her gold and green
> For a coarse merino gown,
> And see her upon the scene
> Of her home, when coaxing down
> Her drunken father's frown,
> In his squalid cheerless den:
> She's a fairy truly, then!

For the most part, however, the tone of the Bab Ballads is gleefully mischievous. In "My Dream" the speaker envisions a land of "Topsy-Turveydom" where "vice is virtue – virtue vice" – and so on. The catalogue of inversions goes pretty far, including gender and sexuality:

> But strangest of these social twirls,
> The girls are boys – the boys are girls!
> The men are women, too – but then,
> PER CONTRA, women all are men.
>
> To one who to tradition clings
> This seems an awkward state of things,
> But if to think it out you try,
> It doesn't really signify.

This actually raises a serious question for satire: can mere and total inversion, in other words nonsense verse, "really signify" a difference with satiric effect? Doubt about this question is one reason we might not want to classify the brilliant comic verse of Edward Lear and Charles Dodgson (Lewis Carroll) as satire *per se*.

Literary Satire

When the character of Reginald Bunthorne sang "Ballad: The Aesthete" in Gilbert and Sullivan's *Patience* (1881), social satire and literary satire were combined and aimed at James Whistler, Algernon Swinburne, Oscar Wilde, and the aesthetic movement in general: "If you're anxious for to shine in the high aesthetic line, as a man of culture rare, / You must get up all the germs of the transcendental terms, and plant them everywhere." But, in fact, the *fin-de-siècle* aesthetes themselves had a satirical bent, perhaps best represented – outside of Wilde's public performances as himself – in Wilde's plays and Max Beerbohm's visual caricatures and essays for the *Yellow Book* (1894–7, and, after the turn of the century, in the collected parodies of *A Christmas Garland*, 1912, and novels such as *Zuleika Dobson*, 1911). Beerbohm once wrote a satiric Latin epigram in his copy of Gilbert's *Songs of a Savoyard* (1890), suggesting in effect that Gilbert had already satirized himself in one well-known song from *Princess Ida* (1884): "I've an irritating chuckle, I've a celebrated sneer." This anecdote usefully illustrates the way in which satiric responses to movements and schools of literature can become part of the process by which those movements and schools get constructed for the canon and literary history. Gilbert's satire of the aesthetes quickly fed into popular and critical ideas of aestheticism, just as Beerbohm's insider parodies in his caricatures of Wilde and the Pre-Raphaelites helped to define later views of *fin-de-siècle* literary style and culture.

Back at the beginning of the nineteenth century, poetry that would later come to be defined as Romantic was satirized in terms that helped to shape critical debate and, when later transvalued, critical constructions of Romanticism itself. Thus parodies of Lake School simplicity and rusticity published in *The Poetry of the Anti-Jacobin* helped to establish by popular laughter, which was later converted to or replaced by critical acclaim, what mattered most about Wordsworth or Coleridge's poetry. Similarly, Shelley's 1821 elegy for John Keats, *Adonais*, provoked parodies that are sometimes precise critical exposures of the most characteristically Romantic qualities of the Shelley circle's verse. William Maginn, for example, despite his class snobbery, caught the essence of the Hunt school's mixture of the homely and the exotically transcendent, along with its appeals to "nature" made from inner London:

> O weep for *Wontner*, for his leg is broke,
> O weep for *Wontner*, though our pearly tear
> Can never cure him. Dark and dimly broke
> The thunder cloud o'er Paul's enameled sphere...
> (Maginn 1821)

An anonymous reviewer in *Blackwood's* was in 1829 still carrying on the class war ("Oh he was great in Cockney Land, the monarch of his kind"), and by then such satires inevitably participated, by way of negative or oppositional definition, in the emergent process of canonization of the Romantics.

A similar effect was produced from within the ranks of the Romantics themselves. Shelley satirized Wordsworth (especially in *Peter Bell The Third*, 1819) in ambivalent terms that would later come to be part of literary history's construction of Romanticism: the solipsism, for example, that was the extreme version of Romantic subjectivity: "He had a mind which was somehow / At once circumference and centre / Of all he might or feel or know" (293–5). And, of course, Byron's frequent anti-Romantic satires of the Lake School, in *Don Juan, Beppo* (1818), "The Vision of Judgment," and other works, set the tone for much that was positive as well as negative in later critical views. When he said of Coleridge, "I wish he would explain his explanation" (Dedication to *Don Juan*, line 16), he was reinforcing the reputation of the "Sage of Highgate" for abstruse metaphysics, poetic symbolism, and mysticism. Byron's early couplet satire, *English Bards and Scotch Reviewers* (1809), however, struck out so broadly and sometimes indiscriminately ("Behold! in various throngs the scribbling crew") that it often seems more a settling of personal scores, personal and political, than a critical judgment.

Even parodies that were fairly light-hearted at the time and contained very little in the way of satiric intent or effect have sometimes, in the course of literary history, come to seem revealing of the essential outlines of a posthumously constructed "movement" such as Romanticism. One popular volume from the early nineteenth century stands out as an example of deft parody that has had as it were a delayed satiric effect: *Rejected Addresses* (1812) by James and Horace Smith. This collection pretended to contain entries in a competition to choose an inaugural address for the new Drury Lane Theatre. Parodic verses as if by Southey, Wordsworth, Coleridge, Byron, Moore, Scott, et al. were taken mostly as backhanded compliments at the time. But however genial in tone, "Cui Bono?" hits dead-on the target of Byron's pose of Romantic ennui:

> Sated with home, of wife, of children tired,
> The restless soul is driven abroad to roam;
> Sated abroad, all seen, yet nought admired,
> The restless soul is driven to ramble home;
> Sated with both, beneath new Drury's dome
> The fiend Ennui awhile consents to pine,
> There growls, and curses, like a deadly Gnome,
> Scorning to view fantastic Columbine,
> Viewing with scorn and hate the nonsense of the Nine.
> (1–9)

Similarly, a "lisping" ballad in the voice of a rustic girl, "Nancy Lake," works to satirize the traits of "simplicity" and "nature" that Wordsworth's harsher critics also attacked, and that his supporters, conversely, valued as characteristic.

At the end of the nineteenth century, Romantic obsessions with nature and subjectivity, by then part of Victorian assumptions about Romanticism and poetry in general, remain the subject of a dark satire by Thomas Hardy, which will serve to close the present survey. In "The Darkling Thrush," quite pointedly composed on the final day of the century ("The Century's corpse outleant"), Hardy stands dry-eyed before every nightingale and skylark poem ever effusively uttered by a nineteenth-century poet. Aeolian music does not play for this speaker – "The tangled bine-stems scored the sky / Like strings of broken lyres" (5–6) – and nature is no longer Romantically organic: "The ancient pulse of germ and birth / Was shrunken hard and dry" (13–14). Ruskin's "pathetic fallacy" and Romantic figurations of nature have in this case merely depressing rather than transcendent results.

> At once a voice arose among
>   The bleak twigs overhead
> In a full-hearted evensong
>   Of joy illimited;
> An aged thrush, frail, gaunt, and small,
>   In blast-beruffled plume,
> Had chosen thus to fling his soul
>   Upon the growing gloom.
>
> So little cause for carolings
>   Of such ecstatic sound
> Was written on terrestrial things
>   Afar or nigh around,
> That I could think there trembled through
>   His happy good-night air
> Some blessed Hope, whereof he knew
>   And I was unaware.
>   (17–32)

Nothing could be more darkly and effectively parodic, in form and satiric intent, of Romantic poetry's imagery and transcendental effusions on nature and human feeling. We are only a short step away, here, in this "blast-beruffled," anti-Romantic poem from the even colder and more thoroughly disillusioned satiric eye of high Modernism.

REFERENCES AND FURTHER READING

Dyer, Gary (1997) *British Satire and the Politics of Style, 1789–1832.* Cambridge: Cambridge University Press.

Henkle, Roger B. (1980) *Comedy and Culture: England 1820–1900.* Princeton, NJ: Princeton University Press.

Jones, Steven E. (2000) *Satire and Romanticism.* New York: St Martin's Press.

——(ed.) (2003) *The Satiric Eye: Forms of Satire in the Romantic Period.* New York: Palgrave Macmillan.

[Maginn, William] (1821) Review of Shelley's *Adonais. Blackwood's Edinburgh Magazine* December: 696–700.

Strachan, John (ed.) (2003) *British Satire, 1785–1840,* 5 vols. London: Pickering and Chatto.

19
Narrative Satire in the Nineteenth Century
Frank Palmeri

In the course of the nineteenth century, narrative satire underwent a period of eclipse by other forms, but it also experienced a return. For many decades, the cultural circumstances were such that satire did not determine the overall genre of narratives. Displaced by other forms, it played almost exclusively a subordinate and episodic role beginning in the 1840s. However, by the late 1880s, works again began to appear with the generic features of narrative satire predominant.

Narrative satire does not merely refer to isolated or episodic satiric attacks in fictional narratives or novels; rather, this genre can be distinguished both from verse satire and from novelistic forms. Whereas verse satire tends to criticize or attack its object from a single perspective in a sermonizing way, narrative satire in its full form criticizes one side of a cultural opposition, but also turns to undermine the position that its previous criticism had seemed to endorse. In this form of satire, neither of the opposite extremes is authorized, but each is parodied or criticized strongly. Moreover, it is also usually difficult to infer a normative position between these extremes. By contrast with the absence of middle grounds in most narrative satire, novelistic forms seek accommodation between the different positions they represent: for example, an individual protagonist and his or her social context (as in the *Bildungsroman*), or the classes represented by a couple who in the end marry (as in dramatic comedy or the comic realistic novel). The lack of authorized moderate positions can often make narrative satire appear intemperate and excessive. In addition, such satire generally pays more attention to the physical processes of the body than do other forms such as comedy, epic, and romance.

To help explain the constriction of the possibilities for satire in mid- and late nineteenth-century narrative, it will be helpful to discuss conditions of fictional publication at the time in Britain, including the dominance of the three-volume novel, as well as the structure and boundaries of the arena for fictional and non-fictional discussions in print. The circulating library that mandated the triple-decker novel exercised a rigorous censorship of references to sexual activities. In addition, the public sphere in mid-Victorian Britain was structured in such a way that extreme positions on both the right and left were discouraged or silenced, while positions in the middle dominated the conversation. Changes in both of these areas in the last two decades of the century help account for the renewal of satiric and ironic energies at that time. While this discussion will concentrate on the history of satiric narrative in Britain, it will also take notice of cognate and influential developments in other European and American cultures. In the United States and France in particular, although the conditions of publication and the workings of the public sphere differed from those in Britain, some parallels existed and so did parallels in the course of narrative satire.

In the late seventeenth and early eighteenth century, both verse and narrative satire flourished and even for a time assumed a predominant position among genres. However, the increasing production and popularity of novels accompanied a decline in the cultural work accomplished by satire. The development of a pluralist public sphere in Britain, including the emergence of a loyal opposition, provided an arena for the expression of disagreements with official policies which therefore no longer had to be couched in indirect, ironic, and satiric terms. Another side of the developing public sphere was the opening up of a private, domestic life outside the reach of government; this dimension became the privileged subject of novelistic representation. By the second half of the eighteenth century, narrative satire had lost the prominent position it had occupied earlier, at least in Britain. The emergence of a pluralistic public arena occurred first in Britain and proceeded further there than on the Continent, and so did the increasing strength and proliferation of novelistic forms and the fading away of satiric narratives (Palmeri 2003).

From the 1790s to the 1830s

In the aftermath of the French Revolution, the political controversies of the 1790s may appear to have halted this development, at least for a time. Many of the radical novels of the decade employ strong satire in inverting social conventions and undercutting political elites. For example, near the end of Elizabeth Inchbald's *Nature and Art* (1796), in a barbed satiric irony, the judge who sentences a ruined young woman to death is the same man who first seduced and abandoned her. Inchbald also has her characters reflect on the constricted public sphere that in the novel favors conservatives and limits liberal characters; the same phenomenon led the author herself to moderate the satire of political authorities in the final, published version of her novel. From an opposing ideological perspective, Elizabeth Hamilton satirizes radicals in *Memoirs of Modern Philosophers* (1800) by showing each of her female protagonists seduced and abandoned by an atheistic villain, and the more highly born, poorly educated by an irreligious father. But, as these typical examples show, most of the novels of the 1790s are not full narrative satires because they carry out an attack on only one position, leaving unquestioned the solid authority of its unsatirized political or cultural opposite. Little irony or ambivalence is to be found in novels from this decade; rather, such works usually read as narrative expansions and expositions of the verse satire in the *Anti-Jacobin* journal. (On the anti-Jacobin novels and the verse satire in the *Anti-Jacobin*, see Butler 1975; Dyer 1997.) One notable instance of double-edged satire in the period is Maria Edgeworth's *Castle Rackrent* (1800), which overtly satirizes the Irish retainer's habits of speech and thought, but also, through his long monologue, paints a devastating portrait of the feckless family of absentee owners for whom he has worked for three generations. Also consistent with the implications of narrative satire in this period are the prints of James Gillray, whose caricatures of the king and queen on their close-stools, or of the younger Pitt as a mushroom (see figure 16.3) seem hardly less vitriolic than his depictions of the revolutionary Parisians as cannibals or of Napoleon as a megalomaniacal midget (see figure 16.9).

Narrative satire did not persist in the works of the most well-known novelists publishing at the time. The narratives of Jane Austen and Walter Scott contain satiric energies, but seek consistently to contain and domesticate them. For example, in *Pride and Prejudice* (1813), Elizabeth Bennett is a satiric observer of individual characters and social conventions whose insightful sharpness will be tamed by her marriage to Darcy. Similarly, characters such as Edie Ochiltree in Scott's *The Antiquary* (1816) serve an important function as witty truth-tellers; in fact, Ochiltree, the king's licensed beggar, resembles a court jester in the way that he can sharply criticize the antiquary to his own face. Still, Edie's independence is somewhat reduced, and he becomes a kind of *genius loci* when he is given a small house to stay in whenever he is in the neighborhood by the young couple whose marriage concludes the work.

Despite these movements toward novelistic accommodation and comedy, narrative satire did persist after the Napoleonic wars, and even flourished for a period in the late 1810s and early 1820s, through three major practitioners and the subgenres in which they worked. Perhaps the most innovative and most popular of these subgenres was the dual media satire in which children's literature was given a political adaptation by William Hone and accompanied by the satiric caricatures of George Cruikshank. Cruikshank and Hone criticized the harshly repressive policies of the government in a series of works that included: *The Political House That Jack Built* (1819), in which the children's rhyme is adapted to express a radical understanding of the political situation, and author and artist present the printing press (such as the press owned by Hone) as the only source of resistance to a universally corrupt political and religious establishment; *The Matrimonial Ladder* (1820), in which they used a children's game to side with the queen against the king who had initiated divorce proceedings against her; and *The Political Showman – At Home!* (1821), which exhibited and described prominent political figures as grotesque reptilian creatures in a cabinet of curiosities. The combination of well-known popular genres with fierce personal caricatures affected the style of satire through the 1820s (Wood 1994: 215–16).

During the same years, another innovative form of narrative satire appeared. The first two cantos of Byron's *Don Juan* were published in 1819, and the poem remained unfinished when he died five years later. Written in a colloquial and versatile ottava rima, the work has none of the characteristics of formal verse satire: it does not take a sermonizing, monological, and conservative approach to moral and social issues; rather, Byron typically uses the couplet at the end of each stanza to puncture conventional pieties and spiritual pretenses with irreverent worldly wisdom about our physical nature. He does not direct his criticism at a single, consistent object of satire (although he does consistently mock Wordsworth and Southey), but the poem does possess a paradoxical coherence and structure deriving from the mercurial narrative voice. The very inconsistencies of that voice are consistent; the digressiveness and lack of structure give the work its structural principle; and the incompleteness of the work indicates its closeness to the open-endedness of life. In all these ways, and in making the narrative voice rather than the title character the real protagonist of his poem, Byron incorporated Romantic irony into narrative satire; he prepared the way for others simultaneously to employ and critique Romantic sensibilities using a satiric form characteristic of the early eighteenth century. Certainly, the narrator of Pushkin's *Evgeny Onegin* (1823–31) reveals a comparably mercurial voice, which includes a wry, unsentimental nostalgia, a mischievousness, and a piercing sense of the frequent lack of accord between our desires and their object. A similar combination of Romantic irony and narrative satire characterizes the *Operette Morali* (1827) of Giacomo Leopardi. Almost all of these short pieces are dialogues in the manner of Lucian, but their tone is dry, open-eyed, stoical, and grim. They set in tension with each other a passionate and disappointed Romantic yearning for understanding on the one hand, and on the other such eighteenth-century forms as a conjectural history of the human race and a dialogue concerning the significance of suffering and evil (similar to Hume's *Dialogues Concerning Natural Religion*, 1777).

The British government made energetic efforts in this period to narrow the sphere of public discussion and to silence dissent. William Hone had to defend himself against three charges of blasphemous libel for parodies he wrote during the time of his collaboration with Cruikshank (Gilmartin 1996: 114–45). Most of Percy Shelley's radical writings were not able to be published in England before his death in 1822. And Byron, although his exile was self-imposed, wrote all of *Don Juan* outside Britain. By contrast, the third kind of satiric narrative that was prominent in this period, the short narratives of Thomas Peacock, did not arouse outrage and efforts at censorship, even though Peacock was a friend of Shelley and a member of liberal literary circles. Perhaps this was because Peacock cast a skeptical light on the enthusiasms and inconsistencies of the Romantics and liberal intellectuals themselves. In *Nightmare Abbey* (1818), he satirizes Shelley's millenarianism and misanthropic alienation from English society as well as the foibles of several members of his circle; in *Crotchet Castle* (1831), he parodies the arguments of political economists and adherents to the cause of progress; in *Melincourt* (1817), he presents an orangutan as a member of Parliament. But in each case his satire is multidimensional. In *Melincourt*, he not only satirizes Lord Monboddo's idea that orangutans are human, he also adopts the idea with a shrug and takes it further, allowing Monboddo to express his arguments at length in the footnotes. In *Nightmare Abbey*, he mocks not only Shelley, but also his antagonist Coleridge, for woolly-headed incomprehensibility. In *Crotchet Castle*, he undermines not only the progressive economists but also the conservative gentry and churchmen who pack away gourmet meals as they refuse to recognize that poor people exist who do not have enough to eat; in addition, he parodically satirizes both the party of progress in the nineteenth century and the partisans of the medieval period who see the pre-modern world as the source of all high and noble values. As in narrative satires by Rabelais and Swift, in Peacock's works, the satiric attacks are wide-ranging and multidirectional: no ideological position is exempt from his examination of intellectual hobbyhorses and foibles. However, it can also seem with Peacock's satires, as it does with Lucian's, that parodically representing multiple sides of every question makes little difference: the talkers around the well-laden table keep talking, the monaural thinkers maintain their fixed ideas, and nothing changes.

The publication of Peacock's narratives from the late 1810s through the 1820s (a last instance, *Gryll Grange*, appeared in 1860 but in a very different cultural moment) indicates the persistence of narrative satire as a cultural force during that time. Thomas Carlyle's first narrative points to the same conclusion. However different it may appear to be from Peacock's sedate conversations, *Sartor Resartus* (1833–4), like other narrative satires, employs extravagant language, pursues large intellectual ambitions, and moves from a resounding negation of the world's emptiness to an answering affirmation of its plenitude, leaving unexplored a possible middle ground between these two extremes. However, the 1830s and 1840s also saw a dramatic displacement of satire by other forms, primarily the comic novel. The passage of the first Reform Bill in 1832 brought to an end a fifty-year period of iron-fisted rule by conservative governments. The Reform Bill did not open up the franchise for workers or women, but it did allow middle-class men with a modest amount of property to participate in the political process. During the four years following the passage of the bill, radicals agitated for repeal of the stamp tax on periodical publications, an instrument employed by government in the earlier part of the century to restrict access to radical newspapers by making them too expensive for workers. In 1836, Parliament voted not to eliminate the stamp tax entirely, but to reduce it from four pence to one penny. Like the Reform Bill, this act strengthened the middle both socially and politically (see Wahrman 1995, on the growing importance of conceptions of the social and political middle in early nineteenth-century Britain). Relieved of most of the tax, middle-ground, established papers, such as *The Times* and the *Morning Chronicle*, could reduce their price and increase their circulation; however, because of such expansions, the tax still made it difficult for a daily radical paper to survive. Extreme perspectives of the left and right were discouraged by the legislation (on the stamp tax, see Wiener 1969).

Thackeray, Dickens, and Trollope

Narrative satire was not displaced or even rendered invisible for a time solely because of the reduction in the stamp tax; however, such legislation can contribute to and serve as a marker of long-range trends. Even before Victoria became queen in 1837, changes in the cultural landscape had begun, with the result that it became a violation of standards of decency to make reference to what Mikhail Bakhtin has called the "material stratum of the lower body," that is, to sexual and excretory processes. But one of the defining traits of satire is that it brings professions of high ideals and spiritual values into contact with these processes on an earthy physical plane in order to demystify them. After Victoria's accession, this trend grew stronger. In addition, the pressures that were moving cultural and political discourse away from polarized extremes and toward the expression of moderate positions also intensified. As Dror Wahrman shows, during the 1830s, it became vital to claim that one's position occupied a middle ground: the middle class was conceived of as the hinge that unified the nation, and moderate positions were associated with the health, strength, and growth of society. Because narrative satire devotes its energies to extremes, in order to parody them, but typically leaves absent the representation of normative middle grounds, the genre must work against the strong current of a cultural framework like that of early and mid-Victorian Britain. Similar regimes of decency and moderation associated with middle-class ascendancy and ideology also obtained in the United States and France at about the same time (on the situation in France, see Cohen 1999).

To see what happens to narrative satire in such cultural circumstances, we might examine some late examples of such satire, in the early career of William Thackeray. The major characters of Thackeray's fiction from the late 1830s to the mid-1840s – from Barry Lyndon and Captain Rook to Bob Stubbs in *The Fatal Boots* (1839) and Brandon in *A Shabby Genteel Story* (1840) – are cruel rogues, seedy spongers, or audacious poseurs, and part of the satire is directed at their moral bankruptcy. But Thackeray also finds the dupes to be somewhat complicit in their own victimization because of their foolish reverence for those who have any acquaintance with titled aristocrats. Moreover, Thackeray indicates that the sycophancy of both the villains and the fools extends through the entire range of classes (excepting the poorest class of workers). The same thesis informs his *Snobs of England*, which appeared serially in *Punch* for fifty-two weeks in 1846–7: from the lowest boarding house widow to the highest peer, the English are defined as being arrogant toward those below them and obsequious to those above; in this way and in others, wealthy aristocrats prove to be the moral equivalents of bankrupt gamblers or the newly rich. Thackeray extends and sharpens this satiric analysis of British society on an epic level in *Vanity Fair* (1847–8). Becky Sharp is a designing, unscrupulous, and unloving climber whose skills as a performer propel her for a short time to the top of the social ladder. Fascinated with her intelligence and sharp observations of others, which resemble his own, the author nevertheless criticizes her scheming heartlessness. On the other hand, it is also clear that he sees no moral superiority in a Lord Steyne or Sir Pitt Crawley. Indeed, the grasping, self-absorbed, and ruthless aristocrats and gentry are even worse than Becky because, no matter how serious their guilt, no one will speak against them, and, unlike the talented and intelligent newcomer, they will always go unpunished. They are too rich and established to be criticized, except in a narrative such as Thackeray's. Moreover, few if any characters occupy an admirable middle ground in the novel: Amelia is mocked for being whimpering and deluded. The decent and good Dobbins comes closest to embodying positive values in the narrative, but he is also pathetic in his early idolizing of Osborne and in his love of Amelia, whom he wins only after he has seen through her.

However, *Vanity Fair* constitutes the last instance and highest accomplishment of narrative satire in early Victorian Britain. After the success of his first full-length novel, Thackeray became much less interested in the schemes of roguish outsiders or the parallels between their doings and the everyday actions of the rich and titled in English society. In *Pendennis* (1848–50), he traces the semi-autobiographical early life and career of a writer, revealing in his preface that he had wanted to represent the typical young gentleman's sexual activities precisely in order to criticize them, but was prohibited from doing so by the canons of decency. Ironically, Thackeray himself had observed and helped shape those canons in his time at *Punch* (Palmeri 2004). In the last quarter of the novel, Thackeray does provide a satiric portrayal of the publishing world of the 1830s, when Pendennis was a journeyman writer, but the main object of his criticism there, apart from unscrupulous authors and publishers, is the aggressively satiric tone of the book reviews at the time. In the same chapters, Pendennis must turn away from a cynical selfishness in order to accept the love of the patient and submissive Laura, and his cynicism is identified with a satiric attitude. Thus, satiric energies in *Pendennis* are directed only against satire itself. The tendency that begins in this work continues in Thackeray's later novels. In *Henry Esmond* (1852), Swift is one of the main historical objects of satire (for example, in Book 3, ch. 5), and in the end the novel traces the protagonist's disillusioned withdrawal from an engagement with public and historical events to the world of his private affairs. In *The Newcomes* (1853–5), criticism of the market for young women in marriage surfaces occasionally, but it is difficult to decide whether or not the narrator, Pendennis, is treated ironically because of his self-satisfied shallowness. Thackeray's novels of the 1850s thus render satire more obscure and subordinate it to other forms. The satiric and skeptical questioning of the moral basis of the British social system that informed *Vanity Fair* goes underground or into eclipse.

By the time *Vanity Fair* was published, Dickens had been the preeminent novelist in England for a decade. Although Thackeray's career may exhibit a clear engagement with and then retreat from the use of satire, Dickens's career is often considered to move in an opposed direction and to demonstrate an increasing prominence of satiric energies after beginning in the genre of the comic with the essayistic *Sketches by Boz* (1836) and, more importantly, the episodic and madcap novel *Pickwick Papers* (1837).

Although narrative satire does not extend beyond passing and localized effects in most of Dickens's novels, satiric social criticism of institutions does play an important role in the plot and the significance of several of them. Nevertheless, even in most of the novels where it is employed, the satire does not exert a constitutive effect on the genre of the narrative. Of the four novels discussed here, the satiric and social critical elements come close to determining the genre and the implications of the narrative only in *Bleak House* (1853).

In *Nicholas Nickleby* (1839), satiric criticism of the Yorkshire schools expressed through headmaster Squeers's sadistic treatment of the unloved boys in his care contributes to the plot and colors the tone of the narrative. At the school, Nicholas meets the brain-damaged Smike, who will prove to be related to the Nicklebys, and the early placement of the episode and Smike's eventual death strike a somber tone, indicating how badly unfortunate children (such as the Nicklebys) could be treated. However, the entire episode takes up only a few chapters of the novel, and most of the rest of the narrative conveys a barely contained exuberance in the invention of characters (such as those in Crummles' theatrical troupe), with their distinctive uses of language, and the description of things (for example, the profusion of objects displayed in London shop windows at the beginning of chapter 32). The narrative rescues both Nicholas and his sister from real degradation or corruption, the villains' plans are foiled, and appropriate marriages for the Nickleby siblings are arranged. In two other works that satirize institutions established for the care and education of children, the satire is also peripheral or unpersuasive. In *Oliver Twist* (1838), the memorable satire of the Poor Law sets up but also gives way to the genre of the criminal novel; and in *Hard Times* (1854), the satiric implication that a utilitarian education will lead children to become amoral embezzlers may connect the children's education to the principal plot, but it also simplifies radically and strains credulity.

Martin Chuzzlewit (1844) strongly satirizes American journalism for being unscrupulous, scandal-driven, and boorish in its loud assertions of American superiority to Britain or any other country. It also exposes swindles in which land sold as prime western real estate turns out to be a pestilential swamp that almost causes Martin's death. But the energies of the novel during all of its second half turn away from such satire and focus on the way in which Martin sheds his egotism as his loyal servant nurses him through his fever, and then on the thwarting of his evil uncle's schemes, the reconciliation with his grandfather, and the requisite marriages of Martin, his servant, and his friend. A similar pattern persists even in *Little Dorrit* (1857), where the satire of British institutions extends to a more searching and somber criticism than the rather high-spirited attack on American ways in *Martin Chuzzlewit*. The portrayal of the Circumlocution Office shows the constricting effects exerted by the government bureaucracy and the emblematic family of the Barnacles on the intellectual and entrepreneurial life of the nation. Moreover, the Marshalsea Prison for debtors comes to represent a microcosm of British society as a place of confinement, at least for those who once had property, but have lost everything including the chance to work to repay their debts (Trilling 1955). Again, however, almost the entire second half of *Little Dorrit* moves away from this harsh criticism of institutions, after William Dorrit receives a large legacy that enables the family to travel on the Continent, where he must learn to deal with riches better than he dealt with poverty. Arthur Clennam has to endure Marshalsea briefly in his turn, but the novel focuses on resolving family mysteries and bringing together Arthur and Amy Dorrit. As the two of them begin their life together, merging into the river of pedestrians outside the prison, the novel concludes with a scene of the comic sublime.

Although satire plays an important role, it remains subordinate to other genres, especially the imperatives of comedy, in *Nicholas Nickleby*, *Martin Chuzzlewit*, and *Little Dorrit*. The narratives in all these works bring together young couples as emblems of the reconciliation of divisions between classes and within families. Even as they include a focus on injustices, cruelties, and swindles, these plots bridge oppositions and point to imagined ways of redressing the consequences of such wrongs. *Bleak House* (1853) does not move toward such an overcoming of contradictions. Although the Court of Chancery did not affect large numbers of people in Britain, Dickens finds in its interminable workings a resonant metaphor for the entanglement of the society's energies in empty, arcane, long-standing, and soul-deadening procedures. Even more than the two institutions in *Little Dorrit*, the law brings into contact characters from across the entire spectrum of English society, and almost everyone whom the legal system touches in this novel is corrupted, destroyed, or driven mad by it. The young couple of Richard and Ada do marry, but since Richard is intoxicated with the prospect of riches from winning the suit, he applies himself to no profession, and dies upon learning that the case has come to an end after the entire estate has been consumed by legal fees. Esther Summerson's contracting of smallpox from the street-sweeper Jo illustrates the relations that exist among all parts of this society, as well as the consequences for other classes of housing the poor in fetid, unhealthy tenements. Moreover, Esther's decision to accept the proposal of marriage from her guardian Jarndyce, who is more than twice her age, indicates an acceptance of an asexual and non-productive life by the protagonist and co-narrator. When the young doctor whom she loves returns from overseas, Jarndyce eventually releases Esther from her promise so she can marry Woodcourt, but the many deaths, the mental impairments, and the physical disfigurements in this narrative work against the weak comic form of the conclusion. *Bleak House* may not be predominantly a satire, but it is a tragic novel that has been extensively shaped by satire. It even includes a dialogue of perspectives in alternating between the first-person narration of Esther's story and the anonymous third-person narration of the rest of the novel. Still, neither of these perspectives embodies a cultural ideology, nor is either parodied or satirized. In fact, Dickens's novels do not generally parody both sides in a cultural position and leave a normative middle ground unspecified. Rather, his satire usually takes the form of a more one-directional attack on a corrupt institution. In Dickens's distinctive blend of satiric forms, the sermonizing perspective resembles that of most verse satire, while the criticism of established institutions is more characteristic of narrative satire.

Some of Trollope's novels more effectively express the doubleness of narrative satire, especially when they concern the actions of women who are stigmatized for failing to conform to the canons of feminine modesty. In *Barchester Towers* (1857), for example, the beautiful, mysterious, and crippled Signora Neroni, née Stanhope, toys with and fascinates to their own embarrassment and loss nearly all the men she encounters in England, thus serving as a foil to the heroine, the timid Eleanor Bold. However, it is only because she intervenes on behalf of the innocent and shy clergyman Francis Arabin that he is able to marry Eleanor and the novel is able to come to a comic conclusion. Despite being condemned by the narrative, Signora Neroni thus advances its resolution. Similarly, *The Eustace Diamonds* (1872) revolves around the question of whether the necklace of the title rightly belongs to the widow of Sir Florian Eustace. Lizzie, who claims her husband gave her the gems, is untrustworthy, unscrupulous, and scandalous in her behavior, including her simultaneous pursuit of more than one potential second husband. The narrator repeatedly expresses strong disapproval of her, and she is punished by having to marry an unctuous clergyman of Jewish background from Eastern Europe. However, late in the novel it emerges that, according to the most authoritative legal mind in England, the diamonds do rightly belong to Lizzie (or would, if they were in her possession – they have been stolen twice by this point). Although the narrative cruelly scapegoats her, Lizzie's position is thus also in at least this one important sense vindicated against the family's lawyer, the common opinion, and the narrator's own repeated condemnations of her. Moreover, Frank Greystoke, who occupies the normative middle ground, exhibits a notable weakness of character: even though he eventually decides to marry the governess who is his fiancée, for most of the novel he ignores her and pays fascinated attention to Lizzie.

If *The Eustace Diamonds* makes use of many elements of narrative satire, *The Way We Live Now* (1875) extends these on a much larger canvas to produce one of the first full-length narrative satires in Britain since *Vanity Fair*. Behind loud protestations of their probity and high-mindedness, almost all the characters in this novel give evidence of financial, moral, or intellectual bankruptcy. Melmotte the financier floats stock for a huge railway scheme in America with no assets to back it up. In a satire of the publishing world that echoes *Pendennis*, reviews by Lady Carbury and others bear no relation to the quality of the books, but provide the means of repaying favors or pursuing personal animosities. Young aristocrats prove to be drunken louts who pay their gambling debts with worthless IOUs; one bungles his elopement with the financier's daughter because of his drinking and gambling. As in Trollope's other novels, a transgressive woman, in this case an American who shot a man in San Francisco, is the object of fascination and anxiety. And as in other narrative satires, a normative middle ground is lacking: Paul Montague is a young man compromised by his relation with Melmotte, and Sir Roger Carbury, the titular head of his extended family, is neither particularly memorable nor particularly strong.

Satire, Novels, and the Public Sphere

Thus, between the 1840s and the 1880s, satire appears in British narratives not as a determining form, but in a subordinate role, in isolated episodes of works shaped primarily by other genres (including children's literature such as *The Water Babies*, 1863, and *Alice's Adventures in Wonderland*, 1865). If *Vanity Fair* is one of the last narrative satires to appear in the early part of this period of eclipse, *The Way We Live Now* is one of the first to appear as the period was coming to an end. One important reason for this occlusion of satire was the reign of Mudie's, the powerful circulating library. Organized in the mid-1840s, Mudie's lent out volumes for a modest annual subscription fee; specializing in the three-volume novel, they were able to lend parts of the same novel to different borrowers simultaneously. By the early 1860s, the library was buying more than one hundred and fifty thousand volumes each year. Mudie excluded works from his library based on rigorously censorious standards that prohibited anything controversial in religion or politics and anything that referred to or even hinted at sexual activities (Griest 1970). By the mid-1860s, Mudie's was joined by W. H. Smith, which served train stations and towns along railroad lines. In addition, many novels of the period were originally serialized in monthly parts, and both the journals and Smith enforced the same standards of decency and conformity as Mudie's (on the tensions between the editors of such journals and their authors, see Maurer 1959). In such a publishing environment, where being banned by Mudie's meant the loss of thousands of copies in sales, the pressures were formidable to meet Mudie's criteria.

As already noted, the standards of Mudie's, Smith, and the magazines worked directly against the most characteristic features of narrative satire: a demystifying attention to the processes of the lower body, and a parodic representation of both sides of a cultural opposition with no clear sign of a normative, mediating term. Mudie's has often been seen as enforcing middle-class values on Victorian literature; it did so by strongly encouraging an uncontroversial cultural politics of the social, political, and religious middle. George Meredith's *Ordeal of Richard Feverel* (1859) was rejected by Mudie's because it deployed irony, satire, and finally tragedy to depict the consequences of a repressive education; and Meredith had to rely on journalism for a time thereafter because of the novel's poor sales. However, by the 1880s, younger novelists were rebelling against the constricting standards of Mudie's, and the circulating libraries and journals began to lose their stranglehold on the cultural politics — and on the form — of fiction. Processes of the body, and especially cultural attitudes outside the middle, began to figure more prominently in later Victorian literature, and so did the form of satire in which such subjects appropriately found their expression.

The constraints effected by the circulating libraries and the journals were not the sole and determining cause of the eclipse of satire; they played their part among a network of contributing and competing pressures. To understand another part of this network, we might look briefly at a passage from John Stuart Mill's *On Liberty* (1859). In the last paragraph of chapter 2, Mill considers the argument that freedom of speech should be allowed as long as the speech is temperate. At first, he is skeptical about the ability to draw a clear line between moderate and immoderate speech. But Mill goes on to offer a crucial insight when he observes that sarcasm, invective, and personal reflections do not persuade the adherents of an established opinion to come over to the side of those who challenge it, whereas the partisans of prevailing views allow themselves a wide latitude in the use of such tactics against their opponents. In Mill's analysis, the extreme rhetoric of sarcasm functions in the public sphere in one direction only – to discredit the positions and characters of dissidents. Still, he suggests that even though they are at a disadvantage, it is in the interest of those who criticize established positions only to employ careful and moderate language themselves. He does not endorse efforts to censor the speech of conservatives, but instead calls on participants on all sides to condemn bigotry, intolerance, and personal attacks whenever they occur. Thus, although he sets out by doubting the possibility of banning immoderate public speech, Mill's understanding of the workings of discursive forms in the public sphere suggests the tactical prudence and even the general desirability of avoiding satiric, personal, or sarcastic forms of speech. The validity of Mill's analysis may not be limited to Victorian society, but it does indicate one of the mechanisms by which the framework of discussion in the public arena tends to pressure participants, especially those who contest established policies, toward the center and away from the satiric focus on extremes.

Although restrictions of space prevent detailed discussion here of the conditions of publication and the sphere of public discussion in other countries during the nineteenth century, some of the most innovative and influential narrative satire of the century was written in Russia, France, and the United States. In his short novels *The Nose* (1836) and *The Overcoat* (1842), Nikolai Gogol pioneered a form of satire that combined bizarre logic and surrealistic dream elements with realistic details of the lives of poor urban Russians to satirize the government bureaucracy and the texture of modern life in the capital (censors originally prevented the publication of *The Nose*). In *Lost Illusions* (1837–43), Honoré de Balzac depicted the compromises and corruption necessary for a successful career as a writer in early nineteenth-century France, in a sharp satire of the publishing industry that parallels Thackeray's representation of English publishing in *Pendennis* later in the decade. Herman Melville, in *The Confidence-Man* (1857), satirized both knavish confidence men and their credulous and foolish marks because both pledge their faith and credit to a commercial system in which all has become external signs and nothing of substance can be found; the novel, Melville's last, sold only about two hundred copies.

The Return of Satire

As already noted, Meredith's *Ordeal of Richard Feverel* suffered a fate similar to Melville's novel for having challenged the canons of decency enforced by Mudie's lending library. Although it took another two decades, by the 1880s other writers were protesting against the constraints placed upon their subject matter and means of expression by the circulating libraries and literary magazines. Among these were George Moore, who wrote *Literature at Nurse, or Circulating Morals* (1885) as a protest against the system, and Thomas Hardy, who repeatedly tangled with the editors of journals over charges of indecency (Maurer 1959). But we might look to an earlier work for a sign that the system that constrained the publication of satiric narrative was beginning to weaken, and for an indication of why. Samuel Butler's *Erewhon* (1872) may appear at first to portray a utopian society, but as the narrative proceeds, it becomes clear that Erewhon is far from ideal, and in fact that it closely and uncomfortably resembles British society of Butler's day. The novel satirizes the hypocritical practice of established religiosity in England as well as the system of higher education. Its method is deeply ironic and ambiguous, citing Erewhonian defenders of their only apparently inverted order. No middle ground between or apart from Erewhonian and British society is present. Perhaps most importantly, through the example of a society that has banished industrial machines, Butler contests the idea that technological advances have led and will continue to lead to progressive improvement in the conditions of life in modern society. He thus fails to provide middle grounds between opposed perspectives, and undermines the ideology of progress of the middle classes. The stasis of his strangely familiar society, based ironically on a Darwinian argument, indicates a weakening of the Whiggish view of history as progressive. Utopias often are based on an underside of satire, and later utopias such as William Morris's *News from Nowhere* (1891) and narratives of the future such as H. G. Wells's *The Time Machine* (1895) express increasing doubts about what had been a narrative of historical progress with its acme in the nineteenth century.

Challenges to the system of publishing helped make possible the reappearance of narrative satire as the dominant, constitutive form of works, and Butler's novel anticipates the direction that would be taken by the genre on its return. The satires that finally emerge after thirty or forty years of fugitive and fragmentary existence generally are skeptical of or oppose the ideology of the middle class, especially the view of that class as the ground of mediation between opposites that guarantees open-ended historical progress. This position holds true not only for British but for continental and American examples of resurgent narrative satire as well. For example, in Flaubert's *Bouvard and Pécuchet* (1881), after retiring to the country, the two copyists of the title attempt to research and apply all the knowledge available in books concerning the various subjects that successively interest them, including agriculture, history, religion, literature, and education. In each case their projects misfire and show the inconsistencies, contradictions, and uncertainties contained in all the disciplines of knowledge. By the end, the hapless but well-intentioned pair are ostracized by their society as dangerous provocateurs; having learned and demonstrated the emptiness of middle-class knowledges, they decide to return to their former occupation of copying. Flaubert's narrative takes the form of an encyclopedic satire of the ideology of progress through increasing knowledge: in his work, no such progress takes place, and the pursuit of it leads to disaster. Nor can one find grounds of mediation or accommodation between opposing values in any cultural field. *Bouvard and Pécuchet* thus constitutes a deliberate, meta-satiric emptying out of middle-class culture and knowledge.

The narrative in Friedrich Nietzsche's *Genealogy of Morals* (1888) similarly overturns established nineteenth-century understandings of history, morals, and religion. Nietzsche finds no improvement in history, rather only the evidence of continuing struggles for power between groups with opposing interests, languages, and views of the world. In the history of morals and religion, it is not a progress but a degeneration from an earlier, healthier, more aristocratic regime that has led to Christian morality, with its emphasis on compassion, self-sacrifice, and asceticism. In astringent and sarcastic language, Nietzsche pursues the kind of unbridled argument that had been avoided by thinkers and writers for most of the preceding century (significantly, in chapter 2 of *On Liberty*, Mill offers a brief critique of Christian morals that anticipates Nietzsche's by several decades, but casts it in reasonable, temperate terms).

Although Mark Twain is not a philosopher of the order of Nietzsche, many of his late works, only published posthumously, exhibit a similarly caustic critique of Christianity (see Twain 1962); others, published at the time of writing, indicate a resurgence of narrative satire in America. *A Connecticut Yankee in King Arthur's Court* (1889), for example, satirizes the ignorance, inequality, and crudity of life in the Middle Ages, as well as the celebration of chivalry by historical novelists beginning with Walter Scott. However, in its last few chapters the satire reverses direction. Rather than ridiculing the medieval past, the satire exposes the Yankee engineer, who can only defend his modern democratic ideas by using dynamite and machine-guns to kill the thousands of knights in England. The past world may have been superstitious and crude, but the modern world seems to excel chiefly in the efficiency with which it brings about the violent deaths of multitudes. In the familiar pattern of narrative satire, there is no normative ground to occupy apart from the unacceptable alternatives represented in the work.

The works of Oscar Wilde that deserve mention in an account of narrative satire in the nineteenth century are not his short novel or stories, but his paradoxical and ironic dialogue-essays, "The Decay of Lying" (1889) and "The Critic as Artist" (1890). Like the works of other satiric thinkers of the time, these dialogues overturn well-established conventions of the century, in this case focusing on the relation between art and life. Wilde argues that each art follows its own history, independent of the times in which it is created, that life imitates art rather than art imitating life; that realism is not the highest goal of art but the death of art; and, finally, that "Lying, the telling of beautiful untrue things, is the proper aim of Art" (Wilde 1968: 195). Like Nietzsche, Wilde questions the reasons for which we claim to possess the truth. He pursues truths through the form of paradox and wit: the apparently upside-down world that he depicts comes to seem recognizable and even familiar, like the world of Erewhon. (On art for art's sake, and the return of wit in England, see Henkle 1980: 296–352).

The weakening of the system of constraints that held back satire in the nineteenth century did not lead to the publication of a large number of indecent or coarse works, but it did allow to be expressed fundamental doubts about the adequacy of dominant middle-class conceptions of the world. Whatever the differences among the works just cited as illustrating the return of narrative satire in various national cultures, they all share an attack on the complacent acceptance of middle-class verities, and a deep skepticism about the inevitability of progress led by middle-class European or American culture. It is for this reason that satire could be associated with other genres so closely at the time: for example, the dictionary of ironic epigrams by Flaubert (*Dictionary of Received Ideas*, 1881) and Bierce (*The Devil's Dictionary*, 1881–1906) inverts or hollows out the clichés of modern conversation; and much science fiction does not celebrate but critiques the effects of modern science and technology (for example, Wells's *Island of Dr Moreau*, 1896). By adopting the pose of the engineer or the scientific observer, late nineteenth-century satirists prepare the way for such turn-of-the-century narrative satires as Alfred Jarry's *Exploits and Opinions of Doctor Faustroll, Pataphysician* (1911, posthumous), which combines a Rabelaisian voyage and exuberance of language with surrealistically exact descriptions of a physics that is contrary to fact in our everyday world; or Thorstein Veblen's *Theory of the Leisure Class* (1899), where the author employs, straight-faced, a woolly language of sociology to explain that a culture of conspicuous consumption, excess, waste, and obsolescence functions to display great wealth in the modern world just as the magnificent expenses of princes and aristocrats did in the Renaissance. By the 1890s and the first decade of the twentieth century, narrative satire had re-emerged as a culturally viable form, but unlike the satire of a hundred years earlier, it often took as the objects of its attacks technological advances and the otherwise unquestioned conventions of modern middle-class life.

References and Further Reading

Bakhtin, Mikhail (1968) *Rabelais and his World*, trans. Hélène Iswolsky. Cambridge, MA: MIT Press.

Butler, Marilyn (1975) *Jane Austen and the War of Ideas*. Oxford: Oxford University Press.

——(1979) *Peacock Displayed: A Satirist in his Context*. London: Routledge and Kegan Paul.

Cohen, Margaret (1999) *The Sentimental Education of the Novel*. Princeton, NJ: Princeton University Press.

Dyer, Gary (1997) *British Satire and the Politics of Style, 1789–1832*. Cambridge: Cambridge University Press.

Gilmartin, Kevin (1996) *Print Politics: The Press and Radical Opposition in Early Nineteenth-century England*. Cambridge: Cambridge University Press.

Griest, Guenevire (1970) *Mudie's Circulating Library*. Bloomington, IN: Indiana University Press.

Habermas, Jürgen (1989) *The Structural Transformation of the Public Sphere: An Inquiry into a Category of Bourgeois Society*, trans. Thomas Burger. Cambridge, MA: MIT Press.

Henkle, Roger B. (1980) *Comedy and Culture: England 1820–1900*. Princeton, NJ: Princeton University Press.

Jones, Steven (ed.) (2000) *Satire and Romanticism*. New York: St Martin's Press.

——(ed.) (2003) *The Satiric Eye: Forms of Satire in the Romantic Period*. New York: Palgrave.

Kelly, Gary (1976) *The English Jacobin Novel, 1780–1805*. Oxford: Oxford University Press.

McCann, Andrew (1996) William Godwin and the pathological public sphere: theorizing communicative action in the 1790s. In Paula Backscheider and Timothy Dykstal (eds), *The Intersections of the Public and Private Spheres in Early Modern England*, pp. 199–222. London: Frank Cass.

Martin, Robert Bernard (1974) *The Triumph of Wit: A Study of Victorian Comic Theory*. Oxford: Clarendon Press.

Maurer, Oscar (1959) "My squeamish public": some problems of Victorian magazine publishers and editors. *Studies in Bibliography* 12, 21–41.

Mill, John Stuart (1989) *On Liberty and Other Writings*. Cambridge: Cambridge University Press (originally published 1859).

Palmeri, Frank (1990) *Satire in Narrative: Petronius, Swift, Gibbon, Melville, Pynchon*. Austin: University of Texas Press.

—— (2003) *Satire, History, Novel: Narrative Forms, 1665–1815*. Newark: University of Delaware Press.

—— (2004) Cruikshank, Thackeray, and the Victorian eclipse of satire. *Studies in English Literature* 44, 753–77.

Russell, Frances Theresa (1920) *Satire in the Victorian Novel*. New York: Macmillan.

Trilling, Lionel (1955) Little Dorrit. In *The Opposing Self: Nine Essays in Criticism by Lionel Trilling*, pp. 50–65. New York: Viking Press.

Twain, Mark (1962) *Letters from the Earth*, ed. Bernard De Voto. New York: Harper and Row.

Wahrman, Dror (1995) *Imagining the Middle Class: The Political Representation of Class in Britain, c.1780–1840*. Cambridge: Cambridge University Press.

Wiener, Joel H. (1969) *The War of the Unstamped: The Movement to Repeal the British Newspaper Tax, 1830–1836*. Ithaca, NY: Cornell University Press.

Wilde, Oscar (1968) *Literary Criticism of Oscar Wilde*, ed. Stanley Weintraub. Lincoln: University of Nebraska Press.

Wood, Marcus (1994) *Radical Satire and Print Culture, 1790–1822*. Cambridge: Cambridge University Press.

20
American Satire: Beginnings through Mark Twain
Linda A. Morris

American satire began in earnest in the early eighteenth century and flourished in the nineteenth century, culminating in the late works of Mark Twain. From the beginning, conditions were ripe for political, social, and religious satire. Satirists poked fun at the Puritans, rude country people, and people who aspired to lives of fashion, as well as at the British, who fought to keep the colonies under their legal and economic control, and at the democratic institutions that arose after the Revolution. Political abuses were frequently the targets of satire, whether in the eighteenth or nineteenth century, no matter the party in power. Writers used their biting humor to attack the institution of slavery as early as 1797 and as late as 1865. Satire focusing on social manners and customs persisted. Women writers in particular, but by no means exclusively, exposed the folly of social excesses and pretensions to gentility, as well as the crudeness of social life on the frontier.

For the purposes of this chapter, literary satire is understood to be work that relies upon humor to expose both human and institutional failures. Often the humor builds upon a sense of authorial indignation targeted at any number of possible human and/or institutional shortcomings: greed, self-indulgence, drunkenness, incompetence, hypocrisy, intolerance, corruption, excesses, or partisanship. Most satire, in spite of the anger that may lie behind it, depends for its success upon a sense of restraint and an underlying, almost always unspoken, sense that there is some hope that exposing society's excesses might lead to reform. American satire of the eighteenth, and especially of the nineteenth century, often relies upon the creation of a naïve persona who inadvertently, and in an understated manner, reveals social truths. Yet, American satire also frequently relies on comic exaggeration. Satire may be stinging and bitter, or good natured and mild. Works may contain satiric moments, may seem to be built upon a satiric impulse, or they may offer sustained critiques of contemporary society. Finally, because satire, to be at all relevant, must be topical and timely, its fine points and even some of its broader strokes may be lost upon modern readers. Nonetheless, the early satirists discussed in this chapter still have the ability to amuse and to expose human and institutional foibles; they can still hit their marks.

The earliest sustained American satire belongs to the seventeenth century; it is a three-volume work written by Thomas Morton and first published in 1637. The explicitly anti-Puritan thrust of this work, *New English Canaan*, was born out of the author's own experience with the Puritans of Plymouth, Massachusetts. Morton came to colonial America from England in 1622 and began to trade with the Indians, who are depicted rather favorably in his satire in contrast with the Puritans, or the "precise Separatists," as he called them. Indeed, the first two of the three books of *New English Canaan* are not particularly satiric in tone, yet they set up, by contrast, the disdain that Morton lays upon the Puritans in the third book.

The most celebrated portion of Morton's *New English Canaan* describes his raising of a maypole at Pasonagessit (renamed by William Bradford "Merry Mount" and by Morton "Ma-re Mount"), the revels that followed, and the Puritans' subsequent determination to capture Morton and deport him to England. In a passage following Morton's quotation of the song the revelers sang as they drank and danced around the maypole, Morton can barely contain his contempt for the Separatists:

> This harmless mirth made by younge men (that lived in hope to have wives brought over to them, that would save them a laboure to make a voyage to fetch any over) was much distasted, of the precise Seperatists: that keepe much a doe, about the tyth of Muit and Cummin [mint and cumin, i.e., trivial matters]; troubling their braines more then reason would require about things that are indifferent: and from that time sought occasion against my honest Host [i.e., Morton] of Ma-re Mount to overthrow his undertakings, and to destroy his plantation quite and cleane. (Morton 1969: 135–6)

The Puritans, led by Miles Standish, set out to ambush Morton at one of his fur-trading posts – from Morton's perspective because they envied his prosperity, and because he adhered to the tenets of the Church of England, and from the Puritan's perspective because he sold guns to the Indians and engaged in lewd conduct – and took him prisoner. He heaps contempt on his captors, calling them colts and a flock of wild geese, and renames Miles Standish "Captain Shrimp." Morton was ultimately deported to England, returned to the Colonies, was again deported (and his plantation burned), whereupon he wrote *New English Canaan* to discredit the Puritans.

Eighteenth-century Satire

With his *Sot-Weed Factor: or, a Voyage to Maryland* (1708), Ebenezer Cooke ushered in eighteenth-century American satire. The poem, which depicts the crude behavior of the Maryland tobacco farmers, is a double-edged sword, for it not only swipes at the farmers but also at characters such as Cooke's persona, a gullible English entrepreneur. In the late nineteenth and early twentieth centuries, critics believed Cooke was satirizing the people and manners of colonial Maryland, while the current prevailing view is that the object of his satire was the immigrant Englishman unprepared for the rigors of colonial life (Micklus 1984: 251–2). There is no doubt that Cooke's persona is gullible and naïve, but the situations and manners he encounters are enough to make any unsuspecting visitor want to flee, as the protagonist does at the end of the poem.

The rural Marylanders whom the narrator encounters have almost no redeeming social graces, except that they welcome any stranger to their table. Their rude country fare is depicted as being nearly inedible. They drink to excess, they are cheats (even a Quaker the narrator encounters makes off with the narrator's large cask of tobacco), and they steal his clothing while he sleeps. The women he encounters are crude – they curse like men and play cards. Judges are illiterate, and the court of law, such as it is, is a drunken free-for-all, offering no justice for a man from outside their community. The strongest condemnation is reserved for the planters, who are almost always depicted as drunken and raucous:

> O'er-whelm'd with Punch, dead drunk, we found;
> Others were fighting and contending,
> Some burnt their Cloaths to save the mending.
> A few whose Heads by frequent use,
> Could better bare the potent Juice,
> Gravely debated State Affairs.
> (Cooke 1708: 16)

It is easy to see how the external and strange world depicted by Cooke is the object of his satire, but it is harder to pinpoint how Cooke tips his hat that the narrator himself is also the butt of the joke, even if he does get into one bad situation after another and is ill equipped to better his financial circumstances. Only his final "curse" upon the New World reveals the full foolish excess of the narrator:

> May Canniballs transported o'er the Sea
> Prey on there Slaves, as they have done on me;
> May never Merchant's trading Sails explore
> This Cruel, this inhospitable Shoar;
> But left abandon'd by the World to starve,
> May they sustain the Fate they well deserve;
> ...
> May Wrath Divine then lay those Regions wast
> Where no Man's Faithful, nor a Woman Chast.
> (Cooke 1708: 26)

For all intents and purposes, Cooke's narrator, and Cooke himself, disappear from public view with this curse, for we know nothing more about Cooke than that he wrote *The Sot-Weed Factor*.

Maryland was the site of another eighteenth-century satiric work, yet in this instance the writer was a staunch defender of the indulgences of some of Maryland's most prominent citizens, members of "The Tuesday Club." The author, Alexander Hamilton, a physician (not to be confused with the famous Secretary-of-Treasury by the same name), emigrated to America from Scotland as a young man, stayed (unlike Cooke apparently), and prospered. In the final years of his life he wrote *The History of the Tuesday Club*, a lengthy work written in the 1750s. Among the many targets of Hamilton's satire was critical pretentiousness:

> Triffles and vanities are but Synonomous terms, and therefore, all that passes in this transitory life, this petty scantling of time, which we have allotted us to peregrinate thro' this absurd worldly wilderness, and to rant our Comical, or (as some are pleased to call it) tragical parts out upon this terrestrial Stage, is but of a triffling nature, why should any saucy, pert, demure, pricise [sic], finical coxcomb of a Clubical [sic] Critic, to say no worse of him, nay, any Chuckleheaded, unexperienced, raw, Saucy Jackanapes pretend to say, that this our famous History, is more triffling than any other history, or this our ancient and honorable Club more triffling in its constitution, government, model, form and Conversation than any other Society whatsoever, great or small, be it Empire kingdom, Commonwealth corporation or Club. (Bakalar 1997: 71)

With such a tone and lively sense of joy, with such playful language typical of much satire, Hamilton wrote the history of his club in a work that was still unfinished at his death.

Writers as varied as Benjamin Franklin, John Trumbull, and Francis Hopkinson satirized the British in their relationship to the Colonies. Franklin's "The Sale of the Hessians" is arguably his most famous satire: short, sharp, to the point, it is written in the form of a letter from the Count of Schaumberge to the Baron Hohendorf, commander of the Hessian troops in America. Franklin assumes the persona of a count, vacationing in Rome in 1777, who is literally profiting from the deaths of Hessian mercenaries hired by George III and sent to fight on behalf of the British in the War of American Independence. He is "compensated" for every Hessian killed and is therefore eager for the total to be large. Extending Swiftian logic, he argues that a wounded soldier should be included in the tally because he is no longer fit for service: "I do not mean by this that you should assassinate them; we should be humane, my dear Baron, but you may insinuate to the surgeons with entire propriety that a crippled man is a reproach to their profession, and that there is no wiser course than to let every one of them die when he ceases to be fit to fight" (Bakalar 1997: 51).

John Trumbull, who passed the Yale entrance exam at the age of seven, eventually studied law in the office of John Adams and became best known for his satiric verse at the time of the Revolutionary War. His *M'Fingal: A Modern Epic Poem in Four Cantos* (1782) was the most popular political satire of the Revolutionary War (Carlisle 1962: 68); it features two narrators, Honorius, a Whig, and M'Fingal, a Tory. It is M'Fingal who bears the brunt of the satire, for he is pompous, self-promoting, renowned for his gift of "second sight," and ultimately ready to abandon his Tory principles to save his own hide. The first canto of the poem describes the defeat of the British troops, with Honorius mocking the British and the Tories for their "crimes." M'Fingal, who fled before the victorious Whigs, rails against the Whigs in the second canto: "Ungrateful sons! A factious band, / That rise against your parent-land!" (Trumbull 1962: 127). In the third canto, M'Fingal is outraged that the Whigs have raised a "liberty pole" and are flying their flag from it. He draws his sword, but he is overpowered by a man wielding a shovel and felled by a blow on his rear. The Whigs tie him up, then string him up "like a keg of ale" to the pole, whereupon he promises to change sides and renounce all his former positions if they will let him down. Instead, he is tarred and feathered (but without apparent pain) and left stuck against the pole. The poem ends with M'Fingal's vision of what is to come: the Whigs will win the day, the rebellion will turn into a revolution, and he himself will abandon his friends and head back to Boston.

Francis Hopkinson reflected his particular zeal for the American Revolution in two pieces, *A Pretty Story* (1774) and *The Battle of the Kegs* (1778), the latter of which rivaled Trumbull's *M'Fingal* in popularity. Hopkinson was the first graduate of a new educational plan devised by his own father and Benjamin Franklin. He tried on several professions as a young man, including a customs collector, a merchant, and a justice of the peace (Zall 1976: 7–10). *A Pretty Story* is an allegory about the treatment of the Americans by the British in the years leading up to the formation of the Continental Congress. It features an Old Nobleman (the King), his Mother-in-law (Parliament), the Steward (the Prime Minister), and Jack (Boston). It begins:

> Once upon a Time, a great While ago, there lived a certain Nobleman, who had long possessed a very valuable Farm, and had a great Number of Children and Grandchildren. Besides the annual Profits of his Land, which were very considerable, he kept a large Shop of Goods; and being very successful in Trade, he became, in Process of Time, exceeding rich and powerful; insomuch that all his Neighbours feared and respected him. (Zall 1976: 37)

The Steward seduces the Mother-in-law, and together they begin to impose more and more requirements on the noble sons, the Colonies, piling on outrage upon outrage. Even so, the fable ends indecisively, leaving the reader to fill in the blanks: "These harsh and unconstitutional Proceedings irritated *Jack* and the other Inhabitants of the new Farm to such a Degree that **********" (Zall 1976: 55).

Hopkinson's most famous poem, *The Battle of the Kegs*, was based on a true incident in which the Americans floated kegs of gunpowder down the Delaware River toward British ships in Philadelphia. The British army, spotting the kegs floating down the river, thought that the Rebels were inside them:

> "Arise, arise!" Sir Erskine cries,
> "The rebels, more's the pity,
> Without a boat are all afloat
> And ranged before the city."
> (45–8)

Hauling out their cannons and small arms, the British begin shooting frantically at the kegs from the shore, with their soldiers showing "amazing courage" and keeping up the firing all day:

> Such feats did they perform that day
>   Against those wicked kegs, sir,
> That years to come, if they get home,
>   They'll make their boasts and brags, sir.
>   (85–8)

With these lines, Hopkinson ended his popular send up of the British troops in the Revolution.

Following the Revolution, toward the end of the eighteenth century, Royall Tyler became known for two full-length satires: one of the first American plays, *The Contrast* (1787), and a novel, *The Algerine Captive* (1797). In his prologue to *The Contrast*, addressing the audience directly, Tyler articulates in a modest fashion the role of satire:

> Still may the wisdom of the Comic Muse
> Exalt your merits, or your faults accuse.
> But think not, 'tis her aim to be severe; –
> We all are mortals, and as mortals err.
> If candour pleases, we are truly blest;
> Vice trembles, when compell'd to stand confess'd.
> Let not light Censure on your faults offend,
> Which aims not to expose them, but amend.
> Thus does our Author to your candour trust;
> Conscious, the *free* are generous, as just.
>   (Tyler 1970: xxxix)

His play has double satiric targets: "fashionable" behavior and courtship conventions. The latter are played out in particular in the engagement of Maria Van Rough to Dimple, a wealthy, foppish young man who courts two other women at the same time. As the play progresses, a sharp "contrast" is set up between her fiancé, Dimple, who has accumulated an astonishingly large debt and who has set out to make Maria hate him so she will break off the engagement, and Col. Manly, an old-fashioned Yankee who courts her with honor and respect. It remained for another playwright, Anna Cora Mowatt, fifty years later, to explore in much greater satiric detail the world of fashionable New York society.

Tyler's *The Algerine Captive, or The Life and Adventures of Doctor Updike Underhill: Six Years a Prisoner Among the Algerines*, was first published anonymously in 1797. The first volume of the novel is presented as an ironic autobiography of Underhill, whose formal, classical education unfits him for life on the family farm, or for any kind of normal conversation with his peers. Beyond the uselessness of Underhill's education, there are multiple targets of the satire in the first half of the narrative: the eccentricity of earlier geniuses, such as Franklin; the museum at Harvard; the life of a country physician, with its poverty, quacks, and puffery; a minister who beats his black servant about the head all the way to church then preaches a sermon on Christian duty; the "dissipated" American South; and, finally, the slave trade. Underhill is recruited to serve as a physician aboard a slave ship:

> As surgeon, it was my duty to inspect the bodies of the slave, to see, as the captain expressed himself, that our owners were not shammed off with unsound flesh.
>
> The man, the affrighted child, the modest matron, and the timid virgin were alike exposed to this severe scrutiny, to humanity and common decency equally insulting. (Tyler 2002: 96)

At this point in the text the tone turns from jocular and ironic to serious, leading into the second volume, in which Underhill is captured by the Algerians and himself enslaved. Much of the remaining volume details his experience in captivity and what he comes to understand about the Muslim faith.

Philip Freneau, like Hopkinson and Trumbull, was also a passionately anti-British poet who wrote a number of satiric verses during the Revolution; his post-Revolutionary satire, moreover, both celebrated the new Republic and warned of the threats to democracy. He was thus a transitional figure between the eighteenth and nineteenth centuries. He served as a seaman during the war and was captured by the British and held prisoner on board a ship in the New York harbor. In the 1780s he became, for a time, a newspaper editor but continued to go to sea at intervals. One of his most important and significant collections of poems, called *A Collection of Poems on American Affairs, and a Variety of Other Subjects, Chiefly Moral and Political; Written Between the Year 1797 and the Present Time*, staunchly defends democracy against the "embryo monarchs" who threatened the new Republic. Nowhere is this expressed more clearly than in his "Reflections on the Gradual Progress of Nations from Democratical States, to Despotic Empires," which begins:

> Oh fatal day! when to the Atlantic shore,
> European despots sent the doctrine o'er,
> That man's vast race was born to lick the dust;
> Feed on the winds, or toil through life accurst;
> Poor and despised, that rulers might be great
> And swell to monarchs, to devour the state.
> (Freneau 1815: 13)

He was scornful, too, of the new capital being built on the banks of the Potomac River because of its grandeur and the initial exclusion of the common man:

> So, bounding on Potowmac's flood,
> Where ancient oaks so lately stood

> An infant city grows apace
> Intended for a ruling race.
>
> Here capitols of awful height –
> Already burst upon the sight.
> And buildings, meant for embryo kings
> Display their fronts and spread their wings.
>   (Freneau 1815: 34)

Nineteenth-century Satire

The nineteenth century, a time of rapid economic, geographic, and social expansion, and a time that saw major reform movements such as abolition and woman's suffrage, was ripe for satire, and writers responded generously. With the national boundaries more or less secure, and indeed expanding, and with democracy safely installed in the states, nineteenth-century satire lacked some of the urgency of the pre-Revolutionary and Revolutionary times, but it flourished. Women entered the political arena through the Abolitionist and the Woman's Rights movements, and they asserted themselves in the literary scene. The first half of the nineteenth century was graced with the highly varied satiric voices of writers such as Washington Irving, Seba Smith, James Russell Lowell, Frances M. Whitcher, and David R. Locke.

In addition to the sketches for which he is justly famous, Washington Irving was the author, with his brother William and with James K. Paulding, of *Salmagundi* (1807–8), and on his own, but in another's voice, of *A History of New York... by Diedrich Knickerbocker*, originally published in 1809. Much of the first part of the book is more a burlesque history than a sustained satire, but over the course of the lengthy work Irving takes aim at theories of how America came to be populated by the Native Americans; the rise of political parties (the Long Pipe, the Short Pipe, and the Quid parties); and especially the vagaries and eccentricities of the early Dutch settlers of New York, given such names as William the Testy, Wouter Van Twiller, and Peter the Headstrong. One nineteenth-century appraisal of the popular book declared it "an original creation, and one of the few masterpieces of humor. In spontaneity, freshness, breadth of conception, and joyous vigor, it belongs to the springtime of literature" (Warner 1891: n. p.).

Several years before, Irving had entered into a collaboration with his brother, William Irving, and with James K. Paulding, and published a series of pamphlets they subsequently collected into a book entitled *Salmagundi* (1807). Their stated intention for the collection echoes the larger purpose of satiric literature:

> Our intention is simply to instruct the young, reform the old, correct the town, and castigate the age; this is an arduous task, and therefore we undertake it with confidence ... should any gentleman or lady be displeased with the inveterate truth of their likenesses, they may ease their spleen by laughing at those of their neighbors – this being what *we* understand by *poetical justice*. (Irving et al. 1860: 14)

By the light of an early critic, they succeeded in their goal:

> A whole bevy of beaux and belles saw themselves reflected in the Ding Dongs and Sophy Sparkles. The base metal of Brummagem adventurers and spendthrifts was nailed to the counter by the satire of Straddles; theatrical critics were silenced by a glance at themselves in the mirror of 'Sbidlikens; fashionable upstarts shrank from the portraits of the Giblets; the small beer of the politician soured at the thundering satire of Dabble; the feathers of the carpet soldiers wilted when they were paraded in the regiment of the Fag-rags. *Salmagundi* was the mild terror of the town when society was not too overgrown an instrument to be played upon by a cunning musician. (Evert Duyckinck in Irving et al. 1860: xii–iii)

James K. Paulding, for his part, wrote a less gentle, broader-stroked satire indicting English visitors to America. His *John Bull in America* (1825) was an ardent defense of democracy, although the means by which Paulding accomplished this aim was through the first-person wild exaggerations of an Englishman reporting on his wholly unpleasant visit to America. From the beginning, it is abundantly clear that the narrator, named John Bull, is prejudiced against the Americans, though he claims not to be; he knows the Americans to be: "altogether barbarous. I also fully believed that the people were a bundling, gouging, drinking, spitting, impious race, without either morals, literature, religion, or refinement; and that the turbulent spirit of democracy was altogether incompatible with any state of society becoming a civilized nation" (Paulding 1825: 2). This satire depends upon gross exaggeration at every turn, all presented by the narrator with a straight face. Southerners engage in cannibalism, with the toes of black slaves turning up in terrapin soup; in one village even the hogs are enfranchised; in the frontier areas most people have only one eye (or none), having had their eyes gouged out; elsewhere people are such dancing fools that they literally wear their feet and legs down to stumps. In spite of the comic exaggeration, or perhaps because of it, there is still a freshness about *John Bull in America*.

The year 1830 ushered in the first in a long series of letters written, ostensibly, by Jack Downing of Downingville, Maine, and published in the Portland *Courier*. Jack's letters, written by the newspaper editor Seba Smith, represented an original voice in American political commentary: a vernacular narrator offering up revealing, but naïve, political satire. Originally Jack was represented as a Yankee peddler, traveling to Portland to sell axe handles, but ultimately he became a confidential adviser to President Andrew Jackson. Ostensibly, Jack could not afford to pay the postage to have his letters sent home to his Uncle Joshua, Cousin Nabby, and Cousin Ephraim, so the editor of the Portland newspaper printed the letters in the paper for the family to read; in "real" life, the Downing letters were widely reprinted in newspapers all over the Northeast. While waiting for the market in axe handles to improve, Jack visits the state legislature and becomes interested in politics, although he clearly does not understand what he sees. All he understands is that the legislators bicker over who is to be seated when there are obviously enough chairs for everyone. He continues to attend sessions of the legislature, where almost nothing happens until the end of the session when the legislators are finally galvanized into action; they begin to think about the planting season and pass bills by the gross: "Till they settled 'em away like a heap of corn at a husking, before a barnful of boys and gals... It seems to me, Uncle Joshua, it costs our farmers a great deal more to husk out their law-corn every winter than it need tu. They let tu many noisy talking fellers come to the husking" (Smith 1973: 75). As this simple example illustrates, the humor is gentle and muted, with Jack's naïveté as much the target as the partisan wrangling in the State House.

Six years after Seba Smith first published his Jack Downing letters in book form, celebrating a vernacular perspective, Caroline Kirkland published *A New Home, Who Will Follow?* (1839) in which she was less than amused by the rustic denizens she encountered in her move to the frontier – western Michigan. While much of the book is a more-or-less realistic depiction of frontier life from a woman's perspective, coming as she did from a middle-class background and from an educated family, Kirkland satirized what she saw as the romanticized versions of frontier life then in vogue.

Of all the challenges Kirkland faces in her "new home," the manners and habits of her neighbors come in for the harshest criticism:

> "Mother wants your sifter," said Miss Ianthe Howard, a young lady of six years' standing, attired in a tattered calico, thickened with dirt; her unkempt locks straggling from under that hideous substitute for a bonnet, so universal in the western country, a dirty cotton handkerchief, which is used, *ad nauseam,* for all sorts of purposes.
>
> "Mother wants your sifter, and she says she guesses you can let her have some sugar and tea, 'cause you've got plenty."
>
> This excellent reason, "'cause you've got plenty," is conclusive as to sharing with your neighbours. (Kirkland 1990: 67)

Repeatedly, Kirkland drives home her point that life on the frontier for an educated woman is a trying affair, a perception she reinforced in a sequel to *A New Home* entitled *Forest Life* (1842).

If Kirkland found the manners and customs of frontier men and women apt material for ridicule, in the same era Anna Cora Mowatt turned her satiric aim against the *nouveau riche* of New York society. Her play *Fashion; or Life in New York* (1845) was produced first at the Park Street Theater and almost immediately became a popular success. *Fashion* is exuberant in its satirizing of the pretentiousness of Americans' attempts to imitate French fashions. In the comedy, the newly rich Mrs Tiffany spends all her husband's earnings attempting to establish herself as a woman of fashion. She hires a black servant, Zeke, whom she renames Adolph, and dresses him in livery. All she knows about French fashion she learns from her maid, Millinette:

Mrs Tif.:	But I hear that nothing is more fashionable than to keep people waiting. None but vulgar persons pay any attention to punctuality. Is it not so, Millinette?
Mil.:	Quite *comme il faut*. Great personnes always do make little personnes wait, Madame.
Mrs Tif.:	This mode of receiving visitors only upon one specified day of the week is a most convenient custom! It saves the trouble of keeping the house continually in order and of being always dressed. I flatter myself that *I* was the first to introduce it amongst the New York *ee-light*. You are quite sure that it is strictly a Parisian mode, Millinette? (Mowatt 1854: 3)

The comedy is carried by dialogues such as this, and by the inability of Mrs Tiffany to tell that a baker who poses as a French count is an obvious fraud; there is also didactic dialogue that articulates specifically what has gone wrong in New York society. Adam Trueman, a farmer and old friend of Tiffany, comes to town, and, in keeping with his name, tells the truth about the Tiffany family:

The *fashion*-worship has made heathens and hypocrites of you all! *Deception* is your household God! A man laughs as if he were crying, and cries as if he were laughing in his sleeve. Everything is something else from what it seems to be. I have lived in your house only three days, and I've heard more lies than were ever invented during a Presidential election! (Mowatt 1854: 17)

In the tradition of Seba Smith, and in contrast with Caroline Kirkland, James Russell Lowell (of the famous New England Lowells) created a vernacular, common-sense Yankee poet, Hosea Biglow, to express his abolitionist and anti-war ideology. Also like Smith, Lowell originally published his satiric pieces in the newspapers, then collected them in book form and called them *The Biglow Papers* (1848). Two other personae appear in the papers: the Rev. Mr Homer Wilbur, who writes prose introductions to Biglow's poems, and Birdofredom Sawin, a common soldier in the Mexican War. In the voice of Homer Wilbur, Lowell, like Tyler before him, articulates the purpose of satire itself:

the aim of the true satirist is not to be severe upon persons, but only upon falsehood, and, as Truth and Falsehood start from the same point, and sometimes even go along together for a little way, his business is to follow the path of the latter after it diverges, and to show her floundering in the bog at the end of it. Truth is quite beyond the reach of satire. There is so brave a simplicity in her, that she can no more be made ridiculous than an oak or a pine. (Lowell 1977: 69)

The first poem in the collection was written by Hosea Biglow in a fit of anger in response to encountering an army recruiter; it weds Lowell's anti-war sentiments with his hatred of slavery, but all in a disarming vernacular voice and rustic poetics:

> Aint it cute to see a Yankee
>   Take sech everlastin' pains,
> All to git the Devil's thankee,
>   Helpin' on 'em weld their chains?
> Wy, it's jes ez clear ez figgers,
>   Clear ez one an' one make two,
> Chaps that make black slaves o'niggers
>   Want to make wite slaves o' you.
>   (Lowell 1977: 52)

Birdofredom Sawin, whose language is as exaggerated as Biglow's, writes about his experience in the Mexican War, where he lost a leg, an eye, and an arm; since he is no longer a viable soldier, and since he has no principles whatsoever, and never did, Sawin plans to run for the office of President of the United States.

Two women writers, from radically different perspectives, wrote widely popular social satire at mid-century: Frances M. Whitcher (the Widow Bedott) and Sara Willis Parton (Fanny Fern). The first of these, Frances M. Whitcher, was from upstate New York; she married an Episcopalian minister when she was in her mid-thirties and moved with him from her home in Whitesboro to Elmira, New York. By then she had already established herself as a humorist, writing sketches in the voice of the Widow Bedott, which were published (anonymously) in *Neal's Saturday Gazette*; through the vernacular perspective of the Widow, she poked fun at husband-hunting, gossiping women and exposed the foibles of small-town life. When she moved with her new husband to Elmira, Whitcher began to write sketches for *Godey's Lady's Book* from the common-sense, humorous perspective of the Widow's fictive sister, Aunt Maguire. Her language softened but her satire became more pointed and biting, targeting in particular hypocrisy, pretensions toward gentility, and women's uncharitable behavior toward one another. Her most famous sketches appeared as a series in *Godey's*, featuring a local church sewing society in which the women spend more time gossiping than sewing, and compete with each other over who can provide the most elaborate tea. They are particularly critical of their minister's wife, who dresses in a plain style and who does not "visit" as much as they would like. The most pointed satire is directed against a woman named Miss Samson Savage:

> She was always a coarse, boisterous, high-tempered critter, and when her husband grow'd rich, she grow'd pompous and overbearin'. She made up her mind she'd rule the roast [sic], no matter what it cost – she'd be the *first* in Scrabble Hill ... Of course, them that thinks money's the main thing (and ther's plenty such here and every where), is ready to flatter her and make a fuss over her, and approve of all her dewin's. If ther's any body that *won't* knuckle tew her, I tell ye they have to take it *about east*. She abuses 'em to their faces and slanders 'em to their backs. (Whitcher 1855: 303)

Within days of the publication of the sketch in *Godey's*, rumor spread that Whitcher was the author of the anonymous sketch featuring Miss Sampson Savage. People in

Elmira "recognized" each other in the characters and were either delighted or outraged. Readers in towns throughout the region thought the sketch was satirizing *their* sewing societies, creating a storm of controversy that would not subside (Morris 1992: 157). The Whitchers were ultimately forced out of Elmira, but Frances Whitcher had the last laugh, so to speak – her *Widow Bedott Papers*, published posthumously in 1855, was immediately a best-selling book.

Celebrated for her newspaper columns, primarily for the New York *Ledger*, Sara Willis Parton (Fanny Fern) was reportedly the best-paid columnist of her day, earning $100 a week in her prime. She subsequently collected her columns into two books for which she earned both fame and relative wealth. In addition, Fern published an autobiographical novel, *Ruth Hall* (1854), which was soundly criticized in her day (and lauded in our own) for its satiric portrayal of her brother and her in-laws. The novel's heroine, Ruth, undergoes a series of personal losses, including the deaths of her first child and her husband. Destitute, she turns to her brother and in-laws for help, but they turn deaf ears. She lives in grinding poverty with her two daughters until she begins to write newspaper columns and earns her own way in the world. Along the way, Fern takes aim at subjects such as hotel life, boarding houses, book-sellers, greedy and dishonest editors, and most emphatically her brother, who is a literary editor, fop, and opportunist.

In her newspaper columns as well, Fern covered a wide range of topics and employed a variety of tones, from sentimental to satiric, and from ironic to sarcastic. In our time, she has been celebrated, fairly, for her proto-feminist stance on subjects such as a double standard for the sexes, men's inflated sense of themselves, their dereliction of duty as husbands, and their smoking; Tabitha Tomkins, for instance, one of her fictional speakers, asks: "Have I...a right to my share of fresh air uncontaminated? Or have I not?...Every man I meet is a locomotive chimney. Smoke – smoke – smoke – smoke –" (Fern 1854: 80). But women, and women's manners, are also targeted in her satire, sometimes without a hint of irony. In a piece on lady doctors, she concedes that it is good that women are able to become doctors – "an honest and honorable deliverance from the everlasting, non-remunerating, consumptive-provoking, monotonous needle" – but she still prefers a male doctor in her sick room; women doctors, she says, would have to have the mirrors taken out of the room if you wanted their undivided attention, and she would have to be sure she had not "come between" that woman and her lover, or that the woman's husband had not "smiled upon" her (Fern 1857: 112). In his obituary for Fanny Fern, her editor at the New York *Ledger*, Robert Bonner, wrote that "she was one of the most humorous and witty of writers, but her humor and wit were never wasted in purposeless display. She always took aim at something that deserved to be hit, and wrote on subjects in which the great masses of people were interested" (Warren 1995: 57).

In a much different vein, William Allen Butler, poet and lawyer, was made famous in his times by a three-hundred line satiric poem about the lengths (and expense) fashionable women go to in their clothes shopping, then declare that they have "Nothing to Wear" (1857). The poem begins:

> Miss Flora M'Flimsely, of Madison Square,
> Has made three separate journeys to Paris,
> And her father assures me, each time she was there,
> That she and her friend Mrs Harris
> ...
> Spent six consecutive weeks without stopping,
> In one continuous round of shopping;
> Shopping alone, and shopping together,
> At all hours of the day, and in all sorts of weather;
> For all manner of things that a woman can put
> On the crown of her head or the sole of her foot,
> Or wrap round her shoulders, or fit round her waist,
> Or that can be sewed on, or pinned on, or laced,
> Or tied on with a string, or stitched on with a bow,
> In front or behind, above or below.
> (Butler 1857: 1–2)

The poem takes an unexpected turn at the end when the narrator warns that when the day comes that the "soul"

> Must be clothed for the life and the service above,
> With purity, truth, faith, meekness, and love;
> Oh, daughters of Earth! Foolish virgins, beware!
> Lest in that upper realm you have nothing to wear!
> (Butler 1857: 68)

Here the implied "right behavior" underlying the satire throughout is made explicit, detracting, perhaps, from the pure pleasure of the comic exaggeration, but no doubt adding to the popularity of the poem among the sterner sex.

At the outset of the Civil War, David Ross Locke began to write editorials for an Ohio newspaper in the persona of Petroleum V. Nasby, of Wingert's Corners, Ohio. Nasby is a blatantly racist, semi-literate, self-serving, corrupt opportunist who, although a Northerner, supports the South in the war. The reader is compelled to understand Nasby's views, so grotesque in their exaggeration, as deeply ironic. President Lincoln, whom Nasby describes as "a goriller, a fiendish ape, a thirster after blud," loved the Nasby columns and read them to his cabinet. On the issue of race and emancipation, Nasby was relentless. Determined to drive all the black people out of Wingert's Corners, Nasby makes these resolutions: "Wareas, Any man hevin the intellek uv a brass-mounted jackass kin easily see that the two races want never intended to live together; and Wareas, Bein in the majority, we kin do as we please, and ez the nigger aint no vote he kant help hisself... Ameriky for white men!" (Locke 1962: 12).

Over the course of the war, Nasby first objects to being drafted and escapes into Canada; when he is caught, he claims to be an Abolitionist. He is drafted into the Union army, but shortly thereafter deserts to the Confederacy. His new uniform is stripped off him and put on by a Southern colonel. In turn, the Confederates strip the clothes off a soldier dying of the fever and give them to Nasby: "There wuz a pair uv pants with the seat entirely torn away, and wun leg gone below the kneed, a shoe with the sole off, and the straw he had wrapped around the other foot, and a gray woolen shirt" (Locke 1962: 17). Shortly after, Nasby deserts from the Confederates when he is down to a blanket and one shoe, strips the uniform off a drunk, and goes home, declaring himself a deserter. His friends take up a collection for him, but they take their money back and call him a swindler when they discover that he has deserted from the Confederate army.

Over the course of a similarly long career and publishing more than twenty novels, Marietta Holley ("Josiah Allen's Wife") wrote satire that struck at most of the prominent social issues of her day – woman's rights, temperance, racial uplift, church reform, and dress reform. Of these, her satire on behalf of women's equality predominated, beginning with her first book, *My Opinions and Betsey Bobbet's* (1873), to her last, *Josiah Allen on the Woman Question* (1914). Holley wrote in the long tradition of American satirists who adopted a rustic persona to deliver up the "truth" about a particular social or political issue; in so doing, she reversed the traditional stereotypes about the sexes. In her novels

> Samantha articulates common-sense arguments in favor of women's political rights, while her "pardner," Josiah, serves as a spokesman for traditional and sentimental male opposition to women's equality. Samantha "soars" in her defense of women and Josiah resorts to clichés that produce comic effects. Nonetheless, each novel is framed by the domestic happiness and stability of the Allen family. No matter how misguided Josiah is on the issues of women's rights, Samantha is devoted to him, as she says, "with a cast-iron affection." (Morris 1988: 150)

Holley understood that her satire against the constraints on women's full equality worked best because it was articulated by a married woman, the wife of a farmer. A second antagonist in the early works is Betsey Bobbet, an aging spinster who wants nothing more than a husband to cling to and thinks women should have no rights at all. Like Josiah, she is a foil to Samantha Allen's proto-feminist views:

> "Yes" says Betsey "men do admire to have wimmen clingin' to 'em, like a vine to a stately tree, and it is indeed a sweet view."
>
> "So 'tis, so 'tis," says I, I never was much of a clinger myself. Still if females want to cling, I haint no objection. "But," says I, in reasonable tones, "as I have said more'n a hundred times, if men think that wimmen are obleeged to be vines, they ought to feel obleeged to make trees of themselves, fo 'em to run up on. But they wont; some of 'em, they will not be trees, they seem to be sot against it." (Holley 1873: 237)

Holley's earliest novels were all published by the American Publishing Company, a subscription press that also featured the works of Mark Twain. In 1905, the *Critic* proclaimed that Holley reached an audience as large as Twain's, and she was called "the Female Mark Twain in the popular press" (Winter 1984: 1). Although her work received little attention in the middle decades of the twentieth century, her skills as a humorist and satirist were once again recognized beginning in the late 1970s, one hundred years after the publication of her first novel.

Mark Twain as Political and Social Satirist

The same year that Holley published her first novel, Mark Twain published his third book, *The Gilded Age* (1873), co-written with Charles Dudley Warner. It was his first foray into political satire, which he did not return to again in earnest until the end of the century. Over the course of his career, in fact, he wrote many pieces that properly can be called satiric; the darkest of these were written in the early years of the twentieth century, with many of them not published in Twain's lifetime. While none of his satires fit into neat categories, it is useful to group the pieces broadly in terms of their primary targets: politics and government, imperialism, war, religion (specifically Christianity), and man's folly and pride. Some of the satiric writings are narrowly focused, such as "The War Prayer," while other works, such as the unfinished "The Chronicle of Young Satan," cut a wide swath through the human landscape. They call upon a variety of techniques and literary personae to do the satiric work, yet all are masterfully done and burn with conviction. Because so much has been written about two of Twain's masterpieces that are often considered to be satires – *Adventures of Huckleberry Finn* (1884) and *A Connecticut Yankee in King's Arthur's Court* (1889) – this chapter will not include them; rather, it will consider one novel briefly, *The Gilded Age*, then move to Twain's late essays and short stories.

There is a playfulness about *The Gilded Age* that both marks it as a relatively early work in Twain's canon and that distinguishes it sharply from the satiric works that followed two decades later. There are multiple targets of satire in the novel (as well as a somewhat conventional set of romantic relations), ranging from Washington society to legislative corruption, from corporate (and individual) greed to influence peddling in Congress. At the center of the novel is a character who was wholly Twain's creation – Col. Beriah Sellers, a hopelessly optimistic dreamer who, among his many schemes, expected to cash in on the westward expansion of the railroads, and who, in his ebullience, has a remarkable ability to persuade others of the value of his schemes and his imagined place in society. The novel follows him from a hamlet in Missouri to Washington, DC, where legislative corruption abounds. Sellers, who is an apologist for the corruption, can only be understood ironically:

> Well, yes; in a free country like ours, where any man can run for Congress and anybody can vote for him, you can't expect immortal purity all the time – it ain't in nature. – Sixty or eighty or a hundred and fifty people are bound to get in who are not angels in disguise, as young Hicks the correspondent says; but still it is a very good average; very

good indeed. As long as it averages as well as that, I think we can feel very well satisfied. Even in these days, when people growl so much and the newspapers are so out of patience, there is still a very respectable minority of honest men in Congress. (Twain and Warner 2001: 364–5)

The heroine of the novel, Laura Hawkins, also Twain's creation, stands to gain a fortune if a particular extremely dubious appropriation bill passes in Congress, and she lobbies very effectively for it; the bill, however, is ultimately defeated because of the scandalous behavior of a Senator Dilworthy, a Western senator, who is exposed for attempting to bribe a legislator to vote with him. Laura, in turn, is undone by an unscrupulous Southern "gentleman" who had earlier seduced her and whom she murders; she is acquitted, but dies shortly thereafter of heart failure. Col. Sellers returns to Missouri, a disappointed man, but Twain brings him back in a successful stage comedy named in his honor.

In 1901, Twain wrote and published another satire, "To the Person Sitting in Darkness," aimed at corrupt and immoral government practices, but in this instance with a bitter, sustained sense of irony and righteous indignation directed against European and American imperialist practices and policies. The essay begins with parallel newspaper articles, one detailing the "havoc and ruin" of life in the East Side of New York City, and the other a report from a missionary to China about the retribution he has exacted upon the Chinese for "damages" incurred in the Boxer Rebellion. The narrator, presumably in the unmediated voice of Twain himself, moves directly into a sardonic discussion about the effects of "extending the blessing of civilization to our Brother who sits in Darkness":

> We have been treacherous; but that was only in order that real good might come out of apparent evil. True, we have crushed and deceived a confiding people; we have turned against the weak and the friendless who trusted us; we have stamped out a just and intelligent and well-ordered republic; we have stabbed an ally in the back and slapped the face of a guest; we have bought a Shadow from an enemy that hadn't it to sell; we have robbed a trusting friend of his land and his liberty; we have invited our clean young men to shoulder a discredited musket and do bandit's work under a flag which bandits have been accustomed to fear, not to follow; we have debauched America's honor and blackened her face before the world; but each detail was for the best. We know this. The Head of every State and Sovereignty in Christendom and ninety per cent of every legislative body in Christendom, including our Congress and our fifty State Legislatures, are members not only of the church, but also of the Blessings-of-Civilization Trust. (Twain 1992: 471)

The essay becomes an extended recitation of the imperialist projects of England, Germany, Russia, and, finally, a stinging indictment of the United States for its entry into the "game" in the Philippines. Twain's satire in this essay is fierce: "it sparked an intense controversy that revitalized the [anti-imperialist] movement and restored some of the momentum it had lost following the election. The country's leading anti-imperialist newspaper, the *Springfield Republican* (Mass.), editorialized that 'Mark Twain has suddenly become the most influential anti-imperialist and the most dreaded critic of the sacrosanct person in the White House that the country contains'" (Zwick 1992: xix).

Twain's anti-imperialist satire is even fiercer in "King Leopold's Soliloquy: A Defense of his Congo Rule" (1905). This relatively long essay, published in Twain's lifetime in pamphlet form, alternates between King Leopold's soliloquies lamenting the ways in which the press and other "busy bodies," such as missionaries, continue to expose the atrocities he is responsible for in the Congo, and extended passages from his critics whom Leopold is in the process of reading. Unlike a dramatic monologue, which would have depended on a fine-tuned sense of irony, Leopold's soliloquizing allows Twain to represent the king's perspective in a straight-forward, unapologetic manner, since he is theoretically speaking only to himself. Thus, he readily owns responsibility for the deaths of 15 million Congolese, and for the mutilation of thousands more. The king brags that he used Christianity to further his own cause, and over twenty years has successfully pursued his nefarious ends without any significant interference from other governments. He delights in the fact that he put one over on the Americans, getting the government to endorse his state:

> Yes, I certainly was a shade too clever for the Yankees. It hurts; it gravels them. They can't get over it! Puts a shame upon them in another way, too, and a graver way; for they never can rid their records of the reproachful fact that their vain Republic, self-appointed Champion and Promoter of the Liberties of the World, is the only democracy in history that has lent its power and influence to the establishing of an *absolute monarchy*! (Twain 1992: 667)

Of all the complaints about the abuses reported by the missionaries, one that particularly galls King Leopold is that *he* is accused of cannibalism simply because his black mercenaries practice it on their victims:

> They report cases of it with a most offensive frequency. My traducers do not forget to remark that, inasmuch as I am absolute and with a word can prevent in the Congo anything I choose to prevent, then whatsoever is done there by my permission is my act, my *personal* act; that *I* do it; that the hand of my agent is as truly *my* hand as if it were attached to my own arm; and so they picture me in my robes of state, with my crown on my head, munching human flesh, saying grace, mumbling thanks to Him from whom all good things come. (Twain 1992: 673)

The piece ends as darkly as it begins, with actual photographs of mutilated Congolese, and with Leopold secure in the knowledge that people do not want to look at the atrocities he has committed: "I know the human race."

An additional piece, "The War Prayer," was written in the same year as "King Leopold's Soliloquy" but was not published until 1923. Fable-like in its form and effect, "The War Prayer" is a cautionary tale. The situation is simple, yet startling.

A congregation gathers, full of patriotic fervor on the eve of an unspecified war, and prays, with the pastor, for "the ever merciful and benignant Father of us all... [to] watch over our noble young soldiers, and aid, comfort, and encourage them in their patriotic work... [and] help them to crush the foe..." (Twain 1992: 653). Then an "aged stranger" enters the church, tells the congregation that he comes directly from God, then proceeds to put into words the implications of the unspoken part of their prayer:

> O Lord, our God, help us to tear their soldiers to bloody shreds with our shells; help us to cover their smiling fields with the pale forms of their patriot dead; help us to drown the thunder of the guns with the shrieks of their wounded, writhing in pain; help us to lay waste their humble homes with a hurricane of fire; help us to wring the hearts of their unoffending widows with unavailing grief... (Twain 1992: 654)

The effect of the stranger is lost upon the immediate audience, who dismiss the old man as a lunatic, but its impact on Twain's readers continues to this day for its trenchant anti-war sentiment.

Satiric essays written by Twain in the final decade of his life are more explicitly aimed at religious beliefs. One in particular, "Letters from the Earth" (1909), takes aim at man's hubris in believing he was made in God's image, when in fact he is just an "experiment." The narrator contends that the biblical stories of the Old Testament are absurd fictions and that the God imagined by man does not resemble the God known to the narrator. The letters all are written by the fallen angel Satan, who has been banished from God's company for a day (a thousand years in earthly time) because he had uttered a sarcasm; he decides to spend that day on Earth to see how the experiment is working, and writes letters back to the angels Michael and Gabriel reporting what he finds. His first impression is that man is insane because he thinks he is God's pet; then the irony increases, and man's religious beliefs, biblical stories, and man's nature are all reported with some amusement by Satan. Throughout, there is an underlying assumption that the three angels know that God is a cynical, cruel, and jealous god. He created all kinds of diseases out of revenge, he invented hell because death alone was too sweet, too easy, and he kills men for trifling reasons. The letters end with Satan quoting, for Gabriel and Michael's amusement, the Beatitudes, which he calls an "immense sarcasm." "Letters from the Earth" was first published in 1939 by Bernard DeVoto, and reissued in 1962 in an expanded collection bearing the same name.

Finally, two longer satires take aim at man's pride. "The Man that Corrupted Hadleyburg" was published in 1899, while "The Chronicle of Young Satan" was left unfinished at Twain's death, but in abbreviated form was the basis for Albert Bigelow Paine's bowdlerized "Mysterious Stranger" manuscript, which until 1963 was widely accepted as being Twain's own work (Camfield 2003: 387). "The Man that Corrupted Hadleyburg" involves a complicated revenge plot set in motion by a stranger who had once "received a deep offense" in Hadleyburg and devises an elaborate scheme to humiliate the entire town. At the heart of the matter is the town's pride in being "the most honest and upright town in all the region round about. It had kept that reputation unsmirched during three generations, and was prouder of it than of any other of its possessions" (Twain 1992: 390). The stranger delivers up a large bag reported to contain 160 pounds of gold, which is to be given to the person who had earlier supposedly given him $20 and a piece of advice. The gold is to go to the citizen who can reproduce that remark, that piece of advice, which is to be revealed in a town meeting. The stranger then writes confidential letters to the nineteen most prominent citizens in the town, repeating the remark; each person in turn half-way persuades himself that he did loan a stranger that money and that he did make a memorable remark, and they all fall to the temptation. The climax of the tale takes place in the town meeting, where one prominent citizen after another is publicly exposed and humiliated when each, in turn, produces the same remark and makes the same claim to an act of charity. Only one man is spared the humiliation and the mockery of the crowd, which turns into a raucous chorus, chanting the "remark" and enjoying every moment of the town's fall from pride:

> The pandemonium of delight which turned itself loose now was of a sort to make the judicious weep. Those whose withers were unwrung laughed till the tears ran down; the reporters, in throes of laughter, set down disordered pothooks which would never in the world be decipherable; and a sleeping dog jumped up, scared out of its wits, and barked itself crazy at the turmoil. (Twain 1992: 420)

The belief held by the town at the beginning of the tale, that it is "incorruptible," is shattered by the actions set in motion by the vengeful stranger. Even the man who is spared, Richardson, is ultimately exposed as one of the corruptible. What makes the satire gentler than it might seem is that the leading citizens, especially Richardson and his wife, are portrayed with some sympathy, and that the tale reads more like a fable than a realistic story – the ultimate target of the humor being hubris. As Gregg Camfield points out, "'Hadleyburg' develops the moral double-vision of many of Twain's late works, recognizing and scorning human shortcomings while simultaneously sympathizing with individual human beings for the impossible demands placed on them by a morally indifferent universe" (2003: 354).

"The Chronicle of Young Satan" may be one of the most bittersweet pieces that Twain wrote. His protagonist, Young Satan, also called Philip Traum, is a charming, magical character who befriends three young Austrian boys in the year 1702. The story is told in the first-person voice of one of those boys, Theodore Fischer. At the same time that Young Satan (the nephew of the fallen angel) entertains the boys with all manner of magical activities, he educates them in the most matter of fact way about the extraordinary limitations of the human race, which commits one act of cruelty after another. Humans, he explains, are inferior to all other animals because humans are cursed with "the mongrel Moral Sense." In his first encounter with the boys, Satan creates out of the dirt a "crowd of little men and women the size of your little finger" – five hundred in number – who proceed to build a tiny castle while the boys look on, enchanted. Two workers begin to quarrel, then fight, and Satan reaches out and squashes them between his fingers; when their relatives gather round and weep and pray, he picks up the board seat of the boys' swing "and mashed all those people into the earth just as if they were flies..." (Gibson 1969: 50). The boys are horrified, but Satan insists that the people were of no consequence.

Satan's most sustained criticism is reserved for the institution of the church, with all its superstitions, with the fear it instills in people, and ultimately for its bloody wars. The Christians, Satan makes clear, are the bloodiest killers in all of history, both past and future. The fate of a given individual, he teaches the boys, is determined by the first act of his life; nothing can alter the course of a life once it is set in motion, like a row of bricks tumbling down as each one strikes the next. Nonetheless, Satan does alter the course of three lives – for the better, he assures Theodore. He allows their friend Nikolaus to drown attempting to save a young girl, Lisa; had Nikolaus lived he would have contracted scarlet fever and spent the rest of his life "in his bed a paralytic log, deaf, dumb, blind, and praying night and day for the blessed relief of death" (Gibson 1969: 118). Lisa's death saves her from a life of pain, destitution, and depravity. He alters the fate, too, of Father Peter, a beloved, good priest, by having him acquitted of a crime that would have sent him to his death, then simultaneously depriving him, forever, of his sanity and thereby making him happy in his delusion that he is the Emperor. "No sane man," says Satan, "can be happy."

Against this increasingly dark vision of human nature, Twain, through Satan, articulates one of the most famous and telling statements about the role of laughter in human society, and by extension, the role of satire as a means of exposing and destroying falsehood:

> For your race, in its poverty, has unquestionably one really effective weapon – laughter. – Power, Money, Persuasion, Supplication, Persecution – these can lift at a colossal humbug, – push it a little – crowd it a little – weaken it a little, century by century: but only Laughter can blow it to rags and atoms at a blast. Against the assault of Laughter nothing can stand. You are always fussing and fighting with your other weapons: do you ever use that one? No, you leave it lying rusting. As a race, do you ever use it at all? No – you lack sense and the courage. Once in an age a single hero lifts it, delivers his blow, and a hoary humbug goes to ruin. (Gibson 1969: 166)

Young Satan is right in his assertion about the power of laughter, but he underestimates the extent to which it was employed in America as a weapon to "lift at a colossal humbug." The history of early American satire is the story of writers who indeed had the "courage" to wield that weapon to great advantage.

Acknowledgment

The research on American satire for this chapter was completed in 2004 as a Fellow at the Library of Congress.

References and Further Reading

Bakalar, Nicholas (ed.) (1997) *American Satire: An Anthology of Writings from Colonial Times to the Present.* New York: Penguin.

Butler, William Allen (1857) *Nothing to Wear: An Episode of City Life.* New York: Rudd and Carleton.

Camfield, Gregg (2003) *The Oxford Companion to Mark Twain.* Oxford: Oxford University Press.

Carlisle, Henry C., Jr (ed.) (1962) *American Satire in Prose and Verse.* New York: Random House.

Cooke, Ebenezer (1708) *The Sot-Weed Factor: or, a Voyage to Maryland.* London: D. Bragg.

Fern, Fanny (1854) *Fern Leaves from Fanny's Port-Folio.* Buffalo: Miller, Orton, and Mulligan.

—— (1857) *Fresh Leaves.* New York: Mason Brothers.

—— (1999) *Ruth Hall and Other Writings*, ed. Joyce W. Warren. New Brunswick: Rutgers University Press.

Freneau, Philip (1815) *A Collection of Poems on American Affairs, and a Variety of Other Subjects, Chiefly Moral and Political; Written Between the Year 1797 and the Present Time*, 2 vols. New York: David Longworth.

Gibson, William M. (ed.) (1969) *Mark Twain: The Mysterious Stranger Manuscripts.* Berkeley, CA: University of California Press.

Hamilton, Alexander (1995) *The Tuesday Club: A Shorter Edition of the History of the Ancient and Honorable Tuesday Club*, ed. Robert Micklus. Baltimore, MD: The Johns Hopkins University Press.

Holley, Marietta (1873) *My Opinions and Betsey Bobbet's.* Hartford: American.

Hopkinson, Francis (1964) *The Battle of the Kegs.* New York: Crowell.

Irving, Washington (2001) *A History of New York from the Beginning of the World to the End of the Dutch Dynasty, by Diedrich Knickerbocker*, 2 vols. Gretna: Firebird.

——, Irving, William, and Paulding, James Kirke (1860) *Salmagundi; or, the Whim-Whams and Opinions of Launcelot Langstaff, Esq., and Others*, with "Preface" by Evert Duyckinck. New York: G. P. Putnam (reprint of 1807–8 edition).

Kirkland, Caroline (1990) *A New Home, Who Will Follow? or Glimpses of Western Life*, ed. Sandra A. Zagarell. New Brunswick: Rutgers University Press.

Locke, David R. (1962) *Civil War Letters of Petroleum V. Nasby.* Columbus: Ohio State University Press.

Lowell, James Russell (1977) *The Biglow Papers {First Series}: A Critical Edition*, ed. Thomas Wortham. DeKalb, IL: Northern Illinois University Press.

Micklus, Robert (1984) The case against Ebenezer Cooke's *Sot-Weed Factor*. *American Literature* 56 (2), 251–61.

Morris, Linda A. (1988) *Women Vernacular Humorists in Nineteenth-century America: Ann Stephens, Frances Whitcher, and Marietta Holley.* New York: Garland.

—— (1992) *Women's Humor in the Age of Gentility: The Life and Works of Frances Miriam Whitcher.* Syracuse: Syracuse University Press.

Morton, Thomas (1969) *New English Canaan.* Amsterdam: De Capo (facsimile of 1637 edition).

Mowatt, Anna Cora (1854) *Fashion; or Life in New York.* Boston: Ticknor and Fields.

Paulding, James Kirke (1825) *John Bull in America; or, the New Munchausen.* New York: Charles Wiley.

Smith, Seba (1973) *The Life and Writings of Major Jack Downing, of Downingville, Away Down East in the State of Maine.* New York: AMS Press (originally published 1833).

Trumbull, John (1962) *The Satiric Poems of John Trumbull: The Progress of Dullness and M'Fingal*, ed. Edwin T. Bowden. Austin: University of Texas.

Twain, Mark (1992) *Collected Tales, Sketches, Speeches, and Essays: 1891–1910*, ed. Louis J. Budd. New York: Library of America.

—— and Warner, Charles Dudley (2001) *The Gilded Age: A Tale of Today.* New York: Penguin.

Tyler, Royall (1970) *The Contrast: A Comedy*, with Introduction by Thomas J. McKee. New York: Burt Franklin (reprint of 1887 edition).

—— (2002) *The Algerine Captive, or The Life and Adventures of Doctor Updike Underhill: Six Years a Prisoner Among the Algerines*. New York: Modern Library.

Warner, Charles Dudley (1891) *Washington Irving* (available at http://www.gutenberg.net/etext02/cwirv11.txt).

Warren, Joyce W. (1995) Uncommon discourse: Fanny Fern and the New York *Ledger*. In Kenneth M. Price and Susan B. Smith (eds), *Periodical Literature in Nineteenth-century America*, pp. 51–68. Charlottesville: University Press of Virginia.

Whitcher, Frances M. (1855) *The Widow Bedott Papers*. New York: J. C. Derby.

Winter, Kate H. (1984) *Marietta Holley: Life with "Josiah Allen's Wife."* Syracuse: Syracuse University Press.

Zall, Paul M. (ed.) (1976) *Comical Spirit of Seventy-six: The Humor of Francis Hopkinson*. San Marino: Huntington Library.

Zwick, Jim (ed.) (1992) *Mark Twain's Weapons of Satire: Anti-Imperialist Writings on the Philippine–American War*. Syracuse: Syracuse University Press.

21
Twentieth-century Fictional Satire
Valentine Cunningham

There was no small disagreement in the twentieth century about satire as a literary kind and literary practice. The continuing existence of any of the traditional genres as fixed and fixable, knowable and bounded literary entities has long been a fraught matter. One may not go so far as to accept Derrida's argument that it is a law of genre that the claimed generic boundaries are all and always unsustainable and will of their very nature be transgressed (Derrida 1992), but it is certainly the case that theoretical and practical attempts to keep up the rigidities of the ancient generic system dramatically collapsed in the early modern period, especially with the Rise of the Novel As We Know It. The novel was, I suppose, the most potent engine, as well as the greatest beneficiary, of this dramatically undoing turn in literary practice. It quickly became the glory of novels that they are wonderfully confused, generically considered, that they mix and match the generic possibilities with extreme plundering relish. And the satirical has been from the novel's start one of the generic pots most regularly plundered.

Difficile est Satyras non Scribere

In one of his characteristic mid-century agonizings, "Juvenal's Error," Theodor Adorno challenges Juvenal's famous allegation, *difficile est satyras non scribere* – it is difficult not to write satires – particularly in the wake of the Hitlerzeit. The modern situation is beyond mockery's reach; irony will not work on targets which embrace cruel, corrupt, wicked action as givens of nature; the traditional power of the satirist's criticism is feeble against the totalitarian's much greater power (Adorno 1978). And these melancholy reflections have their force. But they go too far. Satire flourishes especially in the run-up to and in the aftermath of the great dictators. Twentieth-century fiction has been strongly on Juvenal's side. Twentieth-century fictionists have found it hard to avoid being satirical. "Is satire still possible?" Iain Sinclair asks

J. G. Ballard, dystopian sci-fi novelist, discussing Ballard's momentous 1973 novel *Crash*, about the fetishizing of automobiles and car accidents in the traffic-jammed contemporary urbs, and David Cronenberg's 1996 SM-classic film version of the book. "Why not?" replies Ballard, "I think so. I think anyone in the public eye is – horrible phrase – fair game" (Sinclair 1999: 15). Core inspirations for Ballard's satirizing fetishisms were precisely some celebrity deaths in automobiles, in particular Jayne Mansfield's and President Kennedy's. And offences and offenders in the public eye, from Prime Ministers Thatcher and Blair to headline gangsters like London's Kray brothers and all property developers, keep Sinclair's large roster of fictions and factions in cheerful satiric business. A typical Sinclair "novel" is his *Landor's Tower* (2001), spicing his customary bibliographical japes and psycho-geographical ramblings (around Hay-on-Wye, the Welsh book capital and the Welsh home-scape of poets, scandalous artists and religious crooks, the Vaughan brothers, Eric Gill, "Father Ignatius") with contemporary items such as Beirut kidnapees, the mysterious deaths of employees of the electronics-armaments company, Marconi, and the gay-sex, dog-shooting scandal that brought down Liberal Party leader Jeremy Thorpe. For Sinclair, wide-roaming scrutineer of his times, as for J. G. Ballard and his dystopian sci-fi kind, it is indeed *difficile satyras non scribere*.

Wyndham Lewis – who thought and wrote more extensively than any other twentieth-century writer about the nature and role of satire and the satirist – is emphatically Juvenalian – in every sense. In his (critically satirical) *Men Without Art*, he declared that "there is nothing written or painted today which could not be brought under the head of *satire*" (1934: 12). Arguably, that had been true of much writing for a long time, not least the novel, and twentieth-century fiction's huge investment in the satirical does, as Lewis indicates, more than keep up with this tradition. Numerically, the "wholetime" satirists, as Lewis (1950: 44) calls them, are perhaps not all that many. There is Lewis himself, and Aldous Huxley, Evelyn Waugh, and George Orwell, and just a few others, including, I would say, Kingsley Amis and J. G. Ballard, Martin Amis, Iain Sinclair, and Will Self. Even then, as Lewis nicely puts it (also in *Men Without Art*), "No work of fiction is likely to be only 'Satire,' in the sense that a short epigrammatic piece, in rhyming couplets (an Epistle of Pope) would be" (Lewis 1934: 121). But by the same token – novels consistently refusing, compelled as they are by the mode's developed generic eclecticism, to stick to just one generic impulse – it is hard for novels to keep the satirical impulse at bay. So that part-time satirists, as we may label the generic contemporaries of Lewis's wholetimers, novelists who go in for satire, but patchily and temporarily, as a minor strain or occasional excursion, are almost too numerous to mention.

In his often-quoted essay of 1928 on "Humour and Satire," Father Ronald Knox, part-time satirizer of theologians, textual critics, and ecclesiological change, gloomily suggested that the rising tide of recent humorous writing had rather queered satire's pitch: "our habituation to humorous reading has inoculated our systems against the beneficent poison of satire" (Knox 1928: 42). Beneficent poison: traditional satirical medicine from a Juvenal or a Swift. Knox mentions the manifestly non-Juvenalian

P. G. Wodehouse. But for all Wodehouse's pervasive jokiness, it would be hard to deny a satirical edge or undertow to his comic engagements with Bertie Wooster's dotty aristo clique of club bores, posh idlers, mad aunts, and loopy country-house folk – and all before the terrible Roderick Spode of the ludicrous but sinister neo-fascist Black Shorts movement heaves onto the comic-satiric horizon. Even as Knox was complaining in 1928, Evelyn Waugh's *Decline and Fall* had appeared, the first in his busy conga-line of satires putting humor, the laugh-inducing absurdities of the modern world, especially the world of the English upper-class, foremost.

Comedians Wodehouse and Waugh are clear cases of how satire can work through comedy, which is to say clear cases too of satire's generic generosity, the way it makes itself at home on any and every generic vehicle. Refusing all generic constraints, it will get in everywhere, invading and infecting every brand of twentieth-century fiction: fictions comical and farcical, of course, but also fictions essayistic, elegiac, Gothic, erotic, domestic, historical, topographical, documentary, social- and socialist-realist, magic-realist. Satire pokes through especially dramatically in science fiction, fantasy, detective, and crime fiction (those modes known, curiously, in literary-journalistic jargon as "genre fiction"): futurist fiction in the hands of Brian Aldiss and Michael Moorcock as well as J. G. Ballard; crime as performed by the likes of Derek Raymond and Michael Dibdin. What is Gothic revivalist Patrick McGrath except frequently satirical, or essayistic Julian Barnes, or Jewish urban-mythographer Howard Jacobson? Nor is satire restricted to any one period: the satirical note sounds across all of the twentieth century – among our grand modernists Joyce and Woolf, D. H. Lawrence and E. M. Forster, let alone Wyndham Lewis; in the twenties, when Huxley and Waugh get started; in the social-documentarist thirties with Walter Greenwood, George Orwell, Christopher Isherwood, Henry Green, Lewis Grassic Gibbon; among the moralists of the forties and after (Graham Greene a notorious example); among the Angry Young Men of the fifties (Alan Sillitoe, John Wain, Kingsley Amis) and the mid-century's post-Christian moralists (notably William Golding and Iris Murdoch and Anthony Burgess); as too, among the sixties' and seventies' and eighties' generations of campus novelists (think David Lodge and Malcolm Bradbury), woman-ists and feminists (think Fay Weldon, Angela Carter, Michèle Roberts, Maggie Gee, Jeanette Winterson), post-colonialists (all those immigrating writers and the sons and daughters of the immigrant populations: Sam Selvon, V. S. Naipaul, Caryl Phillips, David Dabydeen, Fred D'Aguair, Abdulrazak Gurnah, Adam Zameenzad, let alone Kazuo Ishiguro and Salman Rushdie), youthies like Irvine Welsh, Alan Warner, Jonathan Coe, and Toby Litt, and the crowd of urbanite protesters against and opponents of Thatcher's Britain and then (on into the nineties) of Blair's Britain (James Kelman, say, or all those novelists associated with the publisher Serpent's Tail, the art terrorist Stewart Home and his kind). And so on and on. Being satirical has come extremely natural to every generation of twentieth-century British fictionists.

At almost any moment in this long period of literary production, a novel might be jogging along in the usual mildly critical vein of much British fiction when there will pop up, almost unprovoked in the context, an outburst of hot spleen against some just perceived abuse or occasion of offence. As in, say, to take almost any old regular and utterly normal bourgeois English novel, *Lucia in London* (1927), one more of E. F. Benson's nicely pottering ribbings of its gang of manipulative bourgeois English culture-vulturesque people from genteel Riseholme (Henry James's Rye) — a novel doing its genial best to be merely diverting — when Lucia, extremest culturata of them all, gets the shock of London's latest artiness full in the teeth.

> Mrs Alingsby was tall and weird and intense, dressed rather like a bird-of-paradise that had been out in a high gale, but very well connected. She had long straight hair which fell over her forehead, and sometimes got in her eyes, and she wore on her head a jockey-cap with an immense cameo in front of it. She hated all art that was earlier than 1923, and a considerable lot of what was later. In music, on the other hand, she was primitive, and thought Bach decadent; in literature her taste was for stories without a story, and poems without metre or meaning. But she had collected around her a group of interesting outlaws, of whom the men looked like women, and the women like nothing at all, and though nobody ever knew what they were talking about, they themselves were talked about. Lucia had been to a party of hers, where they all sat in a room with black walls, and listened to early Italian music on a spinet while a charcoal brazier on a blue hearth was fed with incense... (Benson 1991: 578)

This sharp-tongued bitching is almost worthy of Huxley, or Wyndham Lewis, or Evelyn Waugh. The suddenness of the attack rather takes your breath away. But it is what you have to learn to expect from even the most seemingly genial of twentieth-century English fiction. And, of course, every decade has seen some wholetime satirist or other in action.

Big Canons

It is a notable feature of twentieth-century satirists and satirizers that they write with the great satirical tradition, the satirical canon, much on their minds. For Orwell and his contemporaries, the twentieth century evidently repeats the inciting traumas of the classic satirizing times. At one truly arresting moment in *Lord Rochester's Monkey* (1974), his life of the foulest-mouthed of Restoration satirists, Graham Greene suggests that the post-Dutch-War ennui that fueled Rochester's angers has been repeated for Greene's generation. "Vast hopes disappointed are apt to leave an overmastering weariness behind, and war is not usually followed by peace of mind. The excitement of war is a drug that we miss in the dull days after. Spleen was the disease which ran through the literature of the succeeding quieter years, and my generation is in a good position to understand it" (Greene 1988: 53).

Ronald Knox wants modern satirists to "scourge our vices like Juvenal" and "purge our consciences like Hogarth" (Knox 1928: 40). The title of Aldous Huxley's second novel, *Antic Hay* (1923), comes from the lines from Marlowe's *Edward II* (1593; 1.58–9) which comprise its epigraph: "My men like satyrs grazing on the lawns / Shall with their goat-feet dance the antic hay" – thus announcing that the post-Great War Londoners this satire dyspeptically presents will be updates of the goatish merrymakers whose name was once thought to have given the genre its title and its subject matter. What Jonson and Congreve and Dryden did provides Huxley with a cathartic charter for the modern satirist:

> it is good for solemnity's nose to be tweaked, it is good for human pomposity to be made to look mean and ridiculous... great social function... cruel and unsparing laughter... A good dose of this mockery... should purge our minds of much waste matter... Ben's reduction of human beings to a series of rather unpleasant Humours is sound and medicinal. (Huxley 1971a: 202–3)

Mr Cardan in Huxley's *Those Barren Leaves* (1925) deplores the way casual modern dealings with serious books have turned *Gulliver's Travels* (1726) into a mere children's classic (Huxley 1969b: 55). Wyndham Lewis's touchstones are Ben Jonson, Pope, Hogarth, Swift. Does he give offence in his *The Apes of God* (1931)? Lewis's defense is that he is seeking to imitate Swift. He is aiming for the "special sort of laughter" that "produced the giant maids of Brobdingnag" (Lewis 1934: 109, 110). In his protracted apologia for *The Apes*, he liked quoting Yeats's comment that in it "something absent from all literature for a generation was back again": "We had it in one man once. He lies in St Patrick's now under the greatest epitaph in history" (Lewis 1930: 29). That man is Swift; the epitaph celebrating his *saeva indignatio* now claimed for Lewis. George Orwell's extensive career as satirist is founded on his professed admiration for Swift – "one of the writers I admire with least reserve." In his notorious 1946 "Politics vs Literature" essay on *Gulliver's Travels*, Orwell says that he has read Swift's novel again and again since he was eight years old. He was making sure his readers would recognize the indebtedness of *Animal Farm* (1945), his satirical beast fable and allegory about communism, to the final, animal allegory, section of *Gulliver's Travels*.

Satirists are committed intertextualists. They keep looking back, establishing self-justifying lineages, lineages that keep growing. The satyresque immoralist John Self in Martin Amis's Thatcher-era satire *Money*, which appeared in the momentously Orwellian year of 1984, reads Orwell – *Nineteen Eighty-Four* and *Animal Farm*. Orwell's Swiftian bestialisms leave Self – intended as a Yahoo-like epitome of a Yahoo-like time, the body-pandering, money-materialist eighties – quite cold. He does not get Orwell's allegory. In a novel replete with doubles and doublings, which it is vital to recognize for mere survival's sake, Self cannot recognize himself in the Orwellian-Swiftian mirror. This is perhaps the most crucial of his chain of life-threatening misperceptions – discomfortingly close, as it happens, to his not realizing that he is a sort of remake of John the Savage from Huxley's *Brave New World* of 1932. Self likes *Nineteen Eighty-Four* better than *Animal Farm*, but misreads it too ("welcome sex-interest and all those rat-tortures to look forward to"), even if finding himself in Room 101 of New York's Ashbery Hotel does give him "a jolt" (M. Amis 1985: 210–15, 218, 219–20, 223; see Miller 1985 for the *Doppelgänger* thematic of *Money*).

Monkey Business

Doubling repeats of Swift's uncanny representation of the human as Yahoos — a beastliness and bestialism demonstrated in lowest-of-the-low bodiliness, all unrestrained sexuality and excrementitiousness — are the commonest resort of twentieth-century satire. Monkey business is the modern satirists' usual trade, their regular trope. Modern satire takes up residence on a planet of the apes. Humans have turned everywhere into monkeys — a degree zero of the human animal, devoid of spiritual life and intellectual worth, a parody of civility and culture, repellent, charmless, disgusting. According to Wyndham Lewis's virulent anti-Bloomsbury tirade, *The Apes of God* (1931), the whole culture has gone ape. Culture is in the hands of the philistines, and philistines are all apes, hunting down culture's "great" ones (among whom Lewis includes himself; Lewis 1931b: 127ff). It is a widespread animalization, in which, according to the satirists, nothing is sacred, least of all the sacred. Modern religion is in the hands of Mrs Melrose Ape, according to the religious hand-wringing of Evelyn Waugh's *Vile Bodies* (1930). Mrs Ape, uncouth American evangelist (mocking version of Aimée Semple Macpherson), with her choir of dubious Angels ("Chastity" ends up an international whore and willing army-camp follower), is the antithesis of the good old Christianity of Roman Catholic Father Rothschild and John Wesley, founder of Methodism, whose career gets vividly traduced in a trashy Hollywood film.

Twentieth-century culture thinks it is rather good at producing the Body Beautiful. In his essay "The Beauty Industry" (1931), Huxley cannily put his finger on the modern American model of desirable bodiliness, the cinema-driven cult of cosmetics and other artificial body enhancement (Huxley 1970a: 228–36). It is a ("Manichaean") body fetishism to which he keeps turning with great wryness, culminating in *After Many a Summer (Dies the Swan)* (1939) in which Californian Body *cultisme*, this up-to-date desire for protracted youthfulness, is in the hands of one more Huxleyan mad scientist, Dr Obispo. Obispo is a Sade-loving "apeman." His anti-aging experiments — feeding the intestinal flora of carp to baboons — are utterly personal: he is desperate to stretch out his own sex life. He is aided unexpectedly by visiting English bibliophile, Jeremy Pordage, nostalgic about low-life sex back in London's Maida Vale ("Infinite squalor in a little room!"; Part 1, ch. 9), constantly picking his head-scabs like a monkey ("There! The scab under the right hand had come loose. He pulled it out through the thick tufted hair above his ears and, as he looked at the tiny desiccated shred of tissue, was suddenly reminded of the baboons. But, after all, why not?... Nothing like self-knowledge, he reflected"; Part 2, ch. 1). The old papers Pordage is editing for protracted-sex-life-hungry Hollywood mogul Jo Stoyte (he has got his latest Babe to keep up with) suggest the eighteenth-century Fifth Earl of Gonister had success with the carp treatment. The Californians track him down in his Surrey mansion: caged, two hundred and one years old, "a foetal ape that's had time to grow up," a simian grotesque, naked but for some rags of a shirt, a few tattered nobleman's insignia and his all-over hair, grunting, gibbering, pissing on the floor, pursuing his ancient monkey-woman for one more bout of violent copulation. It is the disgusting apotheosis of modern animalism, a truly horrible update of Swift's Struldbrugs, those ancients in *Gulliver's Travels* living for ever but getting ever more decrepit. Only Jo Stoyte is impressed (he'll have some of *that*! Part 3, ch. 2). It is the grisly end-product of the body-care faddisms, which Orwell kept lampooning: the craving of "health-food cranks" to add a bit to the life of their carcass by vegetarianism, fruit-juice drinking, and the like.

Orwell's food cranks are all leftists, progressives, people of the future. Like Huxley, he blames modern ape-man on modernity. The essence of modernity for Huxley is what the scientific, warmongering, atom-bomb devising apes are up to in his novel *Ape and Essence* (1949). Modernismus fancies its rational, humanist body obsessions are progressive, but in fact they are backward steps for evolution, a terrible regressing. The war-scientists of *Ape and Essence* have wiped out civilization, have regressed the whole culture. Huxley's Californinas have, like the Fifth Earl, effectively gone back down the evolutionary ladder. Which is, in effect, the dyspeptic vision of Huxley's humanity-disliking artist Rampion (a version of Huxley's onetime admiree D. H. Lawrence) in *Point Counter Point* (1928). Rampion has made two Outlines of History after H. G. Wells (ch. 16). One shows humanity's progress from monkey to H. G. Wells, apostle of scientific utopia, and Sir Alfred Mond, modern scientific man himself, clothed in "the radiant mist of prophecy," and heading right off the page "towards Utopian infinity." In the other there are a few human highs, Greek, Florentine, some English and French, but mainly troughs, peopled by the "primeval little monkeys" of medieval monks, the "revolting monsters" of the Reformation, Puritanism, and Methodism, Victorian dwarfs and misshapes, all culminating in the twentieth-century's "abortions": "a diminishing company of little gargoyles and foetuses with heads too large for their squelchy bodies, the tails of apes and the faces of our most eminent contemporaries, all biting and scratching and disembowelling one another with that methodical and systematic energy which belongs only to the very highly civilized."

From primitive monkey all of the way around again to modern fetal monkey. It is an anti-modern grimness turned into black political comedy in *Black Mischief* (1932), Evelyn Waugh's deriding take on the rich newness menu – Bauhaus architecture, birth control, new womanhood, vitamins, nudism – imposed on his African state by sovietizing Emperor Seth, BA Oxon, whose modernized people are actually primitives, savages, animals. In the novel's most memorable scene, Seth's soldiers cook and eat their consignment of boots. "Cook-pots steaming over the wood fires; hand drums beating; bare feet shuffling unforgotten tribal rhythms; a thousand darkies crooning and swaying on their haunches, white teeth flashing in the fire-light" (ch. 5). Not all that far in spirit from all this animalizing is *The Right Honourable Chimpanzee* (1978) by "David St George," in which an Oxford scientist's well-trained chimpanzee is jobbed in as Prime Minister to head a government of National Unity, and gets by nicely, for all that he is obviously a monkey, only ever grunting replies to questions, guzzling handfuls of bananas in public with his toes curled for support around his chair leg, grooming the Chancellor of the Exchequer on the Front Bench of the House of Commons. He likes riding up and down in the dumb waiter during cabinet meetings in the kitchen (a nice parodic reference to Prime Minister Harold Wilson's notorious "Kitchen Cabinet"). "[I]f this was an animal, it was a highly political animal" (St. George 1978: 112). Political animals. The novel's joint authors, journalist David Phillips and the exiled Bulgarian satirical playwright Georgi Markov, knew all about them. As the novel was going to press, Markov was assassinated by Bulgarian agents, stabbed with a poisoned umbrella ferrule at a bus stop in London's Strand – a savage replay of Rochester's being beaten up by royal agents; Markov was wrong in not wearing an equivalent of Defoe's iron-bound head-protecting hat.

The Right Honourable Chimpanzee is Orwell's political Yahoo allegory *Animal Farm* redone under the influence of Huxley and Co.'s extensive simianizing. It is a line of satirical thought with, evidently, great mileage in it. As witness the *Guardian* newspaper's chief cartoonist Steve Bell's wonderfully awing portrayal of US President George Bush as a chimpanzee: "He moved like a chimp, walked like a chimp and even talked like a chimp; George Bush actually was a chimp..." (Bell 2005; see also, Bell 2004). And, of course, Will Self's *Great Apes*. Self's artist-protagonist Simon Dykes has a drugs and drink-induced nightmare of London turned completely ape. Humanity has been replaced by "Chimpunity." Self's anguished vision of modern Western human's degraded bodiliness – orgiastic drinking and coke-snorting in sweaty dives and "shebeens," complexly polyandrous coupling, "conga-lines of buggery" at Oxford Circus, and so on – is accorded what is clearly thought to be its only appropriate Swiftian labeling. Turned ape himself, Dykes pointedly peruses

> a copy of the *Essay of the Learned Martin Scriblerus Concerning the Origin of Sciences*... one of the earliest satires to use the human as a "motionless philosopher"... composed in all probability by Pope and Arbuthnot – among others... the precursor of the grand line of eighteenth-century satires, pitting evolved humans against primitive apes. A line that culminated in Swift's Yahoos. (Self 1997: 273)

At one of the novel's art-gallery events, the male critics and artists urgently display their sex, fight over females, "agitated chimps grooming, drinking, gesticulating and mating. 'Like a bloody *zoo*'" (Self 1997: 180). Only apes could behave like this. This is the satiric mood as a kind of zoophobia, a distress over the animality of the human so fearful it can only conclude that there is an ape beneath the suiting.

Pelting

Here, characteristically of the mood and mode, is Wyndham Lewis's Matthew Plunkett, a very big ape-man in the zoo of twenties' Bloomsbury, feeling hungry at lunchtime, like Joyce's Leopold Bloom in the "Lestrygonians" episode of *Ulysses* (1922; *Apes of God* is, among other things, a satirical parody of *Ulysses*):

He yaw-yaw-yawned with the blank bellow of the great felines, behind their bars at the scheduled feeding-hour (smelling the slaughtered meat for their consumption and sighting the figures of the keepers, moving to be their waiters, at their public table d'hôte, watched by hordes of blanched apes, who had confined them) he roared – disparting and shutting his jaws, licking his lips, baying and, with his teeth, grinding, then again baying, while he stretched the elastic of his muscles elevating his arms with clenched fists, in heavy reproduction of the plastic of the Greek. Then he carried one of his exhausted hands to his head, and scratched it, between two sandy bushes, somewhat sun-bleached. (Lewis 1931a: 59–60)

Strikingly, Plunkett is presented entirely from the outside. This is the constant focal point of *The Apes of God* and of Wyndham Lewis. "For *The Apes of God* it could, I think quite safely, be claimed that no book has ever been written that has paid more attention to the outside of people. In it their shells or pelts, or the language of their bodily movements, come first, not last" (Lewis 1934: 118). Which is satire's way. Satire is, as Lewis insisted, "a great *externalist* art" (1934: 121). It is a visualizing form, the closest an artist in words can get to the plastic artist's efforts. "[I]t is *the shell* of the animal that the plastically-minded artist will prefer" (1934: 120). It is notable how many strong satirists have been pictorial artists – Lewis himself, D. H. Lawrence, Evelyn Waugh. *The Apes* comes illustrated with Lewis's drawings; so do Waugh's *Decline and Fall*, and *Black Mischief*, and *Love Among the Ruins* (1953). Iain Sinclair's texts usually involve collaborations with pictorial artists and photographers. Satire is, as Lewis kept insisting, an art of the eye, an eye fiercely content with the outside of things and people. Lewis sets himself against the impressionism of Bloomsbury's and Virginia Woolf's kind of modernism, her 1919 advice to "Look within..." (Woolf 1966: 2.106). Assailing Plunkett and his kind thus is pointedly one in the eye, as it were, for Bloomsbury. Lewis craves the truth of the materiality Woolf specifically rejected, will deal only in physicality, the realism of the human outside, the overt evidence of human animality, however odd that empiricist insistence might prove in what is, again and again, a warfare of ideas. It is as normal for twentieth-century satirists to challenge ideas they dislike by attacking the bodies of their opponents, as it was for their eighteenth- and nineteenth-century predecessors in the satirical line stretching from Swift to Dickens. So this bodily art is, then, doubly synecdochic. It breaks up opponent bodies into representative bad bits: "The satirist is a bit of a butcher... a full-time satirist is not the most attractive of people" (Lewis 1938: 145). And it tries to make this broken, dismembered bodily stuff stand for the mind, the soul, the ideas of the opposed one. And thus it is doubly traducing: traducing ideas into their alleged bodily manifestation, and then traducing the representative body by caricaturing it, making it as grotesque as could be. Satire is the form of deformation. Characteristically, Dryden once rhymed *reformed* with *deformed*: "And least deform'd because reform'd the least" (*The Hind and the Panther*, 1687, Part 1, line 409). If satire is a reformative art – and that will always be a matter of dispute – it works for its reformations by way of deformations. In other words, it is a catachrestical art. And catachrestical for reasons of hostility and malice. As Lewis repeatedly acknowledged;

the *good* of satire, he said, consists in its "stiffening" of "the grotesque" (Lewis 1934: 121).

One of the "broadcasts" or "gramophone records" of Pierpoint in *The Apes*, as reported by the beastly Horace Zagreus his fellow ape and Jewish shadow, the "split-man" Julius Ratner, is about the laws of satire. The "true satirist . . . must remain upon the surface of existence," and viciously. "True satire must be vicious." "The venom of Pope is what is needed." The laughter of the satirist must have "the metallic bark that kills." "Satire to be good must be unfair and single-minded" (Lewis 1931a: 449, 450, 452). Satire's bodily catachreses are to be motored by disgust; their intention is to disgust: the intention of a Swift – or of those great pictorial German contemporaries of Lewis, the satirical old soldiers from the other side of the trench, Max Beckmann and Georg Grosz. Here is an aesthetics of the turned stomach. Kerr-Orr, the narrator of the stories in Lewis's *The Wild Body* (1927) – the Lewisian satirizing eye inside a disgusting body ("This forked, strange-scented, blond-skinned gut-bag, with its two bright rolling marbles with which it sees, bull's eyes full of mockery and madness") – goes about seeking "sight of some stylistic anomaly that will provide me with a new pattern for my grotesque realism" (Lewis 2004: 6–7). Traveling about pre-1914 Brittany, Kerr-Orr spots many such anomalous bodies – Mademoiselle Peronnete, it might be (disgustingly erotic, "like a mad butcher, who put a piece of bright material over a carcase of pork or mutton, and then started to ogle his customers, owing to a sudden shuffling in his mind of the respective appetites"; 2004: 60–1), or Madame Brotcotnaz ("A sort of scaly rigor fixes the wrinkles of her forehead into a seriated field of what is scarcely flesh . . . Her eyes are black and moist, with the furtive intensity of a rat"; 2004: 133–4). Lewis's skin focus is never pleasant. Like the *Skin, skin, skin* of Watt in Samuel Beckett's *Watt* (1953), *skin* is the rhyming partner of *niks*, or *nix*, the abnegation of the desirable (Beckett 1963: 166). Lewis always looks on darkly at the skin of others – especially if it is black skin. *Négritude* greatly upsets him, as it does Aldous Huxley, both of them keen campaigners against the between-wars sun-bathing cult of white men and white women. *Nigger*-despising, *darkie*-gibing Evelyn Waugh is not far behind those two in this white-ist anxiety. One major reason why Lewis and Huxley and Waugh dislike jazz is that it is black music, the music deplored by Goebbels as *Neger-tanzen* (Goebbels is admired for just that in Lewis's *Hitler*, 1931).

The Other of satire always has a ghastly bodily outside – the outwardly visible sign of badness within, the bad somatic truths which are all that satire's critiques choose to go by. The bad body of the Other might be done amusingly. Wyndham Lewis is, clearly, sometimes trying to be funny. Evelyn Waugh is never not trying, like P. G. Wodehouse, to get a laugh out of his bad bodies. Recall those darkies in *Black Mischief* crooning as they pick juicy bits of stewed boot out of the cooking pot.

Ten men of revolting appearance were approaching from the drive. They were low of brow, crafty of eye, and crooked of limb. They advanced huddled together with the loping tread of wolves, peering about them furtively as they came, as though in constant terror of ambush; they slavered at their mouths, which hung loosely over their receding

> chins, while each clutched under his ape-like arm a burden of curious and unaccountable shape. On seeing the Doctor they halted and edged back, those behind squinting and moulting over their companions' shoulders.
>
> "Crikey!" said Philbrick. "Loonies! This is where I shoot."
>
> "I refuse to believe the evidence of my eyes," said the Doctor. "These creatures simply do not exist."

That is the Welsh brass band at the school sports day in chapter 8 of Waugh's *Decline and Fall* – amusing up to a point, at least if you are not Welsh, nor a brass-band musician (those curiously shaped burdens under those ape-like arms are brass-band instruments). But the comedy's exterminating desire – Philbrick would shoot the bandsmen; the Doctor simply wipes out the sight – rather stifles any rising laugh. And, of course, it is by no means to Lewis's usual purposes, or Huxley's or Orwell's, to play their satirically bad bodies for laughs.

> Glanders, my friends, Glanders – a disease of horses, not common among humans. But, never fear, Science can easily make it universal. Pustules over the whole body. Below the skin hard swellings, which finally burst and turn into sloughing ulcers. Meanwhile the mucous membrane of the nose becomes inflamed and exudes a copious discharge of stinking pus. Ulcers rapidly form within the nostrils and eat away the surrounding bone and cartilage. From the nose the infection passes to the eyes, mouth, throat and bronchial passages. Within three weeks most of the patients are dead.

That is what modern chemical warfare can do in the dystopian vision of the post-nuclear-apocalypse film script in *Ape and Essence*. Not funny, nor intended to be so. It is the modern bad body in wartime *extremis* – that common concern of twentieth-century satire. Basic to the special wartime version of the bad body, though, is the satirists' ongoing horror of the body on the most ordinary of human occasions, at the table, for instance, merely eating and drinking, engaged in the most normal of mouth-work.

Gobstuff

In Part 2 of *The Apes of God*, "The Virgin," Matthew Plunkett plunges into the lunchtime crowd of jostling bodies at the Camden Distillery pub, a throng of biting, chewing, gulping mouths set in animalized faces. "He allowed himself to be revolved half-left, until a magnified jaw, upon the opposite side, came into action, a half-inch from his profile. As the teeth shattered a luncheon biscuit, a mild cerulean eye was dragged open by the rumination, into a cow's sidelong stare and slid shut" (Lewis 1931a: 75). He buys a lager beer, two ham sandwiches and a portion of "British bar-shrimp...upon its finger of damp toast" (1931a: 76).

Brutally Matthew chopped the shrimp and the finger of toast in two with one crash of his ivory-bristling jaw. The half that fell back into his mouth he swallowed. The half that remained in his fingers he regarded with astonishment. After a moment he pushed it into his mouth, and swallowed it, too. Raising the Pilsner heartily to the same place, his tongue laid down like a drugget for its reception, and so into the Red Lane, he washed down the bisected shrimp and its severed raft of damp toast. (1931a: 77)

By their mouth-work shall ye know them. Tongue as drugget, a little carpet, leading into the Red Lane, a kind of anti-red carpet for the gullet. ("'Down the red lane,' as our nurses used to say when they were encouraging us to swallow the uneatable viands of childhood. Down the red lane into the dim inferno of tripes"; Huxley 1970b: 56.) Plunkett's grim luncheon is Lewis's *hommage*, as it were, to the lunchtime horrors of Joyce's Bloom in the "Lestrygonians" episode of *Ulysses*. He is nauseated by the food-shoveling diners in the Burton restaurant, "swilling, wolfing gobfuls." "Gulp. Grub. Gulp. Gobstuff." He meditates on unkosher ham sandwiches ("Ham and his descendants mustered and bred there"); consumes a stinking gorgonzola sandwich, "with relish of disgust, pungent mustard, the feety savour of green cheese." Food with the stink of lower bodily sweat: it is a prelude to Bloom's late-night feast in Dublin's brothel quarter in "Circe," the Nighttown episode, where Bloom drinks urine ("like champagne") and eats shit ("rerererepugnant"; Joyce 1969: 168, 173, 492–3).

Plunkett eats well, i.e., amply, but – in that extended smart verbal play developed in Tom Stoppard's drama *Professional Foul* (1978) – he doesn't eat well. Satirized people tend not to. Waugh's boot-eating darkies are the least of the mode's bad mouth-workers. It is as an utterly characteristic satirist that Waugh disadvantages his subjects precisely by catching them in some disadvantageous eating practice. Like his alter ego Basil Seal in *Put Out More Flags* (1942), who "rejoiced, always, in the spectacle of women at a disadvantage: thus he would watch, in the asparagus season, a dribble of melted butter on a woman's chin, marring her beauty and making her ridiculous, while she would still talk and smile and turn her head, not knowing how she appeared to him" (Part 1, "Autumn," ch. 4). With profound self-consciousness, the satirical bad-mouthing text has its satirical bad-mouther giving bad mouth-work peculiar prominence. Attending like this to bad mouth-work is one of satire's most pointful self-reflexive activities.

Cooking is just a means to a very bad-mouthing end. As George Orwell claimed, in *Down and Out in Paris and London* (1933), to have witnessed it as a *plongeur* in a Parisian hotel's kitchen, public cooked food is inevitably filthy stuff, contaminated by chefs' spittle and waiters' greasy fingers – which only makes it fit for touristic American mouths. "They would stuff themselves with disgusting American 'cereals,' and eat marmalade at tea, and drink vermouth after dinner, and order a *poulet à la reine* at a hundred francs and then souse it in Worcester Sauce. One customer, from Pittsburgh, dined every night in his bedroom on grape-nuts, scrambled eggs and cocoa" (ch. 14). Gentleman George knows about when to eat and drink what. But if Paris hotels and their American customers were ordinarily hostile to good mouth-work, the later thirties turned for Orwell into a veritable mouth-hell. Modernity itself becomes for Orwell and his George Bowling in *Coming Up for Air* (1939) all filth for and in the mouth. Ersatz substitutes for the good, the real, and true are everywhere, summed up in Bowling's frankfurter made of fish: "suddenly – pop! The thing burst in my mouth like a rotten pear. A sort of horrible soft stuff was oozing all over my tongue... That's the way we're going nowadays... Rotten fish in a rubber skin. Bombs of filth bursting in your mouth" (Part 1, ch. 4). Martin Amis's John Self, direst of eighties men, dines on nothing but such filth. He binges on junk food. "I looked in at the Pizza Pouch and had a Big thick Juicy Hot One. Hard by at the Furter Factory I put three nearmeat Long whoppers over my belt, and an American Way." Self's eats are "made of polyester, rayon and lurex." "I am made of – junk, I'm just junk." No wonder his "clothes are made of monosodium glutamate and hexachlorophene" (Amis 1985: 265), and his teeth are so bad ("Minimal vitality," his dentist murmurs; 1985: 76). For their part, the people of Amis's satirical heir Will Self fill their mouths with even worse things. Schizo Ian Wharton in Self's nineties' consumerism satire *My Idea of Fun* (1993) chomps on the penis of a pit-bull terrier he has tortured and cut up (Self 1993: 268 ff). In *Great Apes*, Dr Grebe, eminent linguist (i.e., verbal mouth-work expert) of Exeter College, Oxford (Self's old college), is addicted to shit, sips it constantly, keeps "an extensive personal midden in the college cellars" (ch. 17), which is fitting enough in the college where the dons applaud at dinner as a chimp student drinks his huge sconce of ale spraying his comrades with piss and liquid shit the while, in a novel which is in a way one long replay of Joyce's "Nighttown." Bombs of filth bursting in the mouth indeed: the "tortured mouth-hole" – as Huxley's youthful poet Sebastian Barnack puts it in his very bad poem about Keats's "giant agony of the world" at the beginning of *Time Must Have a Stop* (1945). This agonized orifice is offered as a prevailing condition of the individual subject and his satirizing observer: "Tragical on stilts, bawling sublimities / Through a tortured mouth-hole" (Huxley 1945: 6).

Vile Machinations

And, of course, bad stuff in one orifice, bad stuff out some other. The body of satire is, in those potent and proleptic words of Swift about Belinda's lavatory container in his poem "The Lady's Dressing Room" (1732) poem, a "vile machine": knowable and to be known in its function as a bad economy, a recycler of foodstuffs as truly noxious excrements (line 95). The satirized body is a most unpleasant producer. What comes off it and out of it, in satirical text after text, is filth: sweat, spit, vomit, piss, shit. Here is a very vile body indeed. Waugh's people spit a lot – the Pie-Wie Indians in *A Handful of Dust* (1934), expectably enough from Waugh's point of view, like the Coptic bishops he saw ordaining priests by spitting on their heads, but also the lovely Brenda Last, spitting into her make-up, just like one of the novel's "niggers": "doing her face... Brenda spat in the eye-black" (ch. 2). They vomit a great deal too. Their world is, as they say, too, too sick-making. It is normal, it is implied in *Brideshead Revisited* (1945), to lean out of your college room window to be sick into the quad, should the need arise, except in what is evidently Waugh's old college, Hertford, where drunks in the quad rather lean into a room to vomit (Book 1, "Et in Arcadia Ego," ch. 1). Looking down at the modern landscape from her honeymoon aeroplane (suburbs, arterial roads, bungalows, decaying factories, people miniaturized as "tiny spots") Waugh's Nina feels like being sick (*Vile Bodies*, ch. 12). It is the observing satirist's commonest feeling. In 1923 Huxley found himself typing *Human Vomedy* in error for *Human Comedy*: "Was there ever a criticism of life more succinct and expressive? To the more sensitive and queasy among the gods the last few years must indeed have seemed a vomedy of the first order" (Huxley 1971b: 81–2). A vomedy the satirists cannot stop themselves assisting at.

They have a nose for bad smells. Like the goats on the pseudo Egyptian Public School football field Waugh laughs at in *Labels*, "nosing up morsels of lightly buried refuse" while the boys shout "'ip-'ip-'ooray" every time they kick the ball, satirists keenly nose out the nauseous (Waugh 1930: 69). Orwell's nose for the "feral reek" of the Other, the "spiritual halitosis" of his political enemies, is peculiarly sharp. In fact, everything Orwell opposes stinks: the "smelly little orthodoxies" of his opponents, their bum-sucking, arse-licking, arse-kissing, as he keeps putting it. Now "for a header into the sewage," he will say, venturing onto some repellent political topic. All propaganda is stinking, lying shit. Over the Spanish Civil War, "the newspapers of Left and Right dived simultaneously into the same cesspool of abuse" (*Homage to Catalonia*, 1938; Orwell 2000a: 208). Orwell knows just how Dorothy Hare feels in *A Clergyman's Daughter* (1935), forcing herself to drink from the communion chalice that grotesque old Miss Mayfield's mouth has been at ("The underlip, pendulous with age, slobbered forward, exposing a strip of gum and a row of false teeth as yellow as the keys of an old piano. On the upper lip was a fringe of dark, dewy moustache... not an appetizing mouth"; ch. 1) because he had forced himself to do likewise, on the boyhood train journey he describes in *The Road to Wigan Pier* (1937) – that stink-obsessed map of thirties' proletarian England. He felt morally obliged to "take a swig" from a bottle being passed around by some pig-men. "I cannot describe the horror I felt as the bottle worked its way towards me. If I drank from it after all those lower-class mouths I felt certain I should vomit" (Part 2, ch. 8).

Jonathan Swift's *diseased, depressed* vision gets justified by Orwell for its truth to a necessary disgust with the body ("repulsive and ridiculous" as well as "beautiful"), which quite evidently Orwell passionately shares.

> The sexual organs are objects of desire and also of loathing, so much so that in many languages, if not in all languages, their names are used as words of abuse. Meat is delicious, but a butcher's shop window makes one feel sick: and indeed all our food springs ultimately from dung and dead bodies, the two things which of all others seem to us the most horrible. A child, when it is past the infantile stage but still looking at the world with fresh eyes, is moved by horror almost as often by wonder – horror of snot and spittle, of the dogs' excrement on the pavement, the dying toad full of maggots, the sweaty smell of grown-ups, the hideousness of old men, with their bald heads and bulbous noses. In his endless harping on disease, dirt and deformity, Swift is not actually inventing anything... (Orwell 2000b: 222)

And as a grown-up satirist, Orwell can't turn his face away from deformity, can't put the filthy bottle down, can't help putting his nose into what Wyndham Lewis called "the insanitary trough between the two great wars" (Lewis 1950: 199). Can't, for that matter, stop inspecting close up the bottoms which so repel him.

It is the bottoms of the two leftist "cranks" on a bus in *The Road to Wigan Pier* that peculiarly disgust Orwell:

> One day this summer I was riding through Letchworth when the bus stopped and two dreadful-looking old men got on to it. They were both about sixty, both very short, pink, and chubby, and both hatless. One of them was obscenely bald, the other had long grey hair bobbed in the Lloyd George Style. They were dressed in pistachio-coloured shirts and khaki shorts into which their huge bottoms were crammed so tightly that you could study every dimple. Their appearance created a mild stir of horror on top of the bus. The man next to me, a commercial traveller I should say, glanced at me, at them, and back again at me, and murmured "Socialists," as who should say, "Red Indians." He was probably right – the ILP [Independent Labour Party] were holding their summer school at Letchworth. (Part 2, ch. 11)

(Orwell was himself on his way to it.) Orwell is, of course, entitled to his fun over those bottoms, and "the smell of crankishness which still clings to the Socialist movements," which they give off. As are other satirists. "Bum," Kingsley Amis keeps exclaiming in his letters to Philip Larkin, sharing some dislike or other; for example, about teaching *Ulysses*, "And saying things you don't want to say. Myth bum, interior monologue bum, symbol bum... epic structure bum, in this section over a hundred parts of the body are mentioned bum, Nausicaa bum, *Christ figure bum*, poetic bum, recognition scene bum and all the rest that you know so well" (K. Amis 2000: 564). The best and most sustained jest in Waugh's *Sword of Honour* trilogy (1952–61) about the Second World War is the saga of Apthorpe's "thunderbox," his exotic portable latrine. The absurdities of military life as lavatorial obsession. Meanwhile, back in London, a trio of American journalists pursue their enquiries – Joe, Scab and Bum (Waugh 1955: Book 2, ch. 6). (Compare that trio of porn-stars in Martin Amis's *Money*, Spunk, Sod, and Fart, and poor Spunk's difficulty in grasping the British market's problem with his name; Amis 1985: 125, 200–2.) Wyndham Lewis enjoys jeering, Orwell-like, at men's bottoms in *The Apes of God* and *The Revenge for Love* (1937). But the jokiness (once again) fails to mask a fundamental horror about and neurotic hostility toward the functions of the lower parts of the human body.

The original title of *The Revenge for Love* was *False Bottoms*. False bottoms, literal ones and the frauds, cheats, and fakers they stand for in the worlds of leftwing politics and of art, are everywhere in that novel. For Lewis, the bottom is the zone of especial falsity – namely, the homosexual's treachery toward Lewis's professed heterosexual norms. Lewis hates homosexuals – the likes of author Donald Butterboy, the "world's quean" of the (suppressed) novel *The Roaring Queen* of 1936. They offend him by the "bottom-waggling," which betrays their sexual preferences – Jewish author Julius Ratner in *Apes* giving "his bed-clothed person a horrid homosexual waggle" (Lewis

1931a: 148); fat, buttock-waggling, buttock-swaggering Percy Hardcaster, the fraudulent Communist Spanish Civil War hero in *Revenge*; the "perverse" inhabitants of Weimar Berlin, "Hauptstadt of Vice, the excelsior Eldorado of a sexish bottom-waggling most arch Old Nick sunk in a costly and succulent rut," as described in *Hitler* (Lewis 1931c: 14). It is pretty clear that we are meant to recognize Orwell's pair of horrid-looking socialists as gay men, and be as disturbed by their prominent posteriors as he (like Lewis) is. They are homosexual apes presenting their posteriors as keenly as Will Self's heterosexual ones do.

None of the lower body's sexual potentials fails to disturb the satirical gaze. Down there, clearly, is hell. In the terrible words innocently un-modernist John the Savage borrows from ranting King Lear with, apparently, the support of his author's most intense feelings, to repudiate the sexual advances of uninhibited, modern-body liberated, zippicamiknicks-sporting (and dropping) Lenina in *Brave New World*: "But to the girdle do the gods inherit. Beneath is all the fiends." "There's hell, there's darkness, there is the sulphurous pit, burning, scalding, stench, corruption; fie, fie, fie, pah, pah! Give me an ounce of civet, good apothecary, to sweeten my imagination" (ch. 13; after *King Lear*, 4.6.128–33). Stench. Corruption. They utterly compel the satirist's unsweetened imagination.

Coprophilia

Like Joyce's Leopold Bloom and Will Self's Dr Grebe, the satirist and the satirical text are, in effect, coprophiliacs; they love dwelling on excrement. Waugh's Basil Seal gloomily imagines "a pageant of coprophagists," shit-eaters, as the next stage of Emperor Seth's modernizing future in *Black Mischief* (ch. 5). The Sethized future is coprophagous. At the end of his first book, *Rossetti: His Life and Works* (1928), Waugh talks of the Victorian "romance of decay" – "a sort of spiritual coprophily characteristic of the age" (Waugh 1975: 226). And Waugh patently shared what he recognized as D. G. Rossetti's taste, and so did Waugh's satirical compeers. They are greatly drawn to the allegedly representative activity of the age's representative bodies, namely their "doing dirt" – as D. H. Lawrence put it of pornography, "the attempt to insult sex, to do dirt on it" (Lawrence 1936: 175). Aptly enough, then, they make doing dirt a gist of their writing. Satirical bad mouthing as doing dirt. Or shitting, Yahoo-like, on displeasers and opponents.

In that truly brilliant piece of contemporary sociologizing put into the mouth of sociologist Anthony Beavis in chapter 11 of *Eyeless in Gaza* (1936) – alleged extract from chapter 11 of Beavis's *Elements of Sociology*, and the very best, I think, of the many brilliant analytical essays Huxley seeds his fiction with – Huxley rewrites the Cartesian *cogito ergo sum*, I think therefore I am. The modern self is, by contrast, Beavis argues, all body. "From the Boy Scouts to the fashionable sodomites, and from Elizabeth Arden [the cosmetics leader] to D. H. Lawrence," the self is no longer to be thought of as a thinking, feeling entity but as mere body. And as an exclusively lower-body bodiliness: no longer *homo cogitans*, but *homo cacans, homo eructans, homo futuens*: the shitting, farting, fucking human. Above all shitting. "*Cogito ergo Rothermere* [the newspaper magnate] *est*. But *caco, ergo sum*" (ch. 11). Modernity is full of shit – and so must modern analysis be, the modern sociological text, the text of a satire – like this one of Huxley's. On which reckoning, satire is indeed a caco-poetics – a specialized version of the KAKAO-POETIC announced by Joyce in *Finnegans Wake* (1939) – literally the poetics of wickedness and evil doing (Joyce 1939: 308). Caco-poetic: an aesthetics of bodily waste-matters, of chaos, ruin, refuse, trash. Precisely the "romance of decay." It is no surprise that Waugh should nose out a hotelier called Mr Kakophilos in the travels that comprise *Waugh in Abyssinia* (Waugh 1936: 66–7) – and the basis of so much in *Black Mischief*. Satire trawls in the trash-can of the human, presenting the human as trash-can, and civilization and culture as trashed. "What's he to Hecuba?" sing the four negroes from the dance-band at the cabaret Gumbril and Mrs Viveash go to in Huxley's *Antic Hay* (ch. 15). It is the latest song from the USA. The answer to the repeated refrain is "Nothing at all," for this is the world of "Nil, omnipresent nil, world-soul, spiritual informer of all matter." The world quite emptied of value – emblematized in the crooners' denial of meaning to that version of Hamlet's question (*Hamlet*, 2.2.553), which addressed the power of tragedy and of one of the world's most influential stories, Hecuba's grief at the fall of Troy and the death of her husband. The cabaret ditty represents the *abnihilisation* (to use a word of Joyce's from *Finnegans Wake*; Joyce 1939: 353.22) of the canon, literariness, a whole culture. The moment is akin to the tearing up of Shakespeare and the Shakespearian tradition indicated by "that Shakespehearian rag" pasted into T. S. Eliot's *The Waste Land* (1922). It is an elegy for a culture confirmed by adulterous Mrs Viveash's enthusiasm for the song ("divine tune"), by unfaithful Gumbril's joining in the drama which follows the music, celebrating the "Asses, apes and dogs" of the "social sewer," and by the knowing *roué* Mr Coleman's talk of German research into the joys of sado-masochism and coprophagy to his boy pick-up. The boy shortly afterwards (ch. 16) vomits in Gumbril's rooms. " 'The real charm about debauchery,' said Coleman philosophically [as the youth vomits], 'is its total pointlessness.' "

Bodily wastes in the cultural and moral wasteland: it is a scene of ruination prompted by the Great War, whose despoilings and degradations were quickly recognized as proleptic, the shape of all things to come. Mr Scogan in Huxley's *Crome Yellow* (1921) explains it. Only a few years before the war, news of the treatment of Congo "blackamoors" came as a shock. "Today we are no longer surprised at these things. The Black and Tans harry Ireland, the Poles maltreat the Silesians, the bold Fascisti slaughter their poorer countrymen: we take it all for granted. Since the war we wonder at nothing." "At this very moment... the most frightful horrors are taking place in every corner of the world. People are being crushed, slashed, disembowelled, mangled; their dead bodies rot and their eyes decay with the rest. Screams of pain and fear go pulsing through the air at the rate of eleven hundred feet per second" (ch. 16). Twentieth-century warmongering affirms the satirists' nightmares of universal chaos and waste. The "grimy landscape" of the Orwellian future in *Nineteen Eighty-Four*

(1949), grim setting for an all-enclosing political and moral grimness, only continues a war-ruined present. The novel's hero-victim Winston Smith cannot remember when London was otherwise than a ruined waste.

> Were there always these vistas of rotting nineteenth-century houses, their sides shored up with baulks of timber, their windows patched with cardboard and their roofs with corrugated iron, their crazy garden walls sagging in all directions? And the bombed sites where the plaster dust swirled in the air and the willow-herb straggled over the heaps of rubble; and the places where the bombs had cleared a larger patch and there had sprung up sordid colonies of wooden dwellings like chicken-houses? But it was no use, he could not remember. (Part 1, ch. 1)

The twentieth-century city would always be like this. Shitty City is the post-Orwellian satirist's description: you travel to London in Irvine Welsh's *Trainspotting* (1993) by Inter-Shitty train. You fear for your children playing in Dogshit Park in Martin Amis's *London Fields* (1989). The clock can never be turned back on the excrementitious Hitlerzeit wastings of the human, so awfully fictionalized in Amis's *Time's Arrow: Or, the Nature of the Offence* (1991) — old Jews dunked in vats of shit in Auschwitz ("fiercely coprocentric...made of shit"), while Nazi doctors perform unspeakable operations on healthy bodies turned into sick ones by these terrible medical malpractitioners:

> The *Scheissekommando* was made up of our most cultured patients: academics, rabbis, writers, philosophers. As they worked, they sang arias, and whistled scraps of symphonies, and recited poetry, and talked about Heine, and Schiller, and Goethe...In the officers' club, when we are drinking...and where shit is constantly mentioned and invoked, we sometime refer to Auschwitz as Anus Mundi. And I can think of no finer tribute than that. (M. Amis 1991: 133)

No return to innocence: it is an awing historical point dramatized by Amis's writing his story of these horrors in chunks of narrative proceeding in reverse (those rabbis rise from the excrementitious dead, and so forth). The flow of the story can be reversed but the ruinations of history cannot; the rubbished stay rubbished. (And, not by the way, this highly ironizing novel flatly contradicts Adorno's argument about no irony after Hitler.)

Ruins not Picturesque

Twentieth-century history only confirms the satirists' worst gloomings. It keeps providing the ammunition for satire's tendency to turn into obsequy and elegy, to keep doing threnody and writing elegy. Evelyn Waugh's fictions constantly develop into rituals of mortality, requiems for the lost pasts signified repeatedly in his array of ruined Great Houses: King's Thursday (*Decline and Fall*), Boot Magna Hall (*Scoop*, 1938), Hetton (*A Handful of Dust*), and, of course, Brideshead, the most sadly decrepit of these spoiled houses, requisitioned by the wartime military, its walls, ceilings, rooms marred, its great fountain a wired-off, dried out dump for the cigarette-ends of a heedless soldiery. This modern rot started, for Roman Catholic Waugh, in the Reformation's destruction of the churches and monasteries dwelt on in *Edmund Campion* (1935), when the ruins "were not picturesque...and age had not softened the stark lines of change" (Waugh 1953: 106–7). Now such wrecking is just a norm of modern life; ruination is everywhere. (Waugh's 1953 satire on the post-war Labour government's nationalizations and [for him] socialist devastations is pointedly entitled *Love Among the Ruins* – borrowing its title from the unhappy Robert Browning poem.)

Waugh's *Vile Bodies* ends symptomatically with Adam (modern Adam) sitting "On a splintered tree stump in the biggest battlefield in the history of the world": a "scene...of unrelieved desolation; a great expanse of mud in which every visible object was burnt or broken." Guns are firing; aeroplanes are overhead; he clutches his Huxdane–Halley bomb ("for the dissemination of leprosy germs"). It is a desolation assembled out of Great War components. The awfulness, this affront to the human, is afforced by the presence of Mrs Melrose Ape's onetime Angel Chastity, shagged-out, war-zone whore rising from her torpor to finger optimistically an arriving general's medals. This bad end for everyone and every thing is sited in the novel's last chapter, entitled, with all the irony Waugh can manage, "Happy Ending." Here is apocalypse, the Last Things of Catholic theology, as Hell – cognate with all the bad ends Waugh regularly contrives for his people – shot dead, strangled, killed in car smashes, falling to their death from horses, smashed by bombs, hanging themselves, putting their heads in gas ovens, getting drowned or eaten or imprisoned for life in desolate places. Aimee Thanatogenos (Aimee from Aimée Semple Macpherson of the Four Square Gospel, inspirer of Mrs Melrose Ape; Thanatogenos meaning, roughly, Deathly One), the heart-broken suicide of *The Loved One: An Anglo-American Tragedy* (1948), Waugh's satire on Californian burial customs, ends up in an incinerator intended for animals. She is put there by her treacherous British boyfriend, wartime pilot and minor poet Denis Barlow, an animal mortician with a bright future as an interdenominational pastor. Barlow knocks off elegies. For suicide Francis Hinsley, expatriate scriptwriter, scrapped by Hollywood (his name not a million miles away from Aldous Huxley), Barlow does two elegies, one a parody of Tennyson's great *Ode on the Death of the Duke of Wellington* ("Bury the great Knight / With a studio's valediction / Let us bury the great Knight / Who was once the arbiter of popular fiction"), the other a rewrite of the jazz-standard "St James' Infirmary Blues":

> They told me, Francis Hinsley, they told me you were hung
> With red protruding eye-balls and black protruding tongue;
> I wept as I remembered how often you and I
> Had laughed about Los Angeles and now 'tis here you lie;
> Here pickled in formaldehyde and painted like a whore,
> Shrimp-pink incorruptible, not lost nor gone before.
> (Waugh 1951: 69)

This Blues is a double pastiche, for Waugh is also parodying the ballad "Miss Gee," the sick-joking poem by W. H. Auden (repeatedly lampooned by Waugh as the poet Parsnip) about a spinster who died of cancer, which was itself an earlier parody of "St James' Infirmary." The trashed body of Hinsley, farcically emphasized rather than concealed by the mortician's beautifying efforts, comes in the wrappings of a multiple trashing – the ruination of Tennyson's *Ode* and the undoing of the lovely old elegiacs of the traditional Blues via a farcing rewrite of Auden's farcing.

All things, all mortal remains, end in Waugh's satirical trash-can. Like the red identity disc Waugh's devout soldier Guy Crouchback piously removes from the dead body of a soldier in the Cretan campaign in the *Officers and Gentlemen* volume of *The Sword of Honour* trilogy. The body resembles a dead Christ sculptured in a Deposition scene, or an effigy of a saint, like the effigy of the Crusader knight who so haunts Crouchback, but it is marred by "bluebottles that clustered round his lips and eyes" and proclaimed him mere "flesh." "RC" the disc says, "Roman Catholic." Crouchback prays in the priestly words for the dead, "May his soul and the souls of all the faithful departed in the mercy of God, rest in peace." As he removes the disc from the cold breast, he recalls the military educator advising officers in charge of burial parties to take away the red disc for Records: "The green disc remains on the body. If in doubt, gentlemen, remember that green is the colour of putrefaction" (Book 2, ch. 6). For all the undoubted piety, the sacramentalism even, of this priestly moment, the bluebottles return, and this body will putrefy like all the others. As for the red disc, it never makes it to Records, but only to the waste-bin. Mrs Stitch will chuck it away, a badge of honor dishonoured – refuse, trash, rubbish.

No Deus in this Machina

Satire does not do happy endings. Its wastings and trashings go on irreversibly. *Dei ex machina* steer clear of satirical fictions. Badness is unalleviated. The annihilations just continue. "And presently, like a circling typhoon, the sounds of battle began to return." That is the last, cheerless, line of *Vile Bodies*. It is an endlessness that is utterly grievous for the characters involved. For a Tony Last, it might be, trapped in *A Handful of Dust* in an unending circle of literal and literary hell, doomed to read Dickens to his merciless jungle captor for the rest of his life ("tomorrow, and the day after that, and the day after that. Let us read *Little Dorrit* again"). But paining also for readers. "There are passages in that book I can never hear without the temptation to weep," says Last's tormentor, and these last words of his describe the feelings of the reader at many such passages of Waugh's novels. Surveys show that readers crave a happy ending for *Nineteen Eighty-Four*, greatly desire it that Winston Smith might escape the scrutiny of Big Brother, find a space and place for a private future. But Big Brother's totalitarian regime is total. Smith's succumbing to brainwashing ("the struggle was over... He loved Big Brother") is final. There's no escaping the forebodings that such totalitarian regime managers as Orwell's O'Brien know and exploit to your hurt; they're now and for ever. "*It's all going to happen*," thinks Orwell's war-scared George Bowling in *Coming Up for Air*, "All the things you've got at the back of your mind, the things you're terrified of, the things that you tell yourself are just a nightmare or only happen in foreign countries. The bombs, the food-queues, the rubber truncheons, the barbed wire, the coloured shirts, the slogans, the enormous faces, the machine-guns squirting out of bedroom windows. It's all going to happen" (Part 4, ch. 6). And without let-up. "If you want a picture of the future," O'Brien tells Smith, "imagine a boot stamping on a human face – for ever" (*Nineteen Eighty-Four*, Part 3, ch. 3). And the satirist, imagining it so, invites you to share this disheartening vision.

No *deus ex machina*, then, to alleviate the encircling gloom. Not surprisingly, given that machines are such a main problem of modern satire. No real help for the human comes from the machine. The modernity satirists keep deploring is an infection of the mechanistic, a triumph of the mechanical, of technology. Satire's negative plot machinery is the vehicle of a persistent attack on the mechanistic. Ford is God in the Brave New Huxleyan World. Huxley cannily seized on the Model-T Ford automobile as the emblem of the modern. Everything dates from its invention. Now is not Anno Domini but the Year of Our Ford. Making the Sign of the Cross has given way to the Sign of T. Everything, especially the production of babies, has been Fordized, mechanized, automated, as in Henry Ford's factories (he invented the production-line). Birth is tightly controlled. Genetics are fixable. Pharmaceuticals, the notorious *soma* pills, keep everyone drugged and happy. Sex-hormone chewing-gum is good for you. Music is all synthetic, and so is desire. Lenina's zippicamiknicks sum up the deep intrusion of the manufactured, the machine-made and artificial, into the most intimate as well as the once most messy and random of human activity, the love affair. And science and scientists, the arrangers of this techno-paradise, this utopia per se (the constant references to the contemporary Soviet dream are clear), are by no means benignly inclined. Soma is the dictator's artful tool of people control, the subjugating drug-you-like in the new unthinking life. And chemical weapons, anthrax bombs no less, will keep all external enemies in their place. The aeroplanes which fill the sky are not just for pleasure and utility – aerial taxis and hearses – but for the transporting of high explosive: "$CH_3C_6H_2(NO_2)_3 + Hg(CNO)_2 = $ well, what? An enormous hole in the ground, a pile of masonry, some bits of flesh and mucus, a foot with the boot still on it, flying through the air and landing, flop, in the middle of the geraniums – the scarlet ones; such a splendid show that summer" (ch. 3).

The collusion between science and weaponry, especially chemical weaponry, was a life-long theme with the pacifist Huxley (recall the biologists, pathologists, physiologists of Huxley's *Ape and Essence* going home to hug their wives, romp with their children, listen to chamber music after a hard day's work on glanders and other diseases for weapons: the Auschwitz doctors, done to a T). The Huxdane–Halley leprosy bomb in *Vile Bodies* is Waugh's own gibe at this alliance (the Communist biochemist J. B. S. Haldane and Aldous Huxley's zoologist brother Julian were a pair of campaigning evolutionists and rationalists who collaborated publicly in work on animal biology: Aldous Huxley's anti-scientism was a family affair).

These very modern technological marvels hurt fragile human flesh, and are designed with hurt in mind. Satirists are with Elaine Scarry's frank analysis of weaponry and pain. "The main purpose and outcome of war is injuring...[its] purpose...is to alter (to burn, to blast, to shell, to cut) human tissue, as well as to alter the surface, shape, and deep entirety of the objects that human beings recognise as extensions of themselves" (Scarry 1985: 63–4). This is the kept-up horrified concern of Waugh and Orwell, as well as of Martin Amis and J. G. Ballard. *Vile Bodies* is nothing less than an anti-Futurist tract, devoted to announcing the horrors of mechanically speeded-up modern life and the speed-aesthetic, which T. P. Marinetti and his Fascistic collaborators preached as the glory of twentieth-century technological advance. *"Faster. Faster"* cries the dying Agatha Runcible, smashed up and deranged after her crash in a racing-car of which she lost control. Motor-cars and motorbikes are reckoned as killers, as threatening to people as the more obvious gas ovens that Waugh's suicides like so much. Ballard's novel *Crash* and his manual of modern mechanized violence *The Atrocity Exhibition* (1970), that ongoing tribute to the role of the car-crash in the modern imagination (Ballard actually arranged exhibitions of crashed cars: smashed-up cars as art), are as it were long footnotes to *Vile Bodies*. For its part, Martin Amis's *Time's Arrow*, about the Auschwitz doctors, feelingly continues Huxley's warfare against the technologies of terror, the inhuman pain-dealing efforts of scientists. So do Amis's polemics about the nuclear age and his stories of nuclear-age dementias in *Einstein's Monsters* (1987; see, for example, his introduction and "The Time Disease"). They mightily continue Amis's favorite George Orwell, too, in these regards.

Orwell is, after Huxley, the twentieth-century's main English contender against modernismus as bad mechanismus – the criminal way in which science has transformed the organic real for the worse: the crime of synthetics, of Ersatz.

> Everything slick and streamlined, everything made out of something else. Celluloid, rubber, chromium-steel everywhere, arc-lamps blazing at night, glass roofs over your head, radios all playing the same tune, no vegetation left, everything cemented over... But when you come down to brass tacks and get your teeth into something solid, a sausage for instance, that's what you get. Rotten fish in a rubber skin. Bombs of filth bursting inside your mouth.

That is George Bowling and his modernist distastes in *Coming Up for Air* (Part 1, ch. 4) – those sausage bombs an inevitable prelude to the soon-arriving bomb falling on a Lower Binfield street (one of ours actually, an accident during some bombing practice).

> a frightful smashed-up mess of bricks, plaster, chair-legs, bits of a varnished dresser, rags of tablecloth, piles of broken plates, and chunks of a scullery sink. A jar of marmalade

had rolled across the floor, leaving a long streak of marmalade behind, and running side by side with it there was a ribbon of blood. But in among the broken crockery there was lying a leg. Just a leg, with the trouser still on it and a black boot with a Wood-Milne rubber heel...

I had a good look at it and took it in. The blood was beginning to get mixed up with the marmalade. (Part 4, ch. 6)

Orwell had seen bombed houses in Spain, and would soon see lots more in London. What is daunting is the domestic inclusivity of bombing's chaos-making ruinations. Bombs have no respect of persons. They are as dauntingly inclusive as Orwell's anti-machine-era diatribes. Bowling relishes (Part 2, ch. 4) the old English names of fish, roach, rudd, dace, and so forth, invented, he thinks, by people who hadn't heard of machine-guns, bombing planes, concentration camps, but also of radio, "going to the pictures" and aspirin. Aspirin. Aspirin also gets dismissed in the long discussion toward the end of *The Road to Wigan Pier* (Part 2, ch. 12) about the bad of modern mechanization. "In a healthy world there would be no demand" for it (well, no...), nor for tinned food ("In the highly mechanized countries, thanks to tinned food, cold storage, synthetic flavouring matters, etc., the palate is almost a dead organ"), nor for "gramophones, gaspipe chairs, machine guns, daily newspapers, telephones, motorcars, etc., etc." Factory-produced food-stuffs wrapped in tin-foil ("some slick machine-made article triumphing over the old-fashioned article that still tastes of something other than sawdust"), the "filthy chemical by-product" called beer, aspirins, radio, cinema films, gramophones, newspapers, telephones, motor-cars, Bauhaus-style chairs: they're all lumped in with bombing planes, machine-guns, and poison gas. The common thread is mechanization, industrialization, factory production, and the mass-ness, deindividualization, the loss of human uniqueness in the mechanized world of utopian dream – H. G. Wells-type scientized futures, Sovietization, Socialism. Which is why Orwell spends so much time on the matter in *The Road to Wigan Pier*. He is tilting at the whole worldview of the totalitarian-supporting comrades who nearly cost him his life in Spain, a critique which comes right down to where it affects everybody in ordinary Western bourgeois domestic life as a matter of eating tinned food, sitting in a gaspipe chair and enjoying music from a machine.

Orwell's large allegation is that the machine age softens the whole person, physically, mentally, politically, morally. It is an allegation in which all the satirical voices of Left and Right variously join and converge. Right-wing Wyndham Lewis's campaigns against massness of all kinds. Liberal Huxley's nightmare of person-sapping soma and feelies and dance-halls where the Sixteen Sexophones lull the population with their soothingly mindless sounds. Leftist Orwell's crusades against the media and labor-saving devices, which inevitably lead, he thinks, to thought-control, the brainwashing horrors of Room 101 in *Nineteen Eighty-Four*. Right-wing Waugh's scatter-fire against newspapers, their journalists and owners (Lord Monomark and his gossip columns in *Vile Bodies*; Lord Copper and *The Beast* newspaper's frenzied manipulations of the news in *Scoop* – "Up to a point, Lord Copper"), and cinema (that spoof Hollywood bio-pic about John Wesley in *Vile Bodies*, with the Countess of Huntingdon pursued by Red Indians), as well as against modern design, streamlined buildings, chromium plating and mad Bauhaus architects who mess up, ruin in fact, old country houses, King's Thursday, "finest piece of domestic Tudor in England" (*Decline and Fall*), Gothic Hetton (*A Handful of Dust*). *Decline and Fall*'s Otto Friedrich Silenus, keen on replacing Tudor by ferro-concrete and aluminium, did the décor for a movie with no people in it, rants futuristically about houses as dynamos, and had his rejected design for a chewing-gum factory "featured in a progressive Hungarian quarterly" (Part 2, ch. 1). Which is QED so far as Waugh is concerned.

Eat tinned food, then, sit in a gaspipe chair, and you're more or less supporting chemical warfare. Enjoy jazz? You're as good as endorsing aerial bombing. Watching a movie in your local Odeon you might as well be in Room 101. (John Self, the porno-movie fan turned porno-movie maker, *is* in Room 101.) Buying a newspaper is simply swallowing the dictating magnate's soma pill. *Cogito, ergo Rothermere est*. And so on and so forth. What's more, Orwell urges in *Nineteen Eighty-Four*, we like it. He's with Huxley: our assorted somas are extremely pleasurable. We're softened, brainwashed in effect, by mechanization, and reluctant to go back to the hard, pre-machine world. Orwell's gloomy regret is that we have nothing like a Swiftian energy to resist. "Our attitude towards such things as poison gases *ought* to be the attitude of the King of Brobdingnag towards gunpowder; but because we live in a mechanical and scientific age we are infected with the notion that, whatever else happens, "progress" must continue..." (*Wigan Pier*, Part 2, ch. 12).

Dystopics

Negativity about machines, about the techno-modernity that is the motor of modern utopian visions, is what fires satire's negativity about utopianism. Modern satire is uniformly dystopian. Dystopian form follows dystopian content. It's as if satire had bitten on utopia and found bombs of dystopian filth bursting in its mouth. (As fictional utopias have normally done – and also the human guinea pigs in every utopian experiment known to history.) With the exception of Wyndham Lewis's brief flirtation with Hitlerian futurism in his *Hitler*, no modern satire or satirist has been able to sing along with utopian visionarinesses. Our satirists, given to skepticism about human ambitions and desires, soon perceived modern utopian experiments as totalitarian, dictators' stuff, saw through the grand utopian claims of the Soviet Union, recognized that the utopian things dictators wanted – their politics and civics, their sociology, ethics, aesthetics, their architecture – were all antithetical to human good, and did so long before lots of Western intellectuals and writers got around to sharing their dyspeptic disillusionments (see Rouvillois 2000: 316–31). *Brave New World* appeared in 1932; *Black Mischief*, Waugh's black-comic send-up of Emperor Seth's daft utopia, came out in the same year; Lewis's *Men Without Art* in 1934 – early days for such hostilities. "There is no such thing as a just, humane, and enlightened regime 'just around the corner'... or anywhere in the universe at all" was Lewis's view in *Men Without Art* (1934: 263). These satirists were not at all compelled by the idea of future blessedness on earth. Not least because they could see its promise was usually built on intense misery and cruelty in the present. The great theme of Huxley's *Time Must Have a Stop* is the evil of what has been done to people and is still being done in the name of utopian futures.

> Since I was born, thirty-two years ago, about fifty millions of Europeans and God knows how many Asiatics have been liquidated in wars and revolutions. Why? In order that the great-great-grandchildren of those who are now being butchered or starved to death may have an absolutely wonderful time in AD 2043. And (choosing, according to taste or political opinion, from among the Wellsian, Marxian, Capitalistic or Fascist blueprints) we solemnly proceed to visualize the sort of wonderful time these lucky beggars are going to have. (ch. 30)

Orwell, who had seen Communist utopians in brutal action in Spain, had experienced Big Brother at first hand, escaping only by the skin of his teeth from the unwanted attentions of Stalin's hitmen (as he reports in *Homage to Catalonia*), was skeptical even about socialist utopians' professed good intentions. He has O'Brien, the totalitarians' mouthpiece in *Nineteen Eighty-Four*, openly dismissive of "the stupid hedonistic Utopias that the old reformers imagined... Progress in our world will be progress towards more pain" (Part 3, ch. 3). Orwell's utopians are dystopians by design. As is, in effect, the Stalin of Martin Amis's awed story of the Soviet dictator in his *Koba the Dread* (2002) – yet one more text sealing the link between the satirical gaze and dystopian writing. (What is curious about Fredric Jameson in his *Archaeologies of the Future: The Desire Called Utopia and Other Science Fictions* is not only his general weakness on the satire–dystopia link, but his stumblings and stutterings over Orwell's anti-Communism and anti-Stalinism: like other old Marxist critics, he can't get over the right-wing use of Orwell's work in Cold War jostlings; Jameson 2005: 200–2, passim.)

So satire is commonly stuck between, on the one hand, its melancholy distaste for the present – all bad bodies, disgusting personal behavior, bad media, corrupt intellectuals and artists, in fetid, cramped cities engendering disease and endless misery, all afforded and shaped by the ruinations of the Great War and its aftermaths – and, on the other, its suspicion of the technologized cleaners-up, the gleaming futurological utopian wager and its managers, as, tellingly, and representatively, in Huxley's *Antic Hay*:

> Gumbril looked through the railings at the profound darkness of the park. Vast it was and melancholy, with a string, here and there, of receding lights. "Terrible," he said, and repeated the word several times. "Terrible, terrible." All the legless soldiers grinding barrel-organs, all the hawkers of toys stamping their leaky boots in the gutters of the

Strand; at the corner of Cursitor Street and Chancery Lane, the old woman with matches, for ever holding to her left eye a handkerchief as yellow and dirty as the winter fog. What was wrong with the eye? He had never dared to look, but hurried past as though she were not there, or sometimes, when the fog was more than ordinarily cold and stifling, paused for an instant with averted eyes to drop a brown coin into her tray of matches. And then there were the murderers hanged at eight o'clock, while he was savouring, almost with voluptuous consciousness, the final dream-haunted doze. There was the phthisical charwoman who used to work at his father's house, until she got too weak and died. There were the lovers who turned on the gas and the ruined shopkeepers jumping in front of trains. (ch. 5)

We are made to sympathize with the relishing disgust of Gumbril's father at the "darkness, disorder and dirt" of this civic ruination. He abhors the "wretched human scale, the scale of the sickly body," squalid, ugly, smelly (ch. 11), and we are compelled by his satirical disgust. But the model of an ideal, rebuilt London that he works on obsessively – Christopher Wren's London, reimagined, extended, glamorized – is extremely uncompelling as an alternative, for all its fine piazzas, sumptuous fountains, regulated commercial quarters, noble public buildings, and fine domestic habitations all built symmetrically around the commanding focus of St Paul's Cathedral. It is clean, but impossibly so, and tiny like all models, a dinky parody of a lived-in place, as shrunken indeed as Satan's devilish city Pandaemonium in the Hell of Milton's *Paradise Lost*. It is carefully constructed on a not-at-all-human scale, and is quite empty of human beings, even of simulacra of the human. Empty, in fact, of the people that the terribly angry old man whom Gumbril meets on a train "objects to" because they breed "like maggots" in their "Hideous red cities pullulating with Jews, sir. Pullulating with prosperous Jews" (ch. 16). Dictators knew, as even in 1923 Huxley knew they knew, how to clear away offending humans like that old monster's Jews as a prelude to a Gumbril Senior-like rebuilding of the city, on the lines of Mussolini's Futurist admirers, or the Soviet Union's urban planners, or Hitler's designer of a new Berlin, Albert Speer.

All This Religion

Beastly present, soured futures, the bad ends of dystopian narratives: this is an all-round apocalyptic nightmare. It sounds very Christian, or Christianized, and, of course, it is. Satire after the Reformation is all spilt-theological, and at no time more so than in the twentieth century. "All this religion," sighs Huxley's effete Mr Mercaptan in *Antic Hay* when he is confronted with a Huxleyan range of satirical positionings – Wellsian utopianism, the painter Lypiatt's muscular Christian aesthetic, Coleman's gloomy rants against the copulating urban millions – in which Mercaptan nonetheless joins, with his *dix-huitième* enthusiasms and his little volume of "essays, prose poems, vignettes and paradoxes" on "the pettiness, the simian limitations, the insignificance and the absurd pretentiousness of *Homo* soi-disant *Sapiens*" (chs 4 and 5). And Mercaptan is right about the religion. The satirist's distress leads Waugh to convert to Roman Catholicism; Huxley's pacifism is obviously religious, leading inevitably onto Eastern mysticism and the religiose experiments with LSD. If Communist utopianism is the God that Failed, satiric dystopianism might be thought of as the God that didn't fail – didn't fail Literature, at least.

Our satirists keep finding in the Christian tradition the words with which to make their satirical point. Waugh's irredeemably vile bodies come with irony direct from St Paul. Jesus "will change our vile body, that it may be fashioned like unto his glorious body" (Philippians 3: 21), which does not happen to Waugh's sinful mob. Restless Tony Last is "In Search of a City": the title of chapter 5 of *A Handful of Dust*. The chapter ends (section 4) with Last's fevered dream of arriving at a parody of the Celestial City in Bunyan's *The Pilgrim's Progress* ("The gates were before him and trumpets were sounding along the walls"), but he is still stuck in the Dickens lover's prison. The Bible's Abraham "looked for a city... whose builder and maker is God" (Hebrews 11:10); Last has no idea that that is the city he should be looking for. Waugh's Christians do, however. Uniquely in *Vile Bodies*, it is Father Rothschild who has the recipe for settling the restlessness of the times, a Christian one. Catholic Crouchback finds the *mots justes* for the distresses of modernism and militarism in the words of the Ash Wednesday liturgy, "*Memento homo, quia pulvis es, et in pulverem revertis*" (Remember, O man, that thou art dust, and unto dust thou shalt return). They "echoed dreadfully" in his mind (*Men at Arms*, Book 1, ch. 9). Just so, hymn-writers' perceptions of the hymn-writer precede and inform the Christian satirist's. "Change and decay in all around I see," sings Uncle Theodore in *Scoop* (Part 2, ch. 1), "gazing out of the morning-room window" at Boot Magna: words from H. F. Lyte's famous "Abide with me, fast falls the eventide" ("decay, rather than change, was characteristic of the immediate prospect").

Huxley's Anthony Beavis in chapter 11 of *Eyeless in Gaza* recognizes in the twentieth century's resort to the body as the only ground of confidence about things and self – the body "is indubitably *there*" – a form of Christian heresy. Once upon a time Christians sang about being hidden in the wounded body of Christ, "*Jesu pro me perforatus / Condar intro tuum latus*" (Jesus, pierced for me / let me hide myself in thy side). Now, a skeptical humanity resorts to its own body: "*Condar into MEUM latus!*" (Let me hide myself in MY side): "it is the only place of refuge left to us." You must worship something, advises Huxley's Mr Propter in *After Many a Summer* (in an argumentative move common in twentieth-century apologetics), and if not God, then yourself: "projections" of your own poor ideals – "progress" through "centralization" and "prosperity" through "the intensifying of mass production" (ch. 11). Which is the worship of utopia (Fordism in the terms of *Brave New World*). Which is idolatry, the utopianism that Sebastian Barnack deplores in *Time Must Have a Stop* (ch. 30) as "An idolatrous religion in which time is substituted for eternity." Progress and utopia are both "Molochs, both demand human sacrifice on an enormous scale. Spanish Catholicism was a typical idolatry of past time. Nationalism, Communism, Fascism, all the social pseudo-religions of the twentieth-century, are idolatries of future time."

On these reckonings, the world's wrongings and the world's wrong are, in effect, what the Christian tradition defines as sin, as fallenness. Orwell welcomes Swift's Christianized take on the horrors and pain with which his own, Orwell's, satiric imagining is filled. Swift's

> attitude is in effect the Christian attitude, minus the bribe of a "next world" – which, however, probably has less hold upon the minds of believers than the conviction that this world is a vale of tears and the grave is a place of rest. It is, I am certain, a wrong attitude, and one which could have harmful effects upon behaviour; but something in us responds to it, as it responds to the gloomy words of the burial service and the sweetish smell of corpses in a country church. (Orwell 2000b: 223)

Memento homo... Orwell can't shake the memory. It is strict orthodoxy, of course, that keeps Waugh mindful of what St Paul called his "body of sin" (Romans 6: 6). Georges Bernanos' "sense of sin" is what made his *Journal d'un curé de campagne* "unique," Waugh thought (Waugh 1983b: 209–10). It was a sense Waugh's satirizing, even before his conversion in 1930, could not resist. As neither could Huxley, filtering his bad-body visions through the Manichaean lenses of El Greco's paintings, Baudelaire's poems, and the body theology of Odo of Cluny, who thought his corpse a "sack of shit." Huxley and Orwell and Waugh and, though it might surprise some readers to be told this, Martin Amis, and even Will Self, are actually persistent modern puritans, preachers of righteousness, hostile to what Christians would define as sin. But they are skewed, or exaggerating, puritans, dogged by Manichaean convictions – that ancient heresy, which holds that matter, all materiality, which includes the body, is evil, the devil's bailiwick, beyond the redemptive reach of God. Baudelaire's "theory of love," according to Huxley, "was the theory of those extreme, almost Manichean Christians who condemned indiscriminately every form of physical passion, and regarded even marriage as a sin. Between mind and body, spirit and matter, he had fixed an impassable gulf. Body was wholly bad; therefore, according to the logic of satanism, it had to be indulged as much and above all as sordidly as possible" (Huxley 1937: 308), which is the kind of logic – overtly heretical, consciously Manichaean – which motors, I would say, all of satire's caco-poesis. Joyce liked the thought of *cocoa* not least because its botanical name is *theobroma*, god-food. He has coprophagous, blasphemous, heretical Bloom prepare some for Stephen Dedalus in the "Ithaca" section of *Ulysses* as a mock-eucharist: a cup of cocoa for a blasphemous sacrament, mocking god-food; rhyming pointedly with *caco*, standing for *cack*, the satiric Manichee's satanic tipple.

Sinners in the Hands of an Angry Satirist

But why this extended Manichaean mindfulness, this repeated return to the body-shop of horrors? It is the old, difficult question about what motivates the satirists' obsessive trade in the awfulness which so ghosts them and their texts. Satirists will point, as of old, to the world, to history. Its terrors, they say, are the only source of their dire imaginings. They are only holding up the proverbial mirror. Nothing is invented, they allege. And much, indeed, is not. When J. G. Ballard wants to ransack "a library of extreme metaphors" for his writing, he does not have to look far along the shelf of twentieth-century history. "I'm trying to achieve an elegant weirdness in my work," says Patrick McGrath, and human weirdness is not far to seek (the hero of his *Spider* [1991], for instance, blows up his mother in imitation of the Nazi blitz on London). But still the kind of doubt that circulates around Swift keeps recurring. Why so savage an indignation? Is not the objector in fact implicated in what he deplores by dint of imagining and representing it so strongly? Does not the extent of the savagery, the way the satirist keeps returning to, say, watch the Fascist spanner smashing the victim's face into a blob of strawberry jam, denote some kind of imbalance of mind and spirit, a kind of illness, a Manichaeanism too far? What is at stake is the ethicity of the satiric text as well as the psychic-moral health of the writer. And satirists sometimes recognize this. Orwell certainly does – as in that worrying about the way the anti-Hitler lecturer in *Coming Up for Air* seems possessed by the very violence he is deploring:

> I saw the vision that he was seeing ... It's a picture of himself smashing people's faces in with a spanner. Fascist faces, of course. I *know* that's what he was seeing. It was what I saw myself for the second or two that I was inside him. Smash! Right in the middle! The bones cave in just like an eggshell and what was a face a minute ago is just a great big blob of strawberry jam. Smash! There goes another! That's what's in his mind, waking and sleeping, and the more he thinks of it the more he likes it. And it's all OK because the smashed faces belong to Fascists ... You could hear all that in the tone of his voice. (Part 3, ch. 1)

Satirists are indeed prone to hatred. Spleen is satire's driving emotion. To be effective satire has to be corrosive, as they say, and Orwell is suggesting that such corrosiveness might be corroding the ethicity of the satirist. Orwell's honesty, his way of letting the cat out of the bag like this, was, and remains, disconcerting, but it fits the case.

Huxley was as fond as Orwell of getting our gaze right up to the brutal physical detail: the dying Eustace's vision in *Time Must Have a Stop* (ch. 25) of Japanese bayonets stabbing "again and again," "for ever and ever," into a human face is a kind of proleptic xerox of Orwell's bad dream of the totalitarian boot smashing into the human face for ever, but Huxley is more cynical than horrified about the kind of ethical catch-22 involved. There is a "logical and psychological connection," he observes in his powerful essay on "Ethics" in *Ends and Means* (1937), "between obsession with one's own sins and obsession with the sins of others, between haunting terror of an angry God and an active desire to persecute in the name of that God" (Huxley 1969a: 328). The sin-obsessions of St Augustine, Luther, and their ilk generate religious persecution: the sin-mindful have always wanted to kill off the sinful Other. Huxley can be taken as thinking here about satire. He knows well this tendency in the writings of his friend the ranting Protestant D. H. Lawrence, as his satirizing rendering of D. H. Lawrence as the hate-possessed

Rampion in *Point Counter Point* shows. Rampion is a truthful portrait: splenetic Lawrence was indeed a satirist who liked arranging gleeful annihilations of his satiric targets – recall, for example, the gloating accounts of the drowning bourgeois granny in "The Virgin and the Gypsy" (1930) and the stallion kicking Bright Young Thing Rico in the head in "St Mawr" (1925; see also Paulin 1996: 196–207). Huxley knows too the tendency in himself. His surrogate preacherly analysts and artists, Propter, Barnack, Beavis, are just like traditional Puritan preachers wanting to see sinners placed in the hands of an angry God. Nor is kindliness the going emotion in any of our satirists: not in Wyndham Lewis, or Waugh, or Orwell, or indeed Martin Amis or Will Self.

It well fits Will Self's angry pulpiteering depictions that his artist Simon Dykes in *Great Apes* should get his inspiration for his shocking apocalyptic paintings of London and Londoners destroyed by plane crash, Stock Exchange flood and tube-station fire from John Martin's great nineteenth-century paintings of Biblical apocalyptical destruction, *The Fall of Babylon* and the rest, in the Tate Gallery: "They're essentially paintings of bodily disintegration, destruction... as it were... *dis*corporation... He's taken Martin's apocalyptic paintings as a starting point and produced a series of canvases that depict both imaginary and historical scenes of bodily destruction with a kind of tortured graphicism" (Self 1997: 137). Fittingly central to *Crome Yellow* (1921) is the apocalyptic Reverend Mr Bodiham. His God is the God of Savonarola, excoriator of Florentine vice and frivolity, violent puritanical arranger of bonfires of the vanities. Bodiham tries indeed to make his congregation see "what a fearful thing it is to fall into His hands." Bodiham has published a pamphlet on Matthew 24: 7: "For nation shall rise up against nation and kingdom against kingdom: and there shall be famines, and pestilences, and earthquakes, in diverse places." Huxley quotes the vicar's pamphlet extensively. Most of it is lifted from a 1916 paper on "The War and Signs of the Times, with special reference to our Lord's return," by an evangelical Anglican Bible-Prophecy expositor the Rev. E. H. Horne (Horne 1937: 45–61). Huxley not only quotes it, but supplements it, mightily adding to Horne's already plentiful set of divinely vengeful apocalyptic horrors. Impersonating Bodiham, Huxley really, as they say, gets into it, riffing away with apocalyptic horrors of his own. "In a little while, who knows? the angel standing in the sun may be summoning the ravens and vultures from their crannies in the rocks to feed upon the putrefying flesh of the millions of unrighteous whom God's wrath has destroyed" (ch. 9). The voice and the vision of the preacher are here, literally, Huxley's own. Huxley the satirical preacher of doom in the churchman's pulpit and robes – and the robes sit easily on him.

Arring Writing

Satire is a traditionally malevolent, malignant art. Its muse is rightly thought of as variously snarling, maculate, obscene, cankered, priapic, railing, raging, grotesque-making (Kernan 1950; Henderson 1975; Rhodes 1980; Richlin 1983; Nokes 1985;

Carretta 1993). What unites these malignities is aggressive intent, which originates, evidently, in the satirist himself (usually a he). Fredric Jameson is quite right in *Fables of Aggression* (1979), his book on Wyndham Lewis, to refer to *The Power of Satire: Magic, Ritual, Art* (1960), Robert C. Elliott's classic account of satire's primitive, annihilating desire, its killing force as venom and curse (Jameson 1979: 137–8). The satirical gaze, the eye of the satirist lauded by Lewis, is indeed what we learn from Michel Foucault's *Surveiller et punir* (1975) to read as disciplinary, punitive (Foucault's English title is *Discipline and Punish*). Satirical surveillance is indeed done with an eye to Foucauldian subjugation, the exercise of superior power over subordinated opponents, making victims out of subjects. Satire does catachresis as intellectual, moral, spiritual subjection. It should come as no surprise that Huxley got on to Foucault's great model of subjugatory practice, Jeremy Bentham's panopticon prison, long before Foucault did – and read it, and Bentham's brother Samuel's panopticon factory, as an early example of his dystopian *bête noire*, the sub-human mechanization of the modern world, a precursor of the Nazi concentration camp, of the Fordized means of production, and all in a context of Hogarth's representations of eighteenth-century urban hell, of "senseless evil...chaotic misery...scarcely imaginable refinements of cruelty and obscenity" (Huxley 1950: 194–7).

For as a satirist Huxley is indeed a panopticist. As satirists tend to be. The satiric gaze is nothing if not panoptic, sweeping, dominant. From his vantage point, his privileged height no less, the satirist looks down, defining, controlling, dealing out the analyses that hurt, dishing out the critical medicine, the allegedly cathartic purge Huxley admired in Ben Jonson ("A good dose...should purge our minds of much waste matter"). He is like Waugh's Nina up in her aeroplane, taking in the ruined, depleted, vomit-inducing terrain below, noting and affirming its diminishment, the catachrestic distortions that are inevitable from up where he is, and also dropping bombs of filth, puking and shitting Yahoo-like on the people below, and relishing the pain of that filthifying bombardment.

> Anthony opened his eyes for just long enough to see that the aeroplane was almost immediately above them, then shut them again, dazzled by the intense blue of the sky.
>
> "These damned machines!" he said. Then, with a little laugh, "They'll have a nice God's-eye view of us here," he added.
>
> Helen did not answer; but behind her closed eyelids she smiled. Pop-eyed and with an obscene and gloating disapproval! The vision of that heavenly visitant was irresistibly comic.
>
> "David and Bathsheba," he went on...
>
> A strange yelping sound punctuated the din of the machine. Anthony opened his eyes again, and was in time to see a dark shape rushing down towards him. He uttered a cry, made a quick and automatic movement to shield his face. With a silent but dull and muddy impact the thing struck the flat roof a yard or two from where they were lying. The drops of a sharply spurted liquid were warm for an instant on their skin, and then,

as the breeze swelled up out of the west, startlingly cold. There was a long second of silence. "Christ!" Anthony whispered at last. From head to foot both of them were splashed with blood. In a red pool at their feet lay the almost shapeless carcass of a fox-terrier...

Anthony drew a deep breath; then, with an effort and still rather unsteadily, contrived to laugh. "Yet another reason for disliking dogs," he said... (*Eyeless in Gaza*, ch. 12)

A bomb of canine filth. Doing harm to the human subject with a dead dog. Wishing the death of the dog on some despised persons. One thinks of Flory shooting himself dead after shooting his faithful dog, at the end of Orwell's ranting, filth-obsessed *Burmese Days* (1935): "he fired, blowing her skull to fragments. Her shattered brain looked like red velvet. Was that what he would look like?" (ch. 24). He does look like that – dying like Joseph K at the end of Kafka's *The Trial*, just "like a dog." This is *cynical* writing as Renaissance critics would understand it. "Cynique": dog-like, currish, churlish toward the human; after the Cynic school of Greek philosophers who took their name from the *Kunosarges* gymnasium where Antisthenes taught, but popularly known as the school of the *kun-*, or dog. This is satire making hostile noise, growling, *arring* like a dog, as the old verb had it. *Arring*, making the sound R – the *littera canina*, the dog's letter, of Persius. R for Rochester and Rochesterianism, of course. Writing as *litterae caninae*, then, the literature of the angry, growling, biting, even mad dog.

In his 1947 piece in the Roman Catholic journal *The Tablet*, "Half in Love with Easeful Death: An Examination of Californian Burial Customs," a prequel to *The Loved One*, Waugh imagined being at last up in Heaven and, like Troilus at the end of Chaucer's *Troilus and Criseyde*, being enabled to laugh at the follies below: "standing at the balustrade of heaven among the unrecognizably grown-up denizens of Forest Lawn, and, leaning there beside them, amicably gaze down on Southern California, and share with them the huge joke of what the Professors of Anthropology will make of it" (Waugh 1983a: 337). But meanwhile, before that desired happy release from satirical knowing, he is up in the panoptic heights of his fiction, gazing down with extreme, unamiable, unheavenly, bestializing, Manichaean, cynic viciousness, compiling his blaspheming litanies of the human as dead dog: "Dog that is born of bitch hath but a short time to live, and is full of misery. He cometh up, and is cut down like a flower; he fleeth as it were a shadow, and never continueth in one stay" (Waugh 1951: 96). It is, I'm afraid, what satirists do.

References and Further Reading

Adorno, Theodor (1978) Juvenal's error. In *Minima Moralia: Reflections from a Damaged Life*, trans. E. F. N. Jephcott, pp. 209–12. London: Verso (originally published in 1951).

Amis, Kingsley (2000) To Philip Larkin, 15 December 1959. In *The Letters of Kingsley Amis*, ed. Zachary Leader, pp. 564–7. London: HarperCollins.

Amis, Martin (1985) *Money: A Suicide Note*. Harmondsworth: Penguin (originally published in 1984).

—— (1991) *Time's Arrow: Or, the Nature of the Offence*. London: Jonathan Cape.

Beckett, Samuel (1963) *Watt*. London: John Calder (originally published in 1953).

Bell, Steve (2004) *Apes of Wrath*. London: Methuen/Guardian.

—— (2005) How often does a leader of the free world come along who resembles a monkey in every particular? *Guardian*, *G2* (November 13, 2005): 16–17.

Benson, E. F. (1991) *Lucia Rising*. Harmondsworth: Penguin (originally published in 1927).

Carretta, Vincent (1983) *The Snarling Muse: Verbal and Visual Political Satire from Pope to Churchill*. Philadelphia: University of Pennsylvania Press.

Derrida, Jacques (1992) The law of genre. In *Acts of Literature*, ed. Derek Attridge, pp. 220–52. New York: Routledge (originally published in 1980 as "Loi du genre/Law of genre" in *Glyph* 7).

Greene, Graham (1988) *Lord Rochester's Monkey: Being the Life of John Wilmot Second Earl of Rochester*. Harmondsworth: Penguin.

Henderson, Jeffrey (1975) *The Maculate Muse: Obscene Language in Attic Comedy*. New Haven, CT: Yale University Press.

Horne, E. H. (1937) A war-time address (AD 1916). In *The Significance of Air War*, pp. 45–61. London: Marshall, Morgan and Scott.

Huxley, Aldous (1937) Baudelaire. In *Stories, Essays, and Poems*, pp. 299–316. London: J. M. Dent & Sons (originally published in 1929).

—— (1939) *After Many a Summer: A Novel*. London: Chatto & Windus (republished in the US in 1939 as *After Many a Summer Dies the Swan* [New York: Harper & Row] because US readers were deemed not able to spot the English title's Shakespearian quotation).

—— (1945) *Time Must Have a Stop*. London: Chatto & Windus.

—— (1950) Variations on *The Prisons*. In *Themes and Variations*, pp. 192–208. London: Chatto & Windus.

—— (1969a) Ethics. In *Ends and Means: An Enquiry into the Nature of Ideals and the Methods Employed for their Realization*, pp. 303–30. London: Chatto & Windus (originally published in 1937).

—— (1969b) *Those Barren Leaves*. London: Chatto & Windus (originally published in 1925).

—— (1970a) The beauty industry. In *Music at Night*, pp. 228–36. London: Chatto & Windus (originally published in 1931).

—— (1970b) Meditation on El Greco. In *Music at Night*, pp. 53–68. London: Chatto & Windus (originally published in 1931).

—— (1971a) Ben Jonson. In *On the Margin: Notes and Essays*, pp. 184–202. London: Chatto & Windus (originally published in 1923).

—— (1971b) On deviating into sense. In *On the Margin: Notes and Essays*, pp. 81–6. London: Chatto & Windus (originally published in 1923).

Jameson, Fredric (1979) *Fables of Aggression: Wyndham Lewis, the Modernists as Fascist*. Berkeley, CA: University of California Press.

—— (2005) *Archaeologies of the Future: The Desire Called Utopia and Other Science Fictions*. London: Verso.

Joyce, James (1939) *Finnegans Wake*. London: Faber & Faber.

—— (1969) *Ulysses*. Harmondsworth: Penguin (originally published in 1922).

Kernan, Alvin B. (1950) *The Cankered Muse: Satire of the English Renaissance*. New Haven, CT: Yale University Press.

Knox, Ronald A. (1928) Introduction: on humour and satire. In *Essays in Satire*, pp. 15–43. London: Sheed and Ward.

Lawrence, D. H. (1936) Pornography and obscenity (1929). In *Phoenix: The Posthumous Papers of D. H. Lawrence*, ed. Edward D. McDonald, pp. 170–87. London: William Heinemann.

Lewis, Wyndham (1930) *Satire and Fiction, Enemy Pamphlets No. 1: Scandal of an Attempt to Sabotage a Great Work of Art*. London: Arthur Press.

—— (1931a) *The Apes of God*. London: Nash & Grayson.

—— (1931b) *The Diabolical Principle and the Dithyrambic Spectator*. London: Chatto & Windus.

—— (1931c) *Hitler*. London: Chatto & Windus.

—— (1934) *Men Without Art*. London: Cassell.

—— (1938) *The Mysterious Mr Bull*. London: Robert Hale.

—— (1950) *Rude Assignment: A Narrative of my Career Up-to-date*. London: Hutchinson.

—— (2004) *The Wild Body*. Harmondsworth: Penguin (originally published in 1927).

Miller, Karl (1985) *Doubles: Studies in Literary History*. Oxford: Oxford University Press.

Nokes, David (1985) *Raillery and Rage: A Study of Eighteenth Century Satire*. Oxford: Oxford University Press.

Orwell, George (2000a) *Homage to Catalonia*, ed. Peter Davison. Harmondsworth: Penguin (originally published in 1938).

——(2000b) Politics vs literature: an examination of *Gulliver's Travels*. In *The Collected Essays, Journalism and Letters of George Orwell. Volume 4: In Front of Your Nose 1945–1950*, ed. Sonia Orwell and Ian Angus, pp. 205–23. Boston: Nonpareil Books (originally published in September–October 1946 issue of *Polemic* 5).

Paulin, Tom (1996) Lawrence and decency. In *Writing to the Moment: Selected Critical Essays 1980–1996*, pp. 196–207. London: Faber & Faber.

Rhodes, Neil (1980) *Elizabethan Grotesque*. London: Routledge & Kegan Paul.

Richlin, Amy (1983) *The Garden of Priapus: Sexuality and Aggression in Roman Humor*. New Haven, CT: Yale University Press.

Rouvillois, Frédéric (2000) Utopia and totalitarianism. In Ronald Schaer, Gregory Claes, and Lyman Tower Sargent (eds), *Utopia: The Search for the Ideal Society in the Western World*, pp. 316–31. New York: New York Public Library.

St George, David (1978) *The Right Honourable Chimpanzee*. London: Secker & Warburg.

Scarry, Elaine (1985) *The Body in Pain: The Making and Unmaking of the World*. Oxford: Oxford University Press.

Self, Will (1993) *My Idea of Fun: A Cautionary Tale*. London: Bloomsbury.

——(1997) *Great Apes*. London: Bloomsbury.

Sinclair, Iain (1999) *Crash: David Cronenberg's Postmortem on J. G. Ballard's 'Trajectory of Fate.'* London: British Film Institute.

Waugh, Evelyn (1930) *Labels: A Mediterranean Journal*. London: Duckworth.

——(1936) *Waugh in Abyssinia*. London: Longmans.

——(1951) *The Loved One: An Anglo-American Tragedy*. Harmondsworth: Penguin (originally published in 1948).

——(1953) *Edmund Campion*. Harmondsworth: Penguin (originally published in 1935).

——(1955) *Officers and Gentlemen*. London: Chapman & Hall.

——(1975) *Rossetti: His Life and Works*. London: Duckworth (originally published in 1928).

——(1983a) Half in love with easeful death: an examination of Californian burial customs. In *The Essays, Articles and Reviews of Evelyn Waugh*, ed. Donat Gallagher, pp. 331–7. London: Methuen (originally published in 1947).

——(1983b) Saint's-eye view. In *The Essays, Articles and Reviews of Evelyn Waugh*, ed. Donat Gallagher, pp. 209–10. London: Methuen (originally published 1937).

Woolf, Virginia (1966) Modern fiction. In *Collected Essays*, vol. 2, pp. 103–10. London: The Hogarth Press (originally published in 1919).

22
Verse Satire in the Twentieth Century
Timothy Steele

When we survey twentieth-century verse satire, the prospect does not initially appear promising. Though the poetry of the period offers an astonishing welter of achievements and aberrations, satire does not figure centrally in the spectacle. We do not find major talents devoting themselves to the genre to the degree that Lucilius and Horace, John Donne and Ben Jonson, or John Dryden and Alexander Pope did. Nor does satire enjoy the cachet it held in former times. It is telling that when Calvin Trillin collects into a book the political satires he wrote for *The Nation* magazine in the early 1990s, he entitles the volume *Deadline Poet or, My Life as a Doggerelist* (1994). Though the title reflects Trillin's modesty about the journalistic topicality of his work, it also indicates the view, widely entertained by modern and contemporary poets and critics, that satire is not as serious as other types of poetry. Even those of us who believe that the accomplishments of twentieth-century satirical poets have been underrated must acknowledge the basic accuracy of the gloomy assessment that A. D. Hope, himself a gifted verse satirist, makes in his essay "The Satiric Muse." Alluding to Matthew Arnold's famous statement, "Though they may write in verse, though they may in a certain sense be masters of the art of versification, Dryden and Pope are not classics of our poetry, they are classics of our prose" (Arnold 1953: 318), Hope laments: "By Arnold's day indeed satire had fallen into disrepute and decay as a form of poetry. Neither the nineteenth-century nor the twentieth-century poets have practiced it much and it has come to be classed with comic and occasional verse" (Hope 1970: 61).

The factors that have contributed to the decline of verse satire are complex, but most of them relate to the sea change that occurs in Western poetry during and in the wake of the Romantic movement. For one thing, the Romantic elevation of the spontaneous, subjective emotional lyric produces a concomitant depreciation of the more extended discursive and narrative genres of poetry; and satire, along with epic and romance, has been increasingly obliged to abandon verse for the more pedestrian medium of prose and the prose novel. So, too, the separation, in Kantian and post-Kantian aesthetics, of the Beautiful from the Good and the True — and the identification of poetry with Beauty — negatively affects satire. Though fine satire is beautiful and aesthetically pleasing, it explores manners and morals. It retains the classical view that beauty is an aspect of goodness. Insofar as satire endeavors to teach or to persuade, modern critical judgment is likely to convict it of what Edgar Allan Poe, in his essay "The Poetic Principle," calls "the heresy of *The Didactic*" (Stern 1945: 571).

Satire is undermined as well by the Romantic tendency to regard art as expressive of the artist's internal state rather than as reflective of the external world. Since verse satire is preeminently public, it will not flourish in a culture in which poets look inward more than outward. Similarly, the Romantic concept of the artist as rebel militates against satire, in that the concept encourages poets to think of themselves as working outside or in defiance of conventional norms rather than as speaking from the ethical center of their communities. Even when satirists criticize (as they often do) an established political or social order, they generally launch their attacks from the vantage of a humane mean set against corruptive extremes and abuses of power.

A related development that has hurt verse satire is the radical skepticism of much modern criticism and theory. This skepticism has called into question the very idea of ethical centers and humane means. Many recent writers have questioned whether intellectual objectivity is possible or have denied the existence of stable virtues or values; and in this mistrustful atmosphere, satirical poets have found it difficult to address audiences with the assurance or authority that their predecessors did.

Verse satire is also weakened by the growing indifference or outright hostility to poetic craft. This attitude is evident already in Arnold's disparaging remarks about Dryden and Pope, and it subsequently manifests itself in the twentieth-century vogue of free verse. All poetic genres have been affected by the erosion of the metrical traditions that governed poetic composition for millennia, but satire has suffered more than most. It requires wit and bite, and meter and rhyme greatly aid in securing these qualities. A literary culture that by and large treats verse as, in Edmund Wilson's (1938) striking phrase, "a dying technique," is unlikely to produce excellent satirical poetry.

Yet poetic fashions and trends can never banish vice and folly or diminish our cathartic pleasure at seeing a skillful poet expose and anatomize them. Moreover, poets fortunate enough to live beyond the age of thirty usually discover that the world is as interesting as they are, and want to find ways of writing about it. As W. H. Auden says in his "Letter to Lord Byron" (1937), a satire that he wrote at the age of twenty-nine and that marks a departure from his sometimes obscure and overly compacted earlier verse:

> I want a form that's large enough to swim in,
>   And talk on any subject that I choose,
> From natural scenery to men and women,
>   Myself, the arts, the European news.
>   (1.134–7)

Though the "form" Auden speaks of is the rhyme royal stanza in which he writes his "Letter," the phrase "talk on any subject" reminds us that the Latin word for satire, *satura*, means "medley," and that the word Lucilius and Horace use for their satires, *sermones*, means "talks" or "conversations." Satire has from Roman times been the most capacious and flexible of genres. If it sometimes lacks fiery intensity, it offers a compensatory range of subject and tone; and for this reason, many poets and readers will always be attracted to it.

It should not, then, surprise us that a careful examination of twentieth-century verse will reveal quite a few interesting satirical poems. Though the age is not rich in major figures devoting themselves exclusively or even largely to satire, many gifted poets turn to the form from time to time. In addition, a number of twentieth-century poets, especially those working in the second half of the century, show a keen interest in an important subtype of satire. This is the satirical epistle – the verse letter that the poet writes to a friend, patron, or literary mentor in order to address literary, social, philosophical, or political conditions of the day. Auden's "Letter to Lord Byron" well illustrates this subtype, which is exemplified in Roman verse by Horace's letters to Maecenas (*Sat.* 1.1; 1.6; *Ep.* 1.1; 1.19) and Persius' letter to Caesius Bassus (*Sat.* 6); and it is exemplified in earlier English verse by Thomas Wyatt's "Mine Own John Poyntz," Donne's letter "To Sir Henry Wotton" ("Sir, more than kisses, letters mingle souls"), and Pope's "Epistle to Dr Arbuthnot." Finally, some twentieth-century poets reconcile satire with the modern preference for the short poem by turning their hands to satirical epigrams and satirical lyrics.

Before proceeding to the main body of my remarks, I should acknowledge that I feel, as must anyone who writes about satire, the difficulty of maintaining its boundaries. From the very beginning, no genre has been more narrowly defined or more broadly practiced. On the one hand, most of us will concur with Samuel Johnson's well-known definition that a satire is "a poem in which wickedness or folly is censured." On the other hand, we are well aware that this definition covers only a fraction of the great satires of our literary tradition. Horace's satires, for instance, comprehend not only examinations of vice and stupidity, but also literary essays, dialogues on ethics, and sketches of Roman social life. Moreover, as scholars have long noted, it is not always easy to distinguish conventional satires – poems that embody traditional features of the genre in particular and obvious ways – from poems that are more generally infused with a satirical spirit. For my part, I shall treat the genre liberally. I shall include, under the satirical rubric, not simply poems that excoriate foolishness and evil, but also those wider-ranging essayistic medleys that explore, in the manner of Horace and the great Renaissance satirists, various topics of interest to intelligent women and men.

I should also make a preliminary point about satirical lyrics and satirical epigrams. Though twentieth-century satirists write these more often than their predecessors did, such poems also appear in earlier periods. If we do not always appreciate these earlier efforts or recognize their satirical character, it is because they are overshadowed by the larger satires of their day or of their authors. For example, Walter Ralegh's "The Lie" is one of the greatest of all English satirical short poems, but it appears in neither *The Oxford Book of Satirical Verse* (Grigson 1980) nor *The Penguin Book of Satirical Verse* (Lucie-Smith 1967). Its omission is, however, understandable when one considers that the editors, in selecting material from the Renaissance, necessarily focused on the major satirical works of Wyatt, Donne, and Jonson. By the same token, Donne, Dryden, and Pope all wrote clever satirical epigrams, but these naturally look tangential to the achievements of their longer satires. (Ben Jonson, who called his epigrams "the ripest of [his] studies," is a special case. We do highly and rightly prize his epigrams. However, like Robert Herrick, Walter Savage Landor, and J. V. Cunningham, Jonson uses the form not simply for satirical purposes, but draws on all of its historical associations and functions.)

Satirical Lyrics

We may begin our discussion of twentieth-century satirical lyrics with Thomas Hardy's "Satires of Circumstance in Fifteen Glimpses," which appeared in *The Fortnightly Review* in 1911 and which Hardy collected in his *Satires of Circumstance* in 1914. The sequence consists of fifteen poems, and Hardy uses, in the course of the sequence, several lyric forms, the most common involving *sesta rima* stanzas, the individual lines of which have four beats apiece. Each poem presents a little portrait of weakness, vanity, or folly. For instance, the second poem, "In Church," concerns a minister whose devotion is not to God, but to the rhetorical effects of his sermons. The twelfth, "At the Draper's," depicts a wife who, far from grieving over her husband's imminent death, anticipates the event as an opportunity to purchase chic mourning apparel. Here is the sequence's third poem, "By Her Aunt's Grave," in which a young girl betrays the trust a deceased relative has reposed in her:

> "Sixpence a week," says the girl to her lover,
> "Aunt used to bring me, for she could confide
> In me alone, she vowed. 'Twas to cover
> The cost of her headstone when she died.
> And that was a year ago last June;
> I've not yet fixed it. But I must soon."
>
> "And where is the money now, my dear?"
> "O, snug in my purse... Aunt was *so* slow
> In saving it – eighty weeks, or near."...
> "Let's spend it," he hints. "For she won't know
> There's a dance to-night at the Load of Hay."
> She passively nods. And they go that way.

Hardy locates his satire in the drama – in the circumstance – of what he presents. Though he does not point his moral, he achieves, by means of the dialogue, the satirist's dual function of revealing corrupt behavior and of suggesting a corrective to it. The young woman's self-deception and irresolution are clear not only from her acquiescence to her boyfriend's suggestion, but also from her having procrastinated so long (for over a year!) to order the aunt's headstone. (This technique of dramatizing rather than moralizing appears in most of the other "Satires of Circumstance," as well as in Hardy's often anthologized satirical lyric "The Ruined Maid.") And in exposing the girl's failings, Hardy implicitly encourages us to judge them against the humane mean from which they deviate. He implicitly recommends the virtue of fidelity to the past and to one's family. By the same token, Hardy encourages us to assess the young man's selfishness in light of our duty to respect our fellow humans in life and in death.

William Butler Yeats is more openly didactic when, in the satirical lyrics in his middle period, he ridicules what he regards as the commercialism of modern Irish society and the petty, oppressive piety of the Irish Catholic Church. Against the present times and practices he condemns, Yeats holds up as a standard a past in which superior men and women such as the Fenian patriot John O'Leary devoted themselves to the greater good of their country. "September, 1913," the first stanza of which appears below, well illustrates Yeats' satirical method:

> What need you, being come to sense,
> But fumble in a greasy till
> And add the halfpence to the pence
> And prayer to shivering prayer, until
> You have dried the marrow from the bone?
> For men were born to pray and save:
> Romantic Ireland's dead and gone,
> It's with O'Leary in the grave.

The satirical lyrics of the First World War often feature even bitterer contrasts. Often, fatuous abstractions about martial heroism are juxtaposed with the horrifying particulars of battle in trenches. Wilfrid Owen's "Dulce et Decorum Est" is a terrific poem of this type, though Owen concentrates mainly on the realities of modern warfare and only at the end does he focus on the disparity between the realities of combat and the specious glorification of it. In other poems about the war, however, the satirical contrast not only underscores the poem's message, but also creates its texture and structure. A case in point is Siegfried Sassoon's "They," which satirizes a bishop who imagines that the war is ennobling a generation of young men when it is in fact destroying them.

> The Bishop tells us: "When the boys come back
> They will not be the same; for they'll have fought
> In a just cause: they lead the last attack
> On Anti-Christ; their comrades' blood has brought
> New right to breed an honourable race,
> They have challenged Death and dared him face to face."
>
> "We're none of us the same!" the boys reply.
> "For George lost both his legs; and Bill's stone blind;

>   Poor Jim's shot through the lungs and like to die;
>   And Bert's gone syphilitic: you'll not find
>   A chap who's served that hasn't found *some* change."
>   And the Bishop said: "The ways of God are strange!"

Edwin Arlington Robinson presents a gentler satire in his poems about individuals who cannot or will not adapt to changing conditions in their societies or lives. In "Miniver Cheevy," for example, Robinson portrays a man who finds the modern world dull and drab and who feels an absurdly impractical nostalgia for bygone days. The sixth of the poem's eight stanzas is especially amusing:

>   Miniver cursed the commonplace
>   And eyed a khaki suit with loathing;
>   He missed the mediaeval grace
>   Of iron clothing.

Even more impressive is Robinson's "Veteran Sirens," a portrait of aging *femmes fatales* who cling to a semblance of youth instead of accepting the natural process of aging – a process that, as Robinson suggests, may add some attractions even as it takes away others. Here is the poem's next-to-last stanza, the concluding line of which contains one of Robinson's characteristically acute oxymorons.

>   But they, though others fade and are still fair,
>   Defy their fairness and are unsubdued;
>   Although they suffer, they may not forswear
>   The patient ardor of the unpursued.

Much of T. S. Eliot's work is satirical, including the early Columbo and Bolo verse, the Sweeney poems, and the cancelled white-armed Fresca passage of *The Waste Land* (1922). Like Yeats, Eliot frequently satirizes a sordid present by juxtaposing it with a grand past. However, Eliot customarily associates the greatness of earlier ages not with an historical figure like John O'Leary but with literary works and characters of an ennobling nature. Hence Eliot's satire is more allusive than Yeats's and recalls something of the method and tone of Pope's *Rape of the Lock* (1714). Just as the satire of Pope's mock-heroic mode involves the discrepancy between nobility of style and triviality of subject, the satire of, for example, "Sweeney among the Nightingales" entails the disparity between the large world of Aeschylean tragedy to which the poem alludes and the vulgarity of the poem's protagonist. In *The Waste Land* we see Eliot's satirical technique in miniature in that passage that occurs just after the typist has lost her virginity in a fumbling and chilly sexual encounter with the carbuncular clerk:

>   When lovely woman stoops to folly and
>   Paces about her room again, alone,
>   She smoothes her hair with automatic hand,
>   And puts a record on the gramophone.
>   (253–6)

Eliot satirizes the typist by contrasting her with the heroine of Goldsmith's song. Whereas the latter would die of shame as a result of losing her virtue and being abandoned by her lover, the typist is unfazed by her fall and, in its wake, merely seeks distraction.

A variant of Eliot's technique appears in Philip Larkin's satirical lyrics. These often invoke, by their very titles, romantic or heroic views of life that former poets entertained but that Larkin regards as incompatible with the stinted conditions of the mid-twentieth-century England of which he writes. For instance, Larkin's "Annus Mirabilis" immediately reminds us of Dryden's heroic poem of the same title; as soon as we read Larkin's first stanza, however, we discover that his poem concerns a year whose wonders involve not splendid naval victories or epochal fires, but sexual liberation:

> Sexual intercourse began
> In nineteen sixty-three
> (Which was rather late for me) –
> Between the end of the *Chatterley* ban
> And the Beatles' first LP.

Larkin's "This Be the Verse" and "Sad Steps" work on the same principle. Though the former's title (which comes from a line in Stevenson's ringingly affirmative "Requiem") suggests moral elevation, the poem itself runs:

> They fuck you up, your mum and dad.
>   They may not mean to, but they do.
> They fill you with the faults they had
>   And add some extra, just for you.
>
> But they were fucked up in their turn
>   By fools in old-style hats and coats,
> Who half the time were soppy-stern
>   And half at one another's throats.
>
> Man hands on misery to man.
>   It deepens like a coastal shelf.
> Get out as early as you can,
>   And don't have any kids yourself.

Similarly, in "Sad Steps" (the title alludes to Sidney's great sonnet, "With how sad steps, O Moon, thou climb'st the skies"), Larkin undercuts our initial lofty expectations by offering as his first line, "Groping back to bed after a piss." Like Eliot, Larkin alludes to inspiring poems and times, only to throw into sharp relief a contemporary world in which generation passes misery on to generation, our body decays and shames us, and the highest aim seems to be to have as much sex as you can before you become impotent and die. It is one of the wonders of recent poetry that

Larkin makes such compelling verse out of such doubtful material. ("I Remember, I Remember" is another satirical Larkin lyric that alludes to a celebrated poem of the past to help illuminate an unfortunate condition in the present. In this poem, Larkin paints an amusingly grim view of his childhood, implicitly contrasting it with the happier youth Thomas Hood describes in his poem of the same title. "I Remember, I Remember" also uses the traditional satirical device of an *adversarius*, or interlocutor, who stimulates the poet to indignant speech.)

In Wendy Cope's amusing poems about (and putatively spoken by) the fictional poet Jason Strugnell, Larkin the satirist is himself satirized. Admittedly, Strugnell takes on, in the various poems Cope devotes to him, the characteristics of many different poets; and the Strugnell poems overall lampoon a broad range of fashionable figures and styles of late twentieth-century verse. But Cope's "Mr Strugnell" is clearly a send-up of Larkin's "Mr Bleaney," and Larkin is the principal target of "*From* Strugnell's Sonnets," a sequence of seven sonnets that satirize men who never outgrow the self-centered and gloomy sexual fixations of adolescence. "*From* Strugnell's Sonnets," moreover, exploit the Larkinesque device of alluding to and subverting famous titles or first lines of classic poems. In Cope's sequence, the first lines are variants on the first lines of Shakespeare's sonnets. In one of the funniest, "The expense of spirits is a crying shame," Strugnell bemoans how much he has to spend to get women seducibly drunk. The sonnet concludes with his plaintively unromantic reflection, "I need a woman, honest and sincere, / Who'll come across on half a pint of beer."

Because satire has been written mostly by men, and because male satirists have frequently directed their darts at women, Cope's poems are notable for, among their virtues, giving women a measure of revenge. This is true not only of her Strugnell pieces, but also of "Faint Praise," "Men and their Boring Arguments," and "Tumps" – this last term being short for "Typically Useless Male Poets." Perhaps the best of Cope's satirical lyrics, however, concerns not males or male poets, but the self-obliviousness of the purely practical spirit. This poem is entitled "Engineers' Corner," and bears an epigraph from an advertisement placed in *The Times* of London by the Engineering Council: "Why isn't there an Engineers' Corner in Westminster Abbey? In Britain we've always made more fuss of a ballad than a blueprint... How many schoolchildren dream of becoming great engineers?" The poem imagines a world that richly rewards poets and obliges engineers to dwell impecuniously on the margins of society.

> We make more fuss of ballads than of blueprints –
> That's why so many poets end up rich,
> While engineers scrape by in cheerless garrets.
> Who needs a bridge or dam? Who needs a ditch?
>
> Whereas the person who can write a sonnet
> Has got it made. It's always been the way,
> For everybody knows that we need poems
> And everybody reads them every day.

> Yes, life is hard if you choose engineering –
> You're sure to need another job as well;
> You'll have to plan your projects in the evenings
> Instead of going out. It must be hell.
>
> While well-heeled poets ride around in Daimlers,
> You'll burn the midnight oil to earn a crust,
> With no hope of a statue in the Abbey,
> With no hope, even, of a modest bust.
>
> No wonder small boys dream of writing couplets
> And spurn the bike, the lorry and the train.
> There's far too much encouragement for poets –
> That's why this country's going down the drain.

In her sustained irony, Cope is as memorably effective here as Johnson is in his "Short Song of Congratulation."

Other excellent satirical lyrics include John Betjeman's incisive examination of a real-estate developer, "Executive"; Yvor Winters' "A White Spiritual," a satire against segregationist violence during the Civil Rights Movement; Kingsley Amis's "Shitty," which derides the counterculture of the 1960s; X. J. Kennedy's grimly funny portrait of family dysfunctionality, "Tableau Intime"; Turner Cassity's "Adding Rattles," a mordant meditation on aging; and Richard Wilbur's "A Finished Man," which depicts a plutocrat trying to use philanthropic activity to mask the deficiencies of his character. (Wilbur wrote, as well, some brilliant satirical lyrics, including "Glitter and Be Gay" and "Pangloss's Song," for *Candide*, Leonard Bernstein's comic opera based on Voltaire's novella.) An excellent short satire involving literary life is Gavin Ewart's "2001: The Tennyson/Hardy Poem," in which Ewart imagines himself as an octogenarian writer like Tennyson and Hardy and suggests that one way to achieve literary eminence is just to outlive your contemporaries. In later sections of this chapter, I shall make note of additional satirical lyrics when I speak of poets whose chief contributions to satire consist of extended poems, but who also wrote shorter satirical pieces.

Satirical Epigrams

It is natural that satirically inclined modern poets have often turned to the epigram. The epigram not only suits an age that favors shorter poems over longer ones, but also is historically associated with satire to a degree that no other short form is. We see this association in the definition of "epigram" in *The Random House Dictionary of the English Language*: "a short, often satirical poem dealing concisely with a single subject and usually ending with a witty or ingenious turn of thought." And though epigrammatists have written on many subjects and in many manners, the form, from Roman times in general and Martial in particular, has been first and foremost satirical.

Twentieth-century epigrams include satires on all facets of human experience. We find social satire, for instance, in Sarah Cleghorn's "The Golf Links":

> The golf links lie so near the mill
>   That almost every day
> The laboring children can look out
>   And see the men at play.

And in Countee Cullen's "For a Lady I Know":

> She even thinks that up in heaven
>   Her class lies late and snores,
> While poor black cherubs rise at seven
>   To do celestial chores.

We find satires of politics and political life in Hilaire Belloc's "On a Politician":

> Here richly, with ridiculous display,
> The Politician's corpse was laid away.
> While all of his acquaintance sneered and slanged,
> I wept: for I had longed to see him hanged.

And in Thom Gunn's "Eastern Europe (February, 1990)":

> "The iron doors of history" give at last,
> And we walk through them from a rigid past.
> Free! free! we can do anything we choose
> – Eat at MacDonald's, persecute the Jews.

We find satires on manners and morals in Ogden Nash's "Which the Chicken, Which the Egg?"

> He drinks because she scolds, he thinks;
> She thinks she scolds because he drinks;
> And neither will admit what's true,
> That he's a sot and she's a shrew.

And in X. J. Kennedy's "To Someone who Insisted I Look up Someone":

> I rang them up while touring Timbuctoo,
> Those bosom chums to whom you're known as *Who*?

And also in Henri Coulette's "Overture":

> Stand back and give me room.
> Cogito ergo zoom.

We also find epigrammatic satires on writers and scholars, including Cunningham's distich:

> This Humanist whom no beliefs constrained
> Grew so broad-minded he was scatter-brained.

John Frederick Nims' "Visiting Poet":

> "The famous bard, he comes! The vision nears!"
> Now heaven protect your booze. Your wife. Your ears.

And Helen Pinkerton's "Literary Theorist":

> Abusing its otherness, its soul and wit,
> He rapes the text, claiming its benefit –
> And that, inscrutable, it asked for it.

Among the most powerful satirical epigrams of the twentieth century are those that Rudyard Kipling wrote about the First World War. When the war began, Kipling was zealously patriotic, but after his son John perished at Loos, Kipling reassessed his position and composed the angrily clear-sighted "Epitaphs of the War, 1914–1918." Almost every one of the thirty-odd pieces in this sequence packs a considerable wallop. Three of the best are "The Beginner":

> On the first hour of my first day
>   In the front trench I fell.
> (Children in boxes at a play
>   Stand up to watch it well.)

"Common Form":

> If any question why we died,
> Tell them, because our fathers lied.

And "A Dead Statesman":

> I could not dig: I dared not rob:
> Therefore I lied to please the mob.
> Now all my lies are proved untrue
> And I must face the men I slew.
> What tale shall serve me here among
> Mine angry and defrauded young?

A well-known satirical epigram of the Second World War is Randall Jarrell's "Death of the Ball Turret Gunner," but no epigrammatist as fine as Kipling emerges from that catastrophe. Not until we come to R. L. Barth, who served as a Marine reconnaissance leader during the Vietnam War, do we find a poet who writes epigrams about war that are as consistently incisive as Kipling's. Barth has written several harrowing epigrams about combat, but he is at his most acute when he addresses the political and ideological stupidities and iniquities that have accompanied recent wars conducted by the United States. One of Barth's sharpest epigrams about Vietnam is "Movie Stars":

> Bob Hope, John Wayne, and Martha Raye
> Were dupes who knew no other way;
> Jane Fonda, too, whose Hanoi hitch
> Epitomized protester kitsch.

Another is "Social Darwinism," which refers to the deferments that spared many middle-class and well-to-do young men from military service during the Vietnam era:

> Professionally aided,
> The Privileged became,
> Until the danger faded,
> The weak and halt and lame.

All in all, the twentieth century may have been the greatest age for the satirical epigram in English. The Renaissance is the only other period in our literature that gave us a comparable body of fine epigrams. In addition to the epigrammatists already cited, the following poets wrote first-rate epigrams in the twentieth century: Harry Graham, Edna St Vincent Millay, Dorothy Parker, Louise Bogan, Janet Lewis, Phyllis McGinley, Stevie Smith, Howard Nemerov, Richard Wilbur, Edgar Bowers, Anthony Hecht, Richard Moore, Tony Harrison, Dick Davis, Robert B. Shaw, Vikram Seth, Brad Leithauser, and Gail White.

Epistolary Satires

One type of satire that particularly attracted twentieth-century poets is the verse epistle addressed to a literary mentor or friend. In treating epistolary verse – or at least some epistolary verse – as satire, I should briefly note the close historical connection between the two genres. As scholars from Isaac Casaubon onwards have observed, Horace and his early readers apparently regarded both his *sermones* and his *epistulae* as *satirae*. G. L. Hendrickson, in his classic paper "Are the Letters of Horace Satires?" (1897), provides the relevant evidence. The degree to which the two genres have subsequently overlapped is reflected in, for instance, Ariosto's entitling his collection of verse letters *Satires*. It is also reflected in Pope's great letter to Dr Arbuthnot and in Charles Churchill's "Epistle to William Hogarth" and "Dedication to the Sermons." Such poems are patently satirical in subject and method even as they are cast in epistolary form. The term "epistolary satires," which heads this section of the chapter, I borrow from Wesley Trimpi, who provides, in his *Ben Jonson's Poems* (1962), a searching study of the epistolary tradition.

Auden's "Letter to Lord Byron," which first appeared in 1937 in Auden and Louis MacNeice's *Letters from Iceland*, is perhaps the best known epistolary satire of the twentieth century. The reasons that Auden felt a special kinship with Byron, and addressed his poem to him, are too complex to detail here, though the interested reader can find a good discussion of the issue in Anthony Hecht's *The Hidden Law: The Poetry of W. H. Auden* (1993). For the present occasion, it will suffice to say that Auden's poem is inspired chiefly by Byron's satirical masterpiece, *Don Juan* (1819–24), and that Auden draws on, as Byron did before him, the tradition of Dryden and Pope. More specifically, Auden argues, as Byron had, that Dryden and Pope more richly practiced verse than did the more subjectively emotive poets who followed them. Auden's suspicion of Romantic excess, and his appeal to the great satirists of the Restoration and Augustan periods, is evident in two stanzas from the third canto of his "Letter" where he addresses Byron directly. ("Storm's" refers to a café, popular with tourists in the 1930s, in Keswick in the Lake District.)

> I'm also glad to find I've your authority
>   For finding Wordsworth a most bleak old bore,
> Though I'm afraid we're in a sad minority
>   For every year his followers get more,
>   Their number must have doubled since the war.
> They come in train-loads to the Lakes, and swarms
> Of pupil-teachers study him in *Storm's*.
>
> "I hate a pupil-teacher," Milton said,
>   Who also hated bureaucratic fools;
> Milton may thank his stars that he is dead,
>   Although he's learnt by heart in public schools,
>   Along with Wordsworth and the list of rules;
> For many a don while looking down his nose
> Calls Pope and Dryden classics of our prose.
>   (3.64–77)

One of the many subjects Auden addresses in his "Letter" is the homogenizing tendencies in modern life – the forces driving men and women into social and intellectual conformity – and this is also the subject of his non-epistolary satirical short poem "The Unknown Citizen." (His other satirical short poems include "Under Which Lyre" and "On the Circuit.") Auden wrote additional epistolary satires, including his book-length *New Year Letter* of 1940 and the later "Epistle to a Godson." However, his "Letter to Lord Byron" is his most successful longer work, and no other poem of his has had a greater influence on later satirical verse.

One sees Auden's influence in A. D. Hope's excellent "Letter from Rome," which is dedicated to Leonie Kramer, the distinguished scholar of Australian literature.

Published in 1958, this poem, like Auden's "Letter," draws formal and psychic inspiration from Byron's verse. Hope correlates his impressions on Rome with those that Byron expresses in the Fourth Book of *Childe Harold's Pilgrimage*; and Hope employs the *ottava rima* stanza that Byron used for *Don Juan* and *The Vision of Judgment*. In the passage below, Hope contemplates Rome and suggests that the same spiritual ambience that drew Byron to the great capital has drawn him:

> Which caused him to leave Venice? Well, he said
> He'd like to take a trip and see the Pope,
> Hinted he'd like a rest from too much bed
> With a blonde charmer called the Antelope;
> Writing to Murray for tooth-powder (red)
> He said that Rome had drawn him with the hope
> To make Constantinople's glories pale.
> The poem, I think, tells quite another tale.
> . . .
> It ends with Nemi and the Golden Bough.
> What instinct led him there? I like to think
> What drew him then is what has drawn me now
> To stand in time upon that timeless brink,
> To sense there the renewal of a vow,
> The mending of a lost primordial link.
> These may be only fancies, yet I swear
> I felt the presence of the numen there.
> (425–32, 441–8)

Hope also wrote a substantial piece of Popean pastiche entitled *The Dunciad Minor*. Composed in the early 1950s, though not published till 1970, this satirizes mid-century critics who were, in Hope's view, attempting to turn criticism into a discipline independent of literature. But while its argument is sound – and prescient, in light of the subsequent advent of Theory – the poem lacks the personal wit and feeling that we find in Hope's "Letter from Rome" or in his best satirical lyrics, such as "Imperial Adam."

Hope is Australian, and it is noteworthy that Australia has produced a number of twentieth-century poets interested in and skilled at satire. These include Peter Porter, James McAuley, and Clive James. I cannot explain why twentieth-century Australian poetry is so rich in satirists. It is possible that these poets, hailing from the provinces, so to speak, felt more comfortable with the full range of poetic forms than did their contemporaries from literary capitals like New York and London, where there were greater pressures to be "modern" in obvious experimental ways.

Porter's best satires are short (for example, his adaptations of Martial and his "Made in Heaven," a withering portrait of a marriage of convenience), but both McAuley and James have written interesting extended epistolary satires. McAuley's chief contribution in this regard is his "Letter to John Dryden." Like Dryden, McAuley was a convert to Catholicism, and his epistle is in the spirit of Dryden's *Religio Laici* and *The Hind and the Panther*. McAuley's kinship with Dryden is founded on his admiration for the earlier poet's work and on his sense that he and Dryden face similar situations and share similar goals. Where Dryden was compelled to attack the Dissenting religious tradition, McAuley feels moved to satirize modern society's benumbing materialism and to oppose it with the Judeo-Christian values of charity and community.

> Material interests cannot but divide
> Unless we are of one mind to decide
> Who shall have what, how much, and when, and why.
> We live by spirit; by the flesh we die.
>
> (221–4)

In the mid-1940s, McAuley perpetrated, with Harold Stewart, a notorious hoax when he and Stewart invented, and foisted on a credulous Australian public, a vigorously unhinged modernist poet named Ern Malley. Among the literary hoaxes of the twentieth century, this ranks second only to the Spectra hoax that the American poets Witter Bynner and Arthur Davison Ficke pulled off three decades earlier. Literary hoaxes lie beyond the scope of this chapter; but they deserve mention to the extent that they involve parody and to the extent that parody is a species of satire.

James is the most formally and thematically adventurous satirist of the late twentieth century, and his versatility is especially evident in his verse epistles. For example, "To Pete Atkin: A Letter from Paris" features lively discussion of the virtues and limitations of popular music, and is in *ottava rima*. "To Russell Davies: A Letter from Cardiff" treats a number of topics from life on a film set to the challenges of writing song lyrics and light verse, and is in rhyme royal. "To Prue Shaw: A Letter from Cambridge," a touching meditation of love and marriage, is in *terza rima*. "To Tom Stoppard: A Letter from London" offers a defense of wit and the seriousness of wit, and is in Romance-Six stanzas. James has also written several verse letters in heroic couplets and several shorter satirical poems, including the hilarious "The Book of My Enemy Has Been Remaindered." And he has as well produced several mock-heroic epics, including *Charles Charming's Challenges*, a satire of the British royal family around the time of Prince Charles's engagement and marriage to Diana Spencer. Today, James is best known for his work in television, and some critics have held his media celebrity against him. But he is a considerable poet, and his satirical epistles are especially rewarding.

So are those of John Fuller, who wrote a sequence of five verse letters in Burns stanza that he included in his *Poems and Epistles* of 1973. (James, in introduction to a selection of his own poems entitled *Other Passports*, praises Fuller for producing "urbane and entertaining public verse.") Perhaps the best of Fuller's epistles is that addressed to the historian Angus Macintyre. The poem chiefly criticizes arid specialization in education. Toward the end of his letter, Fuller asserts the perennial value of impassioned and devoted scholarship – scholarship that is true both to the mind and heart, both to the academy and the world:

> Where has the living starlight gone?
> The owls are loud where once it shone.
> We see the archetypal don
> > Pen in his cloister
> A footnote to a footnote on
> *Ralph Roister Doister.*
>
> We need some vision to achieve,
> A heart to wear upon our sleeve,
> We need a holy spell to weave,
> > Some sacred wood
> Where we can teach what we believe
> > Will do us good.

Fuller later collaborated with James Fenton to produce a collection of satirical pieces, *Partingtime Hall* (1987); and Fenton himself has written a lively "Letter to John Fuller," which satirizes the view, advanced by Alfred Alvarez in his *Savage God*, that true poetry requires emotional recklessness, even suicide, of the poet.

Thom Gunn's "To Yvor Winters" is a quiet and contemplative satirical epistle. Addressed to a favorite teacher and fellow poet, the letter suggests that if we are to live full lives we must respect the claims of both instinct and intellect. Gunn writes in carefully flexible heroic couplets in which syntax sometimes ranges over line endings and sometimes focuses into arresting self-contained distichs:

> You keep both Rule and Energy in view,
> Much power in each, most in the balanced two.

Clive Wilmer has written two excellent verse letters, one to Gunn and one to a former teacher, J. A. Cuddon. Both concern matters of writing and literary style, and reflect, as do many satirical epistles, the longstanding association of the form with cultural criticism. Additional verse letters in this old Roman tradition are Robert Lowell's "To Peter Taylor on the Feast of the Epiphany," Donald Davie's "Six Epistles to Eva Hesse," Robert Pinsky's "An Explanation of America: A Poem to my Daughter," and, if I may be allowed an allusion to a poem addressed to me, Charles Gullans's "Diatribe to Doctor Steele."

Having begun this section by discussing Auden's satirical epistle to Byron, I should like to close it by citing Dick Davis's "Letter to Omar," another outstanding poem in which the poet discusses, with a mentor from the literary past, the present state of life and art. As Davis explains in his "Letter," he fell in love at an early age with Edward Fitzgerald's translation of Omar Khayyám's *Rubiáyát* and was moved for that reason to travel, after graduating from Cambridge University, to Iran. There he studied Persian, married an Iranian woman, and taught school during the 1970s before being forced to leave at the time of the Iranian Revolution. Davis contrasts Omar's philosophical and skeptical approach to existence with the unreflective and brutal tendencies of most political leaders. Writing in the *Rubiáyát* stanza, and using double or triple rhymes throughout, Davis moves skillfully back and forth between literary topics and broader issues of politics and culture. Here are three stanzas in which he explains to Omar the ways in which Persia has and has not changed since the medieval poet's day:

> Dear poet-scholar, would-be alcoholic
> (Well, is the wine – or is it not – symbolic?)
> You would and would not recognize the place –
> Succession now is quasi-apostolic,
>
> The palace is a kind of Moslem Deanery.
> But government, despite this shift of scenery,
> Stays as embattled as it ever was –
> As individual, and as sanguinary.
>
> The roaring creeds still rage – each knows it's wholly right
> And welcomes ways to wage the martyrs' holy fight;
> You might not know the names of some new sects
> But, as of old, the nation is bled slowly white.
>
> (53–64)

Traditional Satires

Turning to conventional twentieth-century satires, we may begin with the work of Roy Campbell. Campbell's three principal satires are *The Wayzgoose* (1928), *The Georgiad* (1933), and *Flowering Rifle* (1939). *The Wayzgoose* satirizes the artistic community of the author's native South Africa; and taking a leaf from Pope's *Dunciad*, Campbell describes Dullness as the reigning deity of the community. (Campbell himself cited Churchill's "Prophecy of Famine" and Marvell's "Character of Holland" as models for the poem.) Even if one knows something of the literary controversy that sparked Campbell's ire (he had been editing a literary journal whose financial backer objected to the magazine's progressive views), most readers today will be hard-pressed to follow and sort out the animosities and personalities that figure in *The Wayzgoose*. In its most spirited passages, however, the satire rises to a comprehensive criticism of the provinciality and racism of South Africa in the 1920s. Here is the opening of the poem:

> Attend my fable if your ears be clean,
> In fair Banana Land we lay our scene –
> South Africa, renowned both far and wide
> For politics and little else beside:
> Where, having torn the land with shot and shell,
> Our sturdy pioneers as farmers dwell,
> And, 'twixt the hours of strenuous sleep, relax
> To shear the fleeces or to fleece the blacks:
> Where every year a fruitful increase bears

>   Of pumpkins, cattle, sheep, and millionaires —
>   A clime so prosperous both to men and kine
>   That which were which a sage could scarce define.

Campbell's *Georgiad* is less effective. Written in the wake of his wife's involvement with Vita Sackville-West, this poem attacks the Bloomsbury circle. Though the poem raises serious points about the literary preciosity, hothouse intellectuality, and cliquishness that sometimes afflicted Bloomsbury, Campbell's indignation is rarely accompanied by the kind of wit that redeems even the most rebarbative passages of Pope; nor does Campbell achieve the vividness of characterization that makes Dryden's portraits of, say, Thomas Shadwell and George Villiers so memorably penetrating. *The Georgiad* has good bits — the description of a literary dinner that opens Part Three is especially entertaining — but these effective moments are largely lost in Campbell's shrill fulminations against vegetarians, nancies, and sonneteering poetesses. For those who admire Campbell's talents, *The Georgiad* has a further disturbing aspect. In its virulence, the poem prefigures the reactionary fury that emerges in *Flowering Rifle*.

This latter satire treats the Spanish Civil War and provides an apologia for Franco and the Nationalists. In one of the explanatory footnotes to this poem, Campbell refers to "the meetings and manoeuvres of the left-wing poets to ban and boycott the 'Georgiad', now a classic, and this poem — which soon will be." The passage of time, however, has not borne out Campbell's assessment of his satires, and, concerning *Flowering Rifle* in particular, most readers will likely agree with a comment that John Press makes in his entry on Campbell in the *Oxford Companion to Twentieth-century Poetry* (1994): "*Flowering Rifle*, a strident eulogy of Franco as the upholder of Christian values, is one of the nastiest and worst poems ever written by a man of Campbell's gifts." In another of his explanatory notes, Campbell describes as a "hoax" the aerial bombing of Guernica by the Condor Legion of Hitler's Luftwaffe. Campbell also tries to extenuate the Nationalist slaughter of the Republicans in Granada on the grounds that "the unbelievable babooneries perpetrated by the Reds made them trigger-happy as they rounded up and shot all corrupters of children, known perverts and sexual cranks." Both sides in the war were guilty of terrible atrocities, and it is not to excuse the depredations committed by the Left to say that one feels sickened by Campbell's justifications of the horrors perpetrated by the Right.

I fear that these remarks will leave readers with a very unjust and incomplete impression of Campbell. Though he could be cruelly reactionary and wildly homophobic, he also held, as has been said, humane and progressive views on race relations in his native country; and some of his lyrics about South Africa (for example, "The Zulu Girl") are admirably delicate and clear-sighted. Moreover, once the Second World War began, he enlisted in the British army, and after the war, he produced some superb translations of the poems of Frederico García Lorca, who was gay and was the most famous Republican victim of the *Falange* militia in Granada. Like a number of writers of his era — his friend Percy Wyndham Lewis and Ezra Pound are other examples — Campbell sometimes foolishly imagined that violence and intemperance were manly or purifying.

Ultimately, Campbell's satires hold more historical interest than literary value; his most accomplished satirical works are his excellent translation of Horace's *Art of Poetry* – Campbell is a remarkable translator of verse – and his epigram "On Some South African Novelists":

> You praise the firm restraint with which they write –
> I'm with you there, of course:
> They use the snaffle and the curb all right,
> But where's the bloody horse?

If Campbell in the 1930s writes right-wing satire, Edgell Rickword produces, in the same period, satire from a Marxist perspective. Rickword's principal political satire is "To the Wife of a Non-interventionist Statesman." Composed in March 1938, at the height of the Spanish Civil War and during Neville Chamberlain's attempts to appease Hitler, the poem advocates opposition to European fascism and Nazism. In the following passage, Rickword pleads that the enemy is almost at the gates and has designs on Britain as well as on continental states. The couplet about Saint Paul's dome would prove sadly prophetic when, two years later, Hitler launched the Blitzkrieg on London.

> Euzkadi's mines supply the ore
> to feed the Nazi dogs of war:
> Guernika's thermite rain transpires
> in doom on Oxford's dreaming spires:
> In Hitler's frantic mental haze
> already Hull and Cardiff blaze,
> and Paul's grey dome rocks to the blast
> of air-torpedoes screaming past.
> From small beginnings mighty ends,
> from calling rebel generals friends,
> from being taught at public schools
> to think the common people fools,
> Spain bleeds, and England wildly gambles
> to bribe the butcher in the shambles.

Though Rickword's satirical poems are shorter and more modest in scope than Campbell's, they read better today than the latter poet's. Rickword was a great admirer of Jonathan Swift; and Rickword's octosyllabic couplets have a Swiftian directness and compression. These qualities, which are also apparent in Rickword's social satire "Hints for Making a Gentleman," are a relief after the rambling manner of Campbell's satires or (to cite another notable satire of the 1930s) Wyndham Lewis's *One-way Song*.

The twentieth century produced several interesting satires of literary life that adopt, like Hope's *Dunciad Minor* and Campbell's *Wayzgoose*, the manner of Pope.

One of the best is Yvor Winters' *The Critiad*. Though Winters did not reprint this in either of the two *Collected Poems* he published in his lifetime (the poem first appeared in *New Quarter* in 1926 and was collected in Winters' *The Journey* in 1931), the poem offers a lively survey of the literary critics in the 1920s, and its unconventional judgments evidently contributed to Winters' reputation as a literary maverick – "the maverick's maverick," as Gunn dubs him in his Library of America edition of Winters' poems. As is the case with most satires about literary life, *The Critiad* has with time acquired obscurities, on account of its referring to figures who, though influential in their day, are no longer widely known. Compensating for its obscurities, however, *The Critiad* has several sprightly passages. Here, for instance, is a description of Harriet Monroe drowning in submissions at her office at *Poetry* magazine:

> Our Aunt Maria! With disheveled hair,
> With classic features drooping in despair,
> With voice inaudible, with coat awry,
> With some faint imprecision in her eye,
> But with determination in her tread,
> She moves to judge the living and the dead.
> Let any rival but suggest a name
> That he has published, she's a prior claim.
> But read her paper and you know the worst:
> Her method's to print everybody first.
> The poems, piling deeper on the floor,
> Cover her softly, till she's seen no more;
> Closing above her venerable head,
> They rustle gently, till each author's dead.
> Mistress of error and consistency,
> I trust no critic as I trust in thee!
>
> (98–113)

An even longer satire in Pope's manner is Richard Nason's *A Modern Dunciad*. Published in 1978 by a small press in New York City, this work runs to over one hundred pages and features an extensive prose apparatus. Though Nason's verse is not as sure-footed as Winters', *A Modern Dunciad* thoughtfully criticizes the fashionable obscurantism of late twentieth-century American poetry. The third of the poem's four books, in which the Goddess of Dullness crowns John Ashbery the modern king of dunces, is especially incisive.

Another excellent satire about literary life is R. S. Gwynn's *Narcissiad* (1981, revised and selected version, 2001). This poem concerns contemporary American poetry and has as its protagonist a narcissistic contemporary poet of great ambition and slight abilities. In his portrait of this hapless but energetic anti-hero, Gwynn supplies an acute analysis of the rampant literary careerism that resulted from the institution and proliferation, in the second half of the twentieth century in the United States, of creative writing programs and arts organizations:

> Confident in his art, he knows he's great
> Because his subsidy comes from the State
> For teaching self-expression to the masses
> In jails, nut-houses, worse, in grad-school classes
> In which his sermon is (his poems show it)
> That *anyone* can learn to be a poet.
> With pen in hand he takes the poet's stance
> To write, instead of sonnets, sheaves of grants.
>
> (41–8)

Gwynn also drolly describes the misshapen education that many younger poets received during the vogue of the Confessional Poets:

> Our Younger Poet, weaned early from his bottle,
> Begins to cast about for a role-model
> And, lacking knowledge of the great tradition,
> Pulls from the bookstore shelf a slim edition
> Of *Poems of Now*, and takes the proffered bait,
> And thus becomes the next initiate.
> If male he takes his starting point from Lowell
> And fearlessly parades his suffering soul
> Through therapy, shock-treatments, and divorce
> Until he whips the skin from the dead horse.
> His female counterpart descends from Plath
> And wanders down a self-destructive path
> Laying the blame on Daddy while she guides
> Her readers to their template suicides –
> Forgetting in her addled state, alas,
> Her all-electric kitchen has no gas.
> If undecided, s/he exalts O'Hara
> And, wandering like the flight of a bent arrow,
> Enthralls us in a poetry whose punch
> Lands on such subjects as his bank and lunch,
> What wines he's bought, what headlines he has seen
> Before his train pulls out at 4:18.
>
> (76–97)

It is often said that contemporary poets outnumber their readers, and *The Narcissiad* climaxes when various bards scattered across the country decide, independently, to kill off their competition. Eventually, only two major poets are left. After they destroy each other in a mock-heroic duel, Narcissus alone remains to bear the standard of poetry. His glory, however, is short-lived. As he ascends Olympus in triumphal train, his execrable verses wake Zeus, who devises an ingenious punishment for him and sends him scurrying back down the mountain. Gwynn is one of the best satirists in American literature, and his *Narcissiad*, as well as his funny shorter poems (for example, "Snow

White and the Seven Deadly Sins," "The Professor's Lot," and "Among Philistines"), represent a durable contribution to English-language satirical poetry.

Robert Frost wrote several excellent satires on Horatian models, the best of which is "The Lesson for Today." This poem satirizes those who contend that the modern age is worse than previous ages and that the special difficulties of the modern world render individual achievement difficult or even impossible. The poem employs the familiar satirical form of a discussion between the poet and an *adversarius*. Frost's *adversarius* is Alcuin, the medieval scholar-poet who advised Charlemagne on educational matters and who guided the humanist revival of the Carolingian court. Because Alcuin lived in the Middle Ages – "the world's undebatably dark ages" (7), as Frost puts it – Alcuin has an accurately grim standard against which to judge the miseries of the modern world. Also, since medieval poets suffered, in Frost's phrase, "the fate / Of being born at once too early and late" (11–12) – too early for the great age of modern-language verse and too late for the great age of classical Latin verse – Alcuin should be able, Frost suggests, to sympathize with moderns who feel that their time does not allow their talents to flourish.

More particularly, Frost sees Alcuin as a fitting foil for his ideas because both of them are teachers as well as poets and are thereby concerned not only with their writing, but with their culture. After complimenting Alcuin, "O Master of the Palace School, / You were not Charles' nor anybody's fool" (19–20), Frost formally invites him to debate which is the bleaker and more egregious, the Middle Ages or the Modern Age. In making his invitation, Frost observes another similarity between himself and his medieval counterpart and another reason why it is appropriate for them to weigh the relative badness of their times. Each writer lived or lives toward the end of a millennium, and they are thus near chronological junctions that encourage historical reflection and evaluation. (This last comparison is stretched insofar as Alcuin's dates, 735–804, fall far short of the end of the first millennium AD, whereas Frost – whose dates are 1874–1963 and who first read his "Lesson" in 1941 before Harvard's chapter of the Phi Beta Kappa Society – did in fact live the better part of his life in the final century of the second millennium.)

> One more millennium's about to end.
> Let's celebrate the event, my distant friend,
> In publicly disputing which is worse,
> The present age or your age. You and I
> As schoolmen of repute should qualify
> To wage a fine scholastical contention
> As to whose age deserves the lower mark,
> Or should I say the higher one, for dark.
> (46–53)

Frost takes, in good-humored fashion, both sides of the debate, speaking now for Alcuin, now for himself. And after the passage just cited, Frost goes on to suggest that miseries exist in all times: "There's always something to be sorry for, / A sordid peace or an outrageous war" (55–6). Frost next tells Alcuin that moderns particularly suffer from a sense of cosmological insignificance. Modern physics has informed them that their earth is just a minor planet in a minor solar system in one of many galaxies: "Space ails us moderns," Frost says, "we are sick with space" (68). But he adds that people in the Middle Ages felt small in a different way. They were utterly and trivially corrupt compared to God. And this in turn leads Frost to the idea that the medieval monk and the modern astronomer ultimately find themselves facing the same metaphysical anxiety: "We both are the belittled human race, / One as compared with God and one with space" (77–8). Frost then imagines Alcuin teaching his students the fourteenth ode from Horace's second book of odes and imparting to them the Stoic-Christian moral that life inevitably leads to death and that we must try, while we live, to be honorable and cheerful, even as we face threats, from every quarter, to our decency and integrity:

> O paladins, the lesson for today
> Is how to be unhappy yet polite.
> . . .
> Memento mori and obey the Lord.
> Art and religion love the somber chord.
> Earth's a hard place in which to save the soul.
> (87–8, 96–8)

Subsequently, Frost recurs to this last thought, commenting, "One age is like another for the soul" (113). And he notes that though the external conditions of existence may alter through the ages, human life never changes in one respect: for whatever mysterious reasons, our world is imperfect, and we are always destined to realize only incompletely what we most aspire to do and be:

> We all are doomed to broken-off careers,
> And so's the nation, so's the total race.
> The earth itself is liable to the fate
> Of meaninglessly being broken off.
> . . .
> On me as much as any is the jest.
> I take my incompleteness with the rest.
> God bless himself can no one else be blessed.
> (145–8, 154–6)

And having earlier referred to the famous epitaphs of Charlemagne and Alcuin, Frost takes leave of his medieval *adversarius* and of his own poem by proposing an epitaph for himself:

> I hold your doctrine of Memento Mori.
> And were an epitaph to be my story

I'd have a short one ready for my own.
I would have written of me on my stone:
I had a lover's quarrel with the world.
(157–61)

The last twentieth-century satire I shall discuss is Edgar Bowers' "How We Came from Paris to Blois." A travel poem, set in France in July 1988, it is, like Frost's "Lesson," Horatian in origin and spirit, being modeled on Horace's satire (1.5) describing a journey from Rome to Brundisium in 38 or 37 BC. (Bowers' title recalls Robert Browning's "How They Brought the Good News from Ghent to Aix," though this allusion appears to be simply humorous or ironical: Bowers' journey to Blois is outwardly undramatic and is, as such, utterly different from the wild ride Browning's narrator makes on his stalwart horse.) Just as Horace, in his satire, is accompanied on his way by his friend Maecenas, so Bowers is accompanied, in his poem, by a friend, the poet and translator Robert Wells. And Bowers relates, just as Horace does, the sights he sees and the people he meets on his journey.

Bowers composes his poem in eighteen stanzas of blank verse, each stanza having nine lines and consisting of a single sentence. For the most part, the poem is warmly discursive. The poet discusses subjects from church architecture to European history to French cuisine. Yet the poem features an underlying sense of the fragility of life and culture. This is especially true in a passage in which Bowers, having stopped en route in Saint Benoît-sur-Loire, thinks of Saint Benedict, the sixth-century monk who founded the Benedictine order and in whose work, as Bowers says, "The Mediterranean legacy of art / Number and word persisted" during a period when Europe had, on the whole, lost the rich legacy of antiquity. And this sense of life's fragility comes into beautiful and moving focus when, a little further on, Bowers hears the ringing of the church bells of Saint Benoît. The sound makes him think of his first visit to France in late 1944, when he was with the 101st Airborne Division of the United States Army and when the Germans surprised and inflicted heavy casualties on Allied troops and paratroopers during the Battle of the Bulge:

> Hearing the bells, recalling, then, the Christmas
> Surprise in the Ardennes, myself afraid
> For friends and strangers I feared for as friends
> Caught in their icy holes by Tiger tanks,
> Just boys, with no experience of fear,
> Victims half-trained and leaderless, I saw
> My own division, proud clean uniforms
> Drifting, some dead, some living, to the ground.
>
> Whenever I remember them, I know
> Their guiltless mouths and their intense clear eyes,
> Astonished by the brimming presences
> Of voices, looks and stories, however brief,

> Like none before, never to be again,
> And see in them a cause for the belief
> That nature loves too well the soul it makes
> Willingly to let it pass away forever.
>
> (97–112)

The satire then modulates back to the present and its quotidian incidentals, such as an argument at a hotel between the concierge and a would-be guest without a reservation. The poem closes with the poet and his friend resolving to read, once they get to Blois, Horace's ode. There follows a two-stanza postscript, concerning Max Jacob, the artist and poet and Jewish convert to Christianity, whom the Nazis murdered and whom Bowers sees as another "brimming presence" tragically martyred by the worst aspects and darkest impulses of our species.

Conclusion

Though we often think of our age as one of fragmentation and discontinuity, history has, as Thomas Mann tells us in *Joseph and his Brothers*, a vertical as well as a horizontal dimension. There is a depth of being and experience beneath every moment of our lives. In the literary realm, satire reminds us that we are never entirely cut off from the past. The verse satirists of the twentieth century are of their time, but we hear in their poems the voices and concerns, the metrical techniques and rhetorical strategies, of satirists going all the way back to antiquity. Most fine verse combines traditional elements with new conditions, but this is especially true of satire, which has always encouraged its practitioners to look outward at their communities and the world. In the introduction to this chapter, I noted that many factors in our culture have, in recent times, narrowed the practice and potentials of poetry. Yet the very fact that poets have continued to write satire suggests that there is a healthy resistance to this trend. And while it is too soon to evaluate the significance of twentieth-century satirical poetry, it may represent an effort not only to restore verse satire to its former dignity, but also to correct or balance the aesthetic principles that have dominated verse for the past two hundred and fifty years or so.

Finally, in assembling this chapter, I have on several occasions thought of Burns' satirical epistle to John McMath and of Burns' lament that he did not possess a greater satirical genius to bring to bear against the religious hypocrisy of his day:

> O Pope, had I thy satire's darts
> To gie the rascals their deserts,
> I'd rip their rotten, hollow hearts,
>   An' tell aloud
> Their jugglin hocus-pocus arts
>   To cheat the crowd.
>
> (37–42)

Burns was not Pope. Yet he need not have worried about any authorial inadequacy. He still wrote wonderful satirical poetry and contributed valuably to the art of satire. By the same token, though the twentieth century did not produce a Pope, the poets discussed in this chapter wrote excellent satire and, like Burns, made permanent contributions to the genre. Most important of all, their poems will help poets of the twenty-first century continue to build and to enrich our long and deep tradition of satirical verse.

References and Further Reading

Arnold, Matthew (1953) *Selected Poetry and Prose*, with an introduction by Frederick L. Mulhauser. New York: Holt, Rinehart, and Winston.

Elliott, Robert C. (1974) Satire. In Alex Preminger, Frank J. Warnke, and O. B. Hardison, Jr (eds), *Princeton Encyclopedia of Poetry and Poetics*, enlarged edn. Princeton, NJ: Princeton University Press.

Grigson, Geoffrey (1980) *The Oxford Book of Satirical Verse*. Oxford: Oxford University Press.

Gwynn, R. S. (2001) *No Word of Farewell: Selected Poems, 1970–2000*. Ashland, Oregon: Story Line Press.

Hecht, Anthony (1993) *The Hidden Law: The Poetry of W. H. Auden*. Cambridge, MA: Harvard University Press.

Hendrickson, G. L. (1897) Are the letters of Horace satires? *American Journal of Philology* 18, 313–24.

Hope, A. D. (1970) *The Cave and the Spring*. Chicago: University of Chicago Press.

Lucie-Smith, Edward (1967) *The Penguin Book of Satirical Verse*. Harmondsworth: Penguin.

Nason, Richard (1978) *A Modern Dunciad*. New York: The Smith.

Pearce, Joseph (2004) *Unafraid of Virginia Woolf: The Friends and Enemies of Roy Campbell*. Wilmington: ISI Books.

Piper, William Bowman (1969) *The Heroic Couplet*. Cleveland: Press of Case Western Reserve University.

Press, John (1994) Roy Campbell. In Ian Hamilton (ed.), *The Oxford Companion to Twentieth Century Poetry in English*, pp. 83–4. Oxford: Oxford University Press.

Steele, Timothy (1990) *Missing Measures: Modern Poetry and the Revolt against Meter*. Fayatteville: University of Arkansas Press.

—— (1999) *All the Fun's in How You Say a Thing: An Explanation of Meter and Versification*. Athens: Ohio University Press.

Stern, Philip Van Doren (1945) *The Portable Edgar Allan Poe*. New York: Viking.

Trillin, Calvin (1994) *Deadline Poet or, My Life as a Doggerelist*. New York: Farrar, Straus and Giroux.

Trimpi, Helen Pinkerton (2004) Letter from Palo Alto. *The New Compass* 3, n.p. (available at http://thenewcompass.ca/jun2004/pinkerton.html).

Trimpi, Wesley (1962) *Ben Jonson's Poems: A Study of the Plain Style*. Stanford: Stanford University Press.

Wilson, Edmund (1938) Is verse a dying technique? In Walter Jackson Bate (ed.), *Criticism: The Major Texts*, enlarged edn, pp. 588–96. New York: Harcourt Brace.

23
Satire in Modern and Contemporary Theater
Christopher J. Herr

Just as in *Hamlet*, when Polonius grows breathless describing the various modes in which the visiting actors excel, the general terms "modern theater" and "contemporary theater" (here, a chronological designation for post-1945 theater) barely contain the range of drama and theater developed over the course of the past century and a half. Characterized by rapidly and radically shifting conventions and assumptions, modern and contemporary theater are fields inescapably various in both form and content. From their antecedents in the early nineteenth century, these dramas develop irregularly, often in competition with one another. Realism and naturalism echo the heroic dramas and melodramas of the mid-nineteenth century even as they shift from an emphasis on complex plots and moral simplicity toward a more complex psychology and social investigation; the clear-sighted social drama of Henrik Ibsen and George Bernard Shaw stems partly from a romantic belief in the individual set against the institution. Similarly, early twentieth-century avant-garde movements react against realism's mundane dependence on verisimilitude, but never reject entirely the desire to illuminate social problems. By the middle of the twentieth century, the Absurdist playwrights create dark, ironic forms of expression that reflect a world disillusioned by the horrors of two world wars.

In dramas and theatrical practices so varied, satire takes equally varied forms, though few plays in the modern dramatic canon are purely satirical, partly because satire is hard to market successfully in systems that rely on public patronage. As American playwright George S. Kaufman quipped, "Satire is what closes Saturday night." Also, because most theater depends upon language and bodies in space, there is usually an element of human identification built into audience response. Acting and scenic design may discount the importance of the audience–performer connection, but the presence of human actors on stage fosters sympathy, and thereby weakens the possibility of sardonic detachment. On the other hand, the fact that audiences watch people like themselves on stage gives the theatrical satirist an advantage – it is hard not to recognize oneself even in the most exaggerated characterization.

A common solution to the problem of theatrical satire has been to develop this sympathetic connection between performer and audience by tempering the bitterness of the attack. More Horace than Juvenal, instructing through laughter rather than punishing through scorn, much of dramatic satire serves comic ends. The traditional movement of comedy tends toward the conservative, restoring order and reincorporating outsiders at the close of the action. It gently chastens those who threaten a stable order: the miserly, the mean-spirited, the anti-social, the self-righteous, and the hypocritical. The figures in these comedies – Menander's grouchy Knemon, the senex of Roman comedy, Shakespeare's Shylock and Egeus, even Molière's Tartuffe, Chekhov's hapless intellectuals, and Shaw's narrow-minded burghers – are morally and existentially redeemable, their vices temporary violations of the accepted order. The satire in such comedies may be blistering, but the comic movement is restorative.

The relationship of satire to tragic drama is even more complex. Since the Greeks, tragedy has enjoyed greater regard than comedy, so that satiric attack, no matter how accurate, righteous, or fierce is often marginalized, undercut by subservience to a larger tragic goal. Arthur Miller's *Death of a Salesman* (1949), for example, repeatedly criticizes Willy Loman for chasing a false dream – his hallucinatory visions underscore the unreal nature of capitalism's promises of plenty. Willy is a querulous, helpless braggart, blind to his failings; in short, he is a figure ripe for satire. Still, as Miller repeatedly argued, the play is tragic; it moves us to believe, as Loman's wife tells us, "He's a human being and a terrible thing is happening to him. So attention must be paid." The raised stakes push the satire toward sympathy; our focus shifts from his weaknesses to his struggle to persevere. Nevertheless, Miller's play hints that the intertwining of irony and tragedy is unavoidable. Both work to isolate the individual, strip away the inessential and force them (and us), however painfully, to confront things as they are. *King Lear* is filled with bitter ironies and *Hamlet* with ontologically anxious gallows humor because the irony natural to tragedy carries its horror. Purely satirical drama may not be able to carry tragic weight, but tragedy almost always carries a satirical tone.

In modern and contemporary theater, both comedy and tragedy remain important, but in the mid-twentieth century there is a shift toward black comedy, where grim humor is born from material that was formerly tragic. Human suffering in both Aeschylus and Beckett is inevitable, but in the *Oresteia*, such suffering is tragic; in Beckett, it is ironic. Other twentieth-century experimental practitioners attempt to reduce audience sympathy for the characters by rejecting accepted moral or aesthetic orders. Such playwrights either create characters so unlike human beings or place characters in situations so foreign to our experience that such a connection becomes virtually impossible. For example, Bertolt Brecht's "epic theater" deliberately undercuts the conventions of what he calls "dramatic" theater: suspense, audience identification with the protagonist, causal plot structure, and the psychologically determined character. By foregrounding the artifice of theatrical presentation, Brecht creates a satirical viewpoint for an examination of human behavior and history.

Thus, the satirical vision is present in much of modern and contemporary theater, shifting form in the context of unprecedented cultural and historical changes: the rapid expansion of industrialism, incomprehensible advances in science and technology, two world wars, and the constant threat, after 1945, of nuclear annihilation. Usually, rapid historical and political change is the impetus for theatrical satirists. Ibsen and Shaw pillory the narrow moralizing of their late nineteenth and early twentieth-century societies because they believe that a scientific awakening has created the necessity for new ways of thinking. Almost simultaneously, Surrealists and Expressionists denounce science as a false prophet and depict unchecked capitalism as a devouring machine. The Futurists, Dadaists, and Absurdists go further by not only questioning accepted values, but by attacking the bourgeois forms that earlier satirists use. By the mid-twentieth century, then, ironic drama dominates the theatrical landscape. Moving from the realists' satire as a response to social ills, these later playwrights focus on the inherent absurdity of the human condition.

Seeing with a Clear Eye: Satire in Ibsen, Shaw, Chekhov, and the Realists

In addition to the Romantic influence, the realist theater was heavily influenced by the developing scientific method, believing that the fullest understanding of human behavior would come from the most accurate depiction. Unlike the naturalists, who often saw human behavior as fatally conditioned by heredity and environment, the realists maintained that individual progress was possible. Thus, realist drama is reality shaped toward a higher end; as Ibsen argued, Zola "goes down in the sewer to take a bath: I, in order to cleanse it" (Le Gallienne 1982: ix). But even as these playwrights exposed and examined human folly, many of them refused to be pinned to a particular social agenda. Ibsen never allied himself with a political cause; Chekhov argued in a letter to one of his editors, "You reproach me for objectivity, calling it indifference to good and evil, an absence of ideals and principles, and so forth. When I describe horse thieves, you want me to say stealing horses is evil. But surely that's been known for a long time without my having to say it" (Chekhov to A. S. Suvorin, 1890, quoted in Dukore 1974: 914). Devastatingly accurate observation and description trumped the overt moralizing that had characterized much of mid-nineteenth-century drama.

Ibsen (1828–1906), undoubtedly the most influential playwright of the nineteenth century, began by writing verse dramas and later built a lasting reputation on more realistic dramas – *A Doll's House* (1879), *Ghosts* (1881), *An Enemy of the People* (1882), *The Wild Duck* (1884), and *Hedda Gabler* (1890) – set in middle-class households. While his plays are suffused with a tragic sensibility, Ibsen's depictions of the obstacles to this understanding, bourgeois narrowness and morality, are invariably satirical. These plays were initially castigated as parades of human immorality. His contemporaries saw Ibsen as a pessimistic muckraker, a photographer of social problems grimly airing the culture's dirty linen. But in these plays, humor carries the bulk of his ire. Showing them in the service of old ideas and hypocritical moral systems, he repeatedly exposes to ridicule the established leaders of society: professors, bankers, judges, newspaper editors, and clergymen. In *Hedda Gabler*, George Tesman, a self-absorbed academic, naïvely delights in his slippers and dotes on Hedda, noticing neither her indifference nor her pregnancy. Later, their friend, Judge Brack, blackmails Hedda into an affair, driving her to suicide. When Brack discovers Hedda has killed herself, Ibsen points up his false propriety to end the play: "Good God – But – people don't *do* such things!"

An Enemy of the People is almost wholly satiric, railing against the worship of dead ideals and the morality fostered by majority opinion. In the play, Dr Stockmann attempts to arouse the righteous anger of the public, only to discover that they won't listen. When he discovers that the newspapers will not print the truth about the town's contaminated water supply because the readers won't believe it, Stockmann explodes in rage. Even the most serious of Ibsen's plays are thick with comic characters that drive the central conflicts. Pastor Manders of *Ghosts* is the most fully drawn of Ibsen's buffoonish figures in this tradition, contemptible for both his narrow piety and his hypocrisy, flaws that are comic in themselves but that also help to bring about the tragedy of the play. Furthermore, by foregrounding the metaphors of sickness and health in these two plays, Ibsen once again reaffirms his central dramatic goal: to show life accurately and honestly, to probe the wounds of a sick society and destroy the moral diseases that impede human progress.

A great admirer of Ibsen, Shaw (1856–1950), too, defined the fundamental problem of his time as a slavish devotion to tradition and outmoded institutions. One of his earlier plays, *Arms and the Man* (1898), satirizes romantic attitudes toward war through Captain Bluntschli, a soldier who carries chocolates instead of a gun, and who fights for money, not causes. *Mrs Warren's Profession*, repressed by the English authorities when it was first written in 1894, examines prostitution as a social problem. In the play's climax, Mrs Warren's daughter Vivie rejects the financial support of her mother, a successful brothel owner. It is not the immorality of prostitution that horrifies her as much as the exploitative immorality of capitalism. Shaw's method is discursive rather than incisive; virtually all of these plays, and others such as *Man and Superman* (1902) and *Pygmalion* (1913), climax in long speeches in which characters present opposing ideas until a resolution is reached.

Shaw eschews the tragic tone of Ibsen's mature plays, instead tempering his satiric impulse with comic plots filled with the witty exchange of ideas. In addition, Shaw's method is more overtly political than Ibsen's. A committed Socialist, Shaw believed that art was inherently didactic. Though he admired Ibsen's technique of crafting plays around the discussion of ideas, Shaw makes little pretense of detachment, shaping his plays around a debate of ideas in which unconventional ideas are shown as triumphant and the status quo is exposed as a sham. For example, *Major Barbara* (1905) pits the ideals of Christian charity against the amoral arms manufacturer Andrew Undershaft, who argues that his daughter, a Salvation Army major, perpetuates the "crime" of poverty by pitying it: "I will take an order from a good man as cheerfully as from a bad one. If you good people prefer preaching and shirking to buying my weapons and fighting the rascals, don't blame me. I can make cannons: I cannot make courage and conviction. Bah! You tire me...with your morality mongering" (Act III). The play's end effects a conversion of a different sort: Barbara's fiancé, Adolphus Cusins, inherits the arms factory, and Barbara vows to work on saving the well-fed and prosperous workers in the factory town. Shaw's vision, then, is satirical, his goals didactic; however, his tone remains comic throughout.

After making his literary reputation with his ironic, sympathetic short stories, Anton Chekhov (1860–1904) turned to playwriting later in his life. His five full-length plays are filled with intimate portraits of the hapless and the feckless, idle dreamers, incompetent aristocrats, and lazy intellectuals unable to understand the changes taking place around them. Chekhov thought of the plays as satirical comedies, a portrait of Russian society at a moment when old systems were beginning to crumble, but before the radical changes that would bring the Revolution had grown to ripeness. The plays are plays of mood rather than action, a mood of loss and impotent frustration. Near the end of the third act of *Uncle Vanya* (1899), for example, the title character becomes enraged at his late sister's former husband, a professor. When he attempts to turn his rage into action by shooting the professor, he misses – twice. Vanya's failure is the point of the play, which is filled with characters wasting away in idleness and confusion. Indeed, the structure of the dialogue mirrors this aimlessness; his characters talk at cross-purposes, repeat themselves, mutter to themselves, interrupt one another, or simply lapse into meaningless catchphrases.

Chekhov works largely by indirection and counterpoint, so that his plays often seem plotless, even though suicides, attempted murders, adulteries, and betrayals abound. But in Chekhov's world, these events often take on a satirical cast; they are the desperate acts of characters too befuddled to move forward. The Ranevskayas in *The Cherry Orchard* (1904) are told from the beginning of the play that they will lose their entire estate unless they sell their orchard. They refuse, or rather ignore, the pleas of their friend, and at the end of the play lose everything. Both satirical and sympathetic, Chekhov does not allow any character to escape his critical eye. In *Uncle Vanya*, the professor is a self-righteous charlatan; the doctor Astrov is often crude; Vanya is petulant; Yelena, the professor's wife, is lazy. However, the characters are complex, so their flaws are balanced by positive qualities: Astrov's love of the forests, Vanya's humanity, Yelena's kindness and beauty. The second characteristic that somewhat redeems the characters is the self-consciousness of each. Even when Vanya lays the responsibility for his unproductive life at the professor's feet – "You wasted my life!...If I'd lived a normal life, I might have turned out as a Schopenhauer, a Dostoevsky!" – he immediately recognizes that his claims are preposterous: "I'm talking so much nonsense! I'm going out of my mind!"

While Chekhov's satire is more diffused than either Ibsen's or Shaw's, and the objects of his attack are less obvious, one clear target – a target he shared with other Russian writers, especially Gogol, whose *Inspector General* (1836) is the finest example of dramatic satire in Russia before Chekhov – is the tedious bleakness of Russian provincial life. In *The Three Sisters* (1901), the sisters, educated and sophisticated, long to move to Moscow: as Masha says, "To know three languages in this town is ... some sort of unnecessary appendage, like a sixth finger." But the satire in the play also takes aim at the sisters themselves. Despite having the means to move, at the end of the play they remain in their town, trapped in bad jobs and worse marriages, dominated by their brother's vindictive peasant wife. Chekhov's satire shows that life is difficult and dark and humans are impossibly flawed; nevertheless, his sympathy tempers his criticism and softens the tone.

In addition to these playwrights of the modern theater, satire was important in the works of their contemporaries and followers, both realists and anti-realists. In Ireland, John Millington Synge (*The Playboy of the Western World*, 1907) and Sean O'Casey (*Juno and the Paycock*, 1924) explored the folk traditions and comic pretensions of a country in the throes of revolution. In Italy, Luigi Pirandello (*Right You Are – If You Think You Are*, 1917) wrote a series of plays that focus on philosophical issues of truth and being; in them, the identity of characters is never definitively established, and the possibility of meaning itself is called into question – truth comes to reside in individual perception. In Soviet Russia, Mikhail Bulgakov (*The Crimson Island*, 1928) and Vladimir Mayakovsky (*The Bedbug*, 1928) pointed out the absurdities of the government, to their audiences' delight and to their own peril.

Satire and Anti-realism: From Wilde to Brecht

Other playwrights of the late nineteenth century adopted non-realistic forms for their satires. Perhaps the best known of these is Oscar Wilde (1854–1900), who achieved popular and critical success with his witty plays about the Victorian upper classes. *A Woman of No Importance* (1893) and *An Ideal Husband* (1895) poke fun at political and social maneuvering and achieved moderate success in their day, but Wilde's dramatic reputation rests almost wholly on *The Importance of Being Earnest* (1905), among the finest examples of light satire in modern drama. Wilde's aesthetic intention differs greatly from the realists with whom he was a contemporary; the satire of his play is at once more pervasive and less bitter, more in keeping with the comic operas of Gilbert and Sullivan than the sharp social criticism of Ibsen or Shaw. Wilde pokes fun at the superficial concerns of an aristocratic Victorian society he knew well, but because the dialogue is so witty, even though the characters are trivial, they never lose their attractiveness. Thus, Wilde's wit is both the fuel for his satire and the means of its amelioration.

The Importance of Being Earnest is at all levels parodic and satirical; gleefully undermining both traditional theatrical forms and the assumed certainties of Victorian life, its stated intention is made clear in the subtitle: "A Trivial Comedy for Serious People." The story is a deliberate parody of melodramatic plot conventions and the structure of the well-made play: the outsider Jack is discovered to be of noble birth and to have the "proper" name, Ernest. Thematically, matters of seriousness to Victorian society – marriage, class distinctions, religion, and death – are treated with deliberate triviality, while minor matters – whether to eat teacake or muffins, how to dress, when to serve cucumber sandwiches – are treated by the characters as matters of utmost gravity.

Serving as a vehicle for Wilde's legendary wit, the play is built on an endless chain of paradoxes or inversions of the accepted norm. "To lose one parent," Lady Bracknell tells Jack, a suitor for her niece, "may be regarded as a misfortune – to lose *both* seems like carelessness. Who was your father? He was evidently a man of some wealth. Was he born in what the Radical papers call the purple of commerce or did he rise from the ranks of the aristocracy?" Wilde's deliberate inversion of accepted formulas – "Divorces are made in Heaven," "Illness of any kind is hardly a thing to be encouraged in others," "the home seems to me to be the proper sphere for a man" – sustains the play's mood throughout, mocking Victorian obsessions with appearance and form while sustaining a lightness of mood.

Perhaps the only figures in the late nineteenth century comparable to Wilde are William Gilbert (1836–1911) and Arthur Sullivan (1842–1900), who captivated the British public with their light operas, among them *Patience* (1881), a parody of the aesthetic movement of the 1870s and 1880s, *HMS Pinafore* (1878), *The Pirates of Penzance* (1879), *Iolanthe* (1882), and *Mikado* (1885). Like Wilde, Gilbert and Sullivan gently point out the hypocrisies of Victorian society, especially its regimentation and its emphasis on class distinction. *HMS Pinafore*, their fourth collaboration, tells the story of Little Buttercup, a simple woman in love with the ship's captain. At the same time, the captain's daughter, Josephine, wooed by Joseph Porter, the First Lord of the Admiralty, pines for a common sailor, Ralph. After Porter threatens Ralph with imprisonment for his presumption, Little Buttercup reveals that Ralph and the captain were switched at birth, thereby necessitating a switch in their social positions. The Admiral, no longer able to pursue Josephine because she is below his station, releases the couples to marry.

One of the chief characteristics of Gilbert and Sullivan's work is their witty burlesque of Victorian military prowess and social rectitude. In *HMS Pinafore*, for example, the captain is praised by his men, for "hardly ever" swearing at them: "He's hardly ever sick at sea! / Then give three cheers, and one cheer more, / For the hardy Captain of the Pinafore!" Because they were able to create a popular format in which music and words worked together seamlessly, Gilbert and Sullivan were able to satirize every part of their society with impunity. Queen Victoria herself is reputed to have enjoyed a performance of *The Gondoliers* (1889), another attack on snobbish class distinctions that, in part, parodies royal subservience to parliament.

A few other playwrights in the early twentieth century worked in a vein similar to Wilde and Gilbert and Sullivan, including Noel Coward (1899–1973). But Coward's brittle, cynical comedies about the British upper class – *Hay Fever* (1925), *Private Lives* (1930), and *Cavalcade* (1931), in particular – are often fueled by a bitter postwar view of the world, peopled by characters disaffected and rudderless, but endlessly amusing. Indeed, as it had for Coward, the war brought a change in tone to much of modern drama. By the early 1920s, Bertolt Brecht (1898–1956) and other continental playwrights were trying to find a theatrical language that would express the darker truths about humanity made clear by the horrors of war. His use of epic theater made Brecht the most consistently satirical playwright of his era. It allowed him to attack war, capitalism, bourgeois morality, repressive institutions, and history from a Marxist point of view, without subscribing to the earnest humorlessness of other political drama. He also developed a theory of theater that allowed his influence to spread far beyond his plays, allowing him to become one of the most influential theater practitioners of the twentieth century. In virtually every play, Brecht aimed to undercut the central assumptions of the realistic theater. He employed the alienation effect (*Verfremdungseffekt*) to prevent the audience from becoming passive recipients of theater experience. For example, he projected titles with summaries of the upcoming action, thereby defeating theatrical suspense; he inserted into the play songs only tangentially related to its action; he rejected "dramatic" plots for an episodic structure. Brecht's ultimate goal was to remove the sense of inevitability from dramatic action, to engage audiences' rational faculties and allow them to see that history is created by human beings capable of action and choice.

Brecht's best plays combine a sense of outrage with ironic detachment. He skewers bourgeois assumptions about the world by stripping them of their trappings – and their justification. *The Threepenny Opera* (1928) is a reworking of Gay's *The Beggar's Opera* (1728) that focuses on the immorality of capitalism in Victorian London. In Brecht's play, Macheath is a vicious killer who sees himself as a businessman, while his father-in-law, Jonathan Peachum, is a respectable businessman who makes his living managing a fleet of beggars. The difference between Macheath and Peachum is marginal; it is only social approbation and moral hypocrisy, Brecht shows, that allows Peachum to dictate the laws by which others operate. In the play, Peachum, displeased with the loss of money that has resulted from his daughter's elopement with Macheath, threatens to turn all the beggars loose at the coronation unless the Queen arrests Macheath. However, in a parody of happy endings, Macheath is spared at the last moment by a messenger from the Queen, who rewards him with a baronetcy. Brecht's argument about the vicious nature of capitalism is wittily articulated in both the action and the songs. In "The Second Threepenny Finale," Macheath sings: "What does a man live by? By resolutely / Ill-treating, beating, cheating, eating some other bloke! / A man can only live by absolutely / Forgetting he's a man like other folk!"

Most of Brecht's plays are as relentlessly satirical as *The Threepenny Opera*. Written in 1939, *Mother Courage and her Children* (which was rewritten after Brecht saw that the title character was too sympathetic to audiences) focuses on the interconnection between war and capitalism by following a merchant during the Thirty Years' War. Mother Courage's commitment to her canteen wagon contributes to the deaths of her three children, but at the end she continues on, pulling the wagon by herself, still hoping to gain profit from a war that has robbed her of everything. *The Resistible Rise of Arturo Ui* (1941) parodies the rise of Hitler, rewriting him as a Chicago gangster who tries to corner the cauliflower market by viciously eliminating his opposition. In these plays, as in *The Good Person of Setzuan* (1940) and *The Caucasian Chalk Circle* (1945), Brecht creates fantastical worlds that push the rules of capitalism to their logical conclusions; his satire stems from the method by which he consistently directs audiences to see their own complicity in such a system.

American Conversions: Political Satire in Mid-century American Drama

In the United States, satirical drama tended to focus less on social mores and institutions than on overt political or social commentary. The influence of European dramatic forms, particularly German Expressionist drama, was essential for the development of satirical drama in the United States. German playwrights such as Georg Kaiser (*From Morn to Midnight*, 1916) and Ernst Toller (*Man and the Masses*, 1920) had helped to develop in the 1910s and 1920s a theatrical style that was characterized by episodic structures and telegraphic dialogue rather than character, and unified thematically rather than by plot. Expressionist plays often traced the peregrinations and death of an ordinary individual alienated by the restrictions of a mechanized society. In American drama, Expressionism came late, and, though never a mainstream form, it remained influential throughout the 1920s. Even Eugene O'Neill (1888–1953), whose preoccupation with the conflict between humans and Fate led him toward tragedy and melodrama, drew on Expressionism to offer flashes of satire in *The Emperor Jones* (1920) and in *The Hairy Ape* (1921). Subtitled "A Comedy of Ancient and Modern Life in Eight Scenes," the latter play attacks the mechanization of the modern world (the steamship is contrasted with the wind-driven ships of earlier generations) and the disinterest of the upper classes toward the working class. The protagonist of the play is a Neanderthal-like furnace stoker, Yank, who searches fruitlessly for a place to "belong," until he ends up being killed by an ape at the zoo.

Perhaps the best example of American Expressionism – and one of the most thoroughly satirical plays of the interwar period – is Elmer Rice's *The Adding Machine* (1923). Focusing on the actions of Mr Zero, an accountant who murders his boss, and is convicted and executed, Rice's play satirizes the vague but extravagant promises of modern life by pillorying the deficient human beings it helps to create. Because all they see in their environment is monotony and conformity, Zero, his wife, and their friends are petty, bland, bigoted, and vindictive. The second half of *The Adding Machine* is devoted to an exploration of Zero's fate in the afterworld. Far from being punished for his crime, Zero is afforded the opportunity to live in the Elysian Fields, a happy home for those free enough to enjoy it. But because of his unyielding ordinariness, Zero will not permit himself to stay in such a scandalous place. At the end of the play, he is doomed to be reincarnated as the operator of the newest and greatest adding machine ever, an eternal cog in a great engine.

While Rice, O'Neill, and others infused American drama with a European sensibility, dramatists such as Clifford Odets (1906–63), Tennessee Williams (1911–83), and Arthur Miller (1915–2005) rooted themselves more firmly in the realist tradition of Ibsen and Shaw. Their influence helped keep realism at the fore of mainstream American theater into the 1950s. While each of these playwrights made humorous and pointed attacks on the failures of American democracy, their satirical attacks tended to be blunted by an earnest assertion of utopian promise (Odets) or a claim for tragic dignity (Williams and Miller). Odets, who became the voice of American drama in the Depression, wrote plays critical of American life and politics (*Awake and Sing!* and *Paradise Lost,* both 1935) with exaggerated characters speaking a language filled with wisecracks and cynical epigrams. However, his plays require sympathy for their central characters, so that their satirical moments are overshadowed by the overall romantic movement of the action. Like Odets, Miller revealed the ugly underside of the American dream, but his plays most often subsume the satirical impulse to larger purposes – tragic, as in the case of *Death of a Salesman,* or political, as in *All My Sons* (1947) and *The Crucible* (1953). The horrible ironies of these plays are inescapable, as are the flaws of the central characters, but the central movement is predicated on sympathy rather than laughter. Williams, too, was capable of creating monstrous characters in ridiculous situations, especially in *A Streetcar Named Desire* (1947) and *Cat on a Hot Tin Roof* (1955), but his overall tone is serious rather than comic or satirical.

Of the other American playwrights of this period, George S. Kaufman (1889–1961) is the most consistently satirical, though his work is more in the tradition of Gilbert and Sullivan than Brecht. Perhaps the most successful of his collaborations was with Morrie Ryskind on the musical *Of Thee I Sing* (1931). Complete with a presidential candidate who runs on a platform of love, a Vice-President whom no one recognizes, and a song from the Supreme Court, the musical spoofs the triumph of surface over substance in American elections. Other Kaufman plays, especially *I'd Rather be Right* (1937, with Moss Hart, a parody of Roosevelt's New Deal), expose through laughter the foibles of the American political system, as does Maxwell Anderson's *Both Your Houses* (1933), which chronicles the unsuccessful attempts of a first-term senator to kill an appropriations bill by adding so much spending to it that others would be ashamed to vote for it. Still, despite the success of these plays, satire in American drama only reaches its full flowering after World War II.

From *Ubu Roi* to the Theater of the Absurd

The realist tradition of Ibsen and Chekhov represents one current of satire in modern and contemporary drama, the political anti-realism of Brecht another. In the late nineteenth century, a third variety of satire began to take shape, though it would reach its full importance only after 1950. Like epic theater and Expressionism, the Absurdist movement began in reaction against realistic drama. Arguing that a scientific view of the world took surfaces for realities, theater artists throughout Europe began to experiment with ways to reveal deeper truths about human existence and contemporary life. Still because they were grounded more in the visual arts or in poetry than in theater, Dadaism, Futurism, and Surrealism made no lasting impact on the development of modern drama literature – all were relatively short-lived movements. But their willingness to challenge conventions and to mock the aesthetic, moral, and political assumptions of their world influenced a whole generation of dramatists and theater practitioners. Alfred Jarry's *Ubu Roi* (1896) can be seen as the founding text of Absurdist drama. Originally conceived as a satirical puppet play, *Ubu Roi* traces the rise to power of the corrupt, violent, and stupid Pere Ubu. The play is filled with illogic, grotesque and bawdy humor (the first word of the play, "*merdre*," started a riot in the audience), and broad caricatures of human behavior. It was staged in a style that eschewed all attempt at realism in favor of shock and humor – Ubu's scepter, for example, is a toilet plunger. Part of the goal was to engender outrage at the systematic disordering of theatrical conventions. But its legacy is more lasting than mere outrage. With *Ubu Roi*, Jarry opened the door for the satire of form developed by later playwrights.

Following Jarry's lead and influenced by the upheaval caused by World War I, Futurism called for dynamic new forms of theater that would be quick (their plays are often only one or two pages long), illogical, and filled with movement. Drawing on other theatrical forms – the circus, puppet shows, vaudeville, and burlesque – with a long history of satirical comment, the Futurists mocked conventional plays and encouraged, even demanded, audience participation. From a similar impulse, Dadaism aimed at a systematic rethinking of aesthetic forms. In theater, this meant the incorporation of masks, nonverbal sounds, and nonsensical or simultaneous dialogue directed more toward breaking down conventions than at making meaning. Another movement, Surrealism, attempted a more systematic exploration of the unconscious mind by juxtaposing disparate images on stage to create an illogical, dreamlike world for the audience. Led by Guillaume Apollinaire, whose play *The Breasts of Tiresias* (1917) satirizes the women's movement, and Jean Cocteau (*The Eiffel Tower Wedding Party*, 1921), Surrealism directly influenced Antonin Artaud (1896–1948), who became one of the leading theorists of twentieth-century theater, and Eugene Ionesco, one of the leading playwrights of the Absurdist movement.

As Martin Esslin (1969) argues in his landmark book, the "Theatre of the Absurd" is a loose theatrical movement unifying several different playwrights who display two common traits: first, these playwrights are concerned with the absurdity of human existence; secondly, they structure their plays to mirror their concern with absurdity or meaninglessness – the plays are not just *about* meaninglessness, they are themselves deliberately and irreducibly meaningless, both verbally and visually. It is this latter point that makes the Absurdist playwrights' vision doubly satirical: they not only point out the flaws in human existence, but, like *Ubu Roi*, they point out the flaws in the theater itself. The theatrical form becomes a satire of the possibilities of human communication. As Ionesco argued, "the comic alone is capable of giving us the strength to bear the tragedy of existence. The true nature of things, truth itself, can be revealed to us only by fantasy, which is more realistic than all the realisms" (Esslin 1969: 159).

Samuel Beckett's (1906–89) plays have remained a challenge to critics partly because Beckett rigorously undercut every convention of mainstream theater. *Waiting for Godot* (1953), for example, is built around the conversations of two tramps waiting for a character that may not exist or, if he does exist, may not come. Nothing happens in the play: the characters do not change; the action is limited; and the dialogue is repetitive. Beckett's characters are often trapped in an existence that is seemingly endless, without reward or meaning. But, as Esslin points out, this is precisely the point: the effect of the play is to strip life down to its barest essentials – in *Endgame* (1957), a group of people waiting for a death that can never come – in order to emphasize its absurdity. To reinforce his point, Beckett also strips down the language, relentlessly calling into question the very possibility of making meaning through words:

Hamm: Yesterday! What does that mean? Yesterday!
Clov: (*violently*) That means that bloody awful day, long ago, before this bloody awful day. I use the words you taught me. If they don't mean anything any more, teach me others. Or let me be silent.

The satire in Beckett is pervasive, but not completely cynical – hope exists, though certainty is vehemently denied.

In addition to setting his plays in places only vaguely identifiable and creating characters who are a pastiche of other characters (Vladimir and Estragon in *Waiting for Godot* owe a great deal to vaudeville, while Hamm in *Endgame* speaks in a pastiche of everything from Shakespeare to popular song), Beckett relies on paradox. Every assertion is undercut, every insight qualified – Beckett commented that the most important word in his plays was "perhaps." As Michael Worton has argued, Beckett builds extensively on allusion to other texts, literary and philosophical, but at the same time mocks their claims to truth by rewriting or recontextualizing them. Thus, the biblical assertion to love your neighbor becomes in *Endgame* "Lick your neighbor as yourself," and Shakespeare's "My kingdom for a horse!" becomes Hamm's "My kingdom for a nightman!" (Worton 1994: 82–4). Beckett does not merely desire to shock, as Jarry and the Futurists did; rather, his drama is an existential satire, integrating form and content, but resisting definitive interpretation, even of those texts that Western culture has taken as definitive.

If Beckett's plays create strange worlds somehow familiar to us because they are steeped in cultural tradition, Eugene Ionesco (1909–94) makes mundane moments of human existence – a couple having tea together, a student meeting with her teacher – strange and menacing. *The Bald Soprano* (1950), for example, undercuts all logical expectations and mocks the inability of language to convey real meaning or new ideas. But like all of the Absurdist plays, the black humor carries with it a grain of bleak existential truth; despite the play's humor, Ionesco conceived of it as a "tragedy of language." In the play a couple named Martin talk contentedly to one another for several minutes; eventually, they discover that they are married to one another and have two children. Strange events take place throughout the play, including a clock that strikes twenty-nine times and then "as much as it likes." The play ends in a cacophony of non sequiturs and gibberish. In another play, *The Chairs* (1952), an old couple gather together empty chairs in anticipation of an Orator who will deliver their message to the audience. After leaving their message in his hands, they kill themselves; soon after, it is revealed that the Orator cannot speak. All of Ionesco's plays create bizarre stage worlds that suggest that the means by which human beings make sense of the world – logic, language, social mores, human relationships – are at the same time arbitrary and absurd.

The dark comedy of Beckett and Ionesco is echoed in the work of their contemporaries. Harold Pinter's (1930–) plays offer worlds in which character motivations are only half-revealed, and ordinary events explode into brutality and misunderstanding. *The Birthday Party* (1957), *The Caretaker* (1959), and *The Homecoming* (1964) derive both humor and terror from the same situation: the unmotivated actions and events of simple human existence. As Pinter argued, "everything is funny; the greatest earnestness is funny; even tragedy is funny. And I think what I try to do in my plays is to get to this recognizable reality of the absurdity of what we do and how we behave and how we speak" (Esslin 1969: 238). The audience only dimly grasps what drives these characters, but the full horror of the action is clear. In *The Homecoming*, for example, a visit home by a married man with his wife ends with his wife remaining with the man's two brothers and father – possibly to work as a prostitute – while he happily returns to America. The fundamental inability of Pinter's characters to communicate comes through in the non sequiturs, the extensive pauses, and the repetitions in his dialogue.

Other Absurdists pursue similar themes in different styles. In France, Jean Genet (1910–86) creates fantastical worlds that operate as distorted versions of reality. In *The Balcony* (1957), for example, a brothel serves as a metaphor for institutions of power; its clients pay money to take on the role of bishop, judge, or general, while outside a revolution threatens the real generals and bishops. Genet satirizes the inability of the individual to break free of the institutions that dominate the modern world, while pointing out that both those institutions and our relations to them are built on role-playing and illusion. In the United States, Edward Albee's *The American Dream* (1960) critiques the hope in progress presented by the American dream by using clichéd dialogue vacated of all real meaning. In Friedrich Dürrenmatt's *The Visit* (1964), a wealthy old woman returns to the town where she grew up in order to exact revenge on Alfred Ill, the man who impregnated her and left her years before. She offers the town a gift of one million dollars if someone will kill him. At first, the townspeople refuse; then they begin to spend money recklessly. In the end, they submit and sacrifice Ill – not for money but for justice and conscience, they avow – in an elaborate ritual. They tell the press that Ill died of joy, and the play ends with a mock epic chorus of thanks to their benefactor.

Satire in Contemporary Theater

Along with Brecht and Antonin Artaud (whose call for a theater that would abolish distance and create a communion between performer and audience influenced many of the theater collectives of the 1960s), Absurdist theater remained one of the central influences on theatrical practice throughout the 1960s. After 1968, however, the increasing influence of postmodernism tended to disintegrate distinctions among styles and genres, and plays increasingly mixed varieties of form, genre, performance style, and media. As a result, satirical writing for the theater became more widespread though often less explicit in its criticism; rather, censure in these works is often implied through a non-linear structure, in juxtapositions of disparate scenes or ideas that allow audiences to see multiple connections among them. Western culture is a main target: Aimé Césaire reworks Shakespeare from a Caribbean perspective in *A Tempest* (1969); David Henry Hwang criticizes Western attitudes toward Asia in *M Butterfly* (1988), which rewrites the Puccini text into a drama of international espionage; in their 1981 piece, *Route 1 and 9 (The Last Act)*, the Wooster Group rethinks *Our Town* (1938) to examine questions of race in the United States.

But contemporary satirists also use postmodern techniques of juxtaposition and bricolage to call into question the assumptions of modern society in a way far less despairing than the dark humor of the Absurdists. Caryl Churchill's *Cloud 9* (1979) explores and satirizes the legacy of Victorian attitudes toward sex and power in contemporary Britain. To emphasize her point, Churchill casts many of the roles with actors of the opposite sex or a different race in Act I (an African servant is played by a white actor, a little girl is represented by a doll) in order to call attention to the arbitrary distinctions of gender and race in a patriarchal society. By Act II, however, change is taking place, and the end is hopeful for continued progress.

Other important satirists of the contemporary period include Dario Fo (*The Accidental Death of an Anarchist*, 1970) in Italy, whose frank and imaginative political satires use mime and other elements to attack capitalism and the Catholic Church. In England, Tom Stoppard, heavily influenced by Beckett, has written a series of clever plays (*Travesties*, 1974; *Arcadia*, 1993), which explore the nature and limits of human knowledge. One of his earliest successes, *Rosencrantz and Guildenstern are Dead* (1966), views Shakespeare's *Hamlet* from the point of view of two minor characters, arbitrarily called to the stage and subsequently put to death for reasons they scarcely understand. The two characters' haplessness in the face of their fate is both touching and funny, as they wrestle with their purpose in *Hamlet*: "Our names shouted in a certain dawn...a message...a summons...There must have been a moment, at the beginning, where we could have said – no. But somehow we missed it." Peter Handke (*Offending the*

Audience, 1966; *Kaspar*, 1968), Max Frisch (*Biedermann and the Firebugs*, 1953; *Andorra*, 1961), Wole Soyinka (*King Baabu*, 2001), Gao Xingjian (*The Other Shore*, 1986), and Slawomir Mrozek (*Tango*, 1965) are among the many contemporary playwrights who represent a variety of satirical forms. Handke directs attacks on language as a tool of social control; Frisch uses fables – influenced by the history of Nazism in World War II and the rise of Communism in Eastern Europe – to critique the dangers of capitulation and conformity; and Soyinka borrows from Jarry's *Ubu Roi* to pillory corrupt African dictators.

Dramatic satire has also flourished in the United States in recent decades. Several important playwrights moved away from realism, embracing more experimental forms, while others remained rooted in a realist aesthetic, but borrowed techniques from postmodern experiments. Like Edward Albee, Sam Shepard examines important American myths (the West, the American dream) and finds them virtually empty of meaning. In *True West* (1980), for example, two brothers fight over the rights to a screenplay they have written, but the real question is the possibility of survival in a place where the mythic landmarks are no longer familiar. The West has disappeared; all that is left in its place are cheesy movies or dreams of living in the desert. David Mamet's *Glengarry Glen Ross* (1983) covers related territory – the American dream as a false idol. Mamet's real-estate salesmen scheme to get ahead, willing to do anything to make a sale. The parody of the language of American business, freely interlarded with obscenities, underscores both the violence and the mendacity at the center of all their actions, and by extension, at the center of the dream itself.

Some of the strongest voices in contemporary American satirical drama have come from groups excluded from the mainstream stage until the second half of the twentieth century. Luis Valdez, a Chicano playwright and co-founder of El Teatro Campesino, has emerged as a champion of Latino rights and a severe and funny critic of the Anglo culture. *I Don't Have to Show You No Stinking Badges* (1986) parodies the representations of Latinos in Hollywood movies, while *Los Vendidos* (The Sellouts, 1967) mocks the stereotyping of Latinos for political purposes. Suzan-Lori Parks points out the gaps in American history in *The America Play* (1992). In it, an African-American Abraham Lincoln impersonator, called "The Foundling Father" and "The Lesser Known," searches for identity in the great (w)hole of history. Parks's play is thoroughly postmodern, challenging not only traditional perceptions of historical representation, but also linear structures of theater. Similarly, Tony Kushner's *Angels in America* (1993) points out, with often caustic humor, the ways in which the AIDS crisis reveals America's self-absorption. Other contemporary American playwrights who incorporate satire into their work include Stephen Sondheim (*Assassins*, 1990), Larry Gelbart (*Mastergate*, 1989), Maria Irene Fornes (*Fefu and her Friends*, 1977), and George C. Wolfe (*The Colored Museum*, 1986). Overall, then, the movement of theatrical satire since 1870 from realism through Absurdism to postmodernism suggests that the satiric viewpoint is central to modern theater. With such a rich history and such a multiplicity of forms available to its writers and performers, it seems likely that dramatic satire will continue to flourish.

Rising of 1916 and the execution of its leaders, the War of Independence from the United Kingdom of 1919–21, the declaration of the Irish Free State and its partition from Northern Ireland in 1922, and the Civil War of 1922–3, and these events were followed by several decades of cultural repression and economic depression. Periods of cultural turmoil and political upheaval, during which established institutions are dismantled and new norms and values are established, are typically a breeding ground for Menippean satire, and such was also the case in Ireland. This type of satire is essentially a genre of ideas, and its characters represent specific ideological positions rather than individual opinion. The first hint that satire was becoming less personal and more general came within a theatrical context, in an early play by Eimar O'Duffy, also presented by Edward Martyn's Irish Theatre. While Martyn was fighting past personal battles, O'Duffy was targeting the present and future of the nation.

O'Duffy's *The Phoenix on the Roof* (1915) revolves around the refusal of its middle-class characters – a doctor, a professor, a clergyman, a policeman – to admit that a phoenix has landed on the roof of Dr Westbrook's home in a small Irish town, until the bird's funeral pyre sets the house ablaze. Eimar O'Duffy was a member of the Irish Republican Brotherhood, an outgrowth of the mid-nineteenth-century revolutionary Fenian movement, which included O'Donovan Rossa's literary and political group the Phoenix Society. O'Duffy's phoenix represents the resurgence of the old separatist movement, but his satire also implies that the Irish middle class was in denial about the impending revolution – a point confirmed by the fact that his audience failed to understand the significance of his play.

O'Duffy wrote another satirical play, *Bricriu's Feast* (1919), in which he took aim at, among other targets, the romanticism of the Irish Literary Revival. As a satirist, he may have wanted to model himself on Bricriu "of the poison tongue," a mythological trickster notorious for stirring up controversy, but he eventually realized that the theater was not the ideal medium for his brand of satire. Whereas verse and drama are more properly vehicles for satirical invective, narrative satire is better able to adopt a questioning, critical attitude toward authoritative discourses, and puts to the test, not individual failings or any specific version of the truth, but the nature of "truth" itself, particularly by questioning the legitimacy of those who claim to be the sole possessors of it. Typically, Menippean satire is skeptical of all authoritative pronouncements, including its own. This was the type of satire toward which Irish writers turned from 1916 onward, and especially after the declaration of the Irish Free State in 1922, when they began to voice their frustration, first with the new state's lack of political imagination, and increasingly with a political system that maintained control through censorship and repressive legislation. While the focus of the satirists writing in the decade after 1916 (Darrell Figgis and Eimar O'Duffy) was largely political, by the 1930s this shifted to a concern with personal freedom, particularly freedom of individual and artistic expression, within an increasingly puritanical, authoritarian society that afforded a privileged position to the Roman Catholic Church. This is especially true of the satires of Austin Clarke, Flann O'Brien, and Mervyn Wall.

References and Further Reading

Artaud, Antonin (1981) *The Theatre and its Double*, trans. Victor Corti. London: Calder.

Bigsby, Christopher W. E. (1992) *Modern American Drama, 1945–1990*. New York: Cambridge University Press.

Brandt, George W. (ed.) (1999) *Modern Theories of Drama: A Selection of Writings on Drama and Theatre 1850–1990*. New York: Oxford University Press.

Brecht, Bertolt (1964) *Brecht on Theatre*, ed. and trans. John Willett. New York: Hill and Wang.

Chaudhuri, Una (1995) *Staging Place: The Geography of Modern Drama*. Ann Arbor: University of Michigan Press.

Cohn, Ruby (1980) *Just Play: Beckett's Theatre*. Princeton, NJ: Princeton University Press.

Davis, Tracy C. (1994) *George Bernard Shaw and the Socialist Theatre*. Westport, CT: Greenwood Press.

Dukore, Bernard F. (ed.) (1974) *Dramatic Theory and Criticism: Greeks to Grotowski*. Fort Worth, TX: Harcourt Brace Jovanovich.

Esslin, Martin (1969) *The Theatre of the Absurd*, 2nd edn. New York: Penguin (originally published in 1961).

Gilman, Richard (1974) *The Making of Modern Drama*. New York: Farrar, Straus and Giroux.

Goldman, Michael (1999) *Ibsen: The Dramaturgy of Fear*. New York: Columbia University Press.

Herr, Christopher J. (2003) *Clifford Odets and American Political Theater*. Westport, CT: Praeger.

Homan, Sidney (1989) *The Audience as Actor and Character: The Modern Theater of Beckett, Brecht, Genet, Ionesco, Pinter, Stoppard, and Williams*. Lewisburg: Bucknell University Press.

Innes, Christopher (1993) *Avant Garde Theatre 1892–1992*. London: Routledge.

Kirby, Michael (1971) *Futurist Performance*. New York: Dutton.

Le Gallienne, Eva (ed.) (1982) Introduction. *Henrik Ibsen: Eight Plays*. New York: Modern Library.

Matthews, J. H. (1974) *Theatre in Dada and Surrealism*. Syracuse: Syracuse University Press.

Murphy, Patrick D. (ed.) (1992) *Staging the Impossible: The Fantastic Mode in Modern Drama*. Westport, CT: Greenwood Press.

Orr, John (1991) *Tragicomedy and Contemporary Culture: Play and Performance from Beckett to Shepard*. Ann Arbor: University of Michigan Press.

Peter, John Desmond (1987) *Vladimir's Carrot: Modern Drama and the Modern Imagination*. Chicago: University of Chicago Press.

Steiner, George (1980) *The Death of Tragedy*. New York: Oxford University Press.

Styan, John L. (1968) *The Dark Comedy: The Development of Modern Comic Tragedy*. London: Cambridge University Press.

Tufts, Carol Strongin (1989) Prisoners of their plots: literary allusion and the satiric drama of self-consciousness in Chekhov's *Three Sisters*. *Modern Drama* 32, 485–501.

Valency, Maurice (1980) *The End of the World: An Introduction to Contemporary Drama*. New York: Oxford University Press.

Worton, Michael (1994) *Waiting for Godot* and *Endgame*: theatre as text. In John Pilling (ed.), *The Cambridge Companion to Beckett*, pp. 67–87. Cambridge: Cambridge University Press.

Wren, Gayden (2001) *A Most Ingenious Paradox: The Art of Gilbert and Sullivan*. New York: Oxford University Press.

24
Irish Satire
José Lanters

Ireland has a long and varied satirical tradition, and forms of satire lie at the heart of much of its literature, in the distant past as well as the present. In his seminal work *The Irish Comic Tradition*, Vivian Mercier remarked that "[p]erhaps the most striking single fact about Irish literature in either Gaelic or English is the high proportion of satire which it contains" (Mercier 1962: 105). Irish satire can be broadly divided into two well-established branches. The earliest of these, dating back to the Old Irish period (eighth and ninth centuries) and persisting into modern times, is the type that is initially associated with verbal magic and cursing, and develops over time into the tradition of literary invective and flyting. This form of satire had a strong public and social function within what was essentially a shame culture, that is, a culture preoccupied with reputation, honor, and respect. So important was satire in this regard that the ancient Brehon laws of Ireland made a distinction between lawful and unlawful satire, and made provisions for different kinds of violations, such as slander, a damaging nickname, or making fun of a man after his death. The second branch of satire, following the narrative or Menippean tradition, did not flourish in Ireland until Jonathan Swift's day. Neither as old nor as widespread as the tradition of invective, it experienced something of a revival in the first half of the twentieth century.

According to Robert C. Elliott, "Ireland is the great and fertile source of material on the early relation of satire to magic" (Elliott 1960: 18). The magical maledictions uttered by satirists in the early Irish texts often strike the modern reader as being closer to curses and spells than to "proper" satire, and many such utterances barely rise above the level of name-calling. The very first satire allegedly ever made in Ireland, by satirist Coirpre mac Etaine, invoked a curse on King Bres, who had received the poet at his house with less than customary hospitality: "Without food quickly on a dish; / Without a cow's milk whereon a calf grows; / ... Without paying a company of storytellers – let that be Bres's condition" (Robinson 1912: 111). There is good reason for classifying these types of utterances as satire. The Irish language uses the same terminology for what we would call spells and curses as it does for the more elaborate and sophisticated satire of the later period. There are numerous words for "satire" in Old and Middle Irish – an indicator of the importance and pervasiveness of the genre – but "in their use no distinction is made... between the satire of magic malediction and the satire of mockery or abuse" (Robinson 1912: 104). Some of these terms, such as "cutting," "reddening," or "blemishing," refer to the physical effects caused by the satire, in that a person is literally "defaced," while other words refer to the ridicule and disgrace brought on by mockery. Particularly notorious in this regard was the *glám dícenn* or "destructive satire," a special curse uttered by a poet in a ritual manner, designed to destroy its victim's health and reputation. Sometimes this required the satirist to stand on one leg, with one eye closed and one arm outstretched; in other instances, the curse involved fasting against the victim, and the use of ritual objects like thorns or stones.

No text illustrates more clearly the culture of praise and blame that provided such fertile ground for the growth of satire in Ireland than the great Old Irish epic, the *Táin Bó Cúailnge* or "Cattle Raid of Cooley." Satirists play a crucial role in the outcome of some of its most important battles. In the conflict between Ulster and Connacht, the hero Ferdia is goaded into fighting his best friend, Ulster's Cú Chulainn, when Connacht's Queen Medb "sent poets and bards and satirists to bring the blushes to his cheek with mockery and insult and ridicule, so there would be nowhere in the world for him to lay his head in peace" (Kinsella 1977: 168). When Cú Chulainn realizes the strength and skill of his opponent, he tells his charioteer: "If my defeat seems near at any time, you must abuse and insult and mock me to make my anger rise. But if ever his defeat seems near tell me that, and praise and encourage me to raise my spirits" (Kinsella 1977: 193).

The invective of the Old and Middle Irish tradition is often occasioned by "the same vices and follies which preoccupy Horace and Wyndham Lewis, Rabelais and Pope: stinginess, inhospitality, pride, the inflexibility of those in power" (Elliott 1960: 39). However, in Ireland, satire frequently takes the form of an *ad hominem* attack or condemnation rather than a more general rejection of a particular type of behavior. What is remarkable about this "cursing" or "flyting" branch of the Irish satirical tradition is the extent to which it persists, modified but virtually unbroken, into the contemporary period. The introduction of Christianity into Ireland did nothing to curtail the practice; indeed, the hagiographers who wrote the lives of the early Irish saints "endowed their heroes with fearful powers of cursing" (Power 1991: 38). In the ninth-century *Tripartite Life of Saint Patrick*, for example, Ireland's patron saint is depicted as "a hurler of maledictions," who once cursed an entire hostile clan by pronouncing that "you will be defeated in every engagement you take part in and in every assembly you attend you will be spat on and reviled!" (Power 1991: 39–40).

In spite of the increase of more sophisticated forms of satire in later centuries, "the old conception of the destructive satirist, the poet with superior power, whom it is dangerous to displease, has never disappeared among the Gaels of either Ireland or

Scotland" (Robinson 1912: 127). The belief in the magical power of words survived in Ireland well into the nineteenth century, and as a literary device, satirical invective is still widespread to this day. Mercier (1962) cites an early nineteenth-century example of a beggar man who threatened to satirize a woman to death if she did not give him what he asked for. Another nineteenth-century example is the popular Irish ballad "Nell Flaherty's Drake." The colors of the "drake" represent the green-and-white uniform of the Irish revolutionary nationalist Robert Emmet (1778–1803), who led an uprising against the British presence in Ireland and was subsequently executed for treason. The song curses the villain responsible for the death of Ireland's heroic son:

> That the flies and the fleas may the wretch ever tease,
> May the piercing March breeze make him shiver and shake;
> May a lump of a stick raise the bumps fast and thick
> On the monster that murdered Nell Flaherty's drake.

Curses and maledictions are by their very nature aimed at known individuals or specific groups. As a result of its magical origins, therefore, "Irish satire in Gaelic or English usually has great difficulty in escaping from the personal lampoon towards more generalized satire" (Mercier 1962: 107).

Satirical Invective in Modern Drama and Poetry

Nina Witoszek and Patrick Sheeran argue that "[t]he best confirmation that the tradition of verbal abuse remains as vital and as destructive as ever is to be found in twentieth century Irish literature, especially in drama" (Witoszek and Sheeran 1991: 17). No modern Irish poet has made a career out of satirical verse, with the possible exception of Austin Clarke, the only writer to provide a consistent critique in his work of what he called the Irish "ill-fare state," although some critics find his tone too careful and mild to be called truly satirical. Other poets did not hesitate to adopt a tone of outraged indignation, although they usually reserved their strongest personal vitriol for their literary enemies or rivals rather than for more public targets. The hostile audience reaction to J. M. Synge's play *The Playboy of the Western World* (1907) sparked an angry response from the author in his poem "The Curse," directed at "a sister of an enemy of the author's who disapproved of 'The Playboy' ": "Lord confound this surly sister, / Blight her brow with blotch and blister..." (Synge 1921: 25).

James Joyce wrote several satirical broadsides aimed at the Irish literary world. In "The Holy Office" (1904) he sneered at W. B. Yeats, George Russell, and their followers, whom he accused of lacking the courage of their literary convictions, unlike himself: "Thus I relieve their timid arses, / Perform my office of Katharsis. / My scarlet leaves them white as wool. / Through me they purge a bellyful" (Joyce 1975: 36). In *Gas from a Burner* (1909) Joyce humiliated the printer who, for fear of being accused of printing libelous material, had destroyed the proofs of his short story collection *Dubliners*, by putting words into his mouth:

>   I'll penance do with farts and groans
>   Kneeling upon my marrowbones.
>   This very next lent I will unbare
>   My penitent buttocks to the air
>   And sobbing beside my printing press
>   My awful sin I will confess.
>   (Joyce 1975: 46)

In the 1940s, inspired by Alexander Pope's *The Dunciad*, Patrick Kavanagh wrote a satirical attack on the mediocre poets of his day in "The Paddiad":

>   In the corner of a Dublin pub
>   This party opens – blub-a-blub –
>   Paddy Whiskey, Rum and Gin
>   Paddy Three Sheets in the Wind;
>   Paddy of the Celtic Mist,
>   Paddy Connemara West,
>   Chestertonian Paddy Frog
>   Croaking nightly in the bog.
>   All the Paddies having fun
>   Since Yeats handed in his gun.
>   Every man completely blind
>   To the truth about his mind.
>   (Kavanagh 1972: 90)

Apart from such occasional personal invective, however, there is no sustained satirical voice in modern Irish poetry.

Drama, being a verbal medium, is particularly suited to the expression of personal invective. One reason why such forms of verbal magic and satire still retain their force in Ireland is that the country, especially the rural areas in which many Irish plays are set, has a high residual orality, which means that actions and attitudes are determined by verbal interaction between individuals rather than by predominantly visual impulses from the outside world. Since in oral societies the spoken word is an active event, words can be used to produce tangible effects, including physical harm.

Tom Murphy (1935–) is originally from Tuam, a small town in Co. Galway in the west of Ireland. In his play *The Morning after Optimism* (1971), an adult fairytale that satirizes both the romantic innocence of youth and the knowing cynicism of middle age, the jaded couple Rosie and James engage in elaborate flyting:

>   *James*:   Whore, harridan, slut, shrew! –
>   *Rosie*:   Pencil prick!
>   *James*:   Oh yeah? – Oh yeah?
>   *Rosie*:   Unforgettable pencil prick!
>   (Murphy 1973: 62)

The assault they plot upon their innocent counterparts, Anastasia and Edmund, is likewise a verbal one:

> *James*: I'll tell him about the smells.
> *Rosie*: Garlic!
> *James*: Onions!
> *Rosie*: Parsnips!
> *James*: Worse! – The sweat –
> *Rosie*: Unmentionables!
> *James*: Mention them!
> *Rosie*: The rotten teeth! –
> *James*: The nagging! –
>   (Murphy 1973: 73)

Curses and maledictions are also frequent in Murphy's plays, as when Francisco in *The Sanctuary Lamp* (1976), disillusioned with the spiritual barrenness of the modern Catholic Church, savagely pronounces "a pox, clap, double-clap, crabs on Christianity and all its choirs and ministers – " (Murphy 1976: 16). Witoszek and Sheeran contend that evidence of a similar "rhetoric of violence" may be encountered in plays by Brendan Behan, J. M. Synge, Sean O'Casey, Samuel Beckett, John B. Keane, M. J. Molloy, and T. C. Murray. They take these examples to be evidence of "a culturally encoded, morbid use of the word which functions as a diluted form of murder" (Witoszek and Sheeran 1991: 20).

The Anglo-Irish Narrative (Menippean) Tradition

Whereas *ad hominem* lampoon and invective are extremely widespread in both the early Gaelic and the contemporary English literature of Ireland, more "general" narrative or Menippean satire, the kind that arises from motives such as "selfless indignation and a desire for abstract justice" (Mercier 1962: 184), has virtually no roots in the Gaelic tradition, and is not very common in the Anglo-Irish period. Examples of narrative satire in Irish do exist in medieval Ireland: the twelfth-century *Aislinge Meic con Glinne* ("The Vision of Mac Conglinne") is a satire on gluttony and on the Irish clergy, as well as an elaborate parody of various types of religious discourse. While well known, the text is atypical of satire in Irish, and there exist only a handful of early Anglo-Irish narrative examples: two fourteenth-century texts, "The Land of Cokaygne" and "A Satire on the People of Kildare," and James Farewell's *The Irish Hudibras* (1689).

Why the Anglo-Irish period produced so few examples of formal narrative satire is a matter for speculation. One reason may be that it requires a worthy opponent: there is nothing to be gained by ridiculing the weak, the poor, and the powerless. After the defeat of James II at the Battle of the Boyne in 1690, no power remained in the hands of the native Catholic Irish, who had been subdued by penal legislation. Anglo-Irish literature was written by Protestants of English descent, whose relatively small numbers and marginal status put them in no position to direct their satires at the British government or the Church – the only obvious and legitimate targets. Swift's eccentric personality and the power of his position as Dean of St Patrick's Cathedral allowed him to take risks that others could not afford.

Swift's satire was the kind that, in Pope's phrase, "heals with morals what it hurts with wit" (*Imitations of Horace*, Ep. II. i. 262). Vivian Mercier (1962) proposes that Swift worked very much within the Gaelic tradition of invective and malediction, but that he added a new element, sustained irony, to that tradition, which Mercier considers the basic device of all true satire. Such a reading of Swift makes a connection between his *saeva indignatio* and the savage invective of Gaelic satire, and detects parallels between Swift's work and earlier Irish texts, for example, between the imaginary journey of *Gulliver's Travels* and the fantastic voyage tales of medieval Irish literature. Swift may have known some of this material, but his sources and influences are more likely to have been Classical and European. He was clearly influenced by Rabelais, for example, whom he is known to have admired. Swift also has more in common with a writer like Lucian, whose satirical account in *A True Story* may have served as a model for the fantastic journey in *Gulliver's Travels* (see chapter 11).

The immediate influence of Swift can be detected in the work of Laurence Sterne, another writer and clergyman of Anglo-Irish stock. In *Tristram Shandy* (1760–7), Sterne acknowledges his indebtedness to Lucian, Rabelais, and Cervantes, and puts himself in the company of Swift, suggesting that his own book may swim down the gutter of time along with Swift's *Tale of a Tub* (1704). That journey through time led *Tristram Shandy* eventually to be a major influence on James Joyce's *Ulysses* (1922), which employs many Menippean devices, including parody, a mixture of styles and genres, a juxtaposition of base and lofty subject matter, unusual perspectives, and so on. On the whole, however, Swiftian satire did not have a strong following in Ireland after the eighteenth century – perhaps because there was no such established native tradition, but also because writers in the nineteenth century, who witnessed such catastrophes as the Famine, found it difficult to put enough ironic distance between themselves and the often dire circumstances of their fellow countrymen. In the early nineteenth century, Maria Edgeworth's novel *Castle Rackrent* (1800) employed satire to expose the mismanagement of English and Anglo-Irish estates in Ireland and the complacency and opportunism of the Irish tenants, and there are satirical touches in novels by William Carleton and Marmion Wilme Savage. On the whole, however, there is very little satire of any kind in nineteenth-century Irish literature.

The Satiric Revival of the Early Twentieth Century

The Irish Renaissance of the 1890s and the following decades radically altered the face of Irish literature. While the land wars, the home rule debate, and the Parnell divorce scandal had left the political climate still too sensitive for sustained satirical discourse, developments on the literary front created a new cultural elite (Anglo-Irish by descent but Celtic by spiritual affiliation) that immediately formed a legitimate target for the satirical attacks of dissenting artistic colleagues. The Celtic Revivalists of the turn of the century used Irish mythology and heroic literature as a source of inspiration to establish the idea of a national identity with ancient and noble roots. The Irish Literary Theatre (which after 1904, as the Abbey Theatre, became the national theater of Ireland) was established by W. B. Yeats and Lady Gregory, with the help of Edward Martyn, as an instrument to depict Ireland as "the home of an ancient idealism," and the peasant play, set in the West of Ireland where the true Gaelic spirit was supposed to have been best preserved, became the dominant genre of early twentieth-century Irish drama. The success of the Celtic formula, and the authoritative position held by the Abbey directors in enforcing their artistic vision, sparked numerous satirical responses and counter-responses (often, but not exclusively, in dramatic form) in the decade or so that followed the launch of the Abbey Theatre. These responses were invariably personal in nature.

Bernard Shaw was among the earliest satirists to mock the newly established conventions of the Irish peasant play. In *John Bull's Other Island*, he questions both the British stereotype that the Irish peasant is amusing but ignorant, and the Celtic cliché that he is inherently noble and heroic. The play was offered to the Irish Literary Theatre in 1904, but rejected by Yeats, in part because Shaw makes his Irishman lament that the only way to interest his countrymen in their nation is "to call the unfortunate island Kathleen ni Houlihan [the title of an unashamedly nationalistic play by Yeats and Lady Gregory, staged in 1902] and pretend she's a little old woman. It saves thinking" (Shaw 1962: 131). Edward Martyn also lampooned his former Abbey colleagues, with whom he had come to disagree personally and professionally. His Irish Theatre, established in 1914 specifically to produce non-peasant drama by Irish writers, staged a number of satires that were directly aimed at the philosophy and methods of its more successful and powerful theatrical rival. Martyn's own *Romulus and Remus, or the Makers of Delights* (1916), depicted Remus (W. B. Yeats) and Daisy Hoolihan (Lady Gregory) as creators of perfumes flavored with the essence of dead flies collected from the Dublin slums (that is, plays inspired by folk material collected from the peasant population).

The most elaborate example of early twentieth-century personal satire in prose is undoubtedly George Moore's monumental autobiography *Hail and Farewell*, whose three parts ("Ave," "Salve," and "Vale") were published between 1911 and 1914, and in which he ridiculed both himself and his contemporaries. According to Elizabeth Grubgeld, Moore's self-irony, which creates a distinction between author and narrator, enables him "both to speak as satirist and to appear as the object of satire" (Grubgeld 1994: 108). Grubgeld argues that modern Irish autobiography "may well be rooted more truly in satire than in any other form of discourse"; pointing to the prevalence of satire in ancient Irish society, she claims that "Moore's method brings in precisely those types of satire specifically indicated in ancient laws: a nickname that clings, recitation of a satire in the absence of its subject, satirizing of the face, laughing at all aspects of a subject, sneering at bodily form, and magnifying a blemish!" (Grubgeld 1994: 151). Oliver St John Gogarty (who himself was satirized by James Joyce in the figure of Malachi "Buck" Mulligan in *Ulysses*) wrote in a similar mocking vein in the several volumes of his memoirs, of which the first, *As I Was Going Down Sackville Street* (1937), sparked a successful libel action by one of its victims. Grubgeld links the prevalence of personal satire in Irish autobiography to the fact that it originated in the small, gossipy world of Dublin art and letters, a milieu "of literate satirists who repeated each other's best anecdotes, [and] topped each other's invectives" (Grubgeld 1994: 153).

Many of Moore's contemporaries who were lampooned in *Hail and Farewell* responded by deriding Moore in their own writings. Edward Martyn, Moore's cousin, found himself at the receiving end of much mockery in the autobiographies. In "Ave," Martyn is described as "a pathetic figure" who "believes himself to be the Messiah – he who will give Ireland literature and her political freedom" (Moore 1985: 145). Elsewhere, Moore compares his cousin's mind to the weather in Ireland: "sometimes a muddling fog, sometimes a delicious mist with a ray of light shining through; and that is why he is the most delightful of travelling companions. One comes very soon to the end of a mind that thinks clearly, but one never comes to the end of Edward" (Moore 1985: 150). Martyn's retaliation came in the form of several satirical plays written for his Irish Theatre, which reflect his pique at having been satirized in *Hail and Farewell*.

Hail and Farewell was completed in 1914, and the first play staged that year by the newly established Irish Theatre was Martyn's *The Dream Physician*. While Moore's mockery of Martyn in his autobiography is mostly gentle, Martyn's revenge was more mean-spirited. *The Dream Physician* was designed almost exclusively to make fun of Moore in the figure of George Augustus Moon, a journalist from Mayo, Moore's home county. The character was played in the Irish Theatre production by John MacDonagh, who had been made up to look like Moore. The play presents Moon as a "most egotistical" creature (Martyn n.d.: 30), given to writing preposterous poetry in the guise of a fictitious grand-niece, Martha, otherwise known as "La Mayonaise." Although one character in the play argues that Moon is ultimately more comic than evil, and that his "genius for purging caddishness of its essential offence is [his] chief claim to immortality" (Martyn n.d.: 71), the ridiculing of Moon continues relentlessly to the end of the play.

The Menippean Revival

Personalized satire was an appropriate vehicle for the culture wars that were fought within the very limited, almost incestuous world of Dublin art and literature in the first decade and a half of the twentieth century. The political events that took place in the second and third decades, however, changed the climate and produced a very different kind of satirical discourse. In this period, the country faced the Easter

Darrell Figgis's *The Return of the Hero* (written in 1919, published in 1923) reflects its author's uneasiness with the developing political situation in Ireland after the Easter Rising. Where, at the turn of the century, Yeats and Lady Gregory had sought to bring back to Ireland an "ancient idealism" based on heroic Celtic myth and legend, Figgis's narrative two decades later suggests that true heroism is neither recognized nor valued in an Ireland where idealism is already being replaced by bureaucracy and opportunism. *The Return of the Hero* is based on a number of medieval tales that describe an encounter between Saint Patrick and the pagan hero-poet Oisín, who has miraculously survived into the Christian era. His father was Finn Mac Cumhal, the leader of the Fianna (or Fenians), a legendary band of warriors. In the dialogue between saint and hero, Patrick represents Christian spiritual doctrine, while Oisín is a defiant defender of physical heroic values. While saint and hero are honest and earnest in their debates, Figgis ridicules the rigid and convoluted reasoning of Patrick's self-serving bishops. The book opens with the arrival of the hero in the Christian world, where his first noble deed is to assist a group of men in placing a heavy cornerstone for a new church. The orange of the clearing cut in the gray gravel and the green grass surrounding the location evoke the three colors of the republican flag, which makes it possible to see the church foundations as the basis for the new state, which was founded by modern-day Fenians – a notion also supported by the fact that, according to Figgis himself, the structure of Sinn Féin, the political party representing Irish republicanism, had been modeled on the organization of the early Irish church. Figgis makes Oisín say that the Ireland to which he has returned is a doleful place, "a land blistered by a satire from the gods" (Figgis 1923: 63). It is a country where the leaders eventually refuse to build on the foundations laid by a Fenian hero.

The Return of the Hero can be read as a satirical depiction of the power struggle within the republican leadership in the years after the Easter Rising, as it gradually loses touch with its base and its ideals. In the book, Darrell Figgis, who had spent several years in prison for revolutionary activities, expressed his disillusionment with the authority figures in Sinn Féin, casting himself in the role of Oisín, whose heroic voice of reason is drowned out by the drone of dogma. In typical Menippean fashion, however, the narrative ends inconclusively by undermining its own textual authoritativeness, as conflicting accounts of Oisín's final moments on earth begin to proliferate, and become increasingly nonsensical and incomprehensible. In Menippean satire, according to Mikhail Bakhtin, all endings are merely new beginnings, and, like the embroidery on Oisín's tunic, the narrative of *The Return of the Hero* moves "in sinuous whorls that flowed endlessly and gracefully and returned upon their beginning" (Figgis 1923: 16). The inconclusiveness and ambiguity of the book's ending express the frustration of a revolutionary politician and self-styled hero who had consistently spoken his mind, and whose voice had equally consistently been ignored by those in positions of power.

In the first decade after the founding of the Irish Free State, Eimar O'Duffy produced a trilogy of satirical novels: *King Goshawk and the Birds* (1926), *The Spacious*

Adventures of the Man in the Street (1928), and *Asses in Clover* (1933). As in Figgis, the satire hinges on the juxtaposition of ancient heroic values and the greed and degeneracy of the modern world. In *King Goshawk*, the Old Irish hero Cuchulain (O'Duffy's spelling) is persuaded to return to earth to combat man's wickedness, but the intrusion of the hero into modern society causes more problems than it solves, and he therefore hands over the task to his son, Cuanduine. Both heroes, while acting as vehicles for the satire, are themselves also satirized: a hero is described as "a person of superabundant vitality and predominant will, with no sense of responsibility or humour, which makes him a nuisance on earth" (O'Duffy 1926: 34).

In *King Goshawk*, the spirit of Cuchulain temporarily borrows the body of the Dublin grocer's assistant Aloysius O'Kennedy. In *The Spacious Adventures of the Man in the Street*, O'Kennedy's disembodied spirit drifts off into space and lands in the city of Bulnid on the planet Rathé, which serves as a semi-Utopian inversion of his home town, where he adopts the body of the recently deceased Ydenneko. In this guise, the prototypical man-in-the-street argues with the citizens of Bulnid, whose values are the opposite of his own, about topics as wide-ranging as politics, economics, religion, and sexuality. Sexual morality was a much-debated issue in the Ireland of the late 1920s. The obsession with national purity that came with independence culminated in 1929 in the passing of the Censorship of Publications Act, which not only led to the banning of all books that could be remotely regarded as being, as the law stated it, "in their general tendency indecent," but also to the removal of all nudes from Dublin's Municipal Gallery. The topic of sexuality takes up more than half of O'Duffy's second satirical narrative, in the form of an elaborate analogy between sex and eating: the Bulnidians regard the latter in much the same way as Dubliners consider sex – it takes place in private, diners commit themselves to one food only, and any public mention of the topic fills them with outrage or embarrassment. Having first attempted, unsuccessfully, to alter the monophagous eating habits of the Bulnidians, O'Kennedy launches a campaign to enforce monogamy in marriage, which also fails. A Bulnidian tells him: "Every objection you have made to our institutions simply demonstrates the silliness and malignity of the race from which you spring" (O'Duffy 1928: 183). O'Kennedy's position makes a mockery of the polemic between the two opposed ideologies, and satirizes both positions.

In *Asses in Clover*, the hero sets himself a number of noble tasks involving the distribution of wealth. One is to fulfill the modest dream of a man named Mac ui Rudai ("Mr Thingie," whose name suggests that he is both average and materialistic) to have a cottage, a wife, and a job – a reflection of future Irish president Eamon De Valera's 1928 statement on behalf of the Fianna Fáil party that "there ought to be available for every single man in the country employment which will bring him in enough recompense to enable him to maintain his family, and the whole organisation of the State ought to be to that end." Cuanduine's primary task is to defeat Goshawk, and to liberate the world's songbirds from the cage in which they are being held for the selfish delight of the wife of the world's wealthiest capitalist.

Cuanduine wins both battles but loses the war. When the hero reiterates Mac ui Rudai's dream in a public speech, the latter, now the slick and materialistic owner of a sales empire, heckles him from the audience. The greatest betrayal comes from the songbirds: when Cuanduine rips open their cage, they "would not stir, and pecked him viciously when he tried to shoo them forth" (O'Duffy 1933: 271). Disillusioned with the world, Cuanduine turns his back on it and is never seen again. The final episodes of *Asses in Clover* look at the world from a distant, future perspective: the human race has died out, a consequence of its own destructive habits, and rabbits have inherited the earth. Man "achieved a mastery of natural forces that was marvellous in a race so stupid, but his wickedness and folly were such that it did him more harm than good" (O'Duffy 1933: 330). O'Duffy is neither the first nor the last satirist to suggest, misanthropically, that there is often little to distinguish the victim from the perpetrator, or the hero from the fool.

Austin Clarke's three satirical narratives, all set in the early Middle Ages, focus predominantly on the role of the Catholic Church in shaping Irish attitudes toward sexuality. His prose romances of the 1930s, *The Bright Temptation* (1932) and *The Singing-Men at Cashel* (1936), show a growing bitterness about the dogmatic teachings of the Church, and the complacency of the Irish people in accepting its puritanical and misogynistic values. The Irish bishops had voiced their fears about the decline of sexual morality in a joint pastoral in 1927, in which they warned against indecent books and movies, and immodest female attire, "all of which tend to destroy the virtues characteristic of our race." Clarke's works (his poetry as well as his prose narratives) target the religious insistence on the repression of the physical in favor of the spiritual, and expose the sexual suffering this caused for many of his countrymen and women. When he was in his twenties, Clarke's own traumatic experiences in this regard had led to a mental breakdown. This fact, coupled with the slightly obsessive nature of his writing, provided Samuel Beckett with the ingredients for a merciless satirical portrait of Clarke. In *Murphy* (1938), Clarke appears as the poet Austin Ticklepenny. Ticklepenny is under the impression that his problem is alcohol, but Beckett's narrator argues that it is the poet's own verse rather than drink that has driven him to a mental institution, a view that "will not seem strange to anyone familiar with the class of pentameter that Ticklepenny felt it his duty to Erin to compose...No wonder he felt a new man washing the bottles and emptying the slops of the better-class mentally deranged" (Beckett 1973: 53).

The Sun Dances at Easter (1952), Clarke's most effective narrative satire, carnivalizes the world it depicts by ridiculing the sterile forces of authority and celebrating the fertile powers of nature and the imagination. Unlike straight satire, carnival includes a celebratory aspect: turning the world upside down is associated with the process of death and regeneration. In the plot of Clarke's narrative, a jolly, fat, wandering cleric (who eventually turns out to be the Irish god of love, Aongus, in disguise) promises a childless couple, Orla and Flann, that they will have a son if Orla visits the Well of St Naal (or Natalis). The monk's patchwork outfit and his merriment make him both ridiculous and subversive: his "disgraceful sanctity" (Clarke 1952: 15) unites the sacred with the profane in true carnival fashion. On her journey, Orla teams up with a young scholar, who closely resembles her husband. Orla visits the well, where Flann catches up with his wife, and in due course she gives birth to a boy who looks exactly like his father. The latter's identity is left open to speculation.

The opposite of the "holy show" of the merry pagan monk is provided in the book by the absolute seriousness of the official representative of the Church, the Lord Abbot-Bishop Macuad. The mere presence of this clergyman and his entourage puts the fear of God into the entire natural world: "Behind every bush, as they passed, the birds went into hiding, reeds shook, tiny pleasure-seekers clambered down from the grass-stalks and took to their heels. Every thicket, every pool was still, for the reverend Macuad was the most renowned moralist in Ireland" (Clarke 1952: 171–2). Macuad is a thinly veiled satirical portrait of the Most Reverend John Charles McQuaid, Archbishop of Dublin from 1940 to 1972, who was uncompromising in his views on sexual morality, being an avid opponent of birth control and an advocate of the censorship and banning of what he called impure books. In Clarke's narrative, when Macuad begins to preach to a large public gathering, guffaws interrupt his diatribe against immorality, instigated by the fat monk whose ridiculous figure and infectious merriment soon have the crowd in stitches, as people "staggered into fits of laughter until their legs could support them no more" (Clarke 1952: 174). Carnival laughter of this kind is a reaction to a crisis, in which negative ridicule of the authority figure is fused with positive rejoicing at the renewal of life.

As an alternative to the inflexible morality dictated by the Catholic Church and endorsed by the Irish state, *The Sun Dances at Easter* offers an open-ended, creative position that offers no single answer, but culminates in the symbol of a new beginning. Carnival liberates the imagination for new possibilities that may lead the way to change. This is, of course, a theoretical position. Clarke's third satirical narrative, like the previous two, was banned shortly after its publication. In the decades following the creation of the Irish Free State, many satirical texts were banned by the same authorities they sought to ridicule. Flann O'Brien and Mervyn Wall are two authors whose works reflect the predicament of the satirist who writes in the vacuum created by official censorship, seeking to engage his audience in the dethroning of the very authorities by whom he is deprived of his audience.

In *At Swim-Two-Birds* (1939), Flann O'Brien makes literature itself both the vehicle and the focus of his satirical critique. The protagonist of this complex carnivalized text is a fledgling author whose literary technique is to borrow extensively and randomly from other authors, both real and fictitious. In *At Swim*, books and the activity of writing them are mischievously and ridiculously associated with the forbidden and the indecent, by means of ambiguity and innuendo. If plays are "consumed in wholesome fashion by large masses in places of public resort," the novel, being "self-administered in private," is by implication associated with unwholesome activity (O'Brien 1967: 25). The student narrator of *At Swim* prefers to conduct his writing in the privacy of his bedroom with the door locked; on several occasions, his uncle, with whom he lives, expresses skepticism regarding what goes on behind the closed door. If the uncle tacitly equates writing with masturbation, his nephew connects it in a similarly unspoken fashion with other forms of forbidden sexuality, as when he describes his fellow students as being devoted variously to English letters, Irish letters, "and some to the study and advancement of the French language" (1967: 48). The implicit phrase "French letters" also means "condoms," and birth control was a banned subject in the context of Irish moral legislation.

In *At Swim-Two-Birds*, such tongue-in-cheek self-censorship is paradoxically employed as a critique of censorship. O'Brien makes a sport of including as many forbidden topics as possible without mentioning them, by using the conspicuousness of the absence of a prohibited subject as a means of drawing attention to it. Such an informational lacuna can be found, for example, in an account concerning the cowboy characters borrowed by the book's narrator from western novels. When the gun belonging to one of the cowboys is found in the bed of a scullery-maid, he is unable to explain its presence there but speculates that "she appropriated the article in order to clean it in her spare time in bed (she was an industrious girl) or in order to play a joke." The passage concludes that "the former explanation is the more likely of the two as there is no intercourse of a social character between the men and the scullery-maids" (O'Brien 1967: 55). While the text censors the reader's options by offering only two possible explanations for the incident, the qualifier in the phrase "intercourse of a social character" suggests the possible existence of other types of "intercourse," which the text studiously avoids mentioning.

Flann O'Brien's *The Third Policeman*, which was completed in 1940 but not published until 1967, mixes Menippean characteristics with elements of Kafkaesque menace. The book is set in a cyclical otherworld governed by its own impenetrable logic and ruled by strange policemen, and features a posthumous and nameless protagonist perpetually in search of an elusive box of "omnium," which will allow its possessor to create unimaginable objects and perform unheard-of feats. *The Third Policeman* cannot be called a direct satirical critique of specific aspects of Irish society, except in a very general sense, but its paradoxical construction does reflect both the satirist's desire to escape to some unimaginable otherworld of unlimited possibility, and his realization that he was inexorably confined to the claustrophobic and oppressive reality of 1940s' Ireland.

Like the other satirists of his generation, Mervyn Wall was disconcerted by the stifling atmosphere of Ireland in the decades after the declaration of independence, and the climate of hostility toward literature and the arts. In *The Unfortunate Fursey* (1946) and *The Return of Fursey* (1948), Wall ridiculed the dogmatic and self-serving nature of the medieval church and its pervasive influence on all aspects of life as a means of commenting indirectly on the institutions of his own day. Fursey is a tenth-century monk in the monastic settlement of Clonmacnoise, which one day is invaded by a plague of foreign demons, who settle in the unfortunate brother's cell because his speech-impediment prevents him from uttering a word, let alone a prayer or an exorcism, when he is afraid. Expelled from the monastery for being a harborer of demons, Fursey embarks on a series of adventures designed to question assumed truths about the nature of good and evil. Small and tubby, and more sinned against than sinning, Fursey is an unlikely and reluctant hero who belongs to the category of the wise fool or tragic clown. He serves as a foil for the hypocrisy and selfishness of the rest of humanity in general, and the Irish clergy in particular.

In the Ireland of the 1940s and 1950s, many of the authors whose books were banned (Gide, Hemingway, Sartre, Steinbeck) were among the most important in modern literature. In *The Return of Fursey*, Wall ridicules the Irish Censorship Board's zeal in the figure of the monastic Censor, whose principal qualification for the post "was that each of his eyes moved independently of the other, a quality most useful in the detection of double meanings" (Wall 1985: 82). He burns all manuscripts that do not pass his touchstone – his mother, who is to him "the type of the decent, clean-minded people of Ireland," but who is also completely illiterate: "Whenever I'm in doubt about a word or phrase, I ask myself would such a word or phrase be used by her" (Wall 1985: 83). This method means that virtually all texts, including the great books of Western civilization, are condemned to the flames. When the plundering Vikings set fire to Clonmacnoise, it takes the Censor only a moment to take advantage of the situation: emerging from the manuscript room after a hard day's chasing innuendoes, he "cast one glance at the raging fires which threatened the whole settlement; then he returned and set fire to the library" (Wall 1985: 89). The sight of his subhuman appearance has meanwhile caused the Vikings to retreat in alarm. The Censor's action reflects Wall's conviction that repression did not need to be imposed on the Irish people by the clergy or the government, but came from within Irish society itself.

Both O'Brien and Wall are ultimately aware of the profound paradox of their position: in order for their satire on censorship to be read, it must be able to pass muster with the censor as well as with a potential audience. In such an impossible position, the satirist typically justifies his own lack of principles, and that of his audience, by adopting the mask of misanthropy. Flann O'Brien never rejected the idea of censorship outright, and instead openly questioned whether his fellow human beings were capable of making their own decisions, given their propensity to commit fatal errors of judgment. Mervyn Wall eventually took the view that the only constant characteristic of human beings since the beginning of time is their stupidity. These acerbic views represented the last gasp of a satirical movement that had written itself into a corner and had nowhere else to go. Menippean satire petered out in Ireland in the 1950s. The end of that decade brought a more enlightened government, economic reform, the liberalization of religious thinking, and a relaxation of censorship. With social reform and the decline of narrative satire also came a resurgence of the older satirical tradition of literary invective and personal lampoon, which, in any case, had never really gone away.

References and Further Reading

Beckett, Samuel (1973) *Murphy*. London: Picador.

Booker, M. Keith (1995) *Flann O'Brien, Bakhtin, and Menippean Satire*. Syracuse: Syracuse University Press.

Clarke, Austin (1952) *The Sun Dances at Easter*. London: Andrew Melrose.

Elliott, Robert C. (1960) *The Power of Satire: Magic, Ritual, Art*. Princeton, NJ: Princeton University Press.

Figgis, Darrell (1923) *The Return of the Hero*. London: Chapman and Dodd.

Grubgeld, Elizabeth (1994) *George Moore and the Autogenous Self: The Autobiography and Fiction*. Syracuse: Syracuse University Press.

Joyce, James (1975) *Pomes Penyeach*. London: Faber and Faber.

Kavanagh, Patrick (1972) *Collected Poems*. London: Martin Brian and O'Keeffe.

Kinsella, Thomas (trans.) (1977) *The Táin: Translated from the Irish Epic Táin Bó Cúailnge*. Oxford: Oxford University Press.

Lanters, José (2000) *Unauthorized Versions: Irish Menippean Satire, 1919–1952*. Washington, DC: Catholic University of America Press.

Martyn, Edward (n.d. [1915?]) *The Dream Physician*. Dublin: Talbot Press.

Mercier, Vivian (1962) *The Irish Comic Tradition*. Oxford: Oxford University Press.

Moore, George (1985) *Hail and Farewell*, ed. Richard Cave. Gerrards Cross: Colin Smythe.

Murphy, Thomas (1973) *The Morning after Optimism*. Dublin: Mercier.

——(1976) *The Sanctuary Lamp*. Dublin: Poolbeg Press.

O'Brien, Flann (1967) *At Swim-Two-Birds*. Harmondsworth: Penguin.

O'Duffy, Eimar (1926) *King Goshawk and the Birds*. London: Macmillan.

——(1928) *The Spacious Adventures of the Man in the Street*. London: Macmillan.

——(1933) *Asses in Clover*. London: Putnam.

Power, Patrick C. (1991) *The Book of Irish Curses*. Cork: Mercier.

Robinson, Fred Norris (1912) Satirists and enchanters in early Irish literature. In David Gordon and George Foot Moore (eds), *Studies in the History of Religions*, pp. 95–130. New York: Macmillan.

Shaw, Bernard (1962) *Complete Plays with Prefaces*, vol. 2. New York: Dodd, Mead and Co.

Synge, J. M. (1921) *Poems and Translations*. Dublin: Maunsel and Roberts.

Wall, Mervyn (1985) *The Complete Fursey (The Unfortunate Fursey* and *The Return of Fursey)*. Dublin: Wolfhound Press.

Witoszek, Nina and Sheeran, Patrick (1991) The tradition of vernacular hatred. In Geert Lernout (ed.), *The Crows behind the Plough: History and Violence in Anglo-Irish Poetry and Drama*, pp. 11–27. Amsterdam: Rodopi.

Part IV
The Practice of Satire

25
Modes of Mockery: The Significance of Mock-poetic Forms in the Enlightenment
Blanford Parker

Mockery and the European Genre System

The reader will forgive me if I admit from the beginning that the subject of satirical mockery is too large for the scope or ambition of the present chapter. First, I shall limit myself to mockery of genres and modes – to explicit parody of literary types. In a wider sense all satire is mockery, but the kind of mockery I wish to explicate is not personal lampooning or invective, but the inversion or reversal of expectation in a known literary form. Parody itself is too general a term for what I wish to describe. I will limit myself to that sort of parody that brings to mind the specific literary conventions – the sense of generic decorum in the system of traditional literary kinds.

Every period – I might say every imaginative episteme – carries with it an identifiable hierarchy of modes and styles. There has been a constant assimilation and displacement of generic norms, and only those who know well the literary choices of an earlier age can recognize the effects of mockery. The mock genres and the practice of literary mockery goes back at least as far as the sixth century BCE. "The Battle of the Frogs and the Mice" was believed to be as ancient as the *Iliad* and even the work of Homer himself. There was from the earliest stages of Western and Semitic literature a kind of shadow canon, which served as an ironic or humorous double of the more serious one. But a distinction must be made at the outset, and that distinction is the cornerstone of my argument. Not all ages of literary mockery are the same. The purpose of mockery is constantly shifting. The value that an age puts upon mockery of the literary sort depends on a wide variety of imaginative and moral variables. Surely, the author of "The Battle of the Frogs and the Mice" did not intend either an organized critique of the heroic ideal or a serious lampooning of the limitations of Homeric style. The poem shows in little, and at an ironic distance, the pathos of Homeric fatalism, the hopelessness of the Homeric hero, but the same exact notions may be found in the Homer text itself. The root of the poem's humor is its relative littleness – the unheroic energies of its antagonists. Had it included the sea-wanderings of great whales, the magnificent flight of sea birds, or the strength and cunning of the lion and boar, then it would not have been mockery at all. It would have fallen within the normal metaphoric repertoire of oral epic. But we are supposed to see how strangely frogs and mice fit into the world of preternatural strength and high moral seriousness. "The Battle of the Frogs and the Mice" lacks what Aristotle calls *spoudaios* – high and weighty seriousness. The poem is funny without being profound. More importantly, its irony does not betoken a change of moral consciousness – an anxiety over the efficacy of Homeric poetry. It does not even stress in any positive sense the Hesiodic or practical qualities of the animals. Their rodent industry and persistence is part of the joke. The frog, like every good host of the Homeric epic, asks the stranger mouse to describe his lineage. He receives a marvelous response:

> Why do you ask my race, which is well-known amongst men and gods and the birds of heaven? Crumb-snatcher am I called, and I am the son of Bread-nibbler – he was my stout-hearted father – and my mother was Churn-licker, the daughter of Ham-gnawer the king; she bare me in the mousehole, and nourished me with food, figs and nuts and dainties of all kinds. But how are you to make me your friend who am altogether different in nature? For you get your living in water but I live upon such food as men have. ("The Battle of the Frogs and the Mice," 24–31)

First, it is important to note the twist on the Homeric formula epithet "known among gods and men." The Homeric hero is known by and is sometimes the darling of both gods and men. He is, after all, a link between the human and divine nature, having either an immortal parent or divine protector. But the mouse adds the anomalous phrase "and the birds of heaven." Mice are known by the birds of heaven, either as the bothersome competitors of smaller nesting birds, or the delicious prey of hawks and owls. This added element of the mouse's epithet reduces his grandeur rather drastically. Our translator, Hugh Evelyn-White, has nicely realized the homey and paltry heroic epithets, "bread-nibbler," "churn-licker," and "ham-gnawer" to emphasize the un-Homeric humbleness of the mouse-hero's diet. In fact, the mouse is rather hubristic and claims superiority over the frogs because he lives on "such food as men [the actual phrase implies fighting men] have." Of course, the crumb-snatchers and cheese-grabbers actually live on what can be furtively stolen from men, but this fact is omitted by the proud creature. The mouse recognizes that frogs and mice have very different natures and live in opposing elements. This makes them as far as possible removed from human heroes, who, as we learn in the famous speech of Glaucon to Sarpedon (*Iliad* 7.201–232) are always of the same nature and character. The Homeric and Virgilian heroes are brothers in battle and share the same martial ideals. It is the likeness of Hector and Achilles, Turnus and Aeneas, that leads to the tragic pathos of their conflicts.

"The Battle of the Frogs and the Mice" is in fact the meeting place of the ancient folk fable, which we associate with the name of Aesop (probably a contemporary of the author of "The Frogs and the Mice"), and the narrative and metrical style of oral epic. The fairly sonorous replication of the Homeric hexameter and the other poetic devices of oral epic are out of scale and tone with the folk material. Such a break with verbal and narrative decorum is one of the signs of literary mockery. But the poem is not an attempt of folk consciousness to show the moral inadequacy of the Homeric poem. If anything, it is an attempt to show the inadequacy of folk material to hold up the serious moral demands of the epic.

But it must be understood that at later phases of history the beast fable and folk poetry have very different uses and a very different relation to the "higher genres." This is partly because there has been a broad reconsideration of the relation of animal and human nature (especially since the seventeenth century). Even in later antiquity, Horace had used the Aesopic animal allegory in a new and sophisticated way in his "City Mouse and Country Mouse." There the fable was used to show the moral and political differences between the rural Italian population with its laborious and self-sacrificing values and the corrupt cosmopolitanism of Rome. Virgil, too, in his *Georgics*, following the example of Hesiod, and under the influence of the materialism of Lucretius, had shown human nature in an intimate relation to the world of plants and animals – in a kind of battle against the harsh elements of the natural world. But even in his praise of the social nature of bees (*Georgics* 3) he does not imply any moral equality of man and animal.

Up to the Middle Ages we can expect the use of animal analogy, as in the *Nun's Priest's Tale* of Chaucer, to be an allegorical or parabolic instruction for men. There is no implied question about the place of human nature in the hierarchy of creatures. The medieval mind had constructed a complete animal symbology in which one or another human quality could be represented by animal types. This can be seen in Books of Hours, paintings, poems, and other artistic media. In the mind of many Medievals the animals and all created nature formed a kind of instructive language that could be used for human moral instruction. The same might be said, though more ambiguously, of Humanist imaginative discourse.

But from the middle of the seventeenth century there is a new possibility – something that would have shocked our British and European forebears. From that point forward the space between animal and human nature began to collapse. What Robert Frost called "the downward metaphors," created a new possibility for poetry. John Wilmot, Earl of Rochester's words in the 1670s are representative:

> Were I (who to my cost already am
> One of those strange, prodigious creatures, man)
> A spirit free to choose, for my own share,
> What case of flesh and blood I pleased to wear,
> I'd be a dog, a monkey, or a bear,
> Or anything but that vain animal
> Who is so proud of being rational.
> ("A Satire against Reason and Mankind," 1–7)

Rochester was under the influence of Hobbes's new philosophy in which human and animal nature were closely equated. In the generation after Rochester, Bernard Mandeville was to push the analogy of man and beast further. In "The Grumbling Hive" (1705) and *The Fable of the Bees* (1714), he would push Virgilian metaphors to their logical extreme. According to Mandeville, the same amoral naturalism that controlled the social and physical instincts of animals controlled human ones. In the later years of the eighteenth century, it was a commonplace that animals not only were like humans, but even had virtues that humans lacked. We see in sentimental poets like Thomson, Smart, and Cunningham a kind of cult of the animal nature. In the sentimental age we see for the first time the arguments against hunting, the idealizing of the wilderness, and the early attacks on the use of agricultural livestock for human benefit, which were early stages in the "greening" of modern consciousness. It was only a few more steps from there to Darwinism.

If we were to read a poem today about a battle between frogs and mice we could make several interpretive choices that were not available in antiquity or up to recent times. We could marvel at the real ingenuity and perseverance of the animals and sympathize with their difficult condition (so like our own). Or we could see all of nature from bacteria to the high mammals as engaged in a struggle for survival. In such a world, differences of scale are meaningless. It is now a commonplace that cockroaches have great natural advantages over humans. But all of this was the antithesis of Homeric realism. No reader of "The Battle of the Frogs and the Mice" could have imagined such a collapsing of kinds – such a breach of literary and moral decorum. As in most literary eras, there could be no differentiation between poetic form and subject matter. The resonant oral meter of the epic hexameter was connected to the heroic narrative. The oral formulation was meant to preserve the *kleos* (good fame) of the hero who represented a high possibility of human nature. The humor of the "The Battle of the Frogs and the Mice" was in no way an indication of the decline of Homeric authority.

There have been very few periods of cultural history in which the longstanding norms and conventions of literary practice have been called into question. Even fewer have made a serious break with the generic decorum of the past. The Confucian ideal of poetry, which was based on the verbal and rhythmic model of the great "Book of Odes," was to last more than twelve centuries. Traces of the vocabulary and rhetoric of those ancient models may be seen in the poetry of Chairman Mao. Similarly, the canons of Greco-Roman poetic ideals were preserved as much as possible even in the Middle Ages when access to classical paradigms was difficult. The Humanists re-invented or re-established the canonical critical views of Aristotle, Dionysius, Cicero, Horace, and Quintilian. A part of that classical inheritance was a generic system. Virgil was the most important Roman poet for Europe in late antiquity (we may remember the struggles with the *Aeneid* in *The Confessions* of Saint Augustine), the Middle Ages, and the Renaissance. The tripartite division of his work, as explained by the Roman editor and commentator Servius, became a generic model for later generations. The medieval "wheel of Virgil" granted great importance to the three Virgilian types: pastoral, georgic, and epic. This paradigm became a decisive model for the structure of poetic careers in the early modern period. We can see Ronsard, Sidney, Sannazaro, Spenser, Vida, and Milton (to name a few) attempting to recreate the *cursus poetarum* ("course of the poets") from pastoral to epic. The tripartite division of generic types was widely represented in terms of style and character. The pastoral represented the low or plain end of poetic style, the georgic the middle, and the epic the high. Similarly, the cultural archetypes of character – shepherd, farmer, and soldier – were placed in a hierarchy, though in Christian culture after the thirteenth century the pastoral character became increasingly ambiguous and came to represent in turn the monk, the priest, the poet, and the man of private meditation. In fact, each of the poetic types represented a high ideal. In a poet like Milton, all three must be granted their dignity of kind. Such dignity is derived in part from the authority of Virgil. It would not be an exaggeration to say that the debates about private versus civic or heroic values, so central to the intellectual program of the West, are preserved in and through this generic system. I call it a system because the elements were seen as a constant set of relations – defining and opposing each other.

It is a commonplace of every literary period for the authors of different genres to mock each other. About one-fifth of the Greek lyric poems we have preserved from the period before the fourth century BCE have a distinct disavowal of the heroic ideal. These signature passages mark the territory of moral discourse against the claims of other genres. We find these anti-heroical markers in the poetry of Archilochus, Ibycus, Anacreon, Sappho, and many others. A few famous lines of Sappho are representative: "Some say that the most beautiful thing on the black earth is an army of horsemen, others an army of foot-soldiers, others a fleet of ships; but I say it is the person you love" (*Poetorum Lesbianum fragmenta* 12). Sappho distances herself from the themes and characters of heroic poetry and goes on to talk about the universal power of love. We may see the same pointed oppositional rhetoric concerning war and violence in the famous opening of the oldest of georgic poems, Hesiod's *Works and Days*.

In a very old but generally rejected opening to the *Aeneid*, Virgil himself distinguishes the territory of the epic from that of the pastoral and georgic. "That man am I who having once played his song upon a slender reed, emerging from the woods, compelled neighboring fields to submit even to the greediest farmer, a work welcome to husbandmen, but now Mars' bristling arms and the Man I sing" (Theordorakopoulos 1997: 160). Virgil announces his turn from the subject and decorum of pastoral and georgic to the martial themes of the *Aeneid*. In this brief passage, we see the "slender reed" of the pastoral contrasted with the tougher georgic style of the "neighboring fields" and, finally, the "bristling arms" that represent the high seriousness of the heroic. In a traditional genre structure the author must place him or herself within the boundaries – rhetorical and moral – of a certain literary kind and show that he or she knows the rules of that kind. Nonetheless, such a literary marker of genre is not really a form of mockery. Spenser does not have to mock heroic ideas in *The Shepheardes Calender* (1579). He must only prove that he recognizes the rules of kind and marks of style of the pastoral and its relation to the heroic poetry that helps to define it. Pope moves easily from the idealized landscape of his *Pastorals*

(1709) to the georgic world of "Windsor-Forest" (1713, corrected 1717). The genre system is a differential one; each generic kind is understood in relation to the others.

Pope and Enlightened Mockery

The mock-heroic poetry in Britain after 1660 (or in France after 1640) was not of the playful kind that we see in "The Battle of the Frogs and the Mice." It did not display the marks of differentiation that separated literary kinds in the Renaissance. Mock-heroic writing in the enlightened phase of European culture does not involve itself in a debate over the relative ethical and rhetorical merit or level of different kinds of poetry as was common in medieval and Humanist poems. Its mockery was of a different kind.

Pope's *The Rape of the Lock* (1714) may be a good starting-point for our discussion of the mature stage of Enlightened mockery – a kind of literary mockery distinct from but connected to its Humanist sources. Pope recognized as much as any poet could the whole panoply of metrical and verbal effects, which constituted the horizon of verse writing in the age that preceded him. His youthful imitations of Cowley or Spenser show that he had an ear for the peculiarities of earlier poetic schools – even those like the Metaphysical that he would come to repudiate in poetry and prose. Pope knew that sophisticated literary mockery depends on the recognition of a range of literary markers that determine the rules of kind. He also felt the attraction of a growing current of poetic mockery that had become one of the surest paths to contemporary literary success. No author knew more about the reinvention of satire that had been ushered in by his favorite authors of the previous generation – Butler, Dryden, Denham, and Rochester. No author better recognized the constant refinement of both the four-foot Hudibrastic line and the comic-heroic pentameter of Rochester and Dryden. Pope also kept a close eye on the growth of mock generic writing like that of John Philips and Samuel Garth. These poems had pointed the way to wide (if brief) celebrity in the London circles of refined journalists like Addison and Steele, whose regard Pope coveted. We can see how deeply and precisely he had plumbed the resources of these mock-heroic models. Poems of only moderate success, such as Philips's "The Splendid Shilling" (1701) or Garth's *The Dispensary* (1699–1718), which may now appear to be minor period pieces, were valuable sources in Pope's education. From those authors he gleaned a set of useful verbal and thematic techniques. From Philips he discovered the humorous use of Miltonic *topoi* – the powerful effect of describing everyday objects in terms of the sublime. Philips had brought the involution and Latinity of Milton to the streets of the London ghetto. This is the language he uses to describe the act of smoking a cigarette in his London flat:

> Then solitary walk, or doze at home
> In garret vile, and with a warming puff
> Regale chilled fingers; or from tube as black

> As winter-chimney, or well-polished jet,
> Exhale mundungus, ill-perfuming scent:
> Not blacker tube, nor of a shorter size
> Smokes Cambro-Britain (vers'd in pedigree
> Sprung from Cadwalader and Arthur, kings
> Full famous in romantic tale) when he
> O'er many a craggy hill, and barren cliff...
> High overshadowing rides, with a design
> To vend his wares.
> ("The Splendid Shilling," 17–26, 28–9)

In this passage we see the full repertoire of modern mock-heroic rhetoric. The elaborate syntax of Philips's Miltonic pastiche describes the humble scene of the hack author smoking tobacco in his dingy garret at the end of a busy day. The blackness of the unswept "winter-chimney" (one of the perennial images of London grime) is placed in comparison with "the well-polished jet," a commonplace of idealized Baroque love compliment. The short, loose, dark-paper cigarette of the eighteenth century is compared with the long, black pipe smoked by a Welsh peddler as he travels the mountainous countryside to vend his humble wares. The mock romantic pedigree of the heroes of Wales and England heighten the absurdity and lowness of the poem's situation. They place the objects of the reader's world into the elevated atmosphere of the Arthurian poem. It is natural to see a warrior or prince in a medieval lay connected to a mythic forebear. But here the hack poet and peddler would seem to demand a humbler origin. The sublime of the primitive natural vista of Wales, which was to become a staple of later Romantic landscape, was here an insider's joke about the crudeness and poverty of a typical Welsh peasant. Milton has been brought in to show the intense littleness (and meanness) of a world one shilling short of comfort. The world of eighteenth-century mockery is never metaphorical, but depends on the force of metonymy. Here the single coin represents metonymically the solution to all the problems of embarrassed poverty. It could save the narrator from ignorance, solitude, the weather, and even prison. Pope was to use the same ironic and metonymic formulae, but with much finer effect in *The Rape of the Lock*:

> "Now meet thy fate," incensed Belinda cried,
> And drew a deadly bodkin from her side.
> (The same, his ancient personage to deck,
> Her great great grandsire wore about his neck,
> In three seal-rings; which after, melted down,
> Formed a vast buckle for his widow's gown;
> Her infant granddame's whistle next it grew,
> The bells she jingled, and the whistle blew;
> Then in a bodkin graced her mother's hairs,
> Which long she wore and now Belinda wears).
> (*The Rape of the Lock*, 5.87–96)

The pedigree and origin of the Welshman's family and ancestral briar pipe is loosely suggestive of the elaborate myths of origin in Milton, which were themselves derived from the lineal narratives of Spenser. But the passage in Pope, more interesting both in its literal meaning and in its Homeric analog, has a richness that Philips could not approach. The family history of Belinda's hatpin, here described as "a deadly bodkin," is revealing. Her great-great-grandfather wore three seal or signet rings about his neck, which indicates the trade of a city bureaucrat or banker, who applied a seal to legal or monetary documents. This stamp on official documents (akin to the seal of a modern notary) indicates the source of family wealth at the time of the English Civil War (or three generations before Belinda) and may also imply the capacity of Caroline Catholics to maintain substantial positions in the city. As a young recusant Catholic living under the legal restrictions of the early eighteenth century, Belinda is probably ignorant of the history implied by the object. The transformation of the seal-rings to the hairpin shows the decline from economic power to private adornment. Perhaps we are to imagine that Belinda's great-great-grandfather's widow melted down the valuable silver of a banker's signet to make a buckle to hold up her aging and tattered gown. In the period of the Protectorate she could no longer afford a new buckle. This is a pointed symbol of the social decline of Catholics after 1642 and the harsh restrictions placed upon them by Cromwell's and later governments. In the succeeding generations it declines from a stamp of trade to a baby's toy and in the end to a cosmetic adornment – a hair pin attached to the vaunted lock itself. This is a pregnant history indeed and must be contrasted to the implied source in Homer. In describing the scepter of Agamemnon Homer says:

> Hephaistos gave it to Zeus the king, the son of Kronos,
> and Zeus in turn gave it to the courier Argeiphontes,
> and lord Hermes gave it to Pelops, driver of horses,
> and Pelops gave it to Atreus, the shepherd of the people.
> Atreus dying left it to Thyestes of the rich flocks,
> and Thyestes left it in turn to Agamemnon to carry
> and to be lord of many islands and over all Argos.
> (*Iliad* 2.102–8, trans. Richard Lattimore)

If we leave aside the divine artisan and Zeus, we will notice the same passing of the symbolic object through five hands and four generations. I will not try to summarize the avalanche of horrors that befell all of these descendants of Pelops, but I will make a few relevant comments about Pope's use of literary analogy. Like Belinda's deadly bodkin, the scepter of Agamemnon represents both the vanity and the power of its possessor. In the scene quoted above, Agamemnon is about to pass cruel and unforgiving judgment on Achilles and at the same time alienate by his petty claims of authority all of the Greek captains under his command. "Now meet thy fate" is roughly the opening phrase he will use in passing judgment on his lieutenants. Of course, in one sense he is perfectly justified or at least justifiable. But he lacks the seriousness and intimacy with the gods that we see in the lives of his grandfather and father, Pelops and Atreus, just as Belinda lacks the practical and moral weight of her forebears. His besetting fault is vanity and an unwillingness to forgive Achilles, whose doubtful actions were brought on by the unfairness of Agamemnon himself. This is very like Pope's attitude toward Belinda's petty aggravation over the loss of her hair.

Now it is funny to compare the hairpin of a teenager to the scepter of a legendary prince. But this is not the end of the matter. Pope is using the Homeric analogy primarily to shed light on Belinda. Pope is primarily interested in Belinda, and the passage on the bodkin is meant to show us a new angle on the problems of her character. The bodkin helps us understand the world of Belinda, which is the world of Pope's reader and finally of Pope himself. The Homeric analogy is only relevant if it clarifies the quotidian events of the eighteenth-century courtship plot. In effect, Homer has been dragged into the scene of the card game to illustrate in a gratuitously grandiose way the pettiness of Belinda. The scene of *The Rape of the Lock* is more real, more morally potent, than that of the King of Argos. While the mockery gives Pope's learned audience the pleasure of feeling the disparity between the heroic and the mundane existence, it also permits us to look at the heroic as itself comical. All of this is a stage in preparing the audience for a new imaginative space – urban, bourgeois, practical, and historical. The last word, historical, is important. The scene of epic and pastoral is unhistorical. The epic takes place in an always remote and idealized past – the past of the great martial founders of cities and states. The battlefield of Homer or Virgil is a moral space. It does not recall a familiar territory to the reader. But in the place of modern mockery – London, Dublin, Glasgow, Paris, Rome – we are in historical settings known to the contemporary reader. The burlesque progress of Pope's *Dunciad* (1728) through the streets of London and the detailed realism of leisure at Hampton Court in *The Rape of the Lock* look forward to the encyclopedic realism of Dickens or Balzac. Similarly, the pastoral is an idealized space, outside the accumulated accidents of history. Sometimes, as in Virgil's first and ninth eclogue, the ideal world of love and poetic meditation is threatened by historical events. But the pastoral is suited for a complete and atemporal *allegoresis* of the private man – poet, lover, friend, thinker, griever. I shall say more about how the mockery of Pope's contemporaries transformed the pastoral genre in a moment.

In Samuel Garth's *Dispensary* Pope found a new language to describe the modern urban culture. Garth showed the way to illuminate through irony quotidian and contemporary objects by placing them in the scene – the imaginative field – of the heroic. The world of narrative poetry was for the first time approaching the world of modern prose fiction. The English language culture had only begun to invest its full power in the prosaic world of the mature novel. Garth had labored (and with surprising success) to transform the contemporary conflict between London physicians and druggists into an Homeric *agon*.

> The adverse host for action straight prepare,
> All eager to unveil the face of War.

> Their chiefs lace on their helms, and take the field,
> And to their trusty squire resign their shield:
> To paint each knight their ardour and alarms,
> Would ask the muse that sung the Frogs in arms.
>
> And now the signal moment to the fray;
> Mock falchions flash, and paltry ensigns play.
> There patron god his silver bow-strings twangs;
> Tough harness rustles and bold armour clangs;
> The piercing caustics ply their spiteful pow'r;
> Emetics rough, and keen cathartics scour.
> The deadly drugs in double doses fly;
> And pestles peal a martial symphony.
> Now from their level'd syringes they pour
> The liquid volley of a missive show'r.
> Not storms of sleet which o'er the Baltic drive,
> Pushed on by northern gusts, such horror give.
> (*The Dispensary*, 6th edn, 1706, 5.205–22)

Garth describes the battle of the physicians and druggists over the dispensing of charitable medical aid to the poor of London. Garth was an ardent advocate of charity medicine, but many of his contemporary doctors and nearly all of the apothecaries were bitterly opposed to it. They saw it as cutting into their lucrative fees from city hospitals in dealing with the epidemic of gin drunks and chronically ill street people. Garth ingeniously represents the famous physicians and apothecaries of the day – Millington, Tyson, Brown, Ratcliffe, and others – as heroes gathering their medical forces for a final heroic battle. We see the humorous arming of the doctors after the fashion of the battle preparations of the *Aeneid*, Book 9. The short, sharp blade of the medieval falchion stands for the scalpel, the painted ensigns of battle flags for the trade insignia of the druggists. It was a great convenience to Garth that Mercury, "the patron god" with his "silver bow," was both the guardian of Odysseus in his trials and the conventional symbol for the modern medico. Garth cleverly interweaves the violent and arcane debates of the contemporary medical profession with the relevant passages in Homer, Virgil, and Milton.

But Pope could do more in *The Rape of the Lock*. With a mind replete with relevant set pieces from the heroic tradition and a whole range of effects from early modern literature as well, he constructed a thick web of verbal analogies. But more importantly, he had a voyeuristic fascination for Belinda's world – the world of middle-class courtship, familial machinations, rituals of politics and leisure, and the novel objects of international trade. The poetic world of Philips and Garth was attenuated and shallow. The heroic mockery of their poems has a narrow, argumentative purpose. They were written to make a point at once local and arcane, which, after so many years, must be of little interest to us. Pope had a mind preeminently teachable, for he had learned to write poetry while still a boy by copying out, imitating, and translating set passages from a wide variety of authors (and in three languages). But he also had the most precious sense of the decorum – the verbal and prosodic regimen of English verse of the sixteenth and earlier seventeenth century. He knew which poetic kinds formed the horizon of the central early modern genre system. He recognized that any mockery of kind was perforce a mockery of established taste. He was endowed with a singularly rich and precise sense of poetic decorum. He realized that each poetic kind – eclogue, georgic, epic, tragic, satiric – had developed such arcane and imitable conventions of diction, meter, character, and figurative language that the smallest element of construction could be fruitfully mocked. Sophisticated literary mockery, like that of Pope, depends on recognizable generic markers on several levels. His kind of mockery is most effective for those readers who have a detailed recollection of a number of Latin school texts and who have dabbled in translation or paraphrase. Those who recall that the long vituperative speeches of Dido and Anna in the *Aeneid* are punctuated by the metrical formula *dixit* (either at the end or beginning of hortatory verse paragraphs in the Latin text) will laugh when they read the "She said," that opens Canto 4 of *The Rape of the Lock*. Similarly, only a few will recognize that Pope uses something closely akin to the *hic/ille* construction in Latin for organizing passages in his early poems. The humor involved in such an arcane irony must be invisible to later readers. These small pleasures abound in all the works of Pope, but we are likely to notice only his more obvious acts of parody – mockery of epic invocation, the hero's arming for battle, the references to Eve's temptation in Book 4 of *Paradise Lost*, and the like.

Pope also recognized the hierarchy of kinds that his contemporaries had inherited. It is obvious that he attempted in his *Pastorals* and "Windsor-Forest" to construct a career of the older kind – strictly following the path of the *cursus poetarum* from pastoral to georgic and (if his early aspirations had been fulfilled) to epic. Pope's kind of mockery depends on a recognizable hierarchy of types with respect to genre and character. The satire of *The Rape of the Lock* depends not only on the inversion of the generic position of the heroic, but also on the veiled criticism of the Petrarchan blazon (as in the cosmetic scene in Canto 1), the parody of Latin syntax and diction (in the opening of Canto 3), Shakespearean pastiche (as in the parody of Cleopatra's barge in the opening of Canto 2), and semi-blasphemous biblical allusion. Appreciation of *The Rape of the Lock* depends on a living sense of the constant reversal of aesthetic and moral expectations. Like other jokes, these effects are ruined by explication.

Pope was uncomfortable creating his archetype of the courtship novel, and in the explanatory letters and prefaces to the *Rape*, he pretended that his own aspirations were far above its homely subject matter. In fact, he used the contemporary woman's plot with the intense fascination of a voyeur. His condensed poetic narrative gives as rich a texture of modern fictional realism as anything in Behn or Manly and looks forward to Fielding and Austen. The contemporary novel had not reached canonical stature, and its subjects were not easily incorporated into the poetic genre system that was swiftly becoming moribund. Pope recognized the conventions he was mocking, but he could not really recognize the complete effect that such mockery would have.

His motives for writing a "Heroi-Comical" poem were complex. On the simplest level, he was entertaining his Roman Catholic friends and neighbors (like the Blount family and Caryll). More importantly, he was building on the literary capital, as I remarked above, among important journalists and authors like Addison and Steele, that he had acquired by writing *The Pastorals* and *The Essay on Criticism* (1711). His youth was a professional liability, and he labored to mitigate the natural envy that older authors feel in the presence of a novice with superior talent. But this was a private negotiation. What Pope could not have measured, and what precious few have measured since, is the way his mockery was aiding the destruction of the literary values that he apparently championed. He could not see that the use of Homeric, Petrarchan, Ovidian, and Miltonic materials as an instrument of mockery was bound in the end to contribute to the demise of the Humanist canon that he loved. The subject of *The Rape of the Lock* is Belinda and her world. Whenever epical or supernatural analogies are placed beside this world we see in everyday life, not only the littleness of middle-class society but also the massive irrelevance and hyperbole of the classical and the Baroque become highlighted. Pope was writing one of the first and best chapters in the novel of domestic romance, and no amount of learned mockery should deflect our attention from that fact. The ironic analogy that places a young woman's affections and social relations in the context of the heroic and the supernatural must contribute to the decline of the moral weight, the imaginative charge, that those categories carry. Pope had already shown how the central scene of the romance novel could be mocked with the conventions of the heroic and the supernatural.

In the recent generation of new historicist and late-Marxist scholars, this realization of the domination of the quotidian over the supernatural has been expressed as a symptom of empire or capitalism. It would be more useful to say that the idea and practice of capitalism as we have come to know it (with its casual pragmatic network of associations and its claim to empirical autonomy) was itself made possible by the kind of mocking disinheritance of the old world of moral analogy, theology, and metaphysical hyperbole represented in the satirical works of Pope and Swift. The whole range of the ideal imaginary of the earlier seventeenth century – microcosm, metaphysical essentialism, analogy, and conceit – had to be repudiated to make our modern economy thinkable. And it is important to remember that Pope himself came to have only a nostalgic regard for the whole range of materials that he had used as the tools of mockery. His letters and the part of his intellectual conversation that has been preserved indicate a thoroughly modern set of prejudices. In fact, as we learn from the last lines of the poem, it is Pope's power of fanciful construction alone that will immortalize Belinda. The apotheosis of the lock is a poetic apotheosis, not a spiritual one, and that is the only kind of apotheosis the author could imagine.

What Pope did not recognize was the enormous and acidic effect that the kind of mockery he had mastered was to have on tradition. If we want to understand the effect of Augustan or Enlightened mockery we must make a choice. Do we look at the works of Pope (we could as easily say Swift or Fielding) as preserving or challenging older traditions? Of course, in some sense, they do both. If we say that they preserve traditions, then we will tend to believe that the chief value of these satirical poems is their capacity to preserve Humanistic or Augustan values: high standards of verse-writing against the claims of a growing set of urban hack writers, a defense of late-Tory feudalism and monarchy, the preservation of the classical canon and classical attitudes, and a belief in some form of moderate and balanced traditional moralism. If we make this choice we will see the mockery of Pope and Swift as Humanistic and conservative. We will see them as Horatian gentlemen stemming the tide of modernity. We will believe in the oldest of fictions: that Pope, Swift, and the Scriblerians were on the side of the ancients in the battle of the books.

Some Conclusions

I have tried to indicate by brief examples and a map for reading the traditions of mockery that the role of the satiric inversion of generic types can change violently over time. In antiquity, although there is a strong tendency to differentiate poetic kinds by pointed attacks on or dismissals of the conventions of other genres, there was not a strong tendency toward the use of parody to challenge the authority or subvert the rhetoric of higher modes like epic or tragedy. Where it exists, as in Petronius, it fails to bring under censure the parent genre that it imitates. In fact, it does not even intend to do so. It is indeed difficult to decide how serious (or able) Petronius was as an imitator of Virgil and Lucan. In the Middle Ages, as Bakhtin argues at length, there is a subculture of laughter that uses the various official or high modes of literature as the butt of raucous folk humor. But the Goliard poets, ironic troubadours like Guillaume I, or satiric masters like Villon, do not in any way bring the idealized literature of love or war under disrepute. In fact, the tripartite Virgilian pattern survived even the Rabelaisian burlesque, and was in an odd sense supported by it. Never before had the European literary culture developed such an elaborate hierarchy of verbal and metrical types, nor were the cults of the idealized pastoral lyric and the martial epic ever stronger.

Swift was the culminating example of the acidic and destructive tendencies of generic mockery. If we make a close inspection of his poems, we find in his complicated corpus mockery of every mode and kind of Renaissance literature. In "Baucis and Philemon" (1709) he savagely attacks the cult of Ovid that still flourished in his youth. The old husband and wife are bumpkin Puritan saints who cannot benefit from the gifts of a divine visitor. In his famous prostitute poems and the more serious *Cadenus and Vanessa* (1726), he uncovers the preposterous delusions of the Baroque amatory traditions – compliment, blazon, and conceit. He even mocks the echo poem, amoebic dialogue, and every other characteristic gesture of the pastoral. It was he who invented the "Town Eclogue," a special genre in which the harshest realities of enlightened urban life are set in the language of the *locus amoenus*. It was Swift who prompted his friend, John Gay, to create in *The Shepherd's Week* (1714), a kind of final death-blow in Britain to the perennial cult of the pastoral lyric. From then on the form was under broad critical censure and even the authority of Virgil could not resuscitate it. We see in Swift a wide variety of mock forms – epic, georgic, and lyric. His poetry represents the complete evacuation of the idealizing modes of the Renaissance. *The Tale of a Tub* (1704) and *Gulliver's Travels* (1726) are prose anatomies of the same acidic kind. And though we say he was neo-classical in attitude, the cult of the classical was to fall with the decline of Humanist tastes. This decline was partly spurred on by the wide mockery of the literary kinds I have been describing.

It is no exaggeration to say that Pope's work, though less savage and incisive, is just as deeply involved (though unconsciously) in the repudiation through mockery of the traditional European genre system. As Swift followed the low road of the Hudibrastic tetrameter to deracinate empty traditions, Pope in a suave and Drydenesque heroic line did almost as much damage to the serious literary conventions of the past. Of the works of classical imitation that he created, only "Windsor-Forest" and "The Horatian Poems" (1733–8) could be said to be successful. This is an important point to consider. Pope and his contemporaries were unable to recreate either of the chief forms of Renaissance idealizing – the epic or the pastoral. His pastorals are cold and literary pastiche. For the epic, Pope turned to translation, and his manner of translating, brilliant as it can be, only helped to aggravate the sense that the epic was a thing of the past – something lost to the modern imagination. Pope helped to make those genres literary – part of the five-foot shelf of classics that every enlightened gentleman must appreciate at a distance. "Windsor-Forest" is more successful because it is a poem of the middle – the georgic. The poem ends in a defense of infant capitalism, which is a sign of a new world. It may seem glib to say so, but the wish of Bacon that we moderns discover a "georgics of the mind" to supplant the empty idols of the human imagination has in part come true in the Augustan age of mockery. Only the middle, the realm of the practical and mundane, could hold up under the pressures of Enlightenment. The mockery of epic and pastoral (and a host of other moribund kinds) led to a collapse into a unitary and dominant georgicism. Through the novel, the georgic element could enlarge its domain. This may help us understand the inevitable domination of the novelistic, the descriptive, the historical, and the pragmatic in the age that followed the death of Swift and Pope.

References and Further Reading

Anonymous (1977) The battle of the frogs and the mice, trans. H. G. Evelyn-White. In *Hesiod, The Homeric Hymns and Homerica*, pp. 542–63. Cambridge, MA: Harvard University Press.

Doody, M. (1992) *The Daring Muse*. Cambridge: Cambridge University Press.

Guilhamet, L. (1987) *Satire and the Transformation of Genre*. Philadelphia: University of Pennsylvania Press.

Parker, B. C. (1998) *The Triumph of Augustan Poetics: English Literary Culture from Butler to Johnson*. Cambridge: Cambridge University Press.

Paulson, R. (1967) *Fictions of Satire*. Baltimore, MD: The Johns Hopkins University Press

Purvis, C. J. (1991) *The Offensive Art: The Liberation of Poetic Imagination in Augustan Satire*. Doncaster: Brynmill.

Seidel, M. (1979) *Satiric Inheritance: Rabelais to Sterne*. Princeton, NJ: Princeton University Press.

Theordorakopoulos, E. (1997) Closure: the Book of Virgil. In C. Martindale (ed.), *The Cambridge Companion to Virgil*, pp. 155–60. Cambridge: Cambridge University Press.

Wilding, M. (1987) *The Last of the Epics*. New York: Oxford University Press.

26

Irony and Satire

Zoja Pavlovskis-Petit

Distinctions and Resemblances

There is no necessary connection between irony and satire; indeed, they would seem to exclude each other. Irony works through ambiguity, while satire must be plain and clear (albeit amusing) to make its point. Yet satire often makes irony its instrument or even its substance. Like innocence (which it does not in the least resemble), irony is a characteristic or an attitude; like malice (with which it can indeed have much in common), it is an intention. The word "satire" denotes neither a characteristic nor an intent. It is a way of expressing censure – a form. "I am reading – or writing – satire" is a straightforward statement; one cannot say "I am reading – or writing – irony" without sounding awkward and unclear. Yet "I enjoy irony" is a sentence as viable as "I enjoy satire."

Not everything is satirical; anything and everything can be made ironic or be perceived as ironic. For instance, the "Big Bang" theory aims to provide a scientific explanation of how the universe began; in no way is the theory a piece of satire. However, the Big Bang can abound in irony if that is one's choice. Aside from offering the ultimate instance of cosmic irony as we contemplate the nothingness of ourselves in the face of incomprehensible vastness, the very metaphor of the Big Bang has something inherently ironic about it: who was there to hear the "bang" or measure its scale? There is no end to the ways in which irony can select, seize upon, and manipulate its material by creating ambiguities and contradictions. Satire itself, intentionally ironic or not, may be ironically claimed to be a paradoxical endeavor, for it takes us into its confidence and expects us to share, or at least approve, its author's attitudes and judgments, and to agree with its analyses and criticism of what it regards as wrong – with humanity as a whole or with particular groups within it (such as women, or "dead white males," or clergy, or hypocrites, or cat fanciers – the list is endless) and their proclivities and practices. Yet at the same time, while we, as a satirist's audience, are assumed to be in agreement with what is being said, while the "others" (women, clergy, and so on) are left out of this bond of confidence, we may ask: what good does satire accomplish? After all, its classic professed aim is to improve the world by revealing what is wrong with it and convincing it to better its ways.

Then again, what if a woman does enjoy the wit of Juvenal's sixth *Satire* (directed against women) or a Pole relishes "Polish" jokes? Is not the very undertaking of satire ironically subverted by putting readers in the ambiguous position of standing outside what is being criticized even while they do not cease to be members of categories victimized by the satirist? To view the very undertaking of satire ironically would seem to frustrate it; but, paradoxically, it enriches our experience of it by allowing us to occupy the position of satire's prey, while, at the same time, sharing the joys of the hunter and, thereby, being complicitous in the games satirists play with us, with everyone else, and with themselves. Ultimately, the purpose of satire may be to alleviate a compulsion (or to pretend to): what Juvenal refers to when he says *difficile est saturam non scribere* ("it is difficult not to write satire"). But no matter what satire may or may not achieve, both it and irony are effective in providing an intellectual satisfaction whose important source is watching a subtle interaction between what is said, who says it, and how those addressed (including ourselves) react to it all. Being privy to knowledge not available to all is pivotal to all types of irony and satire.

Is irony a larger category than satire? Perhaps so. What is more important to note is that it is more pervasive. It is the nature of satire to be concerned with the generic. Satire does not allow exceptions to its sweeping pronouncements (such as "it is stupid for an old man to marry a young wife," or "anyone who spends money lavishly will run short," and so on). It would take a singularly dull mind to grapple with the question whether something is satirical or not. Irony, on the other hand, belongs to the individual, not the generic, both on the level of the author and that of the audience. In fact, each member of the latter may be faced with the need to decide for oneself if irony is present. What strikes you as ironic may not seem so to me, or not right now, or not in the same way. And how can you or I tell whether something is ironic? We may ask: is there such a thing as fate? We may allow fate to be a factor of human existence in reality, or only in our suspension of disbelief while reading a work informed by a sense of fate. In either case, we may further ask if fate is ironic. Thus, while reading Hardy's *Tess of the D'Urbervilles* (1891), we may be impressed by, or else indignantly reject, Hardy's adaptation of Greek tragic irony – or fail to note it; or enjoy the irony when re-reading the novel the second time but not the third. Then again, when contemplating our own lives, our view of the intricacies of circumstance and coincidence and causation may not be ironic at all: irony is a mental pleasure, and our feelings may militate against a sense of irony where objectivity and distance are difficult to achieve. No room for satire here either. I, as an individual, am likely to take myself too seriously to assume either the satiric or the ironic stance, separately or in combination – unless and until I fall into a Horatian mode. And yet the persona Horace wears as an ironic satirist is hardly the real Horace. Irony typically likes to conceal itself, unlike the self-assured and belligerent ego of satire.

Origin of Concepts

If we approach the distinction between satire and irony historically, we learn that the word "satire" (*satura*) is Latin (as Quintilian pointed out when he said *satura omnis nostra est*, "satire is entirely our [Roman] own"), while the concept of irony (*eironeia*) originates in ancient Greece. Indeed, effective satire has something Roman about it: the powerful, bold attack, the abundance of crudeness, the strong disapproval and rejection of anything that falls outside norms delineated by what is established as common sense; what works. Classical satire demands conformity to a standard of behavior and a conviction that life will be improved if people do what is right – and there is no doubt that right and wrong can, and should be, clearly defined. The satirist assumes a dictatorial authority; we are expected to believe that the satirist is absolutely right. Satire must have originated when human beings first developed a sense of the ridiculous and began to make fun of one another. Pointing a finger in derision is the most elementary form of satiric expression. The one who points makes a basic dissociation between his own superior character and behavior and those of others. The judge and the judged occupy discrete moral planes, and this difference cannot be ambiguous, just as issues of right and wrong cannot afford to be fuzzy in a court of law. The Roman mentality, with its talent for law and order and its penchant for gruff ridicule, took to satire exceptionally well and cultivated it with zest (for instance, even Roman surnames tended to originate in mockery: Ovid's cognomen Naso was undoubtedly due to an ancestor's extraordinary nose; Plautus' meant "flat-foot"; and so on); and it is for the most part from the Romans that the Western world inherited and derived this splendid way of dealing with whatever we dislike or object to.

Irony, despite its manifold forms, has a more traceable history than satire, and, unlike satire, it is rooted in indirection and subtlety. It is quintessentially Greek and comes in many varieties, as Greek city states did. Any distinction between right and wrong, or any moral sensitivity, has little to do with its genesis. It has proliferated ever since its ancient origins: witness our modern concept of dramatic or tragic irony, which was not formulated as "irony" until the Romantic era; or cosmic irony, also not regarded as such before that period. Originally, the word *eiron* ("ironist" or "ironic person") denoted a rather despicable fellow who would pretend to underestimate himself and seek to dupe others into doing so. Dickens's Uriah Heep can serve as a modern example. Satire seeks to tell the truth, however slanted or exaggerated; irony, even in its somewhat limited origins, was an intentional lie. The pre-Socratic ironist had no admirable or redeeming features. In discussions of human tendencies or peculiarities, he was merely a taxonomic entity. It is in that capacity that he is included in catalogues of excessive forms of behavior, such as those that have come down to us in Aristotle's *Nicomachean Ethics* or Theophrastus's *Characters*. Both these works attest to the endurance of the early type of ironist, whose redemption, however, set in with Socrates.

As Plato presents him in his *Dialogues*, Socrates is the first notable example of an admirable *eiron*, although there are several passages where Plato shows Socrates' exasperated interlocutors testily accusing him of being the earlier type of ironist. The reader, though, knows that, despite Socrates' ironic assertions of ignorance, and thus inferiority, he is yet in his own view superior to other people in that he *knows* he does not know, and they do not possess this knowledge. Thus a paradox is created, and irony becomes profound and worth an intelligent person's effort to create and sustain – or react to and still sustain. Not every paradox can be viewed as ironic (for instance, a mathematical paradox such as a Moebius strip or a Klein bottle is intriguing and self-contradictory but hardly ironic), but the kind basic to Socrates' philosophy presages the classic definition of irony, as formulated by Scaliger among many others: two (or more) equally valid meanings contradicting one another. And still another notable feature of irony becomes first evident with Socrates: puzzled and bewildered when confronted with irony, we may, and often do, take recourse to what we know of the ironist's character and interpret what is said accordingly, although, as we shall see further on, this test may fail us.

It does hold for Socrates, a thoroughly admirable man and a seeker for truth, albeit in ironic ways; but all our enthusiasm for his character still does not obviate difficulties of interpretation. In Plato's *Symposium*, one of the supreme masterpieces of all of literature, and all of philosophy, we find a polyphony (to use a Bakhtinian term) of voices and discourses that contradict one another, yet none of them makes it possible to reject out of hand any of the others. In its own terms, each of the speeches on love makes sense and is a literary masterpiece, even though it would be perverse to insist on being unaware that Plato presents Socrates' speech as the most profound – until it too is ironically undercut by the appearance of the drunk Alcibiades, who makes the subject plummet down from the heights of Diotima's discourse. Still, through its wholehearted esteem and approval of Socrates, and the latter's good-humored acceptance of it, Alcibiades' speech manages to offer the reader yet another marvelously enriching and rewarding view of what love may be. No wonder St Augustine claimed that he was first inflamed with passion for philosophy when he read the *Symposium*.

Horatian *vs* Juvenalian Satire

Still, would anyone call Socrates a satirist? Although Alcibiades likens him to a satyr (and one of the possible etymologies of the Latin word *satura* is derived from the mythical personage), and although Socrates must have attracted a lot of dislike by frequently "showing up" the victims of his relentless dialectic, his aims and methods are not identical with those of the satirist. The victim of Socratic irony is his complicitous – willing or unwilling – interlocutor; the reader as the latter's standby; and also the reader as someone who has been let in on Socrates' game. The philosopher's aim surely is to enlighten and thus improve humanity, and that is the ostensible aim of satire as well. However, he differs from a satirist in questioning rather than prescribing, asking questions rather than laying down the law.

A merger of irony with satire finds its first notable expression in the Roman Horace. Although indebted to earlier satirists such as Lucilius (of whose work only fragments remain), Horace seems to have derived from his beloved *Socratici libri* ("Socratic books," meaning the works of Plato) a way of using irony as a pedagogic tool for showing what is wrong with the world or the many various types of humanity that inhabit it. It is worth noting that Horace called his satires *sermones* ("conversations"), thus avoiding the hodge-podge implications of the Lucilian *satura* (since another possible etymology of *satura* is derived from a mixed salad of some kind) and, perhaps, evoking not only the civilized atmosphere of the Scipionic circle but the urbanity of Plato's dialogues as well. Assuming an ironically self-deprecating stance reminiscent of Socrates', though perhaps not directly inherited from him, Horace makes fun of human beings' folly, and of his own into the bargain. What is perhaps most attractive – and most ironic – about his mode of expression is that he creates a fascinating contradiction between his persona as Horace the protégé of Maecenas, the owner of a modest farm, a man who owns some outspoken slaves and goes for walks in the Forum, where he is victimized by a bore, and so on; and Horace the judge of what is right or wrong behavior. As the latter, he is infallible – but even in that role he gives most of the credit for his powers of discernment to his father (*Serm.* 1.6). The latter, although he no doubt had his son's admiration, we yet know only as a literary device used by the son to explain and validate his abilities and authority. The inherent ironic circularity this creates should be evident and offers, perhaps, the best example of Horace's genius in uniting self-deprecating irony with assured satire. Why should we accept Horace's claim to right judgment when it is not even his own, we might say, but taken from a man who is basically yet another character in Horace's discourse? But even as we enjoy the playful contradiction, it is clear where we stand. Horace is right, and we believe him.

Thus, satire evidently testifies to the fallibility of its author, who engagingly shows he is one of us, a part of imperfect humanity. Still, humanity should be improved by his comments, just as he himself is – but not permanently – by the comments of a recalcitrant slave (*Serm.* 2.7). All the factors in such a complex of ironies seem perfectly arranged for our delectation as we grasp their intricacies and contradictions. But do we? The reader of satire, whom the satirist has taken into his confidence, is assumed to be as intelligent as the writer; but if satire is didactic – and no literary form is more so except straightforward sermons – then the reader may have been duped, or at the very least, the reader's position is ambiguously poised between the author's voice of reason (whatever its origin) and the world's unreason. (For pure reason may be beyond our reach: already in the *Symposium* we find an ascription to higher authority when Socrates claims to be quoting the no-doubt-fictional, divinely inspired Diotima.)

There are two main types of classical satire: the Horatian and the Juvenalian. For reasons discussed above, all satire may be seen as inherently ironic, but the involved and complex ironies of Horace and others who adopt his mode (Erasmus is an example of a Horatian satirist; see below) furnish much greater enjoyment to anyone with a penchant for being teased than do Juvenal and his like (such as Samuel Johnson, to name but one). There is no room for suspecting that the latter type of satirist is hiding behind the Horatian mask of an easy-going, fallible, even friendly, fellow talking to us with ironic humility even while concealing the sharpness of his observation and inveigling us into a belief that all that is going on is a friendly conversation. A Juvenalian voice is that of an unimpeachable judge. Even though the reader is still taken into the satirist's confidence, open and angry indignation rather than crafty indirection is what we are made privy to. We hear a Roman brutality. The satirist is no longer an all-too-human being who inhabits the world he criticizes, although typically he still speaks in the first person or else lets a character do so for him. If one is drawn to irony, one will find it anywhere and everywhere, but the satisfaction of reading Horace with his fusion of Roman directness and Greek subtlety is greater for such a seeker than Juvenal will provide. This is not to say that the one is a more outstanding satirist than the other but that they are different in the degree to which irony is part of their manner.

Increasing Complexity: Irony and Allegory

We have mentioned that satire may pretend to be a monologue by a character the satirist has introduced. Perhaps the most remarkable instance of this device is found in Erasmus' *The Praise of Folly* (1511). Here we have a marvelously intricate interplay among the author of the work, the sharp-witted humanist Erasmus; the allegorical figure of Folly, who serves as his mouthpiece; and the several different roles Folly plays as she delivers her discourse. The stages in her development from a humorous but shallow observer of foibles to a stern and forthright delator, who directs a stream of relentless accusations against the failings of the Church, form a masterpiece of irony in the course of which the very meaning of folly is transformed. The speaker assumes a sequence of personae ranging from a carnivalesque entertainer, who abuses many of the time-honored commonplaces of medieval satire (besotted lovers, drunks, and so on), to a proponent of true Christianity as the highest form of folly, namely, an abandonment of a common-sense kind of reason such as is favored, or at least paid lip service to, by such fools as we all are. Yet, the transformation of the speaker by no means proceeds in a straight line. Even early on there are intimations and anticipatory hints of what is to come, and at the end of the discourse Folly deconstructs the seriousness of her observations by reverting to her role as a typically silly woman. Still, as in Horace's satires, so here, the reader is meant to enjoy the foolery but not expected to be unaware of where the satirist's thrusts are directed, nor miss the difference between right and wrong, of which the satirist is an altogether trustworthy judge. Worthy heir to Socratic and to Horatian subtlety and wit, Erasmus is clearly a Christian believer, and his intent is to enlighten us as believers even while his creature Folly playfully serves this purpose. Horace's principle, *ludentem dicere verum* ("playfully to say what is true"), in an ambivalently self-deprecating way puts Erasmus in the rank of supreme ironists – and satirists. Because the self-deprecation he employs is amusing, it makes the message less offensive. However, we know full well that the dichotomy between the deliberately exploited frailty of the speaker and the correctness of what is said is not intended to mislead us. If it does, we are fools indeed in the most literal sense of the word.

Erasmus uses the medieval allegorical figure of Folly but endows unilinear allegory with a complexity it had not been capable of before. It is basic to allegory that it involves two or more meanings which do not contradict each other; with irony, the meanings always counter one another. Erasmus manages to combine the two mutually exclusive figures. His introduction to *The Praise of Folly* is an ironic masterpiece in itself, playing games with the persona of the author and, at the same time, that of Thomas More, to whom the work is dedicated. This preface allows us to see Erasmus standing outside the satire proper, all of which is spoken by Folly, yet behaving like, and unlike, her. No such concession is allowed to the reader, or to the satirist's own person by himself, in an ironically even more complex satire, Swift's *Gulliver's Travels* (1726). The earlier sections of this book are relatively easy to interpret, but the meaning of the final part, Book IV, is notoriously impenetrable. All we can know for certain is that the Yahoos are disgusting brutes. But, are they not natural? And, is not living in conformity with nature, without the falseness of civilization, one of the most prominent ideals of Swift's time, and indeed prominent throughout Book IV? The Houyhnhnms in their rationality are the complete opposite of the Yahoos and thus admirable. But, is not their totally sound mind pitilessly devoid of charity and difficult, if not impossible and even undesirable, for human beings, flawed as they are? And, is this good or bad, or is the very question irrelevant because it cannot be answered, especially by beings whose reason is imperfect?

It would appear that Gulliver himself, caught up between the two extremes, should represent the quasi-Aristotelian Golden Mean so beloved of classical satire. When we find ourselves facing a pair of extremes that cannot coexist, we desire to find a middle ground. Perhaps the greatest satisfaction classical satire affords is that it elicits and satisfies this need by clearly identifying extreme forms of behavior and then allows us to believe, at least while we are reading, that moderation is possible, and that moderation is for what the world should strive. Even so complex a satire as that which comes out of the mouth of Erasmus' Janus-faced Folly implies the existence of an elusive but nonetheless real Good. Her references to Pauline theology are an anchor that firmly holds Erasmus' satire to Christian convictions, which are one thing of which we can be sure that he is sure of. Swift provides no certainty of that kind. He savagely deprives us of any illusion that there is a right path, even though, like Erasmus, he too uses allegory ironically as his satiric vehicle. But, his allegories are no longer clearly identifiable. They do not bear abstract terms as their names but are identified as hitherto unfamiliar peoples discovered by a European far away from those lands where his and our stereotypes of the French, or the Levantines, or the Chinese, could provide a starting-point for dealing with anything outlandish.

Such a starting-point may be faulty, but to writers and to the audience of satire it is indispensable, for satire of its very nature deals in generalizations. It may reject them in showing how deplorable "type casting" can be, but we are on firm ground because we recognize all the while just what are the accepted, or the rejected, definitions. We do not have that sort of help toward developing a final understanding of the Yahoos or the Houyhnhnms. What we read encourages us to see them as apes and horses, but while the fable has always made use of animal characters for illustrating to what human beings are prone, full-fledged satire is seldom able to sustain such a device. (There are a few exceptions, such as Orwell's *Animal Farm* [1945]. Like Swift, Orwell is bitter and brilliant, but he leaves no doubts about his meaning. *Animal Farm* takes a definite moral stance and is a typical satire in this.) The hopeless, despairing ambiguity of Swift's satire does not even pretend to offer any possibility of hope for the human race. After leaving the island, Gulliver cannot tolerate other humans but sees them as Yahoos; that is, he objectifies himself as them. At the end of the tale, he can endure no society except that of his horses. Is he a bearer of impossibly high ideals or has he sunk to the level of an animal – or both? Like the also deeply ironic Delphic oracle, Swift leaves interpretation entirely up to us. What we make of his ambiguity is a revelation of who we are. Our character is our destiny in our existence as human beings and as critics too (as is that of the dramatically ironic Sophoclean hero). Unlike our position as readers of limpid classical satire, where we enjoy the illusion that the victims of satire are distinct from ourselves, in reading Erasmus, and even more so Swift, we are victims of ironies practiced by the satirist – as is everyone else – and are unable to extricate ourselves. Satire and irony become fused, and our roles as victims of the one coincide with our victimization by the other. There is no way out for Swift or for us. The prevailing mood is despair, rather than the pleasingly constructive programs for improvement favored by either Horace or Juvenal.

Irony in the Satiric Novel

One might think that satiric irony could go no further than it does with Swift. Only half a century later, however, a work such as Laurence Sterne's *Tristram Shandy* (1760–7) raises problems even more bewildering. This is a book full of ironic wit and whimsy. There are many satiric elements in it, such as the fun it makes of recognizable human peculiarities, but does this make it a satire? Notable for raising fragmentation of meaning and of composition to a level unimaginable before and, for this reason, beloved and endlessly imitated by those lovers of the fragmentary, the Romantics, *Tristram Shandy* generously uses satiric caricature and ironically teases the reader while doing so. Much of the pleasure in reading this book results from our enjoyment of being tricked. Sterne asserts his authority by making us his accomplices in flitting from one apparent triviality to another, violating all the while any dictates of time and logic. Our reason is split into two: we distrust such infractions even while we playfully acquiesce to them; in fact, reason is abandoned even while it delights in its own abandonment. Has the high moral intent of satire been given up in favor of flippancy? Is this still satire? But then has not satire always brought up masses of small nothings in order to build up a picture of the real world in all its innumerable details and then attack and tear it apart for its faults? (Juvenal's "light summer ring" in *Sat.* 1.28 is one of a myriad of examples.) And, after all, who is the butt of Sterne's ironic humor? Not the elusive Tristram himself, who is not even born until well into the story and then disappears from it; and the other characters are more amusing than castigated. The irony lies in playing with the text as if it had a stable identifiable meaning, and playing with the reader who, willy-nilly, will seek for meaning, be continuously frustrated, and love being at wits' end. If indeed we choose to read this bewildering book as mainly satirical, the satire may be directed mainly at the processes of writing and reading and the illusions writers and readers are involved in. Irony has grown to the point where even the status and quality of satire become difficult to recognize.

A proto-Romantic book such as *Tristram Shandy*, then, subjects us to a lack of certainty about how to take what we read. Many works of high realism, such as the novels of Tolstoy, or George Eliot, or many others, are, and should be, read as mirrors of identifiable reality; to do otherwise would be perverse. (But see below on Chekhov.) Yet, beginning with the Romantic era and continuing up to the present, links between irony and satire that are patent (though complex) in the earlier periods, and unquestionably intended by the author, come to be left to the reader's discretion. Even a classicizing novelist, such as Jane Austen, a sharp-eyed satirist in the eighteenth-century mode, whose command of irony is the equal of any of her predecessors, surpasses Fielding and his eighteenth-century contemporaries in effective indirection. It is probably an intentional irony on Austen's part that the reader can be gulled into reading her novels primarily as romances. Many of the most devoted "Janeites" read and re-read her, captivated by her marvelous characterizations, lightness and surety of style, entertaining situations, and, finally, the satisfactory resolution of each story as the main female character and her most fitting admirer achieve what we are meant to assume will be a happy marriage.

But it can be argued that we are so enticed by all these delights and become so comfortable in our enjoyment of a quasi-fairytale (and why should we not? as Mary Bennett might ask) that we lose sight of Austen's pitilessly keen view of human nature and human fallibility, which she understands but never forgives. We, however, thankful for the diversion and amusement, are at liberty to be lenient. The heroine of her finest novel, Emma, is very flawed, and so is Fanny of *Mansfield Park*, though less obviously than Emma; and so are all the others, with the possible exception of Elizabeth Bennett, who in true eighteenth-century fashion is no mean satirist herself yet makes horrendous errors in misjudging people. Perhaps the most ironic repercussion of Austen's novels, which, however, does not directly flow out of their inherently ironic manner, is the proliferation of so-called "Regency romances," feeble imitations of some of the most masterly narratives in all of literature. These are popular for the same reasons for which the genuine article is enjoyed by so many: love stories in a genteel setting and with a reassuringly predictable outcome. The kind of romance that Austen parodied has come back full circle to its prototype even as it preserves the trappings of parody that the common reader (and probably the writer) is unaware was there. This is a rather crude but amusing result of the ironic games Austen plays with her readers, sharing her satire with them to the extent of their capacity for irony. It is up to us to be ironically engaged or else remain obtuse. But, can one be obtuse on purpose? As always, the ability to perceive irony is something we either do or do not have. If the latter is the case, we are not conscious of our lack, and is not that a rich source of ironic enjoyment for someone else? Even trickier, we may not know just how much irony is actually there and how much we are entitled to create for ourselves. (As Booth [1974] points out, knowing "where to stop" can be a major problem.)

This brings us to our next example. The traditional reading of Gogol's *The Overcoat*, all through pre-Revolutionary Russian criticism and then during the Soviet era, made much of the social comment the novella makes and the pity it engenders for the oppressed Akaki Akakievich. Gogol's exaggerating humor firmly puts this story, as most of his others, in the category of satire, even while – to refer to Belinsky's perpetually quoted remark – we laugh through tears. By 1842, when Gogol wrote this astonishing masterpiece, classical verse satire, already moribund when modern Russian literature began to develop, was no longer an option for any critic of human folly or social ills, and so in Russia as elsewhere the satiric voice found expression in prose fiction, as well as, in Russia notably, stage works. Readers looked to the novel or the novella for critical comment and exposure of abuses and misuses surrounding them, and Russian literature probably more than any other was dominated by a demand for social consciousness and social responsibility. In reading, one can always find what one looks for; hence, the almost exclusive tendency to see the amusing and fantastical, indeed surreal, *Overcoat* as mainly a plea for the downtrodden and a document advocating more humane treatment of the poor and disadvantaged. It would be foolhardy to argue that such are not some of the most important aims of this perplexingly intricate story, but intricate it is, and critics who concentrate on the most immediately obvious overlay of satire close their eyes to other layers of signification.

It is difficult to miss how Gogol makes Akaki pitiful, but insisting that social conditions alone make him so ignores other, deeply ironic, aspects of the tale. For instance, a reader may experience an ironic split even while accepting the dominant interpretation, but at the same time viewing Akaki as subhuman, a sort of automaton programmed from birth (even his name hints at "shit") to exist devoid of anything that could be seen as mind or soul. The one love of his life is a nonhuman object, a coat! On still another level (and they all are seamlessly fused), the story may be read as a grotesque satire on that figure beloved by the Orthodox Church and by Russian folklore – the *iurodivy* or "fool in Christ," a figure that has more than a little in common with Erasmus' *Folly*. (Both descend from the ironic Pauline passage on faith in Christ as "folly.") If this interpretation runs counter to what is most widely accepted, so much the better. The ironic disagreement among meanings augments and enriches the satire.

From the isolated Akaki of *The Overcoat* it is but a step to Dostoevsky's alienated antihero in *Notes from Underground* (1864), a work not ostensibly satirical but certainly one that invites a lover of satire to see in it a harsh indictment of nihilism, a philosophical position with which the author had a constant love/hate relationship. While Gogol is vastly amusing, Dostoevsky exhibits a bilious attitude toward his "underground" man, who is dead serious about himself. Surely we too are meant to take this unappealing character seriously. Readers may or may not choose to exercise irony here. If we opt for an existential view of the narrator's predicaments and self-analysis, we may find ourselves so caught up in the pain he feels that any sense of drollery or desire to laugh will be difficult to come by. Irony, after all, is a mental pleasure, and if our emotions are strongly worked upon, any access to irony may be blocked. In reading *The Overcoat*, too, we may be so moved as to decide against irony, commiserate with Akaki and indulge in unrealizable hopes that if only he could be better paid, or if only the authorities had taken a more humane view of his plight, he would be all right. This would be a naïve reading, but one not closed to us, although Gogol's zany humor militates against such a limitation.

With *Notes from Underground* we are more likely to get caught up in the central character's sufferings because a feeling of empathy with the narrator is almost inevitable when we are dealing with an account in the first person. Thus, the irony available to us in reading such a work is of a different kind: it is produced by the split between our emotive self, which merges with the tormented speaker, and our critical faculty, which judges him and his words, and our own reactions to it all. And, how are we to tell whether the author of the story is not playing games with us? A neurotic split between perceiving the "underground" man as caught up in the human condition, as we all are, and a dislike and rejection of him (and thus of ourselves?) is probably the most common reaction to the unwholesome narrator. Is such a contradiction irony, or akin to it? As an analogy, we may invoke the existential parables of Kierkegaard, which make the readers their laughingstock but ironically expect the same readers to see through what they are subjected to, and enjoy the derision. Kierkegaard's accomplishments as a satirist, above all in the parables, are considerable, and fraught with irony; in this he can be compared to a philosopher he admired above all, Socrates. The uses of irony in philosophy after Plato deserve a fuller treatment than the scope of the present chapter affords. Let us only say here, that while Socrates is a superb ironist, he is hardly a satirist; on the other hand, Kierkegaard and some others, such as Nietzsche, can claim the double distinction. (It may be noted that in his detestation of Romantic irony, such as that of F. Schlegel in *Lucinde* [1799], and in his biting wit, Kierkegaard represents a latter-day manifestation of a classic type of irony. Romantic irony involves infinite negation, and although this is one of irony's most fascinating forms, it has little to do with satire.)

Irony – Yes; Satire? The Plot Thickens

While misunderstanding a writer's intention, we may ironically see satire where it may not have been intended, or else – and this would be ironic to someone evaluating our response but not to us – we may miss the satire altogether. *Notes from Underground* may be a case in point, but Chekhov's story *Dushechka* (1899, translated as *The Darling* or *The Angel*) can furnish an even more interesting example of such odd but by no means uncommon responses. It would appear, clearly, that the story satirizes a woman's inability to live except for, and through, other people, notably men. But is this, ultimately, clear? Those who know this woman refer to her as a "darling." The Russian word conveys a slight tinge of condescension, but she does not seem to mind. Is it an ironic joke on Chekhov's part to compel us to think of her, and refer to her, as her acquaintances do? Selflessness is her most notable characteristic. She lavishes love and care upon her two husbands, the lover she has after she is widowed a second time, and the lover's child; and is even ready, had she the opportunity, to do the same for the lover's wife. We do not really know their feelings toward the "darling," but they fully accept her kindness. Tolstoy so admired her generous character that he included the story in his *Russian Readers* as an exemplary model of unselfishness, rather than a satire. There can be no doubt of Tolstoy's intelligence, although at the time he was working on these anthologies he was already putting his mind at the service of a set of convictions that among other things led him to reject Shakespeare as immoral. We can make up our own minds about experiencing Chekhov's story in whatever way seems to make most sense to us. What brings irony into play here for many of us is that, with Tolstoy, we admire the "darling," but we also wonder what is to become of her once the child she is caring for will leave her, perhaps to fulfill her dreams for him – to become a respected professional, own an imposing house, and so on. What will keep her going when she no longer has a loved one to fill and mold her life? A feminist reader may go further and experience a reaction completely opposite to Tolstoy's, an urge to cry out to this malleable "darling": "Go get a life!" And this response too is intelligent and aware of the satiric irony that makes this story unforgettable. Which position is the most preferable? The most fully ironic one, harboring irreconcilable opposites without giving up either, is the richest and most rewarding, to an ironist *and* a lover of satire.

So much for the ambivalence of goodness. If selflessness becomes suspect (and what post-Freudian reader, if at all sophisticated, will allow it to be wholly good?), then are we not moving perilously close to cynicism? Can cynicism be a form of irony? Can it be a vehicle for satire? These are questions this chapter cannot afford to deal with, but it may be appropriate to consider at least one work of fiction that skirts satire but is too whimsical to be considered even remotely didactic, as all satire at least purports to be. Isak Dinesen's *The Monkey* (1934), probably the most enigmatic of her tales, is a good example of this sort of narrative. Dinesen has been accused of cynically ignoring meaning; she certainly has a satirist's sharp eye, but what is it she sees, and what does she make us see? Her wondrously satiric sallies and the sly humor that shapes each of the characters and enchants the reader is mystifyingly ironic. Some elements of the story are ironies of a kind that we can readily grasp; for instance, the failure of the genteel cloistered ladies to understand Boris's homosexuality. But the ultimate meaning of this remarkably well constructed narrative hinges on our reaction to the Prioress and her pet, and even while we take in the final transformation, we are left with a sense that what has happened is ineluctable. It is magic. Unless magicians themselves, the audience cannot see through a performer's tricks, only relish their execution – and the fact that they have been taken in. Such pleasures attend our experience of all irony, but not of satire. Satire has an axe to grind, and there can be no uncertainty about what is to fall to the axe; although with some of the satirical works discussed here, what is being chopped down may be not only the tree right in front of our noses but a whole grove. Ironically, though invited to lose sight of the forest while focusing on one tree, we, at the same time, remain aware of the rest of the growth and are, perhaps, even put at a loss as to which of the other trees are doomed to fall, and why and why not, and so on. If Dinesen satirizes anyone at all, it is the reader, who has been hoodwinked into following the tale into its incomprehensible, though pleasing, resolution.

Another ironist, no less fascinating than she, is Vladimir Nabokov. He too creates ambiguities so rich that we cannot be sure of our ability to grasp them fully. At times it is tempting to suspect that the irony may be only in the mind of the reader, but more likely it rests with the author and indeed may never be accessible to anyone else. For this writer is ultimately penetrable only to some depth; for the rest, one would have to become Nabokov himself, that is, possess the same trilingualism (Russian, English, French) and the same backlog of literary culture and references. It is easy to see him deriving a diabolic pleasure from playing cat-and-mouse games in deprecating (that is, satirizing?) his readers' ineptitude more than they are capable of realizing. To limit ourselves to just one example of this kind of sadism, out of an uncountable enormous number: how many English-speaking readers of his *Ada* (1968), written in English, can he have expected to catch the full significance of the reference to an oak that belongs to a species he invents, "*Quercus ruslan* Chât" (Part 2, ch. 7)? This is obfuscation of the highest order. The term *quercus* is the correct taxonomic Latin for an oak, but the other words in this fantastic construct become understandable only if one detects the allusion to a magical cat, playfully translated into French as *chat* (and pretending to be a designation of a cultivar); a cat that is familiar to the Russian (but not the English) speaker as the animal that is chained to an oak in the introduction to Pushkin's poem *Ruslan and Ludmila* – hence the species designation *ruslan*. (I am currently at work on a monograph dealing with Nabokov's multilingualism as a source and form of irony.) Nabokov is having fun hiding behind a mock-scientific allusion that misleads the unwary. But is he satiric? Leaving aside the professed aim of satire to teach humanity what to avoid, Nabokov's private ironies may be seen as satirical because like all satirists he makes fun of ignorance. What is different in his work (and to some extent in Dinesen's) is the lack of assurance to the readers that they occupy a privileged position while being taken into the satirist's confidence. The moment of pleasure experienced at the recognition of a conundrum, such as the one involving the bogus oak, is paid for by the reflection that many, if not most, of the other private jokes Nabokov allows himself are beyond our reach. With Sterne as their precursor, modern writers exemplified by Dinesen and Nabokov are satirists with a difference – taking the readers as the objects of their ridicule – and are certainly ironic.

Some Reflections on the Contemporary Scene

Within the realm of the written word, the non-satirical, or not predominantly satirical, irony is thriving. The contemporary version of nihilism that is deconstruction can be seen as deeply ironic (and is not irony essentially a kind of deconstruction?) because the interplay of potentially infinite meanings creates a vertiginous multitude of alternatives in which, as in Borges' fictional library, the victimized reader is at the mercy of the ironist even while enjoying the victimization, and is everlastingly invited to create his or her own ironies. Whether knowing or unaware, the ironist's audience is always complicitous in what is being perpetrated upon it. It would seem that the territory irony claims for itself becomes wider and wider with time. Cosmic despair was not conceived as ironic before the Romantic age, nor did the concept so familiar to us as "dramatic irony" exist until 1833. (Formulated by Bishop Connop Thirlwall, "On the Irony of Sophocles"; the first sentence of this essay reads: "some readers may be a little surprised to see *irony* attributed to a tragic poet.")

Satire is still with us, and still relatively easy to define, but irony continues to lay claims to territories far away from the satiric, and this tendency may delimit satire. It is possible that the urbanity of ironic satire has largely disappeared with the spread of democracy and universally available schooling. One would be ill advised to fault either of these modern phenomena, but with the shrinking of the highly educated literary elite proportionately to the size of the public addressed by satire, in order to have its desired impact satire cannot afford to be bewilderingly subtle; irony can, for it does not bear a burden of political and social responsibility, which has always been satire's. Hence the increasing use in the past two centuries of pictorial caricature to make a political point; and since the invention of film, that medium too has been utilized with splendid effect to make the sort of comment on human nature, society, and the responsibility of human interactions that used to be confined within the domain of literature. (This is not to discount the importance and effectiveness of pictorial satire in previous ages; for instance, much of Bosch's and Hogarth's work.) Film can be devastatingly ironic in its satire – Luis Buñuel is probably the best example of a director who has effectively expressed his censure ironically – but, by and large, contemporary satire tends toward the Juvenalian rather than the Horatian pole, toward invective rather than self-deprecation. A film such as *Fahrenheit 9/11* (2004), powerful denunciation that it is, and with splendid moments of satirical ridicule, cannot afford even to seem ambiguous. Some of the issues it tackles are inherently ambivalent, but the point of view is clearly defined; the director makes no bones about what he means and leaves the viewer no choice but a very plain one: accept the criticism or not.

REFERENCES AND FURTHER READING

A bibliography of irony must be, ironically, diffuse. Even the link between irony and satire continues to be treated in so many publications that it would be a Herculean task to deal fully with the matter. The most outstanding studies of irony are still those of Wayne Booth, *A Rhetoric of Irony* (Chicago: University of Chicago Press, 1974), and D. C. Muecke, *The Compass of Irony* (London: Methuen, 1969). Richard Rorty has done much with the subject of the role of irony in political versus private life; see especially his *Contingency, Irony, and Solidarity* (Cambridge: Cambridge University Press, 1989). Without sinking into ironic self-deprecation, I would like to mention two of my own publications on the subject of irony and satire: Zoja Pavlovskis, "Aristotle, Horace, and the Ironic Man," *Classical Philology* 63 (1968), 22–41; and *The Praise of Folly: Structure and Irony* (Leiden: Brill, 1983).

27
Mock-biblical Satire from Medieval to Modern
Michael F. Suarez

Until recently, literary historians had not spent much time studying how the Bible has been used as a vehicle for satire. Yet, as the following pages will show, satirists have been adroitly exploiting sacred Scripture for many centuries to make their attacks more forceful, funny, and memorable. This chapter, which aims to provide the reader with a far-ranging introduction to the history and behavior of a most lively (and still living) satirical species, is divided into five parts. It begins with an overview and schematic, historical survey of verbal and visual mock-biblical satires before considering four different ways that the mock biblical operates: by quotation, imitation, transformation, and the creation of typological correspondences. Each mock-biblical method is treated by giving sustained attention to an historical example. This twin method of providing both a comprehensive view and a series of close investigations should help the reader develop a sense of the remarkable breadth and the ingenious inner-workings of the mock biblical.

Overview and Historical Survey

The mock biblical is a rhetorical strategy deploying scriptural quotations, typologies, or tropes for satirical ends. The efflorescence of mock-biblical satire in England was in many ways the product of the Restoration era: the popularization of politics in the late 1670s and 1680s, the formation of political parties, increased pamphleteering, and the burgeoning newspaper trade all meant that Tory and Whig propagandists alike needed to find a satirical vehicle with broad appeal. Being the *lingua franca* of English culture, the Bible suited that purpose better than any other form of established writing because of its unrivaled cultural currency. In contrast, knowledge of Greek and Latin literature was available only to the privileged few. The Bible's vast stock of images, catch phrases, and characters could be easily manipulated to suit almost any situation: the quarrel between Alexander Pope and Lewis Theobald over the editing of Shakespeare, for example, was cast as the episode of Cain and Abel in *Dean Jonathan's Parody On the 4th Chapter of Genesis* (1729), an anonymous work by Edward Roome. Because virtually every person who could read had read the Scriptures – in the Authorized (or King James) Version – all of Roome's audience would have easily perceived that the Pope/Cain character was the villain and the Theobald/Abel figure was the innocent victim. Roome's clever parody of a well-known biblical episode relies on the reader's close acquaintance with the sacred page and exploits that familiarity for comic and satirical ends.

Satirical prints also frequently capitalized on the virtually universal accessibility of biblical images and ideas. The foolishness of George II, for instance, was mockingly portrayed as the wisdom of Solomon in such works as *Court and Country... with the Cheats of Rabbi Robbin{,} Prime Minister to King Solomon* (1735, BM 2140) and *Solomon in his Glory* (1738, BM 2348). In a different vein, the self-serving schemes of the politician Charles James Fox were ridiculed as *The Temptation in the Wilderness* (1783, BM 6278), a satire that characterized the proposals in his India Bill as akin to Satan's attempts to beguile Christ in the desert with false enticements. (Throughout this chapter, the "BM" numbers following the titles of prints refer to Stephens and George [1978], *Catalogue of Prints and Drawings in the British Museum*.)

Because scriptural texts can never be wholly divorced from their authoritative context, appropriating the Bible to satirize the world of human vice and folly typically gives the mock biblical a special sting: the distance between tenor and vehicle, like the two ends of the archer's bow, adds power to the satirist's arrow. Exploiting sacred Scripture both as a satirical vehicle for ridicule and as a normative force for reform, mock-biblical satire frequently bears a double valence that makes it an especially effective polemical weapon. Thus, even though the mock biblical is akin to the mock epic in exploiting disjunctions between text and context, matter and manner, and the ideal versus the real, mock-biblical satire differs significantly from the mock epic in that it rarely ridicules the Bible itself. The normative status of Scripture is most often an essential element in mock-biblical satire, not least because it allows the satirist to enlist the authority of Holy Writ for his own polemical ends.

Mock-biblical satire may be traced back to medieval writings against ignorance and corruption in the Roman Catholic Church, including rhymed sermons, mock prophecies, and even political plainchant. Among the most important scriptural satires of the era are the *Apocalypsis Goliae* (*The Apocalypse of Golias*, twelfth century), an anti-monastic satire based on the Book of Revelation, and the *Evangelium Secundum Marcas Argenti* (*Gospel According to the Mark of Silver*, thirteenth century) – the most famous of the "money-gospels" satirizing ecclesiastical greed because of its inclusion in the *Carmina Burana* (and found in many versions throughout the Middle Ages).

John Skelton's *Speke, Parott* (1522) is one of the earliest sustained instances in English of a satire on secular affairs incorporating biblical images and ideas. During the Reformation, Lucas Cranach ("the Elder") and other artists, working in consort with Luther, effectively deployed the mock biblical against Rome in satirical woodcuts that reached a broad audience. Luther himself authored mock-biblical satires: his parody of the First Psalm, "Blessed is the man that hath not walked in the way of the Sacramentarians, nor sat in the seat of the Zwinglians, nor followed the Council of the Zurichers," engages with the politico-religious controversies of his day. His *Sendbrief vom Dolmetschen* (*An Open Letter on Translating*, 1530), an attack on the Roman Catholic establishment, includes a remarkable passage that cleverly adapts 2 Cor. 11: 16–23 to his own ends. The Roman Catholics replied in kind. Johann Cochlaeus (whom Luther called Dr Rotzlöffel [Dr Snot-nose] in the *Sendbrief*) wrote a parody of the gospel account of the birth of Jesus filled with innuendo about the sexual morality of Luther's mother and the true paternity of his father. Fortunately, most other Counter-Reformation satires in the mock-biblical mode were more theological in their arguments.

The English Civil War, fought both on battlefields and in pamphlets, produced satires invoking the Bible from Parliamentarians and Royalists alike. John Cleveland's *The Rebell Scott* (1647) and the anonymous *Ecce the New Testament of our Lords and Saviours, the House of Commons at Westminster* (1648) are among the most successful of such productions. It is during the Restoration and eighteenth century, however, that the mock biblical reached its apogee as a mode of popular political satire. Just as Cromwell and his followers had employed the Scriptures to establish a divine warrant for his rule, so too did his adversaries marshal biblical blunderbusses against him once the Commonwealth had ended. Of the many Restoration satires, John Dryden's "Absalom and Achitophel" (1681) was especially instrumental in propelling the mock biblical into the mainstream of partisan political writing. A flood of typological political and ecclesiastical satires soon followed Dryden's success – including works by Elkanah Settle, Nahum Tate, Samuel Pordage, Richard Steere, John Tutchin, and Daniel Defoe – even as Dryden's own "MacFlecknoe" (1682), with its ludicrous likening of Shadwell's succession to that of Elisha (2 Kings 2), highlighted the comic dimensions of the genre.

The Bible's plasticity, normativity, and accessibility were satirically exploited by Anglicans, Dissenters, and Roman Catholics alike – as may clearly be perceived in Jonathan Swift's *Tale of a Tub* (1704) and *Drapier's Letters* (1724); Daniel Defoe's *The True-Born Englishman* (1701) and *Jure Divino* (1706); and Alexander Pope's "First Psalm" (1716), "Epistle to Bathurst" (1733), and the conclusion of *The Dunciad* (1728, 1742). The mock-biblical engravings of William Hogarth, including *An Emblematical Print on the South Sea Scheme* (1721) and some aspects of *The Harlot's Progress* (1732), gave popular English expression to a common aspect of seventeenth-century Dutch satirical prints. Mock-biblical satire was so routinely found in the papers of the day – viz., *The Weekly Journal; or British Gazetteer, The Craftsman, The Flying Post; or Post-Master, Fog's Weekly Journal* – that it became part of the eighteenth-century journalistic stock-in-trade. It featured in periodicals with such divergent political sympathies as John "Orator" Henley's pro-government *Hyp-Doctor* (1730–41) and the opposition organ, *The Champion* (1739–43).

The mock biblical figured prominently in newspapers and pamphlets surrounding the Excise Crisis (1733), especially in the form of political sermons, sometimes on genuine passages of Scripture, sometimes on wholly invented "biblical" texts. The Jewish Naturalization Act, or "Jew Bill," (1753) occasioned a flood of satires, many of them anti-Semitic, adducing the Hebrew Bible (Old Testament). Other high-water marks include the "prime ministry" of Lord Bute (1761–3) and the highly contentious Westminster election of 1784. Charles Churchill's *Prophecy of Famine* (1763) and William Blake's *Marriage of Heaven and Hell* (c.1793) and *Book of Los* (1795), among many others, testify to the ongoing importance of this satirical species.

The fashion for pseudo-biblical "Chapters," "Chronicles," "Books," and "Lessons" – inspired by Robert Dodsley's *Chronicle of the Kings of England* (1740) and Horace Walpole's *Lessons for the Day* (1742) – lasted into the nineteenth century. In America, Benjamin Franklin's "A Parable against Prosecution" (c.1755), which purported to be a chapter of Genesis, was widely circulated. The apogee of such ersatz biblical books was in the publication of "The Chaldee MS" (1817) – a trenchant satire in the form of a continuation of the Book of Daniel by James Hogg, John Wilson, and John Gibson Lockhart – published in *Blackwood's Magazine* to a storm of controversy and charges of libel.

In the same year, at the three highly publicized trials of William Hone for seditious and blasphemous libel, Hone read out many mock-biblical satires in his own defense, arguing that because these satires had not been legally actionable, the state had no grounds for convicting him for his writings (although biblical parodies were not actually the central issue in his case). The effect of Hone's legal argument was that long-forgotten Restoration and eighteenth-century mock-biblical texts were suddenly available again to the reading public, though almost exclusively in the best-selling accounts of Hone's trials, which Hone himself published. Thus, the mock biblical, already having a long history as an anti-establishment strategy, came to be associated with the dangers of political radicalism. Keats's sonnet, "Nebuchadnezzar's Dream" (December 1817, or early 1818), which plays with the traditions of the mock biblical, is a tribute to Hone and his victorious defense. Byron's treatment of the late George III in "The Vision of Judgment" (1822), rooted in the Book of Revelation, did nothing to dispel this association.

Although the "Chaldee MS" affair and the three trials of Hone attracted particular attention, readers in the first quarter of the nineteenth century could scarcely have helped notice that the sacred page was routinely employed as a weapon for satirical assaults. Writers for *The Morning Chronicle* and *Morning Herald*, for example, regularly printed mock-biblical satires. In *The True Briton* we commonly find titles such as "A New Chapter from the Book of Daniel" (1800) – which may have inspired Hone – while another journal in the same year published "The Land of Nineveh; A Fragment." Even politicians got in on the act: in 1783, Lord Eldon, when he was merely Mr Scott and in the House of Commons, made a satiric speech in parliament based on verses from the Book of Revelation. Similarly, "The New Morality" (1798), by MP and under-secretary at the Foreign Office George Canning, employs Genesis, Job, and Psalm 48 to lampoon his parliamentary colleagues. Moreover, the most popular creators of satirical prints – Thomas Rowlandson, Isaac and George Cruikshank, William Dent, and James Gillray – also exploited the satirical possibilities afforded by the Scriptures in fashioning the profane wit that made their cartoons so accessible.

In the Victorian period, with its ostensibly more genteel sensibilities, most satirists were careful not to offend their audiences (much less incur charges of blasphemy) by employing the mock biblical. The important exception to this is the large number of election satires, predominantly broadsides and short pamphlets, that make use of the scriptural "chronicle." In the United States, Mark Twain wrote a number of satirical works in the form of fictional diaries by antediluvian figures from the Old Testament (Adam, Eve, Methuselah, Shem), but published only the most mildly satirical of these. During the last decades of the nineteenth century, George Yost Coffin regularly introduced mock-biblical elements into his political cartoons appearing in *The Washington Post*. Clifford Kennedy Berryman's cartoons of the 1930s and 1940s in *The Washington Star* followed a similar pattern, and, to a lesser extent, so too did those of Gib Crockett in the same newspaper some decades later.

Contemporary British political cartoonists as diverse as Christopher Riddell and Steve Bell continue to make use of the mock biblical. A good case in point is Riddell's 1993 cartoon in *The Independent* (for August 23) depicting a burly Bosnian Serb staring defiantly at the reader, a rifle labeled "Ethnic Cleansing" across his lap. The "Bosnia Peace Plan" and a rolled-up map sit on a crate of heavy ammunition beside his jack-boots. Behind the soldier in 28-point capitals we read: "BLESSED ARE THE MEEK FOR THEY SHALL INHERIT THE EARTH." *Private Eye*'s "Book of [former Israeli Prime Minister Ariel] Sharon" (for example, issue 1103, April 2, 2004) is but a recent instance of that periodical's enlisting of biblical idiom for satirical editorializing, especially on the Israel–Palestine conflict.

Among the most accomplished mock-biblical satires of the twentieth century is Stefan Heym's *The King David Report* (German edn, 1972; English edn, 1973). This novel traces the career of Ethan of Ezrah (author of Psalm 89) as he is ordered to become part of a commission to rewrite the history of King David's reign in order to establish the legitimacy of Solomon's rise to power, even though it is clear that Solomon did not have a right of succession to the throne and became king by illegitimate means. Thus, the ideologies and activities of the Communist German Democratic Republic – where the novel was written – and the Soviet Union, especially under Stalin, are reflected in this midrashic morality tale rooted in genuine anomalies and contradictions in 1 and 2 Samuel and 1 Kings. The German text (actually a translation of Heym's English original, but published first) imitates the language of Luther's Bible, just as the English text plays with the cadences and phrases of the Authorized Version. Heym's novel testifies to the ongoing vitality, creative possibilities, and subversive power of mock-biblical satire.

Type 1: Mock-biblical Quotation: William Hone's Attack on Prince George

The most basic form of mock-biblical satire is the quotation of biblical verses out of context in order to apply them to a new situation. When Queen Caroline was officially excluded from the prayers for the Royal Family in the *Book of Common Prayer* because of the future King George IV's estrangement from her, William Hone used a catena of biblical quotations to produce a powerful satire, *The Form of Prayer with Thanksgiving to Almighty God, to be used daily by all devout People throughout the Realm, for the Happy Deliverance of Her Majesty Queen Caroline from the late most Traitorous Conspiracy* (1820). In addition to various hymns, prayers, and collects from the Prayer Book, Hone offers a series of biblical texts to satirize both the Prince Regent and the government that cooperated in his displacement of the Queen. At the beginning of the pamphlet, for example, we read in part:

> *At the beginning of Morning and Evening Prayer the Minister may read with a loud voice some one or more of these Sentences of the Scriptures that follow.* When the righteous are in authority, the people rejoice: but when the wicked beareth rule, the people mourn. *Prov.* xxix. 2.
>
> By reason of the multitude of oppressions they make the oppressed to cry: they cry out by reason of the arm of the mighty. *Job* xxx. 9.
>
> If a ruler hearken to lies, all his servants are wicked. *Prov.* xxix. 12.
>
> The wicked walk on every side when the vilest men are exalted. *Psalm* xii. 8. (p. 3)

The juxtaposition and recontextualization of these verses produce a kind of sermon against those in power, using the Bible's normative power both to instruct and to admonish. The reader of Hone's pamphlet would know that this catena of verses was meant to apply to the Prince Regent and the government ministers who had done his bidding.

Similar concatenations of verses drive Hone's point home, and lead the reader to delight in his manipulation of Scripture to advance his political program against the prince and the government:

> There is a generation that are pure in their own eyes, and yet is not washed from their filthiness. *Prov.* xxx. 12.
>
> Woe unto them that call evil good, and good evil; that put darkness for light, and light for darkness; that put bitter for sweet, and sweet for bitter! *Isaiah*, 5. 20.
>
> * * *
>
> For the congregation of hypocrites shall be desolate, and fire shall consume the tabernacles of bribery. *Job*, 15. 34. (p. 9)

Hone's satire becomes increasingly focused as the "service" progresses, until he delivers this *coup de grace*, a series of biblical exhortations on marital fidelity from Ecclesiastes, Ephesians, and Matthew:

After the Prayer for the King, the Priest may say thus.

Live joyfully with the wife whom thou lovest all the days of the life of thy vanity, which he hath given thee under the sun, all the days of thy vanity: for that is thy portion in this life, and in thy labour which thou takest under the sun. *Eccl.* ix. 9.

So ought men to love their wives as their own bodies. He that loveth his wife loveth himself. *Eph.* v. 28.

Nevertheless let every one of you in particular so love his wife even as himself; and the wife see that she reverence her husband. *Eph.* v. 33.

It hath been said, Whosoever shall put away his wife, let him give her a writing of divorcement:

But I say unto you, That whosoever shall put away his wife, saving for the cause of fornication, causeth her to commit adultery: and whosoever shall marry her that is divorced committeth adultery. *Matt.* 5. 31, 32. (pp. 11–12)

Taken together, these passages serve as a bill of particulars against Prince George. Their cumulative effect is to function as both a sacred lecture and as a Horatian *sermo*, a satirical argument that at once amuses and enlightens.

Several Collects then follow before we come to a devastating coda in the *Versicles* – biblical verses recited aloud by the priest to exhort the congregation – among which we find:

A false witness shall not be unpunished, and he that speaketh lies shall not escape. *Prov.* [x] ix. 5.

As a roaring lion, and a ranging bear; so is a wicked ruler over the poor people. *Prov.* xxviii. 15.

His bones are full of the sin of his youth, which shall lie down with him in the dust. *Job*, xx. 11.

Be wise now therefore, O ye kings: be instructed, ye judges of the earth. *Psalm* ii. 10. (p. 13)

Hone's indictment is absolutely clear and, since none of the words are his own, absolutely protected by law! His "*un*authorized version" co-opts a body of sacred texts commonly employed by the state and its official church to advance and justify hegemony, marshaling them instead as an instrument of subversion. This delightfully seditious dynamic, a common feature of biblical satire in its many forms, helps to account for the popularity of the mock-biblical as an instrument of the opposition: those who lack "official" authority seize an "ultimate" authority and make it their own.

Another example of satirical quotation is found in the anonymous print, *The New Coalition* (1784, BM 6568, figure 27.1). Its scriptural citation reads in part: "'The wolf shall dwell with the lamb...and a *little child* shall lead them' (Isaiah. Chap. xi. [verse]. xvi.)." This passage reflects the bizarre character of the alliance between the king (who may be identified with the lamb) and John Wilkes (akin to the wolf) – formerly political enemies – against Charles James Fox. The text from Isaiah "prophesies" that William Pitt ("the Younger") is the *"little child"* who will lead as the new prime minister. Using an eschatological prophecy (one that tells how things will be at the end time when the kingdom of God is fulfilled) in this way satirically suggests that the order of the world as we have known it in the past has been radically altered and a new era with a different moral calculus is about to begin. Thus, the print comments on the realpolitik of parliamentary alliances at a time of transition.

Figure 27.1 Artist unknown, *The New Coalition*, 1784 (BM 6568), etching (8 9/16 × 7 1/2 in). Courtesy of the Lewis Walpole Library, Yale University

Type 2: Mock-biblical Imitation: Robert Dodsley's *Chronicle of the Kings of England*

A second type of mock-biblical satire is imitation of the sacred page. Many satires of this kind are written in the language of the Authorized Version and masquerade as biblical books, chapters, or chronicles. The most popular work in this vein is Robert Dodsley's *Chronicle of the Kings of England* (1740). Dodsley's history of the English monarchs from William the Conqueror to Queen Elizabeth purports to be the work of one "Nathan Ben Saddi, a Priest of the Jews," who writes "in the Manner of the Ancient Jewish Historians" (title page). Loosely following the idiom of the Authorized Version, Ben Saddi's narrative is ostensibly a modern-day secular version of venerable sacred history: what the Books of Kings and Chronicles were for Judah–Israel, the new work's linguistic register and pattern of allusions suggest, the *Chronicle of the Kings* is meant to be for England. Yet, this is no canonical history because it consistently evinces a jocose and irreverent tone altogether foreign to its alleged exemplars.

One theme recurs again and again in this succinct and eminently readable royal history: the ill fate of the nation when royal favorites are ascendant, and the terrible downfall of such men and the monarchs who foolishly put their trust in them. Thus, the dominant subtext of the *Chronicle* is a satirical attack against Robert Walpole. Although Dodsley's assault on the "prime minister" is sufficiently transparent not to require any special knowledge of the biblical base-texts of his parodic narrative, the force of his satire is considerably amplified if the reader is at least generally familiar with them.

One of the most memorable features of 1–2 Kings is the use of a formulaic statement thirty-four times to refer the reader to two historical sources: "Now the rest of the acts of [King X]..., are they not written in the book of the chronicles of the kings of Israel [or "of Judah"]?" (The same formula, albeit referring to different sources, is repeated eleven times in 1–2 Chronicles.) Ben Saddi repeatedly employs this formula, directing the reader to "the Book of the *Chronicles* of the Kings of *England*" (21, 41, 52), "the Book of *Baker* the Historian" (15, 28), "the Book of *Ashmole* the Herald" (34), and so on. Moreover, just as the primary narrative structure of 1–2 Kings consists in naming Judah's and Israel's monarchs, summarizing the chief incidents of their reigns, and telling how long each king ruled, so too does Ben Saddi's *Chronicle* follow the same principle of organization. The cumulative effect of these parallels between the old and new histories markedly advances Dodsley's satirical design, since the purpose of 1–2 Kings is to explain how the chosen people came to lose the blessings given to them by God and became instead a nation of exiles. The biblical narrator's constant theme is that the infidelity of the kings of Israel and Judah in worshipping idols – practicing the "sins of Jeroboam" and going to the "high places" (pagan sacrificial sites) – led God to ordain national destruction as the only fitting punishment for them, a fate seen most dramatically in Israel's devastation by the Assyrians.

Dodsley's "Jewish Historian" adroitly exploits the theme that *royal idol-worship equals national destruction* by repeatedly treating the topic of monarchical favoritism as a form of idolatry that invariably bears terrible consequences:

> Now *Edward* was a wicked Prince, and did that which was evil in the sight of the Lord.
>
> And he departed from the Worship of his Fathers and made unto himself two Idols [Piers Gaveston and Hugh Le Despencer].
>
> And he set them up in his high Places, and commanded them to be worshipped.
>
> Howbeit certain of the... great Men of the Kingdom refused to bow down before the Idols, which king *Edward* had set up.
>
> And great Tumults ensued, and the Nobles rose up against the King... saying, O King! the Gods which thou hast set up are Idols, which we nor our Fathers never knew, neither will we worship.
>
> Moreover they plucked them down from their high Places, and dashed them in pieces... they took from [Edward] the Crown... (p. 32)

Lest the reader imagine that Edward II is here being singled out for his homosexuality, the story of Mortimer, an important counterpart for Walpole in Opposition satire, immediately follows: Edward III "plucked down the Idol which [his mother Isabella] had set up, and hung it on a Tree, even the Tree of *Tyburn*" (p. 33). Similarly, Richard II "made... Idols... and the thing which he did displeased the People, and they... took the Crown from off his head..." (p. 39).

The force of such satire depends upon more than a clever pun on the phrase "high places" to signify both positions of governmental power and sites of idolatrous abomination. The repeated and insistent reading of excessive court favoritism as a form of idolatry necessarily carries with it notions of something essentially disordered: the betrayal of a national inheritance that must result in disaster. Significantly, Dodsley's persona, Ben Saddi, writes most evidently in the "Jewish" historical (i.e., biblical) manner announced on the work's title page when chronicling the rise and fall of favorite ministers. Only the story of Edmund Dudley and Richard Empsom, officials of Henry VII later executed by Henry VIII, is not told in terms of the idols trope, presumably because of its juxtaposition with the account of Wolsey, which is undoubtedly the culmination of Dodsley's satire:

> And *Henry* made unto himself a great Idol the Likeness of which was not in Heaven above nor in the Earth beneath...
>
> His Legs also were as the Posts of a Gate, or as an Arch stretched forth over the Doors of all the Publick Offices in the Land; and whosoever went out, or whosoever came in, passed beneath, and with idolatrous Reverence... kissed the Cheeks of the Postern.
>
> And all the People both small and great fell down before him and worshipped...
>
> Howbeit he fell down from the Pinnacle of his Greatness, and was dashed in pieces... Wherefore let him that standeth take heed lest he fall. (p. 51)

The notoriously corrupt Wolsey was an excellent analogue for Walpole and was frequently used in satires against the "prime minister." Like Walpole, he had risen from humble beginnings, used his position for self-enrichment, and amassed great personal wealth even as he increased taxes. Shortly before his death, he was arrested for treason. The passage's concluding admonition, "let him that standeth take heed lest he fall," clearly links Walpole with Wolsey.

Evidence that this passage caught the popular imagination may be seen in *Idol-Worship or the Way to Preferment* (1740, BM 2447, see figure 27.2). This satirical print is the reverse of the popular representation of Walpole as Colossus (see, for example, BM 2458). At the bottom of the engraving, the text (hitherto unidentified) is borrowed from the Wolsey-as-idol passage in Dodsley's *Chronicle* and even includes the reference, "Chronicle of the Kings, page 51." The designer of the print emphasizes the satirical theme of Dodsley's text: Walpole blocks the front gate of St James's Palace; no one can have access to the king, the Treasury, the Exchequer, or the Admiralty – the "high places" of preferment – without first doing obeisance to Walpole, whose status as idol associates him with falsity, corruption, and national disaster. In both the *Chronicle* and its derivative print, then, adducing historical precedent in a biblical idiom gives the destructive consequences of royal favoritism prophetic force and allows the Opposition to occupy the high moral ground as the saving voice of truth and orthodoxy.

Dodsley's innovation was to commandeer the notion of writing a canonically sanctioned, authorized version of the nation's past from the historical books of the Bible in order to suggest that his account of history, however schematic and satirically tendentious, could also claim to be a privileged form of truth-telling. The reader of 1–2 Chronicles could scarcely fail to notice its judgmental tenor: only four of the twenty-one kings included in that history receive the approbation of the Levite narrator, a figure akin to Dodsley's Ben Saddi, "a Priest of the Jews." Nor are the approved monarchs wholly exempt from criticism, every hero having vices as well as virtues. As we have seen earlier, 1–2 Kings is similarly critical, charging many of the monarchs with gross infidelities. Thus, the sacred exemplars of Dodsley's *Chronicle* license his praise and blame of royalty while forestalling possible charges of national disloyalty or irresponsible anti-monarchism. Biblical allusion and emulation together confer a kind of critical authority upon the modern-day chronicler; appropriating sacred texts that censure the kings of Israel and Judah makes Dodsley's criticisms more appropriate. Similarly, Dodsley's rhetorical strategy of directing his denunciation of royal favorites through a Levite persona not only serves to distance the author from political controversy, but also establishes a parallel authority to sit in judgment upon England, the new Israel. Moreover, associating his attack on Walpole's excessive power with Old Testament idolatry and its terrible national consequences lends moral and prophetic force to his historical argument. Clothing his distinctly modern interpretation of secular history in ancient religious dress is thus neither merely a droll conceit nor primarily a clever publishing ploy; it is, rather, essential to his political program.

Figure 27.2 Artist unknown, *Idol-Worship or the Way to Preferment*, 1740 (BM 2447), etching and engraving (9⅞ × 13¾ in). Courtesy of the Lewis Walpole Library, Yale University

The Chronicle of the Kings of England is one of the most reprinted mock-biblical satires ever published: during the eighteenth century it was issued nearly thirty times in English from Glasgow to Philadelphia and saw eight foreign language editions. Surprisingly, about one-third of these editions appeared in the last decade of the century, when the mock-biblical chronicle enjoyed a second vogue. The 1821 London edition of Dodsley's *Chronicle* must in some sense be accounted the culmination of this generic trend – it is so extensively annotated with historical and political commentary (in nine-point footnotes) in defense of radical politics that it runs to 286 quarto pages and became a radical handbook of English history.

Type 3: The Satirical Transformation of a Biblical Text: 1 Corinthians 13

Closely allied to mock-biblical imitation is a third type of satire: the transformation of a biblical text by inserting secular elements into what is predominately the original Scripture. A good example is "Lessons for the Evening Service," printed in the *Westminster Journal* for August 21, 1742. The second pseudo-biblical "lesson" casts Lord Chesterfield as St Paul exhorting his beloved community to remain faithful to the truths they have been taught:

> The SECOND LESSON is the First Epistle of CH-ST-RF–LD to the KENSINGTONIANS.
> I. CH-ST-RF–LD, called to be a *Patriot* of his Country, thro' the *Spirit* of *Liberty*, and *Love* to his *Country*,
> II. Unto the late Brethren called *Patriots*, now at the Royal Palace at *K-nsi-gt-n*...
> III. Grace be unto you, to be true and faithful to your Country.
> IV. Now I beseech you Brethren, take heed concerning the Things which I write...
> XXII. Tho' ye spake with the Tongues of Men and of Angels, and have not *true Patriotism*, a *true Love* for your *Country*, ye are all as sounding Brass, and tinkling Cymbals.
> XXIII. And tho' ye have the Gifts of *Treasuryships*, of *Secretaryships*, and have *Knowledge*; and tho' ye have all Faith that ye cou'd remove *Mountains*, and have so little *Patriotism* as to remove them not, ye are as nothing...
> XXV. *Patriotism* is vigilant and persevering: *Patriotism* changeth not: *Patriotism* vaunteth not itself, nor is it puffed up by *Places* or by *Honours*...
> XXX. And now abideth great Eloquence, great Knowledge, and great Patriotism; these three: But the greatest of these is *Patriotism*. (*Westminster Journal* no. 39, August 21, 1742)

The opening verses, most indebted to Romans 1, are unmistakably in the Pauline idiom and register, repeating phrases that recur often in the fourteen letters attributed to him in the Authorized Version. Thus, the lesson's title, the "First Epistle of CH-ST-RF–LD to the KENSINGTONIANS," its language, and an extended allusion to 1 Cor. 3: 4–5 in verses VI–X, all prepare the reader for a satirical climax in which the final nine verses (22–30) strictly parallel chapter thirteen of the First Epistle of Paul to the Corinthians, perhaps the most well remembered words the "Apostle to the gentiles" ever wrote:

> Though I speak with the tongues of men and of angels, and have not charity, I am become as sounding brass, or a tinkling cymbal. And though I have the gift of prophecy, and understand all mysteries, and all knowledge; and though I have all faith, so that I could remove mountains, and have not charity, I am nothing... Charity suffereth long, and is kind; charity envieth not; charity vaunteth not itself, is not puffed up... And now abideth faith, hope, charity, these three; but the greatest of these is charity. (1 Cor. 13: 1–2, 4, 13)

Although the "First Lesson," the "First Chapter of the Last Book of PATRIOTS," primarily targets the former prime minister Walpole, this second lesson raises the indictment that the Patriots have forsaken their lofty ideals at the first prospect of possessing real power. They are no longer Patriots, but "Kensingtonians," having abandoned their old creed and become creatures of George II's court at Kensington Palace.

These passages from the "Epistle of Chesterfield" operate by a method that may be described as the inverse of many other mock-biblical chronicles and lessons. In the case of Dodsley's *Chronicle of the Kings of England*, for example, the author uses a loose biblical idiom and resonance to compose a narrative that is the medium for general understanding; he may produce particular satirical effects, however, through the insertion of specific biblical allusions in the secular text. In other words, the sacred text operates in a secular context, since the reader encounters genuine holy writ only in the midst of what, despite its scriptural guise, is clearly modern and worldly. Constructing an analogy for how such satires operate, we may say that the costumes at the fancy-dress ball occasion passing delight and mirth, but do not deceive; the event becomes socially compelling only when a real duchess enters the hall and begins to dance. The inverse of this imaginative procedure occurs when the author appropriates a substantial biblical passage and embeds secular elements, often of arresting incongruity, into the sacred text. In such instances, the secular elements of the text appear in a sacred context. By way of analogy, we may say that the weekly meeting of the Christian Union is an altogether unremarkable event until someone quite notorious unexpectedly arrives.

In contemporary Great Britain and the United States, mock-biblical satires of the first type are fairly rare, not least because they require a readership well-acquainted with Scripture; the allusions cannot do their satirical work unless they are recognized and, often, mentally resituated in their original contexts. Political satirists of today are much more likely to employ the second kind of mock-biblical "lesson," since the reader need only identify one biblical text and perceive what does not properly belong to it. A good case in point is Steve Bell's "IF..." cartoons in the *Guardian* for September 15–17, 1997 (see figure 27.3). Tony Blair, dressed as a preacher, or perhaps as St Paul, delivers a modified version of 1 Corinthians 13: "Modernity suffereth long, and is kind... modernity vaunteth not itself... When I was old Labour, I spake as old Labour... and now abideth faith, hope, modernity, these three; but the greatest of these is modernity." The substitutions in Blair's mock-biblical text transform Paul's sublime exultation of *caritas* (love) into a farcical party-conference speech. Steve Bell's winningly humorous satire against the prime minister is about far more than his evangelical style, however. Blair's emphasis on new pragmatism over old principles has him supplanting the *summum bonum* of human activity and replacing it with a highly transient value — where there was love now there is modernity. Yet, the preacher of party doctrine is so taken with his own meager invention that he proclaims the "most excellent way" to power with the zeal of one who offers a transcendent and liberating truth, rather than a cynically inspired realpolitik. On its most superficial level, then, the cartoons are simply about "spin," but Bell's adducing of *the* classic formulation of Christian virtue makes them into something far more excoriating as they highlight the gross disorder of privileging expediency and fashion over what is fundamental and genuinely worthy of trust.

Figure 27.3 Steve Bell's "IF ..." cartoons from the *Guardian*, September 15–17, 1997. Used by the kind permission of the artist. © Steve Bell

The text Bell chose for his satire was all the more apposite because Mr Blair had read from 1 Corinthians 13 less than two weeks earlier at the funeral of Diana, Princess of Wales. Thus conflating the political and the liturgical, Bell obliquely suggests that one performance is indistinguishable from another – the sacred and the secular are meaningless distinctions where all is profane and the *kairos* moment of kerygmatic proclamation is reduced to just another media opportunity.

Both the "First Epistle of CH-ST-RF–LD to the KENSINGTONIANS," and Steve Bell's cartoons, two unabashedly secular and satirical lessons, derive a rhetorical claim to be transmitting the truth from their association with the Authorized Version, a text inextricably bound up with the idea of truth-telling and, indeed, of revelation. Written in imitation of the book most widely acknowledged to contain the eternal verities, these satires thus lay claim to temporal legitimacy even as they exploit the disparity between the sacred and the secular, the pregnant inconsistencies between tenor and vehicle.

Type 4: Typological Satire: James Gillray's Satirical Print and Daniel Defoe's *The True-Born Englishman*

A fourth kind of mock-biblical satire uses *typology*, a theory of biblical correspondences in which an earlier historical figure or event is completed or fulfilled by a later. Thus, the type of Isaac carrying the wood for his own sacrifice at the hands of his father Abraham has its corresponding fulfillment (or "antitype") in Jesus carrying the wood of the cross for the sacrificial offering of his life at the will of the Father. Another example is the idea that Eve is the type of Mary: the one brought sin into the world, while the other brought redemption. Dryden popularized, though by no means invented, the satirical application of biblical typologies in "Absalom and Achitophel" (1681), in which modern political figures are portrayed in the characters of biblical men and, hence, are represented as the historical fulfillment of those men. Dryden depicts the Earl of Shaftesbury, for example, as the self-seeking and traitorous Achitophel from 2 Samuel 13–19.

A good example of typological satire may be found in figure 27.4, an untitled print from 1783. Its caption reads: "And Herod and Pilate were made Friends together that same Day; for before they were Enemies one to another... Luke Chap 23 Ver 12." Fox and North had formed an unlikely alliance against the prime minister, Lord Shelburn, and effectively forced him out of office. Accordingly, the unidentified artist (sometimes thought to be James Gillray) depicts Fox and North as Herod and Pilate agreeing to "execute" Shelburn, who thus becomes an innocent victim and Christ-figure as he stands under a gallows reminiscent of the cross. Note that all three sport "Jewish beards" to indicate that they have taken on the characters of their respective New Testament counterparts.

Daniel Defoe's greatest triumph as a writer was his verse satire, *The True-Born Englishman* (1700 [1701]), a publication that conferred on him almost instant celebrity, became one of the very best-selling poems of the first half of the eighteenth century, and gave rise to the appearance of his signature, "By the Author of The True-Born Englishman," on many of his subsequent works. Deploying the typological kind of mock-biblical in *The True-Born Englishman*, Defoe was not only responding to a general trend in what we may call "post-*Absalom and Achitophel*" verse satire; he was also answering an adversary in kind. John Tutchin's political

Figure 27.4 Artist unknown (sometimes attributed to James Gillray), *Fox and North as Herod and Pilate*, 1783 (BM 6194), etching, drypoint and roulette with hand coloring (7 × 6$^{13}/_{16}$ in). Courtesy of the Lewis Walpole Library, Yale University

satire *The Foreigners* (1700) ascribes England's woes to the Whig "junto" and, especially, to the powerful Dutch members of King William's court. Modeled on "Absalom and Achitophel," Tutchin's poem, like so many satires of this period, includes the mock-biblical machinery of Israel, Hebron, Sanhedrin, Judah, and the like. An experienced mock-biblical satirist, Tutchin cleverly casts the Dutch as the Gibeonites: "the remnant of the Amorites" (2 Sam. 21: 2) and neighbors of Israel who tricked Joshua into making a peace treaty with them by pretending that they were "from a very far country," when in fact "they dwelt among them" in adjacent lands (Joshua 9). Joshua and his men erroneously made this compact with a foreign nation because they "asked not counsel at the mouth of the Lord" (Josh. 9: 14b). Tutchin, having thus hit upon an apposite type to reflect his grievances against the English–Dutch alliance so dominant in both domestic and international politics under William, now complains:

> Why should the *Gibeonites* our Land engross,
> And aggrandize their Fortunes with our loss?
> Let them in foreign States proudly command,
> They have no Portion in the Promis'd Land,
> Which immemorially has been decreed
> To be the Birth-right of the *Jewish* Seed.
> How ill do's *Bentir* in the Head appear
> Of Warriours, who do *Jewish* Ensigns bear?
> (Ellis 1970: 238, lines 111–18)

"Bentir," Hans William Bentinck – First Earl of Portland, knight of the garter, and privy councilor – is singled out for special abuse; still worse, the king himself comes under attack in this, one of the more xenophobic poems of William's reign. Politically charged replies, many of them in the mock-biblical mode, were soon in circulation.

The most successful reply to Tutchin, Defoe's *The True-Born Englishman*, self-consciously resists becoming yet another pale imitation of Dryden's typological satire:

> *No Parallel from Hebrew Stories take,*
> *Of God-like Kings my Similes to make:*
> *No borrow'd Names conceal my living Theam;*
> *But Names and Things directly I proclaim.*
> (Ellis 1970: 296, lines 921–4)

Nevertheless, Defoe's poem includes a number of allusions to "Absalom and Achitophel" (see especially lines 267–8, 556–7, 679–82, and 990–1) and unabashedly exploits the mock biblical for some of its most memorable satirical effects. Examining three mock-biblical moments in *The True-Born Englishman* will enable us to consider how creatively Defoe used this popular and powerful satirical form to punctuate his text at several crucial junctures.

Defoe's inversion of Psalm 137

A central theme of *The True-Born Englishman* is the people's insufficient gratitude to William, "their Deliverer" (740), for liberating them from the dangers of Popery and the tyranny of arbitrary government under James II. Ever the loyal Williamite, Defoe reminds his readers: "It was but lately that they were opprest, / Their Rights invaded, and their Laws supprest," until "William *the Great Successor* of Nassau, / Their Prayers heard ... : / [And] ... saw and sav'd them" (Ellis 1970: 288, lines 683–4, 693–5). At first, the citizens appropriately laud their heaven-sent rescuer,

> But glutted with their own Felicities,
> They soon their new Deliverer despise;
> Say all their Prayers back, their Joy disown,
> Unsing their Thanks, and pull their Trophies down:
> Their Harps of Praise are on the Willows hung;
> *For* Englishmen *are ne're contented long.*
> (Ellis 1970: 288, lines 697–702)

Defoe's inversion of Psalm 137 is a fine satirical stroke: the English do not hang their harps upon the willows by the rivers of Babylon because "they that carried us away captive required of us a song; and they that wasted us required of us mirth" (Ps. 137: 3). Rather, Defoe's fellow citizens refuse to extol the very king who has liberated them from the yoke of slavery, freed them from the Babylonian bondage of a Popish oppressor, and preserved Protestant worship in their native land.

The people's wayward and unfaithful behavior, responding to emancipation as if it were captivity, is all the more perverse because England's citizens once knew their glad duty: "God and Him they prais'd; / To This their Thanks, to That their Trophies rais'd" (695–6). The conclusion one must draw is that the people have become oblivious to the immense blessings they have received from God's hand through William. This theme of forgetfulness is particularly ironic in the context of Psalm 137, which is itself a song about remembrance and fidelity. The Israelites pledge their lasting commemoration and faithfulness, asking God's steadfast protection from their enemies in return:

> If I forget thee, O Jerusalem, let my right hand forget her cunning. If I do not remember thee, let my tongue cleave to the roof of my mouth; if I prefer not Jerusalem above my chief joy. Remember, O Lord, the children of Edom in the day of Jerusalem ... [and the] daughter of Babylon, who art to be destroyed. (Ps. 137: 5–7a, 8a)

In the calculus of the psalm, then, Israelite loyalty in the midst of adversity wins the destruction of the nation's enemies; conversely, Defoe's satirical inversion suggests that the English, iniquitous and recreant in an era of national triumph and prosperity, are unworthy of the providential deliverance they heedlessly enjoy.

Defoe's favorable portrayal of Hans William Bentinck, the Duke of Portland, as Hushai

Defoe must have thought it a point of honor to defend Bentinck against Tutchin's libels. Defoe also believed it appropriate to vindicate Portland in the same manner that Tutchin had used to attack him. As we have already noted, Defoe did not want *The True-Born Englishman* to be yet another typological satire after the manner of Dryden and the legion of poets who followed suit; accordingly, Defoe's poem is only intermittently mock-biblical. Turning the potential liability of his audience's over-familiarity with "Absalom and Achitophel" and its poetic progeny into a satirical asset, Defoe boldly uses the very core of the Absalom story (2 Samuel 15–18) to dismantle Tutchin's position with admirable economy and *éclat*. Hearkening back to the reign of James II, Defoe reminds his audience of Bentinck's great service in helping to deliver England from an evil and illegitimate monarch:

> Great *Portland* ne're was banter'd, when he strove
> For Us his Master's kindest Thoughts to move.
> We ne're lampoon'd his Conduct, when employ'd
> King *James*'s Secret Councils to divide:
> Then we caress'd him as the only Man
> Which could the Doubtful Oracle explain:
> The only *Hushai* able to repell
> The Dark designs of our *Achitophel*.
> (Ellis 1970: 298, lines 984–91)

The first couplet leads the reader to recall that Bentinck helped to conclude the Dutch–English peace under Charles and arranged the marriage of William and Mary. Even more importantly, Bentinck prepared the way for the Glorious Revolution, serving as a skillful and trustworthy liaison between William and his English contacts. Moreover, William would never have been able to set sail for England if Bentinck had not successfully negotiated vital diplomatic understandings with the princes of northern Germany, most critically with the elector Frederick III of Brandenburg, heir presumptive of the possessions of the house of Orange. In all these respects, Bentinck helped make "his Master's kindest Thoughts" toward the English a reality; hence, Defoe writes, "he strove / For Us," rendering Bentinck not a rival but a servant of the English people.

Unfortunately, the modern editor of *The True-Born Englishman* failed to understand Defoe's use of the mock biblical in the politically important and satirically accomplished lines that follow. Frank H. Ellis correctly realized that the text plainly identifies Hushai with Bentinck, though it should be noted that Defoe is stretching his point by emphasizing Bentinck's role as Prince William's interloper in the English court. Yet, Ellis wrongly glossed "Oracle" as "William of Orange [?]" and "our Achitophel" as "James II [?]," adding bracketed question marks perhaps to acknowledge that such correspondences render the passage virtually meaningless. The "Oracle" refers to Achitophel, as indicated by 2 Sam. 16: 23, "And the counsel of Ahithophel, which he counselled in those days, was as if a man had inquired at the oracle of God: so was all the counsel of Ahithophel..." Defoe styles him "doubtful" to emphasize his bad policies. Achitophel could not be James II, for in the Scripture he is not a ruler but merely a "counsellor" (2 Sam. 15: 12); rather, treacherous Achitophel should be identified with Robert Spencer, Earl of Sunderland, James's rash and reactionary Secretary of State and lord president of the Privy Council, infamous for his ability to shift allegiances.

Defoe had good reason to despise the man: Sunderland voted in favor of the Exclusion Bill, but later claimed this was merely a tactical maneuver and became James's most important adviser; he urged the severe suppression of the Monmouth rebellion (in which Defoe himself had fought) and promoted Kirke's sanguinary activities at the western assize. Sunderland was primarily responsible for James's radical interference in county commissions of the peace and was one of three officials on the notorious Board of Regulators that set out to purge the local corporations of all possible opposition to the king. A staunch supporter of the pro-Catholic party in the court, he warmly endorsed Jeffreys' scheme for the relief of imprisoned Roman Catholics, placing himself at the service of the queen and her circle, and eventually renouncing his own Protestant faith. It was Sunderland who signed the committal of the Seven Bishops. Thus, according to the logic of the poem, Bentinck is "the only Man, / Which could the Doubtful Oracle [i.e. the counsels of Sunderland] explain" to Prince William just as Hushai made plain to David the treasonous advice Achitophel was giving to Absalom (2 Sam. 17: 15–16).

From the typological correlation of Sunderland with Achitophel, it follows that the Roman Catholic James is none other than Absalom: an evil man who briefly enjoys the prerogatives of kingship, but who has no right to occupy the throne and is deposed by the hand of God working through Hushai/Bentinck. This correspondence highlights Defoe's own deeply held beliefs about the illegitimate and malign character of James's rule. Understanding the new Absalom and Achitophel as James and Sunderland, the reader will quickly apprehend that Defoe's political typology makes William a new David, a young king favored by God to be mighty in war and lead his people in true worship. Using a politico-biblical commonplace in an innovative yet understated fashion, Defoe is thus able simultaneously to address Tutchin's defamation of Bentinck, counterattack with ignominious typologies for Sunderland and James, and further advance the positive political program of his poem by leading his readers to perceive William as God's chosen ruler for England/Israel.

Defoe's negative portrayal of Sir Charles Duncombe as Ziba

Much of *The True-Born Englishman* is taken up with exposing the folly of xenophobia by jocularly demonstrating that, with its long succession of invaders, England is an inescapably mongrel nation. Similarly, the poem argues that the vices most commonly attributed by Englishmen to the citizens of various foreign countries may likewise be imputed to virtually all Englishmen. Bearing in mind particularly the case of England's recent attitude to William and his Dutch retainers, Defoe then maintains that ingratitude, "The basest Action Mankind can commit" (1109), is the particular national vice of the English. This theme lies at the core of the poem's political agenda. Accordingly, the climax of the work is Defoe's satirical portrayal of the Tory MP Sir Charles Duncombe, a prominent financier who was holder of the receivership of customs under Charles II and James II, and receiver-general of excise under William III. Duncombe became one of the wealthiest men in Britain largely by embezzlement, fraud, and what we would describe as "insider trading." He was expelled from parliament in 1698 for forging endorsements on exchequer bills. Much to Defoe's irritation, he then took an active role as a Tory (and, to Defoe's mind, Jacobite) leader in London politics, having been elected sheriff of Middlesex in June 1699. In the closing pages of Defoe's satire, Britannia introduces Duncombe as an epitome of the true-born Englishman, whereupon he makes a crowing yet self-condemnatory "Fine Speech" (lines 1064–190), revealing a life characterized by double-dealing and the betrayal of all those who had helped or placed their trust in him – from the master under whom he served his apprenticeship to the king himself.

Using a strategy rarely found in the mock biblical, Defoe has the rapacious Duncombe compare himself with Judas, boasting that he could have sold Jesus for a far better price (lines 1124–9). Next, he considers "My Cousin Ziba" the "First-born of Treason" who "nobly did advance / His Master's Fall, for his Inheritance" (1132–3). Ziba was King Saul's steward; after the death of Saul and Jonathan, David adopted Jonathan's only surviving son, the crippled Mephibosheth (or Meribaal), giving him all of his grandfather Saul's estates and entrusting the "faithful" Ziba with the running of his household (2 Sam. 9: 1–9). When Absalom revolted against David, Ziba met the fleeing David with provisions he had taken from Mephibosheth's stores for David's army. Ziba deceived David into believing that Mephibosheth had sided with Absalom and, in gratitude for his apparent loyalty, David decreed that Ziba could take possession of all his master's property (2 Sam. 16: 1–4). Thus Ziba defrauded King David, who had generously given Ziba and his family employment after the death of his patron, Saul. In addition, Ziba betrayed his new master, Mephibosheth, who was not only the adopted son of David, but the grandson of his first master. Vaunting in his own selfishness and disloyalty, Duncombe observes:

> *Ziba*'s a Traytor of some Quality,
> Yet *Ziba* might ha' been inform'd by me:
> Had I been there, he ne're had been content
> With half th' Estate, nor half the Government.
> (Ellis 1970: 304–5, lines 1138–41)

Duncombe's cupidity and disloyalty appear to know no bounds. Defoe's use of Ziba as a type for the former receiver-general does more than emphasize his "Ingratitude" as "the worst of Human Guilt" (1108), however.

Commentators on the poem, never having adequately understood the contribution of mock-biblical elements to its overall program, have been unable to attend to the larger political resonances of Defoe's Duncombe–Ziba parallel. The opening verses of 2 Samuel 16 relate two incidents: Ziba, the former steward of Saul, executes a highly opportunistic yet carefully wrought plan to deceive David; then, Shimei, a Benjaminite (and hence from Saul's own tribe), curses David, telling him: "The Lord hath returned upon thee all the blood of the house of Saul, in whose stead thou hast reigned; and the Lord hath delivered the kingdom into the hand of Absalom thy son" (2 Sam. 16: 8). The function of these two incidents in the narrative is to demonstrate the continuing northern and Saulite opposition to David's kingship, a repeated political theme readily apparent to an attentive reader of 2 Samuel.

The once-separated kingdom (southern Judah and northern Israel) that David has labored to unite (2 Sam. 5, *et infra*) still contains deep divisions, so much so that some followers of the previous king refuse to recognize the legitimacy of David's rule and look to an insurrection for his downfall. Like Ziba, Duncombe – who had been the "steward" of Charles II and James II before he came into the service of the new king, William – is a Saulite, a Tory-Jacobite long in the employ of a Whiggish monarch, but who would defraud him at the first opportunity, and perhaps support a revolution to restore the old order. According to the poem, this new Ziba could never be content with "half the Government" because he looks to depose the whole. In other words, both the context of the Ziba story and Duncombe's "fine speech" – reflecting not only avarice for gold but covetousness for government – foreshadow Duncombe's characteristic ingratitude and betrayal carried to its farthest political end by indicating that this true-born Englishman harbors treasonable desires.

Defoe's mock-biblical typology also plays an important structural role in the poem. As we have noted, the scriptural account of Ziba's perfidy (2 Sam. 16) occurs in the midst of the Absalom and Achitophel narrative (2 Sam. 14–18). Thus, Defoe's portrayals of Bentinck as Hushai and of Duncombe as Ziba are linked, not merely because they are the only two extended typological treatments of contemporary political figures in the poem, but also because their stories in the biblical chronicle itself present antithetical renderings of human behavior in the midst of political instability and strife. Hushai hazards all in the hope of saving his master, while Ziba traduces his master in the hope of gaining all. As in the Scripture, so in the "satyr": Bentinck and Duncombe are a converse pair. The Dutchman exemplifies faithful service to king and England, while the Englishman personifies "That Sin alone, which shou'd not be forgiv'n / On Earth" (1114–15): an ingratitude, or selfishness, which takes into account neither personal fealty nor the common good. The typological treatment of these two figures draws them together to highlight their differences, so that the Bentinck passage is more than a reply to Tutchin, just as the Duncombe portrait is more than a counter-example. Taken together, as their allusive, topical, and structural congruence insist they be, this pairing represents a contemporary Choice of Hercules, a modern morality play that calls its spectators to choose the path of public service and personal virtue. Defoe's mock-biblical device of twin typologies allows his most successful poem to enact, rather than merely describe, its moral and political theme: that it is ethical excellence, rather than birth, that makes one a true-born Englishman.

Conclusion

Understanding the variety, extent, and rhetorical strategies of the mock biblical can enrich and complicate our understanding of satire. Scrutinizing works in the newly recovered discursive field of the mock biblical should do much to expand and to deepen the ways in which we comprehend a broad spectrum of satirical texts, both verbal and visual. By attending to the long history of this satirical species as it has evolved and propagated over the centuries, we may begin to trace lines of descent and, increasingly, to discern the emergence and development of hereditary traits. Many of the satires adduced in this brief discussion are "fearfully and wonderfully made," remarkable for their accessibility, inventiveness, and wit. These, and many more like them, deserve further study both in their own right and in relation to other satirical forms.

References and Further Reading

Atherton, Herbert M. (1974) *Political Prints in the Age of Hogarth: A Study of the Ideographic Representation of Politics*. Oxford: Clarendon Press.

Bayless, Martha (1996) *Parody in the Middle Ages: The Latin Tradition*. Ann Arbor: University of Michigan Press.

Carretta, Vincent (1983) *The Snarling Muse: Verbal and Visual Political Satire from Pope to Churchill*. Philadelphia: University of Pennsylvania Press.

——(1990) *George III and the Satirists from Hogarth to Byron*. Athens: University of Georgia Press.

Donald, Diana (1996) *The Age of Caricature: Satirical Prints in the Reign of George III*. New Haven, CT: Yale University Press for the Paul Mellon Centre for Studies in British Art.

Ellis, Frank H. (ed.) (1970) *Poems on Affairs of State: Augustan Satirical Verse: Vol. 6, 1697–1704*. New Haven, CT: Yale University Press.

Fisch, Harold (1964) *Jerusalem and Albion: The Hebraic Factor in Seventeenth-century Literature*. London: Routledge and Kegan Paul.

Gilman, Sander L. (1974) *The Parodic Sermon in European Perspective: Aspects of Liturgical Parody from the Middle Ages to the Twentieth Century*. Beiträge zur Literatur des XV bis XVIII Jahrhunderts, vol. VI. Wiesbaden: Frans Steiner Verlag.

Hallett, Mark (1999) *The Spectacle of Difference: Graphic Satire in the Age of Hogarth*. New Haven, CT: Yale University Press for the Paul Mellon Centre for Studies in British Art.

Harth, Phillip (1993) *Pen for a Party: Dryden's Tory Propaganda in its Contexts*. Princeton, NJ: Princeton University Press.

Jemielity, Thomas (1995) A mock-biblical controversy: Sir Richard Blackmore in the *Dunciad*. *Philological Quarterly* 74 (3), 249–77.

——(2000) Alexander Pope's 1743 *Dunciad* and mock-apocalypse. In C. Ingrassia and C. N. Thomas (eds), *"More Solid Learning": New Perspectives on Alexander Pope's Dunciad*, pp. 166–88. Lewisburg: Bucknell University Press.

Korshin, Paul J. (1982) *Typologies in England, 1650–1820*. Princeton, NJ: Princeton University Press.

Lehmann, Paul J. G. (1963) *Die Parodie im Mittelalter*, 2nd edn. Stuttgart: A. Hiersemann.

Lund, Roger D. (1995) Irony as subversion: Thomas Woolston and the crime of wit. In R. D. Lund (ed.), *The Margins of Orthodoxy: Heterodox Writing and Cultural Response, 1660–1750*, pp. 170–94. Cambridge: Cambridge University Press.

Norton, David (1993) *A History of the Bible as Literature*, 2 vols. Cambridge: Cambridge University Press.

Reventlow, Henning Graf (1985) *The Authority of the Bible and the Rise of the Modern World*, trans. J. Bowden. Philadelphia: Fortress Press.

Scribner, Robert W. (1994) *For the Sake of Simple Folk: Popular Propaganda for the German Reformation*, 2nd edn. Oxford: Clarendon Press.

Stephens, Frederick G. and George, Mary D. (eds) (1978) *Catalogue of Prints and Drawings in the British Museum: Division I. Political and Personal Satires*, 11 vols in 12 parts (1870–1954). London: British Museum Publications.

Suarez SJ, Michael F. (1992) Bibles, libels, and Bute: the development of scriptural satire in the 18th-century political print. *The Age of Johnson: A Scholarly Annual* 5, 341–89.

——(2004) A crisis in English public life: the Popish Plot, *Naboth's Vineyard* (1679), and mock-biblical satire's exemplary redress. *Huntington Library Quarterly* 67 (4), 529–52.

——(2006) "The Most blasphemous book that ever was publish'd": ridicule, reception, and censorship in eighteenth-century England. In W. Kirsop (ed.), *The Commonwealth of Books: Essays and Studies in Honour of Ian Willison*, pp. 47–76. Melbourne: Centre for the Book, Monash University.

——(2007) *The Mock Biblical: A Study in English Satire, 1660–1830*, vol. 1. Oxford: Oxford University Press.

Williams, Aubrey L. (1955) *Pope's Dunciad: A Study of its Meaning*. London: Methuen.

Wood, Marcus (1994) *Radical Satire and Print Culture 1790–1822*. Oxford: Clarendon Press.

Zwicker, Steven N. (1972) *Dryden's Political Poetry: The Typology of King and Nation*. Providence: Brown University Press.

28
The Satiric Character Sketch
David F. Venturo

The satiric character sketch has existed as a genre for over two millennia. This chapter traces the development of the genre from its origins in classical Greece through its renascence in early seventeenth-century England to its long afterlife as an embedded genre from the late seventeenth century to the present. The decline of the satiric character sketch from a discrete genre that described general character types to a genre embedded within larger, more capacious literary forms that portrayed not types but individuals coincides with the shift from Baroque to Augustan culture, which took place in England and Europe after the Thirty Years' War and the English Civil Wars and Interregnum.

The earliest known satiric character sketches were written by the polymath Tyrtamus of Lesbos (c.370–285 BCE), better known by the nickname Theophrastus (the godlike speaker), bestowed on him by his teacher, Aristotle, who is said to have regarded him as his favorite disciple. Theophrastus titled his thirty sketches χαρακτῆρες, commonly known in English as *Characters*. The original meaning of the Greek word *character* was *an engraving* or *an impression*, and Theophrastus' title might more accurately be translated as *traits*, since his brief sketches are efforts to taxonomize human types in terms of a defining trait or cast of mind that can be isolated and analyzed. Not surprisingly, Theophrastus was deeply interested in the natural sciences, including biology, meteorology, and especially botany, and was best known in ancient Greece for his writings on this last subject.

Theophrastus' character sketches describe human beings whose behavior deviates from the ethical norms extolled by Aristotle in his *Nicomachean Ethics*. According to Aristotle, all human virtues may, by deficiency or excess, become vices. Thus, for example, the virtue of courage is an ethical mean, lying between the deficiency of courage, which results in cowardice, and its excess, which leads to rashness. Indeed, Aristotle's *Eudemian Ethics* contains a list and detailed descriptions of traditional virtues and their deficient and excessive vices. In addition to Aristotle's ethical treatises, Theophrastus' character sketches may also be indebted to the New Comedy of Aristophanes with its stock satiro-comic figures, which was immensely popular in fourth-century BCE Athens. Such character types as the boor, the braggart soldier, the suspicious old man, the miser, the country bumpkin, and the wily parasite are the common currency of Theophrastan satire and Athenian comedy.

Theophrastus' characters are not individuals, but types succinctly described, on average, in about 300 words in the original Greek. Each character sketch begins with a one-word title, naming the personality trait to be addressed (for example, "Idle Chatter"). Next, the trait is defined, in general, philosophical terms, in a sentence or two (for example, "Idle chatter is engaging in prolonged and aimless talk"; Theophrastus 1993: 61). Finally, the trait is described through the character's actions and often brought to life with quotations from his speech. These descriptions are lively, detailed, and precise, never general and abstract. Indeed, one can learn a great deal about life in Theophrastus' Athens from the circumstantial details of the sketches.

Theophrastus organized his sketches loosely, the details of each character's behavior accrued with an artful artlessness that gives the reader a feeling of directness and spontaneity:

> The idle chatterer is the sort who sits right down beside someone he doesn't know, and starts out by speaking in praise of his own wife; then he recounts the dream he had the night before; then he relates the details of what he had for dinner. Then, as matters progress, he says that people nowadays are much more wicked than they used to be; that wheat is a bargain in the marketplace; that there are lots of foreigners in town, and that the sea lanes have been open since the festival of Dionysus. And that if it rains more, the soil will be better; that he intends to start a farm next year, and that it's hard to make a living; and Damippos dedicated the biggest torch at the mysteries. "How many pillars are there at the Odeion?" "Yesterday I threw up!" "What day is it today?" And that the mysteries are in the month of Boedromion, and the Apatouria in Pyanepsion, and the country Dionysia in Poseidon. And that if you put up with him, he doesn't stop! (Theophrastus 1993: 61, 63)

Indeed, the colloquial diction, lively tone, and loose structure of the descriptions call to mind the carefully rehearsed efforts of modern stand-up comics to dramatize satirically and with seeming spontaneity character types before a live audience. This sense of spontaneity governs the sketches from beginning to end, which tend to close simply, without a formal, rhetorical flourish.

After Theophrastus' *Characters*, the satiric character sketch disappeared for over 1,900 years as a discrete genre, surviving parasitically, embedded within larger, more capacious literary forms. As critics have often noted, the stock characters of Terence's and Plautus' Roman dramatic comedies are indebted to Theophrastus as well as to Aristophanes. In addition, the verse satires of Horace, Juvenal, and Persius, and the epigrams of Martial are peopled by satiric character types similar to those found in Theophrastus: misers, braggarts, bullies, lechers, flatterers, hypocrites, and parasites, among others. Through the Middle Ages, the satiric character sketch survived in the descriptions of the pilgrims in the prologue to Chaucer's *Canterbury Tales*, the seven deadly sins in Langland's *Piers Plowman*, and in the vices of morality plays. Medieval and early modern homilists frequently employed brief positive and negative character sketches known as *exempla* to illustrate moral and immoral behavior in their sermons. The authors of cony-catching pamphlets and rogue tales in the last decades of the sixteenth century, such as Robert Greene's *Defence of Conny-Catching* (1592) and Thomas Nashe's *Apologie of Pierce Penniless* (1592) and *The Unfortunate Traveller* (1594), relied on versions of the satiric character sketch to people their narratives.

After nearly two millennia, the satiric character sketch as a distinct genre enjoyed a resurgence of popularity in the first half of the seventeenth century, especially in England. The immediate impetus for the revival was the great scholarly edition of Theophrastus' *Characters* by Isaac Casaubon, published in Lyons in 1592, and expanded in the second edition of 1599. The 1592 edition of *Characters* contained 23 satiric sketches; the 1599 edition included five more. (The final two characters were not restored to the Theophrastan canon until the publication of a German edition in 1786.) Casaubon (1559–1614), a French Protestant theologian and classical scholar, was regarded by his contemporaries as one of the most learned and accomplished classicists of the age. Although Casaubon was not the first early modern editor of Theophrastus' *Characters*, he was the most intelligent, astute, and thorough. He corrected many errors of transmission in the Greek text, added Latin translations of every character, and provided an introduction and illuminating commentary on the social world of fourth-century BCE Athens which made it possible to read the *Characters* with real understanding for the first time since classical antiquity. The first English translation of Theophrastus, based on Casaubon's edition, was written by John Healey before 1610, although not published until 1616 (Boyce [1947] 1967: 178).

Within a decade of Casaubon's 1599 edition, short sketches devoted to the description of character types became immensely popular in England. This can be attributed to a confluence of new interests and genres that were developing in the late sixteenth century. I have already mentioned the cony-catching pamphlets and rogue tales with their picaresque heroes and anti-heroes, which had caught on in the 1580s and 1590s. The conduct book, growing in popularity since the mid-sixteenth century, contained examples of appropriate and inappropriate behavior. In addition, the essay, which provides insight into human conduct and character within a short compass, was being pioneered by Francis Bacon in England (Michel de Montaigne was writing longer, more discursive essays in France). In drama, Ben Jonson appropriated the Galenic theory of psychological humors from classical medicine and exploited it in his comedies, beginning with *Every Man Out of His Humour*, in 1598, creating eccentric, "humorous" characters known for an exaggerated trait. Many of Jonson's contemporaries, including Thomas Dekker and John Marston, followed suit in their plays. The extraordinary achievements in both comic and tragic drama at this time reflected the early modern period's fascination with human conduct, motives, and psychology. Indeed, as Stephen Greenblatt (1980) famously noted a generation ago, almost every early modern writer, thinker, and artist seemed to be interested in the fashioning of the human self. In addition, in the controversial climate of the 1590s, formal verse satire rose to prominence, most notably in Joseph Hall's *Virgidemiarum* (1597) and John Marston's *Certaine Satyres* (1598) and *The Scourge of Villanie* (1599). These satires, following the Juvenalian model, contain scabrous character sketches of vices endemic to urban life, and only a licensers' order in 1599 to suppress such satire, temporarily put a halt to the growth of this genre.

The formal character sketch — a short essay focused on the description of a particular character type — was pioneered in English by Joseph Hall (1574–1656), theologian, controversialist, and satirist. Hall began his literary career while still a youthful fellow of Emmanuel College, Cambridge, with a book of Juvenalian verse satires, *Virgidemiarum* (1597), which combined moral earnestness with lofty rhetorical denunciation, then turned to the writing of moral and religious tracts, such as *Meditations and Vowes*. It was just after the third series of *Meditations* was published, in 1606, that Hall took up the Theophrastan character sketch as a vehicle for addressing religious and ethical problems from a practical perspective.

Although most modern critics describe Theophrastus as detached in his attitude toward the vices he depicts in his character sketches, Hall, like Casaubon before him, considered Theophrastus a serious, earnest moralist. His *Characters of Vertues and Vices* (1608) relied on Casaubon's edition of Theophrastus as a model, and Hall, like Casaubon, thought the moralistic preface to Theophrastus' little book, now believed to have been written by another hand, the work of Theophrastus himself. In that preface, pseudo-Theophrastus professes his hope that readers will use his sketches "as a guide in choosing to associate with and become close to the finest men, so as not to fall short of their standard" (Theophrastus 1993: 51, 53). In "The Proome" to his *Characters of Vertues and Vices*, Hall describes Theophrastus as "that ancient Master of Morality" whom he vows to follow in "strip[ping]...Vertue and Vice...naked to the open view, and despoil[ing], one of her rags, the other of her ornaments" (Hall 1948: 146). Like Theophrastus', Hall's 24 characters (later increased to 26) are ethical and occasionally social or professional types. Indeed, some of Hall's types, such as the "Busie-body," the "Male-content," and the "Flatterer," seem to be directly borrowed from the Greek original. But Hall's descriptions of his types, in contrast to Theophrastus', tend to be more general and abstract and are often two to three times longer than Theophrastus'. Also, in contrast to Theophrastus, Hall balances his vicious characters with virtuous ones. The first edition of Hall's book (1608) contains nine virtuous and 15 vicious characters. The author added two more virtuous characters to the second edition (1614; Boyce [1947] 1967: 123–4).

In contrast to Theophrastus', Hall's characters are didactic in purpose and often hortatory in tone. Theophrastus was more detached and descriptive, interested in representing and laughing at humankind's faults. Hall uses his characters to promote religion and morality. Like Samuel Johnson a century and a half later, Hall subsumes and integrates certain elements of classical Stoicism within a Pauline, Christian ethos in which thoughtful self-discipline and contempt for worldly goods are parts of a program designed to dissuade human beings from attaching themselves too passionately to life in a dangerous, frustrating, and ephemeral world.

Hall's *Characters of Vertues and Vices* is divided into two books. In the first, *Characterismes of Vertues*, Hall seeks to paint the "many beauties...and...graces in the face of Goodnesse, [so] that no eye can possibly see it without affection, without ravishment" (Hall 1948: 146). Of Hall's eleven sketches of virtuous types, ten are moral and ethical (for example, "Of an Honest man," "Of a Patient man") and one, social or professional ("Of the good Magistrate"). Hall's virtues are essentially Pauline Christian mixed with elements of Stoic doctrine borrowed from Seneca and Juvenal that were regarded by early modern writers as compatible with Christianity. In addition, Hall occasionally borrows from his own sermons in creating his sketches. The eyes of the "Faithfull man," Hall explains, "have no other objects, but [things] absent and invisible; which they see so cleerly, as that to them sense is blind," echoing the Epistle to the Hebrews, which Hall and his contemporaries attributed to St Paul (Hall 1948: 150). Likewise, Hall relies on allusions to St Paul's Epistle to the Ephesians when he compares, in a series of extended metaphors, the life of the "Faithfull man" to a "warre...perpetuall, without truce, without intermission," in which this moral soldier "ever beares before him...a shield" (Hall 1948: 151). The "Patient man," like the virtuous figure at the end of Juvenal's tenth *Satire*, has "so conquered himselfe, that wrongs cannot conquer him" (Hall 1948: 155). And the "Happy man," like the wise man at the end of Juvenal's Tenth, "walks ever even, in the mid-way betwixt hopes and feares" (Hall 1948: 165). In addition, Hall relies on echoes of the conclusion to the book of Ecclesiastes when he asserts that the "Happy man" should "feare nothing but God...hope for nothing but that which he must have" (Hall 1948: 165).

Hall uses the lofty, sententious rhetoric of Juvenal, who was regarded by early modern readers not so much as a no-holds-barred satirist, but as a serious, even austere moralist and philosopher, to describe his characters. As a result, the descriptions of the virtuous characters are often elaborate, sometimes grandiloquent. The "true Friend," for example, opens with a paradox: "His affections are both united and divided; united to him he loveth; divided betwixt another and himselfe; and his own heart is so parted, that whiles he hath some, his friend hath all" (Hall 1948: 156). Equally memorably, Hall's virtuous sketches, in contrast to Theophrastus', tend to end with a rhetorical flourish. The "Faithfull man," for example, closes with elaborate parataxis and parallelism: "he is rich in works, busie in obedience, cheerfull and unmoved in expectation, better with evils, in common opinion miserable, but in true judgment more than a man" (Hall 1948: 152).

In *Characterismes of Vices*, Hall announces his intention to render vice contemptible. The irony is scornful and lofty – Juvenalian in the same way Samuel Johnson's will be in the eighteenth century. Hall cautions in "The Proome" to *Vices* that his style in this book will be "less grave, more satirical," but it is in fact both grave and satirical, as Juvenal's had been in his *Satires* (Hall 1948: 170). As in the *Vertues*, the *Vices* are rounded and shaped by Hall's elegant, sometimes sharp, occasionally dazzling rhetoric. His description of the unhappiness of the "Male-content" beautifully mixes sentiments found in Bacon's essay "Of Marriage and the Single Life" and Poem 9.359

by Posidippus or Plato Comicus from the *Greek Anthology*: "Every blessing hath somewhat to disparage and distaste it: Children bring cares, single life is wilde and solitary; eminencie is envious, retirednesse obscure; fasting painfull; satietie unwieldy; Religion nicely severe; libertie is lawlesse; wealth burdensome; mediocrity contemptible: Every thing faulteth, either in too much, or too little" (Hall 1948: 178). Hall's characterization of "the Flatterer" appropriates elements from Theophrastus' "Flattery" and Juvenal's acid portrait of Greek sycophants in his third *Satire*:

> In himselfe he is nothing, but what pleaseth his *Great-one*, whose virtues he cannot more extoll, than imitate his imperfections, that he may think his worst gracefull. Let him say it is hot, he wipes his forehead and unbraceth himself; if cold, he shivers, and calls for a warmer garment. When he walkes with his friend, he sweares to him, that no man else is looked at; no man talked of. (Hall 1948: 182)

Hall's *Vices* usually end with a ringing, epigrammatic summation. The "Hypocrite," for example, is disposed of in a copious catalogue of rhetorical contempt as "the stranger's Saint, the neighbour's disease, the blot of goodnesse; a rotten stick in a darke night, a Poppie in a corne field, an ill tempered candle, with a great snuffe, that in going out smels ill; and an Angell abroad, a Devill at home; and worse when an Angell, than when a Devill" (Hall 1948: 172–3). Such summations allow Hall to move beyond Theophrastan description to moral reflection on his characters.

Within a few years of the publication of Hall's *Characters of Vertues and Vices*, the popularity of the genre grew significantly. Interest in it expanded beyond the closets and studies of scholars and divines to the drawing rooms of wits and townhouses of gentlemen. Collections of character sketches appeared with increasing frequency, and although the moral imperative was still an important force in the shaping of these sketches, the emphasis fell on entertainment, rather than moral instruction.

The most popular at the time, and most famous since, of these collections of sketches was attributed to Sir Thomas Overbury and "other learned gentlemen his friends" on the title page when first published in 1614. Overbury (1581–1613), in fact, played a negligible role in the creation of the book of sketches ever since associated with his name. Educated at Queen's College, Oxford, and the Middle Temple, Overbury was a friend of, and adviser to, the ambitious and handsome young Scot, Robert Carr, who parlayed King James I's affection for him into a series of increasingly prestigious titles culminating in the earldom of Somerset. In 1608, Overbury himself was knighted and appointed *sewer*, that is, *server*, to King James, and his future seemed assured. But Overbury's master, Carr, fell in love with Frances Howard, the teenaged Countess of Essex, and although Overbury seems to have been willing to countenance the adulterous liaison of Carr and Howard, he opposed their marriage fearing that it would diminish his own influence over his young friend. He angered and alienated Carr by writing a poem, *A Wife*, intended to discourage Carr from marrying Howard, which he circulated in manuscript at court, and then alienated the king by declining a diplomatic post to Russia offered to him by

James as a way to buy his silence about Carr and Howard, who had managed to have her first marriage annulled and now was preparing to wed her lover. In April 1613, Overbury, out of favor with both King James and Queen Anne, was imprisoned in the Tower of London, where, at what appears to have been the instigation of Frances Howard, he was gradually and surreptitiously poisoned, dying five months later, in September. The circumstances of Overbury's death were at first suppressed, and Carr, lately created Earl of Somerset, and Howard were wed in a lavish ceremony, in December 1613, celebrated by many of England's finest and most ambitious poets, including John Donne and George Chapman. Gradually, however, rumors about the circumstances of Overbury's death began to circulate, and, despite the king's desire that the case not be pursued, a lurid trial began in 1615, with Sir Francis Bacon in his role as attorney general leading the prosecution. The Earl and Countess of Somerset were convicted in 1616 and imprisoned, but ultimately pardoned by King James. Four underlings, however, were convicted and executed.

In 1614, shortly after Overbury's death, his poem, *A Wife*, celebrating female chastity and fidelity, was published in a small commemorative volume along with more than twenty elegies mourning Overbury. The book was immediately popular and within months a second edition appeared containing not only "A WIFE / NOW / *The Widdow* / OF / SIR / THOMAS OVERBURYE, / *Being* / A most exquisite and singular Poem / *of the choice of a Wife*," but also 22 "witty Characters, and conceited / *Newes, written by himselfe and other* / learned gentlemen his / friends," as the title page proclaims (Paylor [1936] 1977: frontispiece). The character sketches, coupled with the sudden notoriety of Overbury's death, spurred sales of the book, and by the time it reached its eleventh edition, in 1622, the number of sketches had reached its final total of 83 (Boyce [1947] 1967: 136). A few of these are probably by Overbury, but most have been attributed to others: 32 new characters of "severall persons, in *severall qualities*" added to the sixth edition (1615) are attributed to playwright John Webster; Thomas Dekker, playwright and pamphleteer, who was imprisoned for debt between 1613 and 1619, probably contributed the six characters on debtors and prisons to the ninth edition (1616); John Donne, according to his son, wrote "The True Character of a Dunce," which first appeared in the eleventh edition (Boyce [1947] 1967: 136; Paylor [1936] 1977: xxxiii). The book remained popular into the Restoration, and, by 1664, had reached its seventeenth edition (Paylor [1936] 1977: xxxiii).

The Overburian characters are distinctive in several ways. First, the sketches tend to be very short, pithy, and witty, "in little comprehending much," as one of the contributors to the volume wrote in a clever, self-reflexive character of the character sketch entitled, "What a Character Is" (Paylor [1936] 1977: 92). In contrast to the more expansive characters of Hall, the Overburian characters, for the most part, range from fewer than 100 to about 500 words in length. Indeed, many are even more succinct than Theophrastus'. In addition, the number and variety of character types in the Overbury collection far exceed what one finds in either Theophrastus or Hall. Perhaps most interestingly, the Overburian characters tend not to focus on a single vice or fault, but describe social or professional character types. These were types and classes of people that one might encounter in one's daily dealings in London: businessmen, such as attorneys and money-lenders; professionals, including judges, scholars, and military officers; providers of goods and services, such as tinkers, tailors, and watermen; artists, entertainers, and athletes, including poets, actors, and fencers; criminals, sharpers, and other figures on the social margins, including bawds, whores, and bullies; law enforcement officers, such as sergeants and jailers; religious outliers, including Jesuits, Puritans, and precisians; domestic workers, such as chambermaids and footmen; foreign émigrés, including a "drunken Dutch-man," French cooks, and button-makers from Amsterdam; and rural visitors, such as franklins, milkmaids, and country gentlemen (Paylor [1936] 1977: i–iii). The list could go on. There are a few ethical types – for example, a proud man, a flatterer, a covetous man, a hypocrite – but they are rare, and the Overburians tend to mix ethical and professional characteristics in these sketches rather than focusing, as Theophrastus had done, on a single moral characteristic. As W. J. Paylor notes, the character of "An Hypocrite," for example, begins as a general study of hypocrisy, but evolves into a satire on Puritan duplicity (Paylor [1936] 1977: 125). Indeed, the Overburians focus on the complex mixture of vices and mannerisms in each social type, very much as do the playwrights, verse satirists, and pamphleteers of the period. In addition, the Overbury collection introduced a new wrinkle on the genre, the character of an institution or place. The six so-called prison characters, which first appeared in the ninth edition (1616), include the character of a prison, and together provide insight into the plight of debtors in early seventeenth-century England (Paylor [1936] 1977: xxv).

Like Hall, the Overburians wrote both exemplary and satirical sketches; and, like Hall, they sometimes produced contrasting characters, such as "A Reverend Judge" and several legal rascals, including "A Fantasticke Innes of Court man." But, in contrast to Hall's, the satirical Overburian sketches far outnumber the exemplary ones. Unlike Hall's, the Overburians' satire is less earnest and didactic – indeed, largely unconcerned with persuading the reader to hate vice and emulate virtue. Instead, the Overburian satiric sketches are distinguished by their witty, punning, and conceit-filled rhetoric, which can, as in "A Foote-Man," take on a life of its own, exploding with puns and conceits about the footman's anatomy, livery, and labor:

> Let him be never so well made, yet his Legs are not matches: for he is still setting the best foot forward. He will never be a staid man, for he has a running head of his owne, ever since child-hood. His mother (which, out of question, was a light-heel'd wench) knew it, yet let him run his race, thinking age would reclaime him from his wilde courses. Hee is very long winded: and, without doubt, but that hee hates naturally to serve on horsebacke, hee had proved an excellent trumpet. Hee has one happinesse above all the rest of the Servingmen, for when he most overreaches [a pun – *cheats* and *arrives ahead of*] his Master, hee's best thought of. Hee lives more by his own heat then the warmth of cloathes: and the waiting-woman hath the greatest fancy to him when he is in his close trouses. Gardes hee weares none: which makes him live more upright then any cross gartered gentleman-usher. Tis impossible to draw his picture to the life, cause

a man must take it as he's running; onely this. Horses are usually let bloud on S. *Stevens* day: on S. *Patrickes* he takes rest, and is drencht for all the yeare after. (Paylor [1936] 1977: 53)

The satire is quite good natured, even comic, with just one anti-Irish barb reserved for the closing sentence. Indeed, the writer appears more intent on showing off his skill as a clever rhetorician than at constructing a convincing portrait of a footman. When the wit is more under control, the satire is sharper, and the short, balanced clauses of the sentences, typical of the Overburian sketches, become more noticeable, as in "An affected Traveller," who

Is a speaking fashion; he hath taken paines to bee ridiculous, and hath seen more than he hath perceived. His attire speakes *French*, or *Italian*, and his *gate* cryes *Behold mee*. Hee censures all things by countenances, and shrugs, and speakes his owne language with shame and lisping: he will choake rather than confesse *Beere* a good drinke: and his pick-tooth is a maine part of his behaviour. Hee chooseth rather to be counted a *Spie*, then not a *Polititian*: and maintaines his reputation by naming great men familiarly. (Paylor [1936] 1977: 11)

Some of the Overburian satires are very sharp. The Juvenalian bitterness of "An old Man" was such that it prompted John Earle to write a positive counterpart, "A good old Man," in *Micro-Cosmographie* (1628). The sketches of Puritans – "A Puritaine," "A Precisian," and "An Hypocrite" – are among the most mordant and hostile of the 83. But, in contrast to the corrosive treatment of dissenters by Samuel Butler in the characters he wrote in the 1660s, these figures are mocked for their personal stubbornness, arrogance, and stupidity rather than attacked for the danger they pose to church and state. The Overbury "Puritaine," for example, is so ridiculously contrary in his mindset that, though annoying, it is difficult to imagine him a serious threat to the civil or religious authorities: "any thing that the Law allowes: but marriage and March beare; Hee murmures at: what it disallowes and holds dangerous make him a disciple. Where the gate stands open he is ever seeking a stile, and where his learning ought to clime, he creepes through" (Paylor [1936] 1977: 26–7). Only the satire in "A Jesuite" reflects deep concern about possible political and religious subversion: "Hee is a false Key to open Princes Cabinets, and pry into their Counsels; and where the Popes excommunication thunders, hee holds no more sinne the decrowning of Kings, then our Puritaines doe the suppression of Bishops" (Paylor [1936] 1977: 76).

The Overburians' exemplary characters reflect a syncretic Christian-Stoic ethos similar to Hall's. "A Noble Spirit," for example, draws on the same philosophico-religious tenets as Hall's "The Valiant Man" and "The True Friend" in its insistence on the steadiness of his disposition despite the mutability of his circumstances: "he is the Steeres-man of his owne destinie. Truth is his Goddesse" (Paylor [1936] 1977: 13). One thinks of Hamlet's famous speech to Horatio: "Give me that man / That is not passion's slave, and I will wear him / In my heart's core, ay, in my heart of heart, / As I do thee" (III. ii. 71–4). The exemplary characters tend to be somewhat more generally drawn than their satiric counterparts: "A Reverend Judge" is praised broadly for his probity, modesty, pity, and forthright conduct; "A vertuous Widdow," lauded as "a mirrour for our youngest dames," and "A Wise-man," celebrated as "the servant of vertue" (Paylor [1936] 1977: 69–70).

The Overburian sketches are the most exuberantly Baroque of those in all the major English characterologies. Although they commonly begin, like Theophrastus', with a definition of a character type, the definitions are so complicated by puns and metaphysical conceits as to give pause and demand solution by the reader before he or she can proceed. The Overburian "Host," for example, is defined as "the kernell of a signe: or the signe is the shell, and mine Host is the Snaile," and the "Souldier" as "the husband-man of valor, his Sword is his plow: which honor and aqua vitae, two fierie mettald jades, are ever drawing" (Paylor [1936] 1977: 20, 24). Such definitions are a far cry from the crisp, categorical efforts of Theophrastus to define, then illustrate with examples. Indeed, it has been argued that such conceited definitions are contrary to the conventional purpose of a definition – to distinguish, categorize, or clarify – by transforming definitions into riddles that must be solved before they can be understood. But if the conceited definition obscures and complicates, it also, at its best, unifies and organizes, by providing a kind of rhetorical structure to each character based on a governing analogy or metaphor – a coherence that is lacking in the more accretively constructed characters of Theophrastus. Likewise, the Overburian sketches usually conclude epigrammatically, on a clever point, as "A Meere Pettifogger": "Only with this, I wil pitch him o'er the Barre, & and leave him; That his fingers itch after a Bribe, ever since his first practicing of Court-Hand" (Paylor [1936] 1977: 65).

John Earle (1601?–65) is by consensus the most accomplished of all character writers. His sketches are remarkably nuanced; they reflect a subtle and profound understanding of human nature. While the Overburian characters focus on external behavior, Earle's characters explore human motives and psychology with extraordinary insight and thoughtfulness. He tends to treat his characters with gentle irony, recognizing the foibles of human behavior but also appreciating the inevitability of such foibles. The humorous irony of the sketches is consistent with descriptions left by his contemporaries of Earle's kind personality. A studious, dedicated Anglican divine, he was a friend of Lord Faulkland and tutor to Charles, Prince of Wales, during the Civil Wars and Interregnum, and he lived abroad, a royalist exile, from the mid-1640s until the Restoration. Yet, he successfully maintained friendships with those on both sides in the wars. Indeed, the Earl of Clarendon, who was a shrewd judge of character, noted in his autobiographical *Life* that Earle "never had nor ever could have an enemy."

Earle's *Micro-cosmographie, or A Piece of the World Discovered in Essayes and Characters*, appears to have been published almost by accident. He wrote his character sketches in the early 1620s while a student at Oxford, where they were circulated among friends and acquaintances. Ultimately, the collection wound up in the hands of Edward

Blount, printer, who was a man of considerable taste, a friend of Christopher Marlowe, and a publisher of Marlowe and William Shakespeare. He brought out the first edition of Earle's book, containing 54 characters, in 1628, crediting himself with "play[ing] the mid-wife's part, helping to bring forth these Infants into the world, which the Father would have smoothered" (Earle 1897/1951: iii). In 1629, a "much enlarged" fifth edition appeared, containing 77 characters; the sixth, "augmented" edition, which added one more, was published in 1633. The book remained popular for decades, achieving its eleventh edition in 1669.

Like the Overburians, Earle kept his characters short, and described both ethical and social or professional types. Also like the Overburians, he wrote a handful of locational characters, including "A Taverne," "A Bowle-Alley," and "Paul's Walk." Earle's range of character types is not as broad as the Overburians', as he draws primarily on his own experience as a student and young Oxford scholar. But his knowledge of human nature is deeper and more insightful, and his plainer, less conceitful prose style, perhaps resulting from his direct knowledge of Theophrastus' Greek, allows him to focus more effectively on the substance of his character types.

His character of "A Child," one of his best known, is gently ironic and slightly melancholy in the fashion of Wordsworth's *Ode: Intimations of Immortality* in its treatment of the child's ignorance of adult sorrow: "Nature and his Parents alike dandle him, and tice him on with a bait of Sugar to a draught of Worme-wood" (Earle 1897/1951: 1). His handling of university figures reveals a generosity commonly lacking in the Overburians, and his satire often metamorphoses into humor. Earle defends the "Criticke," the butt of other characterologists and satirists, as "the Surgeon of old Authors, [who] heales the wounds of dust and ignorance," and confidently predicts that "A Downe-right Scholler," given the appropriate social training "shall out-balance those [fashionable] glisterers [i.e., the wits] as farre as a solid substance does a feather, or Gold Gold-lace" (Earle 1897/1951: 58, 60). Earle's sketches regularly contain moments of keen psychological insight. He understands, for example, the self-lacerating qualities of the "Discontented Man" – "one that is falne out with the world, and will bee revenged on himselfe" – and the "Suspitious, or Jealous Man" – "one that watches himselfe a mischiefe, and keepes a leare eye still, for feare it should escape him" (Earle 1897/1951: 15, 37). Earle's character sketches are deftly organized and sharply focused, without the extraneous details, borne of conceitful exuberance, that sometimes mar the Overburians' characters. Finally, Earle frequently improves on the rhetorical conclusions of Hall's and the Overburians' sketches either by closing – with a jot of wit – with his subject's death, or with the subject's transition from one mode of life to another. Of the former kind are the "Old Colledge Butler," who "spends his age, till the tappe of it is runne out, and then a fresh one is set abroach," and the "Aturney," who "is secure" "for Doomes-day" because "he hopes he has a tricke to reverse judgement" (Earle 1897/1951: 67, 57). Of the latter is the "Young Gentleman of the University" who, having completed his degree, "is now gone to the Inns of Court, where hee studies to forget what hee learn'd before, – his acquaintance and the fashion" (Earle 1897/1951: 64).

In the 1640s, as England plunged into civil war, the character sketch underwent a fundamental transformation, becoming a form of ideological and polemical weaponry in the conflict between royalists and parliamentarians, Anglicans and dissenting Protestants. Increasingly, both sides used the satiric character sketch as a means of caricaturing their enemies. The opponents of the king were stereotyped as short-haired, canting, Bible-toting, sexually promiscuous hypocrites, who professed horror at being forced to compromise their consciences while rebelling against their divinely appointed monarch. Jonathan Swift's caustic depictions of hypocritical dissenting divines in *A Tale of a Tub* (1704) may be regarded as the last, belated chapter in those civil war polemics. In turn, partisans of parliament and dissenting Protestantism mocked their enemies as drinking, swearing, cynical, hedonistic, long-haired, licentious crypto-Roman Catholics. Milton's monstrous "sons / Of Belial, flown with insolence and wine" (*Paradise Lost* 1: 501–2), though described in Old Testament terms, are shadowy types of his enemies from the English Civil Wars.

At about the same time, the character sketch began to reflect the epistemic change from Baroque to Augustan poetics that was then taking place. As the 1640s and 1650s unfolded, the character sketch began to lose much of its typical significance. That is, the character *as type* was replaced by the character *as individual*. Baroque symbolism and analogy were yielding to Augustan literalism and historicism. (It is a paradox that Augustan literature is popularly considered to follow generalizing tendencies when, in fact, it delights in the specificity of detail.) In practical terms, this new mode of writing and its new epistemology were embodied in the emerging biographical/historical character portrait and in a shift from constructing character sketches deductively, in order to illustrate a trait or ethos, to constructing them inductively, based on a writer's knowledge, preferably direct and empirical, of the individual he is seeking to draw. The new character portrait can perhaps be seen most clearly in the writing of later seventeenth-century historians and memoirists such as Edward Hyde, Earl of Clarendon (1609–74). Hyde, in his *History of the Rebellion* and *Life of Edward, Earl of Clarendon*, famously wrote brief sketches of persons he had known from both sides in the Civil Wars. Friends and foes, including John Hampden; Lucius Carey, Lord Falkland; King Charles I; Oliver Cromwell; Thomas Wentworth, Earl of Strafford; and Archbishop William Laud were all vividly sketched by Hyde. Indeed, the character portrait became a staple of later seventeenth-century and eighteenth-century writing, commonly embedded in memoirs, histories, and essays. The most famous examples of such character portraits include Jonathan Swift's satiric portraits of John Churchill, Duke of Marlborough, and Thomas, Earl of Wharton, in his *History of the Four Last Years of the Queen* (written c.1713); Samuel Johnson's intellectual characters of the 52 poets he discussed in *Lives of the Poets* (1779–81), particularly the characters of Milton, Dryden, and Pope; Edward Gibbon's portraits in *Decline and Fall of the Roman Empire* (1776–88), most notably Julian the Apostate; and perhaps most famously, James Boswell's character of Johnson in the closing pages of his *Life of Samuel Johnson* (1791). The theoretical justification of the character portrait is best articulated in Johnson's essay *Rambler* no. 60, with its call for the biographer to describe the distinctive, morally relevant idiosyncrasies of his or her subject. The satiric character portrait continued to flourish into the nineteenth century in the essays and letters of William Hazlitt and Thomas Carlyle.

The embedding of encomiastic and satiric character portraits became a staple of English poetry beginning in the 1650s. Poems such as Andrew Marvell's *The First Anniversary of the Government under His Highness the Lord Protector, 1655*, cast Cromwell in a heroic light, and in the 1660s, Edmund Waller invented a new genre with his panegyrical *Instructions to a Painter* (1666), which was promptly mocked, along with its Caroline heroes, by Andrew Marvell and others in a series of satiric *Instructions to a Painter* poems. Marvell's *The Last Instructions to a Painter* (1667) notably attacks prominent figures from Charles II's court and government with its ironic instructions to a putative painter on how to create portraits that reveal their subjects' allegedly heroic virtues. Interestingly, Dryden's "MacFlecknoe" (c.1678), with its extended satiric portrait of Thomas Shadwell, parodies elements of Marvell's 1655 encomium of Cromwell. As late as 1729, Jonathan Swift, in his typically belated fashion, was writing brief, satiric portrait sketches of the British royal family and Sir Robert Walpole in his Hudibrastic poem *Directions to Make a Birth-Day Song*.

As the Restoration unfolded, even ostensibly typical characters began to be interpreted by readers as portraits of individuals. Horner, the witty, libertine hero of William Wycherley's *The Country Wife* (1675), and Dorimant, the hero of George Etherege's *The Man of Mode* (1676), were popularly regarded as portraits of John Wilmot, Earl of Rochester, wit, poet, and libertine, rather than as imaginative constructions of a character type. The degree to which the character sketch and the character portrait were increasingly confounded under the pressures of early modern individualism and historicism is especially apparent in the poetry of John Dryden (1631–1700) and Alexander Pope (1688–1744). When Dryden's contemporaries encountered the satiric character sketches of Absalom, Achitophel, Zimri, and Corah, for example, in "Absalom and Achitophel" (1681), virtually no one regarded them as generalized types, nor did Dryden encourage such interpretation. Indeed, by creating typological parallels between Old Testament history and the present moment, Dryden encouraged, and very likely expected, readers to seek contemporary equivalents for each character in the Old Testament narrative. Keys to poems such as "Absalom and Achitophel" sold widely as readers tried to determine exactly which of their contemporaries was represented under what biblical guise. (In France, Jean de La Bruyère's prose *Caractères* [first edition 1688] worked in similar fashion. They were given classical names but were often based on real individuals who were identified by writers of popular keys.) One finds even more complicated commingling of satiric character sketches and character portraits in the poetry of Pope. Pope tended to insist that the embedded character sketches in his verse satires represented general, moral types, not individuals, but many of his readers refused to believe him, and Pope's writerly habits did not always bear out his claims. Perhaps most notably, "An Epistle to Dr Arbuthnot" (1735) invited readers to identify the ostensibly typical character sketches of Atticus, Sporus, and Bufo with Joseph Addison, John, Lord Hervey, and

Bubb Doddington by Pope's decision to include himself and John Arbuthnot as named characters in the same poem. Pope regularly slips and slides back and forth between character sketches and character portraits in his verse satires, and often muddies the distinction between the two genres as it suits his purpose. The *Moral Essays*, for example, contain both portraits of real people and generic sketches. The Man of Ross, John Kyrle, appears unambiguously as himself in "Epistle III: To Cobham." But who, if anyone, is represented under the guise of Atossa, Philomede, and Chloe in "Epistle II: To a Lady"? Many of Pope's contemporaries were convinced that the satiric character of Atossa was based on Sarah, Duchess of Marlborough. But the match is imperfect, at best, because elements of the character do not conform to what is known of the life of the duchess, and the story that she bribed Pope not to publish this sketch has been deemed implausible. And yet, Pope's readers were probably correct in discerning elements of eminent women who had crossed him, such as the duchess, in these characters. Likewise, some of Pope's readers regarded the description of Timon's villa in "Epistle IV: To Burlington," as an ungenerous attack on Canons, the estate of James Brydges, Duke of Chandos, who was known to have given Pope a gift of £500. Pope vehemently denied the accusation, insisting that the description of Timon's villa was generic. Pope was undoubtedly telling the truth, yet scholars believe that at least some of the hints for Timon's estate *were* based on Pope's experience with Chandos. Ultimately, Pope's familiar commingling of satiric character and satiric portrait in the same sketch has as much to do with his empirical, inductive Augustan habits of mind as he wrote – constructing his characters from details of persons he knew – as with his attempts to deny responsibility for personal attacks in his satiric poems.

Having examined the relation of the character sketch to its generic cousin, the character portrait, let us now turn to the satiric sketches of the last major characterologist, Samuel Butler (1612–80). The sketches of Butler, better known for the corrosively skeptical satiro-epic poem *Hudibras*, illustrate the last major turning point in the history of the genre. Probably written in the 1660s, though none was published before 1759, Butler's *Characters* are radically different from those of all his seventeenth-century predecessors – not in *form*, but *philosophical perspective*. Formally, Butler's sketches are Theophrastan. He usually begins with a striking phrase built on a conceit that defines the character type, then moves on to examples that illustrate the character's behavior. In addition, like Theophrastus, Butler tends to conclude his character sketches suddenly, without the epigrammatic flourish of Hall, the Overburians, or Earle. In the broad range of figures treated in his sketches – 196 of Butler's characters survive – and in their focus on professional or social figures, Butler's satiric characters follow the models of Hall, the Overburians, and Earle. All previous English characterologists, however, wrote in the Baroque poetic tradition. Butler marks a radical departure from the Baroque. Hall and Earle, in particular, were moderate Anglican theologians prepared to satirize religious vice but tolerant of a broad spectrum of Christian doctrine. Earle's "A Grave Divine," for example, wishes to accommodate all reasonable Christians – dissenting Protestant, Anglican, and

Roman Catholic – who do not run into extremes: "In matters of ceremonie, [the Grave Divine] is not ceremonious, but thinkes hee owes that reverence to the Church to bow his judgement to it, and make more conscience of schisme then a Surplesse. Hee esteemes the Church's Hierarchy as the Church's glory, and how-ever we jarred with Rome, would not have our confusion distinguish us" (Earle 1897/1951: 53).

By contrast, Butler's chief target is the religious mind itself, which he regards as diseased, obsessed, unhinged, and the chief source of all human error. Butler repeatedly defines immoral, insane, or criminal behavior using religious tropes and conceits. A pimp "disguises himself in as many Habits as a *Romish Priest*" and maintains "constant Correspondence and Intelligence...with all [whore] Houses...that is, with all *Lay-Sisters*, and such as are *in voto* only" (Butler 1970: 235). A vintner:

> scores all his Reckonings upon two Tables made like those of the ten Commandments, that he may be put in Mind to break them as oft as possibly he can; especially that of stealing and bearing false Witness against his Neighbour, when he draws bad Wine and swears it is good, and that he can take more for the Pipe than the Wine will yield him by the Bottle, a Trick that a *Jesuit* taught him to cheat his own Conscience with. (Butler 1970: 218)

The list could go on and on. Indeed, for Butler, the Baroque culture that sustained dissenting Protestantism, moderate Anglicanism, and Roman Catholicism alike is dangerous and needs to be suppressed. Butler delights in conflating all religious denominations, and particularly enjoys showing how Roman Catholics and dissenting Protestants are spiritual kin despite their obvious antipathy to one another. "A SILENCED PRESBYTERIAN," for example, "[i]s a seminary Minister, a Reformado reformer, and a *Carthusian Calvinist*; that holds two things by his order, seditious opinions, and his tongue" (Butler 1970: 312).

Butler's characterological world is profoundly Hobbesian in its cynicism, egotism, and contentiousness. It contains no virtuous types, but is bursting with knaves, cheats, madmen, and fools like no previous character writer's. He habitually employs debased, reductive Baroque conceits to describe their behavior. "A DISPUTANT," for example, "takes naturally to Controversy, like Fishes in *India* that are said to have Worms in their Heads, and swim always against the Stream" (Butler 1970: 160). In "A LOVER," romantic passion is reduced to a mental form of venereal disease, "a Clap of the Mind, a Kind of running of the Fancy, that breaks out, if it be not stopped in Time, into botches of heroic Rime" (Butler 1970: 222–3). His longest and most powerful characters, "An Hermetic Philosopher," "A Small Poet," and "An Hypocritical Nonconformist" explicitly attack the Baroque imagination and Baroque art as irrational and insane, and Butler, early modern empiricist that he is, bases his sketches on his knowledge of actual Baroque thinkers and writers, such as Thomas Vaughan and Thomas Benlowes, whom he names directly or indirectly (Butler 1970: 89, 155).

Butler has sometimes been called the last of the Metaphysical or Baroque writers because of his use of the conceited style well into the Restoration. But classifying

Butler as a Baroque writer is to misunderstand his use of the conceit. Unlike Hall, the Overburians, and Earle, whose analogical style of writing reflects a Baroque worldview, Butler employs the Baroque style in order to satirize it. Indeed, as one critic has wryly observed, calling Butler a Metaphysical or Baroque writer is like calling James Joyce a neo-Thomist (Parker 1998: 40). The very analogical style that especially to the Overburians exemplified the liveliness of the literary imagination and the underlying cohesiveness of the world exemplifies only absurdity and madness in life and art to Samuel Butler. Pope's attacks in *Peri Bathous, or the Art of Sinking in Poetry* (1728) and *The Dunciad* (1728, 1729, 1742–3) on the Baroque style and Johnson's criticism of the Metaphysical style in the *Life of Cowley* (1779) emphasize how far out of favor this kind of writing had fallen and how little it was understood within the lapse of three or four generations.

After Butler, the character sketch continued to be practiced, but rarely as a discrete genre. Instead, it took on new life, as it had after Theophrastus' death, as an embedded or inscribed form. This happened first, as we have already seen, in verse satire. But by the mid-eighteenth century, verse satire was in decline. Pope's satiric character sketches are powerful, but often heterogeneous combinations of the character and the portrait – witness his Tibbald and Aristarchus in *The Dunciad*. Samuel Johnson wrote extraordinary portraits and characters at mid-century in "The Vanity of Human Wishes" (1749), but he tended to draw on Joseph Hall's venerable homiletic tradition (as well as on Juvenal), and ceased writing formal verse satire after 1749. Beginning around 1700, the satiric character sketch found new life in a more enduring fashion in the essay and novel. Joseph Addison (1672–1719) and Richard Steele (1672–1729) recognized the essay as a sufficiently flexible medium to accommodate the recurring social and professional characters of Sir Roger de Coverley, Will Honeycomb, Sir Andrew Freeport, Captain Sentry, and Mr Spectator himself in the *Spectator* (1711–12, 1714) series. But their wit was gentle, sentimental, and rarely satirical. Indeed, the discursiveness of the long *Spectator* series points toward the growing vogue of the novel rather than back to the dense, epigrammatic sketches of the seventeenth century.

Samuel Johnson (1709–84) and Oliver Goldsmith (1730?–74) also drew satiric characters in their *Rambler* (1750–2), *Idler* (1758–60), and *Citizen of the World* (1760–1) essays, but these also were loose and discursive, and though didactic, their character sketches were only occasionally satirical, and lacked the epigrammatic wit of their Baroque predecessors. The eighteenth-century author who most effectively drew on the tradition of the satiric character sketch was William Law (1686–1761), Anglican priest and religious writer, who, perhaps not surprisingly, sympathized with the philosophical and theological tenets of the hermetic philosophers and Protestant evangelicals satirized by Butler and his Augustan literary descendants. The character sketches in Law's *A Serious Call to a Devout and Holy Life* (1728) arise out of the same homiletic tradition as the early seventeenth-century characters of Hall and Earle. Like his seventeenth-century predecessors, Law draws both virtuous and vicious character types, with the vicious outnumbering the virtuous. Law's Flatus, the man restlessly in pursuit of schemes of happiness, Negotius, the perpetually occupied businessman, and Matilda, ever conscious of the demands of fashion, are described with a specificity consistent with the conventions of the eighteenth-century novel, yet have a generic quality that renders them moral types of human behavior. The same is true of Law's virtuous characters, such as Miranda, said to be based on Edward Gibbon's pious aunt Hester.

By the mid-eighteenth century, the satiric character sketch had been most noticeably absorbed into the novel – especially into the comic novels of Henry Fielding (1707–54) and Tobias Smollett (1721–71) – who worked best at describing characters from the outside in, rather than the inside out. (John Bunyan's satiric characters in *The Pilgrim's Progress* [1677, 1684] and *The Life and Death of Mr Badman* [1680], sometimes described as proto-novelistic, in fact owe more to the traditions of the morality play and the homiletic exemplum.) This tradition continued into the nineteenth century. Charles Dickens, William Makepeace Thackeray, Anthony Trollope, and George Eliot all tried their hand at the character sketch: Dickens in *Sketches by Boz* (1836); Thackeray in *The Book of Snobs* (1846–7); Trollope in *Hunting Sketches* (1865); and Eliot in *Impressions of Theophrastus Such* (1879). Trollope's affectionate descriptions are the most thoroughly novelized – long and realistic, averaging eight to ten pages each. Dickens's sketches are shorter, but in their realism also tend toward the novelistic. Eliot's character sketches are subsumed within her last novel, although its title pays homage to her ancient Greek predecessor. Only Thackeray, with short, witty sketches of character types of three pages on average, comes close to fulfilling the generic requirements of the traditional form. In the twentieth century, the satiric character sketch appeared with some frequency in the writing of such ironic and satiric novelists as Evelyn Waugh (1903–66) and Thomas Pynchon (1937–). At present, the satiric character sketch survives in dramatic form on television and in film. Comedy, especially situation comedy, with its reductive treatment of character, provides a favorable venue for the continued practice of the satiric character sketch.

References and Further Reading

Aldington, Richard (ed. and trans.) (1928) *A Book of "Characters."* London: Routledge.

Bellany, Alastair (2002) *The Politics of Court Scandal in Early Modern England: News Culture and the Overbury Affair, 1603–1660.* Cambridge: Cambridge University Press.

Boyce, Benjamin (1947) *The Theophrastan Character in England to 1642* (with notes by Chester Noyes Greenough). Cambridge, MA: Harvard University Press (reprinted New York: Humanities Press, 1967).

——(1955) *The Polemic Character, 1640–1661: A Chapter in English Literary History.* Lincoln: University of Nebraska Press (reprinted New York: Octagon Books, 1969).

——(1962) *The Character-Sketches in Pope's Poems.* Durham, NC: Duke University Press.

Breton, Nicholas (1879) *The Works in Verse and Prose of Nicholas Breton,* vol. 2, ed. Alexander B. Grosart (reprinted New York: AMS Press, 1966).

Butler, Samuel (1970) *Characters,* ed. Charles W. Daves. Cleveland: Press of Case Western Reserve University.

Earle, John (1897/1951) *Microcosmography,* ed. Alfred S. West. Cambridge: Cambridge University Press.

Fuller, Thomas (1938) *The Holy State and The Prophane State*, 2 vols, ed. Maximilian Graff Walten. New York: Columbia University Press.

Greenblatt, Stephen (1980) *Renaissance Self-fashioning: From More to Shakespeare*. Chicago: University of Chicago Press.

Hall, Joseph (1948) *Heaven upon Earth* and *Characters of Vertues and Vices*, ed. Rudolf Kirk. New Brunswick: Rutgers University Press.

Lanner, Allen H. (ed.) (1991) *A Critical Edition of Richard Brathwait's "Whimzies."* New York: Garland Press.

Macdonald, Hugh (ed.) (1947) *Portraits in Prose: A Collection of Characters*. New Haven, CT: Yale University Press.

Morley, Henry (ed.) (1891) *Character Writings of the Seventeenth Century*. London: Routledge.

Murphy, Gwendolen (1925) *A Bibliography of English Character-Books, 1608–1700*. Oxford: Oxford University Press.

Parker, Blanford (1998) *The Triumph of Augustan Poetics: English Literary Culture from Butler to Johnson*. Cambridge: Cambridge University Press.

Paylor, W. J. (ed.) (1936) *The Overburian Characters, to which is added "A Wife" by Sir Thomas Overbury*. Oxford: Blackwell (reprinted New York: AMS Press, 1977).

Theophrastus (1993) *Characters*. In Jeffrey Rusten, I. C. Cunningham, and A. D. Knox (eds and trans.), *Theophrastus: Characters; Herodas: Mimes; Cercidas and the Choliambic Poets*. Cambridge, MA: Harvard University Press.

Thompson, Elbert N. S. (1924) *Literary Bypaths of the Renaissance*. New Haven, CT: Yale University Press (reprinted Freeport: Books for Libraries, 1968).

Webster, John (1927) *The Complete Works of John Webster*, vol. 4, ed. F. L. Lucas. London: Chatto and Windus (reprinted New York: Gordian Press, 1966).

29
The Secret Life of Satire
Melinda Alliker Rabb

"Much health, a little wealth, and a life of stealth, that is all we want," wrote Jonathan Swift (*Journal to Stella*, 2. 303). Definitions of satire agree that it must attack someone or something, and therefore must depend on prior phenomena to parody, ridicule, or reform. These qualities, evidence of engagement with "the world," have encouraged an emphasis on satire's "public" status and have obscured the extent to which satire operates by stealth. Before 1688, most English satire circulated in manuscript, the "great majority... issued anonymously... copied by nameless scribes ... [and] distributed surreptitiously" (Lord 1963: xxxii). (The Licensing Act of 1662 referred only to printed texts, thus encouraging a secret manuscript trade.) Swift's *Discourse Concerning the Mechanical Operation of the Spirit* (1710) is preceded by a facetious "Bookseller's Advertisement" claiming that he had "kept it... some years, resolving it should never see the Light." *The Mechanical Operation* begins by promising a revelation: "It is a good while since I have had in my Head something... that the World should be informed in. For, to tell you a Secret, I am able to *contain* it no longer." John Gay's *The Beggar's Opera* (1728) offers a counterbalancing example in its ending: "As for the rest... But at present keep your own secret" (3.17). Effective satirists, furthermore, have been praised precisely for their skill at sleight-of-hand. In the seventeenth century, John Dryden, in his "Discourse Concerning Satire" (1693), articulated an ideal for ironic aggression: "Yet there is still a vast difference between the slovenly butchering of a Man, and the fineness of the Stroak that separates the Head from the Body, and leaves it standing in place" (1974: 71). In the twentieth century, Nelson Algren had similar praise for Don DeLillo's satire in which "wit is so surgical you don't even know an artery has been severed" (Algren 1972).

From Lucilius to DeLillo, from the biblical Book of Revelations to the blotted FBI documents in Michael Moore's film *Fahrenheit 9/11* (2004), satiric writing has a long-standing association with the concept of secrecy. This association can help to bridge the chasm dividing postmodern subjects from millennia of now remote, linguistically inaccessible, or little-studied satirists. A few examples across the centuries begin to suggest some shared concepts. Horace claimed that Gaius Lucilius (180–103 BCE), the writer "uniformly recognized as the founder of literary Satire" (Fairclough 1947: xv), would "trust his secrets to his books, as if to faithful friends, never turning elsewhere for recourse" (*Satires* 2.1.30–2). Swift compared the satirist to a broom that discovers hidden dirt ("Meditation on a Broomstick," 1703), and he characterized the eighteenth-century as an era "full of passages which the curious of another age would be glad to know the secret springs of" (*Prose Works* 8.108). Alexander Pope expressed his frustration at politics and art in this "age of lead" (suggesting not only heaviness but opacity): "Out with it Dunciad! Let the Secret pass, / That Secret to each Fool, that he's an Ass" ("Epistle to Dr Arbuthnot," 1735, 79–80). More recently, American novelist Thomas Pynchon created satiric fictions of paranoia and conspiracy in the postmodern world, in which even apparently normal children live clandestine nocturnal lives: "When their mothers thought they were out playing they were really curled in cupboards of neighbors' houses, in platforms up in trees, in secretly-hollowed nests inside hedges, sleeping, making up for these hours" (Pynchon 1999: 96). We, as citizens of a post-9/11 world, have been forced to reconsider the relationships between the ideas of attack and of secrecy.

In order to investigate these relationships, this chapter will establish some parallels between the great age of satire in the Restoration and eighteenth century and our own time. These parallels will be drawn with reference to several ideas: the technology of information (secrecy's "other"); the effects of injurious language (the means of attack); the historical phenomenon of "secret histories"; the satirist's role as both teller and keeper of secrets; ironic representation of real or imagined conspiracy and paranoia. Invoking parallels may require no further justification than that satire of *all* periods may be compared instructively to that of the eighteenth century. But other parallels between the decades following 1660 in England and those following 1960 in America form a long list: escalating party politics (Whig and Tory; Democrat and Republican); controversial wars (Spanish Succession; Vietnam and Iraq); traumatic public deaths of prominent figures through execution or assassination (Charles I and Monmouth; the Kennedys and Martin Luther King); reapportionment of power (parliamentary rule; the civil rights movement and women's lib); revolutions in scientific knowledge and technology (the microscope, experimental method, and global exploration; antibiotics, computers, space exploration); sexual revolution (libertinism; flower children); changes in marriage practices (companionate marriage; divorce and gay marriage); consumerism (the shop; the mall); and fear of conspiracy (Jacobites; Communists and al-Quaedists). Political events that promised good effects (the end of the Civil Wars and the end of the Cold War) instead ushered in periods of cultural paranoia, uncertainty, and new forms of unrest. The following discussion will focus on secrecy and aggression in satires of the two periods, and a few exemplary texts only (principally from Swift, Pope, Manley, Pynchon, DeLillo, and Moore) will serve as representatives of many other possibilities. They share common themes and strategies of linguistic aggression that this chapter will explore.

Almost all discussions of satire measure it, analyze it, and establish its origins in relation to ancient ritual or classical texts, but one might argue for the limitations of such a perspective in a culture like ours, in which classical education cannot be assumed. Perhaps three or two or even one hundred years ago, given the historical relationship between literacy, class, and canonical learning, most readers brought a background of Latin and perhaps Greek to popular satire. In our current culture, satire continues to flourish in widely disseminated formats and media. But how many admirers of *The Onion* or *The Daily Show* have read Horace, Persius, Varro, or Juvenal? Something else besides classical erudition provides the "hook" that holds readers of satire together in mutual desire for its peculiar pleasures.

Secrets and Information

The Restoration and eighteenth century, like our own time, was an "information age." Print culture and the flourishing marketplace allowed the wide dissemination of texts, a process only recently surpassed by electronic communication and digital encoding. The extraordinary access to ideas made possible by a marketplace of cheap, plentifully published texts can be compared to the technological breakthroughs that have made televisions and computers ubiquitous. Information not only flows, it "streams." Technology would seem to promise greater documentation and openness. But both cultures raise alarms about the "virtuality" of their texts, selves, and spaces. If information technology permits greater connection between its users, it also can cause greater isolation. Hours spent facing a book or a screen replace interactive social endeavors, with consequences for the developing human psyche. Both cultures are equally characterized by horrific failures of communication, by malfunctioning of the "free press," by struggles over the control of information. Thus they also exhibit anxieties over the ease with which information can become misinformation, and when pushed to extremes, with which signs can become emptied of meaning.

Satirists observe this process. The streets of John Dryden's "MacFlecknoe" (1682) are clogged with the "trash" of worthless sheets from booksellers' stalls. Throngs of dunces move through London in the service of the goddess Dulness in Pope's *Dunciad*, until they reach a state of complete intellectual and moral "Anarchy." In Pynchon's *The Crying of Lot 49* (1965), an underground communication system, W.A.S.T.E., constitutes a satiric triumph of chaos and meaninglessness in which the solution to every puzzle merely uncovers another enigma. In DeLillo's *Underworld* (1997), technology's by-product is not information but actual waste. Discarded pollutants sink and accumulate into the ooze of oblivion where excrement mixes with plutonium, "from Pluto, god of the dead and ruler of the underworld" (p. 106). Aptly, both historical periods fixed on the term *hack* or *hacker* to label the abuser of information. In cyberspace, as in the print marketplace, anonymous and unregulated publication could translate into irresponsible junk, or worse, predatory seduction and crass market opportunism. Grubstreet has found its postmodern site in Grubnet.

Like our eighteenth-century predecessors experiencing the proliferation of printed texts, we are caught in an asymptotic relationship in which the amount of retrievable knowledge amasses faster than we can process or disclose it. We speed down the information highway to find ourselves caught, so to speak, in our own "net." We hope for empowerment through access to others, yet we are less able to protect our privacy. Eighteenth-century writers associate information with espionage in popular publications like Ned Ward's *London Spy*, Joseph Addison and Sir Richard Steele's *Tatler* and *Spectator* (*tattle*: "to reveal other people's secrets; tell tales...to reveal [a secret] through gossiping," *Webster's Dictionary*). The narrator of Delarivier Manley's bestselling narrative of political and sexual scandal, *Secret Memoirs of The New Atalantis* (1709), bears the name Intelligence, a word defined in Samuel Johnson's *Dictionary of the English Language* as an "account of things distant or secret." The title of Thomas Sheridan and Jonathan Swift's periodical *The Intelligencer* similarly signifies a messenger or spy. In the twenty-first century, every computer and program seems filled with real and metaphorical spies and spyware, engaging us in a constant struggle to outwit the secret agents who plant "cookies" of surveillance, who intercept our most discreetly transmitted information, and who are determined to pry invisibly into our lives. In this regard, we seem to be ensnared in the consequences of problems set in motion by the seventeenth and early eighteenth centuries. The pursuit of knowledge seems not so much collective or shared but concealed, competitive, and aggressive.

Crucial to these comparisons is information's "other," secrecy. Evelyn Keller writes: "secrets function to articulate a boundary: an interior not visible to outsiders, the demarcation of a separate domain, a sphere of autonomous power" (1992: 40). The advent of print encouraged the belief that "valuable data could be preserved best by being made public" (Eisenstein 1979: 1.116). But public access to information did not always have this effect. A dedicatory poem to John Wilkins's *Mercury, or the Secret and Swift Messenger* (1641) notes the paradox: "*Secrecie's* now publish'd; you reveal / By Demonstration how we can conceal." Early modern schemes for a universal language have certain similarities to international computer-based codes (Knowlson 1975: 26). Universal language was supposed to enable broad and easy communication. Wilkins, in *An Essay Towards a Real Character and a Philosophical Language* (1668), proposes both profit to business and benefit to the soul: "Besides that most obvious advantage which would ensure, of facilitating mutual commerce, amongst the several Nations of the World, and the improving of all Natural Knowledge; it would likewise very much conduce to the spreading of the knowledge of religion" (Epistle Dedicatory). Ironically but aptly, universal language schemes grew out of systems of secret writing in the seventeenth century. That is, political motives to conceal meaning vie with religious motives to regain pre-Babel purity/unity of language (Knowlson 1975: 15–27). Thus Cave Beck, in *Universal Character* (1657), transmutes the Old Testament commandment "honor thy father and thy mother" into "leb2314p2477 and pf2477" (p. 63). But John Wilkins in *Mercury, or the Secret and Swift Messenger* encrypts a much more political phrase, "The souldiers are almost famished; Supply us, or we must yield" into "teoloraelmsfmfesplvoweutelhfudefralotaihd,upysremsyid" (Wilkins 1708: 26). Every language (as computer-users who do not know the "inner springs" of programming can attest) "looks like a secret code to the person who does not know its rules" (Potter 1989: 42).

These problems resonate in satire. In Swift's *A Tale of a Tub* (1704), the three brothers, Martin, Peter, and Jack, blithely mystify the language of their father's will in order to discover a hidden meaning: hoping to defy an obvious injunction against stitching shoulder-knots to their coats, "they fell once more to the Scrutiny and soon picked out S, H, O, U, L, D, E, R." In *The Crying of Lot 49*, the heroine Oedipa Maas struggles to decipher codes and symbols: from a distance, San Francisco seems to resemble the confusing circuitry of a transistor, and a puzzling clue from a seventeenth-century text leads first to the acronym WASTE and ultimately to the enigmatic phrase "We Await Silent Tristero's Empire" (p. 139).

The dissemination of information associated with earlier "print culture" generated its own resistance and was accompanied by new strategies for concealment. These strategies could be ingenious, even bizarre: *The Swift and Secret Messenger* suggests shaving a servant's head, writing a message on the bare scalp, and allowing the hair to grow back before delivering the dermatological missive. Revelations of sordid but entertaining misdeeds of prominent citizens and high-ranking government officials in Manley's *The New Atalantis*, Swift's *Gulliver's Travels* (1726), and Pope's *Dunciad* (1728) often refer to actual secret treaties, clandestine financial scandals, and other personal intrigues, but they are couched in elaborate fictions that protect against libel laws and, to a degree, against personal retaliation.

These misdeeds compare readily to the scandals that have ushered in the new millennium. We seem to be living through enough shocking episodes to supply a third volume of *The New Atalantis*: adulterous ministers, pedophilic clergy, a discarded mistress's description of her lover's secret mark, paid intruders and stolen documents, abusive educators, a romantic tryst ending in the violent death of a princess, a nanny's misconduct and a murdered baby, a widely publicized trial in which a guilty husband goes free – these and other episodes of infidelity, bigotry, lust, greed, and injustice have riveted public attention with disclosed "secrets." Now that an American president has been impeached because of a sexual scandal, we can better appreciate the sexual/political dynamic of Restoration and eighteenth-century satiric fictions of promiscuous desire. The Enron scandal may help us to appreciate the imaginative response by Swift and others to the bursting of the South Sea Bubble (1720–1), the first example of a financial disaster predicated on the secret deals of unscrupulous, self-serving company directors.

Most recently, fear of hidden weapons of mass destruction in Islamic Iraq (weapons so well obscured as to be un-findable and possibly imaginary) have involved the United States in a war through which high-ranking officials benefit financially. We might compare WMD and Haliburton to anti-Jacobite conspiracy theories about invasions by Catholic France or the Pretender, and to the riches amassed during war by powerful insiders like the Duke of Marlborough. Then, as now, a degree of skepticism accompanies even "polite" news about "those who have born the parts of Kings, Statesmen, or Commanders": "the Reader will perhaps conceive a greater Idea of him from those Actions done in Secret, and without a Witness, than of those which have drawn upon them the Admiration of the world" (Thomas Tickell, *Spectator* no. 622, November 19, 1714). Thus, Moore's political satire *Fahrenheit 9/11* lingers on behind-the-scenes shots of government officials being prepared for the camera by make-up artists and hair-stylists, in order to expose the artificiality of public image and to undermine the dignity and veracity of men who vainly request self-concealment by "cosmetic powers" (Pope's phrase for Belinda's transformation in *The Rape of the Lock*, 1714). "Make me look young," they confide. A *paparazzi* factor, a compulsion to get inside the bedrooms of famous people, a lack of respect for office *per se*, distinguishes both periods. D. A. Miller's observation pertains here: "[n]o doubt an analysis of the kinds of knowledge that it is felt needful to cover in secrecy would tell us much about a given culture" (1988: 206). Satire attempts precisely this kind of telling.

Secrecy and Aggression

Like satire, secrecy can be a means of aggression. In a study of the moral and ethical dilemmas in the contemporary world, Sissela Bok analyzes "secrecy [as] central to the planning of every form of injury to human beings" (1984: 26). She contextualizes practices such as government surveillance, investigative journalism, and industrial espionage within the traditions of law, religion, and philosophy. Secrets, she argues, determine power relationships because they "protect the liberty of some while impairing that of others" (1984: xvi): "In this exploring secrecy and openness, I have come up against what human beings care most to protect and to probe: the exalted, the dangerous, the shameful, the sources of power and creation; the fragile and the intimate" (1984: xvii–xviii). Her argument stresses the dangers of concealment for the citizen of a political state. Yet her discussion admits inherent contradictions: the myth of Pandora's box, the Sphinx's riddle, and Faust's quest for knowledge suggest that some secrets, however alluring, are better kept. Similarly, Evelyn Keller discusses the problems inherent in revealing secrets in two seminal modern events: the discovery of the double helix of the genetic code and the discovery of atomic fusion. She writes: "Watson and Crick described themselves as embarking on a quest that they themselves described as a 'calculated assault on the secret of life'... The Manhattan Project... was a secret kept by men – an equally calculated assault on the secrets of death" (1992: 42). Implicit in such rhetoric is the possibility of violence.

Secrecy is a crucial concept to the satirist because of its enormous potential to injure. In his "Discourse Concerning Satire," Dryden hints at the fine art of stealth by means of which words can inflict damage: "a Man is secretly wounded, and though he be not sensible himself, yet the malicious World will find it for him" (1974: 71). Postmodern theorist Judith Butler states the problem this way in *Excitable Speech*: "We ascribe an agency to language, a power to injure... Could language injure us if we were not, in some sense, linguistic beings, beings who require language in order to be? Is our vulnerability to language a consequence of our being constituted within its terms?" (1997: 1–2). The connection between vulnerability and secrecy, and between secrecy and the power/knowledge nexus is worth exploring. To be vulnerable is to be susceptible to wounding (from the Latin *vulnus*, wound), to be unprotected, uncovered, and exposed. Cultural myths offer many examples of exposure as weakness (Adam and Eve unable to hide from God) and concealment as strength (the Trojan Horse). But Georg Simmel reminds us of the ambiguous power dynamic in "that purposive hiding and masking, that aggressive defensive, so to speak, against the third person, which alone is usually designated as secret" (Wolff 1950: 330). One cannot wound what is hidden or unknown, but strategies of discovery exist to remove protective veils and coatings: "The secret puts a barrier between men, but, at the same time, it creates the tempting challenge to break through it, by gossip and confession – and thus challenge accompanies its psychology like a constant overtone" (1950: 334).

These unwelcome revelations make people uncomfortable. Pope took satisfaction in the thought that his enemies feared him: "I must be proud to see / Men not afraid of God, afraid of me" (*Epilogue to the Satires: Dialogue II*, 208–9). He construes his satire as a source of psychological terror that makes others so uneasy that they *tremble* (a word he used almost fifty times as a poet and over two hundred times as a translator): "Hear this, and tremble, you who 'scape the Laws" (*The First Satire of the Second Book of Horace Imitated*, 118). What is the means of arousing such terror? Certainly Pope, a disenfranchised, four-and-a-half-foot Catholic hunchback, could claim neither physical prowess nor political power. Yet he could, in verse, at any time choose to "strip the Gilding off a Knave" (115). For Swift, the successful satiric attack would make others uneasy, anxious, on edge, would "vex the world," as he wrote to Pope (September 25, 1725). The depth of vulnerability, individual and social, that would result from the inability to keep anything hidden, from being "laid open" like the flayed woman and anatomized beau in the "Digression on Madness" (*A Tale of a Tub*, 1704), is painful to contemplate. The satirist's job – to peel away and expose unpleasant truths – is re-enacted in postmodern satire. In Moore's film, for example, we witness the removal of ink from condemnatory and embarrassing words and phrases on official documents that have been blotted over. Here too the probing satirist, who lacks both physical intimidation and official authority, nevertheless has the power to arouse fear and uneasiness; Moore depicts himself as an overweight, slightly clumsy ingénue who nevertheless is threatening enough to make senators nervously rush away and to provoke a visit from the Secret Service police.

The satirist's job, then, to wound with words, depends on our status as linguistic beings. How can this attack take place? A harangue in a crowded public square might attract attention. But how much more terrifying is it to imagine an attacker who does not face us directly, who is privy to our secret weaknesses or misdeeds, and who is concealing the precise mode, timing, and full significance of the eventual onslaught on those vulnerabilities? Who would not feel defensive if this same attacker were telling other people about us? Critics have noticed Swift's affinity for the spider's "large Vein of Wrangling and Satyr," in *The Battel of the Books*. This "Modern" creature lives hidden in the most remote corner of St James library, from which vantage point he can spy on all the books below and store up venom for an opportune moment to bite. No wonder Swift referred to his career as a party-writer as "the life of a spider."

Telling Secrets: Gossip, Gender, and Satire

Telling secrets also suggests a relationship between the satirist and the gossip, another participant in verbal espionage and secret-telling. This relationship allows a rethinking of genre and gender. Theories of satire have been relentlessly masculinist, framing their arguments in figures of male aggression: Saturnian blasts from the Roman god of winter; thrusts of libidinous satyrs; cannibalistic rites of primitive warriors; deft slashes, stabs, barbs, and stings from battling soldiers, swordsmen, wits, and moral scourges. "All satire kills, symbolically at any rate," argues Robert Elliott (1960: 4). Since the Greek Archilochus (seventh century BCE) first "dipt a bitter Muse in snake venom," Ben Jonson claims, verse satirists have hoped to "rime 'hem [their adversaries] to death" (*Poetaster*, "To the Reader," 163). In the seventeenth century, the persistent (mis)spelling of "satyr" suggests a lustful man/beast who threatens nymphs, dryads, and mortal women.

Probably in response to the crisis of authority surrounding the English Civil Wars, many early modern commentators on satire continue an anti-feminine strain by favoring a heroic paradigm, heroism serving as wish-fulfillment for lost patriarchal ideals. John Milton asserts that the weapon of satire "ought...to strike high and adventure dangerously" (*Apology for Smectymnuus*, 1642, section 6). John Oldham writes similarly: "strait to thrusts I go, / And pointed Satyr runs him thro' and thro'" (*Satire Upon a Printer*, 1697). And Samuel Butler observes in his manuscript essay on "Wit and Folly": "Among all Sports and shews that are used [by the satirist] none are so delightful as the Military; that do but imitate and Counterfet Fights"; and in his *Prose Observations*: "A Satyr is a kinde of Knight Errant that goe's upon Adventures, to Relieve the Distressed Damsel Virtue, and Redeeme Honor out of Inchanted Castles, and opprest Truth, and Reason out of the Captivity of Gyants, and Magitians..." (De Quehen 1979: 60, 215).

The frontispiece of the second edition of John Stapleton's *Juvenal's Satires* (1697) depicts Juvenal simultaneously receiving the satyr's mask and the hero's crown of laurels. In Ferrand Spence's *Life of Lucian*, satiric irony borrows qualities of Arthur's Excalibur and Perseus' shield: a "keen and shining weapon in [Lucian's] hand; it glitters in the Eyes of those it kills,...his greatest enemies are not butcher'd by him, but fairly slain: they must acknowledge the Hero in the Stroak" (*Lucian's Works Translated*, 1684).

Jonson is anxious to differentiate satire's noble masculinity from less-valued feminine speech acts like gossip and slander: "Each slanderer bears a whip...Which to pursue, were but a feminine honour, / And farre beneath the dignitie of a man"

(*Poetaster*, 176–9). In the Earl of Mulgrave's *Essay on Poetry* (2nd edn, 1691), war-like aggression "[d]istinguishes [male] Satire from a [female] Scold." In the eighteenth century, Joseph Warton praises the potency of Pope's satire because it makes English "depravity and corruption" seem in contrast "emasculated and debased" (*An Essay on the Genius and Writings of Pope*, 1782). Although many militaristic models have been constructed for satire – swordsmen, knights, heroes – its feminine aspects demand attention, too. The insistence on gender difference in the above remarks suggests that perhaps the dividing lines are not self-evident. If satire can be imagined as the magical curse of warriors who eat their enemies' brains, the "mixed dish" or *lanx satura* can also be a gossip's feast.

Patricia Spacks argues that "gossip gets its power by the illusion of mastery gained through taking imaginative possession of another's experience" (1986: 22). In this sense, it resembles satire. But unlike satire, gossip usually is gendered female. The gossip has little stature (George Meredith defines gossip according to the law of the jungle where females hunt and kill; it is "the beast of prey that does not wait for the death of the creature it devours," 1972: 292). The satirist nears heroic heights ("Satire's my weapon," writes Pope in *Satires* 2.1, the self-styled warrior "arm'd for Virtue when [he] point[s] the pen"). Yet the boundaries between satire, scandal, and gossip are not absolute, and male writers are perfectly capable of indulging in and deploying the power of gossip and scandal in their work. Why are personal letters by women in the Public Record Office catalogued as "gossip about private friends," while gossipy letters by men are dignified as "private news" (Rosenfelt 1998: 27)? We must question the operative assumptions about aggressive language that perpetuate a hierarchy from low/feminine/gossip to high/masculine/satire.

What else do the satirist and the gossip have in common? Both reveal information without their subject's volition. Both can "kill" reputation; both can have effects – both can perform – in the "real" world. Both have the effect of destabilizing and challenging authority with unauthorized discourse; they reveal what an official account might wish to conceal. Both generate alternative versions of things, versions that acquire a kind of underground subversive power and that disperse univocal meaning or interpretation into contending possibilities. Both paradoxically can also create a sense of community through the sharing of secrets. The world of Pope's *Rape of the Lock* can both unite and isolate its inhabitants by saying "horrid things." Gossip has acquired an association with women, but historically the *godsib* (or God-sibling) could be male or female. Thus gossip modifies the insistent macho-masculinity of satire and allows a rethinking of its relation to the feminine. Pynchon intimates this inevitable shift by making the heroine of his satire a woman who discovers an underground communication system, and by naming her Oedipa, the feminine variant of the name of Sophocles' (and Freud's) most famous male hero.

Gradations of aggressive speech, each gradation escalating the repercussions of the relationship between secret and public information, form a kind of continuum, from the most private whisper to the most widely published satire. Gossip about public figures, fascination with revealed "dirt," attacks on the betrayal of public and private promises, representations of violent action, inclusion of women, and an insatiable interest in sexual (especially aberrant sexual) practices constitute key elements of both modes of discourse. Manley's successful Tory satire, *The New Atalantis*, is a case in point. The female narrators move unseen through Angela (a fictionalized England), revealing the misdeeds of thinly disguised public figures. While the women chatter about sexual transgressions, dysfunctional families, failed marriages, and illegal financial schemes, Manley also satirizes the Whig ministry so effectively, according to her contemporaries, that her attack contributed to its fall. Arguably, in a postmodern age, when fewer and fewer people would recognize a reference to Lord Godolphin any more than they would an allusion to Horace, satire's gossipy aggression, among what Swift called "friends laughing in a corner," is its most enduring quality.

Satire's intimacy has interested scholars, such as Michael Seidel (1979), Fredric Bogel (2001), and Christian Thorne (2001), in studies that emphasize the importance of establishing personal relationships between the satirist, the reader, and the object of attack. Seidel, for example, notes "the intertwinement of satirist and reader with satiric object, and the compromising intimacies of irony and parody or satiric mimicry, as essential features of the structure of satire rather than occasional aberrations" (1979: 6). The common emphasis on satire's rhetorical purpose designates its primary function as the arousal of strong feelings by means of speech acts, rather than as performance of action through plot. In fact, Alvin Kernan attempts to argue that "the most striking quality of satire is the absence of plot" (1959: 30). Alternative structures to conventional plot, such as the anatomy, the interpolation, and the digression, have informed studies of Swift and Sterne.

Yet there is irony in Kernan's failure to recognize that certain kinds of "plot" frequently exist in satire, namely, conspiratorial fantasies and seductions, as well as "compromising intimacies" that permit the satirist and the reader to conspire together in the attack on an Other. The speech act of secret-sharing is an important alternative to conventional plot. On one hand, its aggression may be understood as competing with other circulating versions or representations of a person or event; it can "win" the competition for authority, for example, by claiming to drag hitherto hidden things into the light, things often shocking, grotesque, or demeaning. On the other hand, not only do its acts of speech add to the circulation of "dirt" in the world, but also its ability to wound with words depends on an authorial self that is constituted by shocking, grotesque, and demeaning secret knowledge.

Secret History: Its Relation to Satire

Competition for authority over versions of recorded "truth" is an essential aspect of print culture in an information age, and the truth about the past is no exception. The historical period that saw the rise of satire in England also saw the proliferation of books of history, as well as the development of a subgenre called "secret history" or "secret memoirs." Some of these works take the form of scandalous *romans à clef*, that is, racy novels about actual people whose names were changed in the main text but identified in accompanying "keys." (A postmodern example would be the exposé, anonymously published in 1996, of Bill Clinton's administration, *Primary Colors: A Novel of Politics*.) But other secret histories stayed away from the boudoir while offering accounts of current events taking place in parliament, court, or army.

Scores of histories and secret histories of England published between the Restoration and the Georgian era document a struggle over the remembrance of things past. Whig, Tory, Anti-Catholic, Jacobite, and anti-Jacobite writers try to highlight, "spin," or maintain silence on selective details in these narratives. What happened and why did it happen? Was, to cite a popular example, the restored King Charles II planning to bring peace and stability to a riven nation? Or was he selling the country out to France, when he was not too busy dallying with one of his mistresses? And were these mistresses really spies? Was his illegitimate son, the Duke of Monmouth, the future hope for a Protestant monarchy? Or was he a superstitious, gullible, libidinous weakling, ungrateful for his father's kindness? Postmodern news-watchers will recognize parallels, as our perceptions of public events vary widely depending on which news channel we watch or which newspaper we read, or if we tune in to *The Daily Show* at night.

The desire to document the past in order to explain the present motivates the production of history, but history provokes secret history. David Jones, the author of *The Secret History of White-Hall* (1697), offers his readers "new Discoveries of State-Mysteries," despite *"the Objection that I foresee would be made upon this subject,* That all that could be writ has been written already, concerning the late Reigns...." His alternative narration will *"promiscuously... call to mind"* a "Private League," a "secret correspondence," a *"Wife's petition* [and suicide]," the prevention *"of the late queen's being married,"* "unseasonable boasting," "censure," and other tidbits that *"had, in all likelihood, been forever buried in the profoundest Oblivion... [in] Dark and almost inscrutable Recesses"* (A4–5).

Secrets seem to enclose secrets like the layers of an onion. We have a sense of the process of peeling away by following chronologically one sequence of titles. Daniel Defoe's *The Secret History of the White Staff* (1714, on government ministers Robert Harley, Francis Atterbury, and Simon Harcourt) was followed by second and third parts (1715), as well as by John Oldmixon's *A Detection of the Sophistry and the Falsities of the Pamphlet, entitl'd, The Secret History of the White Staff* (1714), William Atterbury's *The History of the Mitre and the Purse in which the first and second parts of the Secret History of the White Staff are fully consider'd* (1714), William Pittis's *A Dialogue between the Mitre and the Purse* (1715), and Defoe's *The Secret History of the Secret History of the White Staff* (1715). Swift casts an ironic but knowing eye upon such competing truths: the narrator of the *Tale of a Tub* has "a Quill worn to the Pith in the service of the State, in the Pro's and Con's upon Popish Plots, and Meal-Tubs, and Exclusion Bills." The postmodern satiric novel recreates this sense of layering and contradiction, as in Oedipa's game of strip Botticelli in *The Crying of Lot 49*. The novel's sixth chapter consists of a secret history of Europe from 1577 to 1789. A sequence of conspiracies conflate sex and politics; people are addicted to sex, television, alcohol, and drugs (evidenced by groups like "Inamorati Anonymous"); sunken bones and code words hide truths; and a clandestine group of postmodern West coast neo-Jacobites seem to be waiting for a latter-day Pretender named Tristero. Unlike a mystery novel in which clues lead to the solution of a crime, here the unknown proliferates, and we are not even sure what crime has occurred.

In earlier centuries, secret history offered "those sorts of Relations, which they fancy containing something more Secret and Particular, than is to be found in the Publick Newspapers" (*Polish Manuscripts, or the Secret History of the Reign of Count Sobieski*, 1700, A2). *The Royal Mistresses of France, or the Secret History of the Amours of All the French Kings* (1695) defends and defines the form in its address "[t]o the reader... who may think these Stories Fabulous":

> For certain it is, that in the Main, the short Stories agree exactly with what they call the Truth of History, and as for the Circumstances which are added, they may be justly thought rather to illustrate the Stories, and discover the Causes of those odd Events, which others only barely or obscurely relate. For example, 'tis assuredly true, that a Prince committed such and such miscarriages, that such and such Persons of no Worth or Merit were advanced to high preferments, and that others greatly deserving of their Prince and Country, fell into Disgrace, while the True Historian (as they call them) is at a loss for the Reason of these Whimseys of Fortune. But here the Riddle is unfolded. (A2–A3)

Equally significant is the fact that women wrote (and read) secret histories; and the most popular (and licentious) were authored by Manley and Eliza Haywood. Although Manley, Haywood, and other women writers have been credited recently with contributing to the development of the novel, their relevance to the development of satire has been too little understood. Like gossips, they were dismissed from the official world of power. But their representations of the ways in which power is negotiated (often by means of sex and money) are highly relevant to satiric practice.

Secret history is important in any criticism or theory of satire after the Restoration. Like satire (and gossip) it is characterized by partisanship, by techniques of exposure and linguistic injury, by challenges to the concept of univocal authority, and by interest in the ways that a *sub rosa* reality seems to run simultaneously alongside an apparent one. Furthermore, secret histories encourage conspiratorial fantasies. They often imply that "great" wielders of power are motivated disingenuously by pettiness, greed, or lust. Or they suggest that people and/or events that seem embarrassingly trivial or immoral or foolish are really serving some clandestine purpose, wittingly or unwittingly. In his facetious *The Key to the Lock*, Pope outrageously asserts that *The Rape of the Lock*, a poem supposedly inspired by a private love-quarrel between two Catholic families, really conceals a secret political history written to abet a Jacobite plot. The poem's heroine Belinda is variously identified in the key as both Queen Anne and the Barrier Treaty; Pope here parodies ludicrous "secret" assertions, even though he suspects or knows that government does indeed function behind closed doors.

Indeed, the convergence of the personal and the political in secret history is a key to understanding the direction satire would take from the age of Swift and Pope to our own time. Arguably, the opening scenes of Moore's *Fahrenheit 9/11* precisely enact the contending versions of the past that are essential to secret history. In order to undermine presidential authority, election night 2000 is represented as several contradictory stories. What, the film insinuates, *really* happened? Why did things turn out the way they did? Historical "facts" are invoked to support an obviously partisan, inflammatory view, and damaging secrets underlying the crucial Florida vote put forward (Bush is brother to the Governor and the head of the recount is politically beholden to him). Moore's narrator continues to instill doubt by suggesting that a different history is hidden behind the public version of the Republican victory, the events of September 11, and the subsequent war on terror. He repeatedly tweaks this possibility: "If the public knew this...," "perhaps the war in Afghanistan was really about something else," "somebody [permitted security infractions] or was something else going on?" DeLillo's *Underworld* even more complexly demonstrates the legacy of an ironic relationship between history and secret history. Historical facts and figures (a missing baseball from the game in which the New York Giants won the pennant in 1951, conflict in Vietnam, FBI director J. Edgar Hoover, the Cuban missile crisis, the comedians Lenny Bruce and Jackie Gleason, the nuclear arms race) are transformed into "family secrets and unbreathable personal tales" that disclose a secret history of the Cold War. Mood swinging between "the unseen something that haunts the day" (1997: 11) and "the excitement of a revealed thing" (1997: 14), the country's chief of espionage realizes that "fame and secrecy are the high and low ends of the same fascination" (1997: 17).

Keeping Secrets: Irony, Conspiracy, and Paranoia

We noted above that satiric attacks, as a consequence of their gossipy and feminine qualities, are able to create a sense of community. A partial explanation of this apparent contradiction between anti-social and social effects lies in the sense of shared experience, in the special intimacy and camaraderie enabled by satiric discourse. The ancient attribution of magical powers to the satirist can take the modern form of the uncanny knowing of the secrets of others. There is a satisfying (although not particularly democratic) sense of inclusion of anyone perceptive enough to penetrate the secrets and concealed meanings of satiric allusions and ironies. Those who survive the attack find themselves members of a conspiratorial cabal. They experience "privity," or knowledge of secrets shared with others (*The Secret History of Queen Zarah and the Zarazians*, 1705, attributed to Delarivier Manley, 2.A4). In this sense, satire is intensely private and even unfathomable except to a select few who share its secret meaning. "Such a jest there is," Swift writes, "that it will not pass out of Covent Garden; and such a one, that is nowhere intelligible but at Hide-Park Corner" (Preface, *A Tale of a Tub*). Or, he contends, "If I ridicule the Follies and Corruption of a Court, a Ministry, or a Senate, are they not amply paid by Pensions, Titles, and Power, while I expect, and desire no other Reward, than that of laughing with a few Friends in a Corner?" Such satire may attack public targets, but, as Thorne observes, the text is represented as "essentially private" and its only noteworthy effects are "wholly intimate" (2001: 537). To be "let into the secret" (a common eighteenth-century expression) is to enter an imaginary but privileged space. "[T]here is no Mystery in it, but the Mystery of I – – – y" was the dry self-assessment of the attack on Sarah Churchill and the Whig ministry (*The Secret History of Queen Zarah and the Zarazians*).

But who can know the full import of a satirist's complex ironies? Continuing debates over the meaning of Gulliver's fourth voyage or over the definitions of happiness in the "Digression on Madness," to cite two of many possible examples, measure the elusiveness of this knowledge. Irony is a secret-keeping mode of discourse; it signifies something beyond the literal, but it does not explicitly reveal or confirm that other meaning. In fact, often *multiple* meanings are activated by irony, in the same way that secret histories activate multiple versions of the same event or person. Because of its dependence on irony, satire is always withholding information, always teasing its readers with hidden possibilities, always suggesting a design or plot beyond, beneath, or behind appearances.

Both its characters and its readers can experience this uncertainty as a kind of paranoia. They feel, at various points, embarrassed by ridicule, complicit in conspiratorial fantasies, uncomfortable in a world of scrutiny and accusation, unsure how to respond to fantasies of persecution, or uncertain about the satirist's deeper, unarticulated aggressions. "Terms that mean in equivocal ways are thus a threat," observes Judith Butler of injurious "excitable" language (1997: 86). Satiric laughter differs from the confident superiority associated with *comic* laughter because we are aware that we do not know everything. We are aware that something may ricochet back upon us, that we may have gotten it wrong, that we will be, as the eighteenth-century liked to say, "bit." Swift aptly teased Stella, his friend and confidante, with irony's power to share and to withhold: "But oo must not know zees sings, zey are Secrets, & we must keep them from naughty dollars" (Williams 1948: 2.503).

Thus the club or cabal of irony has a darker side that belongs to satire's power to injure, pain, and vex the world. Satire, for all its assertive posturing, captures the combination of helplessness, secrecy, paranoia, self-importance, and fear that render individuals vulnerable to conspiracy theories in order to explain a flawed and incorrigible world. Pope jokes that even his most "trivial" mock-epic, *The Rape of the Lock*, conceals "secret satyrs on the State" (*Key to the Lock*, 1714). The narrator of Swift's *Tale of a Tub* enlists Prince Posterity's belief in a plot that destroys Modern works as soon as they appear in a bookseller's stall. And, of course, Gulliver is the frequent victim of conspiracies by Lilliputians, Blefescuans, Brobdingnagians, pirates, Houyhnhnms, and English Yahoos, including his own editor. A survey of satiric writing reveals a long list of such real or imagined conspiracies: the evil enchanter who stalks Don Quixote, Jacobite plots that threaten Whigs in Andrew Marvell's "Last Instructions to a Painter" (1667), Dulness's plan to destroy civilization, a secret empire of underground mail in Pynchon, hidden schemes for oil and money determining American foreign policy according to Moore's film, and the clandestine threats involving assassination and pollution in DeLillo. The list could continue to include many other works by many other satirists, Jonson's *Volpone* (1607), Dryden's "Absalom and Achitophel" (1681), Gay's *The Beggar's Opera*, Sterne's *Tristram Shandy* (1760–7), Byron's *Don Juan* (1819–24), Twain's *Huckleberry Finn* (1884), and Waugh's *A Handful of Dust* (1934) among them.

Conspiracy theory has much in common with satire and satiric irony: both fragment and disorient our sense of certainty and authority. Both examine national, historical, or ethnic identity. Both bring objects of fear or danger into our midst by blurring the distinction between the broom and the dirt it sweeps, between us and them, or self and other. Both generate narratives in which perpetrators of misdeeds and violence are portrayed as sexually promiscuous, or bestial, or mad, or otherwise estranged from the norm. In both, the figure of the aggressor, whether terrorist or satirist, is "a consistently ambivalent, yet infinitely adaptable trope of conspiratorial violence...a prolific and charismatic, yet unreliable and inauthentic source of discourse" (Hantke 1966: 223–4). Both offer us many opportunities to interpret threatening possibilities dismissively, to see, according to Swift's metaphor, other faces in the satiric mirror. Yet both construct fictions that we suspect might contain elements of truth.

Perhaps another way of explaining the paranoia lurking in satire's "life of stealth" is to reconsider its frequent target of overweening pride or ego. One thinks of examples like the parody of the Narcissus myth in *Gulliver's Travels*, or of the town of San Narcisso in *The Crying of Lot 49*. According to Freud, paranoid minds "attach the greatest significance to trivial details in the behavior of others. Details...they interpret and utilize as the basis for far-reaching conclusions...project[ing] into the mental life of others what exists in [their] own unconscious activity" (Brill 1938: 162–3). Fear is "in a hostile manner projected on others" (1938: 575), and while that fear may appear ridiculous to some, it nevertheless provokes anxiety. Satire's many examples of self-absorption and self-destruction take forms of aberration like mental illness and addiction: dullness and madness in Pope and Swift; promiscuity and infidelity in Manley and Byron; or DTs and LSD in DeLillo and in Pynchon who, in the tradition of *The Dunciad*'s apocalyptic psychomachia, predicts the "trembling unfolding of the mind's plowshares."

These insights allow us to make one further challenge to the conventional association of genre and gender. Recalling the insistent masculinity of traditional ideas about satire – the knight errant, the primitive warrior, the god Saturn, the deft swordsman, the *vir bonus* – we also note Freud's belief that paranoia resulted from male repression of homosexual impulses. That is, gender confusion seems to be central to the paranoid experience in which one is both passively persecuted and actively aggressive. With respect to the feminization of satire (through gossipy secret-sharing), we now add the transsexual productivity and instability of irony. This figuration of the satirist as a charismatic seeker of elusive but self-aggrandizing knowledge transcends the sexual exclusiveness of the conventional masculinist images of the warrior, armed for virtue and pointing the pen. Anyone – Oedipus or Oedipa – can be paranoid.

Finally, we can draw significance from the intersection of irony, satire, and paranoia with respect to the satirist him/herself, suggesting another link between early modern and postmodern cultures. Paranoiacs frequently inhabit satire: charismatic, excessive, and often crack-brained characters involve us in ironic fictions about *other* people's problems when often they themselves embody the biggest problem of all. In "A Digression on Madness" in Swift's *Tale*, the narrator ironically dismisses the viability of belief in "things Invisible." For many readers, this phrase has connoted the work's recurrent theme of abuses of religion: true spirituality (things invisible) cannot survive in an increasingly materialistic and mechanistic world. But the ironic injunction to credit things invisible also suggests precisely the paranoid belief that another meaning or plot lies concealed behind the obvious and apparent – not God's one plan but ever-proliferating, doomed human plans. With paranoid efficiency, the *Tale's* narrator (a former inmate of Bedlam) perceives the interconnectedness of all things and urges on us the secrets of his own hidden system of coherence. Segments of tale and digressions equally contribute, for example, to his self-absorbed system in which air explains and unites everything from Christian zeal to a fart. The more he feels persecuted and misunderstood, the more intently he whispers in the reader's ear. Leo Bersani, writing of Pynchon, observes that paranoid fear is a necessary product of all information systems: "Information control is the contemporary version of God's eternal knowledge" (1989: 103). Irony epitomizes human resistance to such control. In the eighteenth century, as in the postmodern age, irony complicates the transmission of information. Its disquieting revelations imply further unknowns, and its energy animates the secret life of satire.

References and Further Reading

Algren, Nelson (1972) A Waugh in shoulder padding. *Los Angeles Times Book Review*, March 26.

Ballaster, Ros (ed.) (1991) *Secret Memoirs from... the New Atalantis* [by Delarivier Manley]. London: Penguin.

Bersani, Leo (1989) Pynchon, paranoia, and literature. *Representations* 25, 99–118.

Bogel, Fredric (2001) *The Difference Satire Makes*. Ithaca, NY: Cornell University Press.

Bok, Sissela (1984) *Secrets: Concealment and Revelation*. London: Oxford University Press.

Brill, A. A. (ed.) (1938) *The Basic Writings of Sigmund Freud*. New York: Modern Library.

Butler, Judith (1997) *Excitable Speech: A Politics of the Performative*. London: Routledge.

DeLillo, Don (1997) *Underworld*. New York: Scribner.

De Quehen, Hugh (ed.) (1979) *Prose Observations* [by Samuel Butler]. Oxford: Clarendon Press.

Dryden, John (1974) *The Works of John Dryden, Vol. IV: Poems 1693–1699*, ed. A. B. Chambers, William Frost, and Vinton A. Dearing. Berkeley, CA: University of California Press.

Eisenstein, Elizabeth (1979) *The Printing Press as an Agent of Change*, 2 vols. Cambridge, MA: Harvard University Press.

Elliott, Robert C. (1960) *The Power of Satire: Magic, Ritual, Art*. Princeton, NJ: Princeton University Press.

Fairclough, H. Rushton (trans.) (1947) *Horace: Satires, Epistles, and Ars Poetica*. Cambridge, MA: Harvard University Press (originally published 1929).

Hantke, Steffen (1966) "God save us from bourgeois adventure": the figure of the terrorist in contemporary American conspiracy fiction. *Studies in the Novel* 2 (82), 219–43.

Keller, Evelyn Fox (1992) *Secrets of Life, Secrets of Death*. New York: Routledge.

Kernan, Alvin (1959) *The Cankered Muse: Satire of the English Renaissance*. New Haven, CT: Yale University Press.

—— (1965) *The Plot of Satire*. New Haven, CT: Yale University Press.

Knowlson, James (1975) *Universal Language Schemes in England and France 1600–1800*. Toronto: University of Toronto Press.

Lord, George de F. (ed.) (1963) *Poems on Affairs of State, 1660–1678*. New Haven, CT: Yale University Press.

Meredith, George (1972) *Diana of the Crossways*. New York: Norton.

Miller, D. A. (1988) *The Novel and the Police*. Berkeley, CA: University of California Press.

Nichols, James W. (1971) *Insinuations: The Tactics of Satire*. The Hague: Mouton.

Potter, Lois (1989) *Secret Rites and Secret Writing: Royalist Literature, 1641–1660*. Cambridge: Cambridge University Press.

Pynchon, Thomas (1999) *The Crying of Lot 49*. New York: Harper Collins (originally published 1965).

Roberts, Marie Mulvey and Ormsby-Lennon, Hugh (eds) (1995) *Secret Texts: The Literature of Secret Societies*. New York: AMS.

Rosenfelt, Deborah S. (1998) The politics of bibliography: women's studies and the literary canon. In Joan Hartman and Ellen Messer Davidow (eds), *Women in Print: Opportunities for Women's Studies Research in Language and Literature*, pp. 11–35. New York: Modern Language Association of America.

Seidel, Michael (1979) *Satiric Inheritance: Rabelais to Sterne*. Princeton, NJ: Princeton University Press.

Spacks, Patricia (1986) *Gossip*. Chicago: University of Chicago Press.

Thorne, Christian (2001) Thumbing our nose at the public sphere: satire, the market, and the invention of literature. *Proceedings of the Modern Language Association* 116 (3), 531–44.

Wilkins, John (1708) *Mercury, or the Secret and Swift Messenger*, 3rd edn. N. p. (originally published in 1641).

Williams, Harold (ed.) (1948) *Journal to Stella* [by Jonathan Swift], 2 vols. Oxford: Clarendon Press.

Wolff, Kurt H. (ed. and trans.) (1950) The secret and the secret society [by Georg Simmel]. In *The Sociology of Georg Simmel*, Part 4, pp. 307–76. New York: The Free Press.

Index

Page numbers in italic denote illustrations

Abbey Theatre 482
Abraham 18, 29
Absurdism 460, 462, 469–73
absurdity 4, 95, 96, 170, 217–18
abuse 34–6, 50; social 129, 133
academic satire 119, 122, 123
Addison, Joseph 506, 562–3, 565, 571
Adorno, Theodor 400, 417
The Adventures of Eovaai 260
adversarius figure 455–7
Aeschylus: *Oresteia* 461
Aesop 147, 172–3, 497
aesthetic movement 358
aesthetics 223, 317, 338, 435
Agamemnon 33
agudeza (conceptual artifice) 95
Ahitophel 18
Aislinge Meic con Glinne 480
Albee, Edward: *The American Dream* 472
Alberti, Leon Battista 123; *Intercenales* 126; *Momus* 125–6
Albigensian Crusade 62
Alciati, Andrea 294–5
Alcibiades/Alkibiades 43, 45, 513
Alcock, Mary 234, 236; "The Chimney-Sweeper's Complaint" 284; "Instructions, Supposed to be Written in Paris" 284
Alcuin 455–7
Aldiss, Brian 402
alexandrines 139–40, 284
Algren, Nelson 568

allegorical beast epic 57–8
allegory 125–6, 151, 515–16
Alonso, Dámaso 93
Altman, Robert 166
Alvarez, Alfred: *Savage God* 449
American Civil War 390
American Publishing Company 391
American Revolution 380–1
Amis, Kingsley 401, 402; letters to Larkin 414; "Shitty" 442
Amis, Martin 196, 401; *Einstein's Monsters* 421; *Koba the Dread* 424; *London Fields* 417; *Money* 404, 412, 414; *Time's Arrow* 417, 421
Amos 19, 27
Anacreon 499
anatomy, satire 7, 131
Anderson, Maxwell: *Both Your Houses* 469
Anderson, William S. 43
Anglo-Irish narrative tradition 480–1
Angry Young Men 402
Anne, Queen 213, 216
Anonymous: "Advice to a Painter" 226; *Ecce the New Testament* 527; "Whii werre and wrake ..." 65
Anstey, Christopher 234, 236; *The New BathGuide* 243–5
anti-British poetry 383–4
anti-Catholicism 79–80, 113–14, 212, 279
anti-clerical satire 122, 155
anti-heroic trend 499, 552
anti-Irish texts 558

anti-Italian literature 82, 83
Anti-Jacobin 342–3, 358, 363
anti-Jacobins 234, 274
anti-Jesuit satire 84, 141
anti-matrimonial satire 67
anti-monastic satire 77–8
anti-Puritanism 378
anti-realism 465–8
anti-scholastic satire 75
anti-Semitism 337
anti-war sentiment 395
anti-women satire 81, 95, 96, 141, 154, 164, 575
ape theme 405–7
Apocalypsis Goliae 57, 61, 526
apocalyptic fiction 425, 429
Apollinaire, Guillaume: *The Breasts of Tiresias* 470
apologiae 40
apologues 126
appearance/reality 83, 97–8, 332
Apuleius 120, 322
Aquinas, Saint Thomas 122
Arbuthnot, John 216; *Peri Bathous* 218
Archilochos/Archilochus 7, 34–5, 499, 575
Archpoet 57
Aretino, Pietro 126–7; *Ragionamenti* 126–7
Ariosto, Ludovico 126–7, 445
Aristophanes 7, 36, 161; *Acharnians* 37–8; Athens 40; *Clouds* 27, 36; *Knights* 36; parody 47; rhetoric 39; stock characters 551
Aristotle 40; *Eudemian Ethics* 550; *Nicomachean Ethics* 512, 550; *Poetics* 36, 140; *Prior Analytics* 122–3; *spoudaios* 496; Theophrastus 550
Arnold, Matthew: "Buried Life" 329; on Dryden and Pope 434; "Stanzas from the Grand Chartreuse" 329
art/life 5, 374
Artaud, Antonin 470
Ashbery, John 453
Astell, Mary 277
Athenis 35
Athens 40
Atterbury, Francis 578
Atterbury, William: *The History of the Mitre and the Purse* 578
d'Aubigné, Agrippa 83, 140; *Confession du sieur de Sancy* 83–4
Aubrey, John 188
Auden, W. H.: "Epistle to a Godson" 446; as influence 446–7; "Letter to Lord Byron" 435–6, 446; "Miss Gee" 419; "Musée des Beaux Arts" 302; *New Year Letter* 446; "On the Circuit" 446; "Under Which Lyre" 446; "The Unknown Citizen" 446
Augustan Age: beauty 223–4; classical models 119–20; general/particular 561; mockery 506–7; Pope 563; Protestantism 223–4; range of 178–9; readership 219; satire 212–16; social/historical context 222
Augustine, Saint 318, 513; *The Confessions* 498
Austen, Jane 236; on Crabbe 251; *Emma* 518; irony 518; *Mansfield Park* 518; *Pride and Prejudice* 24, 25–6, 290, 329, 363; sensibility 274
Australian writers 446–9
Avellaneda 91
Ávila, Bishop of 86

Bacon, Francis 552, 556; "Of Marriage and the Single Life" 554–5
Bage, Robert: *Hermsprong* 273
Baines, Paul 226
Bakalar, Nicholas 380
Bakhtin, Mikhail: carnivalesque 6, 258; language of the marketplace 70; laughter subculture 507; Menippean satire 8, 32, 258, 485; novelistic form 90; sexual/excretory processes 366
ballads 179, 478
Ballard, J. G. 402, 428; *The Atrocity Exhibition* 421; *Crash* 401, 421
Ballaster, Ros 260
Balzac, Honoré de: *Lost Illusions* 372
Bancroft, Richard 108
Barbauld, Anna Laetitia 340; "Eighteen Hundred and Eleven" 344; "The Mouse's Petition to Doctor Priestley" 284
Barber, Mary 282
Barlow, Joel 239–40
Barnes, Julian 402
Baroque period 92–9, 564–5
Barth, R. L.: "Movie Stars" 445; "Social Darwinism" 445
Bartolomeo, Joseph F. 260–1
"The Battle of the Frogs and the Mice" 495–7, 498
bawdiness 36, 104, 132, 134
Beasley, Jerry C. 266, 267
Beaumarchais, Pierre Augustin Caron de: *Le Barbier de Séville* 152; *Le Mariage de Figaro* 152
Beaumont, Francis 162
beauty 223–4

Beavis, Anthony: *Elements of Sociology* 415
Beck, Cave: *Universal Character* 571
Beckett, Samuel 461, 480; *Endgame* 471; *Murphy* 487; *Waiting for Godot* 471; *Watt* 409
Beckett, Thomas 56
Beda 73
Beerbohm, Max 358; *A Christmas Garland* 358; *Zuleika Dobson* 358
Behan, Brendan 480
Behn, Aphra 271; drama 278–80; *The Feign'd Curtezans* 279; "The Golden Age" 281; as influence 280–1; *Love-letters between a Nobleman and his Sister* 259, 285–6; *The Luckey Chance* 163, 278–9; *Oroonoko* 286; *The Roundheads* 163; *The Rover* 276, 278–9; *Sir Patient Fancy* 279; *The Widdow Ranter* 279
Bell, Steve 407, 529, 538–40
Belloc, Hilaire 443
Benavente, Luis Quiñones de 92
Benedictine Rule 77
Benlowes, Thomas 564
Benson, E. F.: *Lucia in London* 403
Benson, Larry D. 64, 66, 67, 68
Bentham, Jeremy 333
Bentinck, Hans William 542, 544–5, 547
Bentley, Richard 204
Bergerac, Cyrano de 84
Bernini, Giovanni 28
Bernstein, Leonard: *Candide* 442
Berryman, Clifford Kennedy 529
Bersani, Leo 583
Betjeman, John: "Executive" 442
Bible: knowledge of 525–6; prophets 8–9; satire 525; satirical prints 526; *see also* mock-biblical genre; individual books
Bierce, Ambrose: *The Devil's Dictionary* 375
Big Bang theory 510
Bildungsroman 329–30, 361
bishops 59–60
Bisset, Robert: *Douglas* 274
black comedy 461, 472
Blackstone, William 214
Blackwood's Edinburgh Magazine 347, 358, 528
Blair, Tony 538–40
Blake, William 284–5, 302, 312, 323; *Book of Los* 528; *The Four Zoas* 330; *Marriage of Heaven and Hell* 528; *Songs of Experience* 329
blame 32–4, 40
Blanchard, W. Scott 8
Bloomsbury circle 451
Blount, Edward 559–60

Boccaccio, Giovanni 126–7
bodily excretions 366, 412–17
body fetishism 405–6
Bogan, Louise 445
Bogel, Fredric 577
Boileau, Nicolas: *Art poétique* 142; *Discours sur la satire* 141, 143; individual targets 143; as influence 151; Juvenal 142; laughter 143; poet/mind 139; *Satires* 84, 139; Voltaire 157
Bok, Sissela 573
"Bonaparte's Coronation" 343
Bonner, Robert 389
book illustrations 363
"Book of Odes" 498
booksellers 214
Booth, Wayne 5
Borges, Jorge Luis 523
Bosch, Hieronymus 302
Boswell, James 254; *Life of Samuel Johnson* 561
Bougainville, Louis Antoine de 154–5
Boupalos 35
Bowers, Edgar 445; "How We Came from Paris to Blois" 457–8
Bowling for Columbine (Moore) 4
Boyle, Robert 204
Boyne, Battle of the 480
Bradbury, Malcolm 402
Brathwait, Richard 115
Brecht, Bertolt 218, 461; *The Caucasian Chalk Circle* 468; *The Good Person of Setzuan* 468; *Mother Courage* 467; *The Resistible Rise of Arturo Ui* 467–8; *The Threepenny Opera* 467
Breton, Nicholas 115
Breughel, Pieter: *Crucifixion* 302; *Fall of Icarus* 302, 304; *Nativity* 302
bribery 54, 67
Brooke, C. N. I. 61
Brooks, Mel: *The Producers* 2
Brown, Capability 250
Browning, Robert 457
Bruce, Lenny 9
Brückmann, Patricia Carr 219
Brydges, James 563
Buchwald, Art 9
Buckingham, Duke of: *The Rehearsal* 165–6
Bulgakov, Mikhail: *The Crimson Island* 465
Buñuel, Luis 523
Bunyan, John: character sketches 566; *The Life and Death of Mr Badman* 566; *The Pilgrim's Progress* 212, 304, 426, 566
Burckhardt, Jacob 118

Burgess, Anthony 402
Burke, Edmund 246, 323; Crabbe 251; epitaph on 246; Gillray 294; graphic images 322; Hastings 255; *Reflections on the Revolution in France* 228, 255
burlesque 162, 166
Burnel the ass 58–9
Burney, Frances: *Camilla* 273, 289; *Cecilia* 273, 289; *Evelina* 272, 276, 288–9; narrative voice 272–3; *The Wanderer* 289–90; *The Witlings* 280, 290
Burns, Robert 235; "Address to the Deil" 253; "Address to the Unco Guid" 253; "The Holy Fair" 253; "Holy Willie's Prayer" 245, 253, 254; as influence 284; "To the Rev. John M'Math" 253–4, 458–9
Burton, Robert 124; *The Anatomy of Melancholy* 133–4
Bus, Gervais du: *Roman de Fauvel* 52
Bush, George 407
Bute, Lord 528
Butler, Judith: *Excitable Speech* 573–4; secrecy 581
Butler, Samuel 558; Baroque culture 564–5; *Characters* 563–5; *Erewhon* 373; *Hudibras* 176, 177, 180–2, 183, 563; influences on 181; prose observations 181–2; religious mind 564; shorter verse satires 181; "Wit and Folly" 575
Butler, William Allen 389–90
Bynner, Witter 448
Byrd, Max 269
Byron, Lord George Gordon 215, 254, 340, 352–3; *Beppo* 359; *Childe Harold's Pilgrimage* 447; *Don Juan* 332, 345, 351–3, 359, 364, 446, 582; *English Bards and Scotch Reviewers* 329, 359; "The Vision of Judgment" 345, 359, 528

C., R. 115
Cain and Abel story 526
Calcagnini, Caelio 126
Calderón de la Barca, Pedro 86
Calvinists 79
Cambridge, Richard Owen 234; *Scribleriad* 238–9
Camfield, Gregg 396
Campbell, Roy: *The Flowering Rifle* 450, 451; *The Georgiad* 450, 451; "On Some South African Novelists" 452; translations of Horace 452; *The Wayzgoose* 450–1; "The Zulu Girl" 451

campus novels 402
Candide 21, 26, 27
Canfield, J. Douglas 161
cannibalism 198, 199–200
Canning, George 342; "The New Morality" 529
capitalism 468
Cardenal, Peire 62
Carême (Lent) 71
Carey, Lucius 561
caricature 265, 308–13, 316, 363
Carleton, William 481
Carlyle, Thomas 329–31, 337, 338, 562; *Sartor Resartus* 329–30, 333–4, 337, 365
Carmina Burana 526
carnivalesque 6, 71, 258, 277
Caroline, Queen 351, 530–2
Carr, Robert 555–6
Carracci, Annibale: *Procession of Bacchus and Ariadne* 305
Carroll, Lewis 357; *Alice's Adventures in Wonderland* 371
Carter, Angela 402
Carter, Elizabeth 282, 285
cartoons 312, 340–1, 529
Casaubon, Isaac 140, 445, 552
Cascales, Francisco 90
Cassity, Turner: "Adding Rattles" 442
Castiglione, Baldassare 131; *Corteggiano* 81–2
Castilian grammar 86
Castillejo, Cristóbal de 93
Castlereagh, Viscount 345, 349
catachresis 408, 430
Catherine de Medici 82
Catholicism 83, 87, 149–50, 153, 157, 346; *see also* anti-Catholicism
Catullus 81
Celtic Revival 482
censorship 171–2, 174, 214–15, 322, 371, 490
Censorship of Publications Act 486
Centlivre, Susannah: *A Bold Stroke for a Wife* 280
Cervantes, Miguel de 257; *Don Quijote de la Mancha* 86, 90, 91, 258–9; *entremeses* 92; indignation 90–1; as influence 180, 267; *Persiles and Sigismunda* 258; *Viaje del Parnaso* 90, 91
Césaire, Aimé: *A Tempest* 473
"The Chaldee MS" 528
Chamberlain, Neville 452
The Champion publication 261, 528
Chancery Courts 369
Chandler, Mary 282–3

Chandos, Duke of 563
Chaplin, Charlie 2
Chapman, George 556
character sketches 565–6; Earle 558–64; Hall 553–5; Overbury 556–9; Theophrastus 512, 550, 551–3; type/individual 561
charity 64–5
Charivari (crowd ritual) 305
Charles I, of England 214, 561
Charles II, of England 161, 178, 183, 187–9, 193, 259, 562, 578
Charles V, Holy Roman Emperor 75–6, 79, 87, 88
Charles IX, of France 83
Charles XII, of Sweden 238
Charnage (meat-eating) 71
Chartist verse 340–1, 347, 348
Chatterton, Thomas 234
Chaucer, Geoffrey: *The Canterbury Tales* 52, 65, 67, 238, 299, 349, 497, 551–2; character types 551–2; irony 64; satire 52, 53; *Troilus and Criseyde* 431
Chekhov, Anton 461, 462, 464–5, 518; *The Cherry Orchard* 464; *Dushechka* 521; *The Three Sisters* 465; *Uncle Vanya* 464
Chernaik, Warren 185
Christianity: Erasmus 77, 87, 123–4; Heine 335–6; Ireland 477; models for satire 298–304; satirized 425–6; Stoicism 553, 554, 558–9; Twain 374; *see also* anti-clerical satire; clergy; mock-biblical genre
1 Chronicles 533, 535
Chudleigh, Lady Mary 277
Churchill, Caryl: *Cloud 9* 473
Churchill, Charles 233, 234–5, 240–1; "The Bard" 241; "The Conclave" 241; "Dedication to the Sermons" 445; "Epistles to William Hogarth" 445; *The Ghost* 241; *Gotham* 242; *The Prophecy of Famine* 242, 450, 528; *The Rosciad* 219, 241–2
Churchill, Sarah (Duchess of Marlborough) 259–60, 386, 563
Cibber, Colley 168, 169, 261
Cicero 45, 145
Cistercians 61
city/country division 249
Clarendon, Earl of 559, 561
Clarke, Austin 478, 484; *The Bright Temptation* 487; *The Singing-Men at Cashel* 487; *The Sun Dances at Easter* 487–8
class factors 259, 375
Cleghorn, Sarah 443

clergy 57, 61, 106, 252–3, 356; *see also* anti-clerical satire
Cleveland, John 179, 181; *The Rebell Scott* 527
Clinton, Bill: *Primary Colors* 578
Close, Anthony 258
Cobbett, William 345
Cochlaeus, Johann 527
Cocteau, Jean: *The Eiffel Tower Wedding Party* 470
Coe, Jonathan 402
Coffin, George Yost 529
Coleridge, Samuel Taylor 238, 332, 365
colonialism 155
Colossians 122
comedy 316–19, 402; ballads 179; character sketches 566; Cicero 145; Dickens 369; drama 139–40, 461; Greek 36; inversion 74; novels 147; poetry 37–8, 357; Roman 39–40
commonplace books 130
communism 424
concepto (conceit) 95–6
conduct book 552
Confucianism 498
Congo 394
Connecticut Wits: *The Anarchiad* 234, 239–40
Conrad, Joseph: *Heart of Darkness* 2
conspiracy 569, 582
consumption 42, 47
conversos 87
Cook, Richard I. 229
Cooke, Ebenezer: *The Sot-Weed Factor* 378–9
Cooper, Anthony Ashley (1st Earl of Shaftesbury) 194, 540
Cooper, Anthony Ashley (3rd Earl of Shaftesbury) 220, 317
Cope, Wendy: "Engineers' Corner" 441–2; "Faint Praise" 441; "Men and their Boring Arguments" 441; Strugnell poems 441; "Tumps" 441
coprophilia 415–17
1 Corinthians 123, 537–40
2 Corinthians 527
Corn Laws 346
Corneille, Pierre 144
corruption 149, 223
cosmopolitanism 330, 337
Cotton, Charles 179
Coulette, Henri 443
Courtenay, John 255
courtiers: Aretino 126–7; flattery 110, 147–8; manual for 131; More 129; Rochester 176; sexuality 184; venality 189

courtship 382
Covent-Garden Journal 272
Coward, Noel 466–7; *Cavalcade* 466; *Hay Fever* 466; *Private Lives* 466
Cowley, Hannah: *The Belle's Stratagem* 280
Cowper, William 235; on Churchill 242; corporate responsibility 250–1; realism 234; *The Task* 246, 248–9; town/country living 249–50
Crabbe, George 215, 234, 235, 236, 349; *The Borough* 251; doctors 252–3; *The Library* 251; *The Newspaper* 251; *The Parish Register* 246, 251; *Tales of the Hall* 251; *Tales in Verse* 251; *The Village* 251–3
Cranach, Lucas 527
Crash (Cronenberg) 401
Crisp, Samuel 280
Critic 391–2
Crockett, Gib 529
Cromwell, Oliver 182, 527, 561, 562
Cronenberg, David 401
Cruikshank, George 312, 345, 363, 364, 529
Cruikshank, Isaac 529
Cú Chulainn 477, 486
Cullen, Countee 443
Cumberland, Richard 173
Cunningham, J. V. 437, 444
curses 18, 191, 194, 476, 477
cynicism 74, 521
Cynics 119, 135

Dabydeen, David 402
Dada movement 9, 462, 470
D'Aguair, Fred 402
The Daily Show 570
Dali, Salvador 316
Daniel, Book of 25, 318
Daniel, Samuel 109
Dante Alighieri: *Inferno* 299
D'Anvers, Alicia: "Academia" 281
Darwin, Erasmus 236
Daumier, Honoré 9, 313, 323; *The Incriminating Evidence* 298
David, King 18, 21, 193–4, 529
Davie, Donald: "Six Epistles to Eva Hesse" 449
Davis, Dick 445; "Letter to Omar" 449–50
Day, Robert Adams 265
De Hooghe, Romeyn 304–5
De Valera, Eamon 486
debtors 368–9
deceit 66, 127

declamatory exercises 42–3
Decretals 80
Defoe, Daniel 215; Bentinck 544–5; Duncombe 545–7; "The Dyet of Poland, A Satyr" 221–2; *Jure Divino* 527; *Psalms* 543; "Reformation of Manners" 306; *Robinson Crusoe* 207, 259; *The Secret History of the White Staff* 578; *The Shortest Way with the Dissenters* 259; *The True-Born Englishman* 231, 259, 527, 540–6
Dekker, Thomas 131, 552, 556
Delicado, Francisco 88
DeLillo, Don 568, 582; *Underworld* 570, 580
Della Cruscan School 349
Demokritos 44–5
Demosthenes 45
Dennis, John 168
Dent, William 529
Derrida, Jacques 400
Descartes, René 206
Desmarets de Saint-Sorlin, Jean 140
Destouches, Philippe 151
Dibdin, Michael 402
Dickens, Charles 290, 312; *Bleak House* 368, 369; character sketches 566; comedy 369; "The Fine Old English Gentleman" 341; *Hard Times* 368; on Hogarth 303–4; *Little Dorrit* 368–9, 419; *Martin Chuzzlewit* 368, 369; *Nicholas Nickleby* 368, 369; *Oliver Twist* 368; *Pickwick Papers* 367; *Sketches by Boz* 367, 566; social satire 342; Uriah Heep 512
didactic satire 98
Diderot, Denis 150–1, 158; *Le Neveu de Rameau* 158–9; *La Religieuse* 154; *Supplément au Voyage de Bougainville* 154–5
Dido, Queen 305–6, 314, 505
Dinesen, Isak 521–2
Diogenes 71, 119, 131, 135
Diomedes 40
disgust 413
D'Israeli, Isaac: *Vaurien* 274
dissent 1, 118
doctors 252–3
Dodd, William 248–9
Doddington, Bubb 563
Dodgson, Charles: *see* Carroll, Lewis
Dodsley, Robert: *Chronicle of the Kings of England* 528, 533–7, 538
La Dolce Vita (Fellini) 298
Dominicans 62

Domitian, Emperor 45–6
Donatus 103
Doni, Anton Francesco 127, 128
Donne, John 103; Carr 556; city 111–12; epigrams 437; letter 436; philosophy 204; rhetoric 114; satire 108, 115; style 113, 114
Doody, Margaret Anne 179, 273
Dorset, Earl of 176, 178
Dostoevsky, Fyodor: *Notes from Underground* 520
Downing, Jack 385–6
Drant, Thomas 102, 103, 107
Drayton, Michael 109
dream visions 119
drinking songs 179
Dryden, John: "Absalom and Achitophel" 9, 176, 181, 193–4, 236, 527, 540, 544, 562, 582; *Annus Mirabilis* 183, 247, 440; Arnold on 434; "Astraea Redux" 180; on Butler 178; *The Conquest of Granada* 165; "Discourse Concerning Satire" 176–7, 192, 277, 568, 573; epigrams 437; heroic drama 165; *The Hind and the Panther* 408, 448; imitations 542; Jonson 193; "MacFlecknoe" 116, 176, 181, 192–3, 527, 562, 570; on Marvell 182; "The Medall" 176, 194; on Oldham 241; range of work 176; *Religio Laici* 448; Rochester 186; theory of satire 142, 176–8
Du Bellay, Joachim 81, 82; *Les Regrets* 82
Dudley, Edmund 534
Duffett, Thomas 166
Duncombe, Sir Charles 545–8
Dürer, Albrecht *301*
Dürrenmatt, Friedrich: *The Visit* 472–3
Dyer, Gary 350
dystopia 401, 423–7

Eagleton, Terry 23
Earle, John 181, 559–60; "A Grave Divine" 563–4; *Micro-Cosmographie* 558, 559–60; religious satire 563–4
Easter Rising 483–4
Ecce Homo model 300, 302, 318
Ecclesiastes 9, 18, 24, 26–7, 124, 530, 531
Ecclesiasticus 18
economics texts 199, 247, 248
Edgeworth, Maria: *Belinda* 290; *Castle Rackrent* 363, 481
education 42–3, 258; for women 277–8, 281, 282
Edward II 66
Egerton, Sarah Fyge: "The Emulation" 277
Egyptian campaign 343–4

ekphrasis 293, 295
Eldon, Lord 528–9
Elijah 16, 20
Eliot, George 518; character sketches 566; *Impressions of Theophrastus* 566
Eliot, T. S. 182, 323; *The Waste Land* 236, 416, 439–40
Elizabeth I 109
Elliott, Ebenezer: *Corn Law Rhymes* 346; satiric verse 340
Elliott, Robert C. 3, 322, 430, 476, 575
Ellis, Frank H. 221, 226, 231, 542, 543, 544–5
emblem 294–5, 323
Emmet, Robert 478
Empsom, Richard 534
Empson, William 322
encomium 121, 187, 562
England: Civil War 306, 527, 575; and France, compared 155–6; Renaissance satire 101–16
Enlightenment 151, 220, 302, 342
Ennius 332
Ensor, James: *Christ Entering Brussels* 302
Ephesians 530, 531
epic works 142, 183, 497; *see also* mock-epic poems
Epicureanism 129
epideictic mock oration 120–1, 123
epigrams 437, 442–5; attacks by name 143; irony 375; Jonson 437; Martial 81; satiric 103–4; war 444–5
epistolary form 261, 445–50
epitaphs 246
Epstein, Julia 272–3
epyllion, erotic 109
Erasmus: *Adagia* 124, 131; Christianity 77, 87, 123–4; *Colloquies* 124; human nature 124–5; as influence 89; *poligrafi* 127; *The Praise of Folly (Moriae Encomium)* 5, 71, 121–2, 123, 124–5, 514, 515–16
Ernst, Max 316
eroticism 127
Esslin, Martin 472; "Theatre of the Absurd" 470
estates satire 64–8
Esther 25
Estienne, Henri 83
L'Estoile, Pierre de 83
Etaine, Coirpre mac 476
Etherege, George 278–9; *The Man of Mode* 163, 164, 185, 562
Eucharist 83
eulogy, satirical 123
Eupolis 38

Euripides: *Bacchae* 49
Evangelium Secundum Marcas Argenti 526
Evelyn-White, Hugh 496
evil 299, 302, 305–6
Ewart, Gavin: "2001: The Tennyson/Hardy Poem" 442
exaggeration 336, 385
Excise Crisis 528
Exclusion Bill 545
exempla 552
Exodus 25
Expressionism 462, 468
Ezekiel 21–2, 24

fables 84, 147
Fahrenheit 9/11 (Moore) 4, 523–4, 568, 573, 574, 580
Fairer, David 246
Falkland, Lord 561
fantasy 21, 28, 151
farces 71
Farewell, James: *The Irish Hudibras* 480
fashion 382–3, 389–90
Feast of the Ass 56
Feast of Fools 56
Fellini, Federico 298, 308
feminist novels 402
feminization of satire 583
Fenton, James: "Letter to John Fuller" 449
Ferdinand of Aragón 87
fertility rituals 35, 36
Fichte, Johann Gottlieb 333
Ficke, Arthur Davison 448
Fielding, Henry 166, 518; adaptations of Molière 169; *Amelia* 264; *The Author's Farce* 169–70, 219; character sketches 566; *Covent-Garden Journal* 272; *The Covent-Garden Tragedy* 171; *Eurydice Hissed* 171; *The Historical Register for the Year 1736* 171, 215; *Jonathan Wild* 261–2, 264; *Joseph Andrews* 7, 245, 262–3; *The Life and Death of Tom Thumb the Great* 170–1, 219; names of characters 287; *Pasquin* 171, 215; play-within-a-play 161, 169–70; *Shamela* 215, 261; *Tom Jones* 263–4; *The Tragedy of Tragedies* 171
Fielding, Sarah: *David Simple* 271, 287; *Volume the Last* 271
Figgis, Darrell 484; *The Return of the Hero* 485
Finch, Anne: "A Nocturnal Reverie" 281; "The Petition for an Absolute Retreat" 281; "Tale of the Miser and the Poet" 281

Fitzgeffrey, Henry 115
Fitzgerald, Edward 449
Fitzherbert, Mrs 351
flattery 110, 147–8, 555
Flaubert, Gustav: *Bouvard and Pécuchet* 373–4; *Dictionary of Received Ideas* 375
Flecknoe, Richard 115–16, 181, 192
flyting tradition 476, 479–80
Fo, Dario: *The Accidental Death of an Anarchist* 473
Folkenflik, Robert 267
folly 123–4
fool of Christ 519–20
fools' plays 71–2
Foote, Samuel 161; *The Minor* 172
Fordyce, Dr 290
Fornes, Maria Irene: *Fefu and her Friends* 474
Forster, E. M. 402
The Fortnightly Review 437
Foucault, Michel: *Discipline and Punish* 430
Fougères, Etienne de: *Livre des manières* 65
Fox, Charles James 526, 531
Fox, Christopher 217
France 70; eighteenth century 150–9; and England, compared 155–6; neo-classical satire 179; *philosophes* 120; Protestants 157; seventeenth century 139–50; *see also* French Revolution
Francis I 70–1
Francis of Alençon 83
Franco, Nicolò 127
Franklin, Benjamin 380; "A Parable against Prosecution" 528
freedom of speech 41, 135, 371–2
French Revolution 254, 273, 274, 322, 336, 340, 362
Freneau, Philip: *A Collection of Poems on American Affairs* 383–4
Fréron, Elie-Catherine 158
Freud, Sigmund 33–4, 322, 582
Frisch, Max: *Andorra* 474; *Biedermann and the Firebugs* 474
the Fronde 143–4, 149
Frost, Robert: downward metaphor 497; "The Lesson for Today" 455–7
Frye, Northrop: anatomy 7; fantasy 28; flexible pragmatism 24–5; object attacked 21; social roles 122; three phases of satire/irony 22–3, 24–8, 319; topicality 10
Fuller, John 448; *Partingtime Hall* 449; *Poems and Epistles* 448–9

Fun magazine 355
Furetière, Antoine 147
future, narratives of 373, 423
Futurism 462, 470

Gadeken, Sara 271
Galen 552
Gao Xingjian: *The Other Shore* 474
Garcilaso de la Vega 86, 92–3
Garnett, Father 190
Garrick, David 234, 247; *Fribbleriad* 239; *Lethe* 172–3; *The Lying Valet* 239
Garrison, David 94
Garth, Samuel 215; *The Dispensary* 212, 231, 500, 503–4
Gascoigne, George 107–8
Gay, John 215; *The Beggar's Opera* 161, 166, 168–9, 218–19, 229, 306, 318, 467, 568, 582; play-within-a-play device 166; *Polly* 169; Scriblerus Club 216; *The Shepherd's Week* 231, 507–8; *Three Hours after Marriage* 166, 168; *Trivia* 231, 285; *The What d'ye Call It* 166–7, 219; *Wine* 231
Gee, Maggie 402
Gelbart, Larry: *Mastergate* 474
gender factors 188, 575–6, 582–3
Genesis 18, 220
Genet, Jean: *The Balcony* 472
genres: blurred 331–2, 400; formalist 31–2; parody 204–5, 495; rhetoric 39
The Gentleman's Magazine 343–4
George I 282
George II 526
George III 254, 312, 345, 528
George IV 530–2
German Democrat Republic 529
Gibbon, Edward 566; *Decline and Fall* 22, 561
Gibbon, Lewis Grassic 402
Gibson, William M. 397
Gifford, William 234, 349; *Epistle to Peter Pindar* 254
Gilbert, W. S. 9; Bab Ballads 355–7; *The Gondoliers* 466; *Iolanthe* 466; *Mikado* 466; *Patience* 358, 466; "Phrenology" 355–6; *The Pirates of Penzance* 466; *Princess Ida* 358; *Songs of a Savoyard* 358
Gillray, James 9, 529; *Britannia* 315; caricatures 363; *Dido in Distress* 314; French Revolution 322; Herod and Pilate print 540, 541; *Pitt the Younger* 296, 312, 322–3;

The Plumb-pudding 313; *Smelling out a Rat* 294, 295, 322, 323
God 17, 18
Goddard, William 104, 111
Godey's Lady's Book 388–9
Godwin, William: *Caleb Williams* 274
Goethe, Johann Wolfgang von 330, 338; *Faust* 332–3
Gogarty, Oliver St John 483
Gogol, Nikolai: *Inspector General* 464–5; *The Nose* 372; *The Overcoat* 372, 519–20
Goldin, Frederick 62
Golding, William 402
Goldsmith, Oliver 234, 235, 246, 247; *The Citizen of the World* 154, 565; *The Deserted Village* 246, 247–8, 251; *Retaliation* 245–6; *The Traveller* 247; *The Vicar of Wakefield* 270, 271
goliardic satire 122, 217, 507
Gombrich, Ernst 293, 316, 323
Góngora, Luis de 86; *Fábula de Píramo y Tisbe* 93–4
Goodchild, Francis 296
"Gospel of Silver Mark" 56, 526
gossip 350–1, 575–6
Gower, John 67
Goya, Francisco de 308, 313, 316, 319
Gracián, Baltasar 95
Graffigny, Françoise de: *Lettres d'une Péruvienne* 154
Graham, George 354
Graham, Harry 445
Greek Anthology 555
Greek literature: comedy 36; satire 82; satyr plays 6
Green, Henry 402
Greenblatt, Stephen 552–3
Greene, Graham 402; *Lord Rochester's Monkey* 403
Greene, Robert 132; *Defence of Conny-Catching* 552
Greenwood, Walter 402
Gregory, Lady 482
Gregory of Pavia 55
Griffin, Dustin 9
Gringore, Pierre 72
grotesque 96, 97, 313–16, 318, 343
Grub Street subculture 222
Grubgeld, Elizabeth 482–3
Guardian 407, 538–40
Guevara, Luis Vélez de: *El diablo cojuelo* 98
Guillaume I 507

Guilpin, Everard 102, 103, 104, 108, 111–12
Gullans, Charles: "Diatribe to Doctor Steele" 449
Gunn, Thom 443, 453; "To Yvor Winters" 449
Gurnah, Abdulrazak 402
Gwynn, R. S.: "Among Philistines" 455; *Narcissiad* 453–5; "The Professor's Lot" 455; "Snow White and the Seven Deadly Sins" 454–5

Hagar 18
Haggerty, George 270
Haldane, J. B. S. 420
Hall, Joseph 108, 181; *Characterismes of Vices* 554–5; *Characters of Vertues and Vices* 553–4, 555; homiletic tradition 565; irony 554–5; religious satire 563–4; style 113, 114; *Virgidemiarum* 102, 109, 112, 113, 553
Haman 25
Hamilton, Alexander: *The History of the Tuesday Club* 380
Hamilton, Emma 314, 318–19, 320; *Memoirs of Modern Philosophers* 362
Hamilton, Lady Anne: *The Epics of the Ton* 350–1
Hampden, John 561
Handke, Peter: *Kasper* 474; *Offending the Audience* 473–4
Hands, Elizabeth 284
Hannibal 45
Hantke, Steffen 582
Harcourt, Simon 578
Hardy, Thomas 373, 511; "The Darkling Thrush" 360; "The Ruined Maid" 438; *Satires of Circumstance* 437–8; "Satires of Circumstance in Fifteen Glimpses" 437; *Tess of the D'Urbervilles* 511
Harington, Sir John: *A New Discourse* 131–2
"Harlequin's Invasion" 343
Harley, Robert 216, 578
Harrison, Tony 445
Hart, Moss 469
Hartley, David 333
Harvey, Gabriel 109–10, 132
Hastings, Warren 255
Hawthorne, Nathaniel 1
Haywood, Eliza 260, 271, 286, 579; *Anti-Pamela* 260–1; *The History of Miss Betsy Thoughtless* 287
Hazlitt, William 562
Healey, John 552
Heartfield, John 316
Hebrew Scriptures 8–9, 16, 19, 21, 22; *see also* Bible; mock-biblical genre

Hebrews, Epistle to 554
Hecht, Anthony 445; *The Hidden Law* 446
Hegel, G. W. F. 331, 335, 339
Heine, Heinrich: *Atta Troll* 338; Christianity 335–6; Goethe 338; Hegel 339; on Kant 334–5; "Religion and Philosophy in Germany" 329, 330–1, 333, 334, 337; Schiller 338
Heller, Joseph 106; *Catch 22* 3–4
Hendrickson, G. L. 6, 445
Henley, John: *Hyp-Doctor* 528
Henri III 143–4
Henri IV 156
Henry II 56, 61
Henry III 83
Herman, Ruth 260
Herodotus 83
heroic drama 165
Herrera, Hernando de 93
Herrick, Robert 104, 437
Hervey, Lord 261, 282, 562–3
Hesiod 497; *Works and Days* 499
Heym, Stefan: *The King David Report* 529
Hipponax 35, 36, 47
history 373, 427–9, 577–80
history plays 109
Hitler, Adolf 2, 468
Hobbes, Thomas 229, 498; *Leviathan* 204–5
Hoch, Hannah 316
Hodgart, Matthew 6
Hoffmann, E. T. A. 336
Hogarth, William: *Analysis of Beauty* 307, 312; *Characters and Caricaturas* 310, 311; *Gin Lane* 303, 304; *A Harlot's Progress* 293, 295–6, 300, 302, 304, 317, 318, 322, 527; *Hudibras and the Skimmington* 305; independence 323; *Industry and Idleness* 296; *The Lottery* 294, 295, 297, 305; *Marriage A-la-mode* 308, 319; mock-biblical engravings 527; *A Rake's Progress* 305–6; *South Sea Scheme* 299, 304–5, 527; training 307
Hogg, James 528
Holcroft, Thomas: *Hugh Trevor* 273–4
Holley, Marietta 391; *Josiah Allen on the Woman Question* 391; *My Opinions and Betsey Bobbet's* 391
Home, Stewart 402
Homer 220; *Iliad* 33–4, 502; *Odyssey* 73; Thersites 47
homilists 552
homophobia 414–15, 451

Hone, William 340, 345, 528; George IV 530–2; libel charges 364; *The Matrimonial Ladder* 363; *The Political House that Jack Built* 345, 363; *The Political Showman – At Home!* 363

Hood, Thomas 331–2; "I Remember, I Remember" 441; "Ode to Mr Graham" 354; *Odes and Addresses to Great People* 354

Hook, Thomas: *Blackwood's Edinburgh Magazine* 347

Hope, A. D.: *The Dunciad Minor* 447; "Imperial Adam" 447; "Letter from Rome" 446–7; "The Satiric Muse" 434

Hopkins, Lemuel 239–40

Hopkinson, Francis 380; *The Battle of the Kegs* 381–2; *A Pretty Story* 381

Hoppe, Art 9

Horace: alexandrines 139–40; *The Art of Poetry* 225; character types 551; "City Mouse and Country Mouse" 497; constructivism 28; Diderot 151; Frye's phases 23; as influence 2, 7, 52, 82, 90, 111–12, 115, 120, 140, 141, 277; irony 511, 514; letters to Maecenas 436; on Lucilius 40, 41, 569; mask/persona 201; patron 42; Priapus 44; Quintilian on 31; satire to amuse 19, 28, 104–5, 514–15; *Satires* 24, 102, 107; self-mockery 47; *sermones* 32, 43, 44, 436, 445, 514; sexual behavior 28, 48; talking animals 21

Horne, E. H. 429

Hosea 25, 29

Hospitallers 61

Howard, Frances 555–6

Howard, Sir Robert 165

Hudibrastics 180, 281, 282, 508

Huguenots 83

human nature 42, 124–5, 220, 221–2

humanism: lampoon/moralizing 90; mockery 500, 506–7; Rabelais 77, 258; Renaissance 119, 120, 124, 130–1

Hume, David 333; *Dialogues Concerning Natural Religion* 364

Hume, Robert D. 169

Humphreys, David 239–40

Hunt, Leigh 342, 358

Hunter, J. Paul 259

Hurd, Richard 235

Hutton, Henry 115

Huxley, Aldous 339, 401, 403–4, 421, 430; *After Many a Summer* 405–6, 426; *Antic Hay* 403, 416, 424–6; *Ape and Essence* 406, 410, 420; "The Beauty Industry" 405; *Brave New World* 128, 404, 415, 420, 423; *Crome Yellow* 416, 429; *Eyeless in Gaza* 426; *Point Counter Point* 406, 429; *Those Barren Leaves* 404; *Time Must Have a Stop* 412, 424, 426, 428

Huxley, Julian 420–1

Hwang, David Henry: *M Butterfly* 473

hybrid satire 119, 130–5

Hyde, Edward: *History of the Rebellion* 561

hyperbole 54–5, 63

hypocrisy 66, 82, 97, 98, 132, 225

iambography 7, 34–6

Ibsen, Henrik 460; *A Doll's House* 462–3; *An Enemy of the People* 462–3; *Ghosts* 462–3; *Hedda Gabler* 462–3; *The Wild Duck* 462–3

Ibycus 499

idealism 333, 334

Idol-Worship print 535, 536

imitation 49–50, 191

Imlay, Gilbert: *The Emigrants* 274

immorality 186–7

impersonation 44

Inchbald, Elizabeth: *Nature and Art* 273, 362; *A Simple Story* 288; *Such Things Are* 280

incongruity 318–19, 328–9, 332

The Independent 529

individuals in society 23, 41, 118, 143

institutions satirized 75, 369–70

intellectuals 126, 129, 131, 132

intelligence 571

The Intelligencer 571

intentional fallacy 196

internal focalization 67–8

intertextuality 48, 404

Invasion of the Body Snatchers 223

invective 5–6, 54, 118, 132, 479

inversion 77, 130, 261–2, 357

Ionesco, Eugene 470, 471; *The Bald Soprano* 471–2; *The Chairs* 472

Ireland: Anglo-Irish texts 480–1; civil war 484; landlords 200; Menippean satire 483–90; poverty 198–9; Renaissance 481–2; sexual behavior 486; *see also individual writers*

Irish Free State 485

Irish Literary Revival 484

Irish Literary Theatre 482

Irish Theatre 482, 483, 484

irony: Austen 24, 25–6, 518; censorship 490; Chaucer 64; cynicism 521; Dinesen 521–2; dramatic 49, 461, 523; epigrams 375; Greek origins 512; Hall 554–5; Hardy 511;

irony: Austen (cont'd)
    Hebrew Scriptures 22; Horace 24, 511;
    Nabokov 522–3; nightmare 29; phases 22–4;
    Romanticism 332, 520; satire 71, 510, 512,
    517–18; secrecy 581; Socrates 513, 520
Irving, Washington 384–5; *A History of New York* 384–5; *Salmagundi* 384–5
Irving, William 384–5
Isabella, Queen 86, 87
Isaiah 27, 28, 530, 531
Isherwood, Christopher 402
Ishiguru, Kazuo 402
Israel 30
Italian Renaissance 118–19, 127–8

Jacob, Max 458
Jacobins 62, 274; *see also* anti-Jacobins
Jacobson, Howard 402
James, Clive 447; "The Book of My Enemy Has Been Remaindered" 448; *Charles Charming's Challenge* 448; *Other Passports* 448; "To Pete Atkin" 448; "To Prue Shaw" 448; "To Russell Davies" 448; "To Tom Stoppard" 448
James I 555–6
James II 178, 212, 259, 281, 286
Jameson, Fredric 424; *Fables of Aggression* 430
Jansenists 149–50
Jarrell, Randall 444
Jarry, Alfred: *Exploits and Opinions of Dr Faustroll* 375; *Ubu Roi* 470, 474
Jemielity, Thomas 8–9; *Satire and the Hebrew Prophets* 18–19, 29–30
Jeremiah 20, 28–9, 344
Jerome, Saint 67
Jerrold, Douglas 355
jesters 8–9
Jesuits 141, 149–50, 153, 190–1
Jesus 20; adulterous woman 305, 318; kingdom of heaven 74; paradoxes 71; pictorial representations 298–9; Samaritan woman 15–16; suffering 299–300
Jewish Naturalization Act 528
Joan, Pope 113
Job 17, 18–19, 26, 530, 531
John, Gospel of 15, 71
John, Saint 57
John Bull 216
John of Garland 53, 54
Johnson, Esther 196
Johnson, Samuel: on Butler 180, 181; Crabbe 251; *Dictionary* 5, 571; *Idler* 565; Juvenal 22, 213–14; *Life of Cowley* 565; *Lives of the Poets* 561; "London" 213–14, 234, 236; *Rambler* 561–2, 565; *Rasselas* 21, 26; on satire 436; "Short Song of Congratulation" 442; on Swift 203; "The Vanity of Human Wishes" 9, 237–8, 271, 565
Johnstone, Charles: *Chrysal* 265
Jonah 20, 25
Jones, David: *The Secret History of White-Hall* 578
Jones, Ernest 340–1; "Song of the Low" 348
Jones, Mary: "An Epistle to Lady Bowyer" 283
Jonson, Ben: *The Alchemist* 104; *Catiline* 190; comical satire 115; Dryden 192, 193; epigrams 437; *Every Man Out of His Humour* 552; gender factors 575–6; Huxley 430; satire/killing 575; "To Penshurst" 112; *Volpone* 104, 162, 582
Joshua 542
journalism 368, 527–8
Joyce, James 132, 402, 415, 427; *Dubliners* 478–9; *Finnegans Wake* 416; *Gas from a Burner* 478–9; Gogarty 483; "The Holy Office" 478; memoirs 483; *Ulysses* 407, 411, 481, 483
Juan de la Cruz, San 86
Julian the Apostate 561
Julius II, Pope 72
justice 55–6
Juvenal 105, 514–15; alexandrines 140; Boileau 142; character types 551; corruption 298; Diderot 150–1; Hall 554; imitated 237; as influence 1, 2, 31, 47, 52, 103, 111–12, 115, 120, 140, 141, 236, 271, 277, 344; lampoons 41; Messalina 21, 22; narrator 32; revenge 42; *Satires* 7, 9, 22, 32, 43, 44–6, 48; Skelton 107; women 37, 48, 140, 511; on writing satire 107, 109, 135, 141, 400, 511

Kafka, Franz: *The Trial* 431
Kaiser, Georg 468
Kallimachos 48
Kant, Immanuel: *Critique of Pure Reason* 334–5
Kaufman, George S. 460–1; *I'd Rather be Right* 469; *Of Thee I Sing* 469
Kavanagh, Patrick: "The Paddiad" 479
Keane, John B. 480
Keats, John: *The Fall of Hyperion* 330; "Nebuchadnezzar's Dream" 528
Keller, Evelyn 571, 573
Kelly, Gary 273, 274
Kelman, James 402
Kennedy, X. J. 443; "Tableau Intime" 442

Kerby-Miller, Charles 216
Kernan, Alvin 6, 103, 298–9, 302–3, 577
Keymer, Thomas 269
Kierkegaard, Søren 520
Kinch, Myra 9
1 Kings 16, 529, 533, 535
2 Kings 527
Kingsley, Charles: *The Water Babies* 371
Kinsella, Thomas 477
Kipling, Rudyard: "Epitaphs of the War, 1914–1918" 444
Kirkland, Caroline 387; *Fashion; or Life in New York* 386; *Forest Life* 386; *A New Home* 386
Kleon 36
Knox, Ronald 403; "Humour and Satire" 401–2
Kramer, Leonie 446
Kratinos 38
Kris, Ernst 316
Kushner, Tony: *Angels in America* 474
Kyrle, John 563

La Bruyère, Jean de 84; *Les Caractères* 148–9, 562
La Fontaine, Jean de 84; *Fables* 147–8, 151
La Grange, Isaac de 140
La Motte, Antoine Houdar de 158
La Rochefoucauld, François de 16, 84
Lake School poets 342, 345, 349, 358, 359
Lamb, Charles 331–2
lampoon 5, 41, 89–90, 162, 186, 193; see also personal satire
"The Land of Cokaygne" 480
Lando, Ortensio 127, 128
Landor, Walter Savage 437
Langland, William 129; *Piers Plowman* 52, 55, 60, 66–7, 552
Larkin, Philip 414; "Annus Mirabilis" 440; "I Remember, I Remember" 441; "Sad Steps" 440–1; "This Be the Verse" 440
Latin satire: see Roman satire
Laud, William 237, 561
laughter 16, 19, 143, 144
Lavaud, René 63
Law, William: *A Serious Call to a Devout and Holy Life* 565–6
Lawrence, D. H. 402; as artist 408; Huxley 428–9; pornography 415; "St Mawr" 429; "The Virgin and the Gypsy" 429
Leapor, Mary 283; "An Epistle to Artemisia" 283; "An Essay on Woman" 283; "Man the Monarch" 283

Lear, Edward 357
Ledger 389
Leibniz, Gottfried Wilhelm 157
Leithauser, Brad 445
Lennox, Charlotte: *The Female Quixote* 271–2, 287–8
León, Fray Luis de 86
Leonardo da Vinci 314
Leopardi, Giacomo 364
Lesage, Alain René 151
Lewis, Esther: "A Mirror for Detractors" 283–4
Lewis, Janet 445
Lewis, Wyndham 402; *The Apes of God* 404, 405, 407–8, 410–11, 414; as artist 408; Hitler 409, 423; Jameson on 430; *Men Without Art* 401, 423–4; *One-way Song* 452; *The Revenge for Love* 414; *The Roaring Queen* 414; *The Wild Body* 409
libel 2, 41, 215, 286, 364, 528, 572
The Liberal 345
libraries, circulating 362, 371, 372–3
Licensing Act 169, 171–2, 174, 204, 214, 261, 568
Lindenberger, Herbert 219
Literary Club 246
literary criticism 142
literary hoaxes 448
literary satire 358–60
Litt, Toby 402
Little, Janet: "Given to a Lady" 284
Little Tract of Garcia 68
Lloyd, Charles: *Edmund Oliver* 274
Lloyd, Evan 234–5, 240; *Conversation* 243; *The Curate* 243; *The Methodist* 242–3; *The Powers of the Pen* 243
Lloyd, Pierson 241
Lloyd, Robert 234–5, 240, 242
Locke, David R. 384, 390
Locke, John 219, 333
Lockhart, John Gibson 528
Lodge, David 402
Lodge, Thomas 108, 110, 111, 131
Longchamp, Nigel (Wireker) 58–61
Longinus 218, 223
The Longman Anthology of British Literature 199
Lorca, Frederico García 451
Lord, George deF. 226
Lord Chamberlain 174
Louis IX 63–4
Louis XII 72
Louis XIV 143, 144, 145

Love, Harold 188
Lovely, Ann 280
Lowell, James Russell 384; *The Biglow Papers* 387–8
Lowell, Robert: "To Peter Taylor" 449
Loyola, St Ignatius 190
Lucian of Samosata: *Charon* 83; as influence 79, 119, 120, 125, 263, 481; inversion 130; *Menippus* 71; *Menippus* 71, 74; rediscovered 87–8; *True Story* 73
Lucilius, Gaius: Boileau on 141; Horace on 40, 41, 569; as influence 7, 31, 45; *saturae* 32, 332, 436, 514
Lucretius 497
Luddism 347
Luke, Gospel of 54–5, 74, 540
Luther, Martin: *Sendbrief vom Dolmetschen* 527
luxury 59–60, 106
Lykambes 7, 35
lyrics, satirical 437–42
Lysistrata 37

MacArthur, David Wilson 337
McAuley, James: "Letter to John Dryden" 447–8
McCabe, Richard 108, 115
MacDonagh, John 483
McGinley, Phyllis 445
McGrath, Patrick 402, 428
Machiavelli, Niccolò: *Il Principe* 82
Mackenzie, Henry: *The Man of Feeling* 271
McLuhan, Marshall 222
MacNeice, Louis: *Letters from Iceland* 446
McQuaid, John Charles 488
madness 123, 204
magic 476, 477
Maginn, William 358
malevolence in writing 429–31
Malley, Ern (hoax) 448
Mamet, David: *Glengarry Glen Ross* 474
Mandeville, Bernard 215; "The Fable of the Bees" 228–9, 498; "The Grumbling Hive" 228, 498
Manley, Delarivier 166, 271; *The New Atalantis* 260, 286, 571, 572, 577; *Queen Zarah* 259–60, 286, 580–1; secret histories 579
Mann, Jill 57–8, 67
Mann, Thomas: *Joseph and his Brothers* 458
Map, Walter 61; *De nugis curialium* 61–2
Maravall, Antonio 90
Mardi Gras 79
Marinetti, T. P. 421

Marivaux, Pierre Carlet de Chamblain de: *La Double Inconstance* 151; *L'Isle des esclaves* 151–2
Markov, Georgi: *The Right Honourable Chimpanzee* 406–7
Marlborough, Duchess of: *see* Churchill, Sarah
Marlborough, Duke of 561, 572
Marlowe, Christopher 109, 133, 403–4, 560
marriage 217–18, 279; marital fidelity 530
Marshalsea Prison 368
Marston, John 108, 552; *Certaine Satyres* 103, 553; comical satire 115; erotic epyllion 109; *The Scourge of Villanie* 113, 553; style 102, 113, 114
Martial 81, 103–4, 442, 447, 551
Martyn, Edward 482; *The Dream Physician* 483; *Romulus and Remus* 482
Marvell, Andrew 101, 103, 178; "Character of Holland" 450; ecclesiastical politics 184–5; *The First Anniversary* 562; "Flecknoe" 115–16, 184; "Last Instructions to a Painter" 176, 182–3, 184, 562, 582; metaphysical poetry 182; as public writer 182;
The Rehearsal Transpros'd 182–3, 185;
"Second Advice to a Painter" 183, 226; style 182–3; "Third Advice to a Painter" 183, 226; verse satires 184; "A Year of Wonders" 183–4
Marx, Karl 129
Mary Magdalen 305
Massys, Q. 302
materialism 333, 497
Matthew, Gospel of 56, 71, 74, 305, 530, 531
Mayakovsky, Vladimir: *The Bedbug* 465
Mazarin, Cardinal 143–4
medieval satire 52–4
melancholy 124
Melville, Herman: *The Confidence-Man* 372
Menander 461
Menippean satire 82; Anglo-Irish narrative tradition 480–1; Bakhtin 8, 32, 258, 485; Blanchard 8; Cynics 7, 119; Ireland 476, 483–90; renaissance of 70–2
Menippus 7, 71
Mercier, Vivian 478, 481; *The Irish Comic Tradition* 476
Mercurius Britannicus 179
Mercurius Pragmaticus 179
Meredith, George 576; *Ordeal of Richard Feverel* 371, 372
Messalina, Empress 21, 22
metamorphosis 316
metaphor 497

Methodism 261
metonymy 293–5, 501
Meun, Jean de: *Roman de la rose* 52, 67, 81
Middleton, Conyers 261
Middleton, Thomas 108
Mill, John Stuart: *On Liberty* 371–2, 374
Millay, Edna St Vincent 445
Miller, Arthur: *All My Sons* 469; *The Crucible* 469; *Death of a Salesman* 461, 469
Miller, D. A. 573
Milton, John 498; *Paradise Lost* 2, 183, 561; pastiche of 500–1; *Readie and Easie Way to Establish a Commonwealth* 179–80; Satan 189–90, 202; Smectymnuan pamphlets 184–5, 575; sonnets 344; wars of truth 179
misogyny 36, 239
mock catechisms 144
mock compendium 131–2
mock encomium 132–3, 190–1
mock prophecies 344
mock wills 144
mock-biblical genre 525–9, 540–8
mock-epic poems 47, 94–5, 351, 508
mockery: Augustan 506–7; conventions 505–6; epic 508; humanism 500, 506–7; *Iliad* 34; literary 495; pastorals 508; Romans 41–2
mock-heroic satire 193, 231, 305–8, 495–7, 500–7
Molière (Jean Baptiste Poquelin) 84, 461; *Le Bourgeois Gentilhomme* 146; *Dom Juan* 146; *L'Ecole des femmes* 145, 146; Fielding's adaptations 169; laughter 144; *Le Malade imaginaire* 146–7; *Le Misanthrope* 146; *The Miser* 162; ridicule 144, 145; *Tartuffe* 145, 146, 151, 162
Molloy, M. J. 480
Momus 125
Monboddo, Lord 364–5
"Money Gospel" 56, 526
money/corruption 55–6, 149
Monmouth, Duke of 259, 578
Monmouth rebellion 545
Montague, Lady Mary Wortley 287–8; "Saturday: The Small Pox" 282; "Verses Address'd to the Imitator" 282
Montaigne, Michel de 128, 552
Montesquieu, Charles-Louis de Secondat 144; *Lettres persanes* 153–4, 159
Moorcock, Michael 402
Moore, George: *Hail and Farewell* 482; *Literature at Nurse* 373

Moore, Michael 4, 568, 573, 574, 580, 582
Moore, Richard 445
Moore, Thomas 346–7; "An Episcopal Address on Socialism" 341; *The Fudge Family in Paris* 349; *The Fudges in England* 349–50; *Intercepted Letters* 349–50; *Irish Melodies* 346; *Odes upon Cash, Corn* 346
moral examples 1–2, 45, 147–8
moral satire 84, 98, 298, 317
morality plays 71
Mordecai 25
More, Hannah: "Slavery, A Poem" 285
More, Thomas 123, 127, 130, 516; *Utopia* 71, 128–30
The Morning Chronicle 341, 365, 528
The Morning Herald 528
Morris, Linda M. 391
Morris, William: *News from Nowhere* 373
Morton, Thomas 378; *New English Canaan* 378
Moses 29
Moussorgsky, Modest 9
mouth-work 410–12
Mowatt, Anna Cora 382
Mozley, J. H. 58, 60
Mrozek, Slawomir: *Tango* 474
Mudie's circulating library 371, 372
Mulgrave, Earl of: *Essay on Poetry* 576
Mullan, John 270
Murdoch, Iris 402
Murphy, Tom 479–80; *The Sanctuary Lamp* 480
Murray, T. C. 480
Murry, Ann: "The Tête à Tête" 285
Mynors, R. A. B. 61

Nabokov, Vladimir 219; *Ada* 522; irony 522–3
Naipaul, V. S. 402
names of characters 287
Nantes, Revocation of the Edict 157
Napoleon 312, 315–16, 323, 340, 343, 363
narrative voice 259, 263–4, 272–3
Nasby, Petroleum V. 390
Nash, Ogden 443
Nashe, Thomas 109–10, 127, 131; *Apologie of Pierce Pennilesse* 552; *The Choice of Valentines* 132; *Lenten Stuff* 132–3; *The Unfortunate Traveller* 132, 552
Nason, Richard: *A Modern Dunciad* 453
The Nation 434
nationalism, satiric 153
Navarre, Henri de 84
Neal's Saturday Gazette 388

Nebrija, Antonio de 86
"Nell Flaherty's Drake" 478
Nelson, Horatio 314, 318–19, *320*
Nemerov, Howard 445
neo-Latin 119
neologisms 132
Nero 314
New, Melvyn 268
The New Coalition print 531–2
New Comedy 550–1
New Quarter 453
New Testament 130
New World 128
Newton, Isaac 204, 206
Nicholas V, Pope 125
Nietzsche, Friedrich 520; *Genealogy of Morals* 374
Nims, John Frederick 444
Nixon, Richard 6
North, Frederick 540
The North Briton 242
The Northern Liberator 347
nostalgia 233
Novalis 333
novels 236; comic 147; form 90; irony 517–18; Paulson 257; picaresque 90, 265, 552; postmodernist 578–9; realism 518; themed 402; women writers 259–61, 271–3; *see also individual authors*

O'Brien, Flann 484, 490; *At Swim-Two-Birds* 488–9; *The Third Policeman* 489
obscenity 23, 28, 108, 188–9
O'Casey, Sean 480; *Juno and the Paycock* 465
Occitan vernacular 62, 63
Odets, Clifford 469
O'Duffy, Eimar: *Asses in Clover* 486–7; *Bricriu's Feast* 484; *King Goshawk and the Birds* 485; *The Phoenix on the Roof* 484; *The Spacious Adventures of the Man in the Street* 485–6
Odysseus 34, 38, 50
Oedipus 25
Oedipus 205
Oisín 485
Old Comedy 7, 36, 37
Old Irish 476
Oldham, John 178, 189–91; curse 194; Dryden on 241; imitation 191; mock encomium 190–1; "Sardanapalus" 189; *Satire Upon a Printer* 575; "Satyr Against Vertue" 191; *Satyrs on the Jesuits* 176, 189–90

Oldmixon, John: *A Detection of the Sophistry and the Falsities* 578
O'Leary, John 438
O'Neill, Eugene: *The Emperor Jones* 468; *The Hairy Ape* 468
The Onion 570
ontology 319
Opie, John 254
opposites juxtaposed 73–4, 75, 79–80
optimism satirized 157
"Ordre de Bel-Eyse" ("Order of Fair Ease") 59
Origen 22
Ortuinus 73
Orwell, George 401, 402; *Animal Farm* 147, 404, 517; *A Clergyman's Daughter* 413; *Coming Up for Air* 411–12, 420, 421–2, 428; disgust 413; *Down and Out in Paris and London* 411; *Homage to Catalonia* 413, 424; *Nineteen Eighty-Four* 29, 128, 303, 416–17, 419–20, 422, 423, 424; *The Road to Wigan Pier* 413, 414, 422, 423; on Swift 427; talking animals 21; totalitarianism 24, 336
Other 409–10, 413
ottava rima 447
Otway, Thomas: *Venice Preserv'd* 163–4
Overburian characters 556–9
Overbury, Sir Thomas 181, 555–6
Ovid 81, 194, 507
Owen, Robert 341
Owen, Wilfrid: "Dulce et Decorum Est" 438
Oxford, Earl of 216
The Oxford Book of Satirical Verse 437
Oxford Companion to Twentieth-century Poetry 451
oxymoron 88, 439

Pacuvius 332
Paine, Albert Bigelow 395–6
Palissot, Charles 158; *Les Philosophes* 158
Palmeri, Frank 362
pamphleteers 345, 525
panopticon 430
pantheism 334, 335
parables 520
paradoxes 71, 187, 471
paranoia 582–3
Parker, Dorothy 445
Parks, Suzan-Lori: *The America Play* 474
Parnell, Thomas: Scriblerus Club 216
parody: *Anti-Jacobin* 342; Aristophanes 47; genres 204–5, 495; hoaxes 448; Jesus's teaching 54–5; Milton 2; novel 90; pictorial

304–6; Pope 239; Sterne 268–9; stylistic 94–5
Parton, Sara Willis 388; *Ruth Hall* 389
Pascal, Blaise 84; *Lettres provinciales* 149, 152–3
pastiche 508
pastorals 112, 508
Patch, Thomas 309
pathetic fallacy 360
Patrick, Saint 477, 485
patronage 42, 125–6
Paul, Saint 122, 123, 426
Paulding, James K. 384; *John Bull in America* 385
Paulson, Ronald: eighteenth-century novels 274; on Fielding 263–4; on Hogarth 322; novels 257; satire 2, 3, 7; on Smollett 265, 266, 267–8
Paylor, W. J. 556, 557, 558
Payne, Deborah C. 161
Peacock, Thomas Love 329; *Crotchet Castle* 364, 365; *Gryll Grange* 365; *Melincourt* 364–5; *Nightmare Abbey* 364, 365
Peel, Robert 341
The Penguin Book of Satirical Verse 437
Perotti, Niccolò 131
Persius 47; alexandrines 139; biography 41; Boileau on 141; character types 551; delusion 42; Diderot 151; imitation 48, 49–50; as influence 7, 31, 82, 277; letters 436; Old Comedy 40; *Satires* 40, 43–4; style/genre 49
personal satire 118, 483–4; avoiding 230–1; *see also* lampoon
Peter, John 53
Peterloo Massacre 344, 345
Petronius 7, 120
Petty, William 199
Phaedrus 147
Philip II 84, 89
Philip IV 98
Philippians 426
Philips, John: "The Splendid Shilling" 500–1
Philistines 18, 21, 25
Phillips, Ambrose 167
Phillips, Caryl 402
Phillips, David: *The Right Honourable Chimpanzee* 406–7
Philodemos 48
philosophes 120, 158
philosophy 204
phrenology 355–6

physicality 96, 97
picaresque novel 90, 265, 552
pictorial satire 293–7; caricature 308–13; Christian models 298–304; grotesque 313–16; Rococo style 306–8; *see also* satirical prints
picturesque 224, 417–19
Pinciano, López 90
Pindar 220
Pindar, Peter: *see* Wolcot, John
Pinkerton, Helen 444
Pinsky, Robert: "An Explanation of America" 449
Pinter, Harold: *The Birthday Party* 472; *The Caretaker* 472; *The Homecoming* 472
Pirandello, Luigi: *Right You Are* 465
Pisani, Ugo 121–2
Pitt the Younger, William 294, 296, 312, 314, 322–3, 363, 532
Pittis, William 578
Pix, Mary 166; *The Spanish Wives* 279
Plato: *Apology of Socrates* 73; divine madness 123; *Republic* 128; Socrates 71, 512–13; *Symposium* 513, 514
Plato Comicus 555
Plautus 39, 551
The Player (Altman) 166
play-within-a-play device 165–6
Pléiade 81, 82
Pliny the Elder 35
Poe, Edgar Allan: "The Poetic Principle" 435
"Poems on Affairs of State" 178
poetry: comic 37–8, 357; Confucianism 498; current 220; women writers 280–5; *see also satura*; verse satire
The Poetry of the Anti-Jacobin 342–3, 358
poligrafi 127–8
polis 37
political cartoonists 293, 312–13
political satire: Carlyle 335–9; Dryden 194; *Gulliver's Travels* 206–9; Heine 335–9; Rabelais 75–6; Shaw 463–4; USA 377; verse 340, 342–8
politics 125–6, 129
Poliziano, Angelo 131; *Lamia* 122–3; *Panepistemon* 122
Pontano, Giovanni 126
Pop Art 9
Pope, Alexander 115, 215; Arnold on 434; Augustan mode 563; *Dialogue II* 20; *The Dunciad* 16–17, 29, 171, 218–19, 223, 225, 227, 234, 240, 335, 503, 527, 565, 570, 572; epigrams 437; *Epilogue to the Satires* 234, 574;

Pope, Alexander (cont'd)
  "Epistle to Bathurst" 527; "Epistle to Burlington" 224, 225; "Epistle to Dr Arbuthnot" 213–14, 562–3, 569; *Epistles to Several Persons* 224, 225–6, 236, 283, 436, 445, 563; *An Essay on Criticism* 220, 506; *An Essay on Man* 22, 220–1, 228, 285; "First Psalm" 527; historical context 213–14; *Imitations of Horace* 224, 508; imitators 235, 239, 254; as influence 234, 439, 452–3, 479, 506–7; *The Key to the Lock* 579–80, 581; *Miscellanies* 218; misconduct 2; mock-heroic satire 500–7; *Moral Essays* 224, 563; parodied 239; *Pastorals* 499–500, 505, 506; *Peri Bathous* 170, 218, 565; persona 225; *The Rape of the Lock* 21, 225, 306–7, 351, 500, 501–3, 504–6, 573, 576; reputation 219–20; Rochester 186; Scriblerus Club 216; Swift's influence 231; and Theobald 526; "Windsor-Forest" 247, 500, 505, 508
Pordage, Samuel 527
pornography 108, 187–9, 239, 415
Porter, Peter: adaptations of Martial 447; "Made in Heaven" 447
portraiture 309, 310, 313, 316
Posidippus 555
postcolonial novels 402
postmodernist novels 578–9
Potter, Thomas 239
Pound, Ezra 236
poverty 141, 151, 198, 249, 250
praelectio 121
praise 121
Priapus 44
Priestley, Joseph 228
Primas 57
printing technology 570
Prior, Matthew 215; "The Country Mouse and the City Mouse" 231; "An Epitaph" 231; "Jinny the Just" 231
Pritchett, V. S. 317, 322
Private Eye 529
The Producers (Brooks) 2
prophets 8–9, 15–16, 20, 344
prostitution 300, 302
Protestants 79, 157, 190–1, 212–13, 223–4
Proverbs 18, 24, 26, 530, 531
Psalms 15, 17–18, 527, 531, 543
pseudo-Theophrastus 553
psychological humors 552
public sphere 362
publishers 214
Punch 340–1, 354–5, 366, 367
Pure, Michel de 142
Puritans 179, 180, 557, 558
Pushkin, Alexander: *Evgeny Onegin* 364; *Ruslan and Ludmila* 522–3
Puttenham, George 191; *The Arte of English Poesie* 101–2
Pye, Henry James: *The Democrat* 274
Pynchon, Thomas: character sketches 566; conspiracy 569; *The Crying of Lot 49* 570, 572, 578–9, 582; secrecy 582
Pyramus and Thisbe 93–4

quatrains 104
Quevedo, Francisco de 86, 91, 93, 95–9; *Discursos* 96; *El sueño del Juicio Final* 97; *Sueños* 96; *Vision of the Catchpole Caught* 98; *Vision of Hell* 98
Quintilian 6–7, 31, 42, 512

Rabelais, François 140, 257–8, 481; on education 258; *Gargantua* 70, 72–3, 75–7, 147, 257; humanism 258; influences on 82; Lyonese period 72–3; *Pantagruel* 70, 72–4, 78–81, 257; Parisian period 72–3; skepticism 72
race factors 327–8, 473
Ralegh, Walter: "The Lie" 436–7
Rameau, Jean-Philippe 158
Randolph, Mary Claire 223, 224
The Random House Dictionary of the English Language 442
Rankins, William 103, 108
Raphael 305, 314; *Dispute on the Nature of the Eucharist* 309; *School of Athens* 309
Rapin, René 140
Rawson, Claude 201
Raymond, Derek 402
readership 56, 202–3, 205–6, 209–10, 219
realism: cinematic 4; drama 462, 469; literary 4; meditative 234; novels 518; Romantics 330
reality: appearance 83, 97–8, 332; art 5; readership 209–10
Recluse of Molliens: *Roman de Carité* 64–5
reference sources 130
reform 102–3, 139, 145
Reform Bill 365
Regency period 350–3, 518–19
Régnier, Mathurin 140–1; *Satire* 82
religious satire 126–7, 377, 425–7, 563–4; *see also* anti-clerical satire

Relihan, Joel C. 7
Renaissance satire 6; classical models 119; England 101; humanism 120, 124, 130–1; sin in art 318; in verse 81–2
responsibility, corporate 250–1
Restoration satire 179; Behn 278–9; character sketches 562–3; comedies 161–2, 162–5; information age 570; legacy of 214; present time 569; witty women 276
Revelation 528, 529
Reynolds, John Hamilton: *Odes and Addresses to Great People* 354
Reynolds, Sir Joshua 309–10
rhetoric 3, 5, 34, 39, 114, 185, 215, 319
Rice, Elmer: *The Adding Machine* 468
Richardson, Jonathan 309
Richardson, Samuel: *Pamela* 215, 260–1; *Sir Charles Grandison* 269
Rickword, Edgell: "Hints for Making a Gentleman" 452; "To the Wife of a Non-interventionist Statesman" 452
Riddell, Christopher 529
ridicule 2, 18, 20, 139, 144, 145, 332, 512
Rigault, Nicolas 140
Riley, E. C. 90
Ripa, Cesare 294
Robbins, R. H. 60–1
Roberts, Michèle 402
Robinson, Edwin Arlington: "Miniver Cheevy" 439; "Veteran Sirens" 439
Robinson, Fred Norris 477, 478
Robinson, Mary: "The Confessor" 349; "Horace Juvenal" 349; "January, 1795" 285; "London's Summer Morning" 285; "Tabitha Bramble" 349
Robinson, Ritchie 337–8
Rochester, Earl of 178, 185–9, 403, 497–8; "Allusion to Horace" 192–3; court satires 176; "The Disabled Debauchee" 187; Dryden 186; "An Epistolary Essay" 187; "The Imperfect Enjoyment" 186; "Letter from Artemiza" 187; obscenity 188–9; Pope 186; pornography 187–9; "A Ramble in St James's Park" 186; "Satyre against Reason and Mankind" 187; *Sodom* 188–9; "Upon Nothing" 187; "A Very Heroical Epistle" 187, 188
Rococo style 306–8, 314, 317
Roger & Me (Moore) 4
Rogers, Pat 222
Rojas, Ricardo de 86

role-playing 122, 124–5
The Rolliad (Fox, Sheridan et al.) 240
Roman satire 31–2, 82; comic drama 39–40; Greek influences 40; human nature 42; as influence 81; intertextuality 48; mockery 41–2; readership 56; themes 58–61
Romans, Epistle to 537
Romanticism 224; genre 331–2; internal/external factors 435; irony 332, 520; satire 328–31; satire *aufgehoben* 331, 336, 339; satirized 359–60; sensibility 364; spontaneity 434–5; Wordsworth 218
Ronsard, Pierre de 140
Roome, Edward: *Dean Jonathan's Parody* 526
Roosevelt, F. D. 312
Roosevelt, Teddy 312
Rosenheim, Edward 316–17
Rossetti, D. G. 415
Roth, Philip 21
Rousseau, Jean-Baptiste 158
Rousseau, Jean-Jacques 158
Rowlands, Samuel 115
Rowlandson, Thomas 312, 314, *315*, 317, 529; *The Anatomist* 321, 322; *Modern Antique* 318–19, *320*
Rump: Or an Exact Collection of the Choycest Poems and Songs relating to the Late Times 179
Rump Parliament 163, 179
rural life 249–50, 251
Rushdie, Salman 402
Ruskin, John 360
Russell, George 478
Russell, Henry 341–2
Russian Orthodox Church 519–20
Rutebeuf 63–4
Ryskind, Morrie 469

Sackville, Charles (Dorset) 176, 178
Sahl, Mort 9
Samaritan woman 15–16
Samson 18
Samuel 20
1 Samuel 18, 21, 25, 529
2 Samuel 529, 540, 542, 544, 545, 546, 547
Santos, Francisco: *Rey Gallo* 99; *Verdad en el potro* 99
Sappho 499
Sarah 18
Sassoon, Siegfried: "They" 438–9
Satan 189–90, 202
Satie, Erik 9

satire: *aufgehoben* 339; definitions 6, 21–2, 31–2; double audience 19; drama 145, 151, 161–2, 460–1, 479, 523; as externalist art 408; irony 510, 512; paranoia 582–3; phases 22–4, 27–8; public function 2–3, 568; punitive 19, 322; social function 32; tone/genre 140; traditional 450–8; *see also satura*; verse satire
"A Satire on the People of Kildare" 480
satiric idiom 219, 220, 227–8
satirical prints 526, 529
satura 54, 129, 436, 512; *lanx satura* 6, 177, 332; Lucilius 32, 332; Marvell 183; narrative satire 304; Quintilian 6–7
saturnalia 6, 56
satyr 183, 575
Satyr Ménippée 84
satyr plays 6, 120, 177
Saul 18, 21
Savage, Marmion Wilme 481
scandal 572
Scarfe, Gerald 316
Scarron, Paul 147, 179; *Mazarinade* 143–4
Scarry, Elaine 421
scatology 23, 74, 265
Schelling, F. W. J. von 334, 338
Schiller, Friedrich: "Aesthetic Education of Man" 332; Heine 338
Schindler's List 28
Schlegel, August Wilhelm 332
Schlegel, Friedrich 331, 332; *Lucinde* 520
Schmitz, Christine 48
scholasticism 122, 124, 257–8
science 203, 462
science fiction 402
Scotland 212–13
Scott, Sarah Robinson: *Millennium Hall* 288
Scott, Walter 237, 374; *The Antiquary* 363
Scriblerian Satire 215–19
Scriblerus, Martinus 215–19
Scriblerus Club 215–19
Scudéry, George de 142
secrecy 571, 572, 573, 574–5, 581
secret history 577–80
Seidel, Michael 577
Sejanus 45
Self, Will 401, 407, 415; *Great Apes* 412, 429; *My Idea of Fun* 412
self-censorship 489
self-interest 129
self-knowledge 78–9
self-mockery 47, 48, 230, 332, 348

self-promotion 37–8, 39, 132
Selkirk, Alexander 259
Selvon, Sam 402
Semonides 36, 37
Seneca 7, 119, 120, 554
sensibility 271, 274, 364
sentimental satire 246, 251–2, 269–70, 327–8
sermones 32, 43, 44, 436, 445, 514
Serpent's Tail publisher 402
sesta rima 437
Seth, Vikram 445
Settle, Elkanah 166, 527
Seven Years' War 265
Seward, Anna: "Colebrooke Dale" 284; "Verses Inviting Stella" 284
sexual politics 283
sexual/excretory processes 366
sexuality 22, 48, 486; Aretino 126; Charles II 189; courtiers 184; deviant 163–4; More 130; women 188
Shadwell, Thomas 116, 163, 192, 193, 527, 562; *The Lancashire Witches* 164–5; *see also* Dryden, "MacFlecknoe"
Shaftesbury, 1st Earl of 194, 540
Shaftesbury, 3rd Earl of 220, 317
Shakespeare, William 109, 115, 461; *Hamlet* 460; *King Lear* 8, 461; *A Midsummer Night's Dream* 162
Shaw, George Bernard 169, 460, 461, 463–4; *Arms and the Man* 463; *John Bull's Other Island* 482; *Major Barbara* 463; *Man and Superman* 463; *Mrs Warren's Profession* 463; *Pygmalion* 463
Shaw, Robert B. 445
Sheeran, Patrick 478, 480
Shelburn, Lord 540
Shelley, Percy Bysshe 364; *Adonais* 358; *The Mask of Anarchy* 344–5; *Prometheus Unbound* 329; sonnets 344; on Wordsworth 359
Shepard, Sam: *True West* 474
Sheridan, Richard Brinsley 166; *The Critic* 173; *The School for Scandal* 173
Sheridan, Thomas 571
Sidney, Sir Philip 109
Sillitoe, Alan 402
Silvecane, Guillaume de 140
Simmel, Georg 574
sin 299, 302, 318, 428–9
Sinclair, Iain 400–1, 408; *London's Tower* 401
sirventes 62
Skelton, John 101, 103, 129; "Colin Clout" 102, 105–6; Juvenal 107; *Speke, Parott* 526–7

Skeltonics 105–6
skepticism 72, 435
slander 575–6
Slater, Niall W. 38
slavery 377
Smallwood, Angela 264
Smart, Christopher 234; *Hilliad* 238
Smith, Charlotte: *The Old Manor House* 288
Smith, Horace: *Rejected Addresses* 359
Smith, James: *Rejected Addresses* 359
Smith, Seba 384, 386, 387
Smith, Stevie 445
Smith, W. H. 371
Smollett, Tobias 234, 236, 264–8; "Advice" 238; character sketches 566; *Ferdinand Count Fathom* 266; *The History and Adventures of an Atom* 265; *Humphry Clinker* 245, 267–8; *Peregrine Pickle* 266; "Reproof" 238; *Roderick Random* 265–6, 274; satire in novel 215; *Sir Launcelot Greaves* 266–7; *Travels through France and Italy* 270
social comment 135
social documentaries 402
social drama 460
social inequalities 152
social justice 284
social protest 233–4
social satire 341, 342, 349–57, 358–60, 368–9, 377
Socialists 414
Socrates/Sokrates 36, 43, 71, 512–13, 520
Solomon, King 529
Sondheim, Stephen: *Assassins* 474
sonnets 93, 95, 109, 344
Sorel, Charles 84, 147
sotties 71–2
South Sea Bubble 304–5, 572
Southey, Robert 345
Soyinka, Wole: *King Baabu* 474
Spacks, Patricia Meyer 2, 576
Spain: Baroque period 92–9; Civil War 452; Golden Age 86–7
Spanish Succession, War of 213
Spectator 565, 571, 573
Spectra hoax 448
Speculum stultorum 58, 60
Spence, Ferrand: *Life of Lucian* 575
Spenser, Edmund 108, 109, 177; *The Shepheardes Calender* 499
Spinoza, Benedict 333, 334, 335
spontaneity 434–5, 551

Springfield Republican 394
"St James' Infirmary Blues" 418–19
Staël, Mme de 336
Stamp Act (1712) 214
stamp tax on periodicals 365
Standish, Miles 378
Stapleton, John: *Juvenal's Satires* 575
Stationers' Company 214
Stedman, Ralph 316
Steele, Richard 170, 506, 565, 571
Steele, Timothy 1, 449
Steere, Richard 527
stereotypes 296, 308
Sterne, Laurence 132; as influence 523; *A Sentimental Journey* 270; *Tristram Shandy* 219, 257, 258, 268–9, 481, 517–18, 582
Stewart, Harold 448
stock characters 7, 551
Stoicism 124, 140, 553, 554, 558–9
Stoppard, Tom: influenced by Beckett 473; *Jumpers* 27; *Professional Fowl* 411; *Rosencrantz and Guildenstern are Dead* 473
Strafford, Earl of 561
Stultitia 123–4
Suárez de Figueroa, Cristóbal 90
sublime 218, 223, 224, 330, 369
Sullivan, A. S. 9, 358, 466; *see also* Gilbert, W. S.
Sunderland, Earl of 545
Surrealism 316, 462, 470
Susannah and the Elders 318
Sutherland, James 212
Swift, Jonathan: *Argument against Abolishing Christianity* 303; *The Battel of the Books* 575; "Baucis and Philemon" 507; "A Beautiful Young Nymph Going to Bed" 230; *Cadenus and Vanessa* 507; "Cassinus and Peter" 230; dangers for 215; "A Description of a City Shower" 230; "A Description of the Morning" 285; *Directions to Make a Birth-Day Song* 562; *Discourse Concerning the Mechanical Operation of the Spirit* 568; disgust 413; *Drapier's Letters* 527; ethnic cleansing 202; evil 305–6; *Gulliver's Travels* 4, 21, 26, 28, 196–8, 206–9, 218–19, 257, 259, 304, 404, 481, 508, 516, 572, 582; *History of the Four Last Years of the Queen* 561; as influence 238, 282, 283, 404; *The Intelligencer* 571; *Journal to Stella* 568; "The Lady's Dressing Room" 230, 412; madness 204; on Marvell 185; "Meditation on a Broomstick" 569; Menippean satire 476; *Miscellanies* 218; misfortune of friends 16;

Swift, Jonathan (*cont'd*)
  A Modest Proposal 20, 28, 196, 197, 198–203; Orwell on 427; persona 201; prostitute poems 507; readership 202–3, 205–6, 209–10; Scriblerus Club 216; "Strephon and Chloe" 230; *A Tale of a Tub* 5, 18, 185, 198, 203–6, 317–18, 481, 508, 527, 561, 572, 574, 581–2, 583; "Town Eclogue" genre 507; universalizing satire 230–1; "Verses on the Death of Dr Swift" 230; Yahoos 404
Swiftian, as term 196–7
Swinburne, Algernon 358
synecdoche 323
Synge, John Millington 480; "The Curse" 478; *The Playboy of the Western World* 465, 478

The Tablet 431
Tahiti 154–5
Táin Bó Cúailnge (Cattle Raid of Cooley) 477
talking animals 88–9, 94, 147
Tarteron, Jérôme 140
Tate, Nahum 527
Tatham, John: *The Rump* 162–3
Tatler 571
Taylor, Charles 331
Taylor, Jane: *Essays in Rhyme on Morals and Manners* 350
Taylor, John 115
Tennyson, Alfred Lord 418, 419
Terence 39–40, 551; *The Mother-in-law* 39
Test, George 9
tetrameters 104
Thackeray, William: *The Book of Snobs* 566; character sketches 566; *The Fatal Boots* 366; *Henry Esmond* 367; *The Newcomes* 367; *Pendennis* 367, 370, 372; *A Shabby Genteel Story* 366; *Snobs of England* 366; *Vanity Fair* 366–7, 370, 371
Thelema 77
Theobald, Lewis 526
theophagy 83
Theophrastus 181, 550; *Characters* 512, 551–3
Thersites 33–4, 45, 47, 50
Thirlwall, Connop 523
Thomas, Artus 83
Thomson, Rodney M. 54–5, 56
Thorne, Christian 577
Tickell, Thomas 573
Tieck, Ludwig 336
The Times 365
Tipper, Elizabeth: "A Satyr" 281

Toledo, Canon of 54, 68, 258
Toller, Ernst 468
Tollet, Elizabeth: "The Microcosm" 285
Tolstoy, Leo 518; *Russian Readers* 521
Tonson, Jacob 186, 193
topicality 10, 377–8
Tories 164–5, 265, 342, 525
totalitarianism 24, 336, 424
Tournai, Bishop of 57–8
"Town Eclogue" genre 507
Townshend, George 312
Tractatus Garcia 54–5
trade 247, 248
Trent, Council of 79
Trillin, Calvin 434
Trimpi, Wesley: *Ben Jonson's Poems* 446
Tripartite Life of Saint Patrick 477
Trollope, Anthony: *Barchester Towers* 370; character sketches 566; *The Eustace Diamonds* 370; *Hunting Sketches* 566; *The Way We Live Now* 370, 371
Trotter, Catherine 166
The True Britain 528
Truman, Harry 6
Trumbull, John 239–40; *M'Fingal* 380–1
Tuesday Club 380
Turner, Francis 184
Tutchin, John 527; Bentinck 545; *The Foreigners* 542
Twain, Mark 377; American Publishing Company 391–2; Christianity 374; "The Chronicle of Young Satan" 392, 395–7; *A Connecticut Yankee* 374, 392; *The Gilded Age* 392–3; *Huckleberry Finn* 327–8, 330, 336, 392, 582; "King Leopold's Soliloquy" 394; "Letters from the Earth" 395; "The Man that Corrupted Hadleyburg" 395; *The Mysterious Stranger* 328; Old Testament diaries 529; sentimental 327–8; "To the Person Sitting in Darkness" 393–4; "The War Prayer" 392, 394–5; *What is Man* 328
Tyler, Royall: *The Algerine Captive* 382–3; *The Contrast* 382
typographic effects 132
typology, mock-biblical 540–8
Tyrtamus of Lesbos: *see* Theophrastus

Union of Parliaments 212–13
United States of America 377, 378–84, 468–9, 474
Urceo, Codro 123
utopia 129–30, 373

Valdés, Alfonso de 88; *Diálogo de Mercurio y Carón* 88
Valdez, Luis: *I Don't Have to Show You No Stinking Badges* 474; *Los Vendidos* 474
Valla, Lorenzo: *Encomion S. Thomas* 122
Van Hamel, A. G. 65
vanity 124, 149
Varey, Simon 262–3, 264
Varro, Terentius 7
Varronian satire 7, 177, 194
Vaughan, Thomas 564
Vauquelin de la Fresnaye, Jean 140
Veblen, Thorstein: *Theory of the Leisure Class* 375
Vega, Lope de 86, 93, 94–5
venality 56, 57–8, 189
vernacular satire 64–8, 119
verse satire 81–2, 107–8, 110–13, 115, 234–5, 435
Versicles 531
Villalón, Cristóbal: *El Crótalon* 88–9
Villiers, George (Duke of Buckingham): *The Rehearsal* 165–6
Villon, François 81, 507
Vincent of Beauvais 54
Virgil: *Aeneid* 498, 499, 504, 505; *Georgics* 497
visions 96–7
Vogelweide, Walter von der 62
Voltaire: *Aventure de la mémoire* 157; *Boileau* 157; *Le Bourbier* 158; *Candide* 156–7; *La Crépinade* 158; *Le Dépositaire* 151; *Dictionnaire philosophique* 157; *Discours de réception à l'Académie française* 157; *L'Ecossaise* 158; *L'Ingénu* 157; *Lettres philosophiques* 155–6; *Mémoire sur la satire* 157; *Micromégas* 156; *Le Monde comme il va* 156; *Regnante puero* 157–8; *Siècle de Louis XIV* 150; *Zadig* 156
Vonnegut, Kurt: *Cat's Cradle* 27; *Mother Night* 21, 29; *Slaughterhouse-Five* 27, 28

Wain, John 402
Walker, George: *Berkeley Hall* 274; *The Vagabond* 274
Wall, Mervyn 484; *The Return of Fursey* 489–90; *The Unfortunate Fursey* 489–90
Waller, Edmund 178; "Instructions to a Painter" 183, 226, 562
Walpole, Horace: *Lessons for the Day* 528
Walpole, Robert 213; Dodsley 533–7; Fielding 171, 215, 261; Gay 169; Haywood 260; Hogarth 306; Licensing Act 214–15, 261
Walter of Châtillon 52, 55, 56

war epigrams 444–5
Ward, Ned: *London Spy* 571
Warner, Alan 402
Warner, Charles Dudley 384, 392
Warren, Joyce W. 389
Wars of Religion 82, 83
Warton, Joseph 235, 576
Warton, Thomas 235
The Washington Post 529
The Washington Star 529
Watteau, Antoine 318; *Comédiens Italiens* 307; *L'Enseigne de Gersaint* 307, 309
Waugh, Evelyn 21, 339, 401; as artist 408; *Black Mischief* 406, 408, 409–10, 415, 416, 423; *Brideshead Revisited* 412–13, 417–18; character sketches 566; conversion to Catholicism 426; *Decline and Fall* 402, 408, 410, 417, 423; *Edmund Campion* 418; *A Handful of Dust* 412, 417, 419, 423, 426, 582; *Human Comedy* 413; *Labels* 413; *Love Among the Ruins* 408, 418; *The Loved One* 418–19, 431; *Put Out More Flags* 411; *Rossetti: His Life and Works* 415; *Scoop* 417, 423; *The Sword of Honour* 414, 419; *Vile Bodies* 405, 413, 418–19, 420, 421, 422; *Waugh in Abyssinia* 416
Webster, John 556
Webster's Dictionary 571
Wedgwood, C. V. 179
Weinbrot, Howard 8
Weldon, Fay 402
Wellek, Rene 332
Wells, H. G. 406; *Island of Dr Moreau* 375; *The Time Machine* 373
Wells, Robert 457
Welsh, Irvine 402; *Trainspotting* 417
Wentworth, Thomas 561
Wesley, John 242–3
Western culture as target 473
Westminster Journal 537
Wharton, Earl of 561
Whicher, George F. 55
Whigs 164–5, 213, 250, 265, 279–80, 373, 525
"Whii werre and wrake ..." 65–6
Whistler, James 358
Whitcher, Frances M. 384; *Widow Bedott Papers* 389
White, Gail 445
White, Sir Herbert 355–6
Whitehead, George 172
Whitgift, John 108
Wilbur, Richard 445; "A Finished Man" 442

Wild, Robert 179
Wilde, Oscar 358; "The Critic as Artist" 374; "The Decay of Lying" 374; *An Ideal Husband* 465; *The Importance of Being Earnest* 465–6; *A Woman of No Importance* 465
Wilkes, John 234–5, 239, 310, 531; *The North Briton* 242
Wilkins, John: *An Essay Towards a Real Character* 571; *Mercury, or the Secret and Swift Messenger* 571
William III 212, 226, 231, 279, 286, 304–5
Williams, Tennessee 469; *Cat on a Hot Tin Roof* 469; *A Streetcar Named Desire* 469
Wilmer, Clive 449
Wilmot, John: *see* Rochester, Earl of
Wilson, David Alec 337
Wilson, Edmund 435
Wilson, John 528
Winters, Yvor: *The Critiad* 453; *The Journey* 453; "A White Spiritual" 442
Winterson, Jeanette 402
Wireker, Nigel (Longchamp) 58–61
wit 276
Wither, George 115
Witoszek, Nina 478, 480
wives 48
Wodehouse, P. G. 402
Wolcot, John 234, 254; *Political and Congratulatory Epistle to James Boswell* 254
Wolfe, George C.: *The Colored Museum* 474
Wollstonecraft, Mary: *The Emigrants* 274; *A Vindication of the Rights of Woman* 290; *The Wrongs of Woman* 274
Wolsey, Cardinal Thomas 106–7, 237, 534–5
women: anti-matrimonial satire 67; Aretino 126–7; education 277–8, 281, 282; equality 391; irrationality 123; Juvenal 37, 140; *Lysistrata* 37; public debate 285; Semonides 36, 37; sexuality 188; as targets 81, 95, 96, 141, 154, 164, 575; wit 276; wives 48
women writers: American 377; attacked 166; novels 259–61, 271–3, 285–90; poetry 280–5; satire 276–7; secret history 579
Wooler, Thomas 345
Woolf, Virginia 402, 408
Wooster Group: *Route 1 and 9* 473
Wordsworth, William 238, 330; *Intimations of Immortality* 560; *The Prelude* 329, 333; Romanticism 218; on satire 246; satirized 359
Worton, Michael 471
Wotton, William 204
Wright, Thomas 65
Wyatt, Sir Thomas 103, 107, 110, 437; "Mine Own John Poyntz" 436
Wycherley, William 278–9; *The Country Wife* 164, 562; *The Plain Dealer* 164
Wylie, Philip 4

Yahweh 22, 25, 29
Yeats, William Butler 404, 482; Joyce on 478; "September, 1913" 438
Yellow Book 358
Young, Edward 213, 215, 282; *Conjectures on Original Composition* 235; *Love of Fame* 224
youth novels 402
Ysengrimus 57–8, 63
Yunck, John 56

Zall, Paul M. 381
Zameenzad, Adam 402
Zink, Michel 64
Zola, Émile 462
Zwick, Jim 394

Printed and bound by CPI Group (UK) Ltd, Croydon, CR0 4YY
20/10/2024
14576622-0002